# THE NATIONAL CURR
# ... AND BEYOND ...

*Pow*

*A Pow Guide
to*
# The National Curriculum
## EXTRA

To prepare students for KS3 NCTs
at tiers 3–5 and 4–6

by

### Barbara Young
*Tarporley High School
Cheshire*

*Illustrators*
Matthew Staff, Jennifer Smith, Luke Young and Joanne Young

**Acknowledgements**
to the students and teachers who trialled this new approach,
who worked with enthusiasm
and made suggestions for improving
both content and presentation.

In particular, thanks to those who criticised and made
so many positive suggestions for improvements to the text:
• Linda Goodwin and Lynne Warren of St. John's School, Episkopi
• Sally Brookes and Fiona Lockerbie of The Salt Grammar School, Shipley
• Sue Rawlingson of The Central Technology College, Gloucester
• Gill Burrows of John Hanson School, Andover
• Ann Russell of Blacon High School, Chester
• Ann Payne, Sue Roch and Hilary Sills of France Hill School, Camberley
• Pat Ashurst, Gill Davies, Nicola Heywood and Sandra Price
of The Deanery High School, Wigan

> But, above all, thanks to the Y9 class at Tarporley High School 1997-8
> who made the course their own and worked so hard to improve it.
> Their ideas were brilliant and they corrected so many errors in the text.
> Thanks to : Jonathan Barnes, Christian Bell, Stephen Berry, Andrew Cadman,
> Jamie Crawford, Darren Dodd, Tracey Griffiths, Vickie Heath, Vickie Holden,
> Pamela Kirk, Holly Latham, Jenny Manley, Kirsty Mullineaux, Ben Murphy,
> Matthew Pearce, Claire Slaney, Matthew Stephens, Craig West

Thanks also to the team at the National Numeracy Project.
Their "Framework to Numeracy" was invaluable
when planning the structured mental arithmetic course.

© The 'Maths Is...' Jugglers
2, Millview Close, Bulkeley, Malpas, Cheshire, SY14 8DB

This edition was first published in Great Britain 1998
British Library Cataloguing–in–Publication Data

ISBN   1 – 874428 – 68 – 9

Printed and bound by PRINTCENTRE WALES, Mold, Flintshire

# THE NATIONAL CURRICULUM ...
# ... AND BEYOND ...
## EXTRA

The EXTRA course :
- has been specially written for low attainers
- is a version of the mainstream course
- has lots of EXTRA practice on all techniques
- can be run alongside the mainstream course
- can stand on its own

Each student:
- takes responsibility for his/her own learning
- can decide how much practice (s)he needs to do for each technique
- can try Star Challenges when (s)he feels ready for them

The authors firmly believe that all students can tackle Levels 3 – 6 in the National Curriculum for Mathematics.

However, some students need :
- more time to get to grips with the ideas and techniques involved
- lots of EXTRA practice
- one idea at a time introduced step–by–step
- to meet ideas and techniques over and over again

Most students in lower sets are underachieving.
This course aims to raise the level of achievement of these students.

*Pow*

# CONTENTS

Strategies for Improving Mental Arithmetic Skills *Part 1*     pp05 – 18

> At the end of *Part 1*, students should move straight onto Topic 2 "Back to Basics". Strategies for Improving Mental Arithmetic Skills *Part 2* should be tackled one section at a time at regular intervals throughout the year. These skills should be tested at the beginning of each lesson using one of the structured mental arithmetic tests that are in the Teachers' Resource Pack.

| | |
|---|---|
| Strategies for Improving Mental Arithmetic Skills *Part 2* | pp19 – 40 |
| Back to Basics | pp41 – 66 |
| Bar Charts and Beyond | pp67 – 88 |
| Working with Numbers | pp89 – 118 |
| Areas, Volumes and Formulae | pp119 – 152 |
| Probability | pp153 – 168 |
| Let's Sort Out Fractions, Decimals and Percentages | pp169 – 204 |
| The Geometry of Angle and Shape | pp205 – 236 |
| Patterns and Rules | pp237 – 248 |
| Coordinates and Graphs | pp249 – 270 |
| ANSWERS | pp271 – 296 |

Teachers may change the order of the topics.

These topics are independent
and so can be done in any order.

At the beginning of each topic,
there is a contents list which is matched to
the levels in the National Curriculum for Mathematics.

> In a class which is being prepared to do NCTs at levels 3–5, there will also be some students who are better or work more quickly than the rest. We found that these students were quite prepared to tackle much of the work at level 6 which is at the end of each topic – and with a fair degree of success. The assessments in the Teachers' Pack are structured so that all students get a mark for levels 3–5, but students who have worked at the level 6 material can also earn a mark for levels 3–6.

# THE NATIONAL CURRICULUM ...
# ... AND BEYOND ...

*Pow*

# Strategies for Improving Mental Arithmetic Skills
## EXTRA

Sections 5–18 should be tackled one section at a time at regular intervals through the school year. They cover all the basic mental arithmetic techniques that students ought to know. All students will be familiar with some of these techniques but there will also be some techniques which are weak or unknown. The aim is to find these gaps and fill them; hence boosting self-confidence as well as improving mental arithmetic expertise.

**Every lesson in Y9 should start with a short mental arithmetic test.** These are provided in the Teachers' Resource Pack. After each section is completed, the class can move onto the next level of test, which will include skills/techniques just reviewed.

§5–§18 Strategies for Improving Mental Arithmetic Skills

| §4 Basic addition and subtraction | | | |
|---|---|---|---|
| §3 Improving multiplication & division | | | |
| | §2 Practising multiplication skills | | |
| §1 Multiplication tables | | | |
| Level 3 | Level 4 | Level 5 | Level 6 |

The Y9 course starts with these four sections which start students off on a multiplication tables improvement exercise.

They also review/establish basic mental arithmetic techniques. At the end of these sections, students move straight onto Topic 2 "Back to Basics".

*A POW GUIDE*

# Strategies for Improving Mental Arithmetic Skills

## Section 1: Multiplication tables

In this section you will improve your recall of multiplication tables.

**Levels 3 & 4**

### DEVELOPMENT

### D1: A game to improve your multiplication tables   *tables cards*

**Task 1:**      **The first mental arithmetic test.**
Your teacher will give you a mental arithmetic test.
This is to establish your base score.
In later tests, you will try to improve this score.

*Idea*

**Task 2:**      **Making the game**
Cut out the 36 cards.
Each one will have a multiplication sum on the front and the answer on the back.

| 2 x 2 | 2 x 3 | 2 x 4 | 2 x 5 | 2 x 6 | 2 x 7 |
|---|---|---|---|---|---|
| 2 x 8 | 2 x 9 | 3 x 3 | 3 x 4 | 3 x 5 | 3 x 6 |
| 3 x 7 | 3 x 8 | 3 x 9 | 4 x 4 | 4 x 5 | 4 x 6 |
| 4 x 7 | 4 x 8 | 4 x 9 | 5 x 5 | 5 x 6 | 5 x 7 |
| 5 x 8 | 5 x 9 | (6 x 6) | (6 x 7) | (6 x 8) | (6 x 9) |
| (7 x 7) | (7 x 8) | (7 x 9) | (8 x 8) | (8 x 9) | (9 x 9) |

If you are fairly good, use all the cards. (Level 4)

If you are not very good, leave out the cards with the looped numbers. (Level 3)

Put them back in when you can do the others easily.

You will need an envelope or an elastic band to keep the cards together.
Each student should have their own set of cards.

**Task 3:**     **Playing the game**     The game is for two players.
One person shuffles the cards and holds them in a stack in his/her hand.
(S)he reads off the first sum. The other person has to give the answer.
If the answer is correct, the card is put down on the table.
If the answer is wrong, or the answer is not known, the person holding the cards reads the answer from the back of the card and **puts the card at the back of the stack**.

It is very important, when an answer is not known, that the reader gives the correct answer without any comment. You can only improve your table skills this way, if there is no fear of getting it wrong.
The whole process must be kept hassle–free.

The process continues until there are no cards left in the stack.
At this point, every card will have been answered correctly once.
Repeat the game with the reader answering the questions.

Play this game during the lesson and at least once every night until you can answer them all quickly. Play with your parents – and test their tables too!

WARNING! – make sure the cards are held so that the answers cannot be seen.

A POW GUIDE              page 6              Strategies for Improving **EXTRA**
                                              Mental Arithmetic Skills

## Star Challenge 1

At the beginning of every lesson you will have a tables test.
A star will be awarded if you get 10 out of 10
OR if you get more than your previous highest score.

*Pow*

**P1: Connect Four**     A game for 1–2 players   counters      Levels 3 & 4

| 45 | 24 | 18 | 10 | 64 | 40 |
|----|----|----|----|----|----|
| 15 | 36 | 9  | 16 | 72 | 4  |
| 27 | 28 | 12 | 14 | 32 | 56 |
| 63 | 49 | 25 | 20 | 12 | 18 |
| 81 | 48 | 30 | 6  | 24 | 35 |
| 8  | 40 | 54 | 16 | 36 | 42 |

Choose two numbers from:
2   3   4   5   6   7   8   9

*The more times you play this, the better your multiplication will get!*

Rules: the first person:

Here, the numbers can be the same!
- chooses two numbers from the list below the table
- says what numbers they are before picking up the calculator
- multiplies them using a calculator
- puts a counter on a square with that answer (if it is still available)

The second person does exactly the same.
The game continues with each person repeating these steps.

**The first person with four counters in a straight line is the winner.**

This is excellent practice for mental arithmetic. If you want to get a counter on a particular square – then you have to work out in your head which numbers you need. You have to say what they are – before you can pick up the calculator.

**Alternative game**: Don't use a calculator. Instead, partner challenges if they think the answer is wrong. Then, partner can put counter on that square, if they get the right pair.
Use calculator as referee!

*A POW GUIDE*     *page 7*     *Strategies for Improving* **EXTRA**
                                *Mental Arithmetic Skills*

# Section 2: Practising multiplication skills

In this section you will:
- review using a table square to multiply numbers;
- do plenty of practice using mental arithmetic.

## DEVELOPMENT

### D1: Using a table square

You need to be good at your multiplication tables. Your skill will improve as you practise with the table cards. But, whilst you are improving, you can use this table square to find any multiples that you cannot remember.

NOTE : You will not be able to take the table square into any exam.

| x | 1 | 2 | 3 | 4 | 5 | 6 | 7 | 8 | 9 | 10 | 11 | 12 | 13 | 14 | 15 |
|---|---|---|---|---|---|---|---|---|---|----|----|----|----|----|----|
| 1 | 1 | 2 | 3 | 4 | 5 | 6 | 7 | 8 | 9 | 10 | 11 | 12 | 13 | 14 | 15 |
| 2 | 2 | 4 | 6 | 8 | 10 | 12 | 14 | 16 | 18 | 20 | 22 | 24 | 26 | 28 | 30 |
| 3 | 3 | 6 | 9 | 12 | 15 | 18 | 21 | 24 | 27 | 30 | 33 | 36 | 39 | 42 | 45 |
| 4 | 4 | 8 | 12 | 16 | 20 | 24 | 28 | 32 | 36 | 40 | 44 | 48 | 52 | 56 | 60 |
| 5 | 5 | 10 | 15 | 20 | 25 | 30 | 35 | 40 | 45 | 50 | 55 | 60 | 65 | 70 | 75 |
| 6 | 6 | 12 | 18 | 24 | 30 | 36 | 42 | 48 | 54 | 60 | 66 | 72 | 78 | 84 | 90 |
| 7 | 7 | 14 | 21 | 28 | 35 | 42 | 49 | 56 | 63 | 70 | 77 | 84 | 91 | 98 | 105 |
| 8 | 8 | 16 | 24 | 32 | 40 | 48 | 56 | 64 | 72 | 80 | 88 | 96 | 104 | 112 | 120 |
| 9 | 9 | 18 | 27 | 36 | 45 | 54 | 63 | 72 | 81 | 90 | 99 | 108 | 117 | 126 | 135 |
| 10 | 10 | 20 | 30 | 40 | 50 | 60 | 70 | 80 | 90 | 100 | 110 | 120 | 130 | 140 | 150 |
| 11 | 11 | 22 | 33 | 44 | 55 | 66 | 77 | 88 | 99 | 110 | 121 | 132 | 143 | 154 | 165 |
| 12 | 12 | 24 | 36 | 48 | 60 | 72 | 84 | 96 | 108 | 120 | 132 | 144 | 156 | 168 | 180 |
| 13 | 13 | 26 | 39 | 52 | 65 | 78 | 91 | 104 | 117 | 130 | 143 | 156 | 169 | 182 | 195 |
| 14 | 14 | 28 | 42 | 56 | 70 | 84 | 98 | 112 | 126 | 140 | 154 | 168 | 182 | 196 | 210 |
| 15 | 15 | 30 | 45 | 60 | 75 | 90 | 105 | 120 | 135 | 150 | 165 | 180 | 195 | 210 | 225 |

EXAMPLE 1    Work out  5 x 13        13
5 — — — — — — — — — — — — — — — — — — — — ○    $5 \times 13 = 65$

*Copy and complete each of these multiplication sums:*

1. 2 x 3   = ...
2. 14 x 3  = ...
3. 7 x 8   = ...
4. 13 x 4  = ...
5. 13 x 14 = ...
6. 12 x 7  = ...
7. 5 x 6   = ...
8. 8 x 12  = ...
9. 11 x 13 = ...
10. 6 x 14 = ...
11. 9 x 6  = ...
12. 7 x 13 = ...
13. 4 x 15 = ...
14. 11 x 14 = ...
15. 5 x 15 = ...
16. 12 x 14 = ...
17. 8 x 9  = ...
18. 5 x 12 = ...
19. 12 x 9 = ...
20. 6 x 9  = ...

Your teacher may make a copy of this table for you to stick in your book.
OR
You may put a copy onto card.

• Check your answers.

A POW GUIDE            page 8            Strategies for Improving    **EXTRA**
                                          Mental Arithmetic Skills

# P1: Multiplication arithmogons

**Level 4**

The number in each ☐ is the **product** of the numbers on either side of it.

2 × 3 = 6
Pow

The **product** of 2 and 5 is 10

*Complete each product arithmogon:*

1. Top: 3; sides: 5, 2
2. Top: 5; sides: 4, 7
3. Top: 4; sides: 8, 6
4. Top: 3; sides: 6, 7
5. Top: 6; sides: 5, 9
6. Top: 8; sides: 7, 9
7. Left box: 8, right box: 28, bottom: 2 — 14 — ○
8. Top: 3; left box: 21, right box: 15
9. Right box: 28; bottom: ○ — 24 — 4
10. Left box: 27; bottom: 3 — 12 — ○
11. Top: 5; left box: 10, right box: 50
12. Left box: 36; bottom: ○ — 28 — 7

• Check your answers.

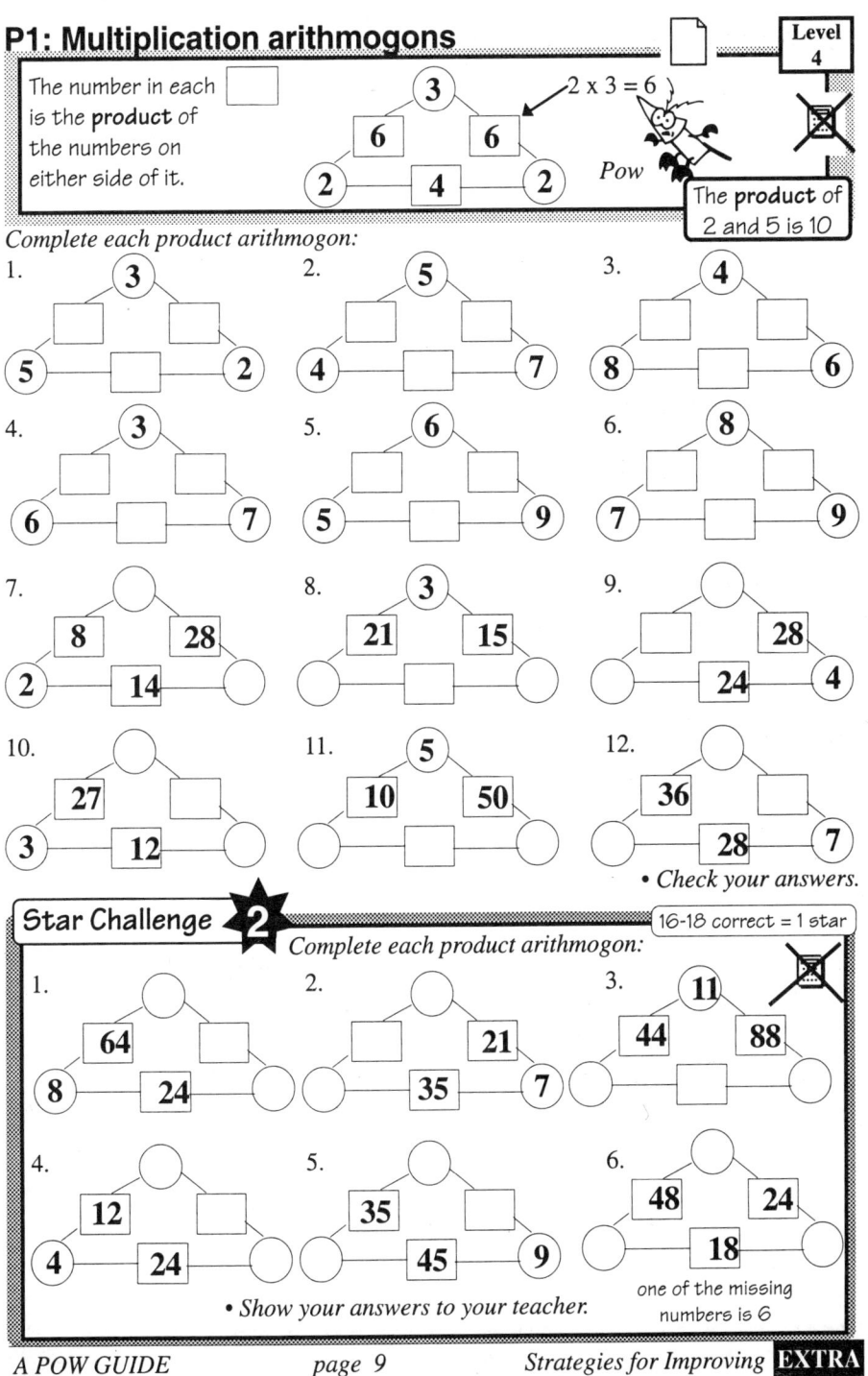

## Star Challenge 2

16-18 correct = 1 star

*Complete each product arithmogon:*

1. Left box: 64; bottom: 8 — 24 — ○
2. Right box: 21; bottom: ○ — 35 — 7
3. Top: 11; boxes: 44, 88
4. Left box: 12; bottom: 4 — 24 — ○
5. Left box: 35; bottom: ○ — 45 — 9
6. Boxes: 48, 24; bottom middle: 18

one of the missing numbers is 6

• Show your answers to your teacher.

A POW GUIDE    page 9    Strategies for Improving Mental Arithmetic Skills    **EXTRA**

# P2: Work out the products

Level 4

| 4 | 6 |
|---|---|
| 3 | 2 |

...  ...

Each number outside the box is **the product** of the two numbers in that row or column.

4 × 3 ⟶

| 4 | 6 | 24 |
|---|---|---|
| 3 | 2 | 6 |
| 12 | 12 | |

*Fill in the missing numbers:*

1.  | 7 | 5 | ... |
    |---|---|---|
    | 3 | 4 | ... |
    ... ...

2.  | 2 | 9 | ... |
    |---|---|---|
    | 6 | 3 | ... |
    ... ...

3.  | 8 | 4 | ... |
    |---|---|---|
    | 5 | 2 | ... |
    ... ...

4.  | 9 | 5 | ... |
    |---|---|---|
    | 7 | 3 | ... |
    ... ...

5.  | 6 | 6 | ... |
    |---|---|---|
    | 4 | 5 | ... |
    ... ...

6.  | 3 | 9 | ... |
    |---|---|---|
    | 4 | 7 | ... |
    ... ...

7.  | 4 | ... | 12 |
    |---|---|---|
    | ... | 8 | ... |
    20 ...

8.  | ... | 9 | 18 |
    |---|---|---|
    | ... | 3 | 15 |
    ... ...

9.  | 6 | ... | 36 |
    |---|---|---|
    | ... | 8 | ... |
    42 48

10. | ... | 7 | ... |
    |---|---|---|
    | 4 | ... | 12 |
    32 ...

11. | 2 | ... | ... |
    |---|---|---|
    | ... | 7 | ... |
    10 63

12. | ... | 3 | ... |
    |---|---|---|
    | 5 | ... | 35 |
    30 ...

13. | ... | 6 | 18 |
    |---|---|---|
    | 8 | ... | ... |
    ... 42

14. | 5 | 9 | ... |
    |---|---|---|
    | ... | ... | 24 |
    40 ...

15. | ... | 9 | ... |
    |---|---|---|
    | ... | 4 | 16 |
    8 ...

## Star Challenge 3

• Check your answers.
22-24 correct = 1 star

*Fill in the missing numbers in each product table:*

1.  | 5 | ... | 40 |
    |---|---|---|
    | ... | ... | 35 |
    ... 40

2.  | 7 | 9 | ... |
    |---|---|---|
    | ... | ... | ... |
    49 72

3.  | ... | ... | 40 |
    |---|---|---|
    | ... | 6 | 18 |
    15 ...

4.  | 5 | ... | 15 |
    |---|---|---|
    | ... | 7 | ... |
    30 ...

5.  | ... | 6 | 18 |
    |---|---|---|
    | ... | 5 | 35 |
    ... ...

6.  | 7 | ... | 49 |
    |---|---|---|
    | ... | 8 | ... |
    42 ...

A POW GUIDE    page 10    Strategies for Improving Mental Arithmetic Skills    EXTRA

# Section 3: Improving multiplication and division

In this section you will:
- look at division in several ways;
- use multiplication facts to do division
- work with multiplication and division together;
- make sensible decisions over remainders in problems involving division.

**DEVELOPMENT**

## D1: Division is sharing

*Counters are optional* — Level 3

EXAMPLE 2  Q: Share 12 counters between 3 people. How many counters does each person get?

A: 12 counters shared between 3 — Ans: 4

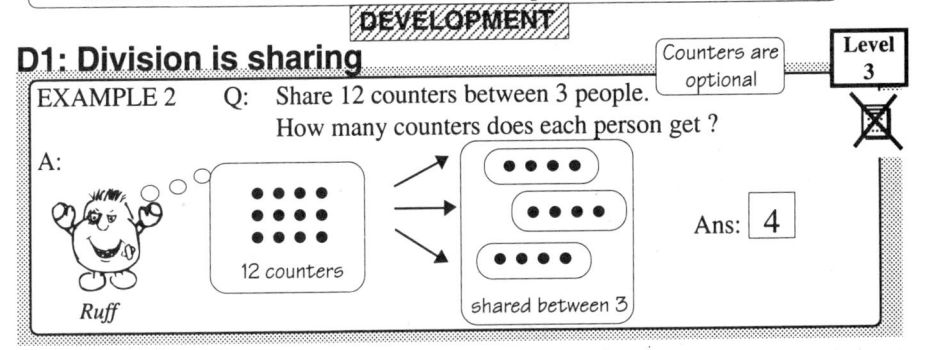

*Ruff*

Work out how many counters each person gets:
1. Share 6 counters between 2 people.
2. Share 6 counters between 3 people.
3. Share 8 counters between 2 people.
4. Share 8 counters between 4 people.
5. Share 10 counters between 5 people.
6. Share 12 counters between 4 people.

• *Check answers.*

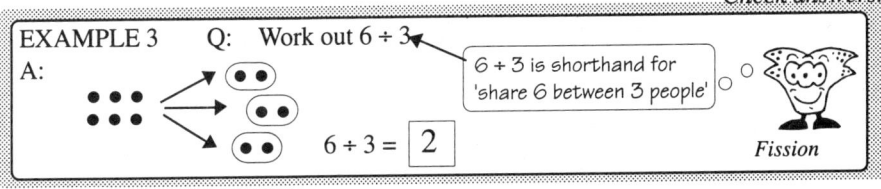

EXAMPLE 3  Q: Work out $6 \div 3$

$6 \div 3$ is shorthand for 'share 6 between 3 people'

A: $6 \div 3 = 2$

*Fission*

Copy and complete:
7. $15 \div 3 = ...$
8. $12 \div 4 = ...$
9. $20 \div 5 = ...$
10. $8 \div 4 = ...$
11. $12 \div 2 = ...$
12. $16 \div 4 = ...$
13. $18 \div 6 = ...$
14. $21 \div 3 = ...$

• *Check answers.*

## D2: Division is 'how many are there in ... ?'

Level 4

EXAMPLE 4  Q: Work out $32 \div 8$

There are four 8's in 32

A: $32 \div 8 = 4$

*Spoton*

Copy and complete:
1. $24 \div 8 = ...$
2. $16 \div 2 = ...$
3. $20 \div 4 = ...$
4. $28 \div 4 = ...$
5. $60 \div 20 = ...$
6. $18 \div 3 = ...$
7. $45 \div 5 = ...$
8. $36 \div 9 = ...$

• *Check answers*

A POW GUIDE — Strategies for Improving Mental Arithmetic Skills — **EXTRA**

## D3: Related x and ÷ statements
**Level 4**

$3 \times 5 = 15$ tells us that
$5 \times 3 = 15$
$15 \div 3 = 5$
$15 \div 5 = 3$

If you are given any one of these statements, you should be able to write down the other three statements.

*Crumbl*

1. $5 \times 6 = 30$ Write down the three number statements related to this.
2. $6 \times 8 = 48$ Write down the three number statements related to this.
3. (a) *Copy and complete this statement:* $7 \times 3 = \ldots$
   (b) Write down the three number statements related to this.
4. (a) *Copy and complete this statement:* $9 \times 6 = \ldots$
   (b) Write down the three number statements related to this. • Check answers.
5. $5 \times 7 = 35$ *Copy and complete:* $35 \div 7 = \ldots$ $\qquad$ $35 \div 5 = \ldots$
6. $9 \times 6 = 54$ *Copy and complete:* $54 \div 6 = \ldots$ $\qquad$ $54 \div 9 = \ldots$
7. $7 \times 6 = 42$ *Copy and complete:* $42 \div 6 = \ldots$ $\qquad$ $42 \div 7 = \ldots$

• Check answers.

### PRACTICE
## P1: Multiplication and division
**Level 4**

**Batch A:** *Copy and complete:*
1. $7 \times 9 = \ldots$
2. $63 \div \ldots = 9$
3. $3 \times \ldots = 24$
4. $30 \div 10 = \ldots$
5. $15 \times 2 = \ldots$
6. $\ldots \times 9 = 18$
7. $6 \times 5 = \ldots$
8. $36 \div 6 = \ldots$
9. $7 \times \ldots = 56$
10. $4 \times 9 = \ldots$
11. $12 \times \ldots = 36$
12. $40 \div 8 = \ldots$
13. Share 30 smarties between 5 people.
14. How many 20s are there in 100 ?

• Check answers.

**Batch B:** *Copy and complete:*
1. $5 \times 8 = \ldots$
2. $40 \div \ldots = 8$
3. $4 \times \ldots = 44$
4. $80 \div 20 = \ldots$
5. $12 \times 3 = \ldots$
6. $\ldots \times 8 = 48$
7. $9 \times 5 = \ldots$
8. $54 \div 6 = \ldots$
9. $9 \times \ldots = 72$
10. $7 \times 9 = \ldots$
11. $32 \div 8 = \ldots$
12. $60 \div 15 = \ldots$
13. Share 36 toffees between 6 people.
14. How many 25s are there in 100 ?

• Check answers.

### Star Challenge 4•4
*Write down the answers:*

14-15 correct = 2 stars
11-13 correct = 1 star

1. Share 12 cakes between 4 people.
2. Share 28 cakes between 4 people.
3. $16 \div 2$
4. $30 \div 3$
5. $4 \times 9$
6. $7 \times 8$
7. $56 \div 8$
8. $6 \times 12 = 72$ Write down the three number statements related to this.

*Copy and complete:*
9. $4 \times \ldots = 28$
10. $40 \div \ldots = 10$
11. $12 \times \ldots = 24$
12. $45 \div 9 = \ldots$
13. $15 \times \ldots = 45$
14. $99 \div \ldots = 11$
15. There are ... 7s in 49.

• *Your teacher has the answers to these.*

A POW GUIDE   page 12   Strategies for Improving Mental Arithmetic Skills **EXTRA**

## D4: Division with remainders

**Level 3**

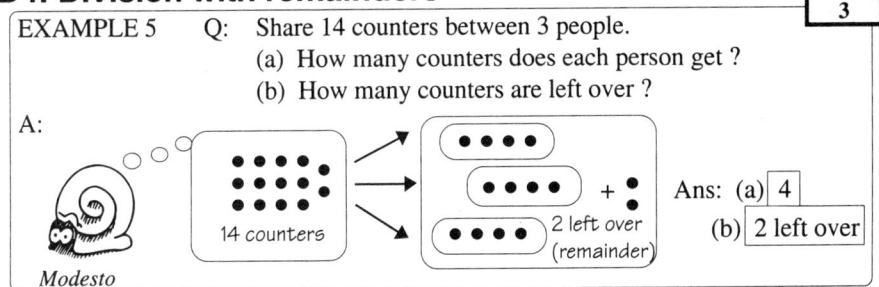

**EXAMPLE 5** Q: Share 14 counters between 3 people.
(a) How many counters does each person get?
(b) How many counters are left over?

A: 14 counters → 4 + 4 + 4 with 2 left over (remainder)

Ans: (a) 4  (b) 2 left over

*Modesto*

In questions 1-6 (a) Work out how many counters each person gets.
(b) How many counters are left over?

1. Share 7 counters between 2 people.
2. Share 10 counters between 3 people.
3. Share 9 counters between 2 people.
4. Share 8 counters between 3 people.
5. Share 11 counters between 5 people.
6. Share 14 counters between 4 people.

• Check answers.

## D5: Practical division problems

**Level 4**

1. 23 people are to be taken from the wedding to the reception.
A taxi can carry up to 5 people. How many taxis will be needed?
2. I collect 19 eggs from my hens. Six eggs go in a box.
How many full boxes do I get? How many eggs are over?
3. I collect 25 eggs from my hens. Six eggs go in a box.
How many boxes do I need to put *all* the eggs in?
4. How many £8 books can I buy with £25?
5. 30 students want to play netball. There are 7 players in a netball team.
How many full teams can be made?
6. Theatre tickets cost £9. How many tickets can I buy with £40?
7. 192 students are going on a day trip to Alton Towers. Each coach takes 52 students.
How many coaches are needed?
8. 56 children want to play rounders. There are 9 players in a rounders team.
(a) How many teams can be made? How many children would be left over?
(b) All the 56 children play rounders. How many teams had 9 players in them and how many had 10?
9. A week is 7 days long. How many full weeks are there in 50 days?
10. A tape cassette costs £1.99. How many can I buy for £10?
Explain how you work it out.
11. How many 26p stamps can I buy for £1?
Explain how you work it out.
12. I sell eggs in dozens. A dozen is 12. How many dozens can I make with 40 eggs?

• *Check your answers.*

# Section 4: Basic addition and subtraction

In this section you will practise adding and subtracting in your head.

### DEVELOPMENT

## D1: Find numbers that add up to ...

Level 3

*Fill in the missing numbers:*

| | | |
|---|---|---|
| 1. 1 + ...... = 8 | 2. ...... + 4 = 7 | 3. 2 + ...... = 9 |
| ...... + 3 = 8 | 2 + ...... = 7 | ...... + 4 = 9 |
| ...... + 2 = 8 | ...... + 6 = 7 | 6 + ...... = 9 |
| 4 + ...... = 8 | 2 + ...... = 6 | 4 + ...... = 11 |

| | | |
|---|---|---|
| 4. 4 + ...... = ☐ | 5. ...... + 5 = ☐ | 6. 3 + ...... = ☐ |
| ...... + 2 = 10 | 3 + ...... = 15 | ...... + 4 = 14 |
| ...... + 5 = ☐ | ...... + 8 = ☐ | 7 + ...... = ☐ |
| 7 + ...... = ☐ | 6 + ...... = ☐ | 9 + ...... = ☐ |

| | | |
|---|---|---|
| 7. 5 + ...... = ☐ | 8. ...... + 7 = ☐ | 9. 3 + ...... = ☐ |
| ...... + 14 = 20 | 9 + ...... = 18 | ...... + 4 = 12 |
| ...... + 17 = ☐ | ...... + 13 = ☐ | 7 + ...... = ☐ |
| 8 + ...... = ☐ | 3 + ...... = ☐ | 9 + ...... = ☐ |

| | | |
|---|---|---|
| 10. 8 + ...... = ☐ | 11. ...... + 6 = ☐ | 12. 10 + ...... = ☐ |
| ...... + 5 = 16 | 2 + ...... = 11 | ...... + 5 = 19 |
| ...... + 7 = ☐ | ...... + 4 = ☐ | 8 + ...... = ☐ |
| 4 + ...... = ☐ | 8 + ...... = ☐ | 6 + ...... = ☐ |

| | |
|---|---|
| 13. 8 + ...... + 4 = ☐ | 14. 7 + 6 + ...... = ☐ |
| 3 + 5 + ...... = ☐ | 2 + ...... + 10 = ☐ |
| ...... + 7 + 7 = ☐ | ...... + 9 + 7 = ☐ |
| 4 + ...... + 9 = 16 | 4 + ...... + 12 = 20 |
| 8 + 6 + ...... = ☐ | ...... + 6 + 9 = ☐ |
| ...... + 2 + 11 = ☐ | 8 + ...... + 8 = ☐ |
| 9 + ...... + 5 = ☐ | 10 + 4 + ...... = ☐ |
| ...... + 8 + 7 = ☐ | |

• *Check your answers.*

A POW GUIDE     page 14     Strategies for Improving **EXTRA**
Mental Arithmetic Skills

## P1: Addition tables

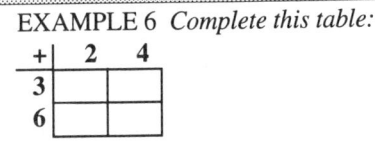

**PRACTICE** — Level 3

EXAMPLE 6 *Complete this table:*

| + | 2 | 4 |
|---|---|---|
| 3 |   |   |
| 6 |   |   |

| + | 2 | 4 |
|---|---|---|
| 3 | 5 | 7 |
| 6 | 8 | 10 |

(3+2) (3+4) (6+4) (6+2)

*Do-med*

*Fill in the missing numbers:*

1. 
| + | 5 | 7 |
|---|---|---|
| 4 |   |   |
| 2 |   |   |

2. 
| + | 6 | 9 |
|---|---|---|
| 2 |   |   |
| 5 |   |   |

3. 
| + | 7 | 3 |
|---|---|---|
| 8 |   |   |
| 4 |   |   |

4. 
| + | 13 | 3 |
|---|---|---|
| 4 |   |   |
| 5 |   |   |

5. 
| + | 5 | 9 |
|---|---|---|
| 5 |   |   |
| 6 |   |   |

6. 
| + | 11 | 6 |
|---|---|---|
| 7 |   |   |
| 4 |   |   |

7. 
| + | 3 | 18 |
|---|---|---|
| 12 |   |   |
| 2 |   |   |

8. 
| + | 15 | 8 |
|---|---|---|
| 4 |   |   |
| 5 |   |   |

9. 
| + | 5 | 3 |
|---|---|---|
| 16 |   |   |
| 11 |   |   |

10. 
| + | 2 | 4 |
|---|---|---|
| 13 |   |   |
| 16 |   |   |

11. 
| + | 4 | 7 |
|---|---|---|
| 12 |   |   |
| 9 |   |   |

12. 
| + | 6 | 5 |
|---|---|---|
| 8 |   |   |
| 7 |   |   |

13. 
| + | 9 | 8 |
|---|---|---|
| 7 |   |   |
| 6 |   |   |

14. 
| + | 9 | 7 |
|---|---|---|
| 9 |   |   |
| 8 |   |   |

15. 
| + | 6 | 8 |
|---|---|---|
| 9 |   |   |
| 4 |   |   |

16. 
| + | ... | 10 |
|---|---|---|
| 6 |   |   |
| 7 | 19 |   |

17. 
| + | 7 | ... |
|---|---|---|
| 14 |   | 20 |
| 12 |   |   |

18. 
| + | 4 | 9 |
|---|---|---|
| ... |   | 17 |
| 7 |   |   |

19. 
| + | 5 | 4 | 2 |
|---|---|---|---|
| 3 |   |   |   |
| 7 |   |   |   |
| 5 |   |   |   |

20. 
| + | 6 | 8 | 3 |
|---|---|---|---|
| 9 |   |   |   |
| 7 |   |   |   |
| 5 |   |   |   |

21. 
| + | 4 | ... | 7 |
|---|---|---|---|
| 3 | 8 |   |   |
| 6 |   |   |   |
| ... |   | 9 |   |

• *Check your answers.*

A POW GUIDE — page 15 — *Strategies for Improving Mental Arithmetic Skills* **EXTRA**

## P2: Row and column additions

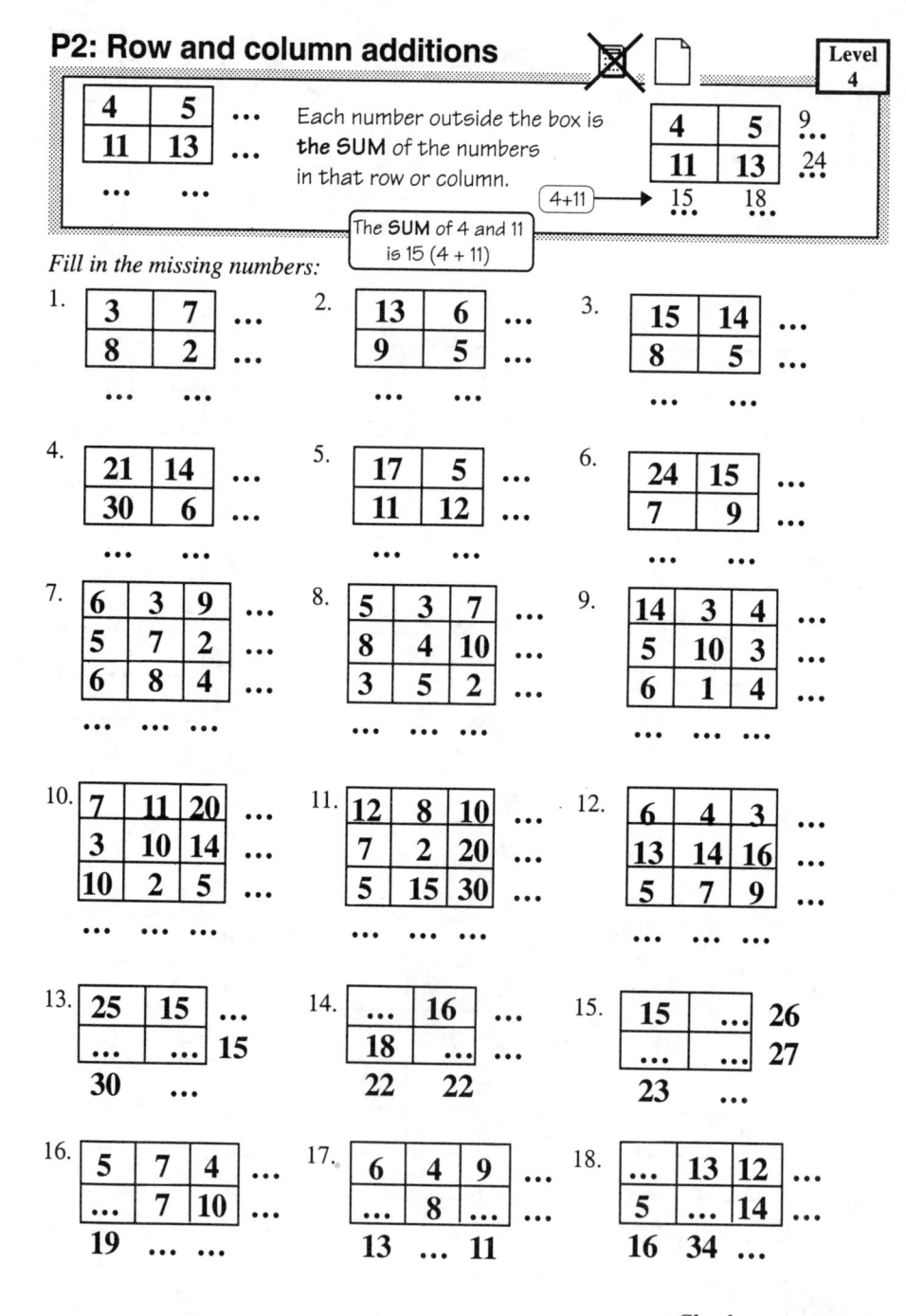

**Level 4**

| 4 | 5 | ... |
|---|---|---|
| 11 | 13 | ... |
| ... | ... | |

Each number outside the box is **the SUM** of the numbers in that row or column.

| 4 | 5 | 9 |
|---|---|---|
| 11 | 13 | 24 |
| 15 | 18 | |

4+11 → The SUM of 4 and 11 is 15 (4 + 11)

*Fill in the missing numbers:*

1.
| 3 | 7 | ... |
|---|---|---|
| 8 | 2 | ... |
| ... | ... | |

2.
| 13 | 6 | ... |
|---|---|---|
| 9 | 5 | ... |
| ... | ... | |

3.
| 15 | 14 | ... |
|---|---|---|
| 8 | 5 | ... |
| ... | ... | |

4.
| 21 | 14 | ... |
|---|---|---|
| 30 | 6 | ... |
| ... | ... | |

5.
| 17 | 5 | ... |
|---|---|---|
| 11 | 12 | ... |
| ... | ... | |

6.
| 24 | 15 | ... |
|---|---|---|
| 7 | 9 | ... |
| ... | ... | |

7.
| 6 | 3 | 9 | ... |
|---|---|---|---|
| 5 | 7 | 2 | ... |
| 6 | 8 | 4 | ... |
| ... | ... | ... | |

8.
| 5 | 3 | 7 | ... |
|---|---|---|---|
| 8 | 4 | 10 | ... |
| 3 | 5 | 2 | ... |
| ... | ... | ... | |

9.
| 14 | 3 | 4 | ... |
|---|---|---|---|
| 5 | 10 | 3 | ... |
| 6 | 1 | 4 | ... |
| ... | ... | ... | |

10.
| 7 | 11 | 20 | ... |
|---|---|---|---|
| 3 | 10 | 14 | ... |
| 10 | 2 | 5 | ... |
| ... | ... | ... | |

11.
| 12 | 8 | 10 | ... |
|---|---|---|---|
| 7 | 2 | 20 | ... |
| 5 | 15 | 30 | ... |
| ... | ... | ... | |

12.
| 6 | 4 | 3 | ... |
|---|---|---|---|
| 13 | 14 | 16 | ... |
| 5 | 7 | 9 | ... |
| ... | ... | ... | |

13.
| 25 | 15 | ... |
|---|---|---|
| ... | ... | 15 |
| 30 | ... | |

14.
| ... | 16 | ... |
|---|---|---|
| 18 | ... | ... |
| 22 | 22 | |

15.
| 15 | ... | 26 |
|---|---|---|
| ... | ... | 27 |
| 23 | ... | |

16.
| 5 | 7 | 4 | ... |
|---|---|---|---|
| ... | 7 | 10 | ... |
| 19 | ... | ... | |

17.
| 6 | 4 | 9 | ... |
|---|---|---|---|
| ... | 8 | ... | ... |
| 13 | ... | 11 | |

18.
| ... | 13 | 12 | ... |
|---|---|---|---|
| 5 | ... | 14 | ... |
| 16 | 34 | ... | |

• *Check your answers.*

A POW GUIDE    page 16    *Strategies for Improving Mental Arithmetic Skills* **EXTRA**

## P3: Connect-4 addition

**Rules**: Each person
- chooses two DIFFERENT numbers from the list on the left of the table
- says what they are <u>before picking up the calculator</u>
- adds them using a calculator
- puts a marker on a square with that sum if there is one available

The first person to get 4 markers in a straight line is the winner.

(OR – use the alternative version of the game described on p7)

**CONNECT FOUR GAME** Level 3

**A +**

| | | | | | | |
|---|---|---|---|---|---|---|
| 34 | 28 | 23 | 9 | 29 | 13 |

| 5 / 7 | 12 | 11 | 22 | 27 | 24 | 20 |
|---|---|---|---|---|---|---|
| 13 / 4 | 24 | 18 | 21 | 35 | 23 | 28 |
| 8 / 16 | 21 | 19 | 20 | 31 | 17 | 26 |
| 19 / 9 | 15 | 14 | 32 | 21 | 25 | 13 |
| 15 | 16 | 23 | 20 | 24 | 17 | 12 |

You have to work out which numbers will give you the total you want, before you are allowed to use a calculator. So, these games will improve your mental arithmetic skills!

**CONNECT FOUR GAME** Level 4

**B +**

| | | | | | | |
|---|---|---|---|---|---|---|
| 60 | 128 | 87 | 90 | 103 | 93 |

| 41 / 35 | 122 | 76 | 113 | 100 | 67 | 73 |
|---|---|---|---|---|---|---|
| 19 / 26 | 106 | 136 | 106 | 57 | 139 | 125 |
| 52 / 71 | 91 | 71 | 158 | 54 | 152 | 78 |
| 38 / 65 | 61 | 79 | 117 | 90 | 97 | 106 |
| 87 | 123 | 64 | 84 | 112 | 45 | 109 |

A POW GUIDE     Strategies for Improving Mental Arithmetic Skills   **EXTRA**

## Star Challenge 5

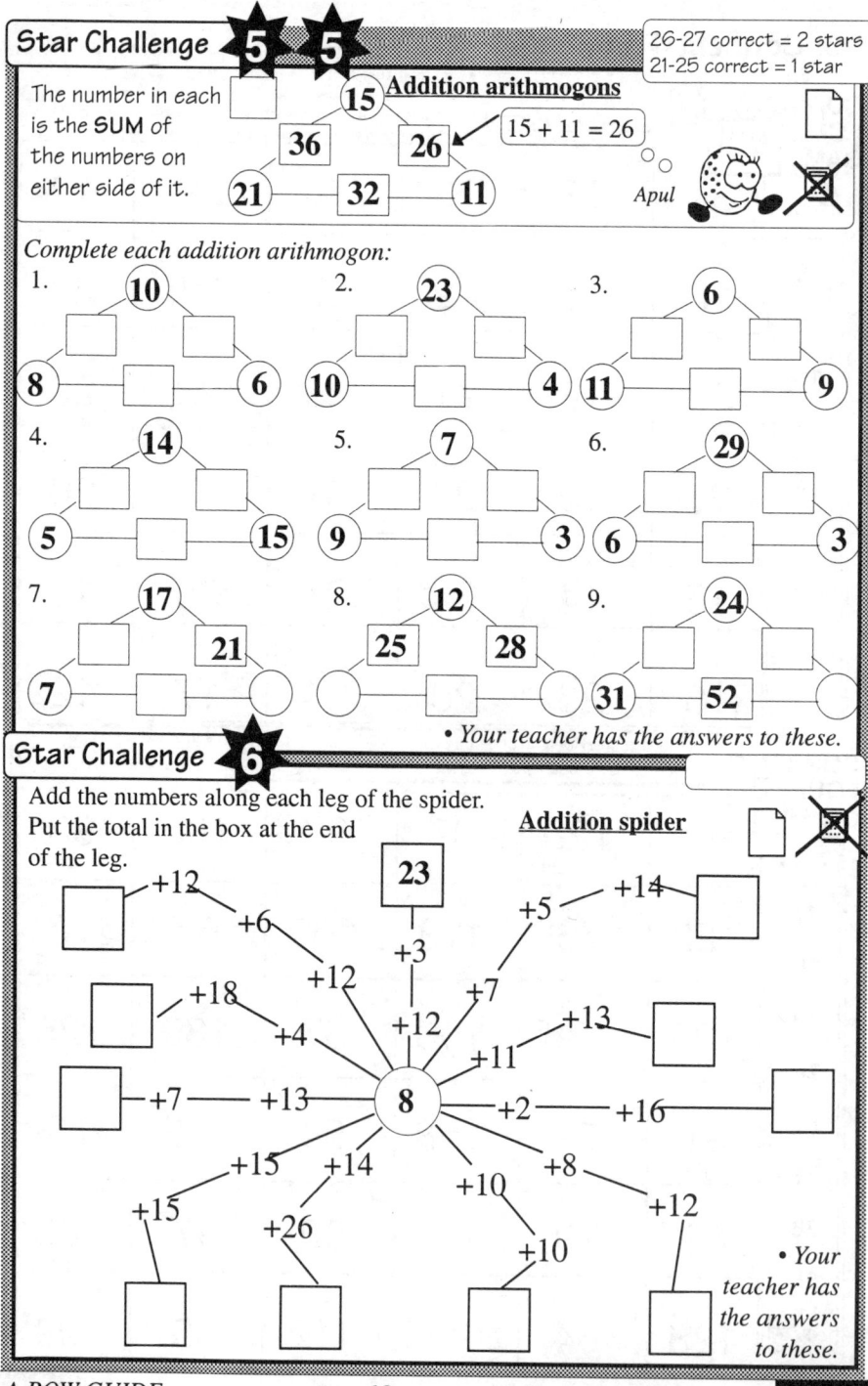

26-27 correct = 2 stars
21-25 correct = 1 star

**Addition arithmogons**

The number in each □ is the **SUM** of the numbers on either side of it.

Arithmogon example: top 15, middle row 36, 26, bottom row 21, 32, 11. $15 + 11 = 26$

Apul

*Complete each addition arithmogon:*

1. top: 10; bottom: 8, __, 6
2. top: 23; bottom: 10, __, 4
3. top: 6; bottom: 11, __, 9
4. top: 14; bottom: 5, __, 15
5. top: 7; bottom: 9, __, 3
6. top: 29; bottom: 6, __, 3
7. top: 17; middle right: 21; bottom: 7, __, __
8. top: 12; middle: 25, 28; bottom: __, __, __
9. top: 24; middle: 31, 52; bottom: __, __, __

• *Your teacher has the answers to these.*

## Star Challenge 6

**Addition spider**

Add the numbers along each leg of the spider. Put the total in the box at the end of the leg.

Center: 8

Legs with operations: +12, +6, +12, +3, +5, +14, +18, +4, +7, +12, +13, +7, +13, +11, +2, +16, +15, +14, +26, +10, +10, +8, +12, +15

Top box: 23

• *Your teacher has the answers to these.*

*A POW GUIDE*   page 18   *Strategies for Improving Mental Arithmetic Skills*   **EXTRA**

# THE NATIONAL CURRICULUM ...
# ... AND BEYOND ...

*Pow*

# Strategies for Improving Mental Arithmetic Skills
# EXTRA
## *Part 2*

> At the end of the first four sections, students should move straight onto Topic 2 "Back to Basics".
> The first topic test is done at the end of "Back to Basics".

### Part 2
### §5–§18 Strategies for Improving Mental Arithmetic Skills

Sections 5-18 should be tackled one section at a time at regular intervals through the school year. They cover all the basic mental arithmetic techniques that students ought to know. All students will be familiar with some of these techniques but there will also be some techniques which are weak or unknown. The aim is to find these gaps and fill them, hence boosting self-confidence as well as improving mental arithmetic expertise.

**Every lesson in Y9 should start with a short mental arithmetic test. These are provided in the Teachers' Resource Pack. After each section is completed, the class can move onto the next level of test, which will include skills/techniques just reviewed.**

| Level 3 | Level 4 | Level 5 | Level 6 |
|---------|---------|---------|---------|

A POW GUIDE

# Section 5: + and − shortcuts

**Level 3**

In this section you will review/learn some shortcuts for addition and subtraction.

### DEVELOPMENT

## D1: Adding tens, nines, elevens …

**Task 1:** *Copy and complete:*
1. 4 + 10 = …
2. 7 + 10 = …
3. 15 + 10 = …
4. 28 + 10 = …
5. 36 + 10 = …
6. 87 + 10 = …
7. 19 + 10 = …
8. 24 + 10 = …

• CHECK YOUR ANSWERS. *Do not go on to Task 2 until you can do these.*

### Task 2 – Adding 9

EXAMPLE 7    26 + 9 = ?    + 9 is the same as + 10 − 1
                            26 + 10 = 36
So   26 + 9 = 35   *Big Edd*    36 − 1 = 35

*Write down the answers to each of these:*
9. 4 + 9    10. 13 + 9    11. 46 + 9    12. 32 + 9    13. 54 + 9
14. 16 + 9    15. 25 + 9    16. 64 + 9    17. 72 + 9    18. 83 + 9

• Check your answers.

### Task 3 – Adding 11

EXAMPLE 8    37 + 11 = ?    + 11 is the same as + 10 + 1
                            37 + 10 = 47
So   37 + 11 = 48   *Pow*    47 + 1 = 48

*Write down the answers to each of these:*
19. 5 + 11    20. 16 + 11    21. 34 + 11    22. 78 + 11    23. 82 + 11

• Check your answers.

### Task 4 – Adding 19

+ 19 is the same as + 20 − 1    OR    + 19 is the same as + 10 + 10 − 1

*Write down the answers to each of these:*
24. 7 + 19    25. 18 + 19    26. 42 + 19    27. 67 + 19    28. 39 + 19

• Check your answers.

## Star Challenge 7

14-15 correct = 1 star

*Write down the answers to each of these:*
1. 7 + 9    2. 15 + 9    3. 36 + 9    4. 56 + 11    5. 18 + 11
6. 17 + 19    7. 35 + 19    8. 43 + 9    9. 43 + 19    10. 43 + 29
11. 84 + 9    12. 67 + 19    13. 28 + 9    14. 37 + 19    15. 72 + 9

• Your teacher has the answers to these.

*A POW GUIDE* — *Strategies for Improving Mental Arithmetic Skills* — **EXTRA**

# D2: Counting on and counting back in tens

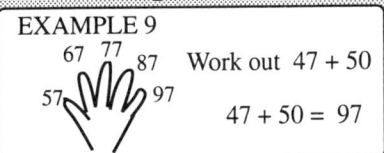

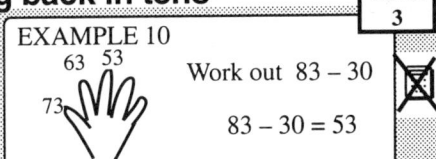

**Level 3**

**EXAMPLE 9**

Work out 47 + 50

47 + 50 = 97

**EXAMPLE 10**

Work out 83 – 30

83 – 30 = 53

**Task 1:** *Copy and complete:*
1. 30 + 20 = ...
2. 59 + 40 = ...
3. 43 + 50 = ...
4. 32 + 60 = ...
5. 90 – 10 = ...
6. 66 – 10 = ...
7. 85 – 30 = ...
8. 97 – 40 = ...
9. 35 + 60 = ...
10. 76 – 20 = ...
11. 38 + 40 = ...
12. 21 + 70 = ...

• Check your answers.

**Task 2: Adding 19, 29, ...**

EXAMPLE 6    34 + 29 = ?

So    34 + 29 = 63

Lubbly

+ 29 is the same as + 30 – 1
34 + 30 = 64
64 – 1 = 63

*Write down the answers to each of these:*
13. 27 + 19
14. 43 + 39
15. 38 + 29
16. 17 + 49
17. 68 + 19
18. 52 + 39
19. 17 + 29
20. 13 + 49
21. 58 + 39
22. 88 + 19

• Check your answers.

**Task 3 : Subtracting 9, 19, 29, ...**

EXAMPLE 11    37 – 19 = ?

So    37 – 19 = 18

Taz

– 19 is the same as – 20 + 1
37 – 20 = 17
17 + 1 = 18

*Write down the answers to each of these:*
23. 55 – 19
24. 83 – 29
25. 93 – 49
26. 66 – 29
27. 71 – 39

• Check your answers

**Task 4: A mixture of these techniques**

*Write down the answers to each of these:*
28. 33 + 40
29. 64 – 19
30. 27 + 59
31. 78 – 29
32. 83 + 19
33. 29 + 29
34. 75 – 49
35. 28 – 19
36. 60 + 39
37. 70 – 20

• Check your answers.

## Star Challenge 8

14-15 correct = 1 star

*Write down the answers to each of these:*
1. 27 – 9
2. 45 + 50
3. 68 + 29
4. 57 – 19
5. 30 + 50
6. 80 – 30
7. 55 + 19
8. 86 – 39
9. 70 + 19
10. 50 – 29
11. 38 + 39
12. 100 – 20
13. 71 + 19
14. 54 – 39
15. 60 + 20 – 39

• Your teacher has the answers to these.

A POW GUIDE          page 21          Strategies for Improving **EXTRA**
                                      Mental Arithmetic Skills

# Section 6: + and − technique review

**Level 3**

In this section you will review some addition and subtraction techniques.

### DEVELOPMENT

## D1: Crossing the tens boundary

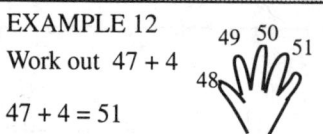

EXAMPLE 12
Work out 47 + 4
49 50 51
48
47 + 4 = 51

EXAMPLE 13
Work out 82 − 4 
80 79 78
81
82 − 4 = 78

Write down the answers to each of these:
1. 56 + 5   2. 28 + 4   3. 36 + 6   4. 16 + 7   5. 38 + 8
6. 23 − 5   7. 42 − 4   8. 65 − 7   9. 91 − 3   10. 46 − 9

• Check your answers.

## D2: Adding by splitting up numbers

EXAMPLE 14  Work out 30 + 56

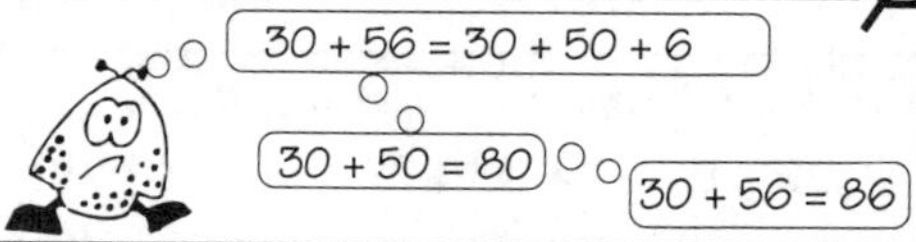

30 + 56 = 30 + 50 + 6
30 + 50 = 80
30 + 56 = 86

So   30 + 56 = 86
*Dwork*

Write down the answers to each of these:
1. 50 + 27   2. 30 + 68   3. 20 + 56   4. 60 + 29   5. 40 + 36

EXAMPLE 15  Work out 43 + 36

43 + 36 = 40 + 3 + 30 + 6
40 + 30 = 70 and 3 + 6 = 9
43 + 36 = 79

So   43 + 36 = 79
*Flumpf*

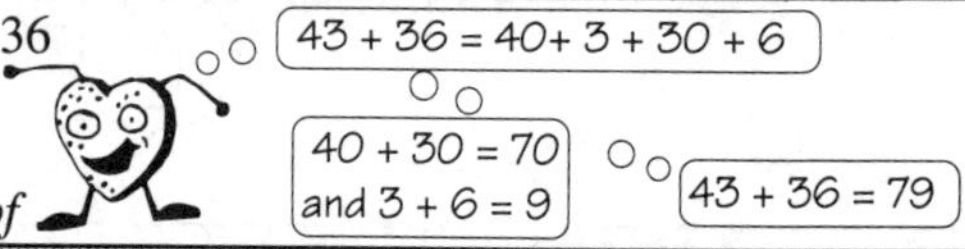

6. 23 + 35   7. 37 + 42   8. 42 + 34   9. 61 + 27   10. 56 + 33
11. 37 + 42   12. 65 + 33   13. 27 + 43   14. 25 + 25   15. 62 + 18
16. 28 + 45   17. 74 + 28   18. 39 + 52   19. 48 + 27   20. 59 + 36

• Check your answers.

## D3: Subtracting by splitting up numbers

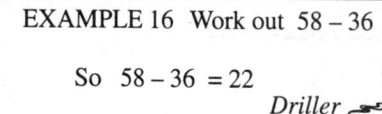

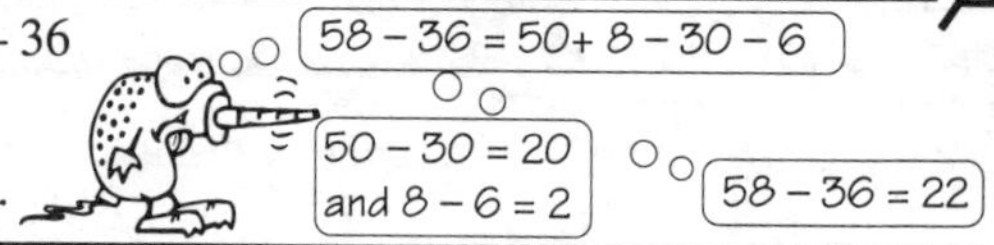

EXAMPLE 16  Work out 58 − 36

58 − 36 = 50 + 8 − 30 − 6
50 − 30 = 20 and 8 − 6 = 2
58 − 36 = 22

So   58 − 36 = 22
*Driller*

Write down the answers to each of these:
1. 49 − 27   2. 65 − 32   3. 28 − 15   4. 46 − 31   5. 69 − 34
6. 36 − 23   7. 97 − 42   8. 75 − 35   9. 93 − 52   10. 76 − 36

• Check your answers

A POW GUIDE      Strategies for Improving **EXTRA**
Mental Arithmetic Skills

## D4: Related number statements

**Level 3**

$3 + 5 = 8$ tells us that
$5 + 3 = 8$
$8 - 3 = 5$
$8 - 5 = 3$

If you are given any one of these statements, you should be able to write down the other three statements.

*Apul*

1. $5 + 6 = 11$
   Write down the three number statements related to this.
2. $12 - 3 = 9$
   Write down the three number statements related to this.
3. (a) *Copy and complete this statement:* $34 + 25 = \ldots$
   (b) Write down the three number statements related to this.
4. (a) *Copy and complete this statement:* $87 - 54 = \ldots$
   (b) Write down the three number statements related to this.

• *Check your answers.*

5. $15 + 7 = 22$
   *Copy and complete:* $22 - 7 = \ldots$   $22 - 15 = \ldots$
6. $32 + 59 = 91$
   *Copy and complete:* $91 - 59 = \ldots$   $91 - 32 = \ldots$
7. $67 - 43 = 24$
   *Copy and complete:* $24 + 43 = \ldots$   $67 - 24 = \ldots$   • *Check your answers.*

### PRACTICE
## P1: Completing number statements

*Copy and complete:*
1. $45 + 14 = \ldots$
2. $37 + \ldots = 49$
3. $65 + \ldots = 98$
4. $59 - 32 = \ldots$
5. $80 - \ldots = 77$
6. $58 - \ldots = 33$
7. $88 - \ldots = 55$
8. $56 + \ldots = 68$
9. $56 - \ldots = 24$
10. $\ldots + 13 = 63$
11. $\ldots - 5 = 35$
12. $21 + 49 = \ldots$
13. $70 + 23 = \ldots$
14. $84 + 8 = \ldots$
15. $72 - \ldots = 68$
16. $73 - 14 = \ldots$

• *Check your answers.*

### Star Challenge 9 9

22-23 correct = 2 stars
18-21 correct = 1 star

*Write down the answers to each of these:*
1. $67 + 6$
2. $41 - 7$
3. $30 + 54$
4. $63 + 26$
5. $57 + 42$
6. $57 - 23$
7. $38 - 14$
8. $85 + 14$
9. $58 - 17$
10. $75 + 16$
11. $91 - 20$
12. $48 + 25$
13. $84 - 22$
14. $65 + 15$
15. $45 + 20 + 25$

*Copy and complete:*
16. $35 + 23 = \ldots$
17. $46 + \ldots = 59$
18. $37 + \ldots = 68$
19. $64 - 32 = \ldots$
20. $77 - \ldots = 53$
21. $39 - \ldots = 13$
22. $65 - \ldots = 50$
23. $29 + \ldots = 44$

• *Your teacher has the answers to these.*

*A POW GUIDE*   page 23   *Strategies for Improving Mental Arithmetic Skills*   **EXTRA**

# Section 7: Doubling and halving

Levels 3 & 4

In this section you will practice doubling and halving.

**DEVELOPMENT**

## D1: Doubling and halving

| Double 20 = 20 + 20 = 40 |   | Half of 40 = 20 |

You need to KNOW the doubles of all numbers up to 20 and the doubles of 25, 30, 35, 40, ...95, 100

Copy and complete:
1. Double 10 = ......
2. Double 4 = ......
3. Double 14 = ......
4. Double 18 = ......
5. Double 6 = ......
6. Double 15 = ......
7. Double 19 = ......
8. Double 55 = ......
9. Double 75 = ......
10. Double 95 = ......
11. Half of 20 = ......
12. Half of 30 = ......
13. Half of 200 = ......
14. Half of 80 = ......
15. Half of 34 = ......
16. Half of 18 = ......
17. Double... = 60
18. Half of ... = 140
19. Double 55 + double 15 = ...
20. Half of 14 + half of 10 = ......
21. Double 6 + double 15 = ......
22. Half of 26 + double 5 = ......
23. Double 35 + half of 50 = ......

• Check your answers.

## D2: Halves of odd numbers and their doubles

| Half of 6 = 3 | Half of 7 = $3\frac{1}{2}$ | Half of 8 = 4 |

You ought to KNOW the halves of all odd numbers up to 30

Copy and complete:
1. Half of 3 = ......
2. Half of 5 = ......
3. Half of 9 = ......
4. Half of 21 = ......
5. Half of 15 = ......
6. Double $2\frac{1}{2}$ = ......
7. Double $3\frac{1}{2}$ = ......
8. Double $5\frac{1}{2}$ = ......
9. Double $10\frac{1}{2}$ = ......

• Check your answers.

## D3: Using doubles as shortcuts

EXAMPLE 17    Work out 30 + 31 using doubles

30 + 31 = double 30 + 1 = 60 + 1 = 61

So 30 + 31 = 61                              Big Edd

Copy and complete:
1. 25 + 26 = double ... + 1 = ......
2. 30 + 40 = double ... + 10 = ...
3. 25 + 30 = double ... + 5 = ...
4. 48 + 50 = double ... − 2 = ...
5. 33 + 30 = double ... + 3 = ...
6. 39 + 41 = double ... = ...

• Check answers.

### Star Challenge 10

Copy and complete:                          All correct = 1 star

1. Double 12 + half of 4 = ...
2. Half of 13 = ...
3. Half of 20 + half of 10 = ...
4. Double 40 = ......
5. Double ... = 130
6. Double $7\frac{1}{2}$ = ......
7. Double ... + 3 = 63
8. Double ... + 5 = 145
9. 21 + 20 = double ... + 1 = ...

A POW GUIDE    page 24    Strategies for Improving Mental Arithmetic Skills    EXTRA

# Section 8: Words and numbers

Levels 3 & 4

In this section you will review some of the problem areas when writing numbers.

## DEVELOPMENT

### D1: What does the ... stand for?

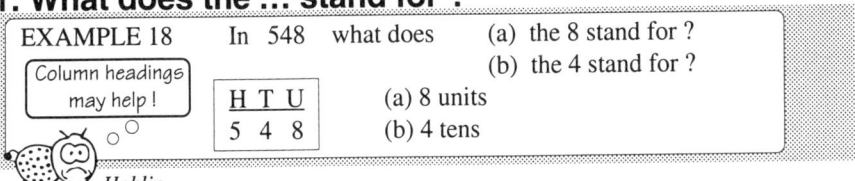

EXAMPLE 18    In 548 what does    (a) the 8 stand for?
Column headings may help!                       (b) the 4 stand for?

| H | T | U |
|---|---|---|
| 5 | 4 | 8 |

(a) 8 units
(b) 4 tens

*Hoblin*

1. In 359 what does (a) the 3 stand for? (b) the 9 stand for?
2. In 407 what does (a) the 7 stand for? (b) the 0 stand for?
3. In 510 what does (a) the 1 stand for? (b) the 0 stand for?
4. In 501 what does (a) the 1 stand for? (b) the 0 stand for?
5. In 2035 what does (a) the 3 stand for? (b) the 0 stand for?    • Check answers.

### D2: Numbers and words

1. Copy and complete this table:

| Th | H | T | U | in words |
|----|---|---|---|----------|
|    | 2 | 0 | 1 | two hundred and one |
|    |   |   |   | two hundred and ten |
|    |   |   |   | three hundred and six |
|    | 5 | 3 | 0 | five hundred and thirty |
|    |   |   |   | six hundred and forty |
|    |   |   |   | seven hundred and fifteen |
|    |   |   |   | nine hundred and six |
|    |   |   |   | nine hundred and sixty |
|    | 7 | 2 | 5 |          |
|    | 4 | 0 | 3 |          |
|    | 6 | 7 | 0 |          |
|    | 7 | 1 | 0 |          |
|    | 9 | 0 | 5 |          |

2. Copy and complete this table:

| Th | H | T | U | in words |
|----|---|---|---|----------|
| 1  | 2 | 0 | 4 | 1 thousand, 2 hundred and 4 |
|    |   |   |   | 2 thousand and 5 |
|    |   |   |   | 2 thousand and fifty |
|    |   |   |   | 3 thousand, 1 hundred and 3 |
|    |   |   |   | 3 thousand, 1 hundred and thirty |
| 2  | 5 | 0 | 0 | 2 thousand 5 hundred |
|    |   |   |   | 2 thousand 5 hundred and 4 |
|    |   |   |   | 2 thousand 5 hundred and forty |
|    |   |   |   | 3 thousand and ten |
| 4  | 0 | 0 | 9 |          |
| 3  | 1 | 0 | 0 |          |
| 7  | 0 | 2 | 3 |          |
| 6  | 0 | 4 | 0 |          |

• Check your answers.

### D3: Reading big numbers

There are two ways of writing big numbers

2,356,741  (gaps every 3 digits) or (commas every 3 digits)  3,578,642

million  thousand
2 million 356 thousand 741

Where the commas/gaps are you say "million" or "thousand"

million  thousand
3 million 578 thousand 642

How would you read each of these numbers?

1. 3 468    2. 2 025    3. 7 990    4. 12 451    5. 25 001
6. 245 346    7. 32 030    8. 1 231 435    9. 2 001 352    10. 25 200 310

• Check your answers.

A POW GUIDE        page 25        Strategies for Improving Mental Arithmetic Skills    **EXTRA**

# Section 9: + and − with 3-digit numbers   Level 4

In this section you will review arithmetic techniques with 3-digit numbers.

## DEVELOPMENT

### D1: + and − single digit numbers to 3-digit numbers

EXAMPLE 19
Work out $365 + 4$
$365 + 4 = 369$

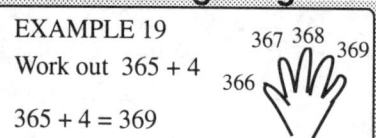

EXAMPLE 20
Work out $248 − 4$
$248 − 4 = 244$

Write down the answers to each of these:
1. $713 + 5$   2. $640 + 4$   3. $258 + 6$   4. $302 + 7$   5. $421 + 8$
6. $648 − 5$   7. $118 − 4$   8. $209 − 7$   9. $194 − 3$   10. $329 − 9$
   • Check your answers.
11. $346 + 6$   12. $218 + 5$   13. $418 + 3$   14. $672 − 3$   15. $496 − 8$
16. $630 − 2$   17. $274 + 7$   18. $312 − 8$   19. $584 + 9$   20. $961 − 7$
   • Check your answers.

### D2: Adding 2-digit numbers to multiples of 100

$200 + 35 = 235$

Copy and complete:
1. $300 + 45 = \ldots$   2. $100 + \ldots = 157$   3. $65 + \ldots = 365$   4. $68 + 400 = \ldots$
5. $91 + \ldots = 791$   6. $75 + \ldots = 775$   7. $600 + \ldots = 645$   8. $72 + 500 = \ldots$
9. $99 + \ldots = 999$   10. $\ldots + 13 = 213$   11. $\ldots + 200 = 271$   12. $\ldots + 87 = 187$
   • Check your answers.

### D3: Adding 3-digit numbers to multiples of 100

EXAMPLE 21   Work out $200 + 376$

$200 + 376 = 200 + 300 + 76$
$200 + 300 = 500$
$200 + 356 = 576$

So $200 + 376 = 576$ 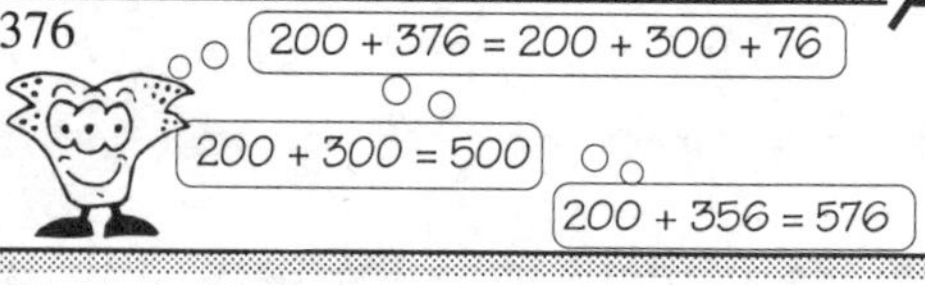
   Fission

Write down the answers to each of these:
1. $500 + 127$   2. $300 + 468$   3. $700 + 261$   4. $600 + 129$   5. $400 + 236$
   • Check your answers.

### Star Challenge 11

13-14 correct = 1 star

Write down the answers to each of these:
1. $267 + 6$   2. $305 + 8$   3. $528 − 3$   4. $600 + 26$   5. $300 + 542$
6. $240 − 3$   7. $721 − 6$   8. $159 + 200$   9. $623 + 100$   10. $325 − 7$

Copy and complete:
11. $400 + \ldots = 472$   12. $\ldots + 700 = 759$   13. $64 + \ldots = 664$   14. $357 + 6 = \ldots$

# Section 10: Crossing the hundreds boundary

In this section you will:
- add and subtract numbers across the hundreds boundary;
- using counting on/back to add or subtract numbers which are close together.

Level 4

## DEVELOPMENT

### D1: With and without number lines

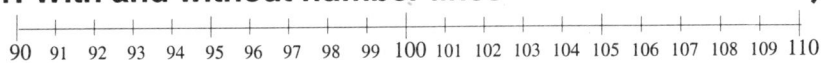

|—+—+—+—+—+—+—+—+—+—+—+—+—+—+—+—+—+—+—+—+—|
90  91  92  93  94  95  96  97  98  99  100  101  102  103  104  105  106  107  108  109  110

*Write down the answers to each of these:*

1. 95 + 6
2. 98 + 7
3. 102 – 5
4. 109 – 10
5. 96 + 11
6. 105 – 10
7. 101 – 4
8. 107 – 8
9. 93 + 8
10. 100 – 6

• Check your answers.

|—+—+—+—+—+—+—+—+—+—+—+—+—+—+—+—+—+—+—+—+—|
290                          300                          310

11. Copy and complete this number line.

*Write down the answers to each of these:*

12. 298 + 5
13. 291 + 12
14. 303 – 6
15. 309 – 10
16. 294 + 7
17. 307 – 8
18. 299 + 11
19. 302 – 8
20. 305 – 9
21. 289 + 15

• Check your answers.

*Write down the answers to each of these:*

22. 505 – 10
23. 497 + 5
24. 392 + 11
25. 795 + 10
26. 797 + 5
27. 603 – 8
28. 402 – 7
29. 408 – 11
30. 495 + 8
31. 896 + 12

• Check your answers.

### D2: Counting on and back when numbers are close together

EXAMPLE 22
388 + ... = 393
Missing number is 5
(400 401 402 399 403)

EXAMPLE 23
Work out 502 – 499 = ...
502 – 499 = 3
(500 499 501)

*Copy and complete:*

1. 276 + ... = 282
2. 605 – ... = 598
3. 703 – 696 = ...
4. 419 + ... = 426
5. 487 + ... = 496
6. 824 – ... = 819
7. 658 + ... = 663
8. 898 + ... = 909

• Check your answers.

### Star Challenge 12

13-14 correct = 1 star

*Write down the answers to each of these:*

1. 96 + 7
2. 101 – 7
3. 406 – 8
4. 798 + 8
5. 731 – 724
6. 701 – 5
7. 642 – 639
8. 97 + 7
9. 401 – 396
10. 325 + 8

*Copy and complete:*

11. 238 + ... = 244
12. ... + 516 = 522
13. 702 + ... = 711
14. 295 + ... = 302

A POW GUIDE        Strategies for Improving Mental Arithmetic Skills        EXTRA

# Section 11: + & − techniques for large numbers

In this section you will:
- add and subtract 10s to/from 2- and 3-digit numbers;
- add and subtract two multiples of 10 crossing the hundreds boundaries;
- add and subtract multiples of 10 to/from 3-digit numbers;
- add and subtract 9, 19, 29, … 11, 21, 31, … to/from 3 digit numbers.

Levels 3 & 4

### DEVELOPMENT
### D1: + and − 10 to/from 2- & 3-digit numbers

65 + 10 = 75     231 + 10 = 241     302 + 10 = 312

Adding 10 puts the tens digit up 1
*Lubbly*

Write down the answers to each of these:
1. 75 + 10   2. 231 + 10   3. 104 + 10   4. 340 + 10   5. 73 + 10
6. 730 + 10   7. 48 + 10   8. 724 + 10   9. 695 + 10   10. 970 + 10

• Check your answers.

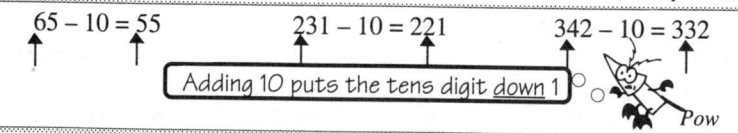

65 − 10 = 55     231 − 10 = 221     342 − 10 = 332

Adding 10 puts the tens digit down 1
*Pow*

Write down the answers to each of these:
11. 84 − 10   12. 478 − 10   13. 124 − 10   14. 560 − 10   15. 198 − 10

• Check your answers.

Copy and complete:
16. 371 + … = 381   17. … + 10 = 598   18. 743 − 10 = …   19. 469 + … = 479
20. 298 + … = 308   21. … + 10 = 706   22. … − 10 = 304   23. 898 + 10 = …

• Check your answers.

### D2: + and − two multiples of 10

40 + 70 = 110    4 + 7 = 11        12 − 4 = 8       120 − 40 = 80
*Spottee*

Write down the answers to each of these:
1. 70 + 20   2. 80 + 20   3. 80 + 30   4. 120 + 40   5. 90 + 60
6. 130 − 20   7. 150 − 40   8. 140 − 50   9. 310 + 50   10. 280 + 40

Copy and complete:
11. 50 + 60 = …   12. 90 + … = 120   13. 120 − 40 = …   14. … + 20 = 110
15. 130 − … = 90   16. … + 50 = 130   17. … − 50 = 60   18. … + 80 = 150

• Check your answers.

A POW GUIDE   page 28   Strategies for Improving **EXTRA**
Mental Arithmetic Skills

## D3: + and − multiples of 10 to a 3-digit number
**Levels 3 & 4**

255 + 30 = 285   281 − 40 = 241   302 + 70 = 372

(Adding 30 puts the tens digit up 3)   (Taking 40 puts the tens digit down 4)   (Adding 70 puts the tens digit up 7)

Write down the answers to each of these:
1. 125 + 30   2. 472 + 20   3. 296 − 30   4. 540 + 50   5. 815 + 60
6. 830 − 20   7. 469 + 30   8. 805 + 80   9. 785 − 60   10. 890 − 80

• Check your answers.

365 + 50 = 415      238 − 40 = 198
(36 + 5 = 41)      (23 − 4 = 19)
*Letmewin*

Write down the answers to each of these:
11. 195 + 30   12. 234 − 40   13. 184 + 50   14. 672 + 30   15. 556 + 80
16. 263 + 50   17. 402 − 60   18. 742 − 50   19. 389 + 20   20. 728 − 40

• Check your answers.

## D4: + and − 9, 19, 29, …
**Task 1: Adding 19, 29, …**

EXAMPLE 24
345 + 29 = ?
So   345 + 29 = 374   *Gizmo*

345 + 29 = 345 + 30 − 1
345 + 30 = 375
345 + 29 = 374

Write down the answers to each of these:
1. 327 + 19   2. 543 + 39   3. 238 + 29   4. 617 + 49   5. 168 + 19
6. 752 + 39   7. 317 + 29   8. 513 + 49   9. 158 + 39   10. 688 + 19

• Check your answers.

**Task 2: Subtracting 9, 19, 29, …**

EXAMPLE 25
471 − 19 = ?
So   471 − 19 = 452   *Frizzbang*

471 − 19 = 471 − 20 + 1
471 − 20 = 451
471 − 19 = 452

Write down the answers to each of these:
11. 255 − 19   12. 183 − 29   13. 593 − 49   14. 266 − 29   15. 871 − 39

• Check your answers.

**Star Challenge**

14-15 correct = 1 star

Write down the answers to each of these:
1. 327 − 9   2. 145 + 50   3. 768 + 29   4. 257 − 19   5. 230 + 50
6. 480 − 30   7. 255 + 19   8. 70 + 70   9. 270 + 19   10. 350 − 29
11. 738 + 39   12. 400 − 20   13. 871 + 19   14. 154 − 39   15. 258 − 39

• Your teacher has the answers to these.

A POW GUIDE   page 29   Strategies for Improving **EXTRA**
Mental Arithmetic Skills

# Section 12: Number pairs

**Levels 3 & 4**

In this section you will:
- recognise number pairs that add up to 10, 100, 1000, 20, 30, ...200, 300 ...
- use number pairs as addition shortcuts.

**DEVELOPMENT**

## D1: Number pairs that add up to 10, 100, 1000

**Task 1:** *Join up any number pairs that add up to 10*

| A | B | C | D |
|---|---|---|---|
| 8  2 / 5 / 3  5 | 7  5 / 4 / 6  3 | 9  8 / 2 / 1  7 | 4  5 / 7 / 3  6  5 |

**Task 2:** *Join up any number pairs that add up to 100*

| E | F | G | H |
|---|---|---|---|
| 55 / 45 / 50  50 | 70  30 / 40 / 80  20 | 40  100 / 60 / 25  75  70 | 40 / 10  50 / 90  80 / 20  60 |

| I | J | K | L |
|---|---|---|---|
| 11  79 / 35 / 65  45  89 | 48  25 / 67 / 77  33 / 52  75 | 19  55 / 9  45 / 72 / 18  28  81 | 51  49 / 29  23 / 61 / 77  59 |

**Task 3:** *Join up any number pairs that add up to 1000*

| M | N | P | Q |
|---|---|---|---|
| 900  800 / 600 / 200  100  400 | 600  300 / 250  800  750 / 200  700 | 50  350  650 / 250  750 / 950  400  600 | 290 / 710  550 / 960  650 / 350  450  40 |

**Task 4:** *Join up pairs that add up to 20*   **Task 5:** *Join up pairs that add up to 30*

| R | S | T | U |
|---|---|---|---|
| 15  17 / 6  10 / 3  5  14 | 4  6 / 13  7  14 / 16  15 | 25  26  8 / 5  16 / 28  14  2 | 5 / 21  25  17 / 13  15  15 / 9 |

### Star Challenge ⭐14⭐14

*Complete these number statements:*

- Check your answers.
- 14-15 correct = 2 stars
- 10-13 correct = 1 star

1. 7 + ...... = 10
2. 15 + ...... = 20
3. 15 + ...... = 30
4. 75 + ...... = 100
5. 25 + ...... = 30
6. 200 + ...... = 1000
7. 26 + ...... = 40
8. 30 + ...... = 100
9. 49 + ...... = 100
10. 150 + ...... = 200
11. 27 + ...... = 50
12. 66 + ...... = 80
13. 19 + ...... = 30
14. 350 + ...... = 1000
15. 930 + ...... = 1000

*A POW GUIDE*   *Strategies for Improving Mental Arithmetic Skills*   **EXTRA**

# D2: The number pair shortcut

**Levels 3 & 4**

**Task 1:** *Join any pairs of numbers that add up to 10. Use the pairs to help you find the SUM of the numbers in the box. The first one has been done for you.*

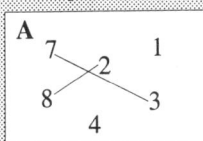

**A** 7, 1, 2, 8, 3, 4   Sum = ...25...

**B** 4, 6, 3, 5, 5, 1   Sum = ........

**C** 4, 8, 7, 2, 6, 3   Sum = ........

**D** 8, 6, 7, 2, 3, 4, 2   Sum = ........

**Task 2:** *Join any pairs of numbers that add up to 10, 20, 30 ... Find the sum of the numbers in each box.*

**E** 17, 8, 2, 24, 6, 3   Sum = ........

**F** 25, 17, 1, 6, 14, 13, 5   Sum = ........

**G** 19, 5, 11, 35, 12, 18, 7   Sum = ........

**H** 19, 11, 5, 6, 3, 27, 14   Sum = ........

**Task 3:** *Join any pairs of numbers that add up to 100. Find the sum in each box.*

**I** 40, 30, 45, 60, 55, 6   Sum = ........

**J** 90, 30, 10, 80, 70   Sum = ........

**K** 50, 50, 75, 25, 40, 100   Sum = ........

**L** 60, 40, 73, 20, 80, 90, 10, 27   Sum = ........

• Check your answers.

## Star Challenge 15

*All correct = 1 star*

Join any pairs of numbers that add up to 10, 20, 30 or 100. Find the sum of the numbers in each box.

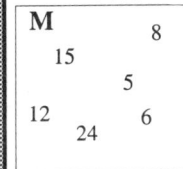

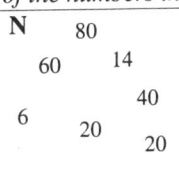

**M** 8, 15, 5, 12, 6, 24   Sum = ........

**N** 80, 60, 14, 40, 6, 20, 20   Sum = ........

**T** 150, 15, 15, 50, 13, 7, 50   Sum = ........

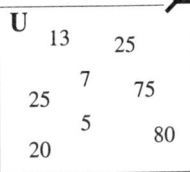

**U** 13, 25, 7, 25, 75, 5, 20, 80   Sum = ........

## Star Challenge 16

*11-14 marks = 1 star*

Circle any pairs of numbers that add up to 10, 20, 30... 100. Write down the total of each set of numbers. The first one has been done for you.

1. (27) + 36 + (13) = 76
2. 5 + 8 + 5 = ......
3. 45 + 5 + 29 = ......
4. 61 + 12 + 4 + 8 = ......
5. 33 + 16 + 17 = ......
6. 38 + 25 + 15 = ......
7. 40 + 29 + 60 = ......
8. 47 + 80 + 20 + 1 = ......

1 mark for correct circling
1 mark for correct answer

A POW GUIDE  page 31  Strategies for Improving Mental Arithmetic Skills  **EXTRA**

# Section 13: Multiplication and division techniques

In this section you will:
- multiply and divide whole numbers by 10, 100, 1000
- multiply by 2, 3, 4, 5 or 10

Level 4

### DEVELOPMENT

## D1: x and ÷ whole numbers by 10, 100, 1000

23 x 10 = 30     23 x 100 = 2300     23 x 1000 = 23000

Copy and complete:
1. 5 x 10 = ...
2. 42 x 10 = ...
3. 6 x ... = 600
4. 83 x 100 = ...
5. 15 x 1000 = ...
6. 17 x ... = 170
7. ... x 100 = 2300
8. 54 x ... = 5400
9. 9 x ... = 9000
10. ... x 58 = 580
11. 101 x 10 = ...
12. ... x 10 = 100

- Check answers.

5700 ÷ 10 = 570     5700 ÷ 100 = 57     30 000 ÷ 1000 = 30

Copy and complete:
13. 60 ÷ 10 = ...
14. 350 ÷ 10 = ...
15. ... ÷ 10 = 49
16. 3100 ÷ 100 = ...
17. 150 ÷ 10 = ...
18. 200 ÷ 10 = ...
19. ... ÷ 100 = 15
20. 7000 ÷ ... = 700
21. 1100 ÷ ... = 110
22. ... ÷ 1000 = 7

- Check answers.

## D2: x 2-digit multiples of 10 by 2, 3, 4 or 5

2 x 3 = 6     4 x 4 = 16
20 x 3 = 60     400 x 4 = 1600

Copy and complete:
1. 50 x 3 = ...
2. 40 x 2 = ...
3. 40 x ... = 120
4. 80 x 2 = ...
5. 120 x 5 = ...
6. ... x 3 = 210
7. 90 x 5 = ...
8. 23 x 3 = ...
9. 110 x 5 = ...
10. 70 x 5 = ...
11. 200 x 4 = ...
12. 600 x 3 = ...

- Check answers.

## D3: x 2-digit number by 2, 3, 4 or 5

21 x 4 = 84     41 x 5 = 205     12 x 3 = 36

Copy and complete:
1. 51 x 3 = ...
2. 44 x 2 = ...
3. 31 x ... = 124
4. 61 x 3 = ...
5. 71 x 5 = ...
6. ... x 3 = 96
7. 91 x 5 = ...
8. 22 x 3 = ...
9. 62 x 4 = ...
10. 54 x 2 = ...
11. 43 x 4 = ...
12. 72 x 3 = ...

- Check answers.

### Star Challenge 17

11-12 correct = 1 star

Copy and complete:
1. 14 x 2 = ...
2. 14 x 10 = ...
3. 1400 ÷ 100 = ...
4. 17 x 2 = ...
5. 200 x 10 = ...
6. ... x 4 = 84
7. 61 x 10 = ...
8. 61 x 4 = ...
9. 25 x 2 = ...
10. 250 ÷ 10 = ...
11. 35 x 10 = ...
12. 81 x 2 = ...

A POW GUIDE     Strategies for Improving Mental Arithmetic Skills     EXTRA

# Section 14: More doubling and halving  [Level 4]

In this section you will:
- extend doubling to bigger numbers;
- use doubling and halving in a variety of ways.

**DEVELOPMENT**

> You need to KNOW the doubles of all numbers up to 50 and the doubles of 10, 20, 30, 40, ...500 and 100, 200, ... 5000

## D1: Doubling bigger numbers

Double 45 = 45 + 45 = 90      Half of 45 = $22\frac{1}{2}$

> You need to KNOW the halves of all odd numbers up to 50 and the halves of 30, 50, 70, 90, ...190 and 300, 500, ... 1900

Copy and complete:
1. Double 40 = ......
2. Double 49 = ......
3. Double 26 = ......
4. Double 42 = ......
5. Double 150 = ......
6. Double 430 = ......
7. Double 4 000 = ......
8. Double 3 700 = ......
9. Half of 800 = ......
10. Half of 750 = ......
11. Half of 29 = ......
12. Half of 45 = ......
13. Double... = 60
14. Half of ... = $17\frac{1}{2}$
15. Double 44 + half 44 = ...
16. Half of 27 + half of 10 = ......
17. Double $2\frac{1}{2}$ + double 15 = ......
18. Half of 70 + double 11 = ......
19. Double 48 + half of 5 = ......

Hint: Double 39 = double 40 – 2

• Check your answers.

## D2: Repeated doubling and halving

EXAMPLE 26    8 x 18 = ?
2 x 18 = 36
4 x 18 = 2 x 36 = 72
8 x 18 = 2 x 72 = 144

EXAMPLE 27    $\frac{1}{4}$ of 36 = ?    $\frac{1}{8}$ of 36 = ?
$\frac{1}{2}$ of 36 = 18
$\frac{1}{4}$ of 36 = $\frac{1}{2}$ of 18 = 9
$\frac{1}{8}$ of 36 = $\frac{1}{2}$ of 9 = $4\frac{1}{2}$

Work out :
1. $\frac{1}{2}$ of 22
2. $\frac{1}{4}$ of 22
3. Double 26
4. 4 x 26
5. 8 x 26
6. $\frac{1}{2}$ of 42
7. $\frac{1}{4}$ of 42
8. $\frac{1}{4}$ of 56
9. $\frac{1}{8}$ of 56
10. 4 x 33
11. $\frac{1}{4}$ of 104
12. $\frac{1}{4}$ of 90
13. 4 x $10\frac{1}{2}$
14. 8 x 15
15. 8 x $5\frac{1}{2}$

• Check your answers.

## D3: Adding near doubles

EXAMPLE 28   Use doubles to work out (a) 160 + 170  (b) 37 + 39
(a)   160 + 170 = double 160 + 10 = 320 + 10 = 330
(b)   37 + 39 = double 40 – 3 – 1 = 80 – 4 = 76

Idea: Double 40 is easier to work with than double 37

Use doubles to work out:
1. 230 + 240
2. 410 + 400
3. 53 + 54
4. 127 + 129
5. 99 + 97
6. 46 + 48
7. 77 + 75
8. 450 + 470
9. 390 + 380
10. 670 + 660

**Star Challenge 18**   Work out:    14-15 correct = 1 star
1. Double 55
2. 4 x 14
3. Half of 47
4. 69 + 70
5. $\frac{1}{4}$ of 46
6. Double 89
7. 8 x 12
8. $\frac{1}{8}$ of 200
9. 17 + 21
10. Half of 27
11. 4 x $6\frac{1}{2}$
12. 123 + 119

• Check your answers.

A POW GUIDE            Strategies for Improving Mental Arithmetic Skills   **EXTRA**

# Section 15: Crossing the thousands boundary

In this section you will develop techniques to work with 3- and 4-digit numbers

**DEVELOPMENT**   Level 4

## D1: Hundreds and thousands

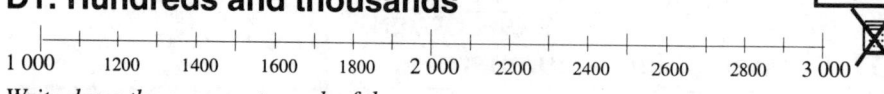

1 000  1200  1400  1600  1800  2 000  2200  2400  2600  2800  3 000

Write down the answers to each of these:

1. 1 800 + 200
2. 1 900 + 500
3. 1 700 + 400
4. 2 400 – 500
5. 2 500 – 800
6. 1 200 + 900
7. 2 400 – 600
8. 1 500 + 1000

• Check your answers.

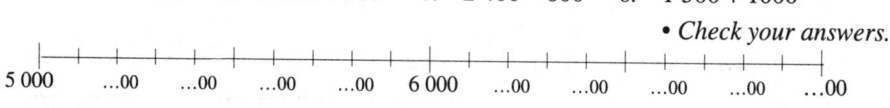

5 000  ...00  ...00  ...00  ...00  6 000  ...00  ...00  ...00  ...00  ...00

9. Copy and complete this number line.

Write down the answers to each of these:

10. 5 500 + 600
11. 5 900 + 100
12. 6 200 – 400
13. 5 800 + 500
14. 6 100 – 300
15. 6 800 – 1000
16. 5 700 + 600
17. 5 500 + 900

• Check your answers.

Write down the answers to each of these:

18. 7 800 + 200
19. 4 800 + 400
20. 7 300 – 500
21. 2 900 + 600
22. 3 400 – 500
23. 7 900 + 800
24. 6 500 + 1000
25. 7 200 – 400

• Check your answers

## D2: Tens and thousands and units

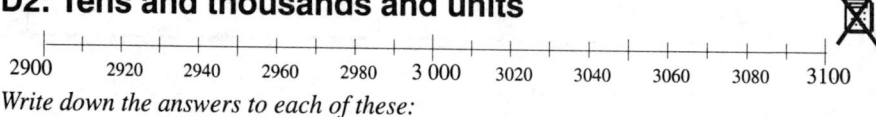

2900  2920  2940  2960  2980  3 000  3020  3040  3060  3080  3100

Write down the answers to each of these:

1. 2 980 + 40
2. 2 960 + 40
3. 2 980 + 50
4. 2 950 + 50
5. 3 010 – 30
6. 3 080 – 100
7. 3 020 – 60
8. 3 010 – 80 + 30

• Check your answers.

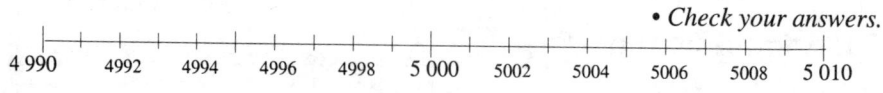

4 990  4992  4994  4996  4998  5 000  5002  5004  5006  5008  5 010

Write down the answers to each of these:

9. 4 996 + 6
10. 4 998 + 5
11. 4 995 + 9
12. 4 993 + 11
13. 5 002 – 5
14. 5 003 – 8
15. 4 999 + 7
16. 5 008 – 12

• Check your answers.

Write down the answers to each of these:

17. 7 900 + 200
18. 3 990 + 15
19. 2 900 + 400
20. 4 990 + 16
21. 2 600 – 800
22. 8 300 – 400
23. 3 980 + 50
24. 8 000 – 500
25. 2 400 – 1 000
26. 2 995 + 6
27. 3 800 + 300
28. 6 500 – 600

• Check your answers

A POW GUIDE                page 34                Strategies for Improving **EXTRA**
                                                   Mental Arithmetic Skills

## D3: Counting on and back when numbers are close together | Level 4

EXAMPLE 29    1279 1280 1281
1277 + ... = 1281    1278
Missing number is 4

Copy and complete:
1. 2999 + 3 = ...    2. 2596 + ... = 2600
3. 1783 + 5 = ...    4. 2779 + ... = 2783
5. 3003 − ... = 2999    6. 3488 + ... = 3495

• Check answers.

## D4: Counting on and back with multiples of 10

643 + 50 = 693
The tens go up by 5

2 156 − 30 = 2 126
The tens go down by 3

Write down the answers:
1. 716 + 40    2. 1 275 + 20    3. 2 478 − 30    4. 895 − 50    5. 7 241 + 40
6. 4 035 + 60    7. 2 509 + 70    8. 1 250 − 30    9. 7 593 + 60    10. 2 267 − 50

• Check your answers.

## D5: Counting on and back with multiples of 100 or 1000

2 463 + 500 = 2 963
The hundreds go up by 5

4 289 + 2 000 = 6 289
The thousands go up by 2

Write down the answers:
1. 2 573 + 200    2. 3 681 − 400    3. 5 420 + 1000    4. 2 895 − 500    5. 8056 − 4000
6. 1 998 + 600    7. 1 859 − 300    8. 6450 − 3000    9. 5 807 + 600    10. 2 357 − 500

• Check your answers.

### Star Challenge 19
8-9 correct = 1 star

1. The year is 1998. What year will it be:
   (a) in 5 years time  (b) in 50 years time  (c) in 500 years time?
2. The year is 1995. What year was it (a) 20 years ago  (b) 200 years ago?
3. My mother was 70 in 1990. In what year was she born?
4. Prince Charles was born in 1948. In what year was he 50 years old?
5. Queen Victoria was crowned in 1837. She was queen until her death 64 years later. In what year did she die?
6. King Arakan of Burma became king in 1279. He died 95 years later. What year was that?

• Your teacher has the answers to these.

### Star Challenge 20
7-8 correct = 1 star

Write down the answers:
1. 4 503 + 30    2. 4 503 + 300    3. 7 829 + 7    4. 7 829 + 70
5. 7 829 + 700    6. 7 829 + 7000    7. 6438 − 20    8. 7149 − 50

• Your teacher has the answers to these.

A POW GUIDE    Strategies for Improving Mental Arithmetic Skills    EXTRA

# Section 16: Decimals and rounding

Levels 3 & 4

In this section you will
- estimate decimal values on a number line;
- write simple fractions as decimals;
- + and − decimals to 1 & 2 d.p.
- x and ÷ decimals by 10 or 100
- round money to work out problems;
- round numbers to nearest 1, 10 or 100

## DEVELOPMENT

### D1: Decimal number lines

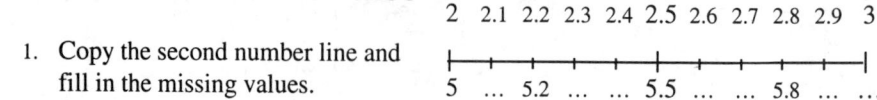

|—+—+—+—+—+—+—+—+—+—|
2  2.1  2.2  2.3  2.4  2.5  2.6  2.7  2.8  2.9  3

1. Copy the second number line and fill in the missing values.

|—+—+—+—+—+—+—+—+—+—|
5  ...  5.2  ...  ...  5.5  ...  ...  5.8  ...  ...

2. Estimate the value of the number that the arrow points to.

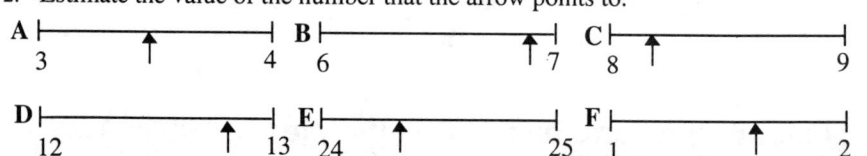

A |———↑————| B |————————↑—| C |——↑————————|
3            4  6              7  8            9

D |—————————↑—| E |—↑——————————| F |————↑————|
12            13  24            25  1            2

• Check your answers.

### D2: Fractions and decimals

| $0.5 = \frac{1}{2}$ | $2.5 = 2\frac{1}{2}$ | $0.25 = \frac{1}{4}$ | $6.25 = 6\frac{1}{4}$ | $0.75 = \frac{3}{4}$ | $4.75 = 4\frac{3}{4}$ |

Write as decimals:
1. $3\frac{1}{2}$   2. $7\frac{1}{4}$   3. $8\frac{3}{4}$   4. $10\frac{1}{2}$

Write as whole numbers and fractions:
5. 5.25   6. 9.5   7. 2.75   8. 25.25

| $0.1 = \frac{1}{10}$ | $0.2 = \frac{2}{10}$ | $0.3 = \frac{3}{10}$ = three tenths | $2.7 = 2\frac{7}{10}$ = 2 and 7 tenths |

Write as decimals:
9. $\frac{3}{10}$   10. $4\frac{6}{10}$   11. $\frac{7}{10}$   12. 9 tenths

Write as whole numbers and fractions:
13. 5.3   14. 0.8   15. 6.1

• Check your answers.

### D3: + and − decimals to 1 d.p.

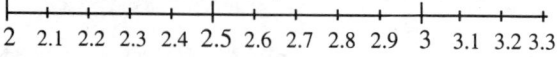

|—+—+—+—+—+—+—+—+—+—+—+—+—|
2  2.1  2.2  2.3  2.4  2.5  2.6  2.7  2.8  2.9  3  3.1  3.2  3.3

Copy and complete:
1. 2.4 + 0.3 = ...   2. 2.5 + ... = 2.9   3. 2.8 + 0.2 = ...   4. 2.8 − 0.6 = ...
5. 2.7 + 0.8 = ...   6. 3.2 − 0.5 = ...   7. 2.9 + ... = 3.5   8. ... − 0.5 = 2.7

• Check your answers.

Copy and complete:
9. 3.5 + 0.2 = ...   10. 6.1 + ... = 6.9   11. 3.7 + 0.2 = ...   12. 4.8 − 0.6 = ...
13. 6.9 + 0.4 = ...   14. 7.1 − 0.4 = ...   15. 8.6 + ... = 9.1   16. ... − 0.3 = 8.7

• Check your answers.

*A POW GUIDE*     page 36     *Strategies for Improving* **EXTRA**
*Mental Arithmetic Skills*

## D4: x and ÷ decimals by 10 and 100    Level 5

To multiply any number by 10 you move the decimal point ONE PLACE to the RIGHT
To multiply any number by 100 you move the decimal point TWO PLACES to the RIGHT

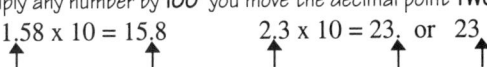

1.58 x 10 = 15.8      2.3 x 10 = 23. or 23

To divide any number by 10 you move the decimal point ONE PLACE to the LEFT
To divide any number by 100 you move the decimal point TWO PLACES to the LEFT

1.58 ÷ 10 = 1.58      2.3 ÷ 10 = .23 or 0.23

*Copy and complete:*
1. 2.4 x 10 = …
2. 4.5 x 10 = …
3. 6.7 ÷ 10 = …
4. 7.1 ÷ 10 = …
5. 6.3 … … = 0.63
6. 27 ÷ 10 = …
7. 12.4 x 100 = …
8. 0.6 ÷ 10 = …
9. 0.04 x 10 = …
10. 3.52 x 100 = …
11. 5 ÷ 10 = …
12. 2.34 ÷ 10 = …

• Check your answers

## D5: Using rounding to work out money problems

EXAMPLE 30   A bag of apples costs £1.45   How many bags can I buy for £5 ?
A:   £1.45 is approx £1.50   3 x £1.50 = £4.50   So, I can buy 3 bags.

1. A cassette tape costs £1.99. How many tapes can I buy for £10 ?
2. A CD costs £11.90.   How many can I buy for £50 ?
3. A pantomime ticket costs £5.95. What will seven tickets cost to the nearest pound?

• Check answers.

## D6: Rounding numbers

1. Round to the nearest whole number   (a) 2.3   (b) 2.7   (c) 2.5   (d) 3.1
2. Round to the nearest whole number   (a) 4.8   (b) 9.4   (c) 11.3   (d) 27.5
3. Round to the nearest ten   (a) 24   (b) 78   (c) 135   (d) 266
4. Round to the nearest hundred   (a) 341   (b) 609   (c) 491   (d) 750

• Check answers.

## Star Challenge

18 correct = 2 marks
15-17 correct = 1 mark

1. *Write as whole numbers and fractions (mixed numbers):*
   (a) 12.5   (b) 3.75   (c) 4.8   (d) 10.3   (e) 9.25
2. *Write as decimals:*
   (a) 7 tenths   (b) 4 and a half   (c) $20\frac{1}{4}$   (d) $\frac{9}{10}$   (e) $3\frac{2}{10}$
3. *Copy and complete:*
   (a) 5.1 + … = 6   (b) 2.4 − 0.5 = …   (c) 6.8 + … = 7.2
4. *Copy and complete:*
   (a) 6.3 x 10 = …   (b) 4.72 x … = 472   (c) 12.75 ÷ 10 = …
5. *Estimate the value of the number that the arrow points to:*
   (a) 7 ——↑—— 8   (b) 23 ——↑—— 24

*A POW GUIDE*     *Strategies for Improving Mental Arithmetic Skills*  EXTRA

# Section 17: Fractions and percentages

Levels 4 & 5

In this section you will
- practise using simple fraction-percentage equivalents;
- find simple fractions and percentages of amounts.

## DEVELOPMENT

### D1: Simple equivalents

$\frac{1}{2} = 50\%$  $\frac{1}{4} = 25\%$  $\frac{3}{4} = 75\%$  $\frac{1}{10} = 10\%$  $\frac{2}{10} = 20\%$

1. A quarter of my friends like playing snooker. What percentage like playing snooker ?
2. 75% of my friends like watching snooker. What fraction like watching snooker ?
3. I saved 50% of my pocket money last week. What fraction did I save ?
4. Bob spent $\frac{3}{10}$ of his saving on a bike. What percentage did he spend ?

• Check your answers.

### D2: Fractions and percentages of amounts

$\frac{1}{2}$ of £40 = £20   to find $\frac{1}{2}$ divide by 2
$\frac{1}{3}$ of £90 = £30   to find $\frac{1}{3}$ divide by 3
$\frac{1}{4}$ of £40 = £10   to find $\frac{1}{4}$ divide by 4
$\frac{1}{10}$ of £40 = £4   to find $\frac{1}{10}$ divide by 10

Work out:
1. $\frac{1}{2}$ of £50   2. $\frac{1}{4}$ of £120   3. $\frac{1}{3}$ of £90   4. $\frac{1}{3}$ of £15   5. $\frac{1}{5}$ of £30
6. $\frac{1}{2}$ of £25   7. $\frac{1}{10}$ of £80   8. $\frac{1}{4}$ of £60   9. $\frac{1}{10}$ of £140   10. $\frac{1}{4}$ of £44

• Check your answers.

50% of £30 = $\frac{1}{2}$ of £30 = £15     25% of 12 smarties = $\frac{1}{4}$ of 12 smarties = 3

Work out:
11. 25% of £20   12. 10% of £30   13. 50% of £22   14. 25% of £84   15. 10% of 90p

• Check your answers.

### D3: Multiples of $\frac{1}{10}$ and of 10%

$\frac{1}{10}$ of £40 = £4
So $\frac{3}{10}$ of £40 = £12   ($\frac{3}{10} = 3 \times \frac{1}{10}$)

10% of £80 = £8
So 40% of £80 = £32   (40% = 4 × 10%)

Work out:
1. 10% of £50   2. 20% of £50   3. 70% of £50   4. 30% of 40p   5. 60% of 20p
6. $\frac{1}{10}$ of 40p   7. $\frac{3}{10}$ of 40p   8. $\frac{9}{10}$ of 40p   9. $\frac{4}{10}$ of £150   10. $\frac{6}{10}$ of £200

• Check your answers.

### Star Challenge 22

9-10 correct = 1 star

1. Sam spent 25% of his money on sweets. What fraction did he spend on sweets.
2. Sara saved $\frac{2}{10}$ of her pocket money. What percentage did she save ?

Work out:
3. 50% of £20   4. 25% of 24p   5. 10% of £450   6. 20% of 60p
7. $\frac{1}{4}$ of 60p   8. $\frac{1}{3}$ of 75p   9. $\frac{1}{10}$ of £300   10. $\frac{7}{10}$ of 30p

• Your teacher has the answers to these.

A POW GUIDE            Strategies for Improving  **EXTRA**
                       Mental Arithmetic Skills

# Section 18: Measurements of length, weight & time

**Level 5**

In this section you will
- change one metric unit to another;
- estimate lengths and use simple map scales;
- do calculations involving time;
- work out fractions of lengths, weights and time.

### DEVELOPMENT

## D1: Changing between cm and mm

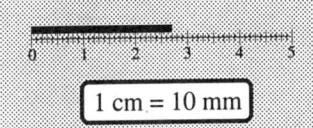

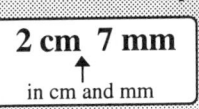

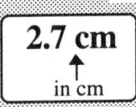

There are three ways of writing the length of this line.

1 cm = 10 mm

| 2 cm 7 mm | 27 mm | 2.7 cm |
| in cm and mm | in mm | in cm |

1. The length of a line is 2 cm 4 mm
   Write this length (a) in mm (b) in cm
2. The length of a line is 36 mm
   Write this length (a) in cm and mm (b) in cm
3. The length of a line is 5.7 cm
   Write this length (a) in cm and mm (b) in mm
4. Write 48 mm (a) in cm (b) in cm and mm
5. Write 9.1 cm (a) in mm (b) in cm and mm
6. Write 3 cm 8 mm (a) in cm (b) in mm • *Check your answers.*

## D2: Changing between m and cm

1 m = 100 cm

*Copy and complete:*

1. 2 m = ...... cm
2. 2 m 40 cm = ...... cm
3. 1 m 25 cm = ...... cm
4. 5 m 12 cm = ...... cm
5. 350 cm = ... m ... cm
6. 405 cm = ... m ... cm
7. 701 cm = ... m ... cm
8. 275 cm = ... m ... cm • *Check answers*

## D3: Changing between kg and g

1 kg = 1000 g

*Copy and complete:*

1. 2 kg = ...... g
2. 3 kg 800 g = ...... g
3. 1 kg 500 g = ...... g
4. 1 kg 50 g = ...... g  ← Hint: think of 50g as 050 g
5. 1200 g = ... kg ... g
6. 2350 g = ... kg ... g
7. 1010 g = ... kg ... g
8. 7250 g = ... kg ... g • *Check answers*

A POW GUIDE — Strategies for Improving Mental Arithmetic Skills — **EXTRA**

## D4: Map scales

This is ⊢—⊣ 1 cm

1. Estimate the length in cm of each of these lines:
   (a) ————    (b) ——————————
   (c) ———————————————
   (d) ⌢⌣⌢    (e) ╱

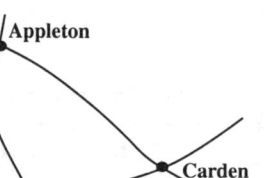

• Check your answers.

2. 

   (a) Estimate the map distance between Box and Carden (in cm).
   (b) Estimate the actual distance between Box and Carden (in km).
   (c) Estimate the actual distance between Appleton and Carden.

Scale : 1 cm to 5 km

• Check your answers.

## D5: Fractions of length, weight and time

| 1 cm = 10 mm | 1 m = 100 cm | 1 kg = 1000 g |

Copy and complete :
1. Half a cm = ...... mm
2. Half a m = ...... cm
3. Half a kg = ...... g
4. $1\frac{1}{2}$ cm = ...... mm
5. $2\frac{1}{2}$ m = ...... cm
6. $4\frac{1}{2}$ kg = ...... g
7. $\frac{1}{4}$ cm = ...... mm
8. $3\frac{1}{4}$ m = ...... cm
9. $1\frac{1}{4}$ kg = ...... g

• Check your answers.

| 1 hour = 60 min | 1 day = 24 hours | 1 min = 60 sec |

Copy and complete :
10. $\frac{1}{2}$ hour = ...... min
11. $\frac{1}{4}$ hour = ...... min
12. $\frac{3}{4}$ hour = ...... min
13. 2 hours = ...... min
14. $1\frac{1}{4}$ hours = ...... min
15. $2\frac{1}{2}$ hours = ...... min
16. $\frac{1}{2}$ min = ...... sec
17. ... min = 15 sec
18. $\frac{1}{2}$ day = ...... hours
19. 3 min = ...... sec
20. 2 days = ...... hours

• Check your answers.

## D6: Time problems

1. The TV news starts at 5.15 and lasts for half an hour. What time does it finish ?
2. Morning registration starts at five to nine. It lasts for a quarter of an hour. What time does registration finish ?
3. The lunch break starts at 12.25 and finishes at 1.20  How long is the lunch break ?
4. A TV programme starts at ten to seven. It lasts for 25 minutes. What time does it finish ?
5. A radio programme starts at half past eight. The programme runs for an hour and a quarter. What time does the programme finish ?

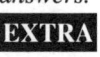

• Check your answers.

A POW GUIDE    page 40    Strategies for Improving  **EXTRA**
Mental Arithmetic Skills

# THE NATIONAL CURRICULUM ...
# ... AND BEYOND ...

*Pow*

# Back to Basics
# EXTRA

| Level 3 | Level 4 | Level 5 | Level 6 |
|---|---|---|---|
| | | §7 Technique review | |
| | §6 Division techniques | | |
| | §5 More multiplication techniques | | |
| | §4 Multiplying by tens ... | | |
| | §3 Pencil-and-paper multiplication | | |
| | §2 Pencil-and-paper subtraction | | |
| | §1 Pencil-and-paper addition | | |

# Back to Basics
## Section 1: Pencil-and-paper addition

Level 4

In this section you will review and practice pencil-and-paper techniques for addition.

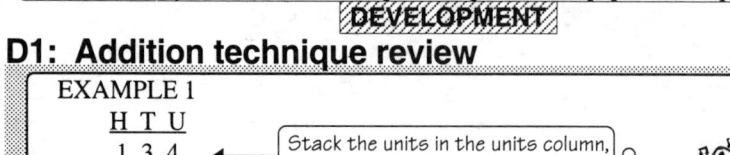

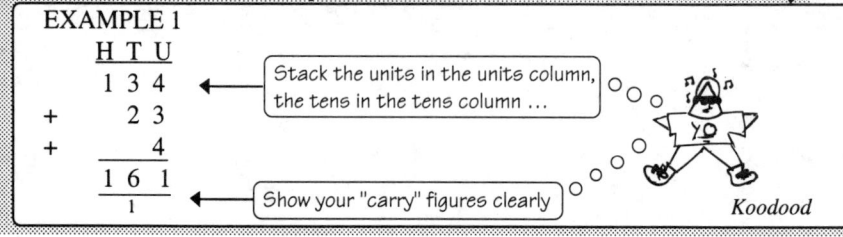

**DEVELOPMENT**

### D1: Addition technique review

**EXAMPLE 1**

```
  H T U
  1 3 4
+   2 3
+     4
  1 6 1
    1
```

← Stack the units in the units column, the tens in the tens column ...

← Show your "carry" figures clearly

Koodood

**Task 1:** Copy and complete these addition sums:

1. H T U        2. H T U        3. H T U        4. H T U        5. H T U
   4 0 3           3 1 4           1 2 6           2 3 4           1 4 5
 +   2 6        + 2 5 3         +   5 6         + 4 7 6         +   2 5
                                                                 +   3 1

CHECK YOUR ANSWERS before you do Task 2.

**Task 2:** Write each of these sums as in example 1.
Stack the numbers in the correct columns.    Work out the answers.

6. 47 + 22      7. 245 + 13 + 21        8. 359 + 9 + 24
9. 72 + 135     10. 264 + 19 + 53       11. 658 + 214 + 5

CHECK YOUR ANSWERS. See your teacher if you have any wrong.

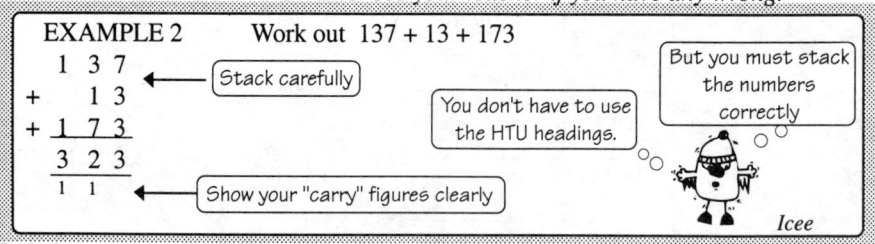

**EXAMPLE 2**       Work out 137 + 13 + 173

```
  1 3 7
+   1 3
+ 1 7 3
  3 2 3
  1 1
```

← Stack carefully

You don't have to use the HTU headings.

But you must stack the numbers correctly

← Show your "carry" figures clearly

Icee

**Task 3:** Write each of these sums as in example 1.
Stack the numbers in the correct columns.    Work out the answers.

12. 342 + 468       13. 91 + 27 + 8         14. 531 + 16 + 160
15. 206 + 26 + 6    16. 357 + 573 + 57      17. 482 + 19 + 84
18. 606 + 212       19. 1739 + 24 + 100     20. 200 + 353 + 17
21. 510 + 332 + 23  22. 345 + 67 + 8

• Check your answers.

A POW GUIDE     page 42     Back to Basics **EXTRA**

## D2: What did they do wrong ?

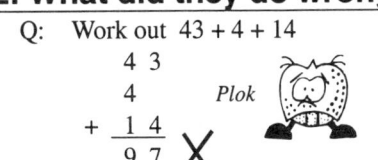

Q: Work out 43 + 4 + 14
```
  4 3
    4      Plok
+ 1 4
  9 7
```
✗

1. Explain what Plok did wrong.

Q: Work out 43 + 4 + 14
```
  4 3
    4
+ 1 4
  5 11
```
✗   Letmewin

2. Explain what Letmewin did wrong.

3. Work out the correct answer to 43 + 4 + 14
   Show your working clearly.

• Check your answers.

### PRACTICE

## P1: Getting different totals

**SHOW ALL WORKING CLEARLY FOR EACH PROBLEM**

1. You can make 6 different addition sums using this and putting **1 2 3** in the three boxes.

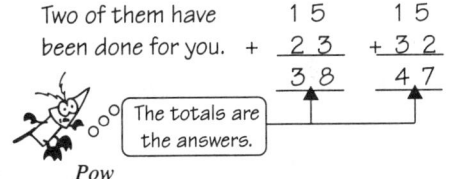

   ```
       ☐ 5
   +  ☐☐
   ```

   Two of them have been done for you.
   ```
     1 5        1 5       2 5      2 5      5        5
   + 2 3      + 3 2     + ___    + ___   + ___    + ___
     3 8        4 7
   ```
   The totals are the answers.   Pow

   Find the other four addition sums. Work out their totals.

2. Make 6 different addition sums using this and putting **5 7 8** in the three boxes.

   ```
      ☐☐
   +  3 ☐
   ```

   Do you get six different totals ?
   What are the totals ?
   What is the largest total ?

   Show all working clearly.

3. Make 6 different addition sums using this and putting **3 6 7** in the three boxes.

   ```
      ☐☐
   + ☐ 8
   ```

   What are their totals ?
   What is the smallest total ?

   Yusual

   • Check your answers.

A POW GUIDE    page 43    Back to Basics **EXTRA**

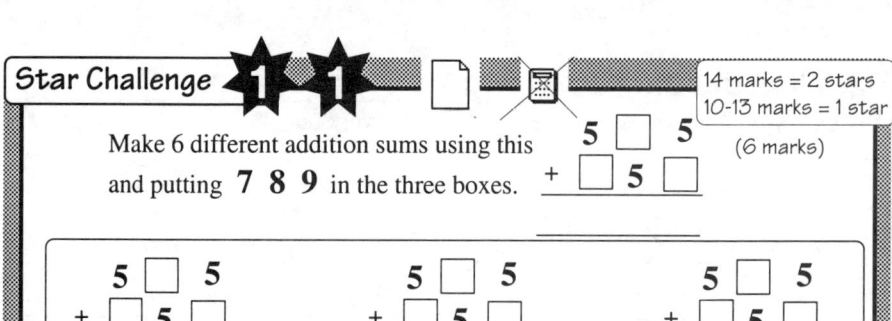

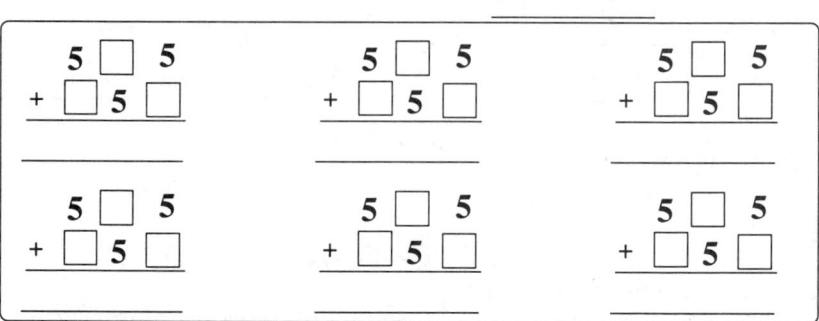

## Star Challenge 1-1

14 marks = 2 stars
10-13 marks = 1 star

Make 6 different addition sums using this and putting **7 8 9** in the three boxes.

```
  5 □ 5
+ □ 5 □
```
(6 marks)

```
  5 □ 5        5 □ 5        5 □ 5
+ □ 5 □      + □ 5 □      + □ 5 □
———————      ———————      ———————

  5 □ 5        5 □ 5        5 □ 5
+ □ 5 □      + □ 5 □      + □ 5 □
———————      ———————      ———————
```

Work out their totals (6 marks)

What is the largest total you can get ? .................... (2 marks)

• *Your teacher has the answers to this.*

## Star Challenge 2-2

60-67 marks = 2 stars
50-59 marks = 1 star

*Stick this worksheet in your book.*
*Show all working out in your book.*

**Across**
1. 27 + 35
2. 29 + 45 + 9
4. 23 + 32 + 17 + 5
6. 257 + 850 + 246 + 921
8. 328 + 49
10. 437 + 523
12. 37 + 37 + 5
13. 56 + 69 + 4
16. 23 + 17 + 14
18. 133 + 269 + 245
20. 17 + 16
21. 45 + 17 + 16
22. 34 + 19 + 5

1 mark for each correct square in grid = total 41 marks
PLUS 1 mark for the working for each sum = 26 marks

**Down**
1. 497 + 106
2. 68 + 14
3. 16 + 17 + 4
5. 387 + 59 + 294
6. 16 + 9 + 2
7. 263 + 175 + 59
9. 329 + 254 + 129
11. 3042 + 2197 + 1714
14. 79 + 14
15. 568 + 727 + 353
17. 59 + 24
18. 33 + 29 + 5
19. 49 + 19

*A POW GUIDE*     page 44     *Back to Basics* **EXTRA**

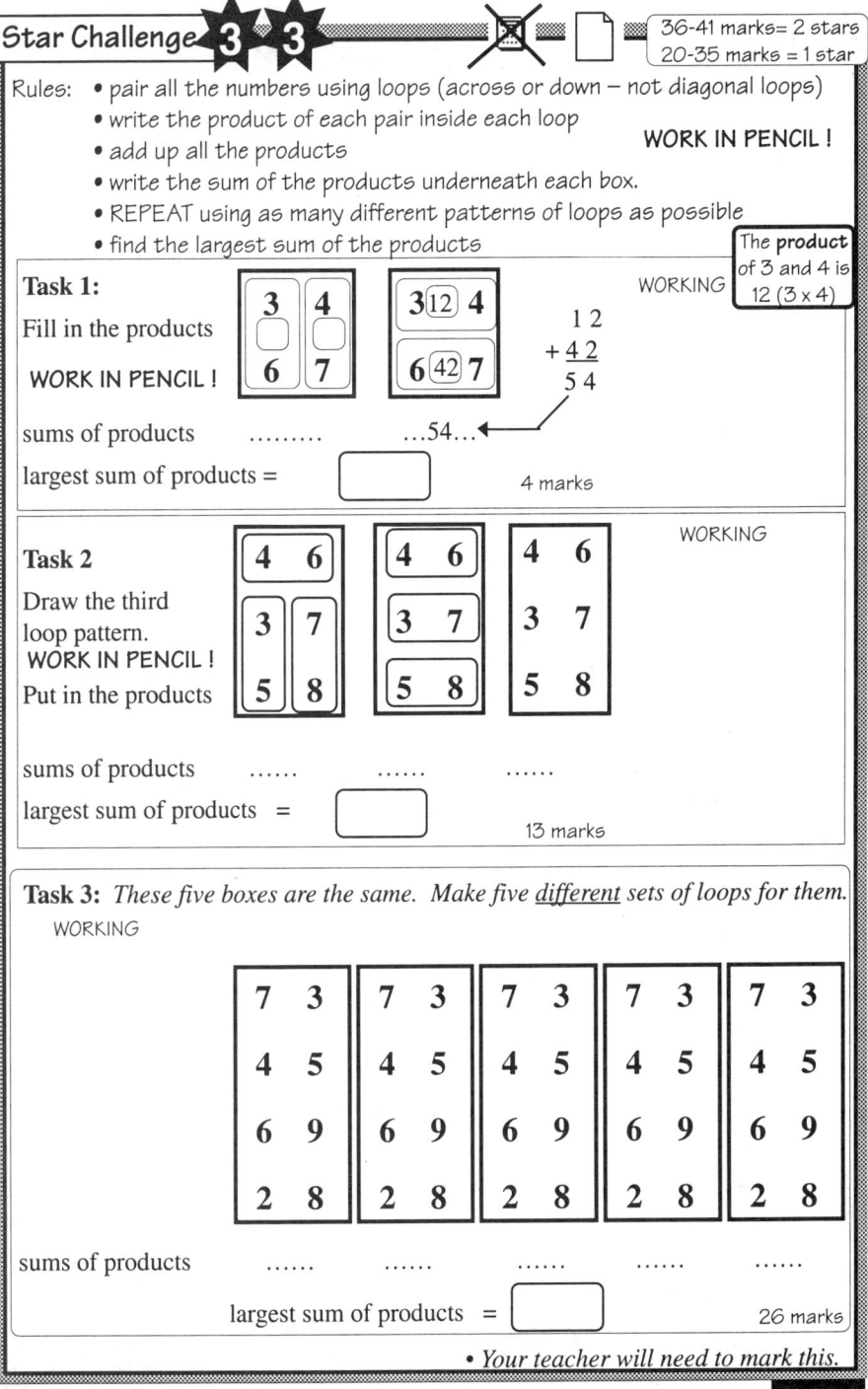

# Star Challenge 3 3

36-41 marks = 2 stars
20-35 marks = 1 star

Rules:
- pair all the numbers using loops (across or down – not diagonal loops)
- write the product of each pair inside each loop
- add up all the products
- write the sum of the products underneath each box.
- REPEAT using as many different patterns of loops as possible
- find the largest sum of the products

**WORK IN PENCIL !**

The **product** of 3 and 4 is 12 (3 x 4)

**Task 1:**
Fill in the products
WORK IN PENCIL !

```
 3   4      3(12) 4
(_) (_)                    WORKING
 6   7      6(42) 7          1 2
                           + 4 2
                           -----
                             5 4
```

sums of products    ………    …54…

largest sum of products = [    ]          4 marks

**Task 2**
Draw the third loop pattern.
WORK IN PENCIL !
Put in the products

```
 4  6     4  6     4  6
 3  7     3  7     3  7
 5  8     5  8     5  8
```
WORKING

sums of products    ……    ……    ……

largest sum of products = [    ]          13 marks

---

**Task 3:** *These five boxes are the same. Make five different sets of loops for them.*
WORKING

```
7 3    7 3    7 3    7 3    7 3
4 5    4 5    4 5    4 5    4 5
6 9    6 9    6 9    6 9    6 9
2 8    2 8    2 8    2 8    2 8
```

sums of products   ……   ……   ……   ……   ……

largest sum of products = [    ]          26 marks

• *Your teacher will need to mark this.*

A POW GUIDE        page 45        Back to Basics **EXTRA**

# Section 2: Pencil-and-paper subtraction

In this section you will:
- review and practice pencil-and-paper techniques for subtraction;
- use + and – techniques together.

**Level 4**

## DEVELOPMENT

### D1: Subtraction technique review

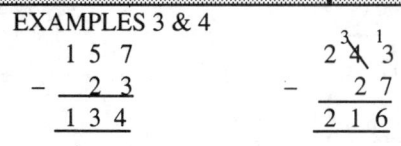

EXAMPLES 3 & 4

```
  1 5 7          2 ⁴̸³ ¹3
-   2 3        -   2 7
  1 3 4          2 1 6
```

You can't take 7 from 3, so you "borrow" a 10 from the tens column

*Do-med*

If you need help with this, ask your teacher.

**Task 1:** Copy and complete these subtraction sums.
Stack the numbers in the correct columns.
Show all working.

```
     T U            H T U          T U           T U          H T U
1.   3 8     2.     1 2 5    3.    6 3    4.     9 2    5.    6 4 2
   - 2 4          -   1 3        - 4 7          - 4 6        - 2 3 7
```

CHECK YOUR ANSWERS before you do Task 2.

**Task 2:** Write each of these sums as in questions 1–5.
Stack the numbers in the correct columns. Work out the answers.
You don't have to use HTU headings.

6. 34 – 12    7. 34 – 15    8. 275 – 64    9. 382 – 75
10. 435 – 117    11. 348 – 55    12. 290 – 24    13. 751 – 336
14. 216 – 109    15. 429 – 137    16. 574 – 53    17. 858 – 519

---

EXAMPLE 5 — two lots of borrowing
```
  ³4̸ ¹⁵6̸ ¹3
-   1 7 9
    2 8 4
```

EXAMPLE 6 — when there are no tens to borrow
```
  ¹9̸ ⁹0̸ ¹5
-     1 7
    1 8 8
```

---

**Task 3:** Write each sum as in the example.
Work out the answer.

18. 433 – 246    19. 762 – 178
20. 455 – 159    21. 238 – 149
22. 642 – 246    23. 377 – 88
24. 525 – 139    25. 526 – 65

**Task 4:** Write each sum as in the example.
Work out the answer.

26. 306 – 19    27. 208 – 119
28. 604 – 86    29. 504 – 218
30. 358 – 92    31. 467 – 83
32. 400 – 15    33. 750 – 408

• Check your answers.

A POW GUIDE      Back to Basics **EXTRA**

## D2: Subtraction mistakes

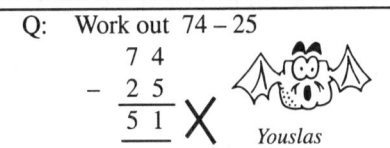

Q: Work out 74 − 25
```
  7 4
−  2 5
  5 1
```
Youslas
1. Explain what Youslas did wrong.

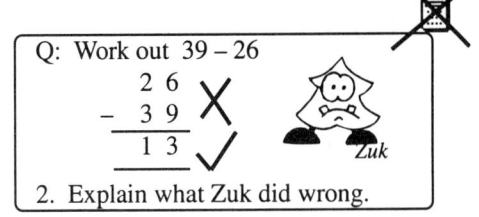

Q: Work out 39 − 26
```
  2 6
− 3 9
  1 3
```
Zuk
2. Explain what Zuk did wrong.

3. Work out the correct answer to 74 − 25.
   Show your working clearly.

• Check your answers.

### PRACTICE

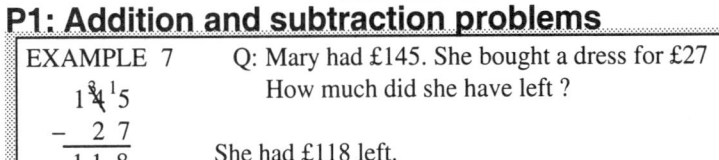

## P1: Addition and subtraction problems

**EXAMPLE 7**   Q: Mary had £145. She bought a dress for £27.
How much did she have left?
```
  1⁴⁵
−  2 7
  1 1 8
```
She had £118 left.

For each problem:
• write down an addition or subtraction sum
• work out the answer to the sum
• write down the answer to the problem

1. Peter had £63. He spent £45. How much did he have left?
2. Mario had £243 in the bank. He puts £28 into his bank account.
   How much does he now have in the bank?
3. Sergio has £317 in the bank. He takes out £40.
   How much has he left in the bank?
4. Sally needs £645 to go on a ski trip. She has earned £562.
   How much more does she need?
5. In Y7, there are 65 girls and 87 boys. How many students are there in Y7?
6. In Y10, there are 5 tutor groups. The numbers in each group are 27, 25, 28, 28, 25.
   How many students are there in Y10?
7. Number of Y8 present : 97    Number of Y8 absent : 45
   How many students are there in Y8?
8. Number in Y9 group : 137    Number of Y9 present : 89
   How many Y9 students are absent?
9. What is the total height of the two boxes?   35 cm / 87 cm
10. What is the size of the gap between the bridge and the top of the bus?   515 cm / 472 cm

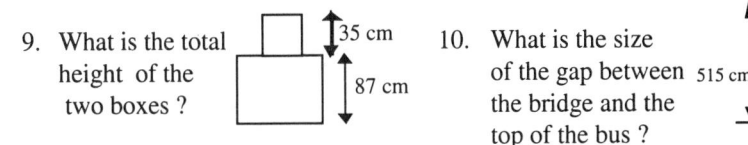

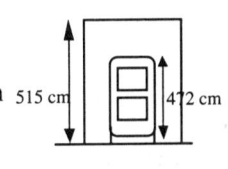

• Check your answers.

A POW GUIDE            page 47            Back to Basics **EXTRA**

## P2: Subtraction snakes

**Level 4**

This is a subtraction snake

15 → [−2] —13→ [−4] —9→ [−3] ..6..

**Task 1:** *Complete each of these subtraction snakes:*

1. 20 → [−4] ······→ [−3] ······→ [−6] ······→ [−5] ······

2. 24 → [−2] ······→ [−7] ······→ [−3] ······→ [−4] ······

3. 50 → [−7] ······→ [−6] ······→ [−9] ······→ [−11] ······

---

**EXAMPLE**

138 → [−14] —124→ [−23] —101→ [−18] → 83

*Show all working clearly*

Working:
```
  1 3 8        1 2 4       1 0 1
-   1 4      -   2 3     -   1 8
  1 2 4        1 0 1       0 8 3
```

*Frizzbang*

**Task 2:** *Complete each of these subtraction snakes. Show all working as in the example.*

4. 246 → [−14] ······→ [−14] ······→ [−40] ······

5. 333 → [−72] ······→ [−13] ······→ [−151] ······

6. 418 → [−22] ······→ [−162] ······→ [−148] ······

7. 765 → [−231] ······→ [−267] ······→ [−139] ······

• *Check your answers.*

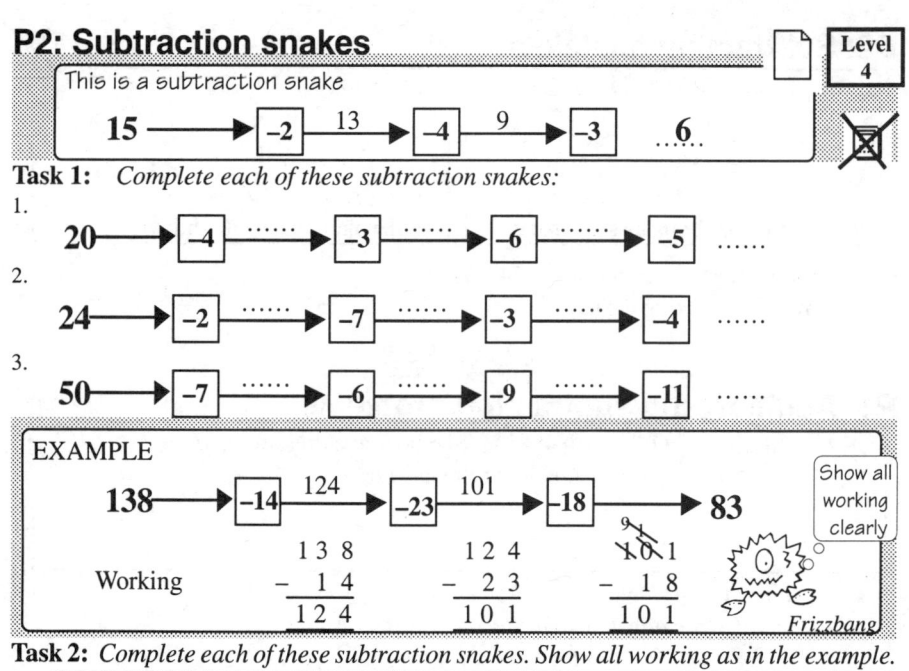

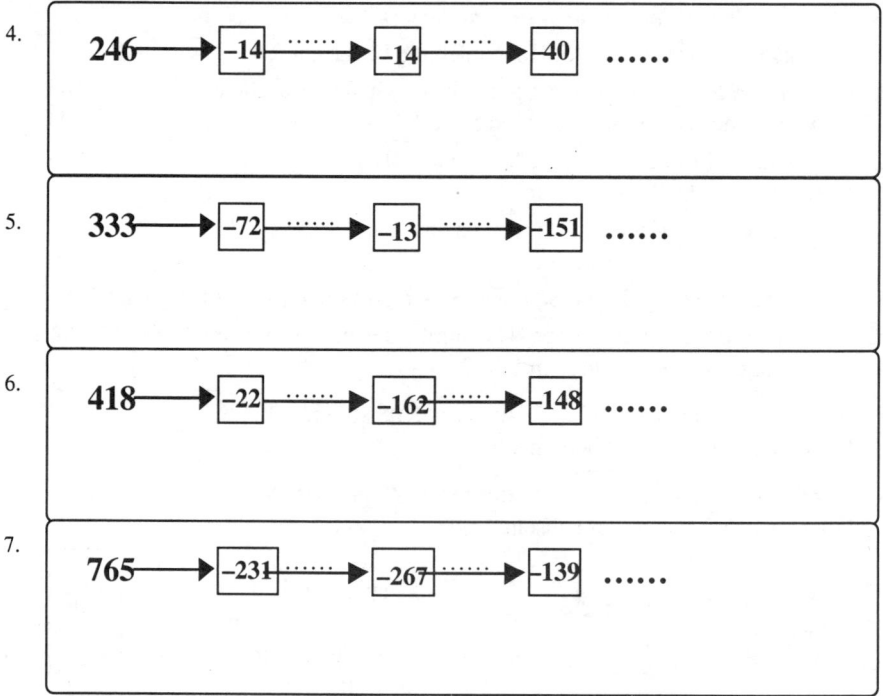

A POW GUIDE    page 48    Back to Basics **EXTRA**

### Star Challenge ★4 ★4

11-12 marks = 2 stars
9-10 marks = 1 star

1. Make three different subtraction sums using and putting **5 5 7** in the three boxes. Work out their answers.

    9☐
    − ☐☐
    ―――
    (6 marks)

2. The digits **2 5 1** go in the three boxes. You can get the answers 63  54⬛   57
What are the three answers under the blot ?
(1 mark for each answer + 3 marks for clear working = total 6 marks)

    7☐
    − ☐☐
    ―――

• Your teacher has the answers to this.

### DEVELOPMENT

## D3: Do you add or subtract ?

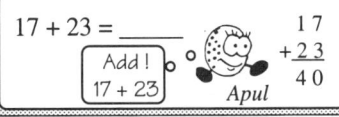

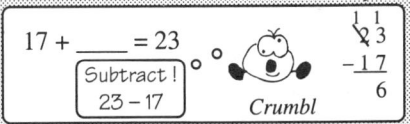

17 + 23 = ___    ┌─────┐    1 7
                 │ Add! │    +2 3
                 │17 + 23│   ―――
                 └─────┘    4 0
                  Apul

17 + ___ = 23   ┌────────┐    ¹ ²̸³
                │Subtract!│    −1 7
                │ 23 − 17 │   ―――
                └────────┘      6
                                Crumbl

**Type 1: using easy numbers**
Find the missing numbers.
Show your working as an addition sum or as a subtraction sum.
1. 15 + 10 = ___   2. 24 + ___ = 41   3. 9 + ___ = 20   4. 25 + 10 = ___
5. 8 + ___ = 20   6. 17 + 7 = ___   7. ___ + 30 = 48   8. 25 + ___ = 33

• CHECK YOUR ANSWERS!

**Type 2: using harder numbers**
Find the missing numbers.
Show your working as an addition sum or as a subtraction sum.
9. 42 + 25 = ___   10. 42 + ___ = 59   11. 32 + ___ = 47   12. 56 + 13 = ___
13. 39 + ___ = 70   14. 51 + 26 = ___   15. ___ + 73 = 98   16. 65 + ___ = 78

• CHECK YOUR ANSWERS!

**Type 3: working with numbers in addition tables**
Find the missing numbers. Complete the table.
Show your working using as addition or subtraction sums.

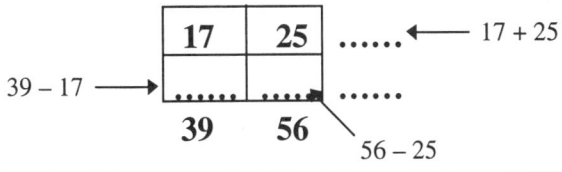

|    | 17 | 25 |
|----|----|----|
|    | 39 | 56 |

...... ← 17 + 25
...... 
56 − 25

39 − 17 →

• Check your answers.

A POW GUIDE          page 49          Back to Basics **EXTRA**

## PRACTICE

## P3: More row and column sums

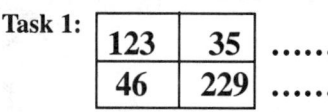

**Task 1:**

| 123 | 35  | ...... |
|-----|-----|--------|
| 46  | 229 | ...... |

...... ......

Working

```
  1 2 3        4 6        1 2 3        3 5
+  3 5      + 2 2 9      +  4 6      + 2 2 9
_____     _____     _____     _____
```

*Complete the sums in the "Working"*
*Fill in the row and column sums in the table.*

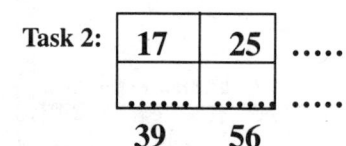

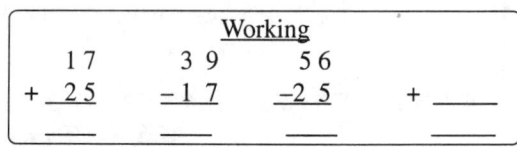

**Task 2:**

| 17 | 25 | ...... |
|----|----|--------|
|......|......| ...... |
| 39 | 56 |        |

Working

```
  1 7        3 9        5 6
+ 2 5      - 1 7      - 2 5      + _____
_____      _____      _____      _____
```

*Complete the table. Show all your working.*

**Task 3:**

| 49 | ...... | 86 |
|----|--------|-----|
| 32 | 65     | ...... |

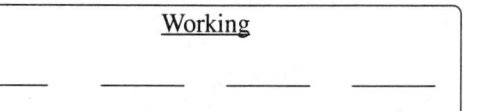

...... ......

Working
_____   _____   _____
_____   _____   _____

*Complete the table. Show all your working.*

**Task 4:**

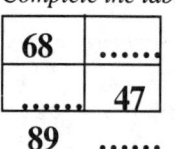

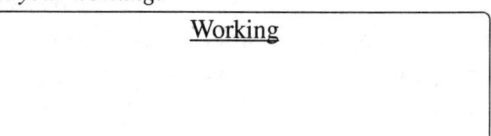

| 68     | ...... | 91 |
|--------|--------|-----|
| ...... | 47     | ...... |
| 89     | ...... |       |

Working

*Complete the table. Show all your working.*

• Check your answers.

### Star Challenge  5 - 5

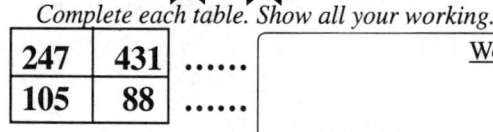

15-16 marks = 2 stars
10-14 marks = 1 star

*Complete each table. Show all your working.*

| 247 | 431 | ...... |
|-----|-----|--------|
| 105 | 88  | ...... |

Working

4 marks for each correct table
4 marks for each set of working

...... ......

| ...... | 76 | 98 |
|--------|----|-----|
| ...... | 33 | 72 |

Working

...... ......

| 97  | ...... | 138 |
|-----|--------|------|
| ...... | 115  | ...... |
| 106 | ...... |      |

Working

*A POW GUIDE*                page 50                *Back to Basics* **EXTRA**

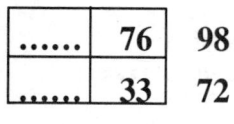

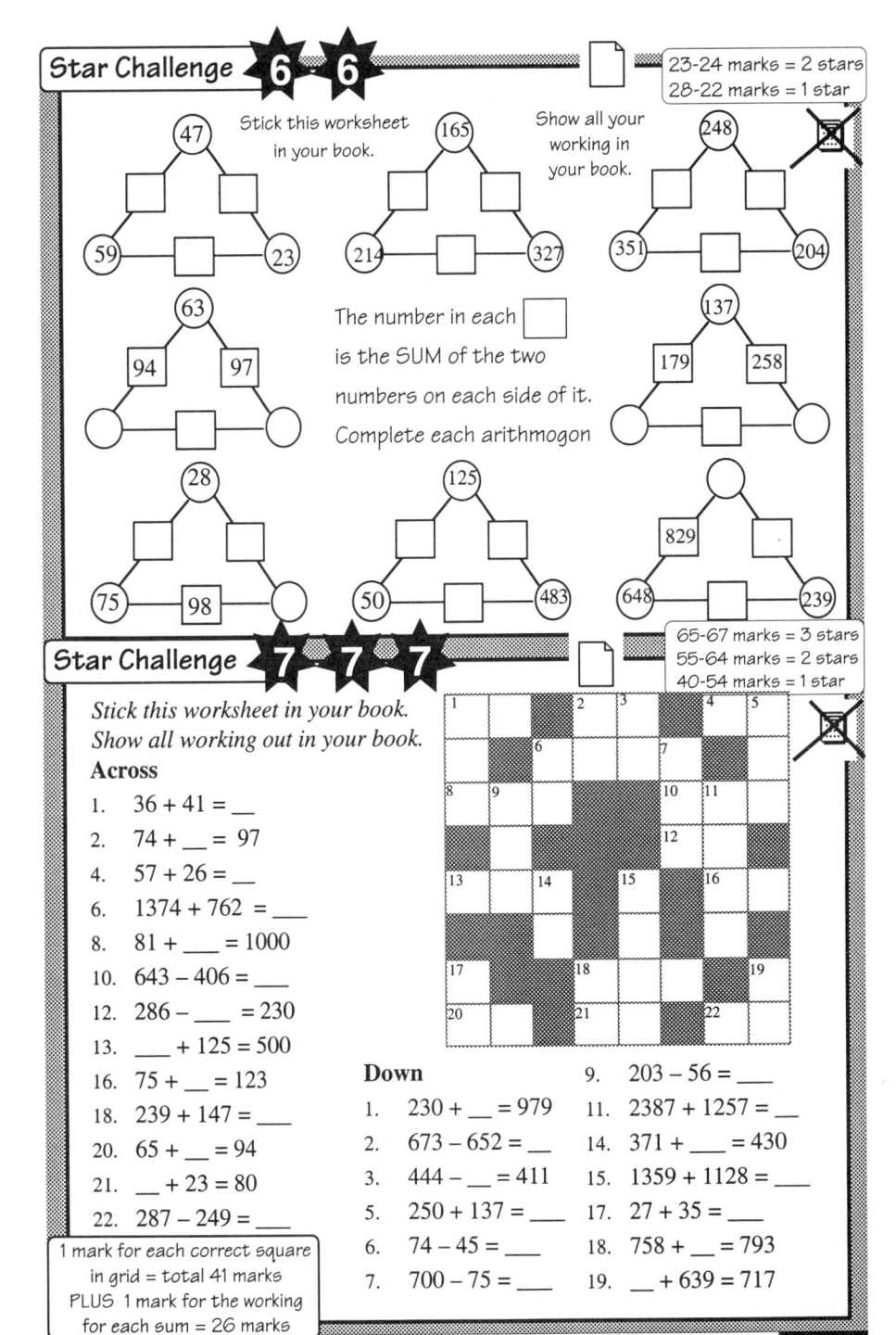

## Star Challenge 6 6

Stick this worksheet in your book. Show all your working in your book.

23-24 marks = 2 stars
28-22 marks = 1 star

(47) — 59, 23
(165) — 214, 327
(248) — 351, 204
(63) — 94, 97
(137) — 179, 258
(28) — 75, 98
(125) — 50, 483
— 829, 648, 239

The number in each ☐ is the SUM of the two numbers on each side of it. Complete each arithmogon

## Star Challenge 7 7 7

65-67 marks = 3 stars
55-64 marks = 2 stars
40-54 marks = 1 star

Stick this worksheet in your book.
Show all working out in your book.

**Across**
1. 36 + 41 = __
2. 74 + __ = 97
4. 57 + 26 = __
6. 1374 + 762 = __
8. 81 + __ = 1000
10. 643 – 406 = __
12. 286 – __ = 230
13. __ + 125 = 500
16. 75 + __ = 123
18. 239 + 147 = __
20. 65 + __ = 94
21. __ + 23 = 80
22. 287 – 249 = __

**Down**
1. 230 + __ = 979
2. 673 – 652 = __
3. 444 – __ = 411
5. 250 + 137 = __
6. 74 – 45 = __
7. 700 – 75 = __
9. 203 – 56 = __
11. 2387 + 1257 = __
14. 371 + __ = 430
15. 1359 + 1128 = __
17. 27 + 35 = __
18. 758 + __ = 793
19. __ + 639 = 717

1 mark for each correct square in grid = total 41 marks
PLUS 1 mark for the working for each sum = 26 marks

A POW GUIDE    page 51    Back to Basics **EXTRA**

# Section 3: Pencil-and-paper multiplication

In this section you will review and practise pencil-and-paper techniques for multiplication

Level 4

## DEVELOPMENT

### D1: Multiplication technique review

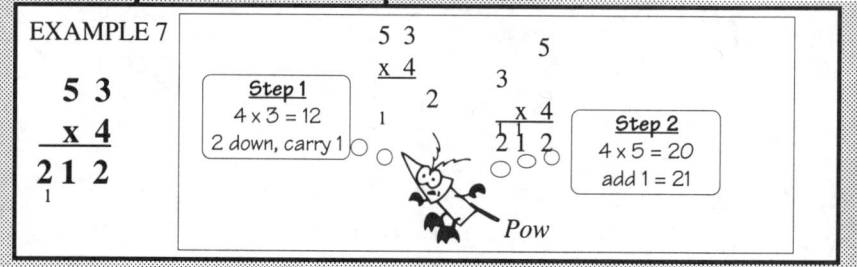

EXAMPLE 7

```
  5 3
x   4
-----
2 1 2
  1
```

Step 1
4 × 3 = 12
2 down, carry 1

Step 2
4 × 5 = 20
add 1 = 21

Pow

Copy and complete the following multiplication sums:

1. 1 2   2. 2 3   3. 4 7   4. 3 6   5. 6 4   6. 8 2
   × 3      × 4      × 2      × 5      × 7      × 3
   ───      ───      ───      ───      ───      ───

• Check your answers.

## PRACTICE

### P1: Multiplication practice

Do the following multiplication sums.

**Set out working as in D1**

CHECK ANSWERS AT THE END OF EACH BATCH.
Do as many batches as you need.

| Batch A | | | | |
|---|---|---|---|---|
| 1. 21 × 4 | 2. 54 × 3 | 3. 72 × 5 | 4. 36 × 8 | 5. 123 × 6 |
| 6. 14 × 3 | 7. 32 × 9 | 8. 28 × 6 | 9. 59 × 7 | 10. 324 × 8 |

| Batch B | | | | |
|---|---|---|---|---|
| 1. 47 × 2 | 2. 33 × 7 | 3. 49 × 6 | 4. 81 × 9 | 5. 410 × 3 |
| 6. 26 × 5 | 7. 82 × 6 | 8. 67 × 9 | 9. 42 × 3 | 10. 125 × 7 |

| Batch C | | | | |
|---|---|---|---|---|
| 1. 82 × 3 | 2. 67 × 3 | 3. 74 × 7 | 4. 29 × 5 | 5. 120 × 6 |
| 6. 19 × 7 | 7. 27 × 6 | 8. 35 × 9 | 9. 52 × 6 | 10. 531 × 5 |

| Batch D | | | | |
|---|---|---|---|---|
| 1. 72 × 4 | 2. 86 × 5 | 3. 47 × 9 | 4. 83 × 8 | 5. 105 × 7 |
| 6. 220 × 3 | 7. 34 × 6 | 8. 29 × 4 | 9. 54 × 9 | 10. 975 × 4 |

A POW GUIDE          Back to Basics **EXTRA**

## P2: Different totals

1. You can make 6 different multiplication sums like this ☐☐
   using **2, 3** and **5**                                    x ☐
   Here are two of them :   2  3           3  2
                                  x  5          x  5       These give totals **115** and **160**
                                  1 1 5        1 6 0
   Find the other four multiplication sums. Work out their totals.

2. Make 6 multiplication sums like this     ☐☐
   using **3, 5** and **7**                             x ☐
   How many different totals can you get ?        Work out the totals.

3. How many different totals can you get using **5, 4** and **4** and ☐☐   ?
   Show all working. What totals do you get ?                            x ☐

4. What is the *largest* multiplication total that
   you can get using   **3, 6** and **8** and   ☐☐?
                                            x ☐

5. What is the *smallest* multiplication total that
   you can get using   **3, 3** and **4** and    ☐☐
                                            x ☐

6. You are going to make multiplication sums like  ☐☐☐
   using the digits **2, 3, 4** and **5**                     x ☐
   Find as many different totals as you can.
   What is the largest total that you can get ?

### Star Challenge ⭐8 ⭐8

*16 marks = 2 stars*
*12-15 marks = 1 star*

1. Make multiplication sums like   ☐☐☐
   using the digits **3  5  7**          x **9**
   Find six different totals.                          (6 marks)
   What is the *largest* total that you can get ?   (2 marks)

2. Make six multiplication sums like  |8|☐☐   (6 marks)
   using **2  4  5**                              x ☐
   What is the *smallest* total that you can get ?    (2 marks)

*A POW GUIDE*          *page 53*          *Back to Basics* **EXTRA**

# Section 4: Multiplying by tens ...

Level 4

In this section you will review and practise multiplying whole numbers:
- by 10, 100, 1000
  - by 20, 30 ... 200, 300 ...

### DEVELOPMENT

## D1: Multiplication by 10, 100 1000

> To multiply a whole number by 10, you add 0
> $2 \times 10 = 20$     $23 \times 10 = 230$

*Copy and complete:*
1. $4 \times 10 = \ldots$   2. $14 \times 10 = \ldots$   3. $37 \times 10 = \ldots$   4. $417 \times 10 = \ldots$

> To multiply a whole number by 100, you add 00
> $3 \times 100 = 300$     $48 \times 100 = 4800$

*Copy and complete:*
5. $5 \times 100 = \ldots$   6. $13 \times 100 = \ldots$   7. $24 \times 100 = \ldots$   8. $40 \times 100 = \ldots$

> To multiply a whole number by 1000, you add 000
> $5 \times 1000 = 3000$     $51 \times 1000 = 51000$

*Copy and complete:*
9. $7 \times 1000 = \ldots$   10. $29 \times 1000 = \ldots$   11. $45 \times 1000 = \ldots$   12. $150 \times 1000 = \ldots$

• Check your answers.

### PRACTICE

## P1: Mixed practice     CHECK ANSWERS AT THE END OF EACH BATCH

**Batch A:**   *Copy and complete:*
1. $7 \times 10 = \ldots$   2. $35 \times 100 = \ldots$   3. $213 \times 10 = \ldots$   4. $9 \times 1000 = \ldots$
5. $35 \times 100 = \ldots$   6. $17 \times \ldots = 1700$   7. $29 \times \ldots = 290$   8. $342 \times 10 = \ldots$
9. $\ldots \times 10 = 150$   10. $\ldots \times 100 = 6200$   11. $73 \times 1000 = \ldots$   12. $27 \times \ldots = 2700$

**Batch B:**   *Copy and complete:*
1. $9 \times 100 = \ldots$   2. $4 \times 1000 = \ldots$   3. $35 \times 10 = \ldots$   4. $19 \times \ldots = 1900$
5. $47 \times 100 = \ldots$   6. $83 \times \ldots = 830$   7. $75 \times \ldots = 7500$   8. $60 \times 10 = \ldots$
9. $\ldots \times 100 = 2500$   10. $\ldots \times 10 = 1050$   11. $222 \times 10 = \ldots$   12. $34 \times \ldots = 3400$

### Star Challenge 9

13-15 correct = 1 star

*Copy and complete:*
1. $7 \times \ldots = 700$   2. $39 \times \ldots = 390$   3. $\ldots \times 100 = 3500$
4. $56 \times 100 = \ldots$   5. $243 \times 10 = \ldots$   6. $77 \times \ldots = 77000$
7. $512 \times \ldots = 5120$   8. $11 \times 1000 = \ldots$   9. $\ldots \times 100 = 6700$
10. $12 \times 10 = \ldots$   11. $120 \times 10 = \ldots$   12. $200 \times 10 = \ldots$
13. $30 \times 100 = \ldots$   14. $\ldots \times 10 = 500$   15. $589 \times 100 = \ldots$

• Your teacher has the answers to these.

A POW GUIDE     page 54     Back to Basics **EXTRA**

## D2: Multiplying in your head

Didi: 7 x 20 = 7 x 2 x 10 = 14 x 10 = 140
So, 7 x 20 = 140

Work out these multiplications in your head. Write down the answers.
1. 6 x 20   2. 7 x 30   3. 7 x 40   4. 8 x 30   5. 5 x 50

Modesto: 3 x 500 = 3 x 5 x 100 = 15 x 100 = 1500
So, 3 x 500 = 1500

Work out these multiplications in your head. Write down the answers.
6. 3 x 400   7. 2 x 700   8. 5 x 600   9. 7 x 300   10. 3 x 600
11. 2 x 3000   12. 5 x 5000   13. 7 x 2000   14. 6 x 6000   15. 8 x 4000

16. 3 x 500   17. 11 x 20   18. 5 x 3000   19. 6 x 30   20. 9 x 20
21. 4 x 2000   22. 7 x 70   23. 6 x 50   24. 8 x 500   25. 6 x 3000

• Check your answers.

## D3: Getting more difficult

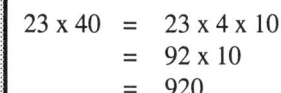

23 x 40 = 23 x 4 x 10
       = 92 x 10
       = 920

```
 23
x  4
 92
  1
```

Spoton: Put your working at the side.

*Copy and complete:*

1. 13 x 30 = 13 x 3 x 10
          =
          =

```
 13
x  3
```

2. 24 x 500 = ... x ... x 100
           =
           =

```
   ......
x ...
```

Work these out. Set out the working as in Q1 & 2.
3. 14 x 40   4. 80 x 60   5. 65 x 50   6. 45 x 80   7. 81 x 90
8. 32 x 700   9. 12 x 3000   10. 95 x 20   11. 43 x 300   12. 70 x 50
13. 15 x 50   14. 20 x 400   15. 72 x 30   16. 93 x 40   17. 60 x 60

• Check your answers.

### Star Challenge 10

8-10 correct = 1 star

Work out these multiplications in your head. Write down the answers.
1. 6 x 100   2. 17 x 10   3. 46 x 100   4. 6 x 20   5. 15 x 300

Work these out. Show all your working.
6. 35 x 50   7. 24 x 200   8. 26 x 70   9. 42 x 200   10. 75 x 50

• Your teacher has the answers to these.

A POW GUIDE — Back to Basics EXTRA

# Section 5: More multiplication techniques

In this section you will review and practise pencil-and-paper techniques for multiplying larger numbers.

## DEVELOPMENT

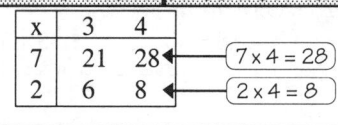

Levels 4&5

### D1: Little multiplication tables

| x | 3 | 4 |
|---|---|---|
| 7 | 21 | 28 | ← 7 x 4 = 28
| 2 | 6 | 8 | ← 2 x 4 = 8

Baggy

Copy and complete these multiplication tables:

1. 
| x | 4 | 5 |
|---|---|---|
| 3 | | |
| 5 | | |

2. 
| x | 10 | 3 |
|---|---|---|
| 7 | | |
| 40 | | |

3. 
| x | 2 | 8 |
|---|---|---|
| 10 | | |
| 20 | | |

4. 
| x | 6 | 9 |
|---|---|---|
| 2 | | |
| 5 | | |

5. 
| x | 3 | 10 |
|---|---|---|
| 10 | | |
| 20 | | |

6. 
| x | 20 | 7 |
|---|---|---|
| 30 | | |
| 2 | | |

7. 
| x | 7 | 4 |
|---|---|---|
| 50 | | |
| 8 | | |

8. 
| x | 40 | 30 |
|---|---|---|
| 30 | | |
| 7 | | |

• Check your answers.

### D2: Another way of setting out multiplication sums

**Old method**  In Section 3, you set out multiplication sums like this:
```
   5 3
 x   4
 2 1 2
   1 1
```

**New method**  53 x 4 = ?

| x | 50 | 3 |
|---|---|---|
| 4 | 200 | 12 |

Step 1

```
 200
+ 12
 212
```
Step 2

Ans: 53 x 4 = 212

Crumbl

**Task 1:** *Copy and complete:*

1. 
| x | 20 | 4 |
|---|---|---|
| 5 | | |

......
+ ......
———

So, 24 x 5 = ......

2. 
| x | 30 | 5 |
|---|---|---|
| 6 | | |

......
+ ......
———

So, 35 x 6 = ......

3. 
| x | 50 | 6 |
|---|---|---|
| 4 | | |

......
+ ......
———

So, 56 x 4 = ......

4. 
| x | 20 | 5 |
|---|---|---|
| 9 | | |

......
+ ......
———

So, 25 x 9 = ......

• Check your answers.

**Task 2:** Use the new method to do these sums. Set out your working as in Task 1.

5. 23 x 4    6. 52 x 7    7. 61 x 9    8. 28 x 5    9. 78 x 3
10. 41 x 8   11. 83 x 2   12. 76 x 3   13. 46 x 8   14. 57 x 5

• Check your answers.

A POW GUIDE    page 56    Back to Basics **EXTRA**

## D3: A useful trick

30 x 20 = 600  (Two 0s)   Work out 3 x 2 = 6 and add 00

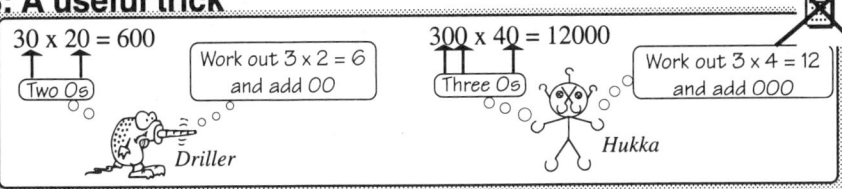

300 x 40 = 12000  (Three 0s)   Work out 3 x 4 = 12 and add 000

*Driller*   *Hukka*

*Copy and complete:*
1. 30 x 50 = ......   2. 40 x 70 = ......   3. 300 x 20 = ......   4. 500 x 30 = ......
5. 70 x 30 = ......   6. 50 x 50 = ......   7. 200 x 70 = ......   8. 600 x 40 = ......

• Check your answers.

## D4: Multiplying bigger numbers

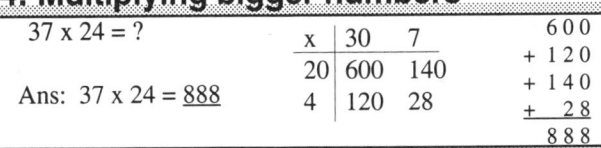

37 x 24 = ?

Ans: 37 x 24 = **888**

| x  | 30  | 7   |
|----|-----|-----|
| 20 | 600 | 140 |
| 4  | 120 | 28  |

```
  600
+ 120
+ 140
+  28
  888
```

**Task 1:** *Copy and complete:*

1.  
| x  | 20 | 3 |
|----|----|---|
| 10 |    |   |
| 5  |    |   |

......
......
+ ......

So, 23 x 15 = ......

2.  
| x | 40 | 5 |
|---|----|---|
| 20|    |   |
| 3 |    |   |

......
......
+ ......

So, 45 x 23 = ......

3.  
| x  | 60 | 2 |
|----|----|---|
| 30 |    |   |
| 7  |    |   |

......
......
+ ......

So, 62 x 37 = ......

4.  
| x  | 70 | 7 |
|----|----|---|
| 20 |    |   |
| 9  |    |   |

......
......
+ ......

So, 77 x 29 = .......

**Task 2:** *Work out each of these. Set out your working as in Task 1.*
5. 32 x 24   6. 72 x 14   7. 68 x 33   8. 49 x 18   9. 67 x 36
10. 59 x 28   11. 47 x 12   12. 84 x 45   13. 83 x 37   14. 71 x 17

• Check your answers.

---

You have to be able to multiply a 3-digit number by a 2-digit number, without a calculator.
There are many possible methods that you could learn.
It does not matter which method you use.
This section has been leading up to one method of doing this, in D5. 
**BUT** – there is a second method of doing it, in D6.
If you find D5 hard, try the other method in D6.
*Idea*   You might find this second method easier.

A POW GUIDE   page 57   Back to Basics **EXTRA**

## D5: Multiplying 3-digit numbers by 2-digit numbers

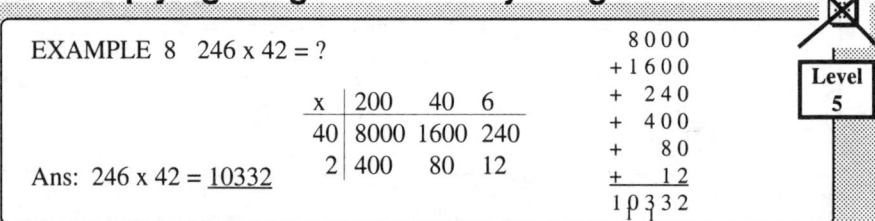

EXAMPLE 8   246 x 42 = ?

| x  | 200  | 40   | 6   |
|----|------|------|-----|
| 40 | 8000 | 1600 | 240 |
| 2  | 400  | 80   | 12  |

```
   8 0 0 0
 + 1 6 0 0
 +   2 4 0
 +   4 0 0
 +     8 0
 +     1 2
 ─────────
   1 0 3 3 2
```

Ans: 246 x 42 = <u>10332</u>

**Level 5**

Work out each of these. Set out your working as in the example.
1. 123 x 13
2. 235 x 25
3. 418 x 33
4. 729 x 18
5. 562 x 36
6. 813 x 27
7. 672 x 73
8. 519 x 48

• Check your answers.

> You only need to know ONE method for multiplying big numbers.
> You can use the method in D5 or the method in D6
> – or another method, if you prefer.
> If you like the method in D5, you do not have to do D6.

## D6: The grating method for multiplication

**Level 5**

EXAMPLE 9   Show that 3 1 2 x 4 9 = 1 5 2 8 8

← first number
← second number

answer → 2 8 8

How is the answer worked out?

You add up along the diagonal lines.

Blurbl     Pow

This method of multiplication was used in the Middle Ages. The earliest record of this is in an Italian arithmetic book published in 1478.

3 x 4   1 x 4   2 x 4
3 x 9   1 x 9   2 x 9

Use the grating method to work out:
1. 435 x 49
2. 248 x 31
3. 872 x 26
4. 592 x 17

• Check your answers.

---

### P1: Multiplication practice

*Use any method. Show all your working out.*
*Check your answers AFTER EACH QUESTION.*
*Do as many batches as you need.*

| Batch A:      | Batch B:      | Batch C:      |
|---------------|---------------|---------------|
| 1. 44 x 12    | 1. 33 x 13    | 1. 25 x 12    |
| 2. 631 x 41   | 2. 437 x 11   | 2. 262 x 22   |
| 3. 754 x 15   | 3. 121 x 63   | 3. 343 x 54   |

**Star Challenge 11**
All correct = 1 star
Use any method.
Show all your working out.
1. 27 x 34
2. 391 x 16
3. 247 x 38

A POW GUIDE          page 58          Back to Basics **EXTRA**

# P2: Using multiplication to solve problems

1. Sport Supply sells ping pong balls to shops.
   They are sold in boxes of 6.

   | Shop A buys 2 boxes. How many ping pong balls do they get ? | Shop B buys 8 boxes. How many ping pong balls do they get ? | Shop C buys 10 boxes. How many ping pong balls do they get ? |

2. Trendy Sports sells ping pong balls to shops.
   They are sold in boxes shaped like pyramids.
   Each box holds 15 balls.

   Shop D buys 5 boxes.
   15
   x 5   *Copy and complete this sum to find how many balls in 5 boxes.*
   ___

   Shop E buys 9 boxes.
   15
   x 9   *Copy and complete this sum to find how many balls in 9 boxes.*
   ___

   Shop F buys 25 boxes. Work out how many balls there are in 25 boxes. Show all your working.

3. The Bulk Sports Factory makes ping pong balls. The balls are packed in boxes of 144. Trendy Sports buys 18 boxes.
   (a) Work out how many ping pong balls there are in 18 boxes. Show all working.

   Sport Supply buys 35 boxes of ping pong balls from The Bulk Sports Factory.
   (b) Work out how many ping pong balls there are in 35 boxes. Show all working.

4. Bill sells TVs in his shop. He buys the TVs from a wholesaler.
   Bill buys some small TVs costing £59 each.
   (a) Work out the cost of 3 of these.
   (b) Work out the cost of 24 TVs at £59 each.

   Bill buys some large screen TVs costing £357 each.
   Work out the cost of (c) 5 TVs     (d) 15 TVs     (e) 75 TVs

   *Show all working*

   • *Check your answers.*
   All correct = 1 star

## Star Challenge

1. To find the number of tiles on this floor, you work out 17 x 6
   Show how to work out the number of tiles.
   (6 by 17)

2. Work out the number of tiles on this floor. Show all working.
   (35 by 12)

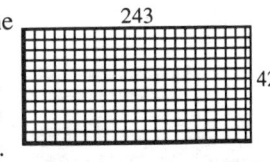

3. Work out the number of tiles on this floor. Show all working.
   (243 by 42)

*A POW GUIDE*     page 59     *Back to Basics* **EXTRA**

# Section 6: Division techniques

In this section you will review and practise techniques for division.

**DEVELOPMENT**

## D1: Division using the table square

Level 3

| x | 1 | 2 | 3 | 4 | 5 | 6 | 7 | 8 | 9 | 10 | 11 | 12 | 13 | 14 | 15 |
|---|---|---|---|---|---|---|---|---|---|----|----|----|----|----|----|
| 1 | 1 | 2 | 3 | 4 | 5 | 6 | 7 | 8 | 9 | 10 | 11 | 12 | 13 | 14 | 15 |
| 2 | 2 | 4 | 6 | 8 | 10 | 12 | 14 | 16 | 18 | 20 | 22 | 24 | 26 | 28 | 30 |
| 3 | 3 | 6 | 9 | 12 | 15 | 18 | 21 | 24 | 27 | 30 | 33 | 36 | 39 | 42 | 45 |
| 4 | 4 | 8 | 12 | 16 | 20 | 24 | 28 | 32 | 36 | 40 | 44 | 48 | 52 | 56 | 60 |
| 5 | 5 | 10 | 15 | 20 | 25 | 30 | 35 | 40 | 45 | 50 | 55 | 60 | 65 | 70 | 75 |
| 6 | 6 | 12 | 18 | 24 | 30 | 36 | 42 | 48 | 54 | 60 | 66 | 72 | 78 | 84 | 90 |
| 7 | 7 | 14 | 21 | 28 | 35 | 42 | 49 | 56 | 63 | 70 | 77 | 84 | 91 | 98 | 105 |
| 8 | 8 | 16 | 24 | 32 | 40 | 48 | 56 | 64 | 72 | 80 | 88 | 96 | 104 | 112 | 120 |
| 9 | 9 | 18 | 27 | 36 | 45 | 54 | 63 | 72 | 81 | 90 | 99 | 108 | 117 | 126 | 135 |
| 10 | 10 | 20 | 30 | 40 | 50 | 60 | 70 | 80 | 90 | 100 | 110 | 120 | 130 | 140 | 150 |

EXAMPLE 10    Work out $65 \div 5$

$$5 \longrightarrow 65$$
with 13 above

$65 \div 5 = \boxed{13}$

*Copy and complete:*

1. $18 \div 2 = \ldots$
2. $12 \div 3 = \ldots$
3. $20 \div 5 = \ldots$
4. $24 \div 6 = \ldots$
5. $32 \div 4 = \ldots$
6. $21 \div 3 = \ldots$
7. $30 \div 6 = \ldots$
8. $56 \div 7 = \ldots$
9. $72 \div 8 = \ldots$
10. $88 \div 8 = \ldots$
11. $63 \div 9 = \ldots$
12. $90 \div 6 = \ldots$

• Check your answers

## D2: It isn't always called division

Level 3

How many 3s are there in 18 ?
Share 18 between 3
Divide 18 by 3
Work out $\frac{1}{3}$ of 18

these all mean $18 \div 3$

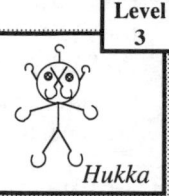

*Hukka*

1. How many 5s are there in 25 ?
2. Share £12 between 4.
3. Work out $\frac{1}{4}$ of 20
4. Divide 12 by 2
5. $16 \div 4$
6. How many 10s are there in 50 ?
7. Share 15 smarties between 3 children
8. Divide 24 by 6
9. $30 \div 5$
10. Work out $\frac{1}{2}$ of 16

• Check your answers.

---

You may use the table square to help you with division.
But, in exams you will not have a table square.
Wherever possible, do division without using the table square.

A POW GUIDE        Back to Basics **EXTRA**

## D3: Setting out division sums

**Level 4**

EXAMPLE 11   Work out  $2\overline{)14}$
A:                       $\phantom{2)}7$  ← answer      *This means 14 ÷ 2*
                      $2\overline{)14}$

*Plok*

*Copy and complete:*

1. $3\overline{)15}$   2. $5\overline{)30}$   3. $6\overline{)48}$   4. $7\overline{)28}$   5. $6\overline{)36}$

6. $4\overline{)36}$   7. $8\overline{)56}$   8. $9\overline{)72}$   9. $11\overline{)99}$   10. $12\overline{)48}$

• *Check your answers.*

## D4: More difficult division sums

*If you need help with this technique, ASK YOUR TEACHER !*

EXAMPLE 12   Work out   $148 \div 4$
A:              $\phantom{4)1}3\phantom{^2}7$
              $4\overline{)14^28}$

*Step 1*: 4 into 1 won't go
*Step 2*: 4 into 14 goes 3 times, with 2 left over. Carry 2 into next column
*Step 3*: 4 into 28 goes 7 times

**Level 4**

*Work out :*

1. $5\overline{)95}$   2. $4\overline{)96}$   3. $5\overline{)255}$   4. $3\overline{)222}$   5. $7\overline{)616}$

6. $5\overline{)525}$   7. $6\overline{)270}$   8. $272 \div 2$   9. $368 \div 4$   10. $276 \div 6$

11. $5\overline{)675}$   12. $3\overline{)243}$   13. $357 \div 7$   14. $138 \div 6$   15. $126 \div 9$

• *Check your answers.*

### PRACTICE

## P1: Division practice

*You must be good at these before you can go on to D5.
Do as many batches as you need.*

*Big Edd*   *At the end of each batch, CHECK YOUR ANSWERS.*

**Batch A:**    Work out :
1. $474 \div 2$   2. $615 \div 5$   3. $665 \div 7$   4. $104 \div 8$   5. $168 \div 7$
6. $750 \div 5$   7. $232 \div 8$   8. $276 \div 6$   9. $153 \div 9$   10. $428 \div 4$

**Batch B:**    Work out :
1. $144 \div 3$   2. $357 \div 3$   3. $574 \div 7$   4. $159 \div 3$   5. $762 \div 6$
6. $496 \div 8$   7. $370 \div 5$   8. $628 \div 2$   9. $540 \div 4$   10. $296 \div 4$

**Batch C:**    Work out :
1. $471 \div 3$   2. $416 \div 8$   3. $635 \div 5$   4. $954 \div 3$   5. $477 \div 9$
6. $448 \div 7$   7. $102 \div 6$   8. $385 \div 7$   9. $468 \div 6$   10. $390 \div 5$

A POW GUIDE            Back to Basics **EXTRA**

**Star Challenge 13-13**

10 correct = 2 stars
8-9 correct = 1 star

1. 544 ÷ 2    2. 228 ÷ 6    3. 366 ÷ 3    4. 328 ÷ 4    5. 189 ÷ 7
6. 414 ÷ 9    7. 268 ÷ 4    8. 520 ÷ 8    9. 203 ÷ 7    10. 342 ÷ 6

• Your teacher has the answers to these.

## P2: Using division to solve problems

1. Share £45 between 5 people. Show how to work it out.
2. Bill buys 6 identical TVs to sell in his shop. They cost him £468. Work out £468 ÷ 6 to find out what each one cost.
3. Bill buys 3 identical TVs. They cost him £828. Work out £828 ÷ 3 to find out what each one cost.

*Show how to work out each answer using a division sum.*

4. I bought 8 pingpong balls. The total cost was 360p. What was the cost of 1 ball?
5. I bought 7 sticky buns. The total cost was 126p. What was the cost of 1 bun?
6. I bought 9 chocolate cakes. The total cost was 252p. What was the cost of 1 bun?

*Ruff*

7. 3 plane tickets to Paris cost £348. Work out the cost of 1 ticket.
8. 8 plane tickets to Madrid cost £928. Work out the cost of 1 ticket.

• Check your answers.

## P3: Division puzzles

1. 2 )☐☐4    How many different answers can you get using the digits **6 & 8**? What are the answers?

2. 3 )☐☐☐    How many different answers can you get using the digits **6, 9 & 9**? What are the answers?

3. 3 )☐☐☐    How many different answers can you get using the digits **5, 6 & 7**? What are the answers?

• Check your answers.

**Star Challenge 14-14**

12 marks = 2 stars
10-11 marks = 1 star

1. 2 )☐☐☐    Use the digits **4, 6 & 8** in this sum. How many different answers can you get? What are the answers?

2. 5 )☐☐☐    Use the digits **3, 5 & 7** in this sum. How many different answers can you get, with no remainder? What are the answers?

• Your teacher has the answers to these.

A POW GUIDE — page 62 — Back to Basics **EXTRA**

## D5: Dividing by large numbers

**DEVELOPMENT** — Level 5

EXAMPLE 7    Work out   $345 \div 23$

A:   $23 \overline{)3\,4^{11}5}$   = 15

*The method is the same as in D4, BUT you can't use the table square*

*Writing out a table like this helps.*

Pow

Make this table by adding 23 each time.
$1 \times 23 = 23$
$2 \times 23 = 46$
$3 \times 23 = 69$
$4 \times 23 = 92$
$5 \times 23 = 115$
...

*Work out the answer to each of these. Show your working.*

1. $11 \overline{)187}$   2. $14 \overline{)322}$   3. $435 \div 15$   4. $504 \div 12$   5. $896 \div 16$
6. $989 \div 23$   7. $837 \div 31$   8. $441 \div 21$   9. $957 \div 11$   10. $756 \div 21$
11. $480 \div 15$   12. $208 \div 16$   13. $793 \div 13$   14. $999 \div 27$   15. $612 \div 12$

• Check your answers.

## P3: Large number division practice

**PRACTICE** — Level 5

*Do as many batches as you need.*
[Show all working.]
*At the end of each batch, CHECK YOUR ANSWERS.*

**Batch A:**   Work out :
1. $165 \div 15$   2. $782 \div 17$   3. $462 \div 21$   4. $156 \div 13$   5. $630 \div 14$
6. $957 \div 33$   7. $473 \div 11$   8. $572 \div 22$   9. $306 \div 18$   10. $732 \div 61$

**Batch B:**   Work out :
1. $663 \div 13$   2. $624 \div 24$   3. $731 \div 17$   4. $923 \div 13$   5. $667 \div 23$
6. $406 \div 29$   7. $897 \div 69$   8. $1008 \div 14$   9. $954 \div 53$   10. $851 \div 37$

### Star Challenge ⭐⭐⭐

20 marks = 3 stars
18-19 marks = 2 stars
13-17 marks = 1 star

*Work each division sum out. Show all working.*

1. $585 \div 15$   2. $918 \div 34$   3. $693 \div 11$   4. $676 \div 52$   5. $868 \div 31$
6. $494 \div 26$   7. $400 \div 16$   8. $475 \div 25$   9. $552 \div 12$   10. $702 \div 54$

• *Your teacher has the answers to these.*

2 marks for each question
: 1 for the answer and 1 for the working

*A POW GUIDE*                          *Back to Basics* **EXTRA**

# Section 7: Technique review

In this section you will:
- do arithmetic totally without a calculator;
- review the arithmetic techniques met in this topic.

Check your answers at the end of each set of problems

## R1: Multiplication and division using a table square

**Level 4**

| x  | 1  | 2  | 3  | 4  | 5  | 6  | 7   | 8   | 9   | 10  | 11  | 12  | 13  | 14  | 15  |
|----|----|----|----|----|----|----|-----|-----|-----|-----|-----|-----|-----|-----|-----|
| 1  | 1  | 2  | 3  | 4  | 5  | 6  | 7   | 8   | 9   | 10  | 11  | 12  | 13  | 14  | 15  |
| 2  | 2  | 4  | 6  | 8  | 10 | 12 | 14  | 16  | 18  | 20  | 22  | 24  | 26  | 28  | 30  |
| 3  | 3  | 6  | 9  | 12 | 15 | 18 | 21  | 24  | 27  | 30  | 33  | 36  | 39  | 42  | 45  |
| 4  | 4  | 8  | 12 | 16 | 20 | 24 | 28  | 32  | 36  | 40  | 44  | 48  | 52  | 56  | 60  |
| 5  | 5  | 10 | 15 | 20 | 25 | 30 | 35  | 40  | 45  | 50  | 55  | 60  | 65  | 70  | 75  |
| 6  | 6  | 12 | 18 | 24 | 30 | 36 | 42  | 48  | 54  | 60  | 66  | 72  | 78  | 84  | 90  |
| 7  | 7  | 14 | 21 | 28 | 35 | 42 | 49  | 56  | 63  | 70  | 77  | 84  | 91  | 98  | 105 |
| 8  | 8  | 16 | 24 | 32 | 40 | 48 | 56  | 64  | 72  | 80  | 88  | 96  | 104 | 112 | 120 |
| 9  | 9  | 18 | 27 | 36 | 45 | 54 | 63  | 72  | 81  | 90  | 99  | 108 | 117 | 126 | 135 |
| 10 | 10 | 20 | 30 | 40 | 50 | 60 | 70  | 80  | 90  | 100 | 110 | 120 | 130 | 140 | 150 |
| 11 | 11 | 22 | 33 | 44 | 55 | 66 | 77  | 88  | 99  | 110 | 121 | 132 | 143 | 154 | 165 |
| 12 | 12 | 24 | 36 | 48 | 60 | 72 | 84  | 96  | 108 | 120 | 132 | 144 | 156 | 168 | 180 |
| 13 | 13 | 26 | 39 | 52 | 65 | 78 | 91  | 104 | 117 | 130 | 143 | 156 | 169 | 182 | 195 |
| 14 | 14 | 28 | 42 | 56 | 70 | 84 | 98  | 112 | 126 | 140 | 154 | 168 | 182 | 196 | 210 |
| 15 | 15 | 30 | 45 | 60 | 75 | 90 | 105 | 120 | 135 | 150 | 165 | 180 | 195 | 210 | 225 |

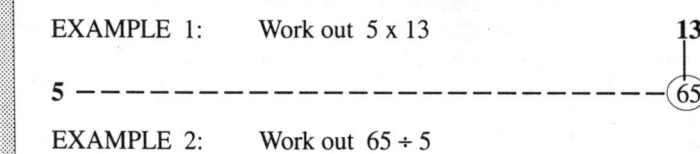

EXAMPLE 1:    Work out  5 x 13       **13**
                                       |
5 — — — — — — — — — — — — — — — — — — — (65)

EXAMPLE 2:    Work out  65 ÷ 5
              Using the diagram above gives

| 5 x 13 = 65 |
| 65 ÷ 5 = 13 |

*Copy and complete each of these sums:*

1. 12 x 3  = ...    2. 42 ÷ 3  = ...    3. 9 x 8  = ...    4. 14 x 4  = ...    5. 52 ÷ 4  = ...
6. 12 x 7  = ...    7. 9 x 6  = ...     8. 108 ÷ 9 = ...   9. 91 ÷ 7  = ...   10. 63 ÷ 9  = ...

## R2: Pencil and paper addition

EXAMPLE 3:    Work out  15 + 130 + 8

```
   15
+ 130
+   8
  153   Pow
    1
```

Stack the numbers with units under units, tens under tens, hundreds under hundreds ...

5 + 8 = 13  Write this as 3 in the units column and carry the 10 as a 1 in the 10s column.

*Work out each addition. Show all working.*   **Level 4**

1. 34 + 2 + 6
2. 163 + 23 + 201
3. 54 + 215 + 3
4. 567 + 120 + 31

*A POW GUIDE*            *Back to Basics* **EXTRA**

## R3: Pencil and paper subtraction

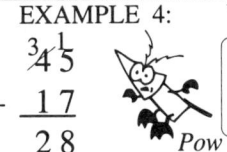

EXAMPLE 4:   Work out  45 – 17

$\overset{3}{4}\overset{1}{5}$
$-\ 17$
$\ \ \ 28$

5 – 7 won't go
So, you borrow a 10 from the tens column to make 15 – 7

Pow

Work out each subtraction. Show all working.

**Level 4**

1. 34 – 23
2. 34 – 15
3. 254 – 126
4. 135 – 63

## R4: Pencil and paper multiplication

**Level 4**

EXAMPLE 5:
Work out  43 x 4

$\ \ 43$
$\underline{x\ \ 4}$
$172$
$\ \ 1$

Step 1
4 x 3 = 12
2 down, carry 1

$\ \ 43$
$\underline{x\ \ 4}$
$\ \ \ 2$
$\ \ 1$

$\ \ 43$
$\underline{x\ \ 4}$
$172$
$\ \ 1$

Step 2
4 x 4 = 16
add 1 = 17

Pow

Work out each multiplication. Set working out as in example 5.

1.  36 x 2   = …
2.  57 x 3   = …
3.  132 x 4  = …
4.  82 x 7   = …

## R5: Pencil and paper division

**Level 4**

EXAMPLE 6:   Work out  2 ) 14

$\ \ \ \ 7$ ← answer
$2\ )\ 14$

This means 14 ÷ 2

Plok

1.  3 ) 210
2.  5 ) 340
3.  3 ) 48
4.  4 ) 208
5.  6 ) 354

## R6: Multiplying whole numbers by 10, 100, 1000

**Level 4**

Rules for whole numbers
   To multiply a whole number by 10, you add 0
   To multiply a whole number by 100, you add 00
   To multiply a whole number by 1000, you add 000

   2 x 10 = 20      3 x 100 = 300      5 x 1000 = 5 000

Copy and complete each of these multiplication sums:

1.  4 x 10     = …
2.  52 x 10    = …
3.  7 x 100    = …
4.  81 x 100   = …
5.  5 x 1000   = …
6.  33 x 10    = …
7.  24 x 100   = …
8.  34 x 10    = …

A POW GUIDE          Back to Basics **EXTRA**

## R7: Multiplication by 20, 30, ... 200, 300, ...

Level 4

EXAMPLE 7:   Q: Work out 23 x 40
A:   23 x 40 = 23 x 4 x 10
              = 92 x 10
              = 920

          2 3
        x   4
        ___
          9 2
          1

*Work out these multiplications. Show all working.*

1. 6 x 20     2. 5 x 30     3. 7 x 200     4. 23 x 300
5. 51 x 200   6. 12 x 4000  7. 72 x 300    8. 47 x 60

## R8: Multiplying by 2-digit numbers

Level 5

EXAMPLE 8:   Q: Work out 312 x 49

You may use any method you choose. Here are two methods of multiplication.

The Table Method

| x  | 300   | 10  | 2  |
|----|-------|-----|----|
| 40 | 12000 | 400 | 80 |
| 9  | 2700  | 90  | 18 |

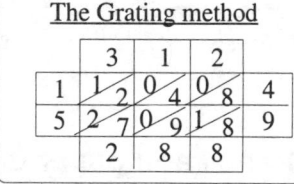

```
  1 2 0 0 0
+   2 7 0 0
+     4 0 0
+      9 0
+      8 0
+      1 8
_____
  1 5 2 8 8
      1 1
```

The Grating method

| | 3 | 1 | 2 | |
|---|---|---|---|---|
| 1 | 1/2 | 0/4 | 0/8 | 4 |
| 5 | 2/7 | 0/9 | 1/8 | 9 |
| | 2 | 8 | 8 | |

Ans: 15288

*Work out these multiplications. Show all working.*

1. 37 x 14    2. 62 x 25    3. 83 x 54    4. 391 x 26    5. 247 x 54

## R9: More difficult division sums

Level 4

EXAMPLE 9: Work out  148 ÷ 4

A:
```
       3 7
    _____
  4 ) 14²8
```

*Work out:*

1. 5)675    2. 3)243    3. 357 ÷ 7    4. 138 ÷ 6    5. 126 ÷ 9

## R10: Dividing by large numbers

Level 5

*Work out the answer to each of these. Show your working.*

1. 13)377    2. 14)336    3. 988 ÷ 26    4. 576 ÷ 12    5. 896 ÷ 16

A POW GUIDE          Back to Basics  EXTRA

# THE NATIONAL CURRICULUM ...
# ... AND BEYOND ...

*Pow*

# Bar Charts and Beyond
## EXTRA

| | | | |
|---|---|---|---|
| | §10 Technique review | | |
| | | | §9 Working with continuous data |
| | | | §8 Constructing pie charts |
| | | §7 Interpreting diagrams | |
| | | §6 Working with averages | |
| | §5 Averages and range | | |
| | §4 Line graphs | | |
| | §3 Grouped data | | |
| §2 Bar charts and pictographs | | | |
| §1 Interpreting tables and diagrams | | | |
| Level 3 | Level 4 | Level 5 | Level 6 |

*A POW GUIDE*        page 67

# Bar Charts and Beyond
## Section 1: Interpreting tables and diagrams

In this section you will:
- interpret information from tables and lists;
- interpret bar charts and pictographs;
- put information from bar charts and pictographs onto tables.

Level 3

### DEVELOPMENT
### D1: From lists and tables

Academy qualification of Pan–Galactic Explorers on Starship 459

| Qualification | 1st class | 2nd class | 3rd class | 4th class |
|---|---|---|---|---|
| PGE Officers | 9 | 11 | 6 | 2 |
| PGE Crew | 2 | 9 | 16 | 21 |

*Gizmo*

1. How many officers have a first class qualification?
2. How many crew have either a first class or a second class qualification?
3. How many officers and crew on this starship have 4th class qualifications?
4. Which have more second class qualifications, officers or crew?
5. Which have more third class qualifications, officers or crew?
6. How many officers are there on board?
7. How many crew are there on board?
8. How many Pan–Galactic Explorers are there on this starship?

*Hukka*

Juno is a planet that was first settled by spaceships from Earth.
Arro and Madria are countries on Juno.

Monthly rainfall in mm

|  | Jan | Feb | March | April | May | June | July | August | Sept | Oct | Nov | Dec |
|---|---|---|---|---|---|---|---|---|---|---|---|---|
| Arro | 72 | 51 | 43 | 50 | 52 | 30 | 56 | 34 | 57 | 70 | 86 | 73 |
| Madria | 0 | 0 | 0 | 0 | 2 | 73 | 246 | 358 | 166 | 82 | 13 | 0 |

9. How much rain falls in Arro in April?
10. Which is the wettest month in Arro?
11. Which is the wettest month in Madria?
12. Which country has a wet season and a dry season?
13. In what months is the dry season?
14. How much rain falls in one year in Arro?
15. How much rain falls in one year in Madria?
16. Which is the driest month in Arro?
17. Which country is more likely to have water shortages?
18. Give a reason for your answer to Q17.

*Frizzbang*

*Yerwat*

*Driller*

• Check your answers.

A POW GUIDE     page 68     Bar Charts and Beyond **EXTRA**

## D2: Pictograph review

Favourite Holiday Planets of the Pan–Galactic Explorers on Starship 310

Holiday Planet:
- Zoom
- Eros
- Zog
- Klar
- Rima
- Other

Key: 1 picture = 2 PGEs

*Sureshot*

1. How many PGEs chose Zoom?
2. How many PGEs chose Zog?
3. Copy and complete this frequency table:

| Holiday planet | Zoom | Eros | Zog | Klar | Rima | Other |
|---|---|---|---|---|---|---|
| Number of PGEs | | | | | | |

4. How many PGEs chose either Klar or Rima?
5. How many PGEs took part in this survey?

*Kooldood*

• Check your answers.

## D3: Bar chart review

Home Planet of New Students arriving at the Pan–Galactic Academy in 2142 AF

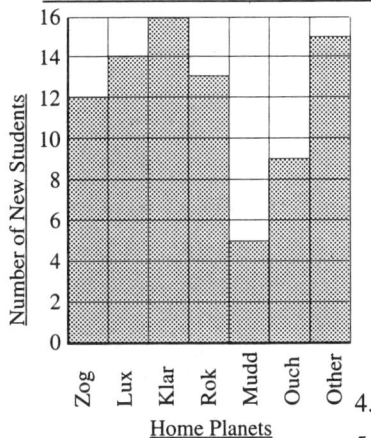

1. How many of them came from Zog?
2. How many of them came from Rok?
3. Copy and complete this frequency table:

| Planet | Frequency |
|---|---|
| Zog | |
| Lux | |
| Klar | |
| Rok | |
| Mudd | |
| Ouch | |
| Other | |

In this case, 'frequency' means the number of new students

(Bar chart x-axis: Zog, Lux, Klar, Rok, Mudd, Ouch, Other — Home Planets; y-axis: Number of New Students, 0 to 16)

*Usu Al*

4. How many New Students were there altogether?
5. Lux and Klar are in the same star system. How many New Students came from Lux or Klar? 
6. From which planet did the most number of students come?
7. Students from Ouch and Rok are insectoid. How many insectoid students are there this time?

Insectoid means 'insect–like'

• Check your answers.

A POW GUIDE     page 69     Bar Charts and Beyond **EXTRA**

# Section 2: Bar charts and pictographs

In this section you will:
- review what must be put onto a bar chart or a pictograph;
- transfer raw data to frequency tables;
- create bar charts and pictographs from frequency tables.

Level 3

## DEVELOPMENT

### D1: What is missing ?

Galacton is very popular board game on Starship 218
This is a **frequency table**.
It gives the number of wins of the best 6 Galacton players.

| PGE | Plok | Do–med | Chyps | Idea | Taz | Dwork |
|---|---|---|---|---|---|---|
| Wins | 6 | 8 | 5 | 4 | 7 | 4 |

This **bar chart** displays the data (information) given in the frequency table.

1. One of the bars is wrong.
   Explain which bar is wrong and what is wrong with it.
2. On this bar chart :
   - the labels on the axes are missing
   - there is no title.
   
   Copy the bar chart. Draw all the bars correctly.
   Put in the missing labels and the title.

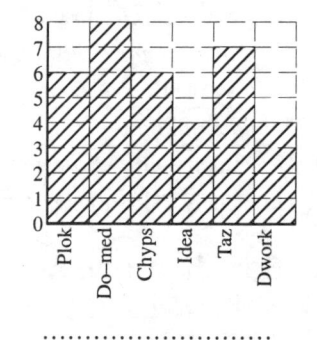

| PGE | Plok | Do–med | Chyps | Idea | Taz | Dwork |
|---|---|---|---|---|---|---|
| Wins | 6 | 8 | 5 | 4 | 7 | 4 |

This **pictograph** displays the data given in the frequency table.

3. There is no key on this pictograph.
   The key says how many wins one symbol stands for.
   What would the key be ?
4. On this pictograph :
   - the label on the axis up the page is missing
   - there is no key
   - there is no title.
   
   Copy the pictograph. Put in the key, the missing label and the title.

• Check answers

## Star Challenge 1

1 star for completely correct bar chart

Survey of favourite music on Starship 218

| Favourite kind of music | Spark | Folk Funk | Klassic | Techno Groove | Wild Beat |
|---|---|---|---|---|---|
| Frequency | 10 | 8 | 12 | 11 | 7 |

Draw a bar chart to show the results of this survey.

• *Your teacher will need to mark this.*

A POW GUIDE — Bar Charts and Beyond **EXTRA**

> **Check List for Bar Charts**
> To earn full marks a bar chart must have:
> - equal width bars (1 mark)
> - labels in the middle of each bar (1 mark)
> - accurate heights of bars (2 marks)
> - sensible scale up the page (2 marks)
> - labels on both axes (2 marks)
> - title (1 mark)

> **Check List for Pictographs**
> To earn full marks a pictograph must have:
> - simple symbols (1 mark)
> - label on the axis (1 mark)
> - correct KEY (1 mark)
> - title (1 mark)
> - correct number of symbols (3 marks) in each line

## D2: Displaying survey results

Taz did a survey on favourite soft drinks on Starship 218.
These are the results:

| M | Z | L | L | S | F |
| F | S | F | L | Z | M |
| L | F | Z | M | S | F |
| S | S | M | L | L | F |
| L | Z | F | S | M | L |

*Taz*

F = Faz
Z = Zorbit
L = Limk
S = Sput
M = Mmm

**Task 1:** Copy and complete this frequency table for the results of the survey.
- Check answers.

**Task 2:** Display this information as a bar chart.

**Task 3:** Display this information as a pictograph.

*Hukka*

| Drink | Tally | Frequency |
|---|---|---|
| Faz | | |
| Zorbit | | |
| Limk | | |
| Sput | | |
| Mmm | | |

• Check your answers.

### Star Challenge 2

1 star for completely correct pictograph

The two most popular snack bars on Starship 218 are Handel Bars and Wizzads

| Survey outcome | Frequency |
|---|---|
| Liked Handel Bars | 16 |
| Liked Wizzads | 14 |
| Liked both | 20 |
| Liked neither | 9 |

*Cringo*

Display this information on a pictograph.
Use 1 symbol = 4 PGEs

• Your teacher will need to mark this.

### Star Challenge 3 & 3

1 star for correct frequency table.
1 star for completely correct bar chart

Favourite Leisure Activities on Starship 218

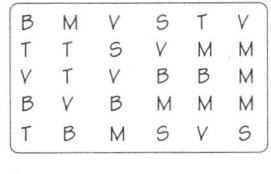

| B | M | V | S | T | V |
| T | T | S | V | M | M |
| V | T | V | B | B | M |
| B | V | B | M | M | M |
| T | B | M | S | V | S |

**Key:** M = Mixit  S = Scord
T = Targ  B = Badminton
V = Volleyball

*Blurbl*

Display this information in a frequency table.
Display this information on a bar chart.

• Your teacher will need to mark this.

# Section 3: Grouped data

In this section you will:
- put data into grouped frequency tables;
- display grouped data using frequency diagrams (bar charts).

Level 4

### DEVELOPMENT

## D1: Working with grouped data

Pan–Galactic Explorers on Starship 218 were asked how many expeditions they had each completed

| 5 | 7 | 23 | 16 | 2 | 0 | 14 | 12 |
| 11 | 22 | 15 | 16 | 6 | 2 | 1 | 18 |
| 12 | 17 | 13 | 21 | 14 | 16 | 0 | 13 |

Number of completed expeditions of crew of SS218

**Task 1:** Tally this data into the grouped frequency table.

Yerwat

| No. of exped. | Tally | Frequency |
|---|---|---|
| 0 – 4 | | |
| 5 – 9 | | |
| 10 – 14 | | |
| 15 – 19 | | |
| 20 – 24 | | |

**Task 2:** Copy and complete this bar chart for the grouped data in this table.

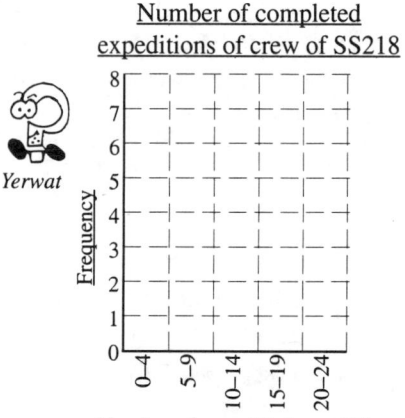

Number of completed expeditions

- Check your answers.

## D2: Choosing the groups

These are the scores in the Pan–Galactic Academy final exam:

68  56  73  47  63  55  86  77  69  84  68  82  57  48  83  66
56  46  82  73  84  41  67  87  73  55  71  77  81  78  71  65

### Grouping data
It is best to divide the data into 4-10 groups.
The groups must all be the same width.
The groups must not overlap – No number can be in two groups.

The smallest number is 41    The largest number is 87

1. Blurbl chose these groups for the frequency table.

Blurbl

| 40 – 50 |
| 50 – 60 |
| 60 – 70 |
| 70 – 80 |
| 80 – 90 |

Explain why these groups won't do.

2. Burga chose these groups for the frequency table.

Burga

| 45 – 50 |
| 51 – 60 |
| 61 – 70 |
| 71 – 80 |
| 81 – 90 |

Explain why these groups won't do.

A POW GUIDE       page 72       Bar Charts and Beyond **EXTRA**

3. Crumbl chose these groups.
   These groups will do.
   Put the exam scores into a grouped
   frequency table using Crumbl's groups.

   | 41 – 50 |
   | 51 – 60 |
   | 61 – 70 |
   | 71 – 80 |
   | 81 – 90 |

   *Crumbl*

   • Check answers.

   *Driller*

4. Copy and complete this bar chart for
   the grouped frequency table in question 3.

   • Check answers before doing Star Challenge 4.

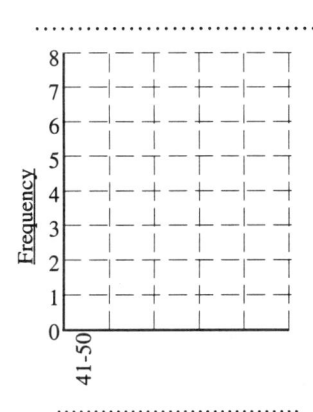

## Star Challenge 4

1 star for correct frequency table.
1 star for completely correct bar chart

### Pan–Galactic Targ Survey
Calling all
you Targ players.
What is the highest Targ
score that you have ever made?

*Hukka*     *Gorbag*

The results of this survey were:

| 14 | 44 | 17 | 41 | 37 | 44 | 34 | 13 | 48 |
| 20 | 34 | 40 | 49 | 42 | 41 | 36 | 24 | 46 |
| 35 | 15 | 25 | 23 | 26 | 43 | 19 | 48 | 25 |
| 42 | 38 | 40 | 34 | 24 | 16 | 39 | 34 | 19 |
| 32 | 45 | 41 | 32 | 19 | 43 | 26 | 41 | 18 |

1. What is the lowest Targ score?
2. What is the highest Targ score?
3. Use these values to help you choose suitable groupings for the data.
   Make a grouped frequency table.
4. Make a bar chart for the grouped data

• *Your teacher will need to mark this.*

A POW GUIDE        Bar Charts and Beyond **EXTRA**

# Section 4: Line graphs

In this section you will work with simple line graphs.

**DEVELOPMENT**

Level 4

## D1: Temperatures on the planet Juno

Arro and Madria are two countries on the planet of Juno. You met them in Section 1: D1

Big Edd

Temperatures in the capital of Arro on 1st May

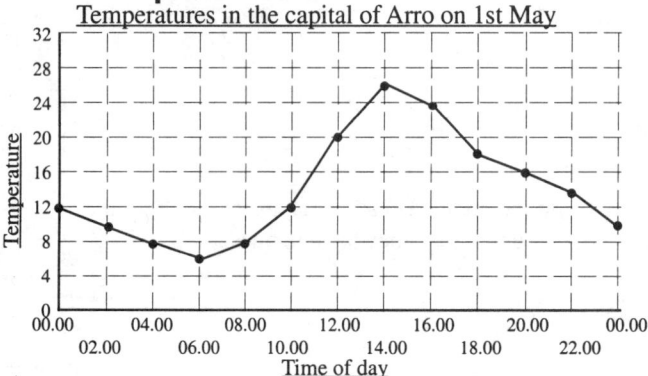

What was the temperature...
1. ... at 08.00 ?   2. ... at 18.00 ?   3. ... at midday ?   4. ... at 06.00 ?
5. At what two times was the temperature 12° ?
6. At what time was the temperature the hottest ?
7. At what time was the temperature the coldest ?
8. What was the highest temperature ?
9. Did the temperature rise or fall between 10.00 and 12.00 ?
10. How many degrees did it rise or fall between 10.00 and 12.00 ?

• Check answers.

**Star Challenge 5**

8-9 correct = 1 star

Temperatures in the capital of Madria on 1st May

Taz

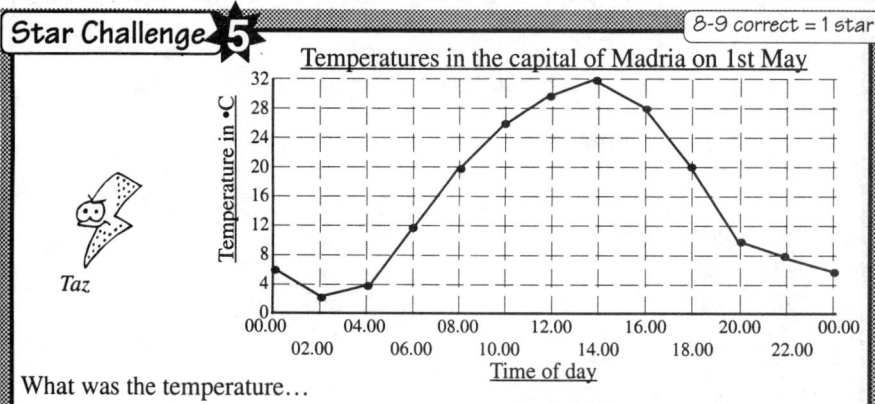

What was the temperature...
1. ... at 16.00 ?   2. ... at 10.00 ?   3. ... at 04.00?   4. ... at 22.00 ?
5. At what two times was the temperature 20° ?
6. What was the highest temperature ?
7. What was the lowest temperature ?
8. At what time was the highest temperature ?
9. Which is the hotter country in May, Arro or Madria ?

• Your teacher has the answers to these.

A POW GUIDE          page 74          Bar Charts and Beyond **EXTRA**

# Section 5: Averages and range

In this section you will :
- work with three measures of average;
- find the mean, mode, median and range of sets of data.

## DEVELOPMENT

The **mode**, **median** and **mean** are three different types of average.
They tell us in different ways where the middle of the data is.

**Level 4**

## D1: The mode

**Mode = most common value**

**EXAMPLE 1**
red, green, green, blue
The mode is 'green'

**EXAMPLE 2**
4, 7, 7, 8, 8, 5
There are two modes.
The modes are 7 & 8

**EXAMPLE 3**
4, 4, 7, 7, 8, 8, 5, 5
There is no mode.
All values are equally common

Find the mode of each set:
1. 2 4 4 5
2. 6 4 4 5 5
3. 7 3 4 8 6
4. 6 9 10 8 6

5. blue green orange blue
6. 3p 10p 5p 5p 20p 10p
7. bird dog cat dog dog cat
8. tiger lion panther

• Check your answers.

## D2: The median

**Level 4**

**Median = middle value or halfway between the two middle values**

**EXAMPLE 4**
4, 5, 6, 7, 7, 8, 8
median is 7

**EXAMPLE 5**
4, 5, 6, 6, 7, 8, 8, 8
median is 6½

Copy each set of data. Find the median.
1. 2 3 3 5 6
2. 2 3 5 5 5
3. 3 4 4 6 7 8

4. 6 7 8 9 9
5. 6 7 8 8 9 9
6. 5 8 10 14 15 15

**EXAMPLE 6**
4, 4, 7, 7, 8, 8, 5, 5
The data must first be put in order : 4, 4, 5, 5, 7, 7, 8, 8
median is 6

Copy each set of data. PUT THE DATA IN ORDER. Find the median.
7. 5 7 3 2 8
8. 3 1 10 5 7
9. 12 6 4 8 10 10

10. 20 26 32 30 21
11. 18 16 6 15 12 15
12. 8 15 10 12 20 12

• Check your answers.

A POW GUIDE        page 75        Bar Charts and Beyond **EXTRA**

## P1: Mode and median practice

*Do as many batches as you need.*
*CHECK ANSWERS at the end of each batch.*

**Batch A:** *Find the mode and median of each set of data:*
1. 2  3  3  5  7
2. –3  –2  –1  0  1  2  3
3. 3  7  8  8  9  9
4. 7  9  10  12  13  13

Mode = most common value    *Put into order first.*    Median = middle value
*Find the mode and median of each set.*

5. 22  19  21
6. 19  20  16  16  16
7. 103  100  99  100
8. 17  25  19  17
9. 60  50  70  80
10. 9  10  9  10  8  6

**Batch B:** *Find the mode and median of each set of data:*
1. 17  18  20  22  25
2. 7  9  14  16  17  20
3. 18  19  19  21  23  23
4. 1  2  9  15  16  16

*Put into order first.*
*Find the mode and median of each set.*

5. 13  15  12  10  8
6. 18  13  13  19  19
7. 65  61  65  31
8. 82  48  60
9. 200  400  100
10. 0  3  4  0  3  8

**Batch C:** *Find the mode and median of each set of data:*
1. 97  98  100  101  101
2. 10  12  12  12  14  14
3. 4  4  4  6  6  8
4. 3  5  7  8  10  20

*Put into order first.*
*Find the mode and median of each set.*

5. 35  30  35
6. 23  27  21  20  23  21
7. 81  83  85  83  87  87
8. 14  10  8  8  10  12  15
9. 150  200  150  200  250
10. 6  7  6  7  6  7  6

## D3: Mean and range

Level 5

Mean = sum of all values / number of all values    *Zuk*

Add them all up.
Divide by how many numbers there are.

EXAMPLE 7   **4, 7, 7, 8, 8, 5**
Sum = 4+7+7+8+8+5 = 39
There are 6 numbers
Mean = 39 ÷ 6 = 6.5

*Work out the mean of each set:*

1. 1  4  4  5  6
2. 2  7  5  10  5
3. 4  4  4  6  6  6
4. 8  9  10  8  7  9
5. 20  10  20  30  5  5
6. 3  9  7  7  3  7
7. 2  8  15  5
8. 5  7  9  10  6  5  7
9. 20  30  14  16  10  9
10. 3  12  15  20  10  3

A POW GUIDE            page 76            Bar Charts and Beyond  **EXTRA**

| Range = largest — smallest | EXAMPLE 8  2, 7, 7, 8, 8, 5 |
|---|---|
| | Largest = 8   Smallest = 2 |
| | Range = 8 – 2 = 6 |

Work out the range of each set:
11.  1   4   4   5   6         15.  3   9   7   7   3
12.  2   7   5   10  5         16.  2   8   15  5
13.  4   4   4   6   6   6     17.  5   7   9   10  6   5   7
14.  8   9   10  8   7   9     18.  20  30  14  16  10  9

Work out the mean and range of each set:
19.  1   4   4   5   6         21.  3   9   7   7   3
20.  3   7   5   10  5         22.  2   8   15  5         • Check answers.

### PRACTICE
## P2: Mean, mode, median and range practice

*Do as many batches as you need. CHECK ANSWERS at the end of each batch.*

**Batch A:**  Find the mean and range of each set of data:
1.  7   3   3   5   7              3.  2   7   8   8   5   6
2.  4   3   10  0   5   7   6      4.  12  8   2   12  15  5

Find the mean and mode of each set of data:
5.  8   4   4   3   11             7.  7   1   6   6   1   3
6.  3   7   2   4                  8.  12  5   10  10  13  8   9

Put into order first. Find the mean and median of each set.
9.  7   9   8                      11. 16  14  16  18
10. 15  20  20  13  17             12. 40  50  90  20

**Batch B:**  Find the mean and range of each set of data:
1.  12  15  6   8   4              3.  10  10  2   3   5   12
2.  6   4   0   3   3   2          4.  20  2   5   6   12

Find the mean and mode of each set of data:
5.  4   3   4   4   5              7.  3   7   6   6   8   5   7
6.  10  9   7   6                  8.  5   5   6   6   13  1

Put into order first. Find the mean and median of each set.
9.  12  14  10                     11. 16  10  20  18
10. 11  13  16  10  10             12. 2   4   2   6   9   4

### ⭐ Star Challenge 6-6 ⭐
30-32 marks = 2 stars
25-31 marks = 1 star

Find the mean and range of each set of data:                (2 marks for each)
1.  20  5   10  25  10             2.  3   12  5   10  5   1
3.  8   4   2   2                  4.  5   7   5   3   8   0   7

Put in order. Find the mean, mode, median and range of each set of data.
5.  6   2   4   4   4              6.  1   1   5   5   2   6   8
7.  8   8   6   6                  8.  2   1   6   6   10
9.  17  14  11                     10. 20  10  20  14       (4 marks for each)

A POW GUIDE              page 77              Bar Charts and Beyond  **EXTRA**

# Section 6: Working with averages

*In this section you will solve problems involving mean, mode, median and range.*

## DEVELOPMENT

### D1: Average problems         Level 5

1. In a test, the marks for one class were
   | 17 | 18 | 15 | 12 | 18 | 16 | 14 | 14 | 15 | 13 |
   
   Work out the mean average test mark.

2. Class 9XY did a survey of the price of a tin of beans in the local shops.
   The prices were: | 24p 25p 26p 27p 24p 25p 26p 26p |
   Work out: (a) the modal price (the mode) (b) the median price (c) the range of prices

3. The weights (in grams) of seven baking potatoes are:
   | 280 g | 225 g | 190 g | 238 g | 220 g | 205 g | 210 g |
   
   Work out: (a) the median weight    (b) the mean weight

4. The number of Ford Escort cars sold by Karmart each month is shown in this table
   
   | Month | J | F | M | A | M | J | J | A | S | O | N | D |
   |---|---|---|---|---|---|---|---|---|---|---|---|---|
   | Number sold | 52 | 45 | 40 | 30 | 28 | 8 | 15 | 82 | 63 | 23 | 12 | 10 |
   
   Work out: (a) the median number sold (b) the mean number sold (c) the range

5. | Boys' Test marks  | 12 | 15 | 18 | 20 | 15 | 17 | 18 | 17 | 19 | 20 |
   | Girls' Test marks | 17 | 13 | 15 | 16 | 18 | 17 | 16 | 16 | 19 | 18 |
   
   Work out the mean of (a) the boys' marks (b) the girls' marks (c) the whole class.

6. During the twelve days of Christmas, the midday temperatures in °C were
   | 2 | 2 | 4 | -2 | 0 | 1 | 5 | 6 | 4 | 1 | 1 | 0 |
   
   Work out : (a) the mean temperature         (b) the median temperature
   (c) the modal temperature (the mode)   (c) the temperature range

   • *Check your answers.*

### D2: Thinking about averages

1. Tom is an estate agent. He earns commission on each house that he sells.
   Tom was paid the following commission on the houses that he sold in April:
   | £150  £200  £540  £700  £430  £850  £360  £280  £120  £650 |

   (a) How many houses did he sell ?

   (b) How much commission did he make altogether ?

   (c) Work out the mean commission.

   (d) What was the lowest commission that he got ?

   (e) What was the highest commission that he got ?

   (f) Work out the range of the commission.

A POW GUIDE          page 78          Bar Charts and Beyond  **EXTRA**

2.

|        | May | June | July | August | Sept | Oct |
|--------|-----|------|------|--------|------|-----|
| Heven  | 22° | 26°  | 29°  | 32°    | 27°  | 20° |
| Helos  | 23° | 27°  | 28°  | 30°    | 24°  | 18° |

Heven and Helos are two holiday islands. The table gives the average midday temperatures during the summer months.

Work out the mean midday temperature for (a) Heven (b) Helos

(c) On Heven, for how many months is the temperature below the mean ?

(d) "The range of temperatures for Heven is greater than the range for Helos." Is this statement correct ? Show how you work it out.

3. A survey was carried out on the shoe sizes of 15 men. The results were:

9  7  6  8  9  8  9  6  10  7  8  10  9  8  9

(a) What is the mode of the shoe sizes ?   (b) What is the median of the shoe sizes ?

(c) "The most common shoe size is ..." What would you put in the gap – the median or the mode ?

• Check your answers.

## D3: Making comparisons

1. The class has five mental arithmetic tests.

Your scores were: 9 3 5 4 6 5
Mean score = 6.6   Range = 6

Your friend's scores were: 7 5 6 5 5
Mean score = 5.6   Range = 2

(a) Who did best in the tests, you or your friend ?
(b) What told you who did best in the test, the mean or the range ?
(c) Who was most consistent in the tests, you or your friend ?
(b) What told you who was most consistent, the mean or the range ?

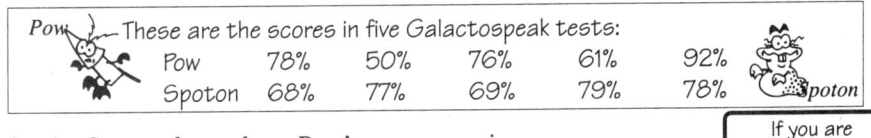

Pow — These are the scores in five Galactospeak tests:

Pow     78%  50%  76%  61%  92%
Spoton  68%  77%  69%  79%  78%

If you are 'consistent' then your marks are fairly close together. The range is small.

2. (a) Copy and complete: Pow's mean score is ............
   (b) Copy and complete: Spoton's mean score is ............
   (c) Which of them did best in the tests ?

3. (a) Copy and complete: The range of Pow's scores is ............
   (b) Copy and complete: The range of Spoton's scores is ............
   (c) Who is the most consistent in these tests ?

• Check answers.

4. (a) Which tells you who is the best in the tests, the mean or the range ?
   (b) Which tells you who is the most consistent, the mean or the range ?

Tamsin says that she is better at maths than her twin Peter.
Tamsin's last five test marks were   64  83  79  62  57
Peter's last five test marks were    65  78  68  66  64

5. (a) Calculate the mean and range of each set of test marks.
   (b) Who has the most consistent set of test marks ? Is it the mean or the range that tells you this ?
   (c) From these marks, who is better at maths ? Is it the mean or the range that tells you this ?

• Check your answers.

A POW GUIDE        page 79        Bar Charts and Beyond  **EXTRA**

**PRACTICE**

## P1: More comparisons

Survey of number of children per family (1997)
1  3  4  2  2  1  3  2  2  2  3  2  4  2  3

1. What is the range of the number of children per family?
2. Work out the mean number of children per family.
3. 

| Number of children per family (1967) | Number of children per family (1997) |
|---|---|
| Range = 6   Mean = 2.7 | Range = ......   Mean = ...... |

Copy these two tables. Complete the second table using your answers to Q1 & 2.

4. Look at the values for the range for 1967 and 1997 (use the tables from Q3). What does this tell you about the changes in family sizes between 1967 and 1997?
5. Look at the values for the mean for 1967 and 1997. What does this tell you about the changes in family sizes between 1967 and 1997?

The main goal scorer in the basketball team is injured. He cannot play in the Cup Final. The captain looks at the records of Peter and Barry, before choosing which one to play.

| In his last 5 matches, Peter has scored | 11 | 14 | 13 | 9 | 13 |
| In his last 5 matches, Barry has scored | 14 | 7 | 3 | 30 | 9 |

6. Work out the mean score for each player.
7. Work out the range of scores for each player.
8. Which player is the most consistent scorer?
9. Which player has the highest average score?
10. Which player has the highest score?
11. Which player would you choose? Explain why, using the means and the ranges.
    [It doesn't matter which you choose. It is your explanation which is important.]

> If you are 'consistent' then your marks are fairly close together. The range is small.

• Check your answers.

### Star Challenge

8 marks = 2 stars
5-7 marks = 1 star

Sally and Kate want to run for their school in the County 100 m race. Only one of them can be chosen. Their last eight times (in seconds) are:

Sally: 10.12  10.15  10.23  10.23
       10.28  10.31  10.37  10.31

Kate:  10.33  10.28  10.29  10.21
       10.31  10.18  10.21  10.27

1. Work out the mean time for each girl. (1 mark)
2. Work out the range of times for each girl. (1 mark)
3. Which girl is the fastest? What tells you this? (2 marks)
4. Which girl is the most consistent? What tells you this? (2 marks)
5. Which girl would you choose. Explain why using the means and the ranges.
   [It doesn't matter which you choose. It is your explanation which earns the marks.]
   (2 marks)

• Your teacher will need to mark this.

A POW GUIDE                page 80                Bar Charts and Beyond **EXTRA**

# Section 7: Interpreting diagrams

Level 5

In this section you will interpret and draw conclusions from diagrams.

### DEVELOPMENT

## D1: Interpreting simple pie charts

1. Copy and complete this frequency table for the pie chart.

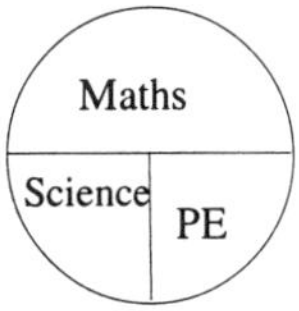

   Survey : Which of these subjects do you prefer ?

   | Subject | Number of pupils |
   |---|---|
   | Maths | |
   | Science | |
   | PE | |
   | Total | 100 |

2. Copy and complete this frequency table for the pie chart.

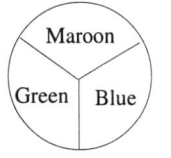

   Survey : Which colour should we have for our school uniform ?

   | Colour | Number of pupils |
   |---|---|
   | Maroon | |
   | Green | |
   | Blue | |
   | Total | 150 |

3. Copy and complete this frequency table for the pie chart.

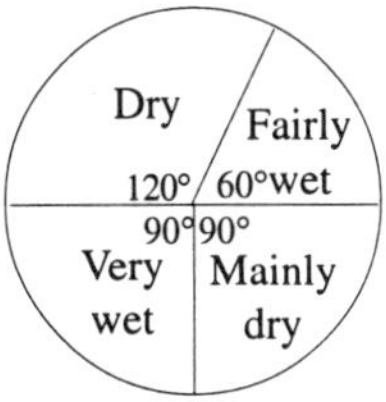

   Weather record

   | Weather | Number of days |
   |---|---|
   | Mainly dry | |
   | Very wet | |
   | Fairly wet | 10 |
   | Dry | |
   | Total | 60 |

4. Match each bar chart to the equivalent pie chart.

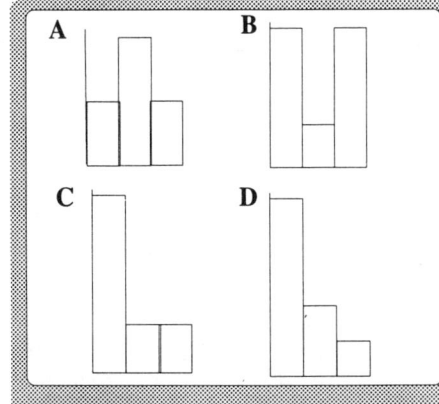

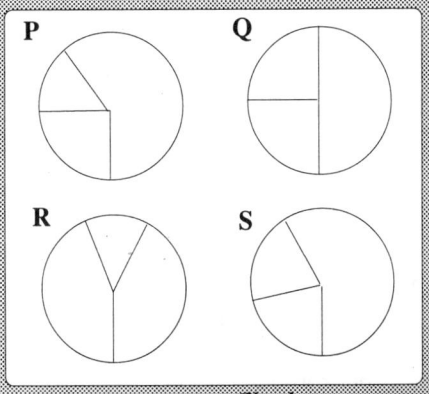

A POW GUIDE     page 81     Bar Charts and Beyond **EXTRA**

# D2: Drawing conclusions

**Level 5**

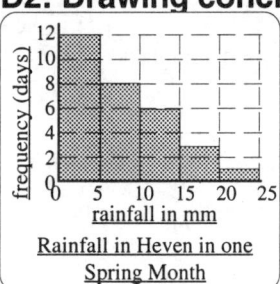

**Rainfall in Heven in one Spring Month** (bar chart: frequency (days) vs rainfall in mm, 0–25)

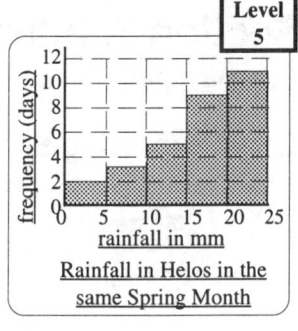

**Rainfall in Helos in the same Spring Month** (bar chart: frequency (days) vs rainfall in mm, 0–25)

1. In Heven, for how many days was there 0-5 mm of rain?
2. In Heven, for how many days was there 5-10 mm of rain?
3. "There are 30 days in the month when this survey was done."
   Explain how you tell that this is true.
4. Copy and complete this table for Helos:

| Rainfall | 0-5 mm | 5-10 mm | 10-15 mm | 15-20 mm | 20-25 mm |
|---|---|---|---|---|---|
| Frequency | | | | | |

5. "The diagram shows that, in Helos, it rained more at the end of the month."
   Explain why the diagram does NOT show this.

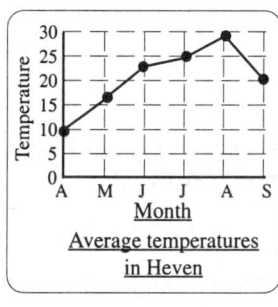

**Average temperatures in Heven** (line graph: Temperature vs Month A M J J A S)

**Average temperatures in Helos** (bar chart: Temperature vs Month A M J J A S)

Say whether each of these statements is true (T) or false (F).

6. It is warmer in Heven than in Helos, in August.
7. It is warmer in Heven than in Helos, in May.
8. It is always warmer in Heven than in Helos.
9. It is warmer in Helos in September than it is in Heven in April.

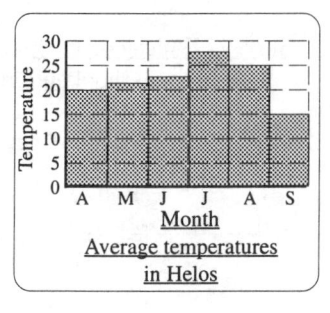

• Check answers.

## Star Challenge 8

*All correct = 1 star*

**How Bob spends his paypacket** (pie chart: Transport, Housing, Heat & light, Food, Other things, Clothes)

**How Fred spends his paypacket** (pie chart: Food, Housing, Heat & light, Other things, Clothes, Transport)

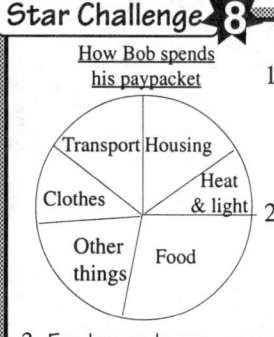

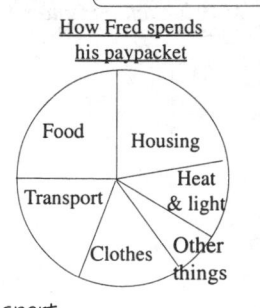

1. Bob spends a larger part of his paypacket on food than Fred does.
   True (T) or false (F)?
2. Bob spends a larger part of his paypacket on housing than Fred does.
   True (T) or false (F)?
3. Fred spends more money on food than he does on transport.
   True (T) or false (F)?
4. Fred spends more money on heat and light than Bob does.
   Explain why this is false.

• Your teacher has the answers to these.

A POW GUIDE        page 82        Bar Charts and Beyond  **EXTRA**

# Section 8: Constructing pie charts

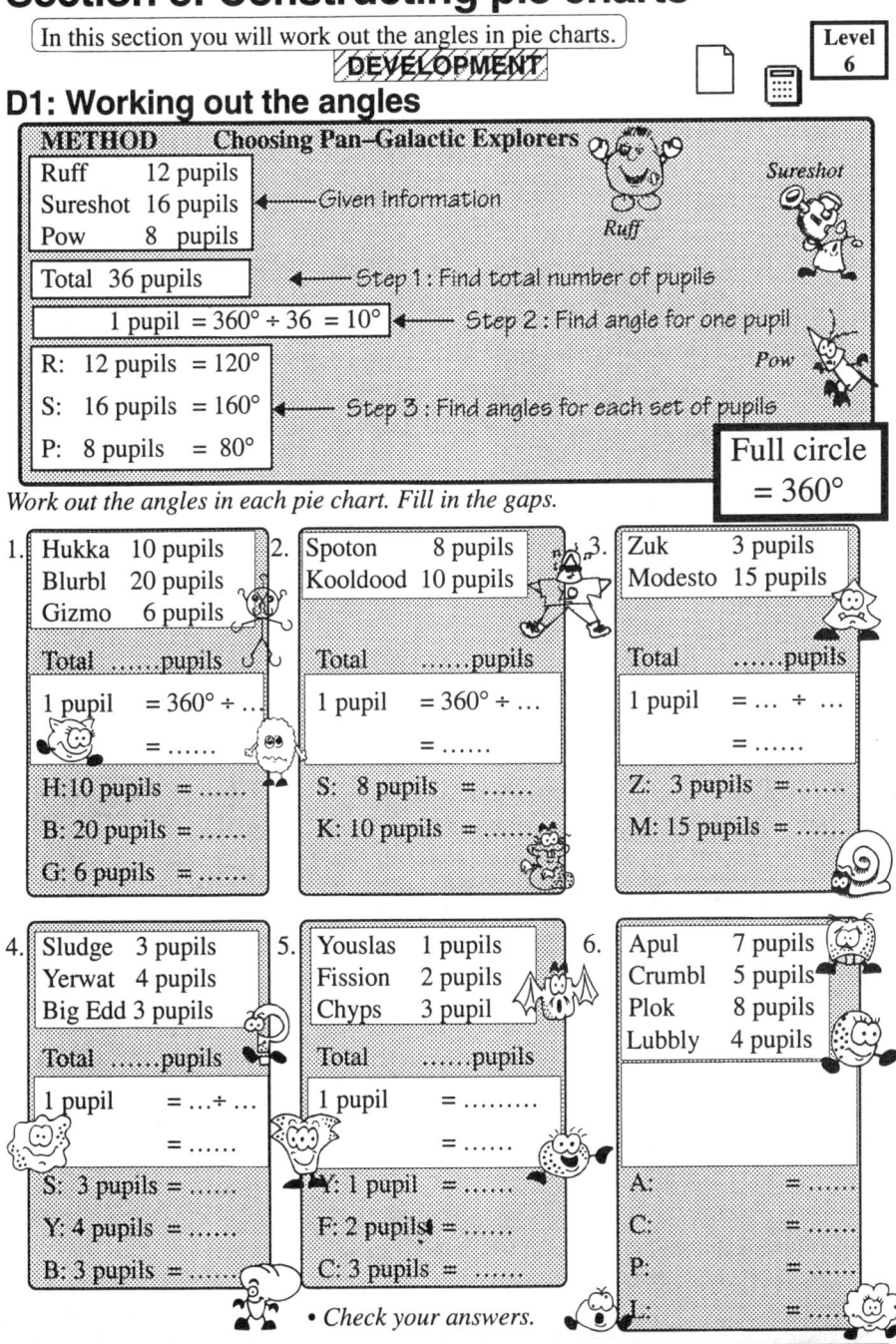

In this section you will work out the angles in pie charts.

**Level 6**

## DEVELOPMENT
## D1: Working out the angles

**METHOD** — Choosing Pan-Galactic Explorers

| Ruff | 12 pupils |
| Sureshot | 16 pupils |
| Pow | 8 pupils |

← Given information

Total 36 pupils ← Step 1: Find total number of pupils

1 pupil = 360° ÷ 36 = 10° ← Step 2: Find angle for one pupil

R: 12 pupils = 120°
S: 16 pupils = 160°
P: 8 pupils = 80°

← Step 3: Find angles for each set of pupils

**Full circle = 360°**

Work out the angles in each pie chart. Fill in the gaps.

**1.**
Hukka 10 pupils
Blurbl 20 pupils
Gizmo 6 pupils

Total ..... pupils

1 pupil = 360° ÷ ...
= ......

H: 10 pupils = ......
B: 20 pupils = ......
G: 6 pupils = ......

**2.**
Spoton 8 pupils
Kooldood 10 pupils

Total ..... pupils

1 pupil = 360° ÷ ...
= ......

S: 8 pupils = ......
K: 10 pupils = ......

**3.**
Zuk 3 pupils
Modesto 15 pupils

Total ...... pupils

1 pupil = ... ÷ ...
= ......

Z: 3 pupils = ......
M: 15 pupils = ......

**4.**
Sludge 3 pupils
Yerwat 4 pupils
Big Edd 3 pupils

Total ..... pupils

1 pupil = ... ÷ ...
= ......

S: 3 pupils = ......
Y: 4 pupils = ......
B: 3 pupils = ......

**5.**
Youslas 1 pupils
Fission 2 pupils
Chyps 3 pupil

Total ..... pupils

1 pupil = ..........
= ......

Y: 1 pupil = ......
F: 2 pupils = ......
C: 3 pupils = ......

**6.**
Apul 7 pupils
Crumbl 5 pupils
Plok 8 pupils
Lubbly 4 pupils

A: = ......
C: = ......
P: = ......
L: = ......

• Check your answers.

*A POW GUIDE* — page 83 — *Bar Charts and Beyond* **EXTRA**

## D2: But what if the number doesn't divide into 360 ?

You need to be able to draw pie charts
when the total number does not divide into 360° exactly. How ?

**EXAMPLE** Work out the angles in the pie chart for the results of this survey

| PGE | Number who chose it |
|---|---|
| Do-med | 9 pupils |
| Chyps | 11 pupils |
| Idea | 7 pupils |
| Total | 27 pupils |

← Given information

← Step 1 : Find total number of pupils

| 1 pupil | = 360° ÷ 27 = 13.3° | ← Step 2 : Find angle for one pupil |
|---|---|---|

Round answer to nearest 0.1°

| Do-med: | 9 pupils | = 120° | [13.3° x 9] |
| Chyps: | 11 pupils | = 146° | [13.3° x 11] |
| Inaspin: | 7 pupils | = 93° | [13.3° x 7] |

Step 3 : Find angles for each set of pupils.
Round answers to nearest degree

Full circle = 360°

Some pupils in Y7 did a survey on "Favourite Pan-Galactic Explorers"

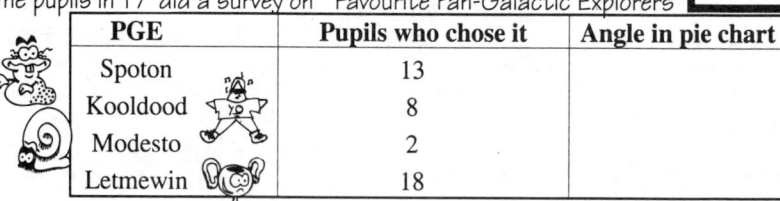

| PGE | Pupils who chose it | Angle in pie chart |
|---|---|---|
| Spoton | 13 | |
| Kooldood | 8 | |
| Modesto | 2 | |
| Letmewin | 18 | |

1. What is the angle for 1 pupil ? [Give your answer to 0.1°]
2. Copy and complete this table. [Give angles to nearest °]
3. Draw and label the pie chart for this survey.

Have you labelled the sectors ?
Have you given it a title ?

*Get your teacher to check your angles
and pie chart before doing the Star Challenge !*

### Star Challenge ⭐ ⭐

1 star for correct angles
1 star for correct pie chart

Pupils in Y9 did a survey on "Which teacher has the worst tutor group ? "
Their results were:

| Teacher | Pupils who chose this teacher | Angle in pie chart |
|---|---|---|
| Mrs. Osborne | 17 | |
| Mr. Percival | 11 | |
| Mr. Navin | 7 | |
| Mrs. Burrows | 4 | |
| Mrs. Young | 13 | |
| | 52 | |

1. What is the angle for 1 pupil ? Give your answer to 0.1°
2. Copy and complete this table.
3. Draw and label the pie chart for this survey.

• *Your teacher will need to mark this.*

A POW GUIDE    page 84    Bar Charts and Beyond  **EXTRA**

# Section 9: Working with continuous data

In this section you will:
- organise continuous data;
- make frequency diagrams for continuous data (histograms).

Level 6

## DEVELOPMENT

### D1: Interpreting frequency diagrams for continuous data

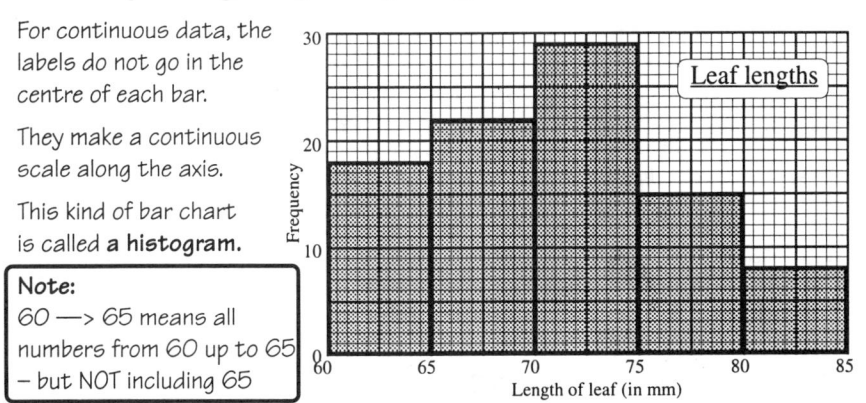

For continuous data, the labels do not go in the centre of each bar.

They make a continuous scale along the axis.

This kind of bar chart is called **a histogram**.

**Note:**
60 —> 65 means all numbers from 60 up to 65 – but NOT including 65

Leaf lengths

Length of leaf (in mm)

1. Copy and complete the frequency table for this histogram:

| Length of leaf (in mm) | Frequency |
|---|---|
| 60 —> 65 | 18 |
| 65 —> 70 | |
| 70 —> 75 | |
| 75 —> 80 | |
| 80 —> 85 | |

2. How many leaves were less than 70 mm long ?

3. How many leaves were more than 75 mm long ?

4. How many leaves were there altogether ?

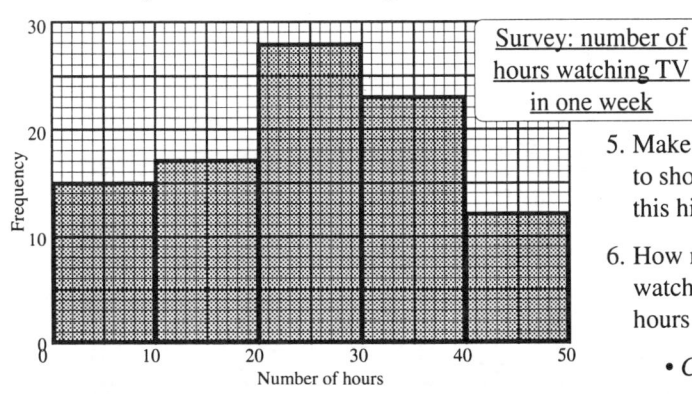

Survey: number of hours watching TV in one week

Number of hours

5. Make a frequency table to show the data from this histogram.

6. How many people watched more than 40 hours TV in that week ?

• Check your answers.

A POW GUIDE    page 85    Bar Charts and Beyond  EXTRA

## D2: Constructing histograms  (graph paper)

There are several methods that are used to label the groups of continuous data.
60 —> 65  means all the measurements between 60 and 65, not including 65
(at least 60 and less than 65) means the same as (60 —> 65)

Survey of train times

| Number of minutes late | Frequency |
|---|---|
| Less than 5 min | 10 |
| At least 5 min and less than 10 min | 8 |
| At least 10 min and less than 15 min | 5 |
| At least 15 min and less than 20 min | 3 |
| At least 20 min and less than 25 min | 1 |

Draw a histogram for this data on a sheet of graph paper.

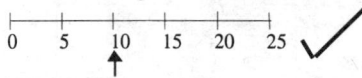

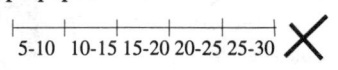

```
|---+---+---+---+---|         |---+---+---+---+---|
0   5   10  15  20  25  ✓     5-10 10-15 15-20 20-25 25-30  ✗
         ↑
```

The scale along the bottom must be continuous.

• Check your answers.

## D3: From data to histogram  (graph paper)

Heights of some Y9 pupils

Height h ( in cm)   123   141   156   132   144   158   140   133
                    145   137   151   159   142   128   131   144
                    139   130   155   158   136   141   149   127

**Remember:  Grouping data**
It is best to divide the data into 4-10 groups.
The groups must all be the <u>same width.</u>

1. Write down the smallest height and the largest height.

2. Make a grouped frequency table (as in D2) for this data.
   The groups chosen can start below the lowest number, if it is more convenient.

3. Draw a histogram for this data on a sheet of graph paper.
   The scale along the bottom must be continuous.

• Check your answers.

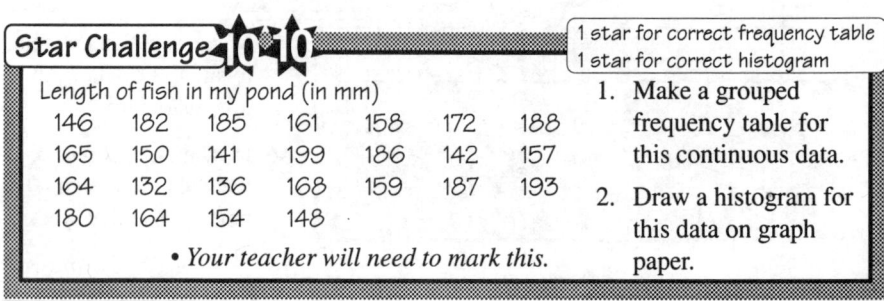

### Star Challenge

1 star for correct frequency table
1 star for correct histogram

Length of fish in my pond (in mm)
146   182   185   161   158   172   188
165   150   141   199   186   142   157
164   132   136   168   159   187   193
180   164   154   148

• Your teacher will need to mark this.

1. Make a grouped frequency table for this continuous data.

2. Draw a histogram for this data on graph paper.

A POW GUIDE            page 86            Bar Charts and Beyond  **EXTRA**

# Section 10 : Technique review

*In this section you will review techniques met in this topic.*

Check your answers at the end of each set of problems

## R1: Extracting information

Level 3

Number of Expeditions of all the new crew members of Starship 218

| Pan-Galactic Explorer | Zuk | Hoblin | Ruff | Taz | Lubbly | Apul |
|---|---|---|---|---|---|---|
| Number of expeditions | 12 | 8 | 16 | 6 | 8 | 10 |

1. Which Starship have these crew members just joined ?
2. How many new crew members are there ?
3. How many of them have done less than 10 expeditions ?
4. How many have done more than 8 expeditions ?

## R2: Drawing bar charts and pictographs

Level 3

**Check List for Bar Charts**
To earn full marks a bar chart must have:
- equal width bars (1 mark)
- labels in the middle of each bar (1 mark)
- accurate heights of bars (2 marks)
- sensible scale up the page (2 marks)
- labels on both axes (2 marks)
- title (1 mark)

**Check List for Pictographs**
To earn full marks a pictograph must have:
- simple symbols (1 mark)
- label on the axis (1 mark)
- correct KEY (1 mark)
- title (1 mark)
- correct number of symbols in each line (3 marks)

Number of Expeditions of all the new crew members of Starship 218

| Pan-Galactic Explorer | Zuk | Hoblin | Ruff | Taz | Lubbly | Apul |
|---|---|---|---|---|---|---|
| Number of expeditions | 12 | 8 | 16 | 6 | 8 | 10 |

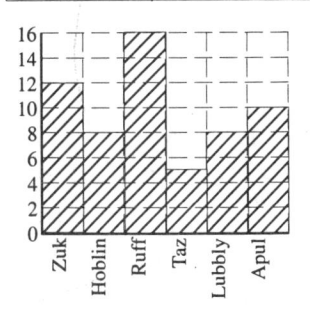

Pictograph

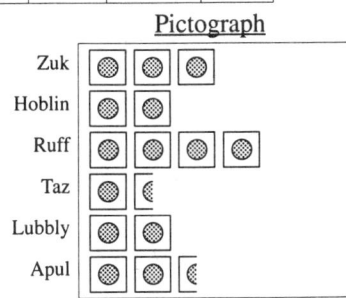

1. This bar chart earned 5 marks out of a possible 9.
   Explain where the 4 marks were lost.
2. The pictograph earned 4 marks out of a possible 7.
   Explain where the 3 marks were lost.
3. Explain why 'pictograph' will not do for a title.

A POW GUIDE   Bar Charts and Beyond **EXTRA**

## R3: Grouped data
**Level 4**

Scord is a Pan-Galactic computer game. It is highly addictive.
Number of games played yesterday by off duty Explorers:

57  35  46  29  17  23  57  40  34  48  33  55  16  36
56  43  51  38  57  29  31  35  (15)  47  29  39  (58)  21
                                    smallest              largest

This data needs to be grouped. Four possible sets of groups have been given.

| Set A | Set B | Set C | Set D |
|---|---|---|---|
| 10 — 19 | 10 — 20 | 15 — 19 | 10 — 19 |
| 20 — 29 | 20 — 30 | 20 — 29 | 20 — 29 |
| 30 — 39 | 30 — 40 | 30 — 39 | 30 — 39 |
| 40 — 49 | 40 — 50 | 40 — 49 | 40 — 49 |
|  | 50 — 60 | 50 — 59 | 50 — 59 |

1. Explain what is wrong with Set A.
2. Explain what is wrong with Set B.
3. Explain what is wrong with Set C.
4. The data is put into the groups in Set D. How many numbers go into the first group ?

## R4: Averages and range
**Level 4** | **Level 5**

**Mode** = most common value
**Median** = middle value
**Range** = largest − smallest

**Mean** = $\frac{\text{sum of values}}{\text{number of values}}$
Add them all up.
Divide by how many numbers there are.

Zuk

**YOU NEED TO LEARN THESE !**

Find the mean and range of each set of data:
1. 14  17  8  10  6
2. 9  7  3  6  6  5
3. 9  9  1  2  4  11
4. 25  7  10  11  17

Find the mean and mode of each set of data:
5. 6  5  6  6  7
6. 7  6  4  3
7. 2  6  5  5  7  4  6
8. 10  10  11  11  18  6

Put into order first. Find the mean and median of each set.
9. 14  16  12
10. 4  6  9  3  3
11. 26  20  30  28
12. 12  14  12  16  19  14

Number of Expeditions of the new crew members of Starship 218

| Pan-Galactic Explorer | Zuk | Hoblin | Ruff | Taz | Lubbly | Apul |
|---|---|---|---|---|---|---|
| Number of expeditions | 12 | 8 | 16 | 6 | 8 | 10 |

13. For the data in this table, work out:
    (a) the mode    (b) the median    (c) the mean    (d) the range

A POW GUIDE         Bar Charts and Beyond  **EXTRA**

# THE NATIONAL CURRICULUM ...
# ... AND BEYOND ...

*Pow*

# Working with Numbers
# EXTRA

| §12 Technique review |||||
|---|---|---|---|---|
| | | | | §11 Working with ratios |
| | | | §10 Checking answers 2 | |
| | | | §9 Metric and Imperial equivalents | |
| | | | §8 Working with negative numbers | |
| | | | §7 Powers | |
| | | §6 Squares and square roots | | |
| | | §5 Factors and prime numbers | | |
| | | §4 Multiples | | |
| | | §3 Checking answers 1 | | |
| §2 Rounding review | | | | |
| §1 Negative number review | | | | |
| Level 3 | Level 4 | Level 5 | Level 6 |

*A POW GUIDE*  *page 89*

# Working with Numbers EXTRA
## Section 1: Negative number review

Level 3

In this section you will review working with positive and negative numbers.

**PRACTICE**

### P1: Temperature changes

| 3°C | −3°C | −5°C | −1°C |
| 21.00 | 00.00 | 06.00 | 09.00 |
| Friday | Saturday | Saturday | Saturday |

1. *Copy and complete:*

   | times | 21.00–00.00 | 00.00–06.00 | 06.00–09.00 |
   |---|---|---|---|
   | temp goes up/down | | | |
   | how much up or down | | | |

2. When I got up, the temperature was −1°C.
   When I went to school, the temperature was 3°C.
   How many degrees had the temperature risen ?

3. When I came home from school, the temperature was 0°C.
   When I went to bed, the temperature was −3°C.
   By how many degrees had the temperature fallen ?

4. The temperature in the garage was −2°C.
   At the same time, the temperature in the greenhouse was −5°C.
   Where was it coldest ?   How much colder ?

5. The central heating broke down. It was very cold when I got up.
   The temperature in my bedroom was −1°C.
   The temperature in the bathroom was −3°C.
   Where was it warmest ?   How much warmer ?

6. The temperature at Manchester airport was 3°C.
   When my plane arrived in Moscow, the temperature was −12°C.
   How much colder was it in Moscow than in Manchester ?

7. The temperature was −15°C when I flew out of Moscow.
   The plane called at Omsk to pick up more passengers.
   The temperature at Omsk was − 20°C.
   Which was coldest, Moscow or Omsk ?   How much colder ?

8. The plane was delayed at Omsk. When we left, the temperature was −18°C.
   Is this warmer or colder than when we arrived ?

9. When we flew out of Omsk, the temperature was −18°C.
   When we arrived at Manchester, the temperature was 10°C.
   How much warmer was it than in Omsk ?

• Check your answers.

A POW GUIDE         page 90         Working with Numbers **EXTRA**

## P2: Work these out with and without a calculator

*Complete:*

| | | | |
|---|---|---|---|
| 1. 5 − 3 = ... | 8. 7 − 2 = ... | 15. 10 − ...... = 7 | 22. 12 − ...... = 5 |
| 2. 3 − 5 = ... | 9. 2 − 7 = ... | 16. 10 − ...... = −1 | 23. 12 − ...... = −2 |
| 3. 6 − 1 = ... | 10. 9 − 10 = ... | 17. 4 − ...... = 1 | 24. 8 − ...... = −1 |
| 4. 1 − 6 = ... | 11. 4 − 6 = ... | 18. 4 − ...... = −3 | 25. 6 − ...... = −4 |
| 5. 10 − 8 = ... | 12. 8 − 2 = ... | 19. 9 − ...... = −1 | 26. 5 − ...... = −5 |
| 6. 3 − 10 = ... | 13. 2 − 9 = ... | 20. 6 − ...... = −2 | 27. 4 − ...... = −3 |
| 7. 5 − 7 = ... | 14. 3 − 10 = ... | 21. 15 − ...... = −5 | 28. 10 − ...... = −10 |

• Check your answers.

## P3: Chart movements

*Complete the chart movement information:*

| Last week's chart | Chart Movement | This week's chart |
|---|---|---|
| 1. Ecstatic | −2 | Falling for You Again |
| 2. Falling for You Again | +1 | Always Wear Black |
| 3. Get Off My Planet | ... | Ecstatic |
| 4. It's Winter Without You | ... | Crispy Bacon |
| 5. Hot Stuff | ... | Hot Stuff |
| 6. Always Wear Black | ... | It's Winter Without You |
| 7. Love Is Mmm! | ... | Hip Hoppity |
| 8. Millennium Fever | ... | Get Off My Planet |
| 9. Hip Hoppity | ... | Love Is Mmm! |
| 10. Crispy Bacon | ... | Millennium Fever |

• Check your answers.

### Star Challenge

All correct = 1 star

*Complete this week's chart :*

| Last week's chart | Chart Movement | This week's chart |
|---|---|---|
| 1. Falling for You Again | −3 | .................. |
| 2. Always Wear Black | +1 | .................. |
| 3. Ecstatic | −7 | .................. |
| 4. Crispy Bacon | +1 | .................. |
| 5. Hot Stuff | −1 | .................. |
| 6. It's Winter Without You | +4 | .................. |
| 7. Hip Hoppity | 0 | .................. |
| 8. Get Off My Planet | −1 | .................. • Show |
| 9. Love Is Mmm! | +4 | .................. your |
| 10. Millennium Fever | +2 | .................. teacher |

A POW GUIDE     Working with Numbers   **EXTRA**

# Section 2: Rounding review

**Level 3**

In this section you will review rounding to the nearest 10, 100, 1000

### DEVELOPMENT

## D1: Rounding to nearest 10 or 100

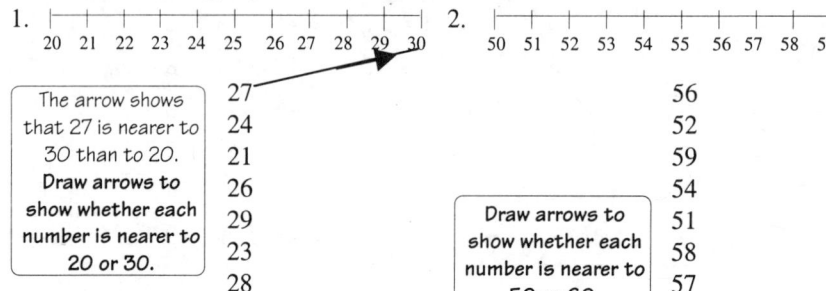

1. ├─┼─┼─┼─┼─┼─┼─┼─┼─┼─┤
   20 21 22 23 24 25 26 27 28 29 30

2. ├─┼─┼─┼─┼─┼─┼─┼─┼─┼─┤
   50 51 52 53 54 55 56 57 58 59 60

The arrow shows that 27 is nearer to 30 than to 20. Draw arrows to show whether each number is nearer to 20 or 30.

27, 24, 21, 26, 29, 23, 28

Draw arrows to show whether each number is nearer to 50 or 60.

56, 52, 59, 54, 51, 58, 57

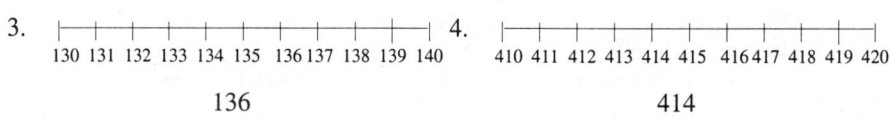

3. ├─┼─┼─┼─┼─┼─┼─┼─┼─┼─┤
   130 131 132 133 134 135 136 137 138 139 140

4. ├─┼─┼─┼─┼─┼─┼─┼─┼─┼─┤
   410 411 412 413 414 415 416 417 418 419 420

Draw arrows to show whether each number is nearer to 130 or 140.

136, 134, 137, 132, 139, 131, 138

Draw arrows to show whether each number is nearer to 410 or 420.

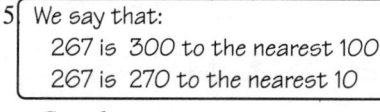

414, 417, 412, 416, 411, 413, 419

5. We say that:
   267 is 300 to the nearest 100
   267 is 270 to the nearest 10

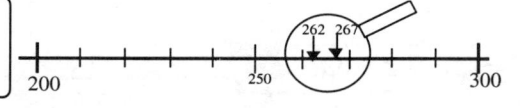

Complete:
262 is ...... to the nearest 100 & 262 is ...... to the nearest 10

6.

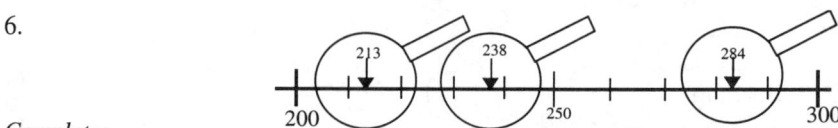

Complete:

| 213 is ......... to the nearest 100 | 238 is ......... to the nearest 100 | 284 ......... to the nearest 100 |
| 213 is ......... to the nearest 10 | 238 is ......... to the nearest 10 | 284 ......... to the nearest 10 |

• Check your answers.

A POW GUIDE — page 92 — Working with Numbers **EXTRA**

## D2: Rules for rounding

65 is midway between 60 and 70. Worldwide, mathematicians have agreed to round up middle numbers.

60 — 60 to the nearest 10
65
70 — 70 to the nearest 10

61, 62, 63, 64 round down to 60 (to nearest 10)

65, 66, 67, 68, 69 round up to 70 (to nearest 10)

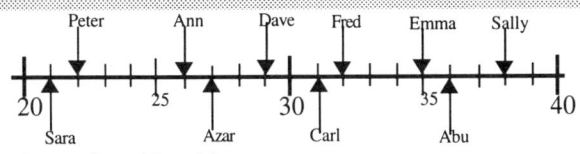

1. Peter, Ann, Dave, Fred, Emma, Sally
   20, Sara; 25, Azar; 30, Carl; 35, Abu; 40

Copy and complete this table:

| Name | Sara | Peter | Ann | Azar | Dave | Carl | Fred | Emma | Abu | Sally |
|---|---|---|---|---|---|---|---|---|---|---|
| Age | | | | | | | | | | |
| Age to nearest 10 years | | | | | | | | | | |

2. The price of this TV is £629
   (a) What is this TV's price to the nearest £100 ?
   (b) What is this TV's price to the nearest £10 ?

3. The price of this TV is £372
   (a) What is this TV's price to the nearest £100 ?
   (b) What is this TV's price to the nearest £10 ?

4. The price of this washing machine is £785
   (a) What is its price to the nearest £100 ?
   (b) What is its price to the nearest £10 ?

5. The price of this washing machine is £384
   (a) What is its price to the nearest £100 ?
   (b) What is its price to the nearest £10 ?

6. The price of a CD player is £176
   (a) What is its price to the nearest £100 ?
   (b) What is its price to the nearest £10 ?

• Check your answers.

A POW GUIDE     Working with Numbers   **EXTRA**

## PRACTICE

## P1: Classes of cars

For most cars, the class of a car is the engine size rounded to the nearest 100 cc. It is given in one of two ways:

Engine size = 1365 cc

Rounded to nearest 100 cc this is 1400 cc

The class of the car is either given as 1400 cc or 1.4l

*Pow*

*Here are some car engine sizes. Work out the class of each car.*
*Give the class in two ways (as above).*

1. Hyundai Coupe (1599 cc)
2. Renault Megane (1998 cc)
3. Austin Maxi (1485 cc)
4. Jaguar XJS3 (3442 cc)
5. Lada Riva (1452 cc)
6. Morris Ital (1695 cc)
7. Metro (1275 cc)
8. Lancia Trevi (1995 cc)
9. Ford Fiesta (1117cc)
10. Opel Senator (2774 cc)
11. Fiat Tipo (1372 cc)
12. Audi Coupe (1984 cc)
13. Ford Puma (1679 cc)
14. Nissan Sunny (1809 cc)

• *Check your answers.*

## P2: Prices of cars

Round the prices of each car to the nearest £1000:

1. Rover 1.4 GTa £9 286
2. Peugot 1.6 GTi £12 835
3. Morgan 1.8 Roadster £19 999
4. Maserati Ghibli £45 995
5. Fiat Punto 55 £8 888
6. Ford Puma £14 550
7. Lotus Elan £25 500
8. Porsche 2.5 Roadster £34 095
9. Alfa Romeo 156 V6 Sport £23 739
10. Rolls Royce Silver Spur £135 240

• *Check your answers.*

### Star Challenge

19-20 correct = 2 stars
15-18 correct = 1 star

*Copy and complete this table of car prices:*

| Car | Price | Price to nearest £1000 | Price to nearest £100 |
|---|---|---|---|
| Daewoo Nexia | £9 445 | | |
| Citroen Xantia 1.6 | £14 240 | | |
| Ford Ka 2 | £8 860 | | |
| Ferrari Spider | £103 735 | | |
| Lada 1.5 SX | £6 445 | | |
| Toyota Corolla 1.6 | £14 144 | | |
| Skoda 1.3 LX | £6 499 | | |
| Saab V6 SE | £25 395 | | |
| Nissan Micra 1.0 S | £9 155 | | |
| Bentley Azure | £222 526 | | |

*A POW GUIDE* • *Working with Numbers* **EXTRA**

# Section 3: Checking answers 1

Level 4

In this section you will use techniques for checking answers

## DEVELOPMENT

### D1: Which is the most likely answer?

1.  24 + 58 = 34 / 62 / 82
    Do NOT work out the answer.
    Which of these is the most likely answer?
    Explain why you think it is.

2.  65 – 37 = 28 / 102 / 58
    Do NOT work out the answer.
    Which of these is the most likely answer?
    Explain why you think it is.

3.  47 x 8 = 55 / 206 / 376
    Do NOT work out the answer.
    Which of these is the most likely answer?
    Explain why you think it is.

4.  85 ÷ 5 = 17 / 425 / 90
    Do NOT work out the answer.
    Which of these is the most likely answer?
    Explain why you think it is.

• Check your answers.

### D2: Working out approximate answers 1

**Technique review**

Work out 30 x 5 in your head

Ruff

30 x 5 = 3 x 10 x 5
     = 3 x 5 x 10
     = 15 x 10
     = 150

Work these out in your head:
1. 20 x 4   2. 50 x 3   3. 300 x 4   4. 200 x 7   5. 40 x 9   6. 8 x 30

• Check your answers.

EXAMPLE 1   Q: A wall is 19 bricks long and 7 bricks high
              Work out how many bricks there are, approximately.   [    ] 7 bricks
        A : Number of bricks = 19 x 7                                19 bricks
            Approximate number of bricks = 20 x 7 = 140
                                            ↑
                                      rounded to
                                      nearest 10

Work out the approximate number of bricks in each of these walls:

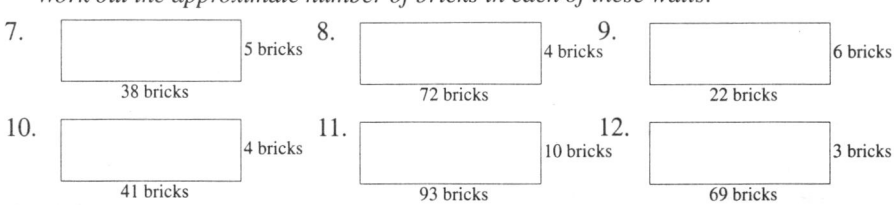

7.  [    ] 5 bricks / 38 bricks
8.  [    ] 4 bricks / 72 bricks
9.  [    ] 6 bricks / 22 bricks
10. [    ] 4 bricks / 41 bricks
11. [    ] 10 bricks / 93 bricks
12. [    ] 3 bricks / 69 bricks

• Check your answers.

A POW GUIDE        page 95        Working with Numbers   **EXTRA**

# Section 4: Multiples

Level 4

In this section you will:
- give multiples of single digit numbers
- recognise the connection between 'multiple of' and 'divisible by'
- recognise numbers which are divisible by 2, 5 or 10

## DEVELOPMENT

### D1: Multiples of numbers

| x | 1 | 2 | 3 | 4 | 5 | 6 | 7 | 8 | 9 | 10 | 11 | 12 | 13 | 14 | 15 |
|---|---|---|---|---|---|---|---|---|---|---|---|---|---|---|---|
| 1 | 1 | 2 | 3 | 4 | 5 | 6 | 7 | 8 | 9 | 10 | 11 | 12 | 13 | 14 | 15 |
| 2 | 2 | 4 | 6 | 8 | 10 | 12 | 14 | 16 | 18 | 20 | 22 | 24 | 26 | 28 | 30 |
| 3 | 3 | 6 | 9 | 12 | 15 | 18 | 21 | 24 | 27 | 30 | 33 | 36 | 39 | 42 | 45 |
| 4 | 4 | 8 | 12 | 16 | 20 | 24 | 28 | 32 | 36 | 40 | 44 | 48 | 52 | 56 | 60 |
| 5 | 5 | 10 | 15 | 20 | 25 | 30 | 35 | 40 | 45 | 50 | 55 | 60 | 65 | 70 | 75 |
| 6 | 6 | 12 | 18 | 24 | 30 | 36 | 42 | 48 | 54 | 60 | 66 | 72 | 78 | 84 | 90 |
| 7 | 7 | 14 | 21 | 28 | 35 | 42 | 49 | 56 | 63 | 70 | 77 | 84 | 91 | 98 | 105 |
| 8 | 8 | 16 | 24 | 32 | 40 | 48 | 56 | 64 | 72 | 80 | 88 | 96 | 104 | 112 | 120 |
| 9 | 9 | 18 | 27 | 36 | 45 | 54 | 63 | 72 | 81 | 90 | 99 | 108 | 117 | 126 | 135 |
| 10 | 10 | 20 | 30 | 40 | 50 | 60 | 70 | 80 | 90 | 100 | 110 | 120 | 130 | 140 | 150 |

1. Multiples of 2 are 2  4  6  8  10 ...   Find them in the table.
   Find the multiples of 3 in the table.
   Write down the first five multiples of 3.
2. Write down the first five multiples of 6.
3. Write down the first three multiples of 10.
4. Is 35 a multiple of 7 ?   How can you tell from the table ?
5. Is 84 a multiple of 7 ?
6. 58 is NOT a multiple of 7. How can you tell from the table ?

*Copy and complete:*

7. The multiples of 2 between 11 and 25 are .................................................
8. The multiples of 3 between 20 and 35 are .................................................
9. The multiples of 8 between 30 and 50 are .................................................
10. The multiples of 7 between 25 and 60 are .................................................
11. Between 10 and 35 there are four numbers which are multiples of both 2 and 3. These are .................................................
12. Which of these numbers are multiples of 9 ?

    27    35    72    99
    80       54    115    135

13. Which of these numbers are multiples of 15 ?

    30    45    85    120
    60       95    135    110

- Check your answers.

A POW GUIDE         page 96         Working with Numbers    EXTRA

## D2: Multiples and divisibility

> 12 is a multiple of 2, 3, 4, 6, and 12
> This also means that
> 12 is divisible by 2, 3, 4, 6, and 12

EXAMPLE 2   Q: Use the table to find out if 84 is divisible by 7

A: The table shows us that 84 is a multiple of 7   So, 84 is divisible by 7

Yes, 84 is divisible by 7

*Ruff*

*Use the table to answer these questions:*
1. Which of these numbers are divisible by 2?
2. Which of these numbers are divisible by 3?
3. Which of these numbers are divisible by 5?
4. Which of these numbers are divisible by 9?

36   18   28   32
30   24   25
42   27   29   9

• Check your answers.

## D3: Rules for divisibility by 2, 5 and 10

A number is divisible by 10 if it ends in 0
A number is divisible by 5 if it ends in 5 or 0
A number is divisible by 2 if it ends in 0, 2, 4, 6 or 8

1. List the numbers in the box that are divisible by 10
2. List the numbers in the box that are divisible by 5
3. List the numbers in the box that are divisible by 2
4. List the numbers in the box that are divisible by 2 & 5

65   30   24
16   52
40   29   15
38   85
258   370   555

• Check your answers.

### Star Challenge 3 ★ 3

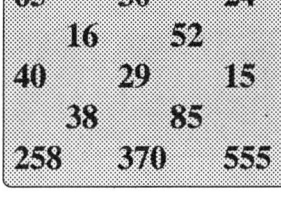

28-30 correct = 2 stars
24-27 correct = 1 star

In the box, find …
1. … three numbers that are divisible by 10
2. … five numbers that are multiples of 5
3. … eight numbers that are divisible by 2
4. … five numbers that are multiples of 9
5. … six numbers that are divisible by 8
6. … two numbers that are multiples of 13
7. … one number that is a multiple of 25

72   81   112
96   130
45   117   16
63   60
24   75   120

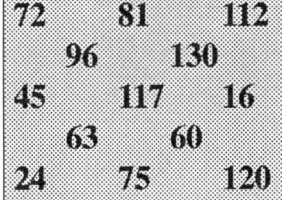

• Your teacher has the answers to these.

A POW GUIDE            Working with Numbers   **EXTRA**

# Section 5: Factors and prime numbers

**Level 4**

In this section you will:
- use a calculator tell whether one number is divisible by another;
- find factors of numbers;
- review prime numbers

**DEVELOPMENT**

## D1: Which answers are whole numbers ?

[377] ÷ [13] = [ 29. ]    Pow

This is **a whole number**.
The calculator writes a whole number with the decimal point at the end.

[377] ÷ [5] = [ 75.4 ]    Plok

This is **NOT a whole number**.
The decimal point is not at the end.

Work out each sum. Say whether each answer is a whole number.

A: 102 ÷ 3     B: 247 ÷ 3     C: 57 ÷ 6     D: 245 ÷ 5     E: 129 ÷ 3
F: 648 ÷ 9     G: 150 ÷ 6     H: 17 ÷ 7     I: 856 ÷ 12    J: 73 ÷ 31

• Check your answers.

## D2: Testing divisibility with a calculator

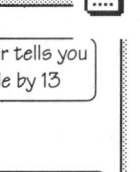

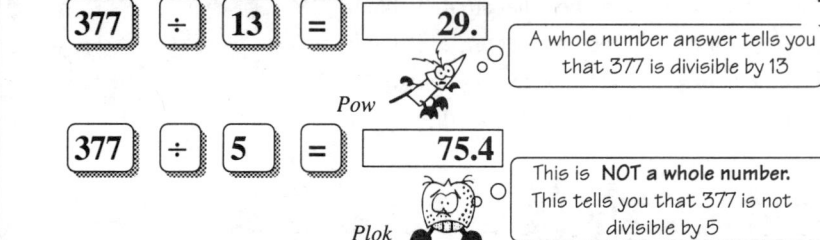

[377] ÷ [13] = [ 29. ]    Pow

A whole number answer tells you that 377 is divisible by 13

[377] ÷ [5] = [ 75.4 ]    Plok

This is **NOT a whole number**.
This tells you that 377 is not divisible by 5

1. Is 235 divisible by 7 ?
2. Is 13 divisible by 1 ?
3. Is 15 divisible by 3 ?
4. Is 568 divisible by 8 ?
5. Is 42 divisible by 6 ?
6. Is 143 divisible by 11 ?
7. Is 246 divisible by 8 ?
8. Is 24 divisible by 9 ?
9. Is 144 divisible by 6 ?
10. Is 402 divisible by 7 ?
11. Is 402 divisible by 6 ?
12. Is 402 divisible by 12 ?

| 133 | 47  | 78  | 35  | 62  | 237 | 512 |
|     | 511 | 89  | 14  | 29  | 161 | 65  |
|     | 314 | 569 | 294 | 82  | 333 | 154 |

13. Seven of these numbers are divisible by 7. Find them.

• Check your answers.

A POW GUIDE     page 98     Working with Numbers   **EXTRA**

## D3: What are factors ?

65 ÷ 5 = 13

A whole number answer tells you that 65 is divisible by 5

We say that 5 is a factor of 65

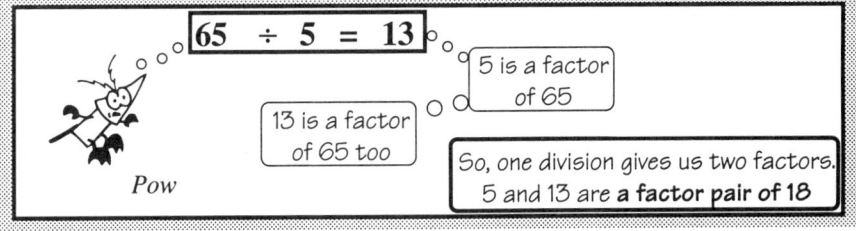

Say whether each statement is true (T) or false (F):
1. 10 is a factor of 30
2. 3 is a factor of 12
3. 5 is a factor of 30
4. 7 is a factor of 28
5. 4 is a factor of 20
6. 7 is a factor of 50
7. 9 is a factor of 35
8. 15 is a factor of 110
9. 8 is a factor of 213

10. 1 is a factor of 3
11. 1 is a factor of 7
12. 1 is a factor of 48
13. 1 is a factor of every number

14. 5 is a factor of 5
15. 23 is a factor of 23
16. 87 is a factor of 87
17. Any number is a factor of itself.

18. 8 has four factors. Find all four factors of 8.
19. 14 has four factors. Find all the factors of 14.
20. 25 has three factors. Find all the factors of 25.

• Check your answers.

## D4: Factor pairs

1. Copy and complete:
   65 ÷ 5 = ......   65 is divisible by 5   ... is a factor of 65
   65 ÷ 13 = ......  65 is divisible by ... ... is a factor of 65

65 ÷ 5 = 13

5 is a factor of 65

13 is a factor of 65 too

So, one division gives us two factors.
5 and 13 are **a factor pair of 18**

2. Copy and complete:
   8 ÷ 2 = ...   2 and ... are a factor pair of 8
   8 ÷ 1 = ...   8 and ... are a factor pair of 8

3. Find two factor pairs of 6
4. Find two factor pairs of 10
5. Find three factor pairs of 18
6. Find three factor pairs of 20
7. Find three factor pairs of 12
8. Find three factor pairs of 28
9. Find two factor pairs of 15
10. Find two factor pairs of 21
11. Find three factor pairs of 50
12. Find three factor pairs of 60

• Check your answers.

## D5: Factor diagrams

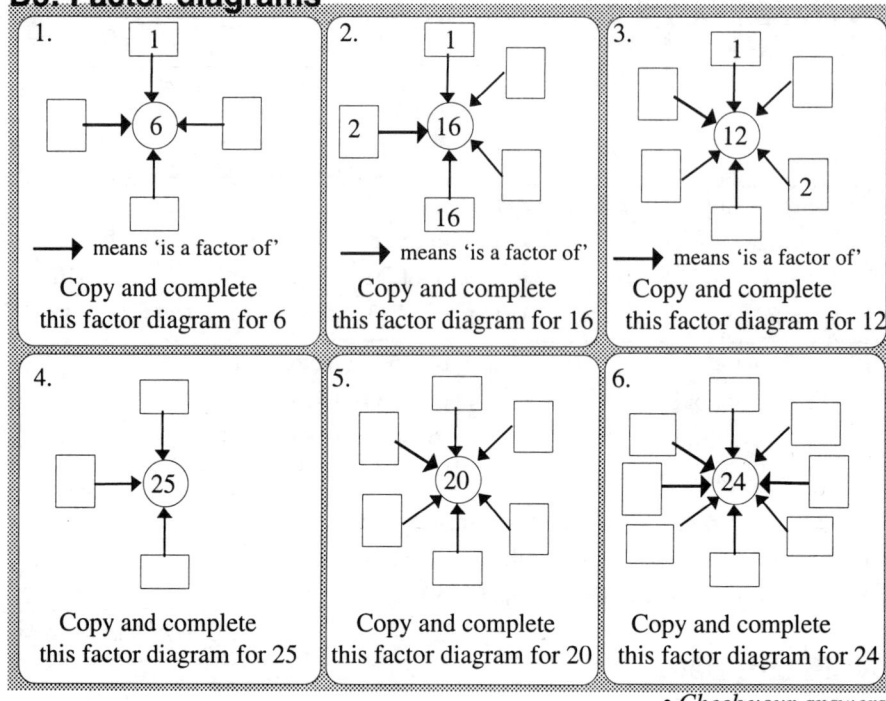

**1.** Copy and complete this factor diagram for 6
⟶ means 'is a factor of'

**2.** Copy and complete this factor diagram for 16
⟶ means 'is a factor of'

**3.** Copy and complete this factor diagram for 12
⟶ means 'is a factor of'

**4.** Copy and complete this factor diagram for 25

**5.** Copy and complete this factor diagram for 20

**6.** Copy and complete this factor diagram for 24

• Check your answers.

## D6: From factors to primes

**Task 1:** Copy and complete this table of factors for numbers 1 – 20

| Number | Factors | How many factors |
|--------|---------|------------------|
| 1 | 1 | 1 |
| 2 | 1, 2 | 2 |
| 3 | 1, 3 | 2 |
| 4 | | |
| 5 | | |
| 6 | | |
| 7 | | |
| 8 | | |
| 9 | | |
| 10 | | |
| 11 | | |
| 12 | | |
| 13 | | |
| 14 | | |
| 15 | | |
| 16 | | |
| 17 | | |
| 18 | | |
| 19 | | |
| 20 | | |

**Task 2:**

> **Prime numbers** have exactly two factors.

*Copy and complete:*

> Prime numbers between 1 and 20 are
> 2,  3,  …  …
> …  …  …  …

• Check your answers.

A POW GUIDE     Working with Numbers **EXTRA**

## EXTENSIONS
## E1: The sieve of Eratosthenes
This is a method for finding all the prime numbers.
It was devised by a Greek mathematician, Eratosthenes.
1. Make a copy of this table of numbers going as far as 102.
   Fill in all numbers up to 102. Cross out 1. It is not prime.
2. 2 is the first prime number.
   Put a circle round it.
   Cross out all the multiples
   of 2 in the table.
3. 3 is the next prime number.
   Put a circle round it.
   Cross out all the multiples
   of 3 in the table.

| 1 | 2 | 3 | 4 | 5 | 6 |
|---|---|---|---|---|---|
| 7 | 8 | 9 | 10 | 11 | 12 |
| ... | | | | | |
| | | | | | |
| | | | | ... | ... |
| | | | | ... | 102 |

4. Continue by circling each prime and crossing out its multiples.
   When you have finished, the numbers left are all prime numbers.
   Up to this point, you may ask your teacher for help.

### Star Challenge 4 4 4
30 correct = 3 stars
28-30 correct = 2 stars
25-27 correct = 1 star

**Prime numbers** have exactly two factors – 1 and the number itself

1. There are 2 prime numbers between 20 and 30. List them. (2 marks)
2. There are 21 prime numbers between 10 and 100. List them (21 marks)
3. An **emirp** is a prime number which is also prime when reversed.
   13 and 31 are emirps.
   There are 9 emirps between 10 and 100 (including 13 and 31).
   Find them. (7 marks)

• *Your teacher has the answers to these.*

### Star Challenge 5 5
5 correct = 2 stars
4 correct = 1 star

The factors of 6 are 1, 2, 3, 6    2 & 3 are prime numbers
We say that 2 & 3 are **prime factors** of 6

1. The factors of 12 are 1, 2, 3, 4, 6, 12
   What are the prime factors of 12 ?
2. The factors of 15 are 1, 3, 5, 15
   What are the prime factors of 15 ?
3. What are the prime factors of 18 ?
4. What are the prime factors of 20 ?         • *Your teacher has the*
5. What are the prime factors of 24 ?           *answers to these.*

A POW GUIDE          page 101          Working with Numbers     **EXTRA**

# Section 6: Squares, square roots and cubes

In this section you will:
- work with squares, square roots and cubes;
- use 'trial-and-improvement' techniques.

Level 4

## DEVELOPMENT

### D1: Squares and square roots

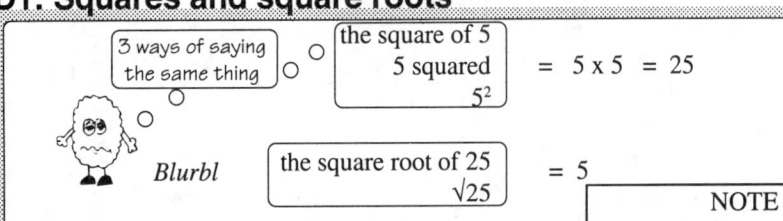

3 ways of saying the same thing:
- the square of 5
- 5 squared
- $5^2$

$= 5 \times 5 = 25$

Blurbl

the square root of 25
$\sqrt{25}$ $= 5$

**NOTE**
we say "square root of 25"
we write it as $\sqrt{25}$
BUT, on a calculator,
we key in [25] [√]

Pow

Write down...
1. ... the square of 3
2. ... $4^2$
3. ... $\sqrt{36}$
4. ... the square root of 9
5. ... 7 squared
6. ... $\sqrt{144}$
7. ... the square of 14
8. ... the square root of 100
9. ... $\sqrt{289}$
10. ... 21 squared
11. ... $16^2$
12. ... the square of 25
13. ... the square root of 2025
14. ... $20^2$
15. ... $\sqrt{64}$
16. ... the square of 40
17. ... $\sqrt{169}$
18. ... 9 squared
19. ... $42^2$
20. ... $\sqrt{1}$

21. Copy and complete this table:

| Number (N)   | 2 | 8 | 12 | 5  |    |     |     | 17 |     |
|--------------|---|---|----|----|----|-----|-----|----|-----|
| Square ($N^2$) | 4 |   |    | 25 | 36 | 121 | 441 |    | 361 |

• Check your answers.

### D2: Square numbers and cube numbers

$5 \times 5 = 25$    so    25 is a square number

16   23   49   81   95   50   1   4   10   64   100

1. Which of these numbers are square numbers?
2. Copy and complete:
   The first ten square numbers are 1  4  9 .................................

$5 \times 5 \times 5 = 125$    so    125 is a cube number

3. Copy and complete:
   $1^3 = 1$ cubed $= 1 \times 1 \times 1 = ...$     $2^3 = 2$ cubed $= 2 \times 2 \times 2 = ...$
4. Work out: (a) 3 cubed  (b) 4 cubed  (c) 5 cubed  (d) 6 cubed
5. Copy and complete:
   The first ten cube numbers are 1  8  27 .................................

• Check your answers.

A POW GUIDE    page 102    Working with Numbers    **EXTRA**

## Star Challenge 6

14-15 correct = 1 star

Write down...
1. ... the square of 5
2. ... 4 cubed
3. ... $\sqrt{36}$
4. ... $5^2$
5. ... $5^3$
6. ...the square root of 100
7. ... 3 cubed
8. ... $6^2$
9. ... 3 squared
10. ...$\sqrt{6.25}$
11. ... the square of 18
12. ... $15^2$
13. ... 8 cubed
14. ... $\sqrt{49}$
15. ... $3^2 + 2^2$

• Your teacher has the answers to these.

## D3: Using trial-and-improvement methods

You may only use these keys

[ x ] [ = ] [ 1 ] [ 2 ] [ 3 ] [ 4 ]
[ 5 ] [ 6 ] [ 7 ] [ 8 ] [ 9 ] [ 0 ]

1. Work out the value of each letter:

$A^2 = 289$   $B^2 = 841$   $C^2 = 1225$   $(A^2 = A \times A)$
$D^3 = 343$   $E^3 = 125$   $F^3 = 1331$   $(D^3 = D \times D \times D)$

In tests and exams you will be asked to show that you have used a 'trial-and-improvement' method. This means that you must show how you work out the answer using a calculator.
You cannot get full marks just giving the answer.
The kind of working out you must give is shown in questions 2 and 3.

2. Copy and complete:
$G^2 = 1681$
10 x 10   =   100   (too small)
25 x 25   =   625   (too small)
45 x 45   =   2025  (too big)
... x ... =   ......(too ......)
... x ... =   ......(too ......)
:
:
Ans : G = .........

3. Copy and complete:
$H^2 = 729$
15 x 15   =   225   (too small)
... x ... =   ......(too ......)
... x ... =   ......(too ......)
... x ... =   ......(too ......)
:
Ans : H = .........

The number of lines will depend on how fast you get the answer.

Work out the value of each letter.
Show how you do it using a trial-and-improvement method.
[Set out your working as in questions 2 & 3.]

4. $J^2 = 324$   5. $K^2 = 1024$   6. $L^3 = 2197$   7. $M^3 = 3375$

• Check your answers.

## Star Challenge 7

20 marks = 2 stars
14-19 marks = 1 star

Work out the value of each letter.
Show how you do it using a trial-and-improvement method.

1. $N^2 = 529$   2. $M^2 = 2304$   3. $P^2 = 3364$   4. $Q^3 = 4913$

• Show your answers to your teacher.

3 marks for working out & 2 marks for answer

A POW GUIDE   Working with Numbers   EXTRA

# Section 7: Powers

Level 5

In this section you will work with powers.

## DEVELOPMENT

### D1: Review of powers

$5^2 = 5 \times 5 = 25$ (read as "5 squared")
$2^3 = 2 \times 2 \times 2 = 8$ (read as "2 cubed")
$3^4 = 3 \times 3 \times 3 \times 3 = 81$ (read as "3 to the power of 4")

The value of $3^4$ is 81

Work out the value of each of these. Copy and complete each expression.
1. $4^2 = ...$  2. $5^3 = ...$  3. $7^2 = ...$  4. $10^3 = ...$  5. $2^5 = ...$
6. $3^3 = ...$  7. $4^3 = ...$  8. $5^4 = ...$  9. $2^6 = ...$  10. $6^3 = ...$

Copy and complete each expression:
11. $2^{...} = 16$  12. $3^{...} = 81$  13. $7^{...} = 343$  14. $9^{...} = 81$  15. $12^{...} = 144$
16. $5^{...} = 625$  17. $8^{...} = 64$  18. $10^{...} = 1000$  19. $5^{...} = 125$  20. $15^{...} = 225$

• Check your answers.

### D2: More difficult powers

To work out $5 \times 2^3$, work out $2^3$ first, then multiply by 5

$2 \times 2 \times 2 \times 5 = \boxed{40}$

Copy and complete:
1. $3 \times 4^2 = ...$  2. $4 \times 3^3 = ...$  3. $2 \times 10^2 = ...$  4. $6 \times 5^2 = ...$

CHECK YOUR ANSWERS before going on.

5. $5 \times 3^2 = ...$  6. $3 \times 7^3 = ...$  7. $4 \times 15^2 = ...$  8. $9 \times 23^2 = ...$
9. $10 \times 11^2 = ...$  10. $7 \times 20^3 = ...$  11. $2 \times 25^2 = ...$  12. $4 \times 34^2 = ...$

Work out any brackets first      $(3^2 + 1)^2 = 10^2 = 100$

$3 \times 3 + 1 = \boxed{10}$
$10 \times 10 = \boxed{100}$

Copy and complete:
13. $(4^2 + 1)^2 = ...$  14. $(2^2 + 3)^2 = ...$  15. $(5^2 + 7)^2 = ...$  • Check your answers.

### Star Challenge ⭐ ⭐

13-14 correct = 2 stars
10-12 correct = 1 star

Copy and complete each expression.
1. $11^2 = ...$  2. $8^3 = ...$  3. $9^4 = ...$  4. $10^5 = ...$  5. $2^4 = ...$
6. $2^{...} = 8$  7. $3^{...} = 27$  8. $6^{...} = 216$  9. $4^{...} = 64$  10. $14^{...} = 196$
11. $6 \times 4^2 = ...$  12. $10 \times 5^2 = ...$  13. $2 \times 4^2 = ...$  14. $(4^2 + 3)^2 = ...$

• Your teacher has the answers to these.

A POW GUIDE            page 104            Working with Numbers    EXTRA

# Section 8: Working with negative numbers

In this section you will:
- review addition of positive and negative numbers;
- review subtraction of positive and negative numbers.

Level 5

## DEVELOPMENT

### D1: Adding positive and negative numbers

EXAMPLE 3   Q: Work out   $5 + (-2)$

A:   $5 + (-2) = 3$

$5F + 2B = 3F$

Big Edd

Copy and complete:
1. $3 + (-2) = \ldots$
2. $1 + (-5) = \ldots$
3. $(-5) + 3 = \ldots$
4. $(-4) + (-3) = \ldots$
5. $7 + 1 = \ldots$
6. $(-3) + 2 + (-1) = \ldots$

- Check your answers

## PRACTICE

### P1: Sums of + and − numbers

Copy and complete each statement. Do as many batches as you need.

**Batch A:**
1. $(-4) + 5 = \ldots$
2. $4 + (-2) = \ldots$
3. $(-2) + (-1) = \ldots$
4. $(-3) + 5 = \ldots$
5. $7 + (-3) = \ldots$
6. $(-2) + (-4) = \ldots$
7. $6 + (-3) = \ldots$
8. $(-4) + 2 + (-3) = \ldots$

**Batch B:**
1. $3 + (-1) = \ldots$
2. $4 + (-5) = \ldots$
3. $(-1) + (-3) = \ldots$
4. $4 + (-6) = \ldots$
5. $3 + (-2) = \ldots$
6. $(-6) + (-2) = \ldots$
7. $(-3) + (-5) = \ldots$
8. $(-5) + 7 + 2 = \ldots$

**Batch C:**
1. $(-1) + (-5) = \ldots$
2. $(-6) + 4 = \ldots$
3. $(-6) + (-3) = \ldots$
4. $(-3) + 7 = \ldots$
5. $5 + (-4) = \ldots$
6. $6 + (-7) = \ldots$
7. $(-3) + (-2) = \ldots$
8. $(-1) + (-2) + 5 = \ldots$

### Star Challenge 9

20-22 correct = 1 star

Copy and complete each of these.
The numbers outside each box are the sums of the rows and columns.

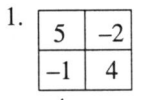

1.
| 5 | −2 | 3 |
|---|---|---|
| −1 | 4 | … |
| 4 | … | |

2.
| −7 | −2 | … |
|---|---|---|
| 3 | 5 | … |
| … | … | |

3.
| −6 | −1 | … |
|---|---|---|
| 2 | 3 | … |
| … | … | |

4.
| −3 | −1 | … |
|---|---|---|
| −2 | 0 | … |
| … | … | |

5.
| −2 | 4 | … |
|---|---|---|
| 3 | −6 | … |
| … | … | |

6.
| −1 | 6 | … |
|---|---|---|
| −5 | 3 | … |
| … | … | |

7.
| 10 | −12 | … |
|---|---|---|
| −8 | −3 | … |
| … | … | |

8.
| 5 | −5 | … |
|---|---|---|
| −3 | 3 | … |
| … | … | |

A POW GUIDE   page 105   Working with Numbers   **EXTRA**

## D2: Subtracting numbers

**Type 1**   $5 - 3 = 2$
              $3 - 5 = -2$

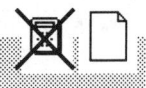

Complete:

1. $5 - 1 = \ldots$   2. $1 - 4 = \ldots$   3. $5 - 3 = \ldots$   4. $12 - 1 = \ldots$   5. $2 - 8 = \ldots$
6. $8 - 2 = \ldots$   7. $2 - 7 = \ldots$   8. $3 - 5 = \ldots$   9. $7 - 3 = \ldots$   10. $1 - 5 = \ldots$

**Type 2**   $-3 - 2 = -5$

"Take 3, take 2" is the same as "take 5"

*Mishrak*

This is a mixture of Type 1 and Type 2 questions.
Complete:

11. $-4 - 1 = \ldots$   12. $-1 - 3 = \ldots$   13. $4 - 1 = \ldots$   14. $-5 - 1 = \ldots$   15. $-2 - 8 = \ldots$
16. $9 - 2 = \ldots$   17. $-3 - 6 = \ldots$   18. $-4 - 2 = \ldots$   19. $2 - 6 = \ldots$   20. $-3 - 4 = \ldots$

**Type 3**

$5 - (-3)$         $-5 - (-3)$
$= 5 + 3$          $= -5 + 3$
$= 8$              $= -2$

Step 1: Change $- (- N)$ to $+ N$
        Leave all other numbers as they are.
Step 2: Add (using steps forward & back)

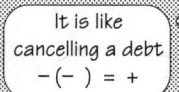

It is like cancelling a debt
$- (-\ ) = +$

*Yerwat*

Fill in the gaps:

21. $3 - (-2)$
    $= 3 + \ldots$
    $= \ldots$

22. $-1 - (-5)$
    $= -1 + \ldots$
    $= \ldots$

23. $2 - (-6)$
    $= \ldots + \ldots$
    $= \ldots$

24. $-3 - (-1)$
    $= \ldots + \ldots$
    $= \ldots$

25. $3 - (-5)$
    $= \ldots + \ldots$
    $= \ldots$

26. $7 - (-2)$
    $= \ldots \ldots \ldots$
    $= \ldots$

27. $-4 - (-1)$
    $= \ldots \ldots \ldots$
    $= \ldots$

28. $-2 - (-2)$
    $= \ldots \ldots \ldots$
    $= \ldots$

29. $6 - (-1)$
    $= \ldots + \ldots$
    $= \ldots$

30. $-2 - (-4)$
    $= \ldots + \ldots$
    $= \ldots$

31. $10 - (-2)$
    $= \ldots + \ldots$
    $= \ldots$

32. $-6 - (-1)$
    $= \ldots + \ldots$
    $= \ldots$

• *Check your answers. DO NOT GO ON UNTIL YOU UNDERSTAND THESE !*

## PRACTICE
## P2: A mixture of all three types

Work out the answer to each sum. For type three subtractions, show your working.
CHECK ANSWERS AT THE END OF EACH BATCH!

| Batch A: | Batch B: | Batch C: | Batch D: |
|---|---|---|---|
| 1. 6 – 3 | 1. 1 – 5 | 1. 1 – (–3) | 1. 7 – (–1) |
| 2. 3 – 6 | 2. 1 – (–5) | 2. 1 – 5 | 2. –3 – (–7) |
| 3. 7 – (–5) | 3. 3 – 7 | 3. –1 – 6 | 3. 4 – 7 |
| 4. 5 – (–7) | 4. 5 – (–2) | 4. 10 – (–2) | 4. –3 – 3 |
| 5. –5 – (–7) | 5. –2 – 6 | 5. –3 – (–7) | 5. 4 – (–6) |
| 6. –7 – (–5) | 6. –7 – (–2) | 6. 21 – (–4) | 6. 10 – (–5) |
| 7. –7 – 5 | 7. –12 – 2 | 7. 3 – 7 | 7. –5 – 7 |
| 8. –4 – (–4) | 8. 10 – (–15) | 8. –4 – (–1) | 8. –5 – (–12) |

### Star Challenge 10 & 10

12 correct = 2 stars
10-11 correct = 1 star

*Copy and complete:*

1. – 1 – 9    = ......
2. – 2 – (–4) = ......
3. 5 – 8      = ......
4. 1 – 5      = ......
5. 10 – (–2)  = ......
6. 6 – (–5)   = ......
7. –10 – 7    = ......
8. 8 – (–2)   = ......
9. –4 – (–6)  = ......
10. 2 – (–4)  = ......
11. –9 – (–1) = ......
12. – 5 – 6   = ......

• Your teacher has the answers to these.

### Star Challenge 11 & 11

12 correct = 2 stars
10-11 correct = 1 star

*This is a mixture of additions and subtractions.*
*Copy and complete:*

1. – 1 + 7    = ......
2. – 3 – 4    = ......
3. 5 + 8 +(–1)= ......
4. 2 – (–5)   = ......
5. 8 + (–2)   = ......
6. –3 + (–2)  = ......
7. –6 – 7 + 1 = ......
8. –2 +(–2)   = ......
9. 5 – (–6) + 3 = ......
10. 2 + (–3) – 1 = ......
11. –8 – (–2) + 1 = ......
12. – 4 + 6 – 3 = ......

• Your teacher has the answers to these.

### Star Challenge 12

8-9 correct = 1 star

EXAMPLE 4  Q: Work out the mean of these numbers  4  5  7  8

A:   Mean = $\frac{4 + 5 + 7 + 8}{4}$ = 24 ÷ 4 = 6

*Add up all the numbers.*
*Divide by how many there are.*

*Work out the mean of each of these sets of numbers:*

1. 7  9  10  6
2. 6  5  10  4  5
3. 0  7  7  5  1
4. 2  –1  3  6  0
5. –4  3  –2
6. 5  –3  4  –2
7. –2  –3  6  2  2
8. 4  –5  –2  –3  1
9. –3  –3  –4  –5  10

*Pow*

• *Your teacher has the answers to these.*

A POW GUIDE          page 107          Working with Numbers  **EXTRA**

# Section 9: Metric & Imperial equivalents

Level 5

In this section you will:
- use approximate equivalent measurements to solve problems.

**DEVELOPMENT**

## D1: Using equivalent values to solve problems

1. | Yeast 30g | Yeast 60g | Yeast 100g |   **1 ounce ≈ 25 g**

   The recipe calls for 2 ounces yeast.   ≈ means "approximately equal to"
   Which of these packets is nearer to 2 ounces ?

2. | Icing sugar 100g | Icing sugar 200g | Icing sugar 300g |

   The recipe calls for 8 ounces of icing sugar. Which packet should I buy ?

3. | Brown sugar 200g | Brown sugar 250g | Brown sugar 300g |

   The recipe calls for 12 ounces of brown sugar. Which packet should I buy ?

4. **12 inches = 1 foot  ≈ 30 cm**

   Mavis wants to buy jeans when on holiday in France.
   In England she looks for 36 inch hip size.
   What size should she look for in France ?

5. Ellen knows that the socks she used to buy were size "9 inch".
   The store she buys from have changed to metric measurements.
   | Socks 15-17 cm | Socks 18-20 cm | Socks 21-23cm | Socks 24-26 cm |   Which size socks should she buy ?

6. **1 kg ≈ 2 pounds**

   Sam wants to buy half a pound of meat.
   He goes shopping at the Belgian camp–site shop.
   What fraction of a kilo should he ask for – a half, quarter or three-quarters ?

7. The next day, Sam is sent to buy one and a half pounds of meat.
   He goes shopping at the same Belgian camp–site shop.
   What should he ask for – a kilo, a quarter kilo, a half kilo or three-quarters of a kilo?

8. The instruction book says "Cook the chicken for 20 min for every pound weight".
   This means that a 3 pound chicken must be cooked for 60 min (3 x 20 min).
   How long do I cook a chicken that weighs
   (a) 4 pounds   (b) 2 kg   (c) 3 kg   (d) $4^{1}/_{2}$ kg   ?

9. Dave is sent to buy flour. His mother says his birthday cake needs 1 pound of flour.
   By mistake, he buys 1 kg of flour.
   How many cakes could his mother make with this amount of flour ?

A POW GUIDE   page 108   Working with Numbers **EXTRA**

10. | 1 inch ≈ 25 mm |

| Frame 1 | Frame 2 | Frame 3 | Frame 4 |
|---|---|---|---|
| 75 mm x 150 mm | 100 mm x 130 mm | 100 mm x 150 mm | 100 mm x 160 mm |

My photo-frame has been broken. I need to replace it.
The size on the back is 4 inches x 6 inches.
Which of these four frames should I buy ?

11. Barbara is buying some wood. She needs pieces that are as near as possible to 2 inches by 2 inches, 2 inches by 1 $\frac{1}{2}$ inches, 3 inches by 1 inch.
At the woodyard, all the wood is measured in mm.

| Wood for sale | | |
|---|---|---|
| 75mm by 40mm | 50mm by 50mm | 50mm by 60 mm |
| 75mm by 25 mm | 50mm by 40mm | 60mm by 60 mm |

Which three sizes did she buy ?

12. | 5 miles ≈ 8 km |

The distance from Artemare to Libos is 40 km.
How far is that roughly in miles ?

13. The distance from Dunkeld to Amultree is 10 miles.
How far is that roughly in kilometres ?

14. Duncan lives in Scotland. His village is 35 miles from the nearest town, Inverness. His cousin, Alan, lives in Australia. His farm is 52 km from the nearest town, Perth. Which one of them lives furthest away from the nearest town ? Explain how you know.

15. | 1 metre ≈ 1.1 yards |

My mother sent me to buy 5 yards of material to make some curtains.
The shop sells the material in metres, not yards.
Should I buy 5m or 6m ? Explain why.

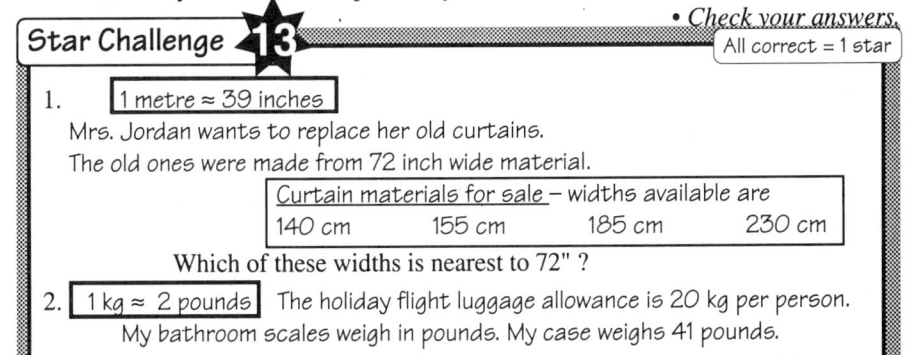

• Check your answers.

## Star Challenge 13

All correct = 1 star

1. | 1 metre ≈ 39 inches |

Mrs. Jordan wants to replace her old curtains.
The old ones were made from 72 inch wide material.

| Curtain materials for sale – widths available are | | | |
|---|---|---|---|
| 140 cm | 155 cm | 185 cm | 230 cm |

Which of these widths is nearest to 72" ?

2. | 1 kg ≈ 2 pounds | The holiday flight luggage allowance is 20 kg per person.
My bathroom scales weigh in pounds. My case weighs 41 pounds.
Is it under or over the luggage allowance ? Show how you work it out.

A POW GUIDE    page 109    Working with Numbers  **EXTRA**

# Section 10: Checking answers 2

**Level 5**

In this section you will:
- check answers using inverse operations;
- check answers using approximations;
- review pencil-and-paper multiplication techniques and check answers.

## DEVELOPMENT

### D1: Checking using inverse operations

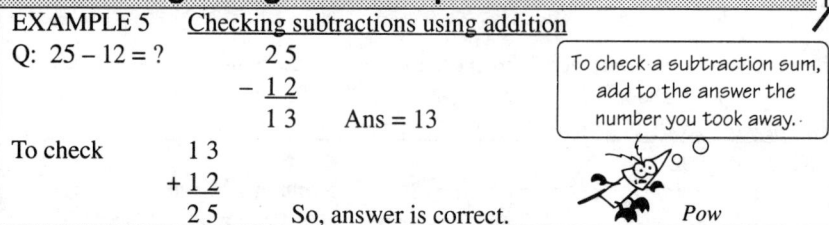

**EXAMPLE 5** — Checking subtractions using addition

Q: 25 − 12 = ?

```
  2 5
− 1 2
  1 3     Ans = 13
```

To check a subtraction sum, add to the answer the number you took away.

To check:
```
  1 3
+ 1 2
  2 5     So, answer is correct.
```

*Pow*

Work out each subtraction sum. Set the sum out as in the example.
Check your answer by adding.

1. 38 − 23
2. 46 − 14
3. 18 − 15
4. 54 − 32
5. 76 − 35
6. 49 − 36

Take care. You will need to 'borrow' to do these subtractions.

7. 45 − 26
8. 63 − 25
9. 12 − 9
10. 24 − 18
11. 235 − 127
12. 62 − 48

• **CHECK YOUR ANSWERS!**

**EXAMPLE 6** — Checking additions using subtraction

Q: 25 + 10 = ?

```
  2 5
+ 1 0
  3 5     Ans = 35
```

To check an addition sum, take away from the answer the number you added.

To check:
```
  3 5
− 1 0
  2 5     So, answer is correct.
```

*Modesto*

Work out each addition sum. Set the sum out as in the example.
Check your answer by subtracting.

13. 35 + 23
14. 126 + 52
15. 12 + 24
16. 35 + 28
17. 48 + 34
18. 126 + 42

• Check your answers.

---

### Star Challenge 14

1 mark for each correct answer

Work out each sum.
Set each sum out as in the examples.
Show how you check your answer.

1 mark for each correct check

16-20 marks = 1 star

1. 37 + 12
2. 58 + 21
3. 27 − 15
4. 46 − 25
5. 145 + 24
6. 53 + 28
7. 95 − 23
8. 246 + 134
9. 326 − 119
10. 546 + 245

A POW GUIDE — Working with Numbers **EXTRA**

# D2: Working out approximate answers 2

**Technique review**

Work out 60 x 40 in your head

*Chyps*

$$60 \times 40 = 6 \times 10 \times 4 \times 10$$
$$= (6 \times 4) \times (10 \times 10)$$
$$= 24 \times 100$$
$$= 2400$$

Work these out in your head:
1. 20 x 40    2. 40 x 30    3. 60 x 40    4. 20 x 70    5. 40 x 50    6. 70 x 30

• *Check your answers.*

**EXAMPLE 7**   Q: A wall is 58 bricks long and 37 bricks high
Work out how many bricks there are, approximately.      37 bricks

A:   Number of bricks = 58 x 37                58 bricks
     Approximate number of bricks = 60 x 40 = 2400
                                    ↑        ↑
                                 rounded to
                                 nearest 10

58 lots of 37 bricks = 58 x 37
*Pow*

Work out the approximate number of bricks in each of these walls:

7. [  ]  12 bricks    8. [  ]  18 bricks    9. [  ]  31 bricks
   48 bricks             81 bricks             73 bricks

10. [  ]  28 bricks   11. [  ]  39 bricks   12. [  ]  47 bricks
    89 bricks             63 bricks             94 bricks

• *Check your answers.*

**Technique review**

Work out 40 x 30 in your head

*Modesto*

$$400 \times 30 = 4 \times 100 \times 3 \times 10$$
$$= (4 \times 3) \times (100 \times 10)$$
$$= 12 \times 1000$$
$$= 12\,000$$

Work these out in your head:
13. 200 x 40    14. 500 x 30    15. 400 x 40    16. 200 x 60    17. 400 x 20

• *Check your answers.*

**EXAMPLE 8**   Q: A wall is 389 bricks long and 23 bricks high
Work out how many bricks there are, approximately.      23 bricks

A:   Number of bricks = 389 x 23              389 bricks
     Approximate number of bricks = 400 x 30 = 12 000
                                    ↑         ↑
                                 rounded to  rounded to
                                 nearest 100 nearest 10

389 lots of 23 bricks = 389 x 23
*Pow*

Work out the approximate number of bricks:

18. [  ]  51 bricks   19. [  ]  69 bricks   20. [  ]  24 bricks
    243 bricks            538 bricks            619 bricks

• *Check your answers.*

A POW GUIDE        page 111        Working with Numbers   **EXTRA**

# D3: Using approximations to check answers

1. This area is to be covered in paving slabs.

   Sludge works out 47 x 21 and gets 987

   Dwork works out 47 x 21 and gets 1410

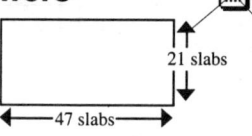

   *Sludge*

   *Dwork*

   Work out the approximate number of slabs.

   Say which you think is probably right, Sludge or Dwork

   (21 slabs, 47 slabs)

2. Four Pan-Galactic trainee explorers got 4 different answers to a question in an exam.

   | Letmewin | Meedy Oker | Pow | Idea |
   |---|---|---|---|
   | Answers: 4 219 | 421 195 | 42 195 | 4 195 |

   The sum they worked out was 485 x 87

   DO NOT WORK OUT THE ANSWER TO THIS SUM.
   Use approximations to check which answer seems the most reasonable.
   Who you think had the right answer. Explain how you know.

3. Sum: **339 x 71**

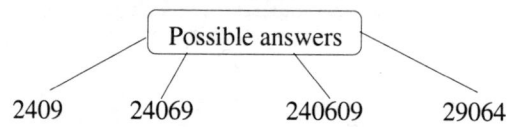

   Possible answers

   2409   24069   240609   29064

   Use approximations to decide which answer is the most reasonable.
   Which do you think is the right answer. Show how you work it out.

---

≈ means 'is approximately equal to'

For each of these multiplications, work out which is the most reasonable approximation.
Show how you work it out.

4. 39 x 19 ≈ 80 / 400 / 800 / 8 000

5. 73 x 23 ≈ 14 / 140 / 1400 / 14 000

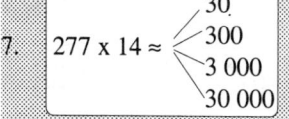

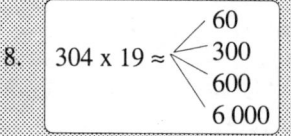

6. 39 x 47 ≈ 200 / 1 600 / 2 000 / 4 000

7. 277 x 14 ≈ 30 / 300 / 3 000 / 30 000

8. 304 x 19 ≈ 60 / 300 / 600 / 6 000

9. 388 x 32 ≈ 120 / 600 / 6 000 / 12 000

• *Check your answers.*

A POW GUIDE  page 112  Working with Numbers  **EXTRA**

## Star Challenge 15

**5-6 marks = 1 star**

1. A wall is 82 bricks long and 13 bricks high. Which of these is the most reasonable estimate of the number of bricks in the wall?

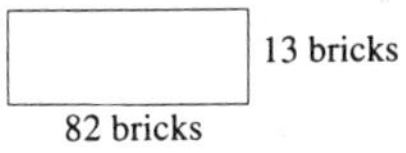

   [ 800 ]   [ 900 ]   [ 1600 ]

   Show how you worked it out.   (1 mark for answer, 2 marks for working out)

2. The volume of air in this hall is given by
   $V = 73 \times 32 \times 12$ m$^3$

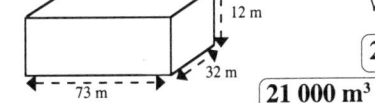

   12 m, 32 m, 73 m

   [ 210 m$^3$ ]   [ 2 100 m$^3$ ]
   [ 21 000 m$^3$ ]   [ 210 000 m$^3$ ]

   Which is the most reasonable estimate of the volume of air in the hall?
   Show how you worked it out.   (1 mark for answer, 2 marks for working out)

   • *Your teacher will need to mark this.*

## D4: Multiplying and checking

You need to be able to multiply a 3-digit number by a 2-digit number *and* check whether your answer is reasonable (likely to be right).

**Technique review (met earlier in Back to Basics)**

Method 1

| x | 200 | 40 | 6 |
|---|-----|-----|-----|
| 40 | 8000 | 1600 | 240 |
| 2 | 400 | 80 | 12 |

246 x 42 = 10332

```
  8000
+ 1600
+  240
+  400
+   80
+   12
 10332
   1 1
```

Method 2

| | 2 | 4 | 6 | |
|---|---|---|---|---|
| 1 | 0⁄8 | 1⁄6 | 2⁄4 | 4 |
| 0 | 0⁄4 | 0⁄8 | 1⁄2 | 2 |
| | 3 | 3 | 2 | |

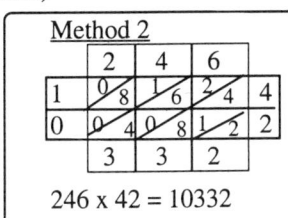

246 x 42 = 10332

Check: 246 x 42 ≈ 200 x 40 = 8 000   (8 thousand)
Since the answer we got is just over 10 thousand, it is roughly the same size as the approximation, so the answer is reasonable (likely to be right).

*For each of these multiplications, work out the answer, using any method. Then use approximations to check whether your answer is reasonable.*

1. 28 x 12   2. 15 x 23   3. 47 x 14   4. 77 x 99   5. 123 x 11   6. 341 x 33

## Star Challenge 16

• *Check your answers.*
**All correct = 1 star**

There are 32 biscuits in a box. There are 48 x 32 biscuits in 48 boxes.

(a) Multiply 48 by 32 to work out how many biscuits there are.
   Show how you worked it out. You may use any pencil-and-paper method.

(b) Work out an approximate answer for 48 x 32

(c) Show how you can use it to check if your answer is correct.

A POW GUIDE   page 113   Working with Numbers  **EXTRA**

# Section 11: Working with ratios

**Level 6**

*In this section you will solve real-life problems involving ratios.*

## DEVELOPMENT

### D1: Applications of ratio

Scientists are developing two new glues. Each glue comes in two tubes – a resin and a hardener. Separate, they are liquids. When mixed, they set very quickly.

> GLU–IT is mixed in a ratio of resin : hardener = 1 : 2
> This means that you use two drops of hardener to every drop of resin
> or two spoonfuls of hardener to every spoonful of resin.

1. With GLU–IT, how much hardener do you mix with 3 *ml* of resin?
2. With GLU–IT, how much resin do you mix with 1 teaspoon of hardener?

> The second glue, STIK–IT is mixed in a ratio of resin : hardener = 4 : 5

3. For STIK–IT, complete this table:

| Resin | 4ml | 8ml |  |  |
|---|---|---|---|---|
| Hardener |  |  | 20ml | 25ml |

> Concrete is made from three ingredients – cement, sand & aggregate (small stones)
> For a general purpose concrete, the mix is in the proportion 1 : 2 : 3
> (1 bucket of cement to 2 buckets of sand to 3 buckets of aggregate)

4. General purpose concrete (1 : 2 : 3)
   (a) How many spadefuls of sand and aggregate do you need with one spadeful of cement?
   (b) A load of concrete is made using 12 barrowloads of aggregate. How much cement and sand are used?
   (c) Another load is made using 12 buckets of sand. How much cement and aggregate are used?

5. For foundations the mix is 2 : 5 : 7    *Copy and complete this table.*

| Cement | 1 | 2 | 3 | 4 | 5 | 6 | 7 |
|---|---|---|---|---|---|---|---|
| Sand |  |  |  |  |  |  |  |
| Aggregate |  |  |  |  |  |  |  |

6. For paving the mix is 2 : 3 : 5    *Copy and complete this table.*

| Cement | 1 | 2 |  |  |  |
|---|---|---|---|---|---|
| Sand |  |  | 3 | 6 |  |
| Aggregate |  |  |  | 20 | 25 |

• Check answers.   24 correct = 2 stars
                   20-23 correct = 1 star

### Star Challenge

| Cider strogonoff – Ingredients: for 6 people | 720g chuck steak | 450g mushrooms |
|---|---|---|
|  | 3 medium onions | 270ml dry cider |
|  | 75g butter | 240ml soured cream |

Write out the amounts of each ingredient needed to make this dish for
   (a) 12 people    (b) 2 people    (c) 3 people    (d) 4 people

• Your teacher has the answers to these.

# E1: Ratio problems

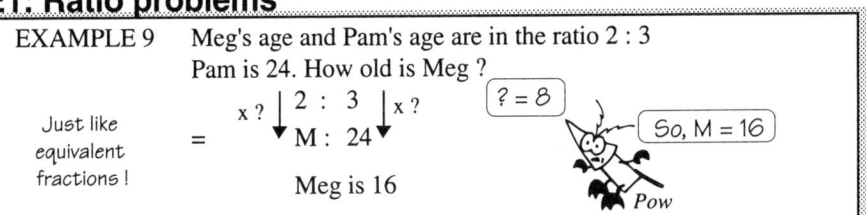

**EXAMPLE 9**  Meg's age and Pam's age are in the ratio 2 : 3
Pam is 24. How old is Meg ?

Just like equivalent fractions !

x ? | 2 : 3 | x ?
   M : 24
Meg is 16

? = 8
So, M = 16
Pow

1. The lengths of two pencils are in the ratio 2 : 3. The smaller pencil is 16 cm long. How long is the other one ?

2. The ratio of David's and his father's heights is 4 : 5. David's father is 180 cm tall. How tall is David ?

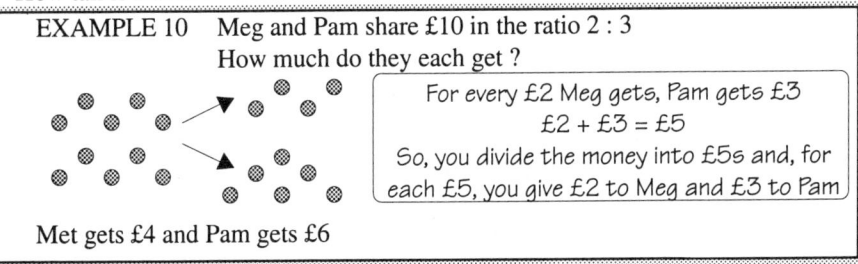

**EXAMPLE 10**  Meg and Pam share £10 in the ratio 2 : 3
How much do they each get ?

For every £2 Meg gets, Pam gets £3
£2 + £3 = £5
So, you divide the money into £5s and, for each £5, you give £2 to Meg and £3 to Pam

Met gets £4 and Pam gets £6

3. Share £25 in the ratio 2 : 3
4. Share £50 in the ratio 1 : 4
5. Share £35 in the ratio 2 : 5
6. (a) Mary and Ann buy a car. Mary pays two thirds of the price. Ann pays the rest. What is the ratio of what they each pay for the car ?
   (b) They later sell the car for £3 600. They share the money in the same ratio as they paid for it. How much does Mary get ?
7. Martin and Asif get paid £60 for clearing a garden. They share the money in the ratio 5 : 7.
   (a) Does Martin get five twelfths of the money or five sevenths?
   (b) How much does Martin get ?
8. A piece of string 40 cm long is cut so that the two pieces are in the ratio 3 : 5.
   (a) What fraction of the original piece of string is the shorter piece ?
   (b) How long is the shorter piece ?
9. Share 70p in the ratio 1 : 2 : 4.
10. Share £80 in the ratio 3 : 7.
11. In one class, the ratio of girls to boys is 2 : 1. What fraction of the class is boys ?
12. In another class, five eighths of the class are boys. What is the ratio of boys to girls?

• Check your answers

A POW GUIDE     Working with Numbers  **EXTRA**

# Section 12 : Technique review

In this section you will review techniques met in this topic.

Check your answers at the end of each set of problems

## R1: Negative numbers
*Level 3*

1. The midnight temperature was 4°C. By next morning the temperature had fallen to −5°C. How many degrees had it fallen?
2. The temperature when I went to bed was −1°C. When I woke up, the temperature was 4°C higher. What was the temperature when I woke?
3. The temperature in the fridge was 1°C. The temperature in the freezer was −6°C. What is the difference in the temperatures?

## R2: Rounding numbers
*Level 3*

*Copy and complete:*
1. 641 is ...... to the nearest ten
2. 641 is ...... to the nearest hundred
3. 1 087 is ...... to the nearest ten
4. 1 087 is ...... to the nearest hundred
5. The price of a CD player is £255.
   (a) What is its price to the nearest £100?  (b) What is its price to the nearest £10?
6. The price of a Ford Ka is £8 860.
   (a) What is its price to the nearest £100?  (b) What is its price to the nearest £1000?

## R3: Checking answers
*Level 4*

1. *Work out:*  (a) 50 x 7    (b) 300 x 6    (c) 30 x 40
2. Work out the approximate number of tiles in this floor.

   29 tiles | 7 tiles

3. 39 x 23 = ⟵ 62 / 427 / 897    Do NOT work out the answer. Which of these is the most likely answer? Explain why you think it is.

## R4: Multiples and divisiblity
*Level 4*

1. Write down the first five multiples of 6.
2. Write down the multiples of 5 between 17 and 41.
3. Which of these numbers are divisible by 5?   36  14  85  90  257  375

   12 is a multiple of 1,2,3,4,6,12
   This means that it is divisible by 1, 2, 3 ,4, 6, 12

4. How do you know if a number is divisible by 10?
5. How do you know if a number is divisible by 5?
6. How do you know if a number is divisible by 2?
7. 35 is a multiple of 7. Is 35 divisible by 7?

Gizmo

A POW GUIDE    page 116    Working with Numbers  **EXTRA**

## R5: Whole number answers and divisiblity
*Level 4*

*Work out each sum. Say whether each answer is a whole number:*
1. $561 \div 3$  2. $561 \div 5$  3. $561 \div 11$

$$561 \div 17 = 33.$$

A whole number answer tells you that 561 is divisible by 17

*Gizmo*

4. Is 561 divisible by 11 ?  5. Is 386 divisible by 2 ?  6. Is 195 divisible by 13 ?

## R6: Factors
*Level 4*

Since 561 is divisible by 17 we say that 17 is **a factor** of 561

1. Is 14 a factor of 28 ?
2. 6 has four factors. Find the four factors of 6.
3. 14 has four factors. Find the four factors of 14.
4. 30 has eight factors. Find the eight factors of 30.

## R7: Prime numbers
*Level 4*

A prime number has only two factors – 1 and itself.

1. Which of these are prime numbers ?   7   9   15   17   23   36
2. There are four prime numbers between 10 and 20. List them.

## R8: Squares, square roots and cubes
*Level 4*

The square of 5 = 5 squared = $5^2$ = 5 x 5 = 25

The cube of 4 = 4 cubed = $4^3$ = 4 x 4 x 4 = 64

The square root of 25 = $\sqrt{25}$ = 5

*Write down ...*
1. ... the square of 7
2. ... six squared
3. ...the square root of 16
4. ... $10^2$
5. ... $\sqrt{9}$
6. ...the square of 9
7. ... 2 cubed
8. ... the cube of 3
9. ...11 squared

10. Copy and complete:
The first ten square numbers are 1, 4, 9, ..., ..., ..., ..., ..., ..., ...

11. $N^2 = 256$  Use a 'trial-and-improvement method' to find the value of N. Show how you work it out.

12. $M^3 = 729$  Use a 'trial-and-improvement method' to find the value of N. Show how you work it out.

A POW GUIDE        Working with Numbers **EXTRA**

## R9: Powers

*Level 5*

Copy and complete each expression.
1. $5^2 = $ ......
2. $6^3 = $ ......
3. $2^4 = $ ......
4. $10^3 = $ ......
5. $5^{...} = 125$
6. $2^{...} = 8$
7. $3^{...} = 81$
8. $10^{...} = 100$
9. $3 \times 6^2 = $ ......
10. $(3^2 + 1)^2 = $ ......

## R10: Working with negative numbers

*Level 5*

$3 + (-1) = ?$
$3 + (-1) = 2$   (3F + 1B)

Copy and complete:
1. $5 + (-2) = $ ...
2. $-1 + (-2) = $ ...
3. $-3 + 4 = $ ...
4. $-2 + (-4) + 1 = $ ...

| Type 1 subtraction | Type 2 subtraction | Type 3 subtraction |
|---|---|---|
| $5 - 3 = 2$ | $-2 - 3 = -5$ | $5 - (-3)$ |
| $3 - 5 = -2$ | | $= 5 + 3 = 8$ |

Copy and complete:
5. $7 - 3 = $ ...
6. $-7 - 3 = $ ...
7. $2 - 6 = $ ...
8. $6 - (-2) = $ ...
9. $-5 - (-3) = $ ...
10. $1 - (-3) = $ ...
11. $-3 - 5 = $ ...
12. $1 - 5 = $ ...

13. Copy and complete this table. The numbers outside the box are the sums of the rows and columns.

| 5 | −1 | ... |
|---|---|---|
| −2 | −3 | ... |
| ... | ... | |

## R11: Metric and Imperial equivalents

*Level 5*

You need to **LEARN** the basic equivalents.
≈ means 'is approximately equal to'

These statements are all given in Section 9.
Copy and complete each statement.
**LEARN EACH STATEMENT.**

1. 1 ounce ≈ ......... g
2. 1 kg ≈ ......... pounds
3. 1 pound ≈ ......... kg
4. 1 foot ≈ ...... cm
5. 1 metre ≈ ......... yards
6. 1 inch ≈ ...... mm
7. 5 miles ≈ ......... km
8. 1 mile ≈ ...... km
9. The distance from Chester to Tarporley is roughly 15 miles. How far is that in km?
10. The distance from Chester to Wrexham is roughly 16 km. How far is that in miles?

A POW GUIDE     Working with Numbers **EXTRA**

# THE NATIONAL CURRICULUM ...
# ... AND BEYOND ...

*Pow*

# Areas, Volumes and Formulae
## EXTRA

| Level 3 | Level 4 | Level 5 | Level 6 |
|---------|---------|---------|---------|
| | | §12 Technique review | |
| | | | §11 The area of a circle |
| | | | §10 Problems involving rounding |
| | | | §9 The circumference of a circle |
| | | §8 Altogether now … | |
| | | §7 Area of any triangle | |
| | §6 Parallelograms | | |
| | §5 Right-angled triangles | | |
| | §4 Volumes | | |
| | §3 Areas of rectangles | | |
| | §2 Perimeter review | | |
| | §1 Area Review | | |

*A POW GUIDE*      *page 119*

# Areas, Volumes and Formulae
## Section 1: Area review

Level 4

In this section you will review:
• what area is;
• using the most common units of area.

**DEVELOPMENT**

### D1: What is area ?

> The **area** of a shape is how much space it covers.
>
> The area of this shape is 4 squares
> Area = 4 squares

Write down the area of each shape.
Write each answer in the form   Area = ...... squares

1.   2.   3.   4.   5.   6.

• Check your answers.

### D2: The most common unit of area

1 cm   The most common unit of area is 1 $cm^2$ ← read as 1 centimetre squared
1 cm
The area of this shape is $2\frac{1}{2}$ $cm^2$    Pow

Write down the area of each shape.
Write each answer in the form   Area = ...... $cm^2$

1.   2.   3.   4.

5.   6.   7.   8.

9.

• Check answers.

A POW GUIDE   page 120   Areas, Volumes and Formulae **EXTRA**

# Section 2: Perimeter review

In this section you will review:
- what perimeter is;
- working out perimeters of shapes.

**DEVELOPMENT**

Level 4

## D1: Distance round the outside

*Measure the sides of each shape.*
*Write your measurements on the diagrams.*
*Work out the distance round the outside of each shape.*

A
A: Distance round
= ......... cm

B
B: Distance round = ......... cm

C
C: Distance round
= ......... cm

D
D: Distance round = ......... cm

E
E: Distance round =
......... cm

F
F: Distance round
= .........

G
G: Distance round
= ......... cm

H
H: Distance round = ......... cm

I
I: Distance round
= ......... cm

- *Check your answers.*

A POW GUIDE    page 121    Areas, Volumes and Formulae **EXTRA**

## D2: Perimeter

**Perimeter** = distance round the outside of a shape

*Ruff*

Copy this into your book. Highlight it.

The length of the side of 1 square is 1 unit.
The perimeter of this shape is 10 units.

Perimeter = 10 units

*Write down the perimeter of each shape.*
*Write each answer in the form   Perimeter = ...... units*

1.   2.   3.   4.   5.

*Each small square below is 1 cm long.*
*Write down the perimeter of each shape.*
*Write each answer in the form   Perimeter = ...... cm*

6.   7.   8.

9.   10.   11.

• Check your answers.

### Star Challenge 1

9-10 correct = 1 star

*Work out the perimeter and area of each of these shapes.*
*Copy and complete the table.*

A   B   C   D   E

| Shape | A | B | C | D | E |
|---|---|---|---|---|---|
| Perimeter (in units) | | | | | |
| Area (in squares) | | | | | |

• Your teacher has the answers to these.

A POW GUIDE        page 122        Areas, Volumes and Formulae  **EXTRA**

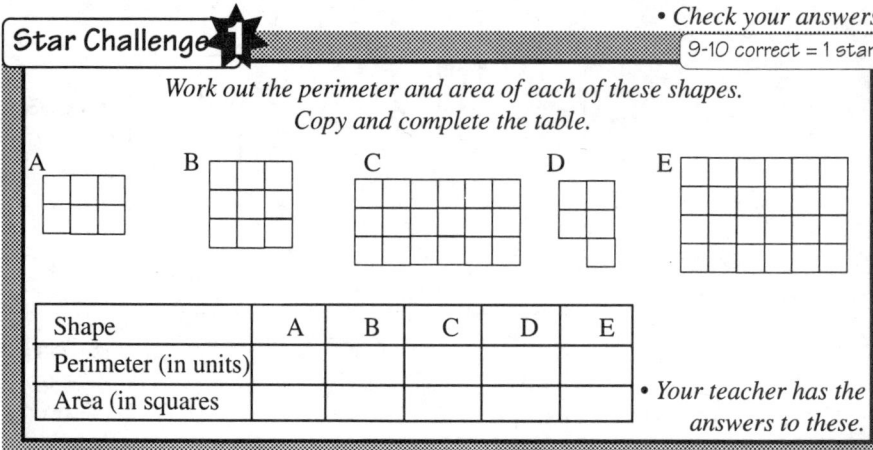

# Section 3: Areas of rectangles

In this section you will work out the area of rectangles:
• by counting squares;
• by using a rule.

**DEVELOPMENT**

Level 4

## D1: Rules for areas of rectangles

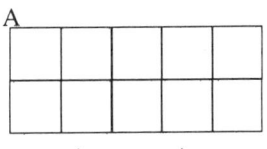

Assume each square has side 1 cm

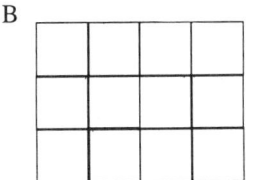

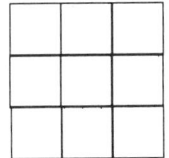

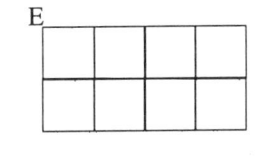

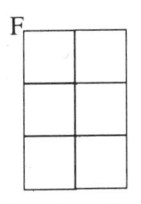

G : rectangle with length = 10 cm width = 4 cm

H : rectangle with length = 6 cm width = 5 cm

**Task 1:** *Copy and complete this table for rectangles A, B, C, D, E, F, G, H*

| Rectangle | length in cm | width in cm | area in cm² |
|---|---|---|---|
| A | 5 | 2 | |
| B | | | |
| C | | | |
| D | | | |
| E | | | |
| F | | | |
| G | 10 | 4 | |
| H | 6 | 5 | |

**Task 2:** Explain how to work out the area of a rectangle with length 7 cm and width 2 cm without drawing it.

**Task 3:**

Rule 1:
Area of rectangle = length + width

Rule 2:
Area of rectangle = length x width

Rule 3:
Area of rectangle = $\frac{1}{2}$ (length x width)

Which of these rules is the correct one ?   • Check your answers.

A POW GUIDE   page 123   Areas, Volumes and Formulae **EXTRA**

## PRACTICE
## P1: Areas of rectangles using the rule

> **Area of rectangle = length x width**
> 
> Copy this into your book. Highlight it.
> 
> Sureshot

Use the rule to work out the area of each of these rectangles.

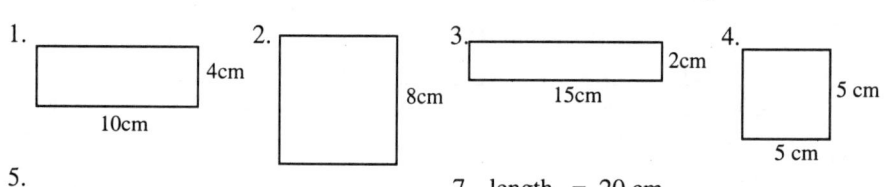

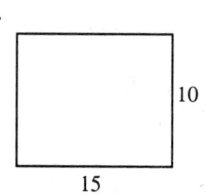

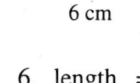

1. 10cm × 4cm
2. 8cm square
3. 15cm × 2cm
4. 5cm × 5cm
5. 15 × 10

6. length = 7 cm
   width = 5 cm

7. length = 20 cm
   width = 4 cm

8. length = 6 cm
   width = 6 cm

• Check answers.

## DEVELOPMENT
## D2: Units of area

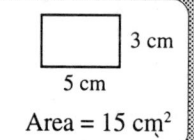

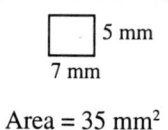

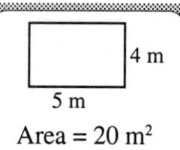

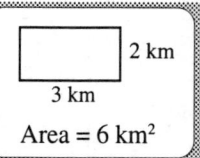

| 5 cm × 3 cm | 7 mm × 5 mm | 5 m × 4 m | 3 km × 2 km |
|---|---|---|---|
| Area = 15 cm² | Area = 35 mm² | Area = 20 m² | Area = 6 km² |

Work out the area of each rectangle. Each answer must have the correct unit of area.

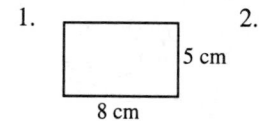

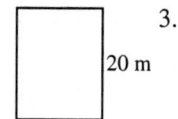

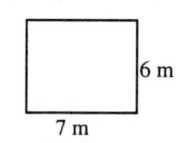

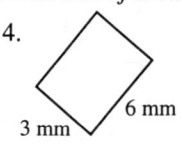

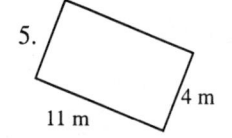

1. 8 cm × 5 cm
2. 9 m × 20 m
3. 7 m × 6 m
4. 3 mm × 6 mm
5. 11 m × 4 m

6. length = 4 cm
   width = 10 cm

7. length = 5 km
   width = 2 km

8. length = 6 mm
   width = 9 mm

9. length = 2 m
   width = 7 m

10. length = 4 mm
    width = 6 mm

11. length = 2 km
    width = 1 km

• Check your answers.

A POW GUIDE     page 124     Areas, Volumes and Formulae **EXTRA**

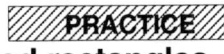

## P2: Areas of measured rectangles

*Measure the sides of each rectangle.*
*Write your measurements on the diagrams.*

*Work out the area of each rectangle.*
*Each answer must have the correct unit of area.*

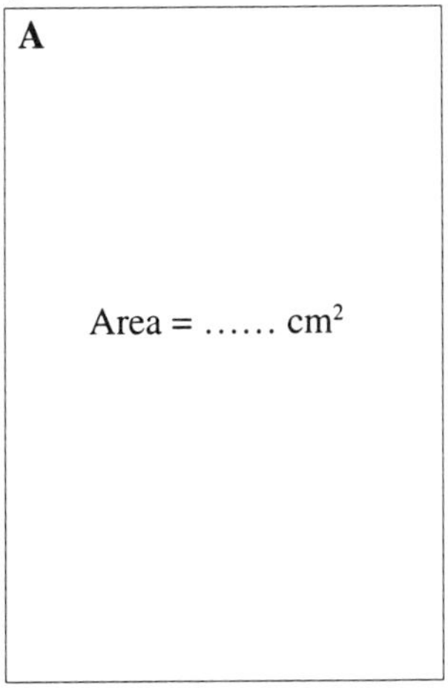

**A**

Area = ...... cm²

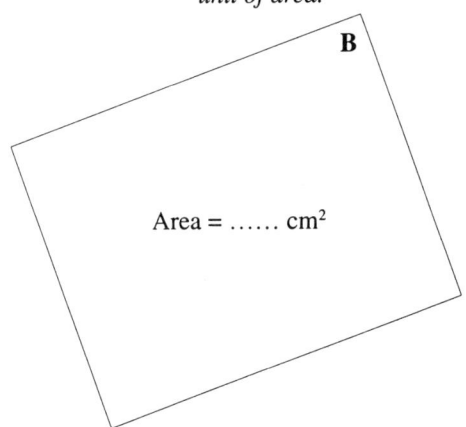

**B**

Area = ...... cm²

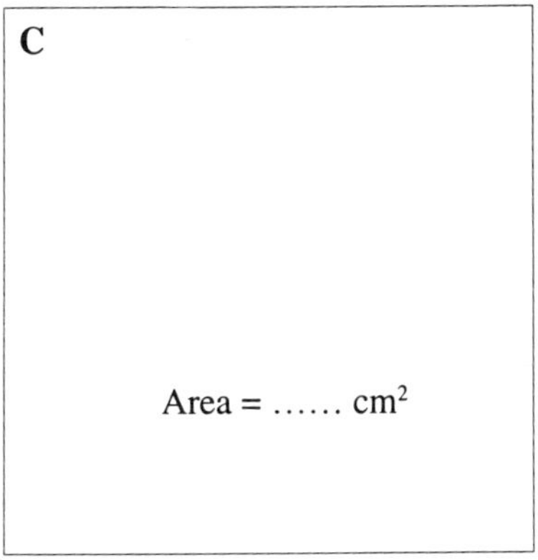

**C**

Area = ...... cm²

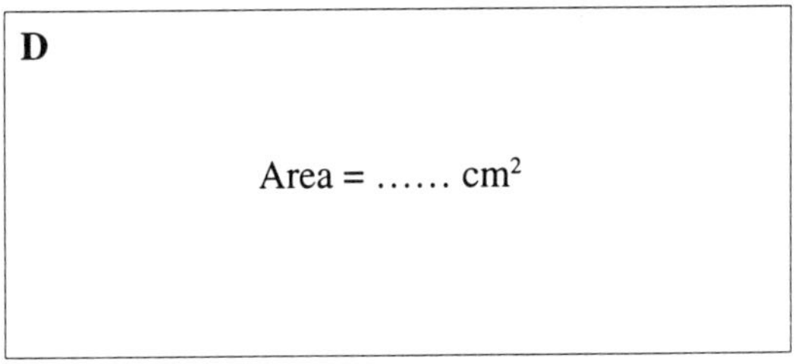

**D**

Area = ...... cm²

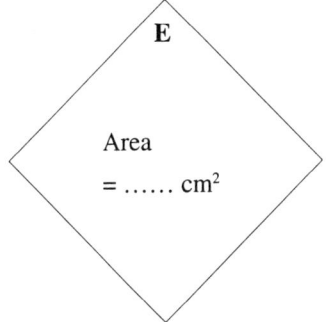

**E**

Area = ...... cm²

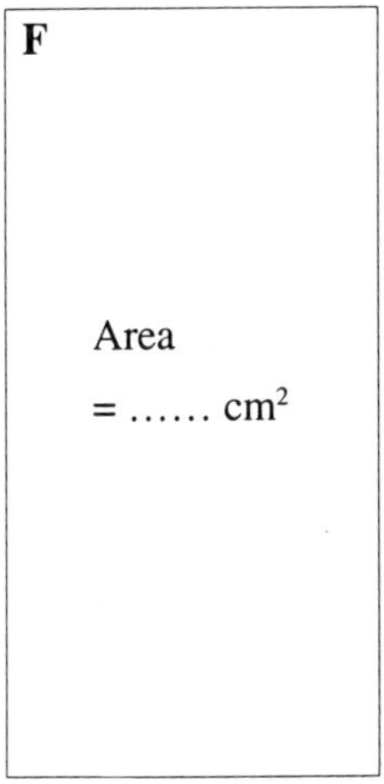

**F**

Area = ...... cm²

• *Check your answers.*

A POW GUIDE   page 125   Areas, Volumes and Formulae **EXTRA**

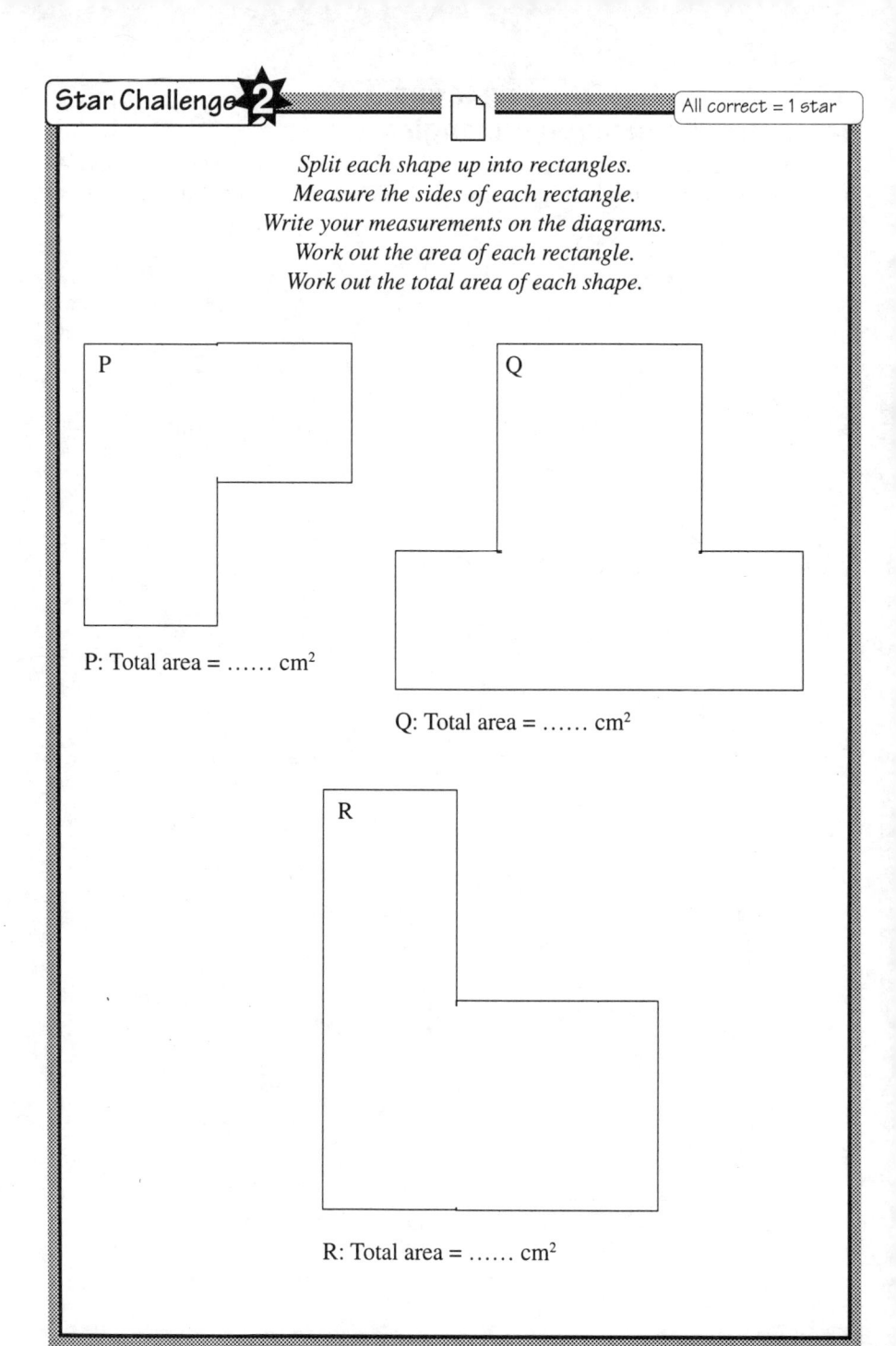

# Star Challenge 2

All correct = 1 star

*Split each shape up into rectangles.*
*Measure the sides of each rectangle.*
*Write your measurements on the diagrams.*
*Work out the area of each rectangle.*
*Work out the total area of each shape.*

P

Q

P: Total area = ...... cm$^2$

Q: Total area = ...... cm$^2$

R

R: Total area = ...... cm$^2$

A POW GUIDE　　　page 126　　　Areas, Volumes and Formulae **EXTRA**

### EXTENSION
# E1: Keeping area or perimeter fixed

**Task 1:** *Copy this table. Do not fill it in yet.*

|           | Area = 12 squares |     |     | Area = 16 squares |     |     | Area = 24 squares |     |     |     |
|-----------|-----|-----|-----|-----|-----|-----|-----|-----|-----|-----|
| length    | 12  | ... | ... | 16  | ... | ... | ... | ... | ... | ... |
| width     | ... | ... | ... | ... | ... | ... | ... | ... | ... | ... |
| perimeter | ... | ... | ... | ... | ... | ... | ... | ... | ... | ... |

**Task 2:** Draw 3 different rectangles with an area of 12 squares.
Put the details of these rectangles onto the table.

**Task 3:** Draw 3 different rectangles with an area of 16 squares.
Put the details of these rectangles onto the table.

**Task 4:** Draw 4 different rectangles with an area of 24 squares.
Put the details of these rectangles onto the table. • *Check your answers.*

---

## Star Challenge 3 3

24 marks = 2 stars   20-23 marks = 1 star
3 marks for each rectangle

**Task 5:** There are 3 different rectangles you can make with an area of 20 squares. Draw them.

**Task 6:** There are 5 different rectangles you can make with an area of 36 squares. Draw them.

**Task 7:** Make a table to show the length, width and perimeter of each rectangle.
• *Your teacher has the answers to these.*

---

## Star Challenge 4 4

18-24 marks = 2 stars
12-17 marks = 1 star

**Task 1:** A piece of wire 10 cm long is used to make a rectangle.
(6 marks) Make 2 different rectangles with the wire.
Draw sketches of the rectangles.
Show the length and width of each rectangle.
Work out the area of each rectangle.

**Task 2:** A piece of wire 24 cm long is used to
(18 marks) make a rectangle.
Make 6 different rectangles with the wire.
Draw sketches of the rectangles.
Show the length and width of each rectangle.
Make a table showing the length, width and area of each rectangle.

• *Your teacher has the answers to these.*

A POW GUIDE   page 127   Areas, Volumes and Formulae   **EXTRA**

# Section 4: Volumes

In this section you will :
- find volumes by counting cubes;
- find and use the formula for finding the volume of a cuboid.

Level 4

## DEVELOPMENT

### D1: What is volume ?

**The volume** of a shape is the number of cubes needed to make the shape.

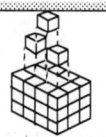

Make each of these shapes.
Write down the volume of each shape.
Write your answers in the form   Volume of A = ......... cubes

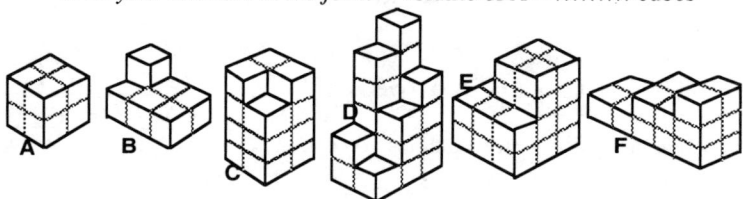

• Check your answers.

### D2: Making cuboids with a given volume

**Task 1:** You can make 4 different cuboids with a volume of 12 cubes. 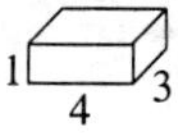
Here are two of them 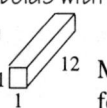
Make all four cuboids.

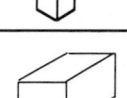

**Cuboids** are boxes – like this.

Copy and complete this table:

| length ($l$) | breadth ($b$) | height ($h$) | Volume ($V$) |
|---|---|---|---|
| 4 | 3 | 1 | 12 |
|  |  |  | 12 |
|  |  |  | 12 |
|  |  |  | 12 |

**Task 2:** Make 4 different cuboids with a volume of 20 cubes.
Make a table like the one in Task 1. Fill in the table.

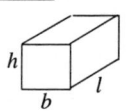

**Task 3:** Make 6 different cuboids with a volume of 24 cubes.
Make a table like the one in Task 1. Fill in the table.

**Task 4:**  Rule 1: Volume of cuboid = *length* + *breadth* + *height*
           Rule 2: Volume of cuboid = *length* x *breadth* x *height*

Which of these rules is the correct one ?
• Check your answers.

A POW GUIDE           page 128           Areas, Volumes and Formulae **EXTRA**

## D3: Volumes of cuboids

**Volume of cuboid = length x breadth x height** ← The rule in words  **Level 4**

$$V = l \times b \times h$$ ← The rule in algebra (shorthand)  **Level 5**

Copy these into your book. Highlight them.

*Taz*

---

**EXAMPLE 1** Work out the volume of this cuboid.

$V = l \times b \times h \Rightarrow V = 10 \times 5 \times 4 = 200 \text{ cm}^3$

If the sides are in cm, then the volume is in $cm^3$
If the sides are in m, then the volume is in $m^3$ .........

4 cm, 10 cm, 5 cm

Work out the volume of each cuboid.
Each answer must have the correct unit.

1. 5 cm, 3 cm, 3 cm
2. 6 cm, 3 cm, 2 cm
3. 10 cm, 5 cm, 4 cm
4. 20 cm, 4 cm, 3 cm
5. 20 m, 4 m, 10 m
6. 25 cm, 4 cm, 4 cm
7. 12 mm, 5 mm, 4 mm
8. 9 m, 3 m, 2 m

• Check your answers.

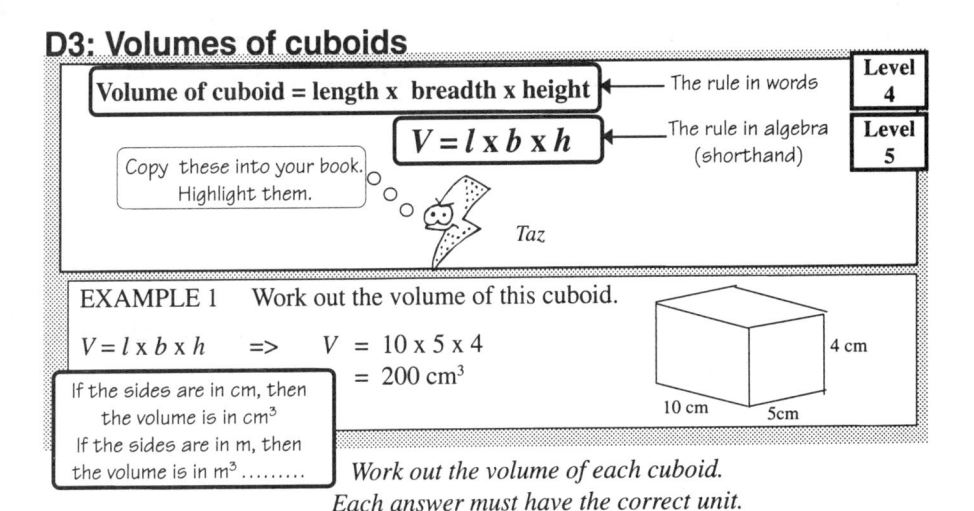

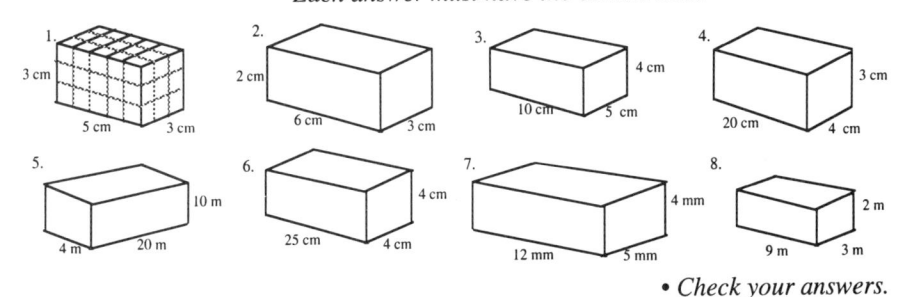

### PRACTICE

## P1: Picking the right information  **Level 5**

$$V = l \times b \times h$$

There is a very common mistake that many students make. They just multiply together all the numbers on the diagram. What they should do is work out the values of *l*, *b* and *h* and multiply these together.
THIS EXERCISE IS TO TRY AND STOP <u>YOU</u> MAKING THIS MISTAKE.

Each of these measurements are in cm.

<u>BUT – in many of the diagrams, too much information has been given.</u>

Find the volume of each cuboid, in $cm^3$.

A: 4, 2, 5
B: 4, 6, 3, 6
C: 3, 3, 5, 2
D: 10, 4, 2, 2
E: 4, 8, 3, 4, 8
F: 4, 4, 4, 4

• Check your answers.

A POW GUIDE        page 129        Areas, Volumes and Formulae **EXTRA**

### Star Challenge 5

All correct = 1 star

The volume of each of these cuboids is 40 cm³. Each of the measurements is in cm.
Find the measurement that each letter stands for.

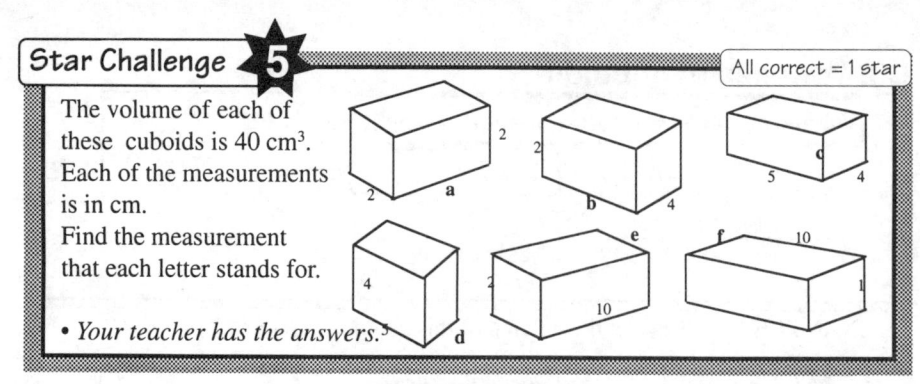

• Your teacher has the answers.

*EXTENSION*

## E1: Compound cuboids

1. This solid can be split into two cuboids like this. Work out the volumes of A and B.
   Work out the volume of the original solid.

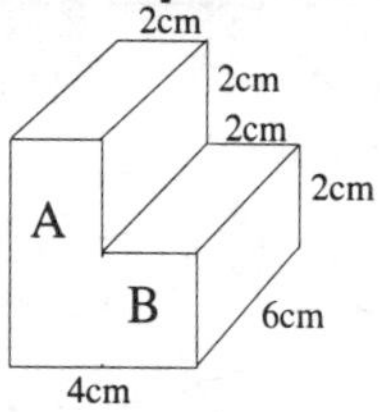

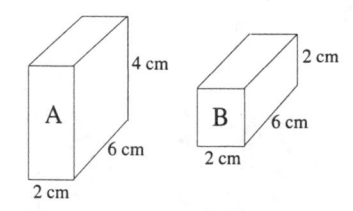

*Split these solids into cuboids. Work out the volume of each solid.*

2. 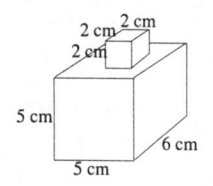
3. 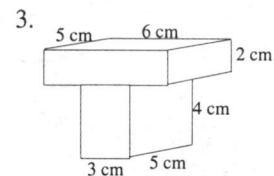
4.

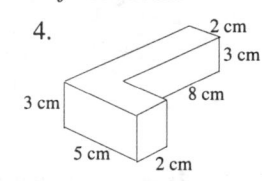

• Check your answers.

### Star Challenge 6

6 correct = 2 stars
4-5 correct = 1 star

1. A box is 12 cm long, 5 cm wide and 4 cm high. What is its volume?
2. A box is 2 m long, 1m wide and 1.5 m high. What is its volume?
3. Our sports hall is a very large cuboid. It is 120 m long, 50 m wide and 35 m high. What volume of air does it contain? 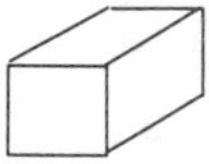
4. A box is 15 cm long and 4 cm high. Its volume is 180 cm³. How wide is the box?
5. A box has a square end. The sides of the square are 10 cm. The box is 24 cm long. What is the volume of the box?
6. The box on the right is a cube of side 1 m. Its volume is 1 m³. Work out its volume in cm³.

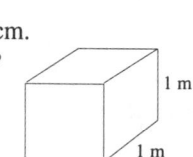

• Your teacher has the answers to these.

1 m (100 cm)

A POW GUIDE        page 130        Areas, Volumes and Formulae   **EXTRA**

# Section 5: Right-angled triangles

In this section you will :
- find the connection between the areas of rectangles and right-angled triangles;
- work out the areas of right-angled triangles.

**Level 4**

## DEVELOPMENT

### D1: Squares and half squares

1. The area of ☐ is 1 cm². What is the area of ◺ ?

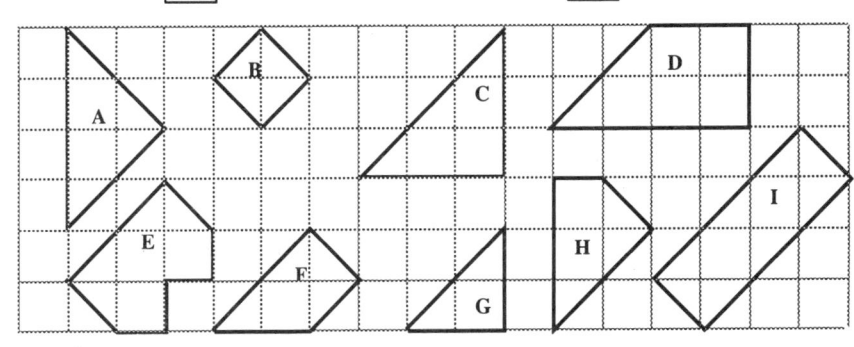

2. Copy this table. Fill in the area of each shape. (Count squares and half squares.)

| Shape | A | B | C | D | E | F | G | H | I |
|-------|---|---|---|---|---|---|---|---|---|
| Area  |   |   |   |   |   |   |   |   |   |

• Check your answers.

### D2: Rectangles and right-angled triangles

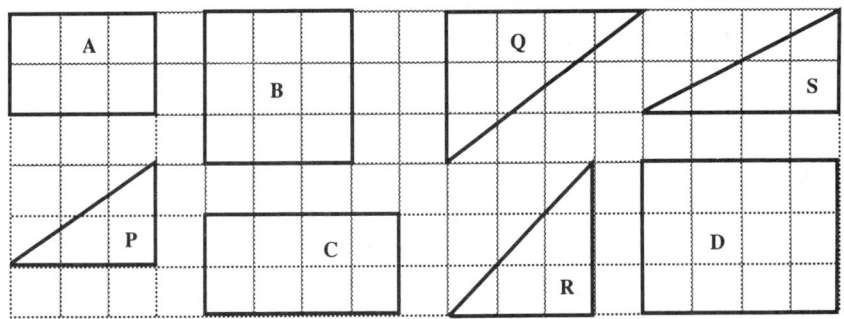

Each triangle is half the area of one of the rectangles.

△ P is half the area of rectangle A

Match up each rectangle and the triangle which is half its area.

*No need to count squares. Which triangle will cover half the rectangle when placed on top of it ?*

• Check your answers.

A POW GUIDE     page 131     Areas, Volumes and Formulae **EXTRA**

## D3: Areas of right-angled triangles     Level 5

△ = half of ▭

### Rule
Area of triangle = $\frac{1}{2}$ (*base* x *height*)

$A = (b \times h) \div 2$

*Copy this into your book. Highlight it.*

*It is easier to work out if written like this.*

**Idea**

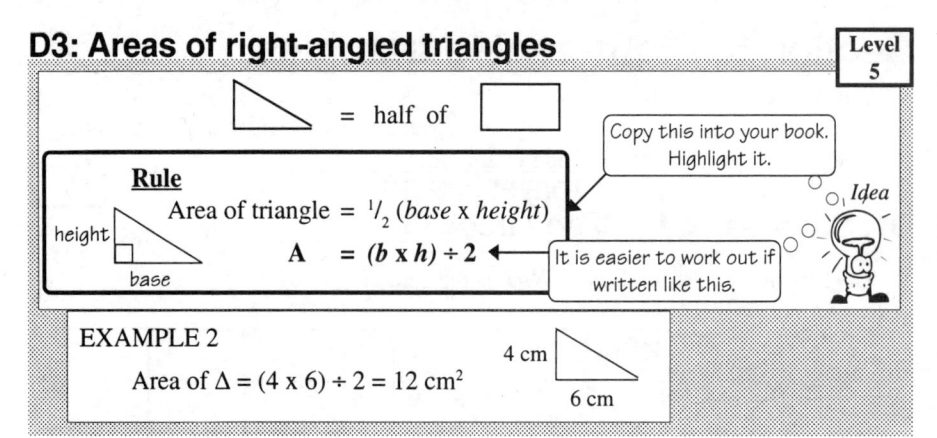

**EXAMPLE 2**
Area of △ = (4 x 6) ÷ 2 = 12 cm²
(4 cm, 6 cm)

*Work out the area of each triangle:*

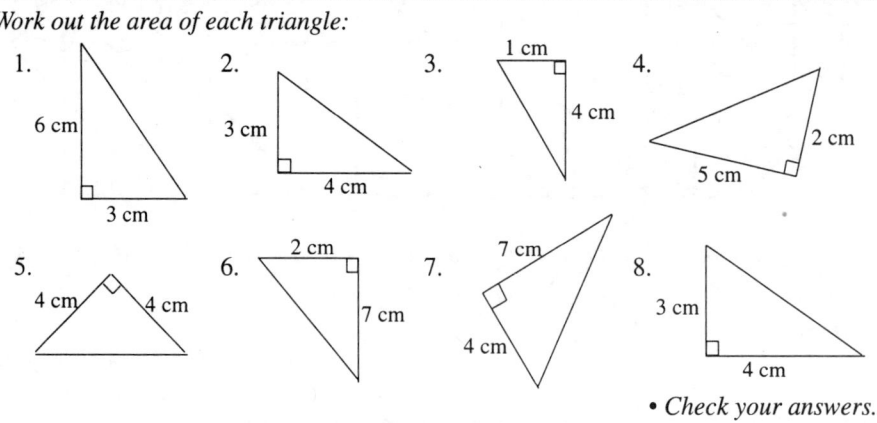

1. 6 cm, 3 cm
2. 3 cm, 4 cm
3. 1 cm, 4 cm
4. 5 cm, 2 cm
5. 4 cm, 4 cm
6. 2 cm, 7 cm
7. 7 cm, 4 cm
8. 3 cm, 4 cm

• Check your answers.

### PRACTICE

## P1: Too much information

*Here, you are given too much information.*
*Choose the correct information and work out the area.*

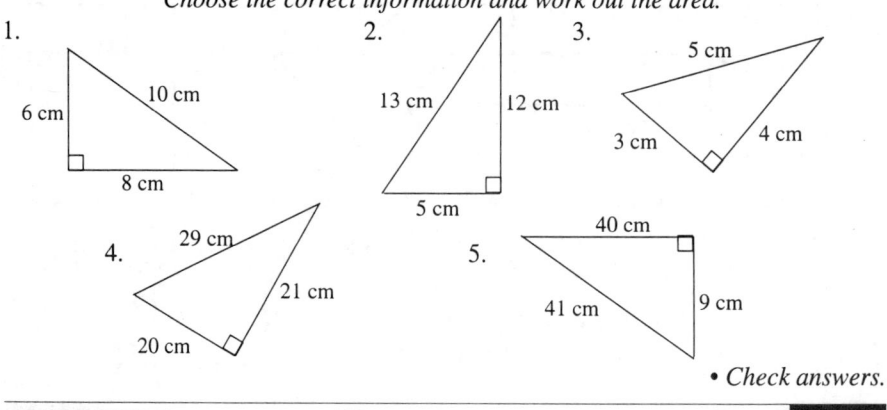

1. 6 cm, 10 cm, 8 cm
2. 13 cm, 12 cm, 5 cm
3. 5 cm, 3 cm, 4 cm
4. 29 cm, 21 cm, 20 cm
5. 40 cm, 41 cm, 9 cm

• Check answers.

A POW GUIDE        page 132        Areas, Volumes and Formulae   **EXTRA**

# P2: Areas of measured triangles

*Measure the base and height of each triangle.*
*Write your measurements on the diagrams.*
*Work out the area of each triangle.*
*Each answer must have the correct unit of area.*

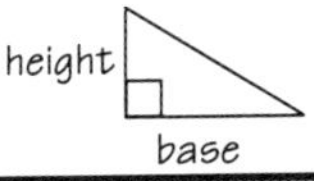

Level 5

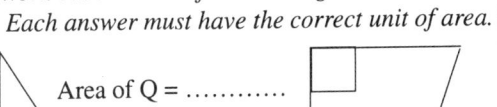

$A = (b \times h) \div 2$

height
base

Area of Q = ...........
P

Area of R = ...........
T
Area of U = ...........
R
U

Q
S

Area of P = ...........

Area of T = ...........

Area of S = ...........
X

V
Area of X = ...........

Area of V = ...........

Area of W = ...........
W

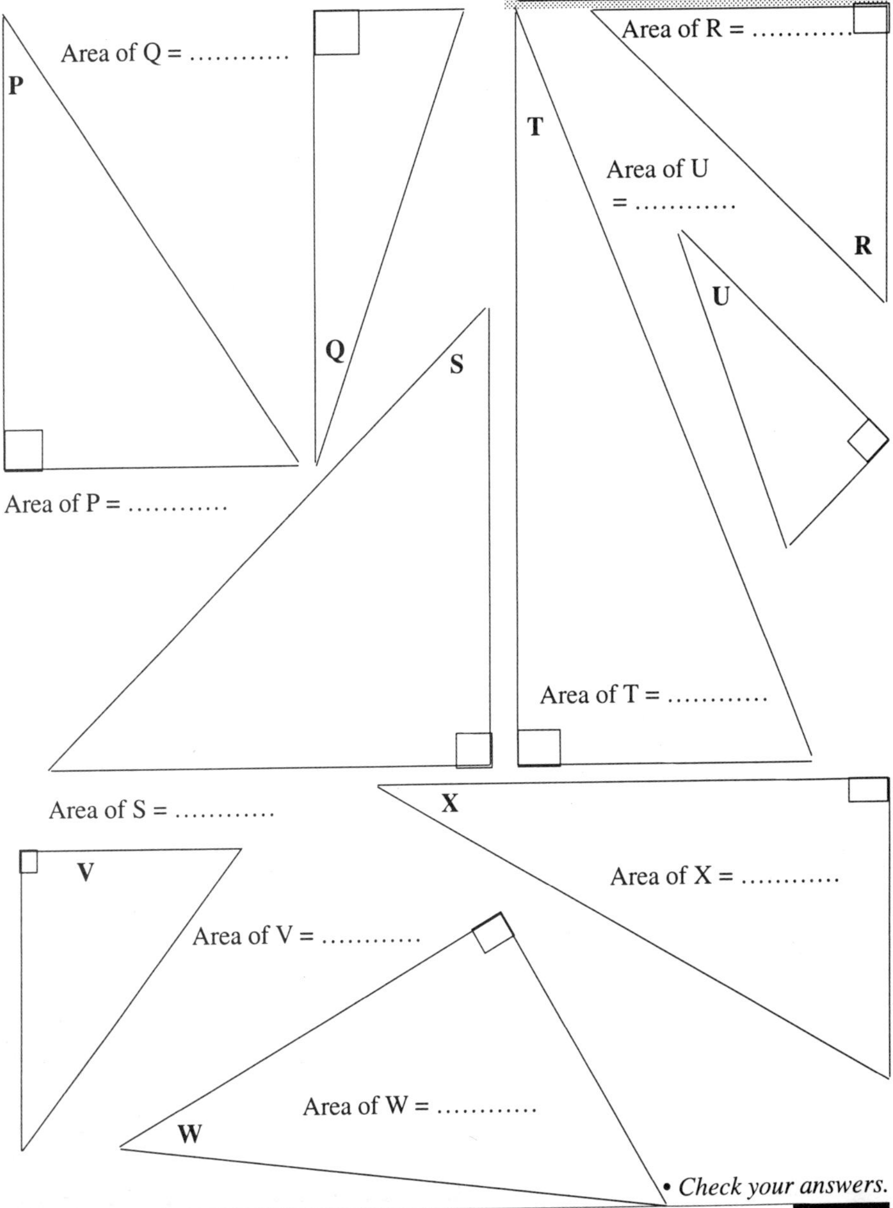

• *Check your answers.*

A POW GUIDE     page 133     Areas, Volumes and Formulae  **EXTRA**

# P3: Areas of rectangles and triangles

**Level 5**

$A = l \times w$  $A = (b \times h) \div 2$

*Work out the area of each rectangle:*

1. 8 cm × 3 cm
2. 5 cm × 5 cm
3. 8 cm × 6 cm
4. 7 cm × 1 cm

*Work out the area of each triangle:*

5. base 8 cm, height 3 cm
6. base 6 cm, height 6 cm
7. base 3 cm, height 6 cm
8. base 8 cm, height 5 cm

*Work out the area of each shape:*

9. 9 cm × 5 cm rectangle
10. triangle base 6 cm, height 3 cm
11. 5 cm × 2 cm rectangle
12. triangle base 6 cm, height 4 cm
13. triangle base 10 cm, height 6 cm
14. 5 cm × 10 cm
15. 9 cm × 11 cm
16. triangle 4 cm and 8 cm

• Check your answers.

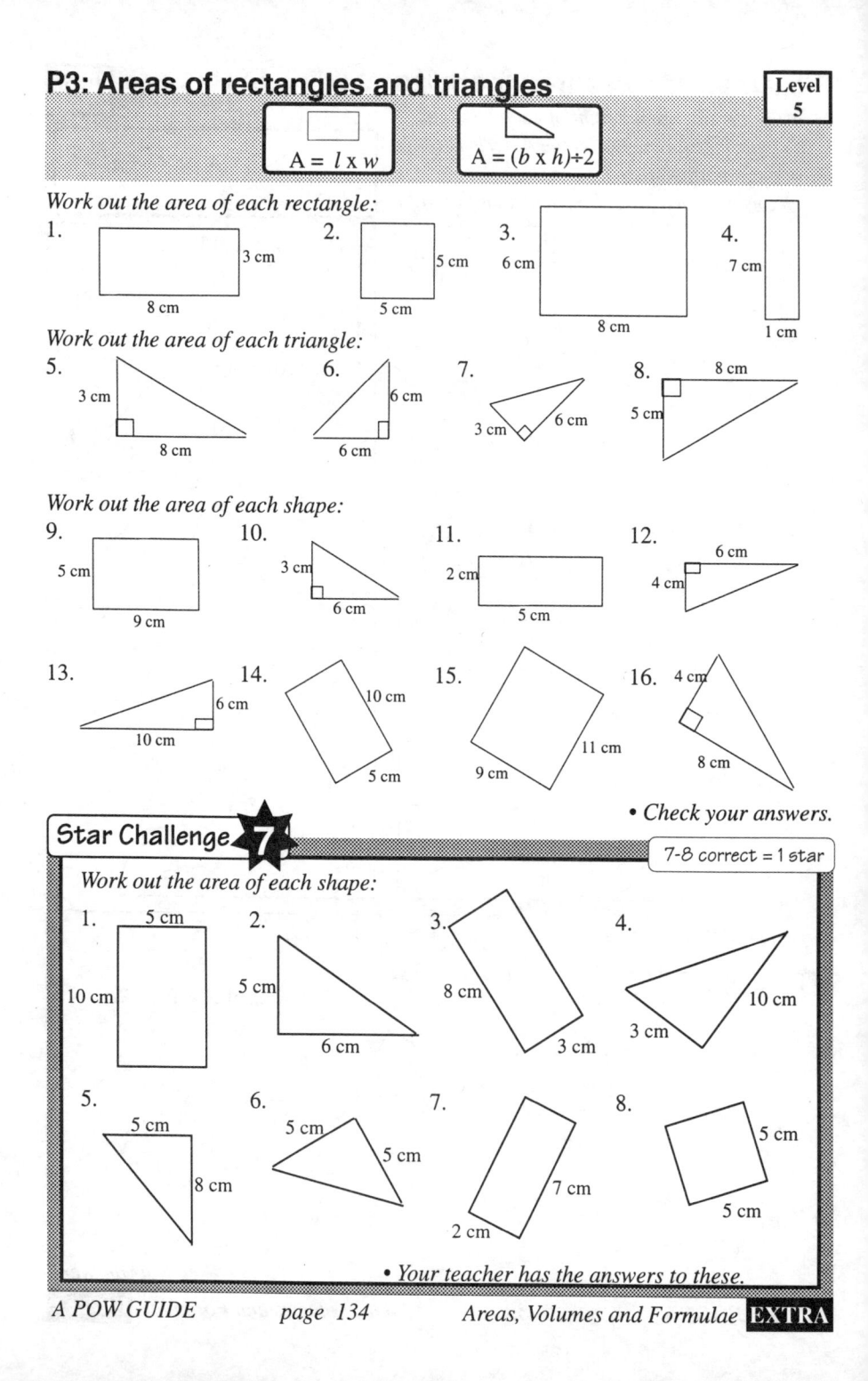

## Star Challenge 7

7-8 correct = 1 star

*Work out the area of each shape:*

1. 5 cm × 10 cm rectangle
2. triangle base 6 cm, height 5 cm
3. 8 cm × 3 cm
4. triangle 3 cm and 10 cm
5. triangle 5 cm and 8 cm
6. triangle 5 cm and 5 cm
7. 7 cm × 2 cm
8. 5 cm × 5 cm square

• Your teacher has the answers to these.

A POW GUIDE    page 134    Areas, Volumes and Formulae  **EXTRA**

# Section 6: Parallelograms

In this section you will :
- work out the area of some easy parallelograms by counting squares ;
- use the rule for working out the area of a parallelogram;
- measure parallelograms and work out their areas.

## DEVELOPMENT

### D1: Areas of some parallelograms

Level 4

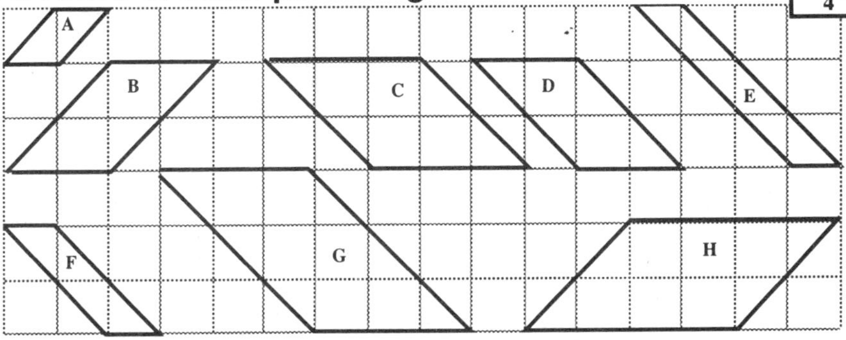

1. Copy and complete this table for the parallelograms. (Count squares and half squares.)

|   | length of base | height | area |
|---|---|---|---|
| A |   |   |   |
| B |   |   |   |
| C |   |   |   |
| D |   |   |   |
| E |   |   |   |
| F |   |   |   |
| G |   |   |   |
| H |   |   |   |

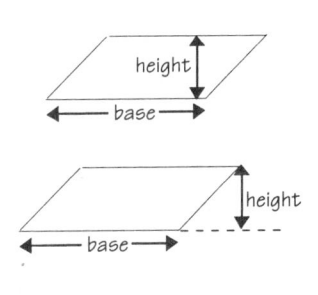

2. What is the rule for working out the area from the length of base and the height ?

• Check your answers.

### D2: What have they done wrong ?

1. 3 cm, 5 cm
The area is 3 cm + 5 cm = 8 cm² ✗
What did Youslas do wrong ?

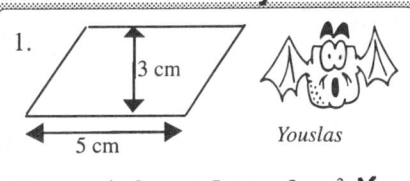

*Youslas*

2. The area is 5 cm x 4 cm = 20 cm² ✗
4 cm, 5 cm
What did Letmewin do wrong ?

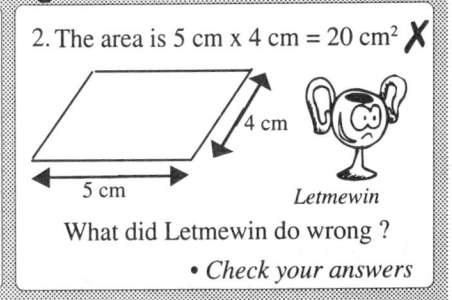

*Letmewin*

• Check your answers

*A POW GUIDE*    page 135    *Areas, Volumes and Formulae* **EXTRA**

## D3: Using the rule to work out the area
**Level 5**

The height must be perpendicular to the base.

Area of parallelogram = base × perpendicular height
$A = b \times h$

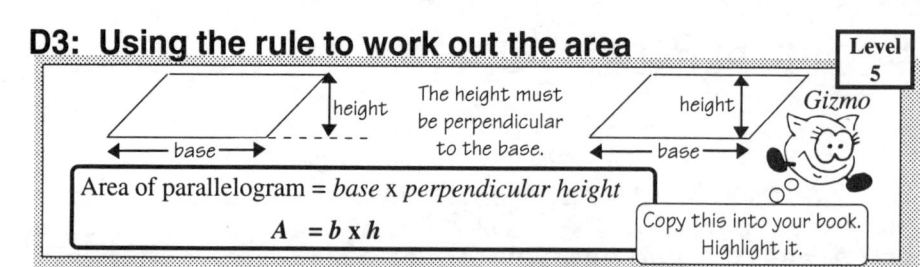

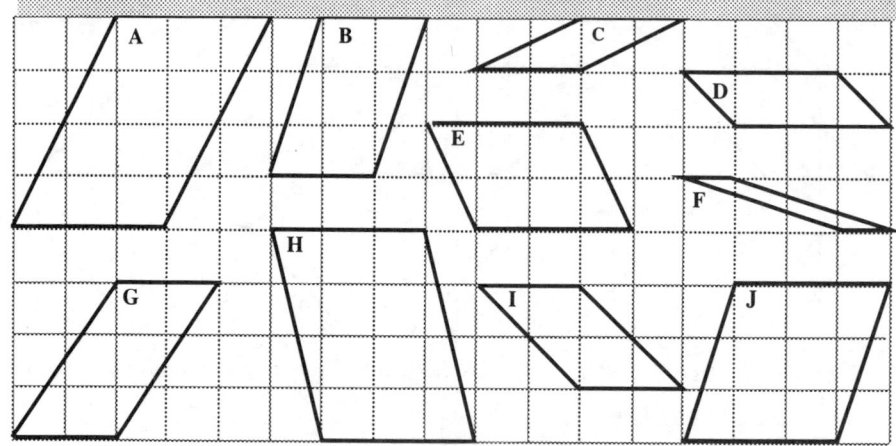

Copy this into your book. Highlight it.

*Parallelograms labelled A, B, C, D, E, F, G, H, I, J shown on grid.*

1. Copy and complete this table for the parallelograms above. Use the rule to work out the areas.

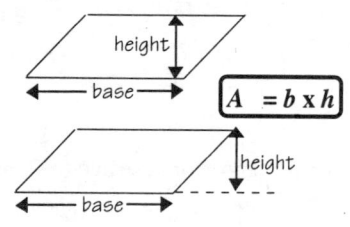

$A = b \times h$

| | length of base | height | area |
|---|---|---|---|
| A | | | |
| B | | | |
| C | | | |
| D | | | |
| E | | | |
| F | | | |
| G | | | |
| H | | | |
| I | | | |
| J | | | |

Work out the area of the parallelograms described below.
Each answer must have the correct unit of area.

2. base = 3 cm    height = 2 cm
3. base = 11 mm   height = 4 mm
4. base = 5 m     height = 3 m
5. base = 20 cm   height = 3 cm
6. base = 5 mm    height = 7 mm
7. base = 3 m     height = 1 m

Area of parallelogram = base × perpendicular height

Copy and complete the data for the following parallelograms:

8. base = 5 cm    height = ... cm    area = 20 cm²
9. base = ... cm  height = 6 cm      area = 60 cm²

• Check your answers.

A POW GUIDE    page 136    Areas, Volumes and Formulae **EXTRA**

## P1: No measurements given

**Task 1:** *Copy the table.*
  *Do not fill it in yet.*

**Task 2:**

*For each parallelogram:*
- *measure the base and height;*
- *work out the area;*
- *complete the table.*

**PRACTICE**

$A = b \times h$

| Parallelogram | A | B | C | D | E | F | G | H |
|---|---|---|---|---|---|---|---|---|
| base | | | | | | | | |
| height | | | | | | | | |
| area | | | | | | | | |

• *Check your answers.*

A POW GUIDE — Areas, Volumes and Formulae **EXTRA**

**Star Challenge** 8 8  $A = b \times h$  7-8 correct = 2 stars
6 correct = 1 star

*Work out the area of the parallelograms described below.*
*Each answer must have the correct unit of area.*

1. base = 4 cm   height = 6 cm
2. base = 5 mm   height = 5 mm
3. base = 8 m    height = 10 m
4. base = 6 cm   height = 3 cm
5.

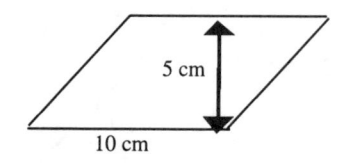

   5 cm
   10 cm

6.

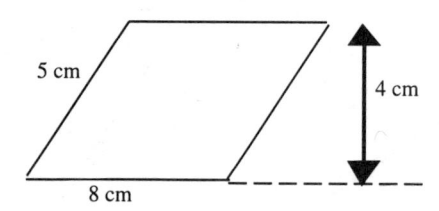

   5 cm   4 cm
   8 cm

7. Measure the base and height.
   Work out the area.

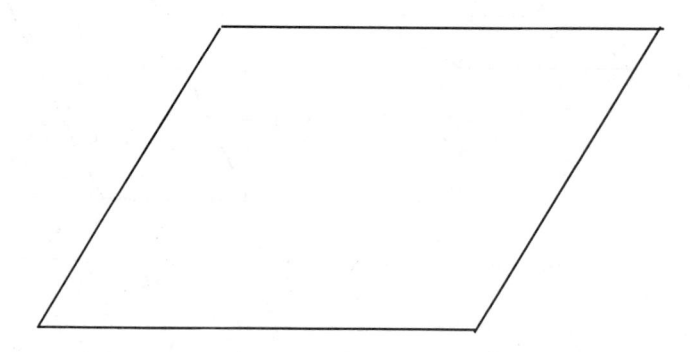

8. The base of a parallelogram is 8 cm. Its area is 40 cm². What is its height ?

   • *Your teacher has the answers to these.*

A POW GUIDE          page 138          Areas, Volumes and Formulae **EXTRA**

# Section 7: Area of any triangle

In this section you will :
• find the connection between the areas of parallelograms and triangles;
• work out the area of any triangle.

## DEVELOPMENT

### D1: Parallelograms and triangles

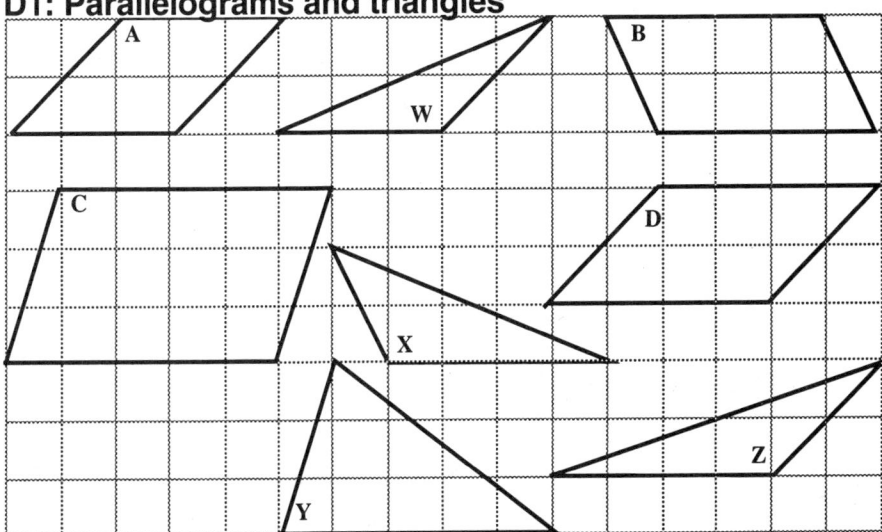

Each triangle is half the area of one of the parallelograms.
△ W is half the area of parallelogram A

Match up each parallelogram and the triangle which is half its area.

Which triangle will cover half the parallelogram when placed on top of it ?

• Check your answers.

### D2: Rule for area of any triangle

**Level 5**

△ & ◸ are half of ▱

**Rule**
Area of triangle = $\frac{1}{2}$(base × perpendicular height)
A = (b × h) ÷ 2

Copy this into your book. Highlight it.

The height must be perpendicular to the base.

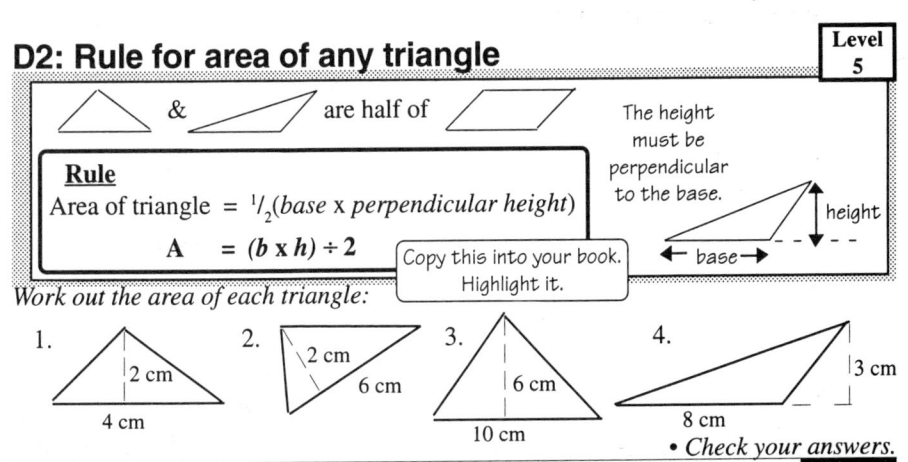

← base →
height

Work out the area of each triangle:

1. base 4 cm, height 2 cm
2. base 6 cm, height 2 cm
3. base 10 cm, height 6 cm
4. base 8 cm, height 3 cm

• Check your answers.

A POW GUIDE     page 139     Areas, Volumes and Formulae **EXTRA**

**PRACTICE**

Level 5

## P1: Areas of triangles

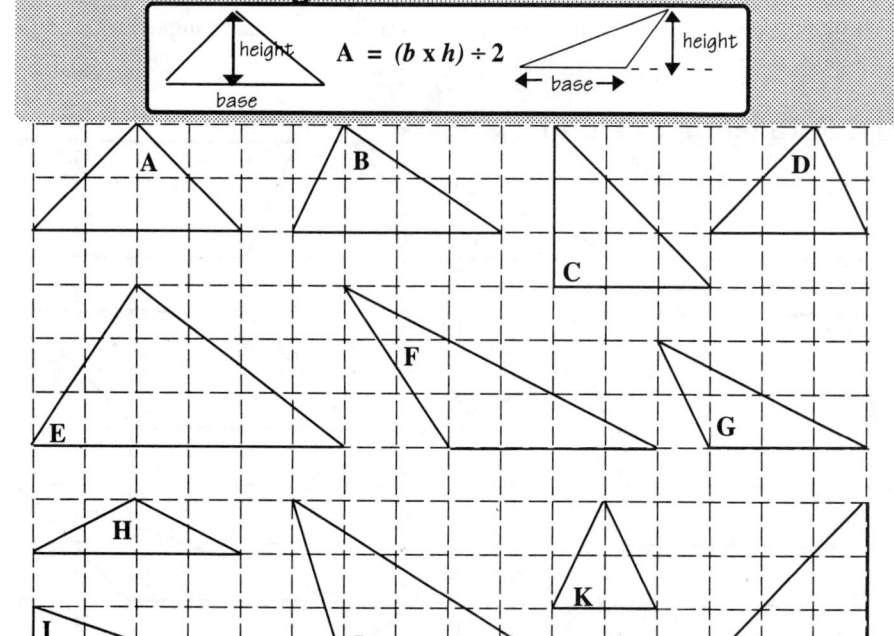

$A = (b \times h) \div 2$

Use the formula to work out the area of each triangle.
Each square is 1 cm long.

• Check your answers.

## P2: Triangles at all angles

*Work out the area of each triangle.*
*For some of the triangles, too much information has been given.*

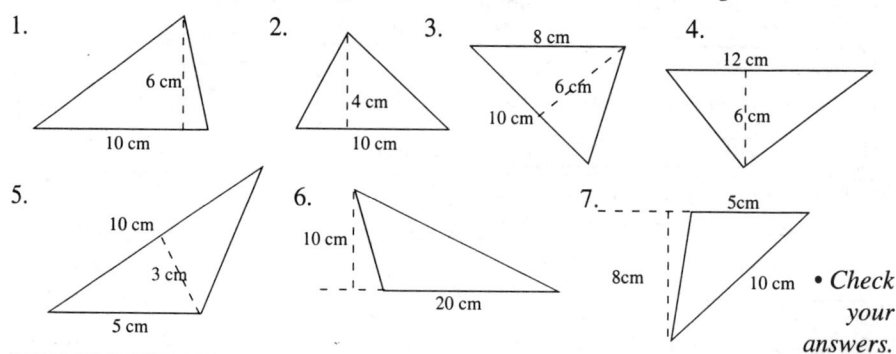

1. 6 cm, 10 cm
2. 4 cm, 10 cm
3. 8 cm, 6 cm, 10 cm
4. 12 cm, 6 cm
5. 10 cm, 3 cm, 5 cm
6. 10 cm, 20 cm
7. 5 cm, 8 cm, 10 cm

• Check your answers.

A POW GUIDE        page 140        Areas, Volumes and Formulae  **EXTRA**

# P3: You will need to measure these triangles

**Level 5**

$A = (b \times h) \div 2$

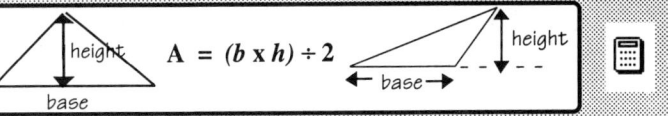

**Task 1:** *Copy this table.*

| Δ | P | Q | R | S | T | U | V | W |
|---|---|---|---|---|---|---|---|---|
| base | 2.8 | | | | | | | |
| height | | | | | | | | |
| area | | | | | | | | |

**Task 2 :** *For each triangle:*
- *Measure the base. Put it onto the diagram.*
- *Draw in the height. Measure the height. Put it onto the diagram.*
- *work out the area*  • *put the base, height and area onto the table.*

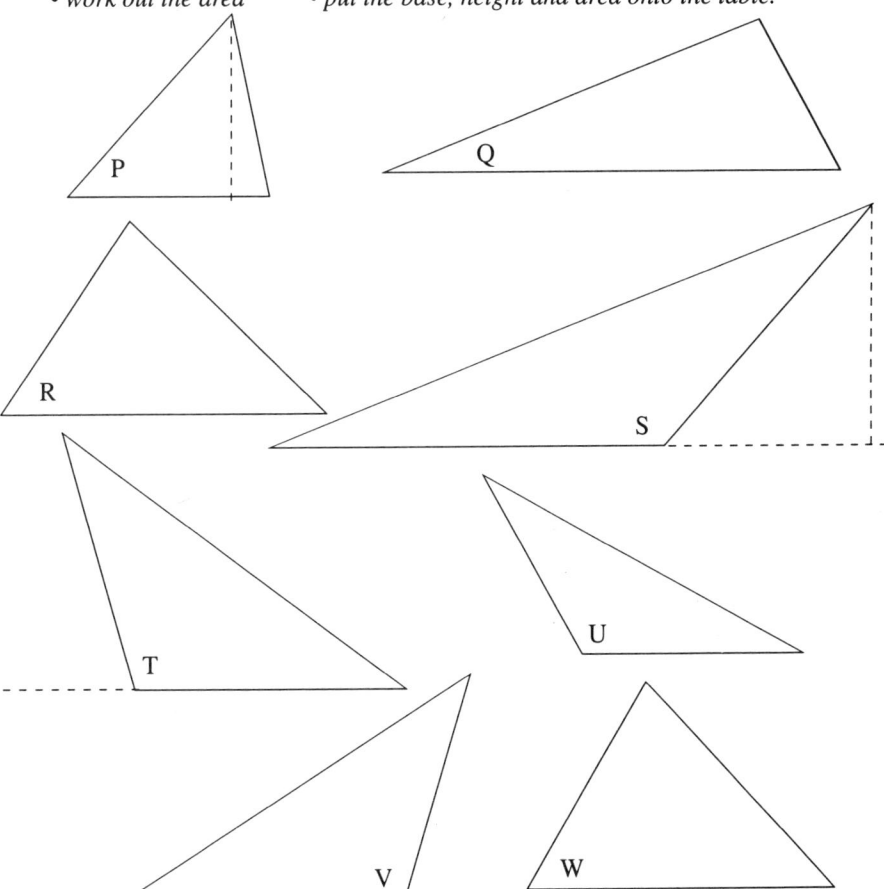

• Check your answers. If any of your areas are wrong, ask your teacher to check your measurements – before you do the Star Challenge.

*A POW GUIDE*  page 141  *Areas, Volumes and Formulae* **EXTRA**

# Star Challenge 9

12 marks = 2 stars
8-11 marks = 1 star

3 marks for each triangle

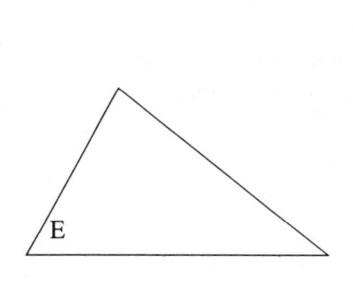

*For each triangle:*
- *measure the base and height;*
- *work out the area;*
- *put all your results into a table.*

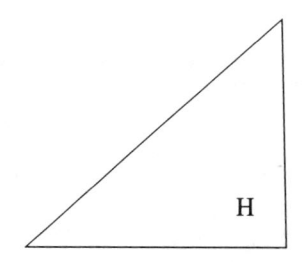

*A POW GUIDE*     page 142     *Areas, Volumes and Formulae* **EXTRA**

# Section 8: Altogether now ...

**Level 5**

In this section you will:
- calculate areas of rectangles, parallelograms and triangles;
- work out areas where too much information is given.

## PRACTICE

### P1: Areas of rectangles, parallelograms and triangles

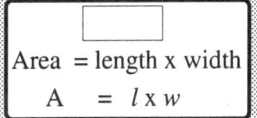

| Area = length x width | Area = $\frac{1}{2}$ (base x height) | Area = base x height |
|---|---|---|
| A = $l \times w$ | A = $(b \times h) \div 2$ | A = $b \times h$ |

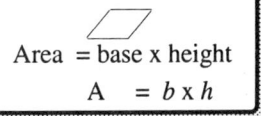

### LEARN THESE RULES !

Work out the area of each shape.
For some shapes you have been given too much information.
You have to choose the information you need.

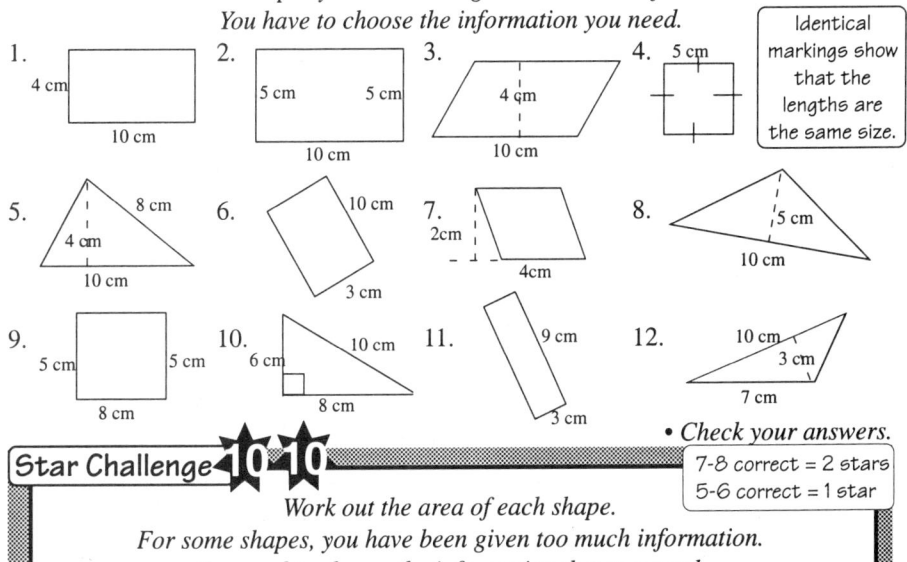

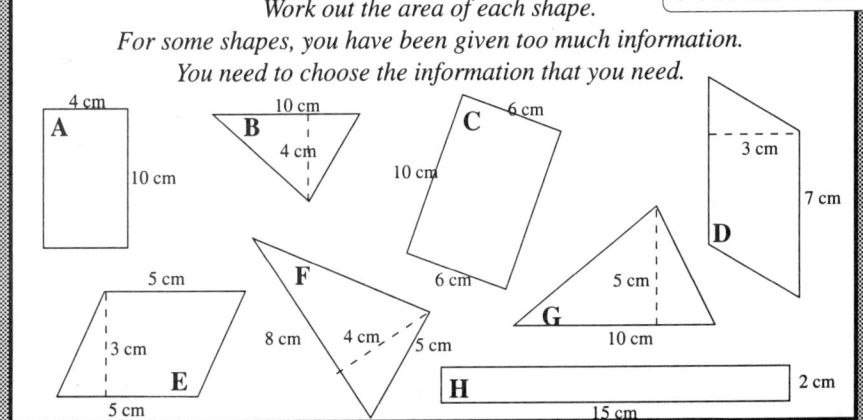

Identical markings show that the lengths are the same size.

1. 4 cm, 10 cm
2. 5 cm, 5 cm, 10 cm
3. 4 cm, 10 cm
4. 5 cm
5. 8 cm, 4 cm, 10 cm
6. 10 cm, 3 cm
7. 2 cm, 4 cm
8. 5 cm, 10 cm
9. 5 cm, 5 cm, 8 cm
10. 6 cm, 10 cm, 8 cm
11. 9 cm, 3 cm
12. 10 cm, 3 cm, 7 cm

• Check your answers.

7-8 correct = 2 stars
5-6 correct = 1 star

## Star Challenge

Work out the area of each shape.
For some shapes, you have been given too much information.
You need to choose the information that you need.

A: 4 cm, 10 cm
B: 10 cm, 4 cm
C: 6 cm, 10 cm
D: 3 cm, 7 cm
E: 5 cm, 3 cm, 5 cm
F: 8 cm, 4 cm
G: 6 cm, 5 cm, 10 cm
H: 15 cm, 2 cm

A POW GUIDE       page 143       Areas, Volumes and Formulae **EXTRA**

# Section 9: The circumference of a circle

In this section you will work out the circumference (perimeter) of a circle.

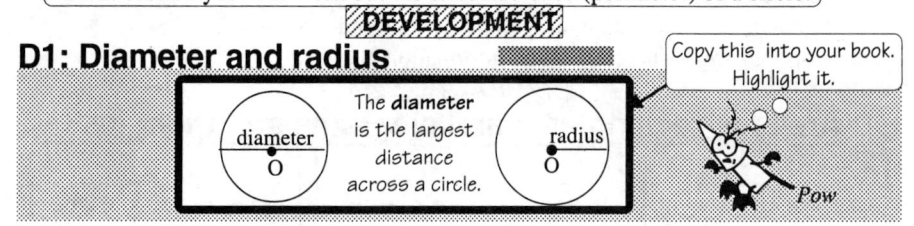

**DEVELOPMENT**

## D1: Diameter and radius

The **diameter** is the largest distance across a circle.

Copy this into your book. Highlight it.

**Task 1:** *Copy the table. Find the missing measurements and put them into the table.*

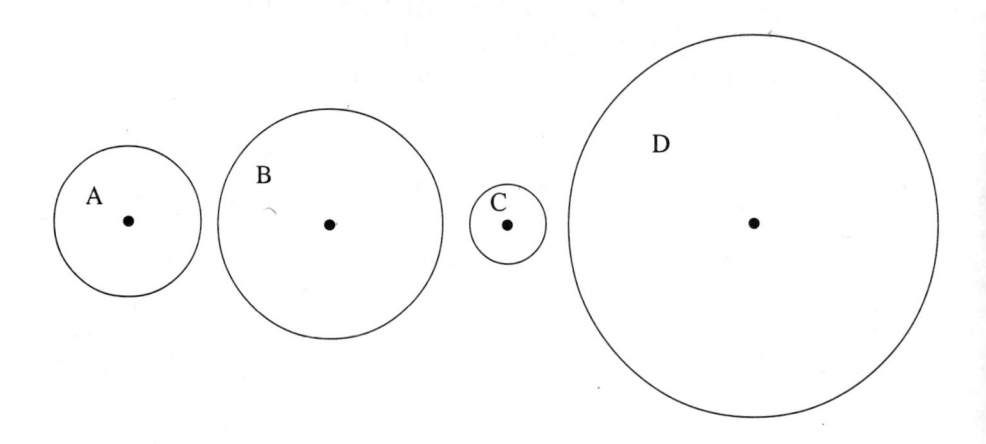

| Circle | A | B | C | D | E | F | G |
|---|---|---|---|---|---|---|---|
| Diameter (*d*) | 2cm | | | | | | 4.4cm |
| Radius (*r*) | | 1½cm | ½cm | | | | |

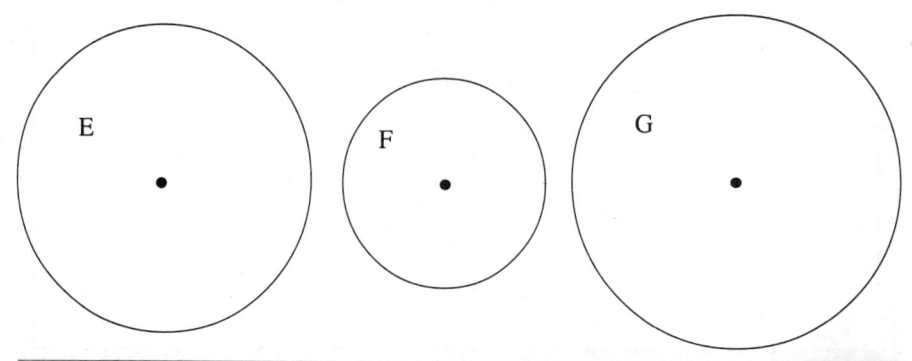

A POW GUIDE      page 144      Areas, Volumes and Formulae **EXTRA**

**Task 2:**

diameter = 2 x radius

1. The radius of circle H is 10 cm. What is its diameter?
2. The diameter of circle J is 12 cm. What is its radius?
3. The diameter of circle K is 16 cm. What is its radius?
4. The radius of circle L is 7 cm. What is its diameter?
5. The radius of a circle M is 6 m. What is its diameter?
6. The diameter of a circle N is 6 m. What is its radius?

**Task 3:** *Copy the table. Work out the missing measurements and put them into the table.*

| Circle   | P    | Q    | R     | S   | T     | U     | V     | W     | X   |
|----------|------|------|-------|-----|-------|-------|-------|-------|-----|
| Radius   | 5 cm | 3 mm |       | 4 m |       |       | 10 cm |       | 1 m |
| Diameter |      |      | 20mm  |     | 14 cm | 100 m |       | 22 cm |     |

• Check your answers.

## D2: Circumference of a circle

Level 6

The perimeter of a circle has a special name.
The perimeter of a circle is called **the circumference**.

It has been known for at least 4000 years that
the circumference = a constant value x the diameter

$$C = \pi \times d$$

$\pi$ is read as 'pi'

The value of $\pi$ has been calculated to over 200 billion decimal places.
Here, we shall use the value 3.14 for $\pi$.

We shall use the formula $C = 3.14 \times d$

Copy. Highlight. Learn.

**EXAMPLE 3** *Work out the circumference of a circle with diameter 20 cm*

$C = 3.14 \times d$

3.14 x 20 = 62.8

$\underline{C = 62.8 \text{ cm}}$

Pow

A POW GUIDE   page 145   Areas, Volumes and Formulae  **EXTRA**

> Read C = 3.14 d as
> 'circumference equals
> 3.14 times diameter'.
> The rule sticks better
> if you do this.

*Work out the circumference of a circle ...*
1. ... with diameter 10 cm
2. ... with diameter 4 cm
3. ... with diameter 2.5 cm
4. ... with diameter 5 m
5. ... with diameter 12 mm
6. ... with diameter 3 km
7. ... with diameter 6.4 cm
8. ... with diameter 1.02 m

---

**EXAMPLE 4** *Work out the circumference of a circle with radius 3 cm*

radius = 3 cm   so   diameter = 6 cm   ← *Work out the diameter first !*

$C = 3.14 \times d$     [3.14] [x] [6] [=]   [18.84]

$C = 18.84$ cm           *Idea*

---

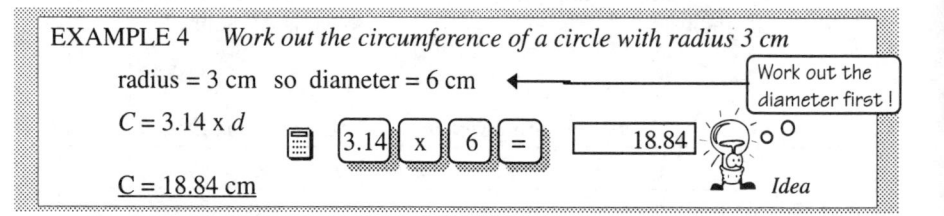

9. Copy and complete:
   radius = 3 cm
   diameter = ...... cm
   C = ......... cm

*Work out the circumference of a circle with radius :*
10. 8 cm     11. 4.5 cm     12. 5.3 m

• *Check your answers.*

## Star Challenge 11·11

7 correct = 2 stars
5-6 correct = 1 star

*Work out the circumference of a circle ...*
1. ... with radius 4 cm
2. ... with radius 10 cm
3. ... with diameter 14 cm
4. ... with radius 14 cm
5. ... with diameter 9 cm
6. ... with radius 11 cm

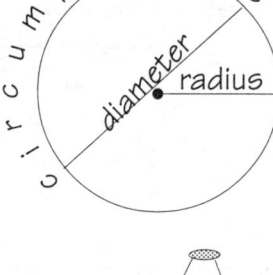

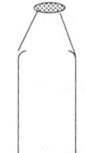

7. The diameter of a milk bottle is 7.4 cm.
   Work out its circumference.

---

A POW GUIDE     page 146     Areas, Volumes and Formulae   **EXTRA**

# Section 10: Problems involving rounding

In this section you will:
- review rounding techniques;
- use the value of π on a scientific calculator;

Level 6

## D1: Rounding to nearest whole number

Round **34.671** to the nearest whole number
To the nearest whole number this is either 34 or 35
If the first decimal place is 0 1 2 3 or 4, the number is rounded <u>down</u> to 34
If the first decimal place is 5 6 7 8 or 9, the number is rounded <u>up</u> to 35

**34.671**
The first decimal place is 6, so the number rounds <u>up</u> to 35

**EXAMPLE 5** My wedding ring has diameter 14 mm.
Work out the circumference of my ring to the nearest mm.

C = π × d

| π | × | 14 | = |   43.982297

C = 43.98... mm  ≈ 44 mm to the nearest mm

(this means that you round up)

**C = π × d**

1. A circle has diameter 8 cm. Kriss works out that the circumference is 25 cm to the nearest cm. Show how he works this out.
2. A cake tin has diameter 18 cm. Work out the circumference to the nearest cm.
3. A circular flower bed has diameter 2.5 m. Work out the circumference of the flower bed, to the nearest m.
4. A circular paddling pool has diameter 160 cm. Work out the circumference of the pool to the nearest cm.

• *Check your answers.*

## D2: Rounding to 2 decimal places (2 d.p.)

Round **34.6716** to 2 d.p.
To 2 d.p., this is either 34.67 or 34.68
The 3rd decimal place is 1, so we round <u>down</u>, to 34.67

1. A circle has diameter 6.55 cm. Show that the circumference is 20.58 cm, to 2 d.p.
2. A circle is painted with white paint on a sports field. The diameter of the circle is 14.25 m. What is the length of the painted line, to 2 d.p. ?
3. Bob's bicycle has wheels of radius 28.64 cm.
   (a) Work out the diameter of each wheel.
   (b) Work out the circumference, to 2 d.p.

• *Check your answers.*

A POW GUIDE        page 147        Areas, Volumes and Formulae **EXTRA**

# Section 11: The area of a circle

**Level 6**

In this section you will :
- meet and use the formula for the area of a circle;
- look at some of the common mistakes in calculating the area of a circle.

## DEVELOPMENT

### D1: Exploring the result of a practical task

Seven children each drew a circle on squared paper. Each one worked out the area by counting squares. Adi and Carol got these results.

|  | Radius | Area |
|---|---|---|
| Adi | 3 cm | 28 cm² |
| Carol | 4 cm | 50 cm² |

$\pi = 3.14$

Teacher says that the formula for the area of a circle is $A = \pi r^2$

1. Adi checks his area by putting $r = 3$ into the formula $A = \pi r^2$

   [3.14] x [3] x [3] = [28.26]

   28.26 is approximately 28, so Adi's area is correct.

   Do what Adi does and show that he gets the result $A = 28.26$ cm²

2. Use the same method to calculate the area of Carol's circle.
   (a) What area do you get ?
   (b) Is Carol's area correct ?

The other children got these results.

|  | Radius | Counted Area |
|---|---|---|
| Karl | 5 cm | 78 cm² |
| Yusuf | 6 cm | 101 cm² |
| Ben | 8 cm | 202 cm² |
| Sara | 10 cm | 315 cm² |
| Milo | 12 cm | 450 cm² |

*Spoton*

3. (a) Check each of the other areas using the same method.
   *Copy and complete this table:*

| Child | Adi | Carol | Karl | Yusuf | Ben | Sara | Milo |
|---|---|---|---|---|---|---|---|
| Radius | 3 | 4 | 5 | 6 | 8 | 10 | 12 |
| Measured area | 28 | 50 | 78 | 101 | 202 | 315 | 450 |
| Calculated area | 28.26 | | | | | | |

4. One child had counted squares and got the wrong area. Which child was it ?

   $A = \pi r^2$     [3.14] x [r] x [r] =

5. The radius of a circle is 15 cm. Work out the area of this circle.
6. Work out the area of a circle with radius 6.5 cm.
   Give your answer to the nearest cm²
7. A circle has diameter 12 cm. Work out its radius. Calculate the area of this circle.

• Check your answers.

A POW GUIDE     page 148     Areas, Volumes and Formulae **EXTRA**

## P1: Area practice

**PRACTICE** — Level 6

$A = \pi r^2$ 　 [🖩] [3.14] x [ r ] x [ r ] = [　　]

1. Work out the area of these two circles.
   *[You have been told the area that you should get. If you cannot get the correct area, ask you teacher what you are doing wrong.]*
   (a) circle with radius 9 cm   [Area = 254.34 cm²]
   (b) circle with radius 21 cm  [Area = 1384.74 cm²]

2. Work out the area of each of these circles:
   (a) 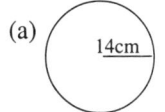 14cm   (b) 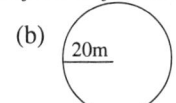 20m   (c) 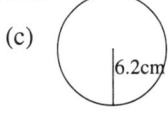 6.2cm   (d) circle with radius 2.5 m

3. (a) What is the radius of this circle?  4 m
   (b) Calculate the area of the circle.

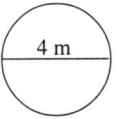

4. The diameter of a circle is 50 cm.
   (a) Work out the radius of the circle.   (b) Work out the area of the circle.

*Work out the area of each of these circles. Each answer must have the correct unit.*

5. 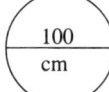 100 cm   6. 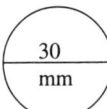 30 mm   7. 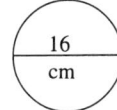 16 cm

*Work out the area of each of these circles. Each answer must have the correct unit.*

8.  20 cm   9. 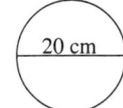 20 cm   10. 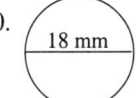 18 mm   11. 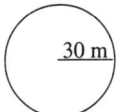 30 m

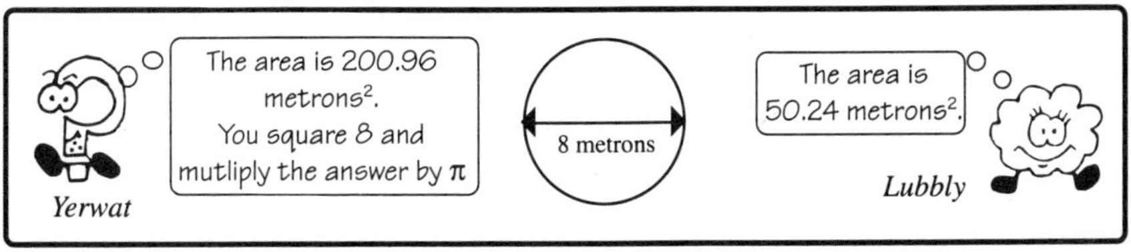

---

Yerwat: The area is 200.96 metrons². You square 8 and mutliply the answer by π.

8 metrons

Lubbly: The area is 50.24 metrons².

---

12. Explain what Yerwat did wrong.

13. Explain how Lubbly worked out the correct answer

• *Check your answers.*

A POW GUIDE　　page 149　　Areas, Volumes and Formulae **EXTRA**

# P2: Area and circumference practice

$A = \pi r^2$   3.14 × r × r =

$C = \pi d$   3.14 × d =

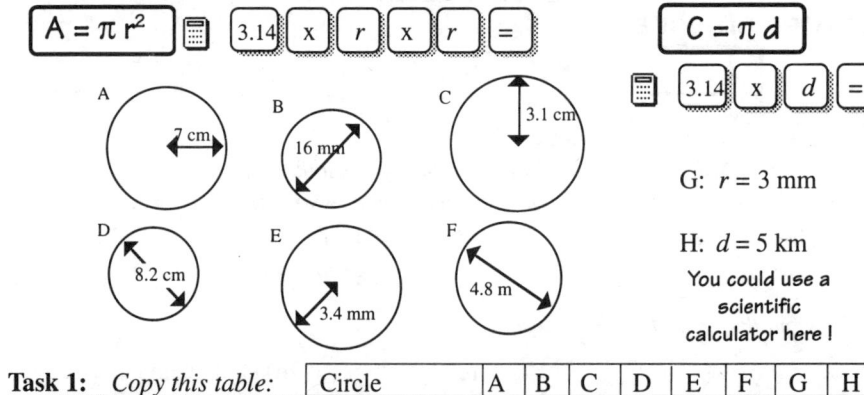

A: 7 cm (radius)
B: 16 mm (radius)
C: 3.1 cm (diameter)
D: 8.2 cm (radius)
E: 3.4 mm (diameter)
F: 4.8 m (diameter)
G: $r = 3$ mm
H: $d = 5$ km

You could use a scientific calculator here !

**Task 1:** Copy this table:  *Give all answers to 2 d.p.*

| Circle | A | B | C | D | E | F | G | H |
|---|---|---|---|---|---|---|---|---|
| Circumference | | | | | | | | |
| Area | | | | | | | | |

**Task 2:** Work out the circumference of each circle. Put the answers into the table.

**Task 3:** Work out the area of each circle. Put the areas into the table.

**Task 4:**

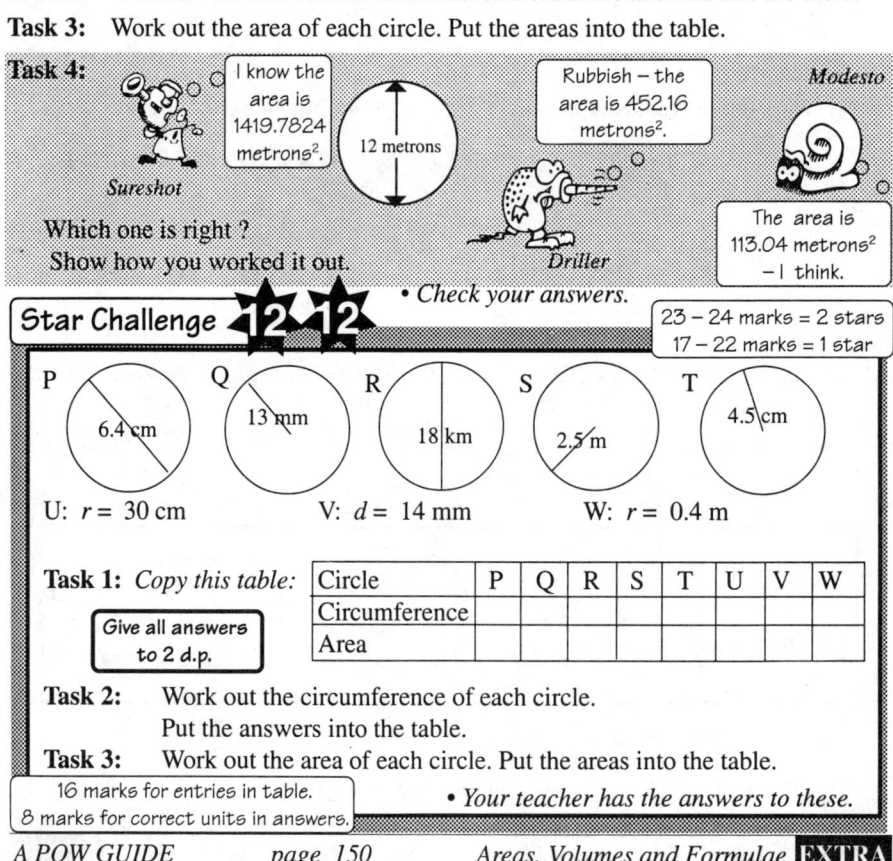

*Sureshot:* I know the area is 1419.7824 metrons².

(12 metrons diameter circle)

*Driller:* Rubbish – the area is 452.16 metrons².

*Modesto:* The area is 113.04 metrons² – I think.

Which one is right? Show how you worked it out.

• Check your answers.

## Star Challenge

23 – 24 marks = 2 stars
17 – 22 marks = 1 star

P: 6.4 cm (diameter)
Q: 13 mm (diameter)
R: 18 km (diameter)
S: 2.5 m (radius)
T: 4.5 cm (radius)
U: $r = 30$ cm
V: $d = 14$ mm
W: $r = 0.4$ m

**Task 1:** Copy this table:  *Give all answers to 2 d.p.*

| Circle | P | Q | R | S | T | U | V | W |
|---|---|---|---|---|---|---|---|---|
| Circumference | | | | | | | | |
| Area | | | | | | | | |

**Task 2:** Work out the circumference of each circle. Put the answers into the table.

**Task 3:** Work out the area of each circle. Put the answers into the table.

16 marks for entries in table.
8 marks for correct units in answers.

• Your teacher has the answers to these.

A POW GUIDE   page 150   Areas, Volumes and Formulae   **EXTRA**

# Section 12: Technique review

In this section you will review the formulae and techniques met in this topic.

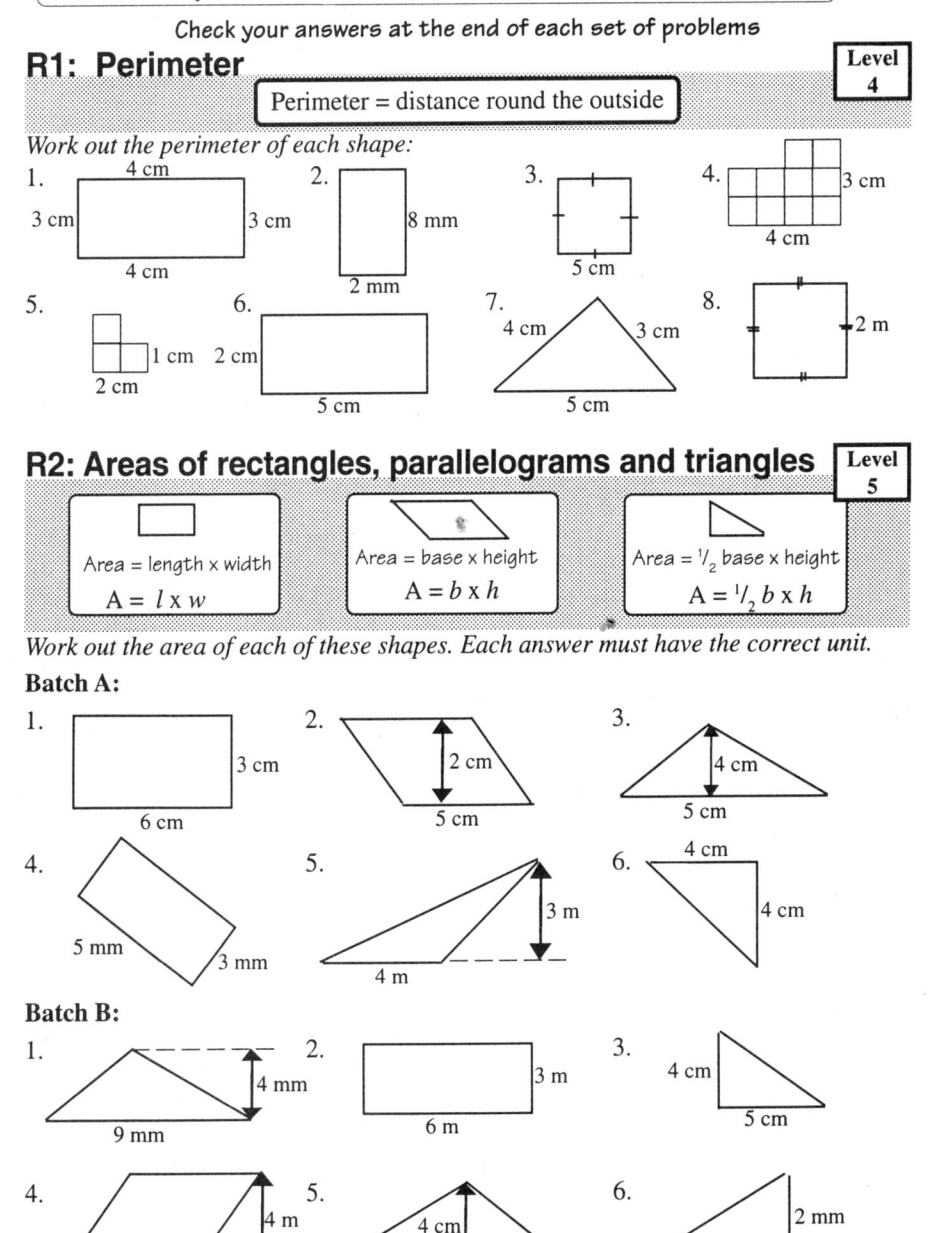

Check your answers at the end of each set of problems

## R1: Perimeter
Level 4

Perimeter = distance round the outside

Work out the perimeter of each shape:
1. rectangle 4 cm × 3 cm
2. rectangle 3 cm × 8 mm / 2 mm
3. square 5 cm
4. shape 3 cm / 4 cm
5. shape 2 cm / 1 cm / 2 cm
6. rectangle 5 cm
7. triangle 4 cm, 3 cm, 5 cm
8. square 2 m

## R2: Areas of rectangles, parallelograms and triangles
Level 5

Area = length × width    Area = base × height    Area = $\frac{1}{2}$ base × height
A = $l \times w$         A = $b \times h$        A = $\frac{1}{2} b \times h$

Work out the area of each of these shapes. Each answer must have the correct unit.

**Batch A:**
1. rectangle 6 cm × 3 cm
2. parallelogram base 5 cm, height 2 cm
3. triangle base 5 cm, height 4 cm
4. rectangle 5 mm × 3 mm
5. triangle base 4 m, height 3 m
6. triangle 4 cm × 4 cm

**Batch B:**
1. triangle base 9 mm, height 4 mm
2. rectangle 6 m × 3 m
3. triangle 4 cm, 5 cm
4. parallelogram base 10 m, height 4 m
5. triangle base 10 cm, height 4 cm
6. triangle base 8 mm, height 2 mm

A POW GUIDE    page 151    Areas, Volumes and Formulae **EXTRA**

## R3: Too much information

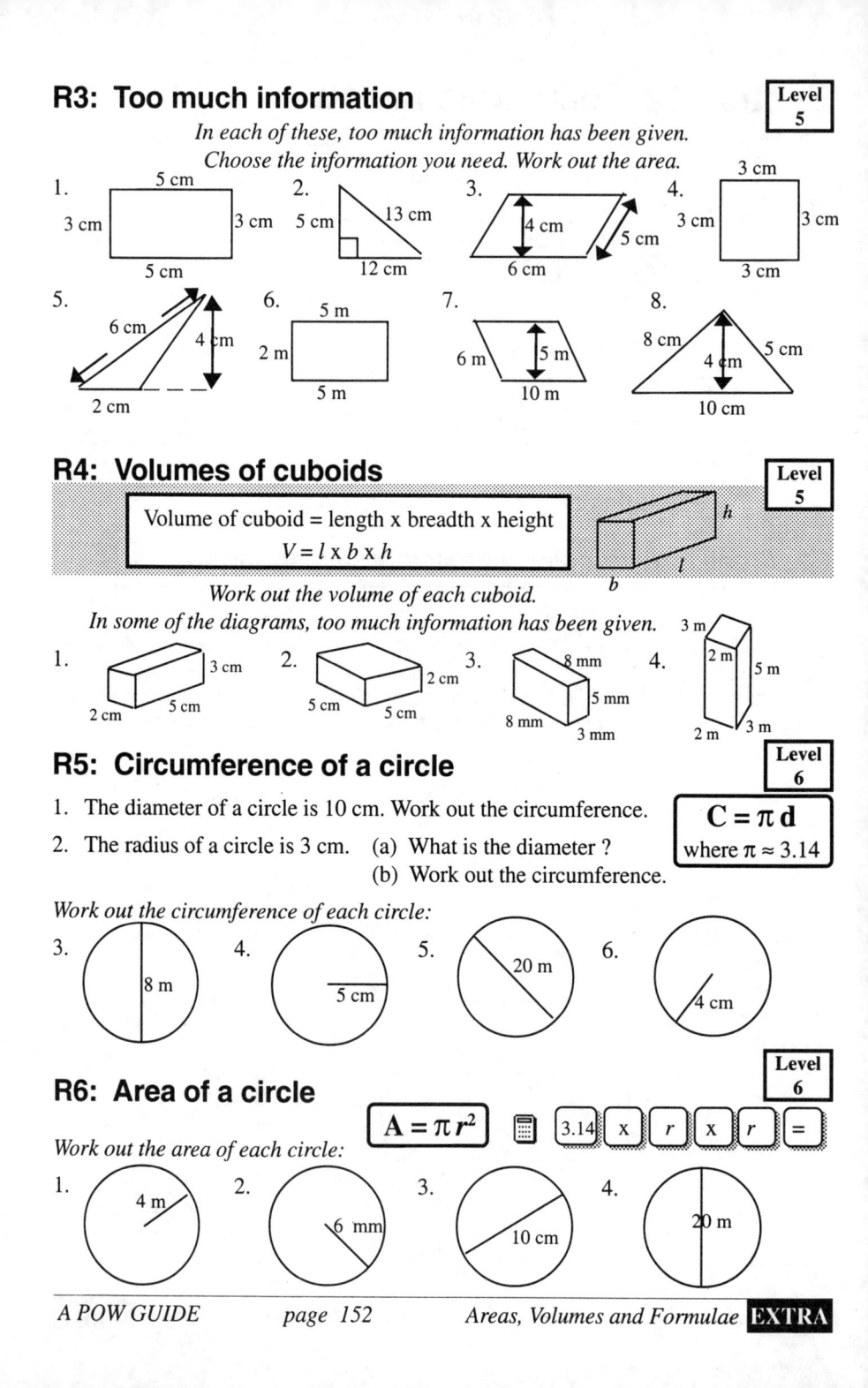

**Level 5**

*In each of these, too much information has been given.
Choose the information you need. Work out the area.*

1. Rectangle: 5 cm by 3 cm (5 cm shown twice)
2. Right triangle: 5 cm, 12 cm, 13 cm
3. Parallelogram: base 6 cm, side 5 cm, height 4 cm
4. Square: 3 cm
5. Triangle: sides 6 cm, base 2 cm, height 4 cm
6. Rectangle: 5 m by 2 m
7. Parallelogram: base 10 m, side 6 m, height 5 m
8. Triangle: sides 8 cm, 5 cm, base 10 cm, height 4 cm

## R4: Volumes of cuboids

**Level 5**

Volume of cuboid = length x breadth x height
$$V = l \times b \times h$$

*Work out the volume of each cuboid.
In some of the diagrams, too much information has been given.*

1. 2 cm x 5 cm x 3 cm
2. 5 cm x 5 cm x 2 cm
3. 8 mm x 3 mm x 5 mm
4. 3 m x 2 m x 5 m (with 2 m)

## R5: Circumference of a circle

**Level 6**

$C = \pi d$ where $\pi \approx 3.14$

1. The diameter of a circle is 10 cm. Work out the circumference.
2. The radius of a circle is 3 cm. (a) What is the diameter?
 (b) Work out the circumference.

*Work out the circumference of each circle:*

3. diameter 8 m
4. 5 cm
5. 20 m
6. 4 cm

## R6: Area of a circle

**Level 6**

$A = \pi r^2$    3.14 x r x r =

*Work out the area of each circle:*

1. 4 m
2. 6 mm
3. 10 cm
4. 20 m

A POW GUIDE        page 152        Areas, Volumes and Formulae  **EXTRA**

# THE NATIONAL CURRICULUM ...
# ... AND BEYOND ...

*Pow*

# Probability
# EXTRA

| | | | |
|---|---|---|---|
| | | §7 Technique review | |
| | | | §6 Combined events |
| | | | §5 Events and non-events |
| | | §4 Estimating probabilities | |
| | | §3 Equally likely outcomes | |
| | | §2 The probability scale | |
| | §1 How Likely ? | | |
| Level 3 | Level 4 | Level 5 | Level 6 |

*A POW GUIDE*

# Probability

## Section 1: How likely ?

Level 4

*In this section you will review words and phrases used with probability.*

**DEVELOPMENT**

### D1: Fair game ?

A teacher plays two games with the class. Some cards are put into a bag. Each card has either "B" or "G" written on it. One card is taken out of the bag without looking. If "B" is drawn, the boys get a point. If "G" is drawn, the girls get a point.

| Cards for Game 1 | Cards for Game 2 | Cards for Game 3 |
|---|---|---|
| B B B B <br> B B B B | B B B B <br> G G G G | B B B B <br> G G G G <br> G G G G |

1. Which game are the boys *certain* to win ?
2. Which game are the girls *most likely* to win ?
3. Which game are the boys *least likely* to win ?
4. Which game is it *impossible* for the girls to win ?
5. For which game is it *equally likely* that the boys or the girls win ?
6. Which game is *fair* ?

• *Check your answers.*

### D2: Order of likelihood

1. In this drawer there are red, black, green and white socks. You take one sock out of the drawer in the dark.

   8 red socks
   2 white socks
   1 green sock
   4 black socks

   (a) What colour are you most likely to get ?
   (b) Put the colours into order:   Most likely ..................
   ..................
   ..................
   Least likely ..................

2. Badges are being sold at a Spice Girls concert. You walk through the crowds at the concert.

   I love Ginger Spice — 100 sold
   I love Baby Spice — 200 sold
   I love Posh Spice — 50 sold
   I love Sporty Spice — 130 sold
   I love Scary Spice — 300 sold
   I hate the Spice Girls — 20 sold

   (a) Which badge are you *most likely* to see first ? Say why.
   (b) Which badge are you *least likely* to see first ? Say why.

• *Check your answers.*

A POW GUIDE     page 154     Probability EXTRA

# Section 2: The probability scale

Level 5

In this section you will:
- make estimates of probability;
- use the probability scale 0 to 1.

## DEVELOPMENT

### D1: The probability scale of 0-1

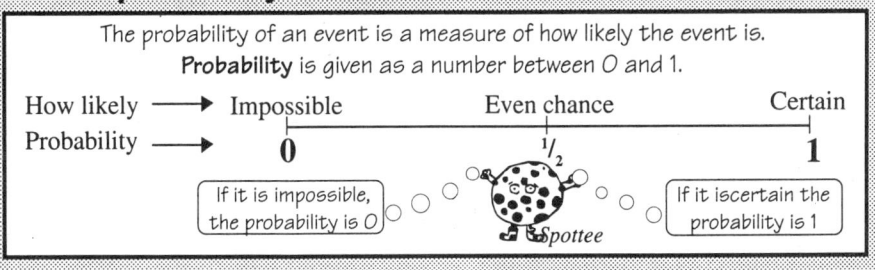

The probability of an event is a measure of how likely the event is.
**Probability** is given as a number between 0 and 1.

How likely ⟶ Impossible | Even chance | Certain
Probability ⟶ 0 | $\frac{1}{2}$ | 1

If it is impossible, the probability is 0

*Spottee*

If it is certain the probability is 1

---

**Task 1:** A raw egg, a boiled egg and a sausage are dropped onto a tiled floor.

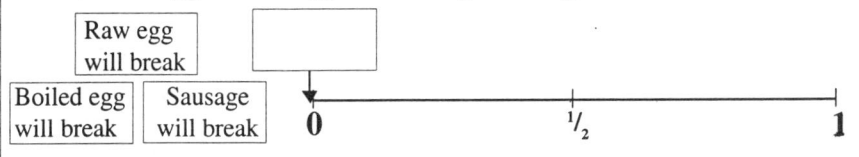

| Raw egg will break |
| Boiled egg will break | Sausage will break |

0 — $\frac{1}{2}$ — 1

1. Which of these three labels will go into the empty box?
2. **Copy the probability line.** Put the other two labels where you think they should go.

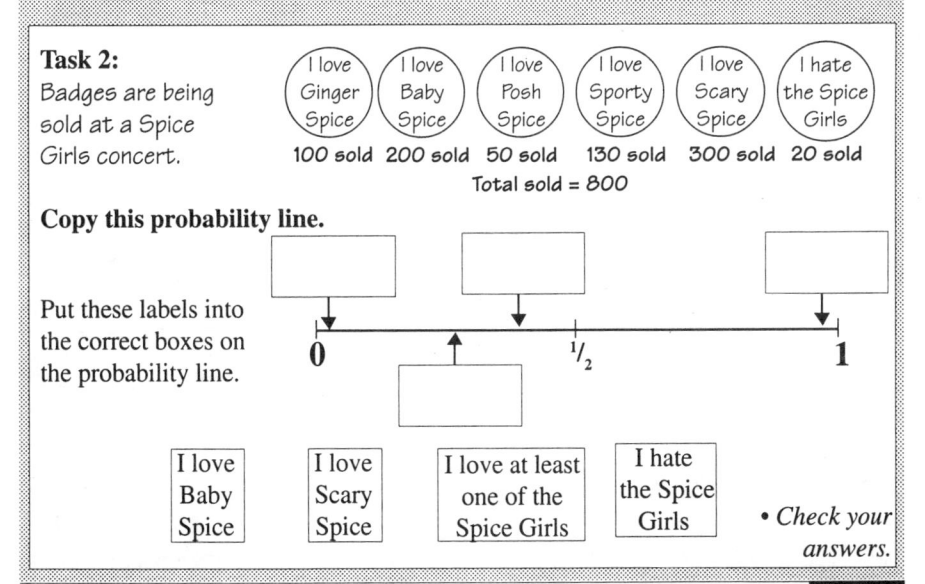

---

**Task 2:**
Badges are being sold at a Spice Girls concert.

I love Ginger Spice — 100 sold
I love Baby Spice — 200 sold
I love Posh Spice — 50 sold
I love Sporty Spice — 130 sold
I love Scary Spice — 300 sold
I hate the Spice Girls — 20 sold

Total sold = 800

**Copy this probability line.**

Put these labels into the correct boxes on the probability line.

0 — $\frac{1}{2}$ — 1

| I love Baby Spice | I love Scary Spice | I love at least one of the Spice Girls | I hate the Spice Girls |

• Check your answers.

A POW GUIDE     page 155     Probability **EXTRA**

# P1: Nick's socks

**Level 5**

**PRACTICE**

Nick is 4 year's old. Every morning he used to argue with his mother over what colour socks he would wear. She invented a game to stop the arguments.

> The game: Each morning Nick picks one sock from the drawer with his eyes shut. He then wears that colour – and a matching tee shirt.

1. On <u>Monday</u> there are 4 red and 4 blue socks in the drawer.

   | 8 socks |
   |---|
   | 4 red (R) → 4 out of 8 are red = $4/8$ |
   | 4 blue (B) → 4 out of 8 are blue = $4/8$ |

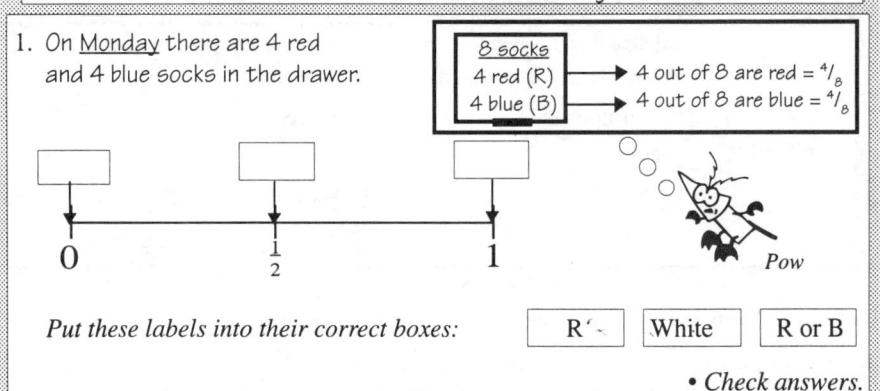

   0 — $\frac{1}{2}$ — 1    *Pow*

   Put these labels into their correct boxes:   | R | | White | | R or B |

   • Check answers.

For each set of socks, put the labels into the correct boxes.
CHECK YOUR ANSWERS AFTER EACH QUESTION.

2. <u>Tuesday</u>

   | 4 socks |
   |---|
   | 3 red (R) → = $3/4$ |
   | 1 white (W) → = $1/4$ |

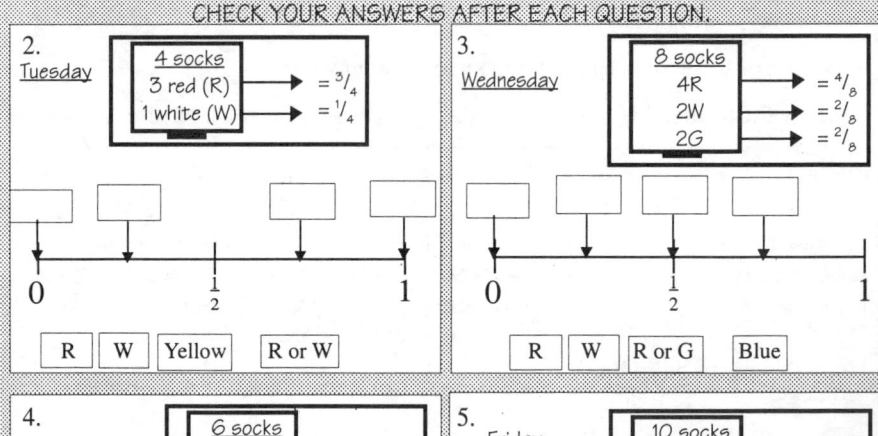

   0 — $\frac{1}{2}$ — 1

   | R | | W | | Yellow | | R or W |

3. <u>Wednesday</u>

   | 8 socks |
   |---|
   | 4R → = $4/8$ |
   | 2W → = $2/8$ |
   | 2G → = $2/8$ |

   0 — $\frac{1}{2}$ — 1

   | R | | W | | R or G | | Blue |

4. <u>Thursday</u>

   | 6 socks |
   |---|
   | 3G → = $3/6$ |
   | 2W → = $2/6$ |
   | 1B → = $1/6$ |

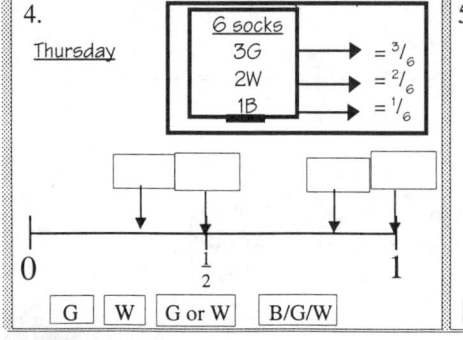

   0 — $\frac{1}{2}$ — 1

   | G | | W | | G or W | | B/G/W |

5. <u>Friday</u>

   | 10 socks |
   |---|
   | 5B → = $5/10$ |
   | 2R → = $2/10$ |
   | 3G → = $3/10$ |

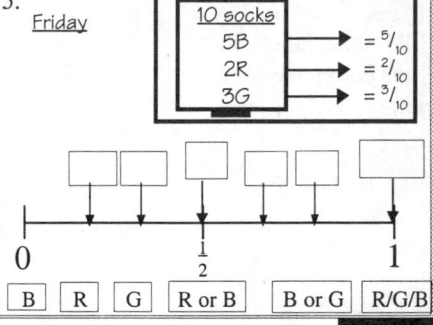

   0 — $\frac{1}{2}$ — 1

   | B | | R | | G | | R or B | | B or G | | R/G/B |

A POW GUIDE        page 156        Probability **EXTRA**

6.

*Put each label in its correct box.*

| 16 socks | |
|---|---|
| 8R | → = $^8/_{16}$ |
| 4G | → = / |
| 2B | → = / |
| 2Y | → = / |

```
[ ]  [ ]  [ ]      [ ]      [ ]      [ ]
 ↓    ↓    ↓        ↓        ↓        ↓
─┼────┼────┼────────┼────────┼────────┼──
 0    1/4           1/2      3/4      1
Impossible                         Certain
```

| R | G | R or G | Y | R/G/B | Orange |

---

7.

*Put each label in its correct box.*

| 12 socks |
|---|
| 6 purple |
| 3 white |
| 2 green |
| 1 orange |

```
[ ][ ] [ ]        [ ]                [ ]
 ↓ ↓    ↓          ↓                  ↓
─┼───────────────┼───────────────────┼─
 0    ↑         1/2         ↑        1
Impossible    [ ]          [ ]    Certain
```

| P | G | W | Red | 0 | P/W | P/W/0 |

---

## Star Challenge

All correct = 1 star

| Socks |
|---|
| 3 Green (G) |
| 4 Red (R) |
| 1 White (W) |

*Put each label in its correct box.*

```
                         [ ]
[ ]   [ ]       [ ] [ ]   [ ]            [ ] [ ]
 ↓     ↓         ↓   ↓     ↓              ↓   ↓
─┼─────┼─────────┼───┼─────┼──────────────┼───┼─
 0    1/4           1/2         3/4           1
Impossible                                 Certain
```

| G | R | W | R or G | R or W | R/G/W | G or W | Yellow |

• *Your teacher has the answers to these.*

*A POW GUIDE*     *page 157*     *Probability* **EXTRA**

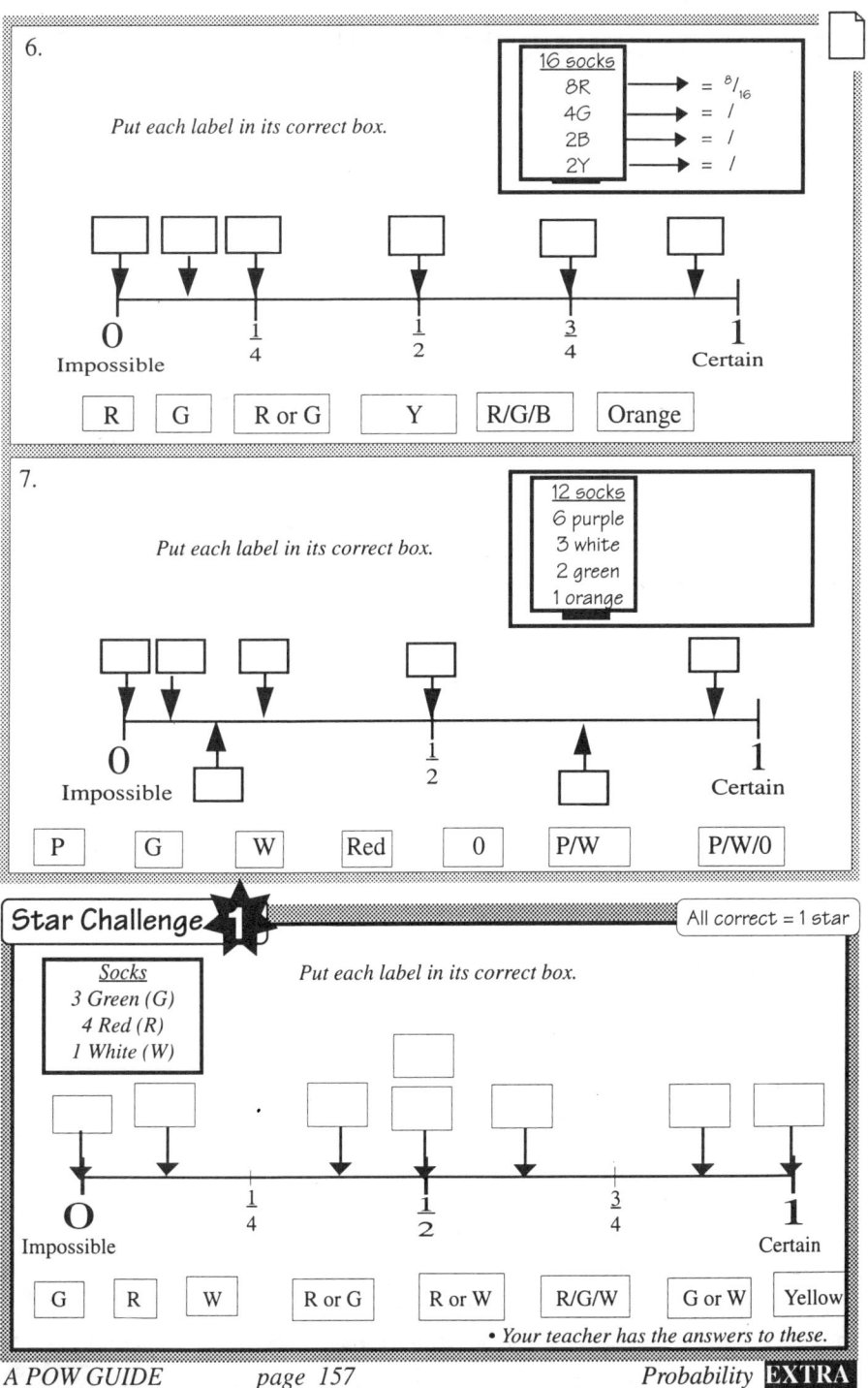

# Section 3: Equally likely outcomes

Level 5

In this section you will :
• decide whether outcomes are equally likely;
• calculate probabilities for equally likely outcomes.

## DEVELOPMENT

### D1: Are the outcomes equally likely ?

A bag contains 3 red counters and 3 blue counters. One counter is drawn. The outcomes are 'red' and 'blue'. These outcomes <u>are</u> equally likely.

A bag contains 5 red counters and 3 blue counters. One counter is drawn. The outcomes are 'red' and 'blue'. These outcomes <u>are not</u> equally likely.

For each situation and set of outcomes, state whether YES or NO should go in the last column.

| | Situation | Set of outcomes | Equally likely ? |
|---|---|---|---|
| 1. | Toss a coin | head, tail | |
| 2. | Weather tomorrow | wet, dry | |
| 3. | Drop a drawing pin | ⊥ , ⋋ | |
| 4. | Throw a dice | 1, 2, 3, 4, 5, 6 | |
| 5. | Throw a dice | 6, not a 6 | |
| 6. | Throw a dice | odd score, even score | |
| 7. | Throw dart at dartboard | hit board, miss board | |
| 8. | Penalty shot at goal | goal, miss | |
| 9. | Football match | home win, away win, draw | |
| 10. | Drop coin onto this board. Outcome is colour covered by most of coin. [red|red / blue|red] | red, blue | |
| 11. | Drop coin onto this board. Outcome is colour covered by most of coin. [red1|red2 / blue|red3] | red1, red2, red3, blue | |
| 12. | Toss 2 coins | HH, HT, TH, TT | |
| 13. | Toss 2 coins | 2 heads, 2 tails, one of each | |
| 14. | Pick a counter out of bag containing (blue 1)(blue 2)(green) | blue, green | |
| 15. | Get home late | mother cross, mother not cross | |

• Check your answers. ASK YOUR TEACHER ABOUT ANY YOU GOT WRONG !

# D2: Probabilities of equally likely outcomes  Level 5

**What do we know?** We know that...
... if an event is impossible, its probability is 0.
... if an event is certain, its probability is 1
... if an event is uncertain, its probability is a number between 0 and 1.

### EXAMPLE 1

probability of getting a grey counter is 1
*or*     prob(grey) = 1     [shorthand]

probability of getting a striped counter is 0
*or*     prob(striped) = 0     [shorthand]

### EXAMPLE 2

chance of getting a striped counter is 2 out of 5
*or*     prob(striped) = $2/5$     [shorthand]

chance of getting a grey counter is 3 out of 5
*or*     prob(grey) = $3/5$     [shorthand]

*Fill in the gaps:*

1. chance of getting a striped counter is ...... out of ..........
   prob (striped) = .........

   chance of getting a grey counter is ...... out of ..........
   prob (grey) = .........

2. chance of getting a striped counter is ...... out of ..........
   prob (striped) = .........

   chance of getting a grey counter is ...... out of ..........
   prob (grey) = .........

3. chance of getting a striped counter is ...... out of ..........
   prob (striped) = .........

   chance of getting a greycounter is ...... out of ..........
   prob (grey) = .........

4. prob (striped) = .........
   prob (grey) = .........

5. prob (striped) = .........
   prob (grey) = .........

6. prob (striped) = ......     prob(black) = ......     prob (grey) = ......

7. prob (striped) = ......     prob(black) = ......     prob (grey) = ......
   prob(white) = ......     • *Check your answers.*

*A POW GUIDE*     *page 159*     *Probability* **EXTRA**

## PRACTICE

## P1: Random choices

You have been choosing counters at random.
"At random" means that each item is equally likely to be chosen.

The letters of each word are put onto cards and shuffled. One letter is chosen at random.
Copy and complete:

1. S C A R Y     chance of getting a Y is ...... out of .........
   prob(Y) = .........   prob(A) = .........   prob(R or Y) = .........

2. G I N G E R     chance of getting a G is ...... out of ......
   prob(G) = .........   prob(I) = .........   prob(R or G) = .........

3. S P O R T Y S P I C E
   prob(S) = ......   prob(T) = ......   prob(A) = ......   prob(S or P) = ......

4. B R I L L I A N T
   prob(B) = ......   prob(I) = ......   prob(Q) = ......   prob(L or I) = ......

5. P R O B A B I L I T I E S
   prob(S) = ......   prob(I) = ......   prob(B) = ......   prob(B or I) = ......

• *Check your answers.*

## P2: Probability practice

1. You choose a letter from the word I D I O T.
   What is the probability that you choose an I ?
2. You buy one raffle ticket. 100 tickets have been sold.
   What is the probability that you win ?
3. You buy 5 raffle tickets. 50 tickets have been sold.
   What is the probability that you win ?
4. You toss a coin. What is the probability that you get a head ?
5. What is the probability that time will run backwards ?
6. You want to choose someone from Bob, Ellie, Sandra and Bill.
   You put their names into a hat and one name is chosen.
   (a) What is the probability that Sandra is chosen ?
   (b) What is the probability that Bob or Bill is chosen ?
7. What is the probability that next week is 7 days long ?
8. You buy this 'scratch card'. You can only scratch one square.
   (a) What is the probability of winning if there is one winning square ?
   (b) What is the probability of winning if there are two winning squares ?

• *Check your answers.*

A POW GUIDE     Probability **EXTRA**

# P3: Probabilities with a dice

**Level 5**

> One dice is tossed.
> The equally likely outcomes are 1 2 3 4 5 6

> The chance of getting 2 is 1 out of 6.
> prob(2) = $1/6$

> The chance of getting 3 or 5 is 2 out of 6.
> prob(3 or 4) = $2/6$

What is the probability of getting ...

1. ... 3 ?
2. ... 1 ?
3. ... an even score ?
4. ... 4 or 5 ?
5. ... a score less than 3 ?
6. ... a score more than 2 ?
7. ... 7 ?
8. ... 1, 2 or 5 ?
9. ... a score of 4 or more ?

• Check your answers

# P4: Nick's sock game

The game:
Each morning 4 year-old Nick picks one sock from the drawer with his eyes shut.
He then wears socks of that colour – and a matching tee shirt (and no arguments).

1. 4 red socks
   6 black socks

   What is the probability
   that Nick picks...
   (a) ...a red sock
   (b) ...a black sock

2. 6 red socks
   6 green socks

   What is the probability
   that Nick picks...
   (a) ...a red sock
   (b) ...a green sock

3. 3 blue socks
   2 yellow socks

   What is the probability
   that Nick picks...
   (a) ...a blue sock
   (b) ...a yellow sock

4. 5 red socks
   5 black socks
   2 white socks

   What is the probability
   that Nick picks...
   (a) ...a red sock
   (b) ...a black sock
   (c) ...a white sock

5. 3 red socks
   2 green socks
   4 white socks

   What is the probability
   that Nick picks...
   (a) ...a red sock
   (b) ...a green sock
   (c) ...a white sock

6. 5 pink socks
   1 orange socks
   4 purple socks

   What is the probability
   that Nick picks...
   (a) ...a pink sock
   (b) ...a purple sock
   (c) ...a black sock

• Check your answers.

## Star Challenge 2

7-8 correct = 1 star

1. A dice is tossed. What is the probability of getting   (a) a 4   (b) a 5 or 6 ?
2. One letter is chosen at random from the letters **F A N T A S Y**
   What is the probability of getting   (a) a T   (b) an A or a T   (c) an S or a Y
3. I buy 5 raffle tickets. 47 tickets have been sold.
   What is the probability that I win ?
4. 10 yellow counters
   7 blue counters
   3 red counters

   This is a box of counters. A counter is chosen at random.
   What is the probability of choosing
   (a) a red counter   (b) a yellow counter

A POW GUIDE        page 161        Probability **EXTRA**

# P5: Probabilities with a pack of cards

**Level 5**

### PACK OF CARDS

| | | | | | | | | | | | Court Cards | |
|---|---|---|---|---|---|---|---|---|---|---|---|---|
| **RED** Hearts | Ace | 2 | 3 | 4 | 5 | 6 | 7 | 8 | 9 | 10 | Jack Queen King |
| **RED** Diamonds | Ace | 2 | 3 | 4 | 5 | 6 | 7 | 8 | 9 | 10 | Jack Queen King |
| **BLACK** Clubs | Ace | 2 | 3 | 4 | 5 | 6 | 7 | 8 | 9 | 10 | Jack Queen King |
| **BLACK** Spades | Ace | 2 | 3 | 4 | 5 | 6 | 7 | 8 | 9 | 10 | Jack Queen King |

**Thinking about the pack.   How many ...**
1. ... cards are there in the pack ?
2. ... hearts are there in the pack ?
3. ... spades are there ?
4. ... black cards are there ?
5. ... 2s are there ?
6. ... Kings are there ?
7. ... court cards are there ?
8. ... black court cards are there ?

prob (red card) = $^{26}/_{52}$ or $^{1}/_{2}$

prob (black Jack) = $^{2}/_{52}$ or $^{1}/_{26}$

CHECK YOUR ANSWERS TO THE FIRST 8 QUESTIONS.
Copy and complete these probabilities.
CHECK YOUR ANSWERS AT THE END OF EACH BATCH.

**Batch A:**
1. prob (black card)    = ......
2. prob (a spade)       = ......
3. prob (a 3 of spades) = ......
4. prob (a 4)           = ......
5. prob (a red 4)       = ......
6. prob (Queen)         = ......
7. prob (Jack or Queen) = ......
8. prob (7 or 9)        = ......
9. prob (6, 7 or 8)     = ......
10. prob (a court card) = ......

**Batch B:**
1. prob (a 2)           = ......
2. prob (2 of clubs)    = ......
3. prob (a black 2)     = ......
4. prob (2, 4, 5 or 6)  = ......
5. prob (King)          = ......
6. prob (a black King)  = ......
7. prob (a red Jack)    = ......
8. prob (Jack of Spades) = ......
9. prob (a black 3)     = ......
10. prob (red 5 or black 6) = ......

## Star Challenge 3

*9-10 correct = 1 star*

Copy and complete these probabilities:
1. prob (10 or Queen)                     = ......
2. prob (10, Jack or King)                = ......
3. prob (a red 4)                         = ......
4. prob (black Jack or black Queen)       = ...
5. prob (black Queen)                     = ......
6. prob (2, 3, 4 or 5)                    = ......
7. prob (red 2 or red 3)                  = ......
8. prob (black 3 or black 5)              = ......
9. prob (red 7)                           = ......
10. prob (the 7 of hearts)                = ......

• *Your teacher has the answers.*

A POW GUIDE        page 162        Probability **EXTRA**

# Section 4: Estimating probabilities

*Level 5*

In this section you will look at different ways of estimating probabilities.

**DEVELOPMENT**

## D1: Methods for estimating probabilities

Here are four different ways of estimating probabilities.

METHOD A:   Use equally likely outcomes
The probability of rolling a 3 on a dice is $\frac{1}{6}$
This is because there are six equally likely outcomes.

So far, the outcomes have been equally likely. When they are not, other methods must be used.

*Meedy Oker*

METHOD B:   Look at statistical data
If I wanted to estimate the probability of a car being stolen on a Saturday night in Birmingham, I would need to look at police crime records.

METHOD C:   Do an experiment to collect data
If I wanted to estimate the probability of a buttered slice of bread landing buttered side down, I could do an experiment.

METHOD D:   Carry out a survey to collect data
If I wanted to estimate the probability that the next car passing my school would only have one occupant, I could do a survey.

Look at each of the following situations.
*For each, say which of these methods you could use to estimate the probability.*

1. The probability that a pupil chosen at random from Year 9 in your school is left-handed.
   [If a pupil is chosen "at random from Y9" then it will have been arranged so that any pupil in Y9 is equally likely to be chosen.]
2. The probability that the top card in a well-shuffled pack is the Ace of Spades.
3. The probability that it will snow next Christmas Day.
4. The probability that the River Dee will flood its banks sometime in the last week of October.
5. The probability that a drawing pin will land point upwards when dropped.
6. The probability that a C60 audio tape will last exactly 60 minutes.
7. The probability that a ruler dropped from a height of 10 m would shatter.
8. The probability that any pupil in the school, chosen at random, would be an only child.
9. The probability that I will win a raffle if 800 tickets are sold and I have 5 of them.
10. The probability that the volcano, Mount Helena, will erupt sometime next year.

• *Check your answers.*

# Section 5: Events and non-events

Level 6

In this section you will use the knowledge that the total probability of all outcomes of an event is 1.

**DEVELOPMENT**

## D1: Sums of probabilities

1. One of these socks is chosen at random.
   Write down the probability of getting
   (a) a red sock   (b) a black sock

   | 4 red socks |
   | 6 black socks |

2. The probability of getting a red sock or a black sock is 1. Explain why.

   > For any one event, the sum of the probabilities is 1
   > prob (something NOT happening) = 1 − prob (it happens)

3. A drawer has blue socks and white socks in it.
   The probability of getting a blue sock is $3/4$.
   What is the probability of getting a white sock?

4. A glass is dropped. The probability that it will break is $2/3$.
   What is the probability that it will not break?

5. The probability that it will snow on Christmas Day is 0.1
   What is the probability that it will not snow?

6. When I come home late, the probability that Mum will moan is 0.8
   What is the probability that she will not moan?

7. A bag contains red, white and blue counters. A counter is picked at random.
   The probability that it is red is 0.5   The probability that it is blue is 0.1
   What is the probability that it is white?

8. A box contains these snooker balls.
   One ball is taken out at random.
   *Write down the probability that it is:*
   (a) black       (b) not black
   (c) red         (d) not red
   (e) red or blue (f) not red or blue   (g) not blue

   | 6 red balls |
   | 1 yellow balls |
   | 2 blue balls |
   | 1 black ball |

   • Check your answers.

### Star Challenge 4

All correct = 1 star

1. The probability that we will have Fish and Chips on Friday is 0.8.
   What is the probability that we do not have Fish and Chips on Friday?

2. There are traffic lights at the end of my road.
   The probability that I have to stop at these lights is $3/4$
   What is the probability that I do not have to stop?

3. A jar contains red beans, white beans and dried peas. I take one out at random.
   The probability that I get a dried pea is 0.2. The probability that I get a red bean is 0.5   What is the probability that I get a white bean?

A POW GUIDE     Probability EXTRA

# Section 6: Combined events

Level 6

*In this section you will list outcomes of combined events.*

**DEVELOPMENT**

## D1: Listing outcomes of two events

1. A coin and a dice are tossed together. One possible outcome is a head and a 6. I can write this as (H,6). List all the possible outcomes in this way.

2. In the hospital waiting room I go to buy drinks for Mum and me from the machine.
The chocolate has run out.
The possible combinations of drinks I could buy are:

   TEA, TEA     COFFEE, TEA
   TEA, COFFEE     COFFEE, COFFEE

   On our second visit, all three drinks are available. I buy two.
   List all the possible combinations of drinks I could buy.

3. (a)   (H)   (T)    If I toss two coins, there are four equally likely outcomes. One of them is HT.
   List the 4 equally likely outcomes.

   (b)   (H)   (H)   (T)    If I toss three coins, there are 8 equally likely outcomes. One of them is HHT.
   List the 8 equally likely outcomes.

4. A red dice and a blue dice are tossed. This is a table to list all the possible ways of getting each total score.

   | Total | Outcomes |
   |---|---|
   | 2 | (1,1) |
   | 3 | (1,2), (2,1) |
   | 4 | |
   | 5 | |
   | : | |
   | : | |
   | 12 | |

   *Remember – You cannot get (1,7) !*

   (a) Copy and complete this table.
   (b) How many equally likely outcomes are there ?
   (c) What is the probability of getting a 7 ?
   (d) What is the probability of getting a double six ?

   • *Check your answers.*

A POW GUIDE     page 165     Probability **EXTRA**

# D2: Systematic methods of getting all outcomes

**Level 6**

1. | Bob | Tim | Mary | Jane | Sue |

   One boy and one girl are to be chosen from these.
   *Copy and complete:*

   Bob + ………    Bob + ………    Bob + ………
   Tim + ………    Tim + ………    Tim + ………

   > Take one boy.
   > Put this boy with each girl.
   > Repeat with the second boy and each girl.

2. | Sally | Mandy | Clare | Fred | Bill | Sam |

   One girl and one boy are to be chosen from these.
   Make a list of all the possible outcomes.

   *Pow*

3. This table shows <u>the sum of the scores</u> when two dice are thrown. It is not complete.

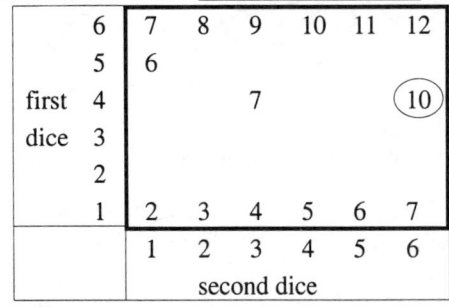

   |  | 6 | 7 | 8 | 9 | 10 | 11 | 12 |
   |---|---|---|---|---|---|---|---|
   |  | 5 | 6 |  |  |  |  |  |
   | first | 4 |  |  | 7 |  | 10 |  |
   | dice | 3 |  |  |  |  |  |  |
   |  | 2 |  |  |  |  |  |  |
   |  | 1 | 2 | 3 | 4 | 5 | 6 | 7 |
   |  |  | 1 | 2 | 3 | 4 | 5 | 6 |

   second dice

   > Each entry in the table is an outcome.
   > These outcomes are equally likely.

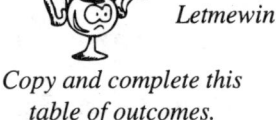

   *Letmewin*

   *Copy and complete this table of outcomes.*

   There are 36 equally likely outcomes.
   prob(3) = $^2/_{36}$    prob(2) = $^1/_{36}$    prob(2 or 3) = $^3/_{36}$

   *Copy and complete these probabilities. Use the table you made in question 3.*

   4. prob (11) = ……
   5. prob (10) = ……
   6. prob (10 or 11) = ……
   7. prob (7) = ……
   8. prob (4) = ……
   9. prob (less than 6) = ……
   10. prob (1) = ……
   11. prob (5 or 10) = ……
   12. prob (6 or less) = ……
   13. prob (9) = ……
   14. prob (more than 9) = ……
   15. prob (an odd sum) = ……

## Star Challenge ★ ★

18 marks for table
1 mark for each question

• Check your answers.
25-26 marks = 2 stars
20-24 marks = 1 star

1. Make a table, like the one above, showing the <u>difference in the scores</u> when two dice are thrown.

   > The DIFFERENCE between 3 and 5 is 2

   *Copy and complete these probabilities. Use the table you made in question 1.*

   2. prob (0) = ……
   3. prob (3) = ……
   4. prob (2 or 3) = ……
   5. prob (5) = ……
   6. prob (6) = ……
   7. prob (5 or less) = ……
   8. prob (an odd number) = ……
   9. prob (even number) = ……

   • *Your teacher has the answers to these.*

A POW GUIDE    page 166    Probability **EXTRA**

# Section 7: Technique review

*In this section you will review the techniques met in this topic.*

Check your answers at the end of each set of problems

## R1: Words and phrases

Level 4

1. A sock is chosen at random from this drawer.
   (a) Which colour are you *most likely* to get?
   (b) Which colour are you *least likely* to get?

   4 red socks
   6 green socks
   10 black socks

2. Describe how likely each event is using one of the words from the box.
   (a) The day that follows Monday will be Tuesday.
   (b) Teacher will give us no homework this term.
   (c) I will have my hair cut this month.
   (d) Tomorrow, a helicopter will land in the school yard.

   certain
   likely
   unlikely
   impossible

## R2: The probability scale

Level 5

A counter is chosen at random from this box of counters.

5 red counters ➤ = $5/10$
3 blue counters ➤ = $3/10$
2 white counters ➤ = $2/10$

**Copy this probability line.**
Put the labels into the correct boxes on the probability line.

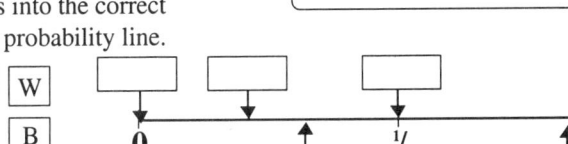

| R, W or B | W |
| R or B | B |
| Green | R |

0 ——— $1/2$ ——— 1

## R3: Equally likely outcomes

Level 5

*For each situation and set of outcomes, say whether the outcomes are equally likely:*

1. Sit an exam          Pass, fail
2. Jump over a log      Land on your feet, fall over
3. Toss a coin          Heads, Tails
4. Throw a dice         1, 2, 3, 4, 5, 6
5. Throw a dice         3, not a 3

## R4: Working out probabilities

Level 5

1. You choose a letter at random from the word  R  E  V  I  E  W
   What is the probability that you choose  (a) R   (b) E   (c) I, E or W?
2. What is the probability that tomorrow is 24 hours long?
3. What is the probability that you get a 3 when you throw a dice?
4. What is the probability that you get a red card when you choose a card from an ordinary pack of cards?

A POW GUIDE          page 167          Probability  **EXTRA**

5. You buy 2 raffle tickets. 120 tickets have been sold.
   What is the probability that you win ?
6. You buy 10 lottery tickets. 50 000 lottery tickets have been sold.
   There is 1 big winner. What is the probability that it is you ?
7. A pack of 52 cards is shuffled. You take the top card.
   What is the probability that it is  (a)  a club   (b) a Jack   (c) the Jack of Clubs ?
8. These tins of soup have lost their labels.
   Bob knows that 2 of them are tomato soups.
   He opens one tin.
   What is the probability that he gets one of the tomato soups ?

## R5: Estimating probabilities           Level 5

| Method A: Use equally likely outcomes | Method B: Look at statistical data |
| Method C: Do an experiment            | Method D: Carry out a survey       |

*Which method would you use to estimate the probability in each case:*

1. The probability that a dropped piece of bread will land butter-side down.
2. The probability that your aunt's newborn baby will be a girl.
3. The probability that the next car to drive in the car park will be white.
4. The probability that the top card in a pack is the Ace of Hearts.

## R6: To happen or not           Level 6

1. The probability that I will get up when Mum calls is $1/_4$
   What is the probability that I do not get up then ?
2. The weather forecast says that the probability of snow tomorrow is 0.2
   What is the probability that it will not snow ?
3. I have to drive through two sets of traffic lights on my way to work.
   The probability that I have to stop at both sets of lights is 0.1
   The probability that I get stopped at just one set is 0.6
   What is the probability that I do not have to stop at all ?

## R7: Listing combined outcomes           Level 6

1. Nick has some new Tee-shirts and shorts.

   | Tee-shirts | Red    |
   |            | Orange |
   |            | Green  |

   | Shorts | Black |
   |        | Blue  |

   List all the combinations of colours he could wear.

2. These two spinners are spun and the result recorded.
   One of the outcomes is (3, +).
   List all the possible outcomes.

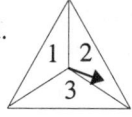

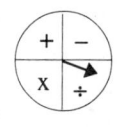

A POW GUIDE          page 168          Probability **EXTRA**

# THE NATIONAL CURRICULUM ...
# ... AND BEYOND ...

*Pow*

# Let's Sort Out Fractions, Decimals and Percentages
# EXTRA

| Level 3 | Level 4 | Level 5 | Level 6 |
|---|---|---|---|
| | | §12 Technique review | |
| | | | §11 Equivalent fractions decimals & % |
| | | | §10 From decimals to fractions |
| | | | §9 Making equivalent fractions |
| | | §8 Fractions and percentages of amounts | |
| | §7 Fractions and percentages of shapes | | |
| | §6 + and – decimals | | |
| | §5 Decimals | | |
| | §4 Number lines | | |
| | §3 Picturing fractions | | |
| | §2 Basic fraction review | | |
| §1 Decimals in everyday life | | | |

*A POW GUIDE*     page 169

# Let's sort out fractions, decimals and percentages

Many of the problems students have with fractions are caused by poor understanding of some of the basic ideas. Sometimes too little time was spent on early fraction work. Sometimes students missed some early work through absence. Often students' understanding is good in most of the early work, but the 'gaps', the small things that they do not fully understand or have forgotten, cause problems in later work.

To remedy this, we have gone right back to the beginning and gone through all the simple ideas and techniques that you ought to know. Much of it you will be able to do already, but there will be little things that you are unsure about and need to get sorted. Also, going back over the basics that you already understand is a memory-jogger which will help when tackling the more difficult techniques.

## Section 1: Decimals in everyday life

Level 3

In this section you will:
- work with decimals in money;
- meet, and learn to avoid, the most common mistakes;
- review techniques for doing money problems using a calculator.

**DEVELOPMENT**

### D1: Money

£2.47 = 247p

*Write in pence:*
1. £1.25    2. £23.14    3. £5.03    4. £6.30    5. £0.35    6. £0.04

346p = £3.46

*Write in pounds:*
7. 273p    8. 540p    9. 102p    10. 75p    11. 20p    12. 5p

• CHECK YOUR ANSWERS *before going on.*

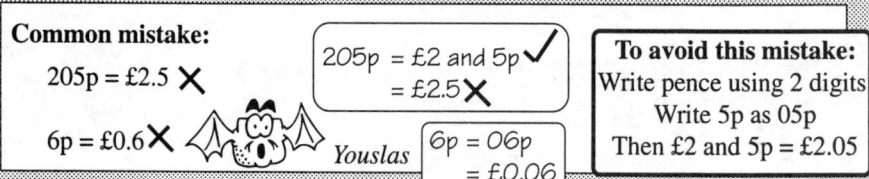

**Common mistake:**
205p = £2.5 ✗

6p = £0.6 ✗

*Youslas*

205p = £2 and 5p ✓
      = £2.5 ✗

6p = 06p
   = £0.06

**To avoid this mistake:**
Write pence using 2 digits
Write 5p as 05p
Then £2 and 5p = £2.05

*Write in pounds:*
13. 1p    14. 10p    15. 104p    16. 30p    17. 8p    18. 2p

*Add up each set of coins. Write the total in pounds:*

19. £1, £1, £1, 20p, 20p

20. 50p, 50p, 20p, 5p, 5p, 10p

21. £1, 5p, 5p, 20p

22. 2p, 2p, 5p

• *Check your answers.*

A POW GUIDE    page 170    Let's Sort Out Fractions, Decimals **EXTRA**
and Percentages

## D2: Money and the calculator

1. **£1.45 + £2.15 = ?**  Use a calculator to work out this sum.
   Write the answer (a) as it appears on the calculator
   (b) using money notation.

2. **£3.24 + £1.16 = ?**

   *Pesymistic* worked it out on a calculator.
   *Pesymistic* wrote
   the answer as **£4.4**

   *Optymistic* worked it out on a calculator.
   *Optymistic* wrote
   the answer as **£4.40**

   Which one of them wrote the answer correctly using money notation?

   *Work these sums out using a calculator. Write the answers using money notation.*
   3. £2.43 + £1.27    4. £3.47 – 2.07    5. £5.21 + £2.93 – £3.64
   
   • Check your answers.

## D3: Money sums with mixed units

*Work out, without a calculator. Write your answers as pounds.*
1. 80p + 25p    2. £1.60 + 50p    3. £2.20 – 30p    4. £3 – 65p

*Work out, using a calculator. Write your answers as pounds.*
5. 75p + 45p    6. £2.57 + 65p    7. £8.17 – 95p    8. £4 – 87p

• Check your answers, before going on.

Some people have problems with sums like this when using a calculator.
To avoid this problem, put each amount of money as pounds before doing the sum.

£3.52 + 87p        [Write as pounds.]
= £3.52 + £0.87   [Use a calculator.]
= £4.39

*Driller*

*Rewrite each sum using pound notation. Use a calculator to work out the answer.*
9. 92p + £3.21    10. £10.02 + 69p    11. £3.45 – 94p
12. £5.10 – 36p    13. £5.03 + £2.30 – 65p    14. £18.64 – £9.05 + 76p

15. *Rewrite each bill with each item written in £.*
    *Work out the total for the bill and the change.*

| First bill | |
|---|---|
| Meal | £21.96 |
| Wine | £9.65 |
| Coffee | 85p |
| Soft drink | 70p |
| Change from £40 | |

| Second bill | |
|---|---|
| Newspapers | £4.58 |
| Delivery charge | 80p |
| Birthday card | 99p |
| Stamps | 52p |
| Sweets | 15p |
| Change from £10 | |

*Work out using a calculator.*
*Just write down the answer.*
16. £3.25 + 85p
17. £1.78 – 82p + £1.35
18. 72p + 47p + 38p – £1.14
19. 43p + £2.61 – 5p
20. £10.50 – 95p + 7p

• Check your answers.

*A POW GUIDE*       page 171      *Let's Sort Out Fractions, Decimals* **EXTRA**
*and Percentages*

# Section 2: Basic fraction review

Level 4

In this section you will review:
- writing fractions using words and numbers;
- recognising fractions of shapes;
- recognising simple equivalent fractions.

**PRACTICE**

## P1: Shaded fractions

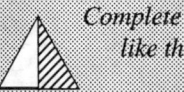

*Complete each statement like the example.*

1 out of 2 parts has been shaded
$1/2$ has been shaded
one half has been shaded

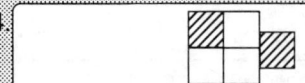

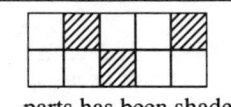

1. 1 out of ...... parts has been shaded
...... has been shaded
one ............... has been shaded

2. ...out of ...... parts has been shaded
......... has been shaded
....................... has been shaded

3. ...... out of ...... parts has been shaded
...... has been shaded
....................... has been shaded

4. ... out of ...... parts has been shaded
......... has been shaded
....................... has been shaded

5. ...... out of ...... parts has been shaded
...... has been shaded
....................... has been shaded

• Check your answers.

## P2: Fractions <—> words

1. Complete each statement:

three quarters = $\frac{3}{4}$

five eighths =

one seventh =

................... = $\frac{1}{10}$

................... = $\frac{4}{5}$

one and a half =

• Check answers.

2. Draw lines connecting matching words and fractions.

one third     $2/8$

two eighths     $1\frac{1}{4}$

five sixths     $2\frac{3}{4}$

one and a quarter     $1/3$

one and a fifth     $1\frac{1}{5}$

two and a third     $2\frac{1}{3}$

two and three quarters     $5/6$

A POW GUIDE    *Let's Sort Out Fractions, Decimals and Percentages* **EXTRA**

# P3: What fraction ...

Level 4

EXAMPLE 1  What fraction has been shaded ?
What fraction has not been shaded ?

$3/7$ shaded    $4/7$ not shaded

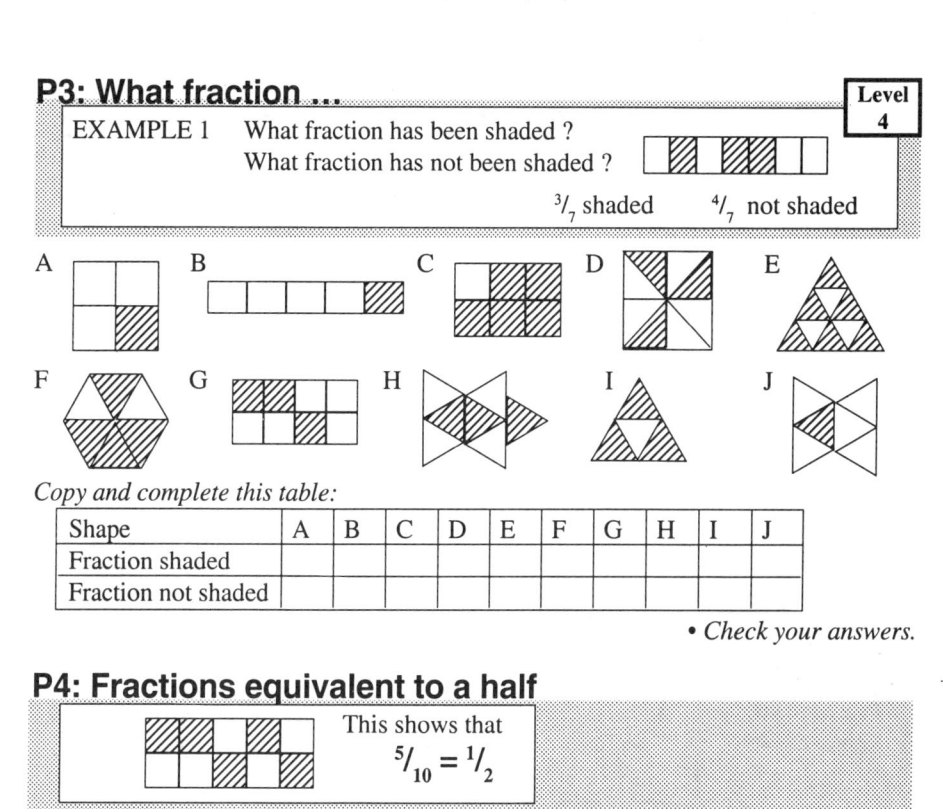

A  B  C  D  E
F  G  H  I  J

*Copy and complete this table:*

| Shape | A | B | C | D | E | F | G | H | I | J |
|---|---|---|---|---|---|---|---|---|---|---|
| Fraction shaded | | | | | | | | | | |
| Fraction not shaded | | | | | | | | | | |

• *Check your answers.*

# P4: Fractions equivalent to a half

This shows that
$$5/10 = 1/2$$

*For each diagram, copy and complete the fraction statement.*

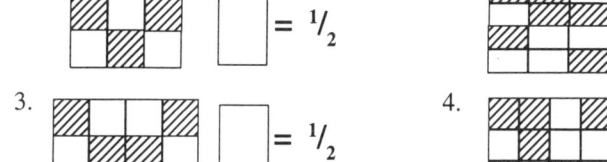

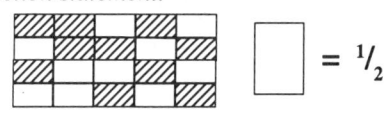

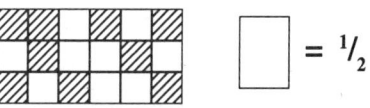

1.  ☐ = $1/2$
2.  ☐ = $1/2$
3.  ☐ = $1/2$
4.  ☐ = $1/2$

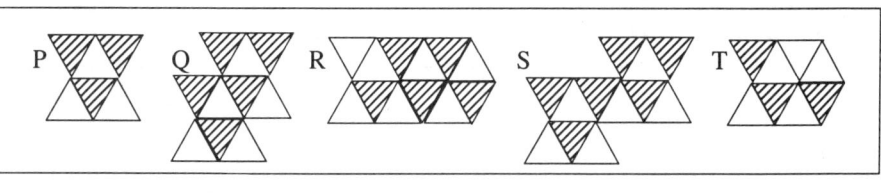

P    Q    R    S    T

5. (a) Which three of these shapes are half shaded ?
   (b) For those that are half shaded, write a statement like those in questions 1-4.
   (c) For the two shapes which are *not* half shaded, say what fraction *is* shaded.
   (d) For the two shapes which are *not* half shaded, say whether each shape is less than or more than half shaded.

• *Check your answers.*

A POW GUIDE    page 173    *Let's Sort Out Fractions, Decimals and Percentages*  **EXTRA**

## P5: Half or not a half ?

**Level 4**

$$\frac{1}{2} = \frac{3}{6} = \frac{25}{50} = \ldots$$ Look ! The bottom number is always twice the top number.

**Task 1** *Put a ring round each fraction equivalent to* $^1/_2$

$\frac{2}{4}$  $\frac{15}{20}$  $\frac{20}{40}$  $\frac{21}{42}$

$\frac{2}{5}$  $\frac{25}{50}$  $\frac{50}{100}$  $\frac{4}{9}$  $\frac{11}{22}$

$\frac{17}{34}$  $\frac{16}{35}$  $\frac{15}{20}$  $\frac{24}{44}$  $\frac{46}{96}$  $\frac{56}{112}$

$\frac{48}{96}$  $\frac{13}{25}$  $\frac{28}{56}$  $\frac{12}{42}$  $\frac{16}{32}$

**Task 2** *Put a number in each box to make a fraction equivalent to* $^1/_2$

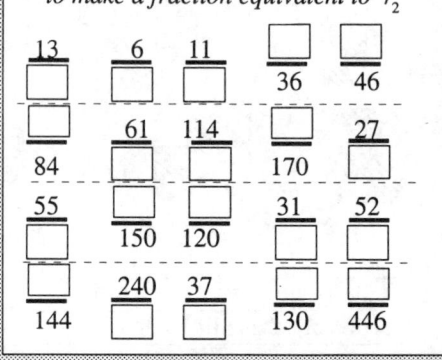

$\frac{13}{\Box}$  $\frac{6}{\Box}$  $\frac{11}{\Box}$  $\frac{\Box}{36}$  $\frac{\Box}{46}$

$\frac{\Box}{84}$  $\frac{\Box}{61}$  $\frac{\Box}{114}$  $\frac{\Box}{170}$  $\frac{27}{\Box}$

$\frac{55}{\Box}$  $\frac{\Box}{150}$  $\frac{\Box}{120}$  $\frac{31}{\Box}$  $\frac{52}{\Box}$

$\frac{\Box}{144}$  $\frac{\Box}{240}$  $\frac{37}{\Box}$  $\frac{\Box}{130}$  $\frac{\Box}{446}$

## P6: More simple equivalent fractions

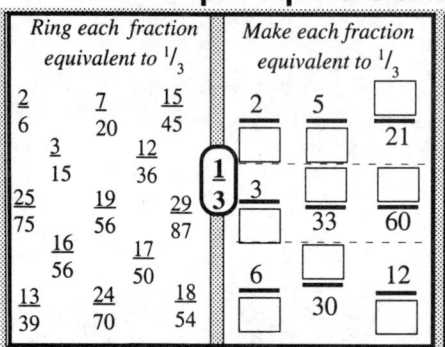

| *Ring each fraction equivalent to* $^1/_3$ | *Make each fraction equivalent to* $^1/_3$ | *Ring each fraction equivalent to* $^1/_4$ | *Make each fraction equivalent to* $^1/_4$ |
|---|---|---|---|

*Ring each fraction equivalent to* $^1/_3$:

$\frac{2}{6}$  $\frac{7}{20}$  $\frac{15}{45}$

$\frac{3}{15}$  $\frac{12}{36}$

$\frac{25}{75}$  $\frac{19}{56}$  $\frac{29}{87}$

$\frac{16}{56}$  $\frac{17}{50}$

$\frac{13}{39}$  $\frac{24}{70}$  $\frac{18}{54}$

*Make each fraction equivalent to* $^1/_3$:  $\boxed{\frac{1}{3}}$

$\frac{2}{\Box}$  $\frac{5}{\Box}$  $\frac{\Box}{21}$

$\frac{3}{\Box}$  $\frac{\Box}{33}$  $\frac{\Box}{60}$

$\frac{6}{\Box}$  $\frac{\Box}{30}$  $\frac{12}{\Box}$

*Ring each fraction equivalent to* $^1/_4$:

$\frac{2}{8}$  $\frac{15}{60}$  $\frac{9}{40}$

$\frac{3}{12}$  $\frac{50}{150}$  $\frac{22}{90}$

$\frac{16}{64}$  $\frac{13}{52}$

$\frac{12}{48}$  $\frac{23}{96}$

$\frac{7}{28}$  $\frac{15}{44}$  $\frac{42}{168}$

*Make each fraction equivalent to* $^1/_4$:  $\boxed{\frac{1}{4}}$

$\frac{4}{\Box}$  $\frac{\Box}{32}$  $\frac{\Box}{12}$

$\frac{5}{\Box}$  $\frac{\Box}{100}$  $\frac{\Box}{60}$

$\frac{6}{\Box}$  $\frac{14}{\Box}$  $\frac{\Box}{120}$

## Star Challenge

• *Check your answers.*
41-45 correct = 2 stars
35-40 correct = 1 star

| *Make fractions equivalent to* $^1/_2$ | *Make fractions equivalent to* $^1/_3$ | *Make fractions equivalent to* $^1/_4$ | *Make fractions equivalent to* $^1/_5$ | *Make fractions equivalent to* $^1/_6$ |
|---|---|---|---|---|

$\frac{4}{\Box}$  $\frac{15}{\Box}$

$\frac{\Box}{12}$

$\frac{\Box}{10}$  $\frac{\Box}{50}$  $\frac{12}{\Box}$

$\frac{\Box}{16}$  $\frac{\Box}{28}$  $\frac{\Box}{14}$

---

$\frac{3}{\Box}$  $\frac{\Box}{\Box}$

$\frac{\Box}{45}$  $\frac{\Box}{12}$

$\frac{7}{\Box}$  $\frac{\Box}{50}$  $\frac{\Box}{36}$

$\frac{13}{\Box}$

$\frac{\Box}{27}$  $\frac{\Box}{42}$

---

$\frac{\Box}{\Box}$  $\frac{5}{\Box}$

$\frac{8}{\Box}$  $\frac{\Box}{60}$

$\frac{7}{\Box}$  $\frac{\Box}{25}$

$\frac{\Box}{160}$

$\frac{8}{\Box}$  $\frac{21}{\Box}$

$\frac{\Box}{52}$

---

$\frac{\Box}{\Box}$  $\frac{4}{\Box}$

$\frac{10}{\Box}$  $\frac{\Box}{25}$

$\frac{\Box}{\Box}$  $\frac{\Box}{12}$

$\frac{35}{\Box}$  $\frac{\Box}{100}$

$\frac{\Box}{\Box}$  $\frac{6}{\Box}$  $\frac{25}{\Box}$

$\frac{\Box}{40}$

---

$\frac{\Box}{\Box}$  $\frac{15}{\Box}$  $\frac{2}{\Box}$

$\frac{18}{\Box}$

$\frac{\Box}{10}$

$\frac{24}{\Box}$  $\frac{\Box}{30}$

$\frac{6}{\Box}$  $\frac{\Box}{\Box}$  $\frac{7}{\Box}$

$\frac{\Box}{72}$

*A POW GUIDE*     page 174     *Let's Sort Out Fractions, Decimals and Percentages*   **EXTRA**

# P7: Comparing fractions

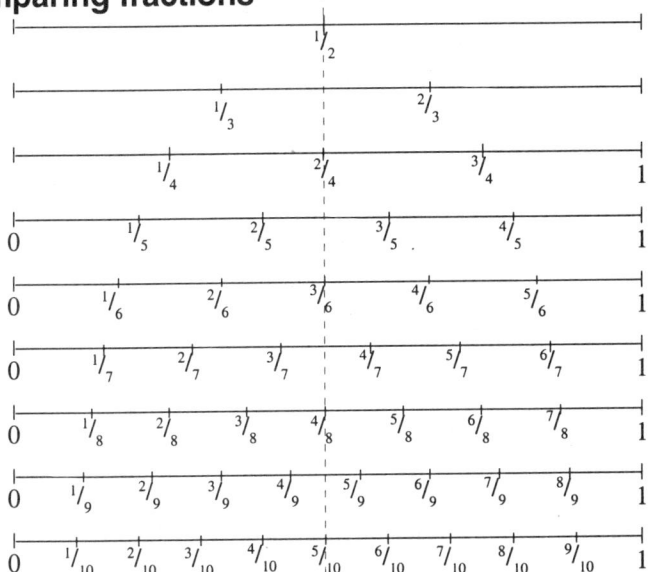

Level 4

[Fraction number lines from halves through tenths]

1. Is $1/8$ bigger or smaller than $1/9$ ?
2. Is $1/6$ bigger or smaller than $1/5$ ?
3. Is $2/7$ bigger or smaller than $1/5$ ?
4. Is $2/3$ bigger or smaller than $3/4$ ?
5. Is $7/9$ bigger or smaller than $7/8$ ?
6. Is $3/10$ bigger or smaller than $1/3$ ?
7. ( $2/7$  $3/5$  $1/10$  $5/9$  $3/8$  $6/10$  $2/3$ )
   Which of these fractions are smaller than $1/2$ ?
8. ( $3/7$  $2/5$  $1/4$  $2/9$  $4/5$  $3/10$  $1/5$ )
   Which of these fractions are smaller than $1/3$ ?
9. Which four fractions in the diagram are equal to $1/2$ ?
10. Which two fractions in the diagram are equal to $2/3$ ?   • Check your answers.

## Star Challenge 2

5-6 correct = 1 star

EXAMPLE 2  Is $3/8$ bigger or smaller than $1/2$ ?
$1/2 = 4/8$ and $4/8$ is bigger than $3/8$ so $3/8$ is smaller than $1/2$

1. Is $3/5$ bigger or smaller than $1/2$ ?
2. Complete this statement: $1/2 = ?/20$   Is $11/20$ bigger or smaller than $1/2$ ?
3. Complete this statement: $1/2 = ?/50$   Is $24/50$ bigger or smaller than $1/2$ ?
4. Is $5/12$ bigger or smaller than $1/2$ ?
5. Is $10/22$ bigger or smaller than $1/2$ ?
6. Is $17/30$ bigger or smaller than $1/2$ ?    • Your teacher has the answers to these.

A POW GUIDE    page 175    Let's Sort Out Fractions, Decimals and Percentages  **EXTRA**

# Section 3: Picturing fractions

**Level 4**

In this section you will :
- work with diagrams and fractions;
- work out how many halves, thirds, quarters … there are in …
- change top heavy fractions into whole numbers/mixed numbers;
- work with fractions that add up to whole numbers;
- share with fraction answers.

*DEVELOPMENT*

## D1: Multiples of simple fractions
*Copy and complete both words and pictures:*

1. 
   - 4 quarters = 1 ; 4 x $\frac{1}{4}$ = ……
   - 5 quarters = $1\frac{1}{4}$ ; 5 x $\frac{1}{4}$ = ……
   - 6 quarters = …… ; 6 x $\frac{1}{4}$ = ……
   - 7 quarters = …… ; 7 x $\frac{1}{4}$ = ……

2. 
   - 3 thirds = 1 ; 3 x $\frac{1}{3}$ = ……
   - 4 thirds = $1\frac{1}{3}$ ; 4 x $\frac{1}{3}$ = ……
   - 5 thirds = …… ; 5 x $\frac{1}{3}$ = ……
   - 6 thirds = …… ; 6 x $\frac{1}{3}$ = ……

3. 
   - 5 fifths = 1 ; 5 x $\frac{1}{5}$ = ……
   - 6 fifths = $1\frac{1}{4}$ ; 6 x $\frac{1}{5}$ = ……
   - 7 fifths = …… ; 7x $\frac{1}{5}$ = ……
   - 8 fifths = …… ; 8 x $\frac{1}{5}$ = ……

• *Check your answers.*

## D2: How many … ?

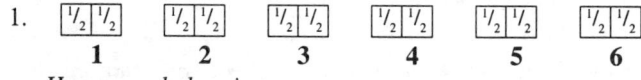

1. How many halves in …
   (a) …1   (b) …$1\frac{1}{2}$   (c) …$2\frac{1}{2}$   (d) …4   (e) …$3\frac{1}{2}$   (f) …$5\frac{1}{2}$

2. How many thirds in …
   (a) …1   (b) …$1\frac{1}{3}$   (c) …$2\frac{1}{3}$   (d) …$1\frac{2}{3}$   (e) …2   (f) …$2\frac{2}{3}$

3. How many fifths in …
   (a) …1   (b) …$1\frac{2}{5}$   (c) …$1\frac{4}{5}$   (d) …2   (e) …$2\frac{3}{5}$   (f) …3

4. How many quarters in …
   (a) …1   (b) …$1\frac{1}{4}$   (c) …$1\frac{3}{4}$   (d) …2   (e) …$2\frac{1}{4}$   (f) …$2\frac{1}{2}$

5. How many tenths in …
   (a) …1   (b) …$1\frac{1}{10}$   (c) …$1\frac{7}{10}$   (d) …2   (e) …$2\frac{3}{10}$   (f) …$3\frac{1}{10}$

• *Check your answers.*

A POW GUIDE   page 176   Let's Sort Out Fractions, Decimals and Percentages   **EXTRA**

## D3: Whole numbers —> top heavy fractions        Level 4

$2 = \frac{8}{4}$

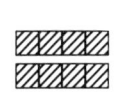

whole number → top heavy fraction

In 2 whole ones there are 8 quarters.

*Ruff*

*Copy and complete:*

1. (a) $1 = \frac{...}{2}$  (b) $2 = \frac{...}{2}$  (c) $5 = \frac{...}{2}$  (d) $7 = \frac{...}{2}$

   How many halves in 1 whole one?   How many halves in 2 whole ones?

2. (a) $1 = \frac{...}{3}$  (b) $2 = \frac{...}{3}$  (c) $4 = \frac{...}{3}$  (d) $3 = \frac{...}{3}$

3. (a) $1 = \frac{...}{4}$  (b) $3 = \frac{...}{4}$  (c) $4 = \frac{...}{4}$  (d) $5 = \frac{...}{4}$

4. (a) $2 = \frac{...}{6}$  (b) $3 = \frac{...}{5}$  (c) $5 = \frac{...}{6}$  (d) $4 = \frac{...}{5}$

• *Check your answers.*

## D4: Mixed numbers —> top heavy fractions

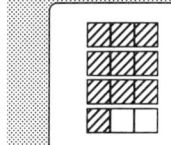

$3\frac{1}{3} = \frac{10}{3}$

mixed number → top heavy fraction

In $3\frac{1}{3}$ there are 10 thirds.

*Icee*

*Copy and complete:*

1. (a) $1\frac{1}{2} = \frac{...}{2}$  (b) $3\frac{1}{2} = \frac{...}{2}$  (c) $5\frac{1}{2} = \frac{...}{2}$  (d) $7\frac{1}{2} = \frac{...}{2}$

2. (a) $1\frac{2}{3} = \frac{...}{3}$  (b) $2\frac{1}{3} = \frac{...}{3}$  (c) $3\frac{1}{3} = \frac{...}{3}$  (d) $5\frac{2}{3} = \frac{...}{3}$

**EXAMPLE 3**   Change $1\frac{4}{5}$ into a top heavy fraction

$1\frac{4}{5} = \frac{9}{5}$

This tells you to change it into fifths

*Modesto*

*Change into top heavy fractions:*

3. $2\frac{1}{2}$   4. $1\frac{1}{4}$   5. $2\frac{2}{3}$   6. $1\frac{3}{4}$   7. $3\frac{1}{10}$   8. $6\frac{1}{2}$   9. $2\frac{3}{4}$

10. $2\frac{1}{5}$   11. $1\frac{3}{4}$   12. $3\frac{2}{3}$   13. $3\frac{3}{5}$   14. $2\frac{3}{10}$   15. $2\frac{1}{7}$   16. $3\frac{2}{9}$

17. $1\frac{7}{8}$   18. $2\frac{2}{5}$   19. $5\frac{2}{7}$   20. $3\frac{3}{8}$

• *Check your answers.*

A POW GUIDE            Let's Sort Out Fractions, Decimals **EXTRA** and Percentages

## D5: Top heavy fractions –> whole or mixed numbers  Level 4

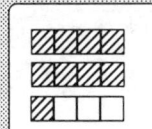

$\frac{8}{4} = 2$ (whole number)    $\frac{9}{4} = 2\frac{1}{4}$ (mixed number)   *Pow*

Change into whole numbers:
1. $\frac{6}{3}$   2. $\frac{10}{2}$   3. $\frac{15}{3}$   4. $\frac{12}{4}$   5. $\frac{14}{2}$   6. $\frac{20}{5}$

Change into mixed numbers:
7. $\frac{8}{3}$   8. $\frac{11}{2}$   9. $\frac{7}{3}$   10. $\frac{9}{4}$   11. $\frac{17}{3}$   12. $\frac{11}{8}$

Change into whole numbers or mixed numbers:
13. $\frac{12}{4}$   14. $\frac{13}{4}$   15. $\frac{16}{5}$   16. $\frac{11}{4}$   17. $\frac{18}{5}$   18. $\frac{22}{6}$
19. $\frac{10}{3}$   20. $\frac{26}{5}$   21. $\frac{12}{10}$   22. $\frac{9}{8}$   23. $\frac{17}{7}$   24. $\frac{13}{6}$

• *Check your answers.*

## D6: Adding up to whole numbers

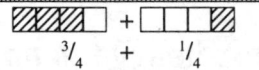

EXAMPLE 4    $\frac{3}{4} + \frac{1}{4} = 1$

Copy and complete the word statements:
1. $\frac{2}{3} + \frac{1}{3} = \ldots$   2. $\frac{3}{5} + \ldots = 1$
3. $\frac{5}{7} + \ldots = 1$   4. $\frac{7}{8} + \ldots = 1$
5. $\frac{3}{10} + \ldots = 1$   6. $\frac{4}{6} + \ldots = 1$
7. $\frac{10}{12} + \ldots = 1$   8. $\frac{14}{16} + \ldots = 1$

|  | $\frac{3}{4} + \frac{1}{4} = 1$ |  | $1 - \frac{1}{4} = \frac{3}{4}$ |
|---|---|---|---|
| so | $1\frac{3}{4} + \frac{1}{4} = 2$ |  | $2 - 1\frac{3}{4} = \frac{1}{4}$ |
| and | $3\frac{3}{4} + 1\frac{1}{4} = 5$ |  | $5 - 3\frac{1}{4} = 1\frac{3}{4}$ |

Copy and complete:
9. $1\frac{1}{4} + \ldots = 2$   10. $1\frac{1}{3} + \frac{2}{3} = \ldots$
11. $2\frac{3}{4} + \ldots = 3$   12. $2\frac{3}{5} + \ldots = 3$
13. $1\frac{3}{8} + \ldots = 2$   14. $2 - \frac{1}{4} = \ldots$
15. $2 - 1\frac{1}{3} = \ldots$   16. $3 - 2\frac{1}{5} = \ldots$
17. $3 - 2\frac{1}{8} = \ldots$   18. $2 - \ldots = \frac{1}{3}$

• *Check your answers.*

A POW GUIDE    page 178    *Let's Sort Out Fractions, Decimals* **EXTRA** *and Percentages*

## D7: Sharing sums with fraction answers

**Level 4**

EXAMPLE 5   Share 9 cakes between 4 people.

$$9 \div 4 = \frac{9}{4} = 2\frac{1}{4}$$

1. Share 5 cakes between 2 people.
2. Share 11 cakes between 3 people.
3. Share 7 chocolate bars between 4 people.
4. Share 8 chocolate bars between 5 people.
5. Share 13 packets of sweets between 4 people.

*Work out:*
6. $15 \div 2$   7. $6 \div 5$   8. $4 \div 3$   9. $9 \div 8$   10. $11 \div 4$
11. $9 \div 5$   12. $10 \div 3$   13. $13 \div 10$   14. $5 \div 3$   15. $17 \div 10$
16. $8 \div 3$   17. $14 \div 5$   18. $16 \div 3$   19. $21 \div 4$   20. $27 \div 10$

• Check your answers.

### Star Challenge ⭐⭐

16-17 correct = 2 stars
12-15 correct = 1 star

1. How many halves in $3\frac{1}{2}$ ?   2. How many quarters in $2\frac{3}{4}$ ?

*Change into whole numbers or mixed numbers:*
3. $\frac{7}{3}$   4. $\frac{13}{4}$   5. $\frac{12}{3}$   6. $\frac{11}{5}$   7. $\frac{31}{6}$

*Change into top heavy fractions:*
8. $3\frac{2}{3}$   9. $1\frac{3}{7}$   10. $4\frac{3}{4}$   11. $2\frac{3}{5}$   12. $2\frac{5}{8}$

*Work out:*
13. $13 \div 5$   14. $17 \div 4$   15. $19 \div 10$   16. $23 \div 7$   17. $41 \div 8$

• Your teacher has the answers to these.

### EXTENSION

## E1: Halves of fractions

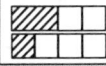

This shows that $\frac{1}{2}$ of $\frac{1}{2} = \frac{1}{4}$

*Copy and complete:*
1. 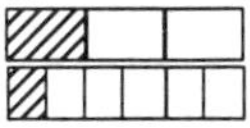 $\frac{1}{2}$ of $\frac{1}{3}$ = ......   2. $\frac{1}{2}$ of $\frac{1}{4}$ = ......

*Work out:*  3. $\frac{1}{2}$ of $\frac{1}{5}$ = ......   4. $\frac{1}{2}$ of $\frac{1}{6}$ = ......   5. $\frac{1}{2}$ of $\frac{1}{7}$ = ......
6. $\frac{1}{2}$ of $\frac{1}{8}$ = ......   7. $\frac{1}{2}$ of $\frac{1}{10}$ = ......   8. $\frac{1}{2}$ of $\frac{1}{20}$ = ......

$\frac{1}{2}$ of $\frac{1}{2} = \frac{1}{4}$   so   $2 \times \frac{1}{4} = \frac{1}{2}$

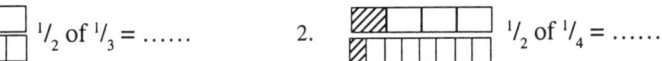

*Work out:*   9. $2 \times \frac{1}{6}$ = ......   10. $2 \times \frac{1}{8}$ = ......   11. $2 \times \frac{1}{10}$ = ......

• Check your answers.

A POW GUIDE       page 179       Let's Sort Out Fractions, Decimals and Percentages   **EXTRA**

# Section 4: Number lines

**Level 4**

In this section you will work with decimals and fractions on number lines.

**DEVELOPMENT**

## D1: Half and quarter jumps

1. Complete this number line.  CHECK YOUR ANSWERS.

2. Start at 0. Make alternate jumps of $\frac{1}{2}, \frac{1}{4}, \frac{1}{2}, \frac{1}{4}, \ldots$ Label the end of each jump.

3. Start at 0. Make alternate jumps of $\frac{1}{2}, \frac{3}{4}, \frac{1}{2}, \frac{3}{4}, \ldots$ Label the end of each jump.

4. What number is halfway between ...

   | A | B | C |
   |---|---|---|
   | 3 and 4 ......... | $2\frac{1}{2}$ and 3 ......... | $3\frac{1}{2}$ and $4\frac{1}{2}$ ......... |
   | D | E | F |
   | $3\frac{3}{4}$ and $4\frac{3}{4}$ ......... | $1\frac{1}{4}$ and $2\frac{3}{4}$ ......... | $2\frac{3}{4}$ and $4\frac{1}{4}$ ......... |

5. Complete this number line (fractions and decimals).  CHECK YOUR ANSWERS.

6. Start at 0.25. Make alternate jumps of 0.5, 0.25, 0.5,... ($\frac{1}{2}, \frac{1}{4}, \frac{1}{2} \ldots$)
   Label the end of each jump.

7. Start at 0. Make alternate jumps of 0.5, 0.75, 0.5,... ($\frac{1}{2}, \frac{3}{4}, \frac{1}{2} \ldots$)
   Label the end of each jump.

8. What number is halfway between ...

   | A | B | C |
   |---|---|---|
   | 2 and 5 ......... | 1.5 and 3.5 ......... | 2.25 and 3.25 ......... |
   | D | E | F |
   | 0.25 and 1.75 ......... | 1.75 and 2.75 ......... | 1.5 and 4 ......... |

   • Check your answers.

A POW GUIDE   page 180   Let's Sort Out Fractions, Decimals and Percentages   **EXTRA**

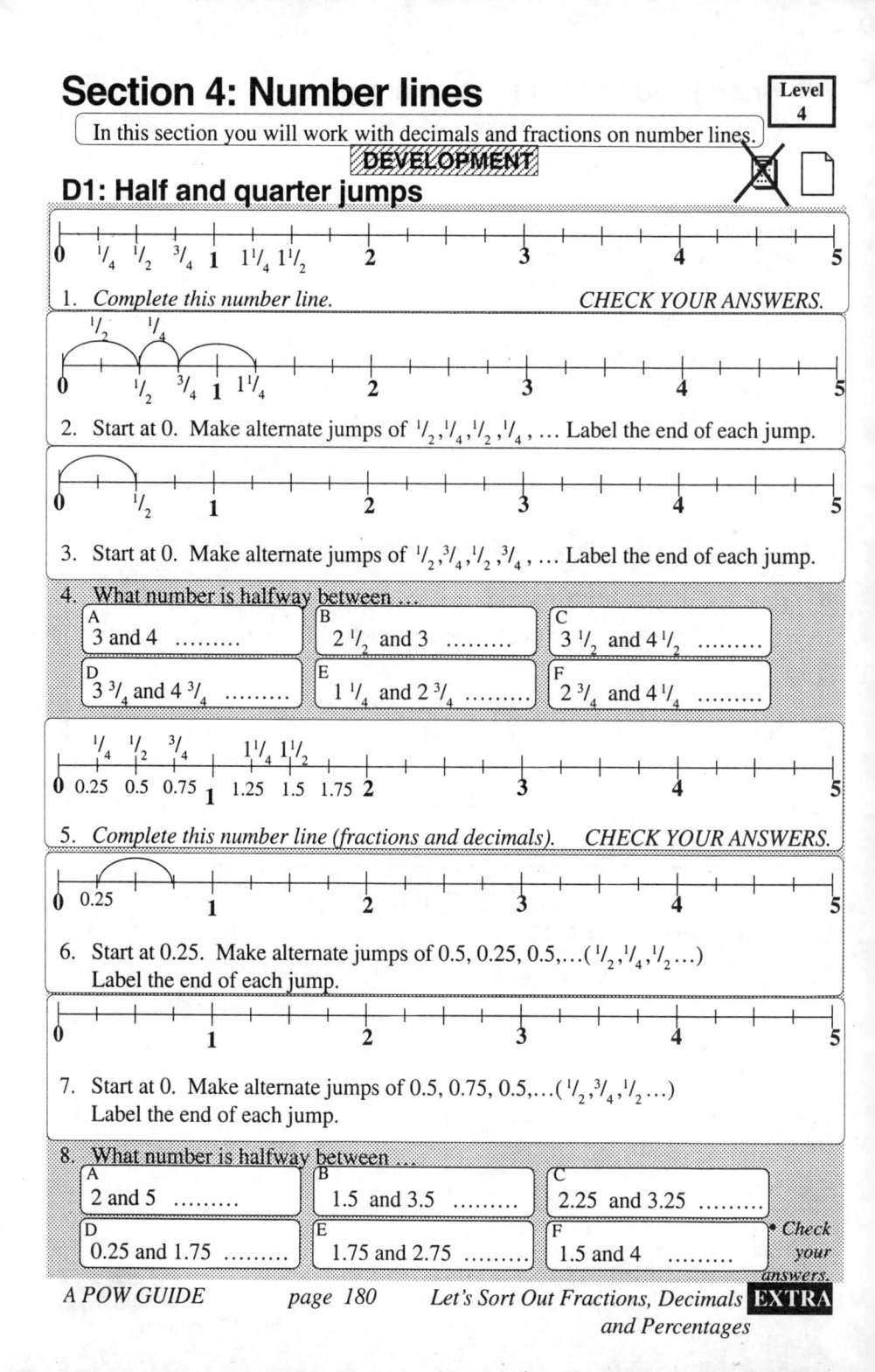

# D2: Adding the same amount each time

Level 4

## Task 1: Adding 0.5

1. $\boxed{7}$ + $\boxed{0.5}$ = $\boxed{7.5}$   $\boxed{7.5}$ + $\boxed{0.5}$ = $\boxed{8.}$

   7   7.5   8   ...   ...   ...   ...   ...   ...   14

2. Add 0.5 each time.

   23   ...   ...   ...   ...   ...   ...   30

3. Add 0.5 each time WITHOUT A CALCULATOR.

   4   ...   ...   ...   ...   ...   ...
   
   • Check answers.

## Task 2: Adding 0.1

4. Add 0.1 each time.

   5   ...   ...   ...   ...   ...

5. Add 0.1 each time.

   9   ...   ...   ...   ...   ...

6. Add 0.1 each time WITHOUT A CALCULATOR.

   3   ...   ...   ...   ...   ...

7. Add 0.1 each time WITHOUT A CALCULATOR.

   12   ...   ...   ...   ...   ...

• Check answers.

## Star Challenge 4

15-16 correct = 1 star

Write in the number that each arrow points to.

1   ...   ...   1.6   ...   2

5   ...   ...   ...   ...   6

8   ...   ...   ...   ...   9

12   ...   ...   ...   ...   13

*A POW GUIDE*   page 181   *Let's Sort Out Fractions, Decimals and Percentages*   **EXTRA**

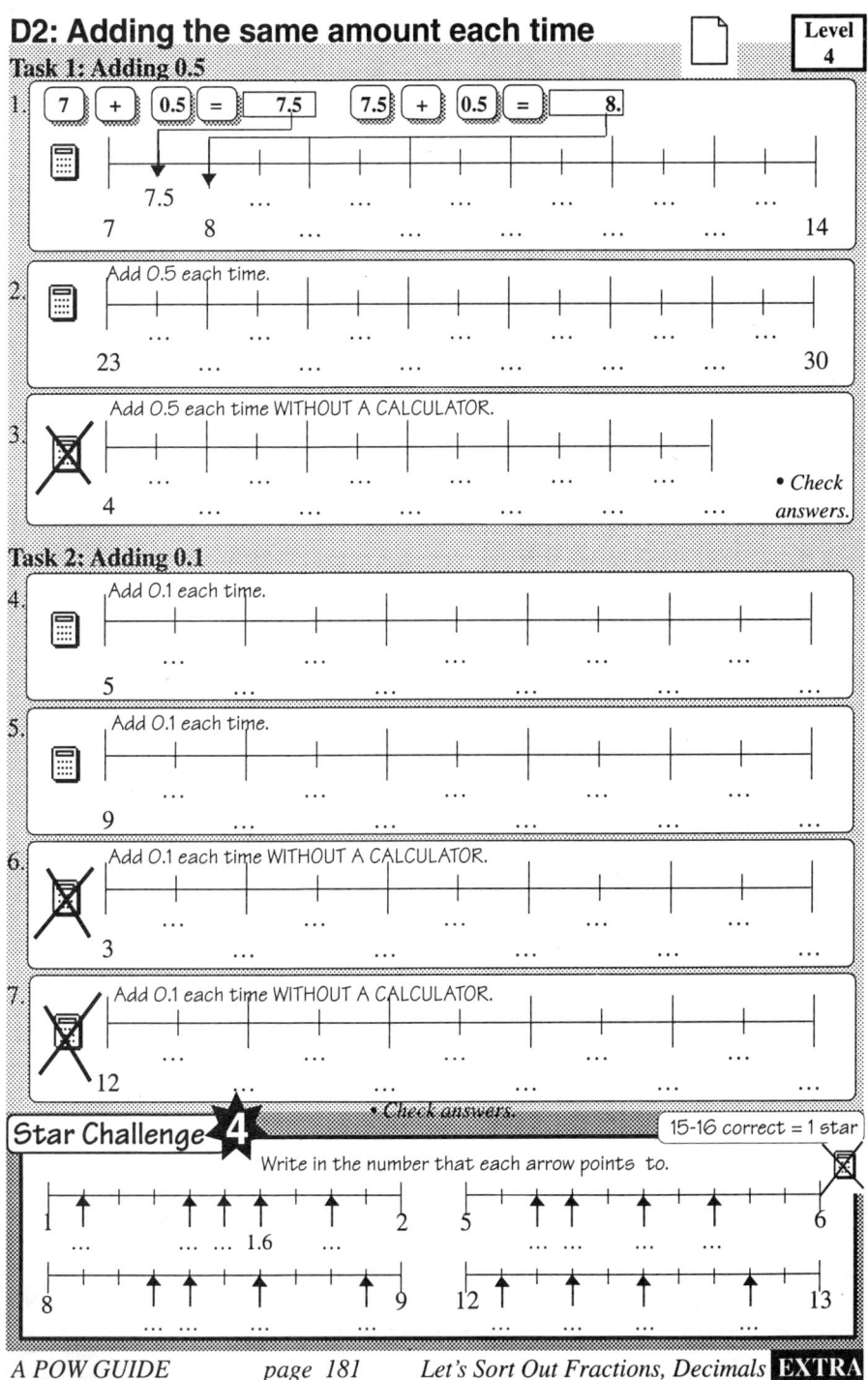

# D3: Getting closer in

Level 4

## Task 1: Adding 0.05

1. Add 0.05 each time.
   3   3.05   ......   ......   ......   ......   ......   ......   ......   ......

2. Add 0.05 each time.
   7   ......   ......   ......   ......   ......   ......   ......   ......   ......

3. Add 0.05 each time WITHOUT A CALCULATOR.
   2   ......   ......   ......   ......   ......   ......   ......   ......   ......

• Check answers.

## Task 2: Adding 0.01

4. Add 0.01 each time.
   3.6   ......   ......   ......   ......   ......   ......   ......   ......   ......

5. Add 0.01 each time.
   4.3   ......   ......   ......   ......   ......   ......   ......   ......   ......

6. Add 0.01 each time.
   6.8   ......   ......   ......   ......   ......   ......   ......   ......   ......

7. Add 0.01 each time WITHOUT A CALCULATOR.
   2.7   ......   ......   ......   ......   ......   ......   ......   ......   ......

8. Add 0.01 each time WITHOUT A CALCULATOR.
   8.61   ......   ......   ......   ......   ......   ......   ......   ......   ......

• Check answers.

## Star Challenge

All correct = 1 star

1. *Fill in the missing numbers:*

   4   4.1   4.2   4.3   4.4   4.5   4.6   4.7   4.8   4.9   5
         4.15        ......        ......        ......   ......

2. *Fill in the missing numbers:*

   7.5   7.51   ......        ......              ......   ......   7.6

3. *Tick the correct one:*

   | 1.2 ↑ 1.3 |   | 1.2      ↑1.3 |
   |    1.21   |   |        1.21   |

   | 1.2    1.3 |
   |   1.21    |

4. *Two of these are correct. Tick them.*

   | 2.6  ↑  2.7 |   | 2.6      ↑2.7 |
   |    2.65     |   |       2.68    |

   | 2.6    2.7 |
   |  ↑        |
   |  2.66     |

A POW GUIDE   page 182   *Let's Sort Out Fractions, Decimals and Percentages*   **EXTRA**

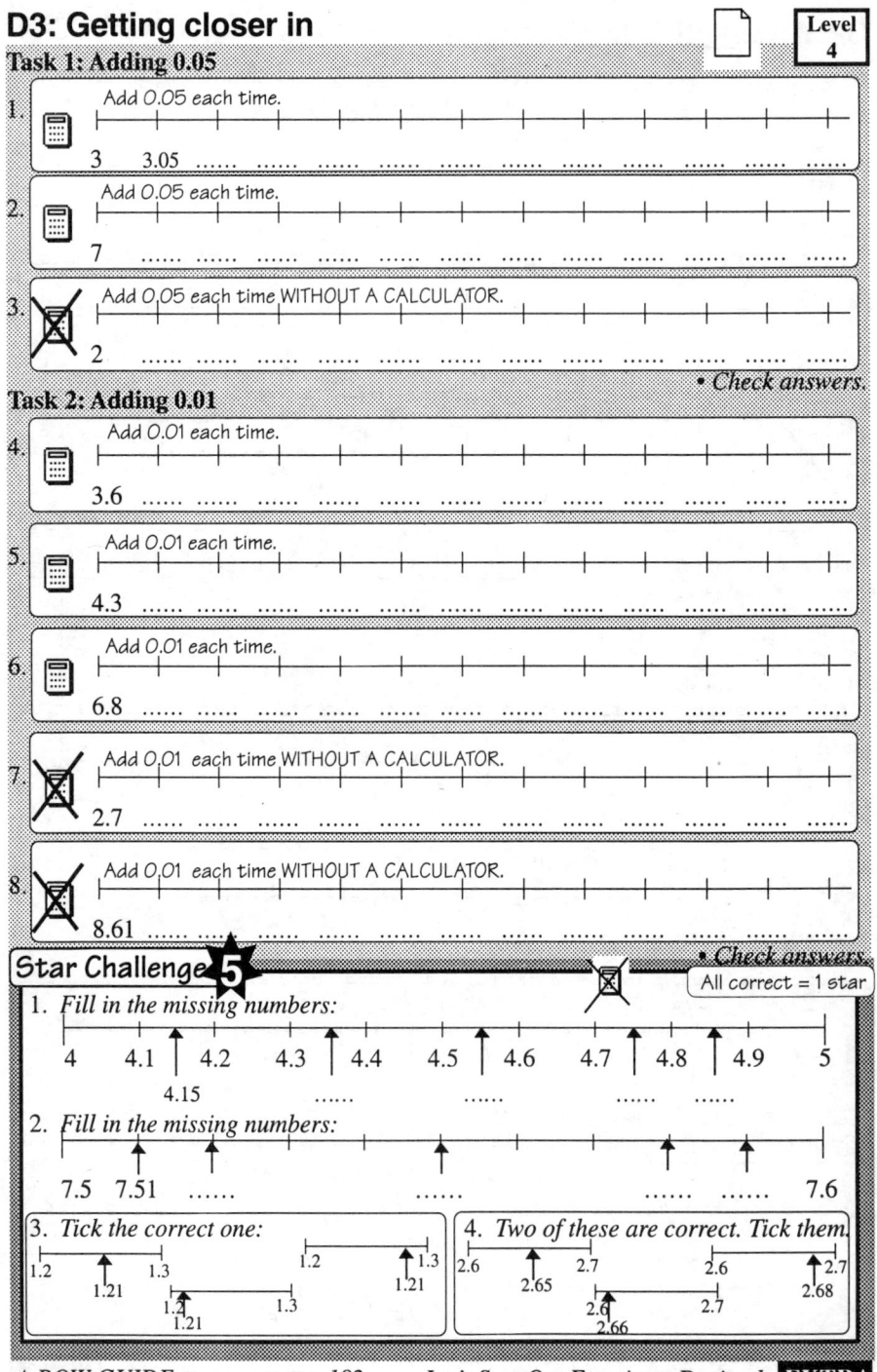

# Section 5: Decimals

In this section you will:
- change decimals into fractions;
- look at equivalent ways of writing decimals;
- x and ÷ decimals by 10, 100, 1000;
- x decimals by whole numbers.

Level 4

## DEVELOPMENT

*The decimal point separates the whole numbers from the bits of numbers.*

## D1: Equivalent decimals and fractions

| Thousands T | Hundreds H | Tens T | Units U | . | tenths t | hundredths h | thousandths th | | |
|---|---|---|---|---|---|---|---|---|---|
| | | | 0 | . | 3 | | | = | $3/10$ |
| | | | 0 | . | 0 | 6 | | = | $6/100$ |
| | | | 0 | . | 0 | 0 | 7 | = | $7/1000$ |
| | | | 3 | . | 9 | | | = | $3\,9/10$ |
| | | | 0 | . | 4 | 8 | | = | $48/100$ |

*Copy and complete this table:*

| Thousands T | Hundreds H | Tens T | Units U | . | tenths t | hundredths h | thousandths th | | |
|---|---|---|---|---|---|---|---|---|---|
| | | | 0 | . | 8 | | | = | ...... |
| | | | 0 | . | 0 | 2 | | = | ...... |
| | | | 0 | . | 0 | 0 | 4 | = | ...... |
| | | | 3 | . | 7 | | | = | ...... |
| | | | 0 | . | 2 | 9 | | = | ...... |
| | | | 0 | . | | | | = | $3/100$ |
| | | | 0 | . | | | | = | $8/10$ |
| | | | 0 | . | | | | = | $3/1000$ |
| | | | 0 | . | | | | = | $61/100$ |
| | | | 0 | . | | | | = | $54/1000$ |
| | | | ... | . | | | | = | $1\,7/10$ |
| | | | | . | | | | = | $2^{13}/100$ |
| | | | | . | | | | = | $6\,72/1000$ |
| | | | 0 | . | 0 | 2 | 8 | = | ...... |
| | | 2 | 3 | . | 7 | 4 | 9 | = | ...... |

*Just keep looking at the labels at the top of the table.*

Hukka

A POW GUIDE        page 183        Let's Sort Out Fractions, Decimals and Percentages  **EXTRA**

# D2: Equivalent ways of writing decimals

**Level 4**

There are often several ways of writing decimal numbers.
When checking answers, you need to know if your answer is right.
For example
    Your answer is  0.40     The answer in the book is  0.4
                    These answers are equivalent.
                    So, you are right.

**Type 1:**  37.0 = 37. = 37 most usual form

All of these mean 3 tens and 7 units

*Copy and complete this table:*

| Book answer (most usual form) | Your answer | ✓ if your answer is right  ✗ if your answer is wrong |
|---|---|---|
| 23 | 23.0 | |
| 41 | 041 | |
| 58 | 5.8 | |
| 27 | 27.00 | |
| 4 | 4. | |

*Pow*

**Type 2:**  0.40 = 0.400 = 00.4 = .4 = 0.4 most usual form

All of these mean 4 tenths

*Copy and complete this table:*

| Book answer (most usual form) | Your answer | ✓ if your answer is right  ✗ if your answer is wrong |
|---|---|---|
| 0.5 | .5 | |
| 0.31 | 00.31 | |
| 0.62 | 0.620 | |
| 0.3 | 0.300 | |
| 0.35 | .305 | |
| 0.46 | .460 | |
| 0.74 | 7.4 | |
| 0.125 | .125 | |
| 0.258 | 00.258 | |

*Driller*

Why do we write 0.2 instead of just .2 ?

If we just write .2, it is very easy to miss the decimal and read the number as 2. The 0 before the point (0.2) draws attention to the decimal point.

## Types 1 & 2 mixed

*Copy and complete this table:*

| Book answer (most usual form) | Your answer | ✓ if your answer is right  ✗ if your answer is wrong |
|---|---|---|
| 27 | 27. | |
| 2.7 | .27 | |
| 3.8 | 03.8 | |
| 0.02 | .02 | |
| 10 | 10.0 | |
| 6 | 6.0 | |

*Icee*   • Check your answers.

A POW GUIDE          page 184          Let's Sort Out Fractions, Decimals and Percentages  **EXTRA**

## D3: Multiplying decimals by 10, 100, 1000 — Level 5

To multiply any number by 10,
you move the decimal point ONE PLACE to the RIGHT.

1.58 x 10 = 15.8     2.3 x 10 = 23. or 23 or 23.0

**Remember:** if the decimal point is not shown, it is at the end of the number.

**Set A:** *Copy and complete:*
1. 3.15 x 10 = ......
2. 61.357 x 10 = ......
3. 2.005 x 10 = ......
4. 3.02 x 10 = ......
5. 5.6 x 10 = ......
6. 24.56 x 10 = ......
7. 5.034 x 10 = ......
8. 37.12 x 10 = ......
9. 1.25 x 10 = ......

• Check your answers.

0.04 x 10 = 00.4 or 0.4     0.43 x 10 = 04.3 or 4.3

**Set B:** *Copy and complete:*
1. 0.1 x 10 = ......
2. 0.25 x 10 = ......
3. 1.003 x 10 = ......
4. 0.02 x 10 = ......
5. 0.003 x 10 = ......
6. 0.105 x 10 = ......
7. 0.048 x 10 = ......
8. 2.001 x 10 = ......
9. 0.035 x 10 = ......

• Check your answers.

To multiply any number by **10**, you move the decimal point **1 PLACE to the RIGHT**.
To multiply any number by **100**, you move the decimal point **2 PLACES to the RIGHT**.
To multiply any number by **1000**, you move the decimal point **3 PLACES to the RIGHT**.

2.25 x 100 = 225. or 225     2.6 x 1000 = 2600. or 2600

If there are not enough digits to move the correct number of decimal places, add some 0s to the original decimal.

**Set C:** *Copy and complete:*
1. 3.41 x 10 = ......
2. 3.41 x 100 = ......
3. 3.41 x 1000 = ......
4. 0.356 x 10 = ......
5. 0.356 x 100 = ......
6. 0.356 x 1000 = ......
7. 11.17 x 10 = ......
8. 11.17 x 100 = ......
9. 11.17 x 1000 = ......
10. 3.01 x 100 = ......
11. 4.5 x 1000 = ......
12. 19.7 x 100 = ......

• Check your answers

### Star Challenge 6

*Copy and complete:*     14-15 correct = 1 star

1. 2.95 x 10 = ......
2. 0.03 x 100 = ......
3. 1.01 x 10 = ......
4. 0.05 x 1000 = ......
5. 1.2 x 100 = ......
6. 5.75 x 100 = ......
7. 4.8 x 1000 = ......
8. 0.02 x 10 = ......
9. 3.03 x 1000 = ......
10. 12.5 x 100 = ......
11. 16.1 x 10 = ......
12. 12.6 x 100 = ......
13. 0.07 x 100 = ......
14. 3.2 x 1000 = ......
15. 0.01 x 100 = ......

• Your teacher has the answers to these.

A POW GUIDE     Let's Sort Out Fractions, Decimals **EXTRA** and Percentages

## D4: Dividing decimals by 10, 100, 1000

**Level 5**

To divide any number by **10**,
you move the decimal point **ONE PLACE to the LEFT**.

$12.5 \div 10 = 1.25$  $\qquad$ $3 \div 10 = .3$ or $0.3$

**Remember:** if the decimal point is not shown, it is at the end of the number.

**Set D:** *Copy and complete:*

1. $12.14 \div 10 = \ldots$
2. $5 \div 10 = \ldots$
3. $0.013 \div 10 = \ldots$
4. $25 \div 10 = \ldots$
5. $38.1 \div 10 = \ldots$
6. $0.015 \div 10 = \ldots$
7. $21.375 \div 10 = \ldots$
8. $3.1 \div 10 = \ldots$
9. $352 \div 10 = \ldots$

• *Check your answers.*

To divide any number by **10**, you move the decimal point **1 PLACE to the LEFT**.
To divide any number by **100**, you move the decimal point **2 PLACES to the LEFT**.
To divide any number by **1000**, you move the decimal point **3 PLACES to the LEFT**.

$2 \div 100 = 002 \div 100 = 0.02$  $\quad$ If there are not enough digits to move the correct number of decimal places, add some 0s in front of the original number.

**Set E:** *Copy and complete:*

1. $6 \div 10 = \ldots$
2. $35.21 \div 100 = \ldots$
3. $0.06 \div 10 = \ldots$
4. $0.04 \div 100 = \ldots$
5. $35.6 \div 100 = \ldots$
6. $0.52 \div 100 = \ldots$
7. $371 \div 100 = \ldots$
8. $15 \div 1000 = \ldots$
9. $2.04 \div 1000 = \ldots$
10. $0.2 \div 100 = \ldots$
11. $0.8 \div 10 = \ldots$
12. $7.5 \div 100 = \ldots$

• *Check your answers.*

**Set F:** *Copy and complete:*

1. $14.35 \div 10 = \ldots$
2. $2.35 \div 100 = \ldots$
3. $0.021 \div 10 = \ldots$
4. $354 \div 100 = \ldots$
5. $23.6 \div 1000 = \ldots$
6. $6.71 \div 100 = \ldots$
7. $0.356 \div 10 = \ldots$
8. $5 \div 100 = \ldots$
9. $0.01 \div 10 = \ldots$

• *Check your answers*

### Star Challenge 7

*Copy and complete:*

All correct = 1 star

1. $2.95 \div 10 = \ldots$
2. $4.9 \div 100 = \ldots$
3. $0.03 \div 10 = \ldots$
4. $7 \div 100 = \ldots$
5. $15.9 \div 1000 = \ldots$
6. $1.06 \div 100 = \ldots$
7. $0.472 \div 10 = \ldots$
8. $9 \div 100 = \ldots$
9. $6.8 \div 100 = \ldots$

• *Your teacher has the answers to these.*

### Star Challenge 8

*Copy and complete:*

11-12 correct = 2 stars
9-10 correct = 1 star

1. $6.3 \times 10 = \ldots$
2. $6.3 \div 10 = \ldots$
3. $0.05 \times 10 = \ldots$
4. $4.5 \div 100 = \ldots$
5. $0.01 \times 1000 = \ldots$
6. $27 \div 10 = \ldots$
7. $17.95 \div 100 = \ldots$
8. $16 \div 10 = \ldots$
9. $19.3 \times 100 = \ldots$
10. $0.7 \times 100 = \ldots$
11. $0.6 \div 100 = \ldots$
12. $13.8 \div 100 = \ldots$

• *Your teacher has the answers to these.*

A POW GUIDE $\qquad$ *Let's Sort Out Fractions, Decimals and Percentages* **EXTRA**

## D6: Multiplying decimals by whole numbers  *Level 5*

```
    5          0.5  ← 1 decimal place in question means
  x 3         x 3      ┐ 1 decimal place in answer
  ---         ----
   15          1.5
```
↑ units in answer go under units in question   ↑↑ Put decimal point in answer under the decimal point in the question

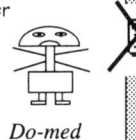

*Do-med*

*Copy and complete:*

1. 0.2     2. 0.4     3. 0.5     4. 0.6     5. 0.3
   x 3        x 2        x 7        x 8        x 6
   ---        ---        ---        ---        ---
   .          .          .          .          .

6. 1.2     7. 3.4     8. 6.2     9. 7.4    10. 4.9
   x 2        x 3        x 7        x 5        x 3
   ---        ---        ---        ---        ---
   .          .          .          .          .

• Check your answers with a calculator.

```
   0.05  ← 2 decimal places in question       1.13
   x 3        means                           x 5
   -----                                      -----
   0.15  ← 2 decimal places in answer         5.65
```
*Icee*

*Copy and complete:*

11. 4.71    12. 3.12    13. 0.45    14. 0.03    15. 0.21
    x 2         x 2         x 3         x 4         x 8
    ---         ---         ---         ---         ---
    .           .           .           .           .

16. 0.32    17. 6.42    18. 3.17    19. 0.48    20. 3.05
    x 7         x 6         x 5         x 4         x 8
    ---         ---         ---         ---         ---
    .           .           .           .           .

• Check your answers.

## P1: Multiplying decimals practice

*Set out sums as in D6*
**CHECK YOUR ANSWERS AT THE END OF EACH BATCH.**

**Batch A:** *Work out:*
1. 0.3 x 7    2. 0.2 x 8    3. 1.3 x 5    4. 6.1 x 7    5. 3.4 x 9
6. 2.1 x 8    7. 0.03 x 2   8. 3.01 x 6   9. 4.12 x 5   10. 6.1 x 3

A POW GUIDE     page 187     Let's Sort Out Fractions, Decimals and Percentages **EXTRA**

**Batch B:** *Work out:*
1. 0.6 x 4   2. 1.5 x 7   3. 2.3 x 4   4. 6.2 x 5   5. 3.7 x 2
6. 4.34 x 2   7. 6.71 x 6   8. 5.01 x 4   9. 1.32 x 7   10. 6.04 x 8

**Batch C:** *Work out:*
1. 2.4 x 7   2. 3.5 x 6   3. 4.1 x 9   4. 6.3 x 2   5. 0.4 x 9
6. 0.05 x 5   7. 0.35 x 7   8. 2.05 x 9   9. 7.11 x 8   10. 2.37 x 4

## P2: Mixed practice

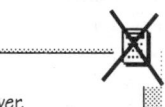

EXAMPLE 6   3.7 x 10 = 37   ← For questions like these, you
   2.54 ÷ 10 = 0.254   ← may just write down the answer.

*Work out:*
1. 7.2 x 10   2. 0.356 x 100   3. 0.02 x 10   4. 34.56 ÷ 10   5. 0.04 x 100
6. 0.03 x 1000   7. 6.1 ÷ 10   8. 0.2 ÷ 10   9. 23.5 ÷ 100   10. 365.7 x 100

EXAMPLE 7   3.7 x 4
$$\begin{array}{r} 3.7 \\ \times 4 \\ \hline 14.8 \end{array}$$
For questions like these, you MUST show the working.

*Work out:*
11. 8.2 x 3   12. 3.15 x 3   13. 5.01 x 7   14. 0.31 x 8   15. 6.23 x 5

Here are a mixture of questions. Work them out. Show your working when like Ex 7.
16. 5.3 x 5   17. 5.3 x 10   18. 5.3 ÷ 10   19. 9.1 x 4   20. 3.75 ÷ 10
21. 8.11 x 6   22. 0.21 x 10   23. 0.41 x 4   24. 0.41 ÷ 10   25. 6.4 x 9

• Check your answers.

### Star Challenge 9

15 correct = 2 stars
12-14 correct = 1 star

*Work these out. Show your working.*
1. 2.6 x 2   2. 2.63 x 10   3. 3.62 x 5   4. 7.14 x 10   5. 18.25 ÷ 10
6. 4.33 x 6   7. 5.19 x 2   8. 0.07 x 2   9. 3.46 x 8   10. 0.2 x 10
11. 7.5 x 5   12. 0.75 x 3   13. 5.75 x 8   14. 5.75 ÷ 10   15. 5.75 x 10

• Your teacher has the answers to these.

### Star Challenge 10

10-12 marks = 1 star

Write each problem as a sum. Work out the answer to the problem.
For each question, there is 1 mark for the working and 2 marks for accuracy.
1. Work out the cost of 5 CDs at £11.55 each.
2. Work out the cost of 10 pairs of trainers at £27.65 each.
3. Work out the cost of 4 goldfish at £1.69 each.
4. The cost of sending a parcel is £5.90.
   Work out the cost of sending 6 of these parcels.

• Your teacher has the answers to these.

# Section 6: Adding and subtracting decimals

In this section you will add and subtract decimals given to 1 or 2 d.p.

**Level 4**

### DEVELOPMENT

## D1: Simple + and − decimals given to 1 d.p.

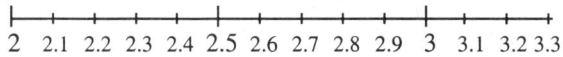

```
2  2.1  2.2  2.3  2.4  2.5  2.6  2.7  2.8  2.9  3  3.1  3.2  3.3
```

*Copy and complete:*
1. 2.1 + 0.3 = ...
2. 2.8 − 0.5 = ...
3. 2.7 + 0.4 = ...
4. 2.3 − 0.2 = ...
5. 2.5 + 0.5 = ...
6. 2.8 + 0.3 = ...
7. 2.7 + ... = 3
8. 3.2 − ... = 3

• Check your answers.

9. 0.7 + 0.3 = ...
10. 1 − 0.2 = ...
11. 3.4 + 0.5 = ...
12. 4.2 − 0.2 = ...
13. 5.9 + 0.4 = ...
14. 2 − 0.9 = ...
15. 5.7 + ... = 6
16. 4.1 − ... = 3.9

• Check your answers.

## D2: Adding and subtracting by stacking

| Type 1: both numbers to 1 d.p. | | Type 2: both numbers to 2 d.p. | |
|---|---|---|---|
| 2.3<br>+ 1.8<br>―――<br>4.1<br>  1 | 3.5<br>− 1.4<br>―――<br>2.1 | 3.24<br>+ 2.05<br>―――<br>5.29 | $4\cancel{5}.^14\,5$<br>− 0.64<br>―――<br>4.81 |

Stack the decimal points underneath each other!

Stack each of these sums as above. Work out the answers.
1. 2.7 + 1.2
2. 7.54 + 2.35
3. 5.4 − 1.3
4. 4.2 − 1.4
5. 2.5 + 3.5
6. 8.25 + 1.08
7. 6.47 − 2.51
8. 12.4 − 3.5

• Check your answers.

## D3: Adding and subtracting a mixture of decimals

| Type 3: 1 d.p. and 2 d.p. | | Type 4: whole numbers and decimals | |
|---|---|---|---|
| 5 + 2.4 = ?<br>5.0<br>+ 2.4<br>―――<br>7.4 | 0.75 − 0.6 = ?<br>0.75<br>− 0.60<br>―――<br>0.15 | 3 + 2.12 = ?<br>3.00<br>+ 2.12<br>―――<br>5.12 | 5 − 1.4 = ?<br>$4\cancel{5}.^10$<br>− 1.4<br>―――<br>3.6 |

Add extra zeros to make both numbers have the same number of decimal places!

*Work out the answers.*
1. 3.6 + 7
2. 2.4 + 1.12
3. 3.66 − 1.2
4. 7.69 − 2.5
5. 3.75 + 4.6
6. 4.35 − 2
7. 0.85 − 0.41
8. 1.2 − 0.75

• Check your answers.

### Star Challenge

15-16 correct = 2 stars
12-14 correct = 1 star

*Work out the answers.*
1. 4.5 + 0.2
2. 6.4 + 3.13
3. 6.95 − 2.5
4. 4.05 + 3.25
5. 6.3 + 2.65
6. 1 − 0.6
7. 4 + 3.1 + 0.5
8. 3.2 − 0.4
9. 2.7 + 4.6
10. 3 + 5.2
11. 2 − 1.2
12. 6.7 + 0.3
13. 7.54 + 1.4
14. 5.5 − 2.25
15. 2.9 + 4 + 1.4
16. 5 − 3.25

• Your teacher has the answers.

A POW GUIDE     page 189     Let's Sort Out Fractions, Decimals and Percentages   **EXTRA**

# Section 7: Fractions and percentages of shapes

In this section you will use fractions and percentages to describe parts of a whole.

**DEVELOPMENT**

Level 4

## D1: The sack race

Copy and complete this table:

| Fraction of race completed | $1/2$ | $3/4$ | $9/10$ | $1/3$ | $1/4$ | $2/5$ |
|---|---|---|---|---|---|---|
| Name | | | | | | |

• Check your answers.

## D2: What percentage is shaded?

10% shaded    25% shaded    50% shaded    75% shaded

Look at each shape below. Estimate what percentage of each is shaded. Use the diagrams above to help you.

1.    2.    3.    4.

• Check your answers.

Look at each shape below. Estimate what percentage of each is shaded.

5.    6.    7.    8.

• Check your answers.

## D3: Percentages of circles

Estimate the percentage of each circle that has been shaded:

1.    2.    3.    4.

5.    6.    7.    8.

• Check your answers.

A POW GUIDE     page 190     Let's Sort Out Fractions, Decimals and Percentages  **EXTRA**

# Section 8: Fractions and percentages of amounts

In this section you will work out fraction and percentage parts of quantities.

**DEVELOPMENT**

## D1: Halves of amounts     Level 5

EXAMPLE 8

56 ÷ 2

$\frac{1}{2}$ of £56 = £28     Pow

Copy and complete these. You may use a calculator.

1. $\frac{1}{2}$ of £12 = ......
2. $\frac{1}{2}$ of £36 = ......
3. $\frac{1}{2}$ of £58 = ......
4. $\frac{1}{2}$ of 44p = ......
5. $\frac{1}{2}$ of £30 = ......
6. $\frac{1}{2}$ of 16p = ......
7. $\frac{1}{2}$ of £78 = ......
8. $\frac{1}{2}$ of £104 = ......
9. $\frac{1}{2}$ of 28p = ......
10. $\frac{1}{2}$ of £54 = ......
11. $\frac{1}{2}$ of 72p = ......
12. $\frac{1}{2}$ of £46 = ......

• Check your answers.

Copy and complete these. You may NOT use a calculator.

13. $\frac{1}{2}$ of £6 = ......
14. $\frac{1}{2}$ of 8p = ......
15. $\frac{1}{2}$ of 14 sweets = ......
16. $\frac{1}{2}$ of £10 = ......
17. $\frac{1}{2}$ of 18 girls = ......
18. $\frac{1}{2}$ of £50 = ......
19. $\frac{1}{2}$ of £20 = ......
20. $\frac{1}{2}$ of 16p = ......
21. $\frac{1}{2}$ of £100 = ......

• Check your answers.

## D2: Simple fractions of amounts

EXAMPLE 9

39 ÷ 3

$\frac{1}{3}$ of £39 = £13

EXAMPLE 10

56 ÷ 4

$\frac{1}{4}$ of £56 = £14

Copy and complete these. You may use a calculator.

1. $\frac{1}{3}$ of £21 = ......
2. $\frac{1}{3}$ of £66 = ......
3. $\frac{1}{3}$ of 72p = ......
4. $\frac{1}{3}$ of £57 = ......
5. $\frac{1}{4}$ of 80p = ......
6. $\frac{1}{4}$ of £64 = ......
7. $\frac{1}{4}$ of £96 = ......
8. $\frac{1}{4}$ of £240 = ......
9. $\frac{1}{3}$ of 99p = ......
10. $\frac{1}{4}$ of 32p = ......
11. $\frac{1}{3}$ of 69p = ......
12. $\frac{1}{4}$ of £72 = ......

• Check your answers.

Copy and complete these. You may use a calculator.

13. $\frac{1}{2}$ of £48 = ......
14. $\frac{1}{3}$ of £48 = ......
15. $\frac{1}{4}$ of £48 = ......
16. $\frac{1}{6}$ of £48 = ......
17. $\frac{1}{5}$ of £25 = ......
18. $\frac{1}{4}$ of 20p = ......
19. $\frac{1}{6}$ of £24 = ......
20. $\frac{1}{3}$ of 21p = ......
21. $\frac{1}{8}$ of 16 = ......
22. $\frac{1}{9}$ of 45 = ......
23. $\frac{1}{5}$ of 75 = ......
24. $\frac{1}{10}$ of £50 = ......

• Check your answers.

Copy and complete these. You may NOT use a calculator.

25. $\frac{1}{3}$ of £21 = ......
26. $\frac{1}{8}$ of 40 = ......
27. $\frac{1}{4}$ of £12 = ......
28. $\frac{1}{10}$ of 70 = ......
29. $\frac{1}{5}$ of 30p = ......
30. $\frac{1}{7}$ of £14 = ......

A POW GUIDE     page 191     Let's Sort Out Fractions, Decimals **EXTRA**
and Percentages

## D3: More complex fractions of amounts

**Level 5**

**EXAMPLE 11** Work out $^3/_4$ of £20

$^1/_4$ of £20 = £5

$^3/_4 = 3 \times ^1/_4$

So $^3/_4$ of £20 = 3 × £5 = £15

Work out $^1/_4$ then multiply by 3

*Chyps*

1. (a) Work out $^1/_4$ of £8 (b) Work out $^3/_4$ of £8
2. (a) Work out $^1/_3$ of £21 (b) Work out $^2/_3$ of £21
3. (a) Work out $^1/_5$ of £10 (b) Work out $^2/_5$ of £10
4. (a) Work out $^1/_6$ of £18 (b) Work out $^5/_6$ of £18
5. (a) Work out $^1/_{10}$ of £30 (b) Work out $^7/_{10}$ of £30

Some people find counters help with these.

• *Check your answers.*

*Copy and complete:*

6. $^3/_4$ of 12 = ...... 9. $^1/_3$ of £15 = ...... 12. $^1/_5$ of 30 = ......
7. $^3/_4$ of 100 = ...... 10. $^2/_3$ of £15 = ...... 13. $^2/_5$ of 30 = ......
8. $^3/_4$ of 16 = ...... 11. $^2/_3$ of 24 = ...... 14. $^4/_5$ of £30 = ......

• *Check your answers.*

*Copy and complete:*

15. $^2/_3$ of £60 = ...... 17. $^3/_5$ of 50 = ...... 19. $^5/_6$ of 24 = ......
16. $^2/_7$ of £21 = ...... 18. $^3/_8$ of £16 = ...... 20. $^5/_8$ of 40 = ......

• *Check your answers.*

## D4: Using fractions to find percentages of amounts

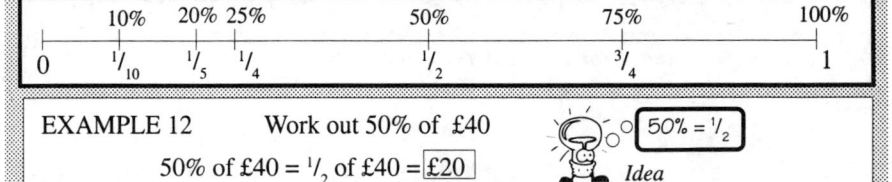

```
     10%  20% 25%        50%            75%              100%
0    1/10  1/5 1/4        1/2            3/4               1
```

**EXAMPLE 12** Work out 50% of £40

50% of £40 = $^1/_2$ of £40 = £20

50% = $^1/_2$

*Idea*

*Copy and complete:*

1. 50% of £20 = ...... 2. 50% of £14 = ...... 3. 50% of £5 = ......

25% = $^1/_4$

4. 25% of 12p = ...... 6. 25% of 48 = ...... 8. 25% of £20 = ......
5. 25% of 60p = ...... 7. 25% of £200 = ...... 9. 25% of £120 = ......

20% = $^1/_5$

10. 20% of 15p = ...... 12. 20% of £10 = ...... 14. 20% of £20 = ......
11. 20% of £25 = ...... 13. 20% of £50 = ...... 15. 20% of £35 = ......

16. 50% of 40p = ...... 18. 25% of 40p = ...... 20. 20% of 40p = ......
17. 25% of £80 = ...... 19. 20% of £45 = ......

• *Check your answers.*

*A POW GUIDE* page 192 *Let's Sort Out Fractions, Decimals and Percentages* **EXTRA**

## P1: Practice and extend the ideas

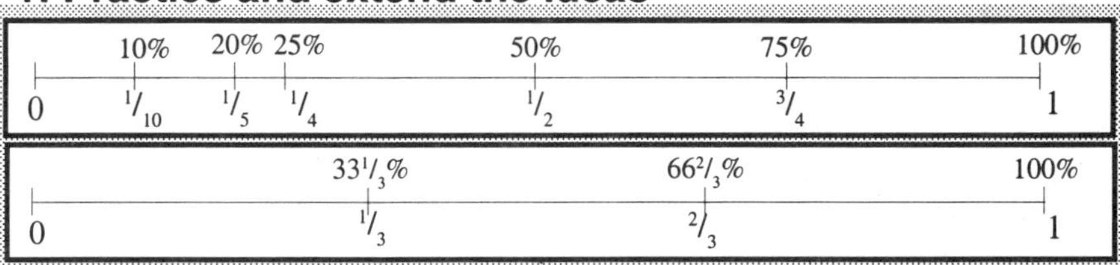

**PRACTICE** — Level 5

[Number line: 0 — 10% (1/10) — 20% (1/5) — 25% (1/4) — 50% (1/2) — 75% (3/4) — 100% (1)]

[Number line: 0 — 33⅓% (1/3) — 66⅔% (2/3) — 100% (1)]

*Copy and complete:* [ 33⅓% = 1/3 ]   [ 66⅔% = 2/3 ]

1. 33⅓% of £21 = ......
2. 33⅓% of £15 = ......
3. 33⅓% of 12p = ......
4. 66⅔% of £30 = ......
5. 66⅔% of 12p = ......
6. 66⅔% of £9 = ......

• Check your answers.

7. 25% of 60p = ......
8. 75% of 60p = ......
9. 50% of £25 = ......
10. 33⅓% of 15p = ......
11. 50% of £16 = ......
12. 20% of £55 = ......
13. 20% of £120 = ......
14. 25% of £16 = ......
15. 33⅓% of £36 = ......

• Check your answers.

## P2: Reducing prices

**CD £12** — SALE PRICE 25% off
1. How much is the price reduced by?
2. What is the sale price of the CD?

**Trainers £60** — SALE PRICE 33⅓% off
3. What is the reduction?
4. What is the sale price?

**TV £200** — SALE PRICE 10% discount
5. What is the discount?
6. What is the new price?

**Video tape £10** — SALE PRICE Price reduced by 10%
7. What is the reduction?
8. What is the sale price?

**Shirt £20** — SALE PRICE 1/4 off
9. What is the reduction?
10. What is the sale price?

**Jacket £20** — SALE PRICE 20% off
11. What is the price reduced by?
12. What is the sale price?

• Check your answers.

A POW GUIDE        page 193        Let's Sort Out Fractions, Decimals and Percentages     **EXTRA**

# P3: Tricks with $1/_{10}$ and 10%

Level 5

EXAMPLE 13  Work out $3/_{10}$ of £20
$1/_{10}$ of £20 = £2    So   $3/_{10}$ of £20 = 3 x £2 = £6

Remember :
$1/_{10}$ of £40 = £4
$1/_{10}$ of £400 = £40
$1/_{10}$ of £4000 = £400

Copy and complete these. You may NOT use a calculator.

1. $1/_{10}$ of £20 = ......
2. $1/_{10}$ of £50 = ......
3. $1/_{10}$ of £200 = ......
4. $3/_{10}$ of £200 = ......
5. $4/_{10}$ of £20 = ......
6. $7/_{10}$ of £40 = ......
7. $3/_{10}$ of £300 = ......
8. $8/_{10}$ of £200 = ......
9. $2/_{10}$ of £50 = ......
10. $9/_{10}$ of £300 = ......
11. $2/_{10}$ of £70 = ......
12. $9/_{10}$ of £1000 = ......

• Check your answers.

$10\% = 1/_{10}$

13. (a) Work out 10% of £30     (b) 20% = 2 x 10% so work out 20% of £30
14. (a) Work out 10% of £500    (b) Work out 30% of £500
15. (a) Work out 10% of £60     (b) Work out 70% of £60
16. (a) Work out 10% of £80     (b) Work out 5% of £80

HINT: Work out (b) from (a)

Copy and complete these. You may NOT use a calculator.         Spottee

17. 10% of £120 = ......
18. 20% of £120 = ......
19. 40% of £120 = ......
20. 60% of £600 = ......
21. 30% of £70 = ......
22. 90% of £40 = ......
23. 20% of £150 = ......
24. 70% of £300 = ......
25. 60% of £2000 = ......

• Check your answers.

## Star Challenge 12-12

15-16 correct = 2 stars
12-14 correct = 1 star

Work these out WITHOUT a calculator.

1. $1/_2$ of 44p
2. $1/_4$ of £200
3. $1/_3$ of 60p
4. $2/_3$ of 60p
5. 25% of 40p
6. 10% of 70p
7. $3/_4$ of £100
8. 20% of £15
9. $2/_3$ of £60
10. $5/_8$ of £24
11. $3/_5$ of £50
12. $7/_{10}$ of £50
13. 75% of 60p
14. 10% of 60p
15. 90% of 30p
16. $33 1/_3$% of 60p

• Your teacher will need to mark these.

## Star Challenge 13-13

16-18 correct = 2 stars
12-15 correct = 1 star

Work these out. You may use a calculator.

1. $1/_2$ of £2.74
2. $1/_3$ of £375
3. $1/_4$ of £6.72
4. $3/_4$ of £82
5. 50% of £12.98
6. 25% of £6.40
7. $2/_3$ of £120
8. $33 1/_3$% of £72
9. 20% of £1.75
10. $3/_8$ of £4
11. $2/_5$ of £2.70
12. 30% of £40
13. 5% of £2
14. 20% of £3.40
15. $2/_3$ of 87p
16. 25% of £6.48

17.  CD  £11.40   Sale price is 25% off the normal price.
(a) What is the reduction ?  (b) What is the sale price ?

• Your teacher will need to mark these.

A POW GUIDE        page 194        Let's Sort Out Fractions, Decimals and Percentages   EXTRA

# Section 9: Making equivalent fractions

**Level 6**

In this section you will create equivalent fractions.

### DEVELOPMENT

## D1: A rule for making equivalent fractions

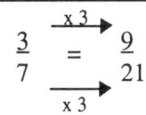

$$\frac{3}{7} \xrightarrow{\times 3} \frac{9}{21}$$
(×3 on bottom)

Equivalent fractions can be made by multiplying the top and bottom by the same number.

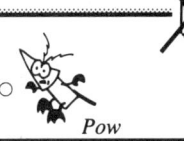

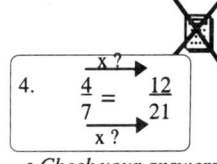

Pow

*Copy and complete:*

1. $\frac{2}{5} \xrightarrow{\times 3} \frac{}{\phantom{0}}$ (×3)
2. $\frac{1}{4} \xrightarrow{\times 2} \frac{}{\phantom{0}}$ (×?)
3. $\frac{2}{3} \xrightarrow{\times 5} \frac{}{\phantom{0}}$ (×?)
4. $\frac{5}{6} \xrightarrow{\times 2} \frac{}{\phantom{0}}$ (×?)

5. $\frac{2}{3} \xrightarrow{\times 3} \frac{}{\phantom{0}}$ (×3)
6. $\frac{1}{2} \xrightarrow{\times 2} \frac{}{\phantom{0}}$ (×?)
7. $\frac{1}{3} \xrightarrow{\times 4} \frac{}{\phantom{0}}$ (×4)
8. $\frac{1}{4} \xrightarrow{\times 5} \frac{}{\phantom{0}}$ (×5)

• *Check your answers.*

## D2: What do you multiply by?

*Copy and complete:*

1. $\frac{1}{2} \xrightarrow{\times ?} \frac{4}{8}$ (×?)
2. $\frac{2}{5} \xrightarrow{\times ?} \frac{6}{15}$ (×?)
3. $\frac{3}{10} \xrightarrow{\times ?} \frac{30}{100}$ (×?)
4. $\frac{4}{7} \xrightarrow{\times ?} \frac{12}{21}$ (×?)

• *Check your answers.*

### PRACTICE

## P1: Making equivalent fractions

**Batch A:** *Copy and complete:*

1. $\frac{3}{4} \xrightarrow{\times ?} \frac{6}{\phantom{0}}$ (×?)
2. $\frac{2}{3} \xrightarrow{\times ?} \frac{}{9}$ (×?)
3. $\frac{3}{5} \xrightarrow{\times ?} \frac{30}{\phantom{0}}$ (×?)
4. $\frac{2}{3} \xrightarrow{\times ?} \frac{}{6}$ (×?)

5. $\frac{2}{8} \xrightarrow{\times ?} \frac{}{16}$
6. $\frac{4}{5} = \frac{8}{\phantom{0}}$
7. $\frac{1}{3} = \frac{}{15}$
8. $\frac{4}{9} = \frac{}{18}$

9. $\frac{2}{7} = \frac{6}{\phantom{0}}$
10. $\frac{5}{6} = \frac{}{24}$
11. $\frac{5}{10} = \frac{20}{\phantom{0}}$
12. $\frac{7}{8} = \frac{21}{\phantom{0}}$

**Batch B:** *Copy and complete:*

1. $\frac{2}{7} = \frac{8}{\phantom{0}}$
2. $\frac{2}{5} = \frac{}{10}$
3. $\frac{3}{8} = \frac{15}{\phantom{0}}$
4. $\frac{6}{13} = \frac{}{26}$

5. $\frac{5}{8} = \frac{}{24}$
6. $\frac{6}{10} = \frac{24}{\phantom{0}}$
7. $\frac{1}{9} = \frac{}{36}$
8. $\frac{2}{11} = \frac{}{33}$

9. $\frac{4}{15} = \frac{8}{\phantom{0}}$
10. $\frac{5}{8} = \frac{}{40}$
11. $\frac{7}{9} = \frac{21}{\phantom{0}}$
12. $\frac{5}{12} = \frac{15}{\phantom{0}}$

• *Check answers.*

A POW GUIDE   page 195   *Let's Sort Out Fractions, Decimals and Percentages*   **EXTRA**

## DEVELOPMENT

## D3: Using division to make equivalent fractions

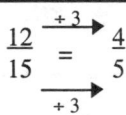

Level 6

$$\frac{12}{15} \xrightarrow{\div 3}_{\div 3} = \frac{4}{5}$$

Equivalent fractions can also be made by DIVIDING the top and bottom by the same number.

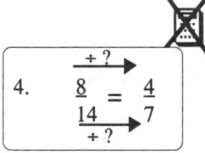

Pow

Copy and complete:

1. $\dfrac{8}{10} \xrightarrow{\div 2}_{\div 2} = \dfrac{\_}{\_}$
2. $\dfrac{6}{9} \xrightarrow{\div 3}_{\div 3} = \dfrac{\_}{\_}$
3. $\dfrac{12}{15} \xrightarrow{\div 3}_{\div 3} = \dfrac{\_}{\_}$
4. $\dfrac{5}{25} \xrightarrow{\div 5}_{\div 5} = \dfrac{\_}{\_}$

5. $\dfrac{6}{15} \xrightarrow{\div 3}_{\div 3} = \dfrac{\_}{\_}$
6. $\dfrac{4}{8} \xrightarrow{\div 2}_{\div ?} = \dfrac{\_}{\_}$
7. $\dfrac{4}{12} \xrightarrow{\div 4}_{\div 4} = \dfrac{\_}{\_}$
8. $\dfrac{10}{15} \xrightarrow{\div 5}_{\div 5} = \dfrac{\_}{\_}$

• Check your answers.

## D4: What do you divide by?

Copy and complete:

1. $\dfrac{3}{9} \xrightarrow{\div ?}_{\div ?} = \dfrac{1}{3}$
2. $\dfrac{4}{20} \xrightarrow{\div ?}_{\div ?} = \dfrac{1}{5}$
3. $\dfrac{15}{20} \xrightarrow{\div ?}_{\div ?} = \dfrac{3}{4}$
4. $\dfrac{8}{14} \xrightarrow{\div ?}_{\div ?} = \dfrac{4}{7}$

• Check your answers.

## PRACTICE

## P2: Making equivalent fractions using division

Copy and complete:

1. $\dfrac{6}{10} = \dfrac{3}{\_}$
2. $\dfrac{9}{12} = \dfrac{\_}{4}$
3. $\dfrac{6}{18} = \dfrac{1}{\_}$
4. $\dfrac{8}{12} = \dfrac{\_}{3}$

5. $\dfrac{4}{16} = \dfrac{\_}{8}$
6. $\dfrac{40}{50} = \dfrac{4}{\_}$
7. $\dfrac{7}{21} = \dfrac{\_}{3}$
8. $\dfrac{4}{14} = \dfrac{\_}{7}$

9. $\dfrac{6}{16} = \dfrac{3}{\_}$
10. $\dfrac{8}{24} = \dfrac{\_}{3}$
11. $\dfrac{5}{10} = \dfrac{1}{\_}$
12. $\dfrac{77}{88} = \dfrac{7}{\_}$

• Check your answers.

## P3: Mixed practice

Copy and complete:

1. $\dfrac{8}{20} = \dfrac{2}{\_}$
2. $\dfrac{4}{7} = \dfrac{\_}{35}$
3. $\dfrac{9}{18} = \dfrac{1}{\_}$
4. $\dfrac{15}{20} = \dfrac{\_}{4}$

5. $\dfrac{4}{20} = \dfrac{\_}{5}$
6. $\dfrac{2}{3} = \dfrac{14}{\_}$
7. $\dfrac{2}{9} = \dfrac{\_}{36}$
8. $\dfrac{1}{25} = \dfrac{\_}{75}$

9. $\dfrac{3}{8} = \dfrac{12}{\_}$
10. $\dfrac{8}{32} = \dfrac{\_}{4}$
11. $\dfrac{5}{11} = \dfrac{15}{\_}$
12. $\dfrac{13}{15} = \dfrac{26}{\_}$

• Check your answers.

A POW GUIDE    page 196    Let's Sort Out Fractions, Decimals **EXTRA** and Percentages

# P4: Equivalent fraction spiders

*The fractions in each spider are equivalent. Complete each spider.*

Level 6

1. Spider with center $\frac{2}{3}$: $\frac{8}{\square}$ (×4), $\frac{24}{\square}$, $\frac{33}{\square}$ (×11), $\frac{\square}{21}$, $\frac{\square}{48}$, $\frac{20}{\square}$, $\frac{\square}{18}$, $\frac{30}{\square}$

2. Spider with center $\frac{2}{5}$: $\frac{4}{\square}$, $\frac{20}{\square}$, $\frac{35}{\square}$, $\frac{\square}{20}$, $\frac{\square}{30}$, $\frac{18}{\square}$, $\frac{\square}{15}$, $\frac{\square}{10}$

3. Spider with center $\frac{3}{4}$: $\frac{9}{\square}$, $\frac{12}{\square}$, $\frac{\square}{32}$, $\frac{\square}{40}$, $\frac{\square}{48}$, $\frac{21}{\square}$, $\frac{33}{\square}$, $\frac{\square}{20}$

*You can put in x... boxes if you want.*

4. Spider with center $\frac{5}{8}$: $\frac{10}{\square}$, $\frac{20}{\square}$, $\frac{\square}{40}$, $\frac{\square}{80}$, $\frac{\square}{72}$, $\frac{35}{\square}$, $\frac{\square}{48}$, $\frac{15}{\square}$

5. Spider with center $\frac{3}{7}$: $\frac{9}{\square}$, $\frac{24}{\square}$, $\frac{\square}{49}$, $\frac{\square}{63}$, $\frac{\square}{35}$, $\frac{18}{\square}$, $\frac{\square}{14}$, $\frac{30}{\square}$

6. Spider with center $\frac{4}{9}$: $\frac{8}{\square}$, $\frac{20}{\square}$, $\frac{\square}{36}$, $\frac{\square}{27}$, $\frac{\square}{99}$, $\frac{24}{\square}$, $\frac{\square}{81}$, $\frac{40}{\square}$

• *Check answers.*

## Star Challenge 14

14-16 correct = 1 star

Spider with center $\frac{1}{3}$: $\frac{12}{\square}$, $\frac{4}{\square}$, $\frac{\square}{15}$, $\frac{\square}{33}$, $\frac{\square}{6}$, $\frac{7}{\square}$, $\frac{6}{\square}$, $\frac{\square}{9}$

*The fractions in each spider are equivalent. Complete each spider.*

Spider with center $\frac{3}{5}$: $\frac{24}{\square}$, $\frac{15}{\square}$, $\frac{\square}{30}$, $\frac{\square}{20}$, $\frac{\square}{45}$, $\frac{6}{\square}$, $\frac{\square}{60}$, $\frac{9}{\square}$

A POW GUIDE     page 197     *Let's Sort Out Fractions, Decimals and Percentages*   **EXTRA**

# Section 10: From decimals to fractions  [Level 6]

In this section you will:
- write fractions in simplest form;
- change decimals to fractions or mixed numbers;
- change decimals to fractions or mixed numbers in simplest form;

**DEVELOPMENT**

## D1: Simplifying fractions

The **simplest form** of a fraction is the equivalent fraction with the smallest possible top and bottom.

$\frac{18}{24} = ?$

What divides into both 18 and 24?

6 divides into both 18 and 24

$\frac{3}{4}$ is the simplest form of $\frac{18}{24}$

So $\frac{18}{24} = \frac{3}{4}$

Sureshot

Find the simplest form of each of these fractions:
1. $\frac{15}{20}$   2. $\frac{7}{14}$   3. $\frac{9}{15}$   4. $\frac{21}{35}$   5. $\frac{10}{15}$   6. $\frac{9}{24}$   7. $\frac{20}{25}$   8. $\frac{10}{30}$

• Check your answers.

**PRACTICE**

## P1: Simplifying practice

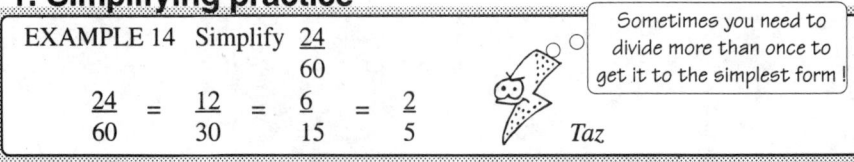

EXAMPLE 14   Simplify $\frac{24}{60}$

$\frac{24}{60} = \frac{12}{30} = \frac{6}{15} = \frac{2}{5}$

Sometimes you need to divide more than once to get it to the simplest form!

Taz

Find the simplest form of each of these fractions. Show all working.

**Batch A:** 1. $\frac{8}{24}$   2. $\frac{20}{40}$   3. $\frac{15}{50}$   4. $\frac{24}{36}$   5. $\frac{25}{40}$   6. $\frac{12}{48}$   • Check answers

**Batch B:** 1. $\frac{7}{21}$   2. $\frac{12}{15}$   3. $\frac{25}{100}$   4. $\frac{9}{36}$   5. $\frac{12}{18}$   6. $\frac{16}{48}$   • Check answers

### Star Challenge

10-12 correct = 2 stars
7-9 correct = 1 star

Find the simplest form of each fraction. Show all working.

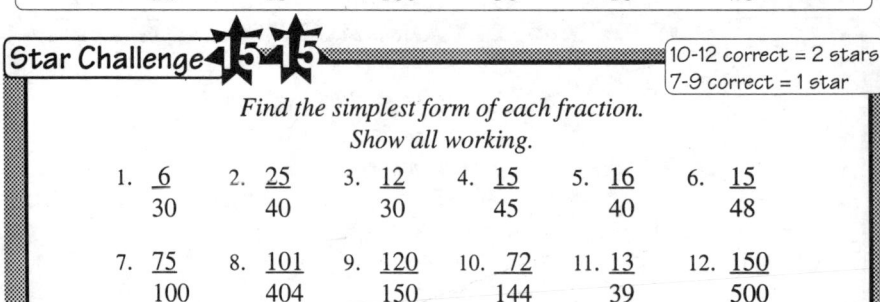

1. $\frac{6}{30}$   2. $\frac{25}{40}$   3. $\frac{12}{30}$   4. $\frac{15}{45}$   5. $\frac{16}{40}$   6. $\frac{15}{48}$

7. $\frac{75}{100}$   8. $\frac{101}{404}$   9. $\frac{120}{150}$   10. $\frac{72}{144}$   11. $\frac{13}{39}$   12. $\frac{150}{500}$

• Your teacher has the answers to these.

A POW GUIDE        page 198        Let's Sort Out Fractions, Decimals and Percentages   **EXTRA**

**DEVELOPMENT** — Level 6

## D2: Changing decimals to fractions or mixed numbers

**EXAMPLE 15**
Q: Write 0.6 as a fraction

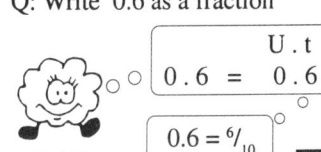

$0.6 = \dfrac{\text{U . t}}{0 . 6}$

$0.6 = {}^6/_{10}$

Lubbly

**EXAMPLE 16**
Q: Write 0.21 as a fraction

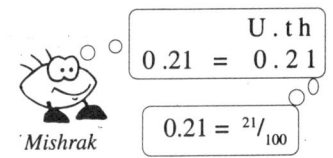

$0.21 = \dfrac{\text{U . t h}}{0 . 2 1}$

$0.21 = {}^{21}/_{100}$

Mishrak

T U . t h th

Write these decimals as fractions:

1. **0.3**  2. **0.07**  3. **0.005**  4. **0.23**  5. **0.013**  6. **0.37**
7. **0.09**  8. **0.036**  9. **0.126**  10. **0.057**  11. **0.001**  12. **0.201**

• Check your answers.

**EXAMPLE 17**
Q: Write 3.17 as a mixed number

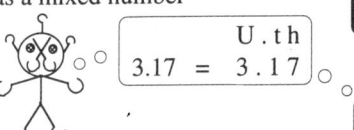

U . t h
3.17 = 3 . 1 7

A **mixed number** is a whole number and a fraction.

$3.17 = 3^{17}/_{100}$

Hukka

Write these decimals as fractions or mixed numbers

13. **2.01**  14. **1.3**  15. **4.31**  16. **3.703**  17. **0.083**  18. **2.67**
19. **6.741**  20. **1.057**  21. **2.05**  22. **7.6**  23. **4.07**  24. **12.309**

• Check your answers.

### Star Challenge 16 — 13-15 correct = 1 star

Copy and complete:

1. 0.3 = ……    2. 0.005 = ……    3. 1.1 = ……
4. …… = $3^1/_{10}$    5. …… = $^{49}/_{100}$    6. …… = $2^3/_{100}$
7. 0.77 = ……    8. 2.39 = ……    9. …… = $3^{13}/_{1000}$
10. …… = $1^{11}/_{100}$    11. 0.049 = ……    12. 6.07 = ……
13. 2.01 = ……    14. …… = $7^{23}/_{100}$    15. 8.035 = ……

• Your teacher has the answers to these.

A POW GUIDE    Let's Sort Out Fractions, Decimals and Percentages    **EXTRA**

## D3: Decimals to fractions in simplest form

**Level 6**

You know how to:
- change decimals into fractions;
- simplify fractions.

*Headbanger*

You are now going to apply both of these techniques.

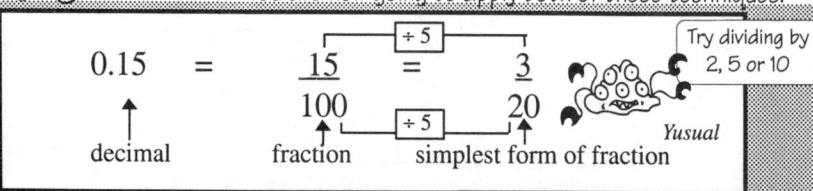

$$0.15 = \frac{15}{100} \xrightarrow{\div 5} \frac{3}{20}$$

↑ decimal    ↑ fraction    ↑ simplest form of fraction

Try dividing by 2, 5 or 10

*Yusual*

**Copy and complete:**

1. $0.35 = \frac{\ldots}{100} = \frac{\ldots}{20}$
2. $0.46 = \frac{\ldots}{100} = \frac{\ldots}{50}$
3. $0.44 = \frac{\ldots}{100} = \frac{\ldots}{20}$
4. $0.28 = \frac{\ldots}{100} = \frac{\ldots}{20}$
5. $0.45 = \frac{\ldots}{100} = \frac{\ldots}{\ldots}$
6. $0.36 = \frac{\ldots}{\ldots} = \frac{\ldots}{\ldots}$
7. $0.75 = \frac{\ldots}{\ldots} = \frac{\ldots}{\ldots}$
8. $0.006 = \frac{\ldots}{\ldots} = \frac{\ldots}{\ldots}$

• Check your answers.

**PRACTICE**

## P2: Decimal to fraction practice

*Write each decimal as a fraction in its simplest form.*
CHECK YOUR ANSWERS AT THE END OF EACH BATCH.

**Batch A:**
1. **0.8**   2. **0.2**   3. **0.06**   4. **0.64**   5. **0.04**   6. **0.85**

**Batch B:**
1. **0.4**   2. **0.08**   3. **0.25**   4. **0.88**   5. **0.6**   6. **0.42**

**Star Challenge 17**

5-6 correct = 1 star

*Write each decimal as a fraction in its simplest form.*

1. **0.04**   2. **0.48**   3. **0.806**   4. **0.68**   5. **0.82**   6. **0.24**

• Your teacher has the answers to these.

A POW GUIDE    page 200    Let's Sort Out Fractions, Decimals and Percentages    **EXTRA**

# Section 11: Equivalent fractions, decimals & %

*In this section you will work with equivalent fractions, decimals and percentages.*

**DEVELOPMENT**

## D1: Equivalent decimals and percentages

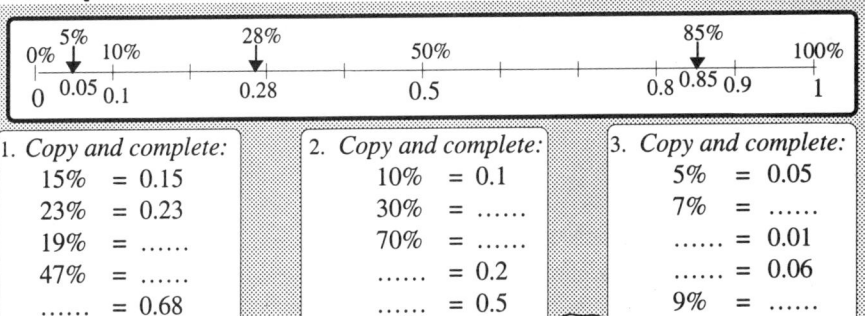

Level 6

```
0%   5%  10%        28%           50%                    85%       100%
|----↓---|-----------↓-------------|----------------------↓---|-------|
0  0.05 0.1         0.28          0.5                   0.8 0.85 0.9  1
```

1. *Copy and complete:*
   15% = 0.15
   23% = 0.23
   19% = ......
   47% = ......
   ...... = 0.68
   ...... = 0.92
   ...... = 0.81

2. *Copy and complete:*
   10% = 0.1
   30% = ......
   70% = ......
   ...... = 0.2
   ...... = 0.5
   
   10% = 1/10 = 0.1

3. *Copy and complete:*
   5% = 0.05
   7% = ......
   ...... = 0.01
   ...... = 0.06
   9% = ......
   
   Think of 5% as 05%

   *Big Edd*

*Copy and complete:*
4. 0.4 = ......%      5. 0.02 = ......%     6. 0.47 = ......%     7. ...... = 13%
8. ...... = 80%       9. ...... = 8%        10. ...... = 18%      11. 0.36 = ......%
12. 0.07 = ......%    13. 0.2 = ......%     14. ...... = 52%      15. 0.9 = ......%

• *Check your answers.*

## D2: Changing fractions into decimals

$$\frac{3}{5} = 3 \div 5 = 0.6$$

Change fractions to decimals by dividing.

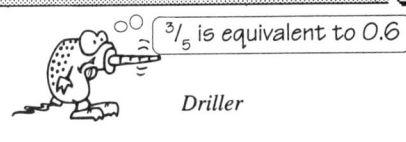

$3/5$ is equivalent to 0.6

*Driller*

*Copy and complete:*

1. $\frac{1}{2}$ = 1 ÷ ... = ...         2. $\frac{4}{5}$ = 4 ÷ ... = ...

3. $\frac{1}{8}$ = ... ÷ ... = ...       4. $\frac{3}{8}$ = ... ÷ ... = ...

5. $\frac{5}{16}$ = ......... = ...      6. $\frac{7}{20}$ = ......... = ...

7. $\frac{13}{50}$ = ......... = ...     8. $\frac{11}{40}$ = ......... = ...

*Change into decimals:*
9. $\frac{1}{4}$   10. $\frac{5}{8}$   11. $\frac{9}{20}$   12. $\frac{3}{4}$   13. $\frac{19}{50}$   14. $\frac{23}{40}$

• *Check your answers.*

A POW GUIDE          *Let's Sort Out Fractions, Decimals and Percentages*   **EXTRA**

## D3: Changing fractions into percentages

**Level 6**

Now we put together the techniques in D1 and D2.

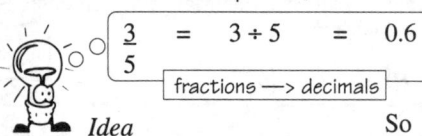

$$\frac{3}{5} = 3 \div 5 = 0.6$$

fractions —> decimals

$$0.6 = 60\%$$

decimals —> percentages

*Idea*

So $^3/_5 = 60\%$

*Change these fractions into percentages:*

1. $\frac{1}{2}$  2. $\frac{3}{4}$  3. $\frac{4}{5}$  4. $\frac{7}{20}$  5. $\frac{6}{15}$  6. $\frac{6}{25}$  7. $\frac{1}{20}$

• *Check your answers.*

**PRACTICE**

## P1: Percentage test marks

*Dwork*

1. Dwork got $^{14}/_{20}$ in the Survival Skills exam. What percentage mark did Dwork get?

2. Sludge got $^{51}/_{60}$ in the Bio-Farming exam. What percentage mark did Sludge get?

*Sludge*

3. *Work out the percentage mark for each of these exams:*

| PGE | Zuk | Modesto | Do-med | Spottee | Gorbag |
|---|---|---|---|---|---|
| Exam | Weapon Repairs | Space Navigation | Electronics | Astronomy | Galacto-speak |
| Mark | $^{36}/_{40}$ | $^{24}/_{30}$ | $^{63}/_{84}$ | $^{36}/_{75}$ | $^{28}/_{80}$ |
| % mark | | | | | |

• *Check your answers.*

### Star Challenge

11 correct = 2 stars
9-10 correct = 1 star

**Fractions**

$\frac{3}{10}$  $\frac{1}{2}$  $\frac{3}{5}$  $\frac{9}{10}$
$\frac{1}{4}$  $\frac{5}{8}$  $\frac{1}{8}$
$\frac{3}{8}$  $\frac{4}{5}$  $\frac{5}{16}$  $\frac{2}{5}$  $\frac{3}{4}$

**Percentages**

75%  37.5%  30%
60%  31.25%  25%
40%  50%  80%
62.5%  12.5%  90%

$^1/_2 = 50\%$   Find eleven more matching pairs of fractions and percentages.

• *Your teacher has the answers to these.*

A POW GUIDE   page 202   *Let's Sort Out Fractions, Decimals and Percentages*   **EXTRA**

# Section 12: Technique review

*In this section you will review the techniques met in this topic.*

Check your answers at the end of each set of problems

## R1: Money sums    Level 3

Write as pounds.      £3.52 + 87p
Use a calculator.   = £3.57 + £0.87
                    = £4.39

*Work out:*
1. £2.53 + 50p   2. £3.20 – 70p   3. £5.05 + 27p – £1.20   4. £2.36 – 85p

## R2: How many ... ?    Level 4
1. How many halves in   (a) 2   (b) $3\frac{1}{2}$
2. How many thirds in   (a) 1   (b) $2\frac{1}{3}$
3. How many quarters in (a) 2   (b) $1\frac{3}{4}$

## R3: Mixed numbers <—> top heavy fractions    Level 4

Change $1\frac{4}{5}$ into a top heavy fraction    $1\frac{4}{5} = \frac{9}{5}$
Modesto    *This tells you to change it into fifths*

*Change into top heavy fractions:*
1. $2\frac{1}{2}$   2. $1\frac{1}{4}$   3. $2\frac{2}{3}$   4. $1\frac{3}{4}$   5. $3\frac{1}{10}$   6. $6\frac{1}{2}$

*Change into whole numbers or mixed numbers:*
7. $\frac{12}{4}$   8. $\frac{13}{4}$   9. $\frac{16}{5}$   10. $\frac{11}{4}$   11. $\frac{18}{5}$   12. $\frac{22}{6}$

## R4: Multiplying and dividing by 10, 100, 1000    Level 5

To multiply any number by **10**, you move the decimal point **1 PLACE to the RIGHT**.
To multiply any number by **100**, you move the decimal point **2 PLACES to the RIGHT**.
To divide any number by **10**, you move the decimal point **1 PLACE to the LEFT**.
To divide any number by **100**, you move the decimal point **2 PLACES to the LEFT**.

*Work out:*
1. 3.5 x 10   2. 41.35 ÷ 10   3. 0.7 x 100   4. 0.6 ÷ 100   5. 2.468 x 100

## R5: Decimal arithmetic    Levels 4&5

*Work out:*
1. 0.3 x 7    2. 4.5 x 3    3. 7.1 x 5
4. 0.3 + 0.5  5. 2.5 – 0.3  6. 3.4 + 1.5
7. 1.9 + 0.4  8. 2.1 – 0.5  9. 2 + 1.5
10. 4.05 + 3.1  11. 5 – 0.4  12. 5 – 3.25

```
 0 . 0 5   ← 2 decimal places in question
   x 3       means
 0 . 1 5   ← 2 decimal places in answer

 4 . 5 0   If needed, add extra zeros to
+3 . 1 5   make both numbers have the
 7 . 6 5   same number of decimal places
```

A POW GUIDE    page 203    *Let's Sort Out Fractions, Decimals and Percentages*  **EXTRA**

## R6: Fractions of amounts

**Level 5**

$\frac{1}{3}$ of £12 = £4   (£12 ÷ 3)
So $\frac{2}{3}$ of £12 = £8   ($\frac{2}{3} = 2 \times \frac{1}{3}$)

*Work out:*
1. $\frac{1}{2}$ of £20   2. $\frac{1}{3}$ of £21   3. $\frac{1}{5}$ of 30p   4. $\frac{1}{10}$ of £200   5. $\frac{1}{6}$ of £30
6. $\frac{1}{4}$ of £40   7. $\frac{3}{4}$ of £40   8. $\frac{2}{3}$ of £12   9. $\frac{3}{10}$ of £50   10. $\frac{3}{5}$ of £20

## R7: Percentages of amounts

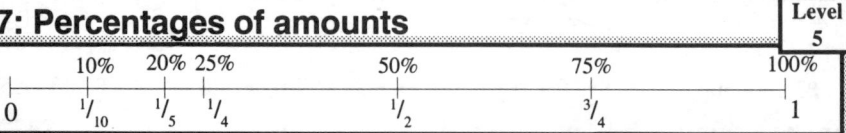

**Level 5**

```
       10%  20% 25%           50%           75%          100%
   |----|---|-|--------------|--------------|-------------|
   0   1/10 1/5 1/4          1/2            3/4           1
```

50% of £40 = $\frac{1}{2}$ of £40 = £20

*Work out:*
1. 50% of £14   2. 25% of 12p   3. 10% of £80   4. 20% of £35   5. 75% of £40

## R8: Equivalent fractions

**Level 6**

$\frac{3}{7} \xrightarrow{\times 3} \frac{9}{21}$  
$\times 3$

Equivalent fractions can be made by multiplying or dividing the top and bottom by the same number.

*Pow*

1. $\frac{2}{7} = \frac{8}{\_}$   2. $\frac{2}{5} = \frac{\_}{10}$   3. $\frac{3}{8} = \frac{15}{\_}$   4. $\frac{6}{\_} = \frac{12}{26}$
5. $\frac{5}{8} = \frac{\_}{24}$   6. $\frac{6}{10} = \frac{24}{\_}$   7. $\frac{1}{9} = \frac{\_}{36}$   8. $\frac{2}{11} = \frac{\_}{33}$

## R9 : Simplest form

**Level 6**

The **simplest form** of a fraction is the equivalent fraction with the smallest whole numbers on the top and bottom.

*Find the simplest form of each of these fractions:*
1. $\frac{15}{30}$   2. $\frac{7}{21}$   3. $\frac{9}{12}$   4. $\frac{14}{35}$   5. $\frac{10}{25}$   6. $\frac{8}{24}$

## R10: Changing decimals to fractions in simplest form

**Level 6**

*Write each decimal as a fraction in its simplest form:*
1. 0.6   2. 0.02   3. 0.75   4. 0.64   5. 0.2   6. 0.62

## R11: Changing fractions to decimals or percentages

**Level 6**

*Change into decimals:*
1. $\frac{3}{5}$   2. $\frac{5}{8}$   3. $\frac{3}{4}$   4. $\frac{7}{20}$   5. $\frac{13}{40}$   6. $\frac{7}{35}$

*Change into percentages:*
7. $\frac{2}{40}$   8. $\frac{3}{10}$   9. $\frac{2}{5}$   10. $\frac{17}{50}$   11. $\frac{24}{60}$   12. $\frac{12}{200}$

A POW GUIDE     page 204     *Let's Sort Out Fractions, Decimals and Percentages*   **EXTRA**

# THE NATIONAL CURRICULUM ...
# ... AND BEYOND ...

*Pow*

# The Geometry of Angle and Shape
## EXTRA

| Level 3 | Level 4 | Level 5 | Level 6 |
|---|---|---|---|
| | | §17 Technique review | |
| | | | §16 Enlargements |
| | | | §15 Quadrilaterals |
| | | §10 Classifying triangles | §14 Parallel and perpendicular lines |
| | | §9 Making accurate drawings | §13 Special triangles |
| | | | §12 Triangles |
| | | §8 Measuring angle sizes | §11 Angle properties |
| | | §7 Estimating angles sizes | |
| | | §6 Classifying angles | |
| | §4 Labelling and measuring lines | §5 Labelling angles | |
| | §3 Congruence | | |
| | §2 Symmetry review | | |
| §1 Classifying shapes | | | |

*A POW GUIDE*        *page 205*

# The Geometry of Angle and Shape
## Section 1: Classifying shapes

In this section you will:
- review some properties of 2-D and 3-D shapes;
- review some words used in geometry.

**DEVELOPMENT**

### D1: Properties of 2-D shapes

Level 3

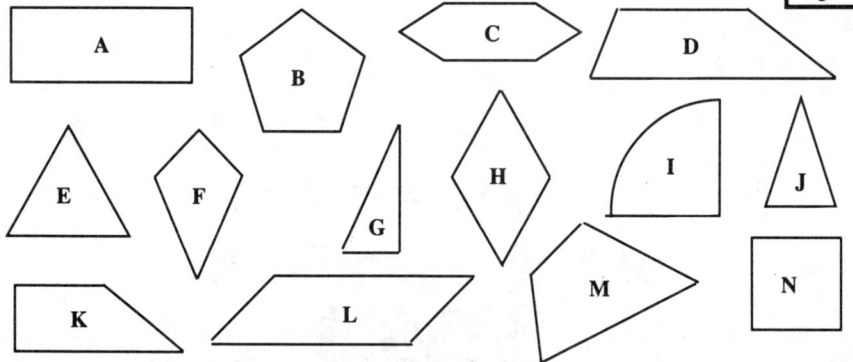

*For each question, list the letters of the shapes that are its answers.*

1. List the shapes that have mirror symmetry.
2. Just <u>one</u> of these shapes has 3 lines of symmetry. Which one is it?
3. Quadrilaterals have 4 sides. A is a quadrilateral. There are 7 other quadrilaterals. List the 7 quadrilaterals.
4. Five of these shapes have at least one right-angle. A is one of them. List the other four shapes with at least one right-angle.

    right-angles

5. Two shapes have 4 right-angles. Which shapes are they?
6. Triangles have 3 sides. Find three triangles.
7. Shapes with all sides equal are called equilateral. Shape H is equilateral. Which other 3 shapes are equilateral?
8. D has one pair of parallel sides. Name one other shape with 1 pair of parallel sides.

    parallel lines

9. L has 2 pairs of parallel sides. Name 3 other shapes with 2 pairs of parallel sides.
10. L has 2 pairs of equal sides. Name four other shapes with 2 pairs of equal sides.
11. Which one shape has 2 pairs of equal sides and none of the sides are parallel?
12. Which two of these shapes have just two equal sides?
13. A polygon is a flat shape with straight sides. Which of these shapes is <u>not</u> a polygon?

• Check your answers.

A POW GUIDE    The Geometry of Angle and Shape **EXTRA**

# D2: Properties of 3-D shapes

Level 3

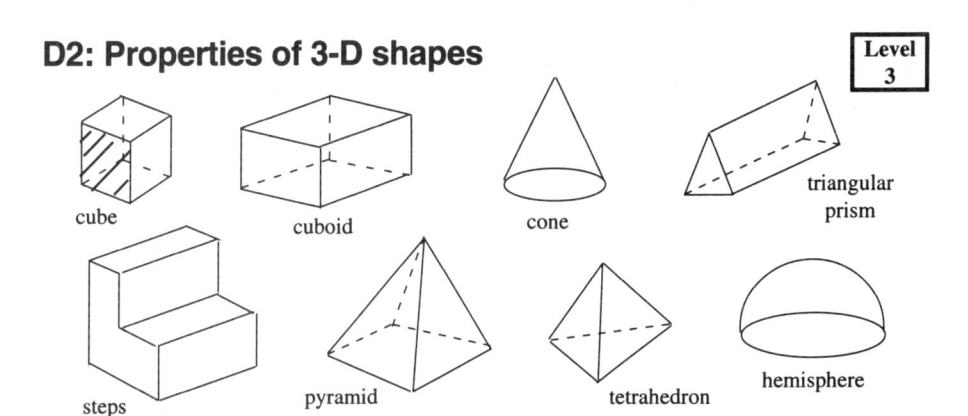

cube, cuboid, cone, triangular prism, steps, pyramid, tetrahedron, hemisphere

*For each question, list the names of the shapes that are its answers.*

1. A cube has 6 faces. One of the faces is shaded. What shape is each face?
2. Which one other shape here has 6 faces?
3. Which two shapes have 5 faces?
4. Three of these shapes have some triangular faces. Which are they?
5. One shape is made from triangular faces only. Which is it?
6. Which two of these shapes have curved faces.
7. Which one shape has faces that are four triangles and a square?
8. The triangular prism has the same cross-section all the way through. If you cut it parallel to an end, the cut face is the same shape as the end. Which three other shapes have the same property?
9. An edge is where two faces meet. A cube has 12 edges. How many edges has
   (a) the cuboid   (b) the triangular prism
   (c) the pyramid  (d) the steps
   (e) the tetrahedron (f) the hemisphere?
10. A vertex (or corner) is where two or more edges meet. A cube has 8 vertices. [1 vertex but many vertices (say as 'ver-ti'sees')] How many vertices has
    (a) the cuboid   (b) the triangular prism
    (c) the pyramid  (d) the steps
    (e) the tetrahedron (f) the hemisphere?
11. For a cube, three edges meet at a vertex? True or false?
12. For a pyramid, three edges meet at a vertex. True or false?
13. A hemisphere has two faces. True or false?
14. The only shape here with a curved face is the hemisphere. True or false?

• *Check your answers.*

A POW GUIDE    page 207    The Geometry of Angle and Shape **EXTRA**

# Section 2: Symmetry review

Level 4

In this section you will review mirror symmetry and rotational symmetry.

**DEVELOPMENT**

## D1: Lines of symmetry

mirror

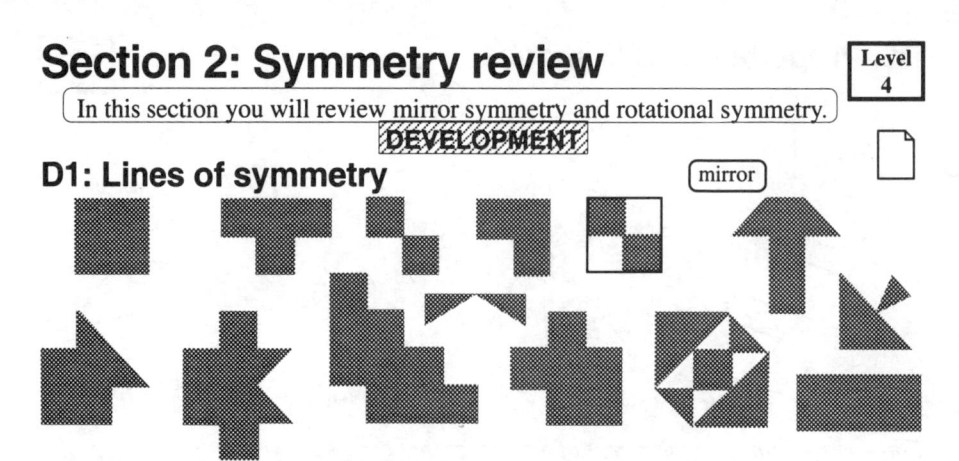

Draw in all the lines of symmetry of each shape.

• *Check your answers.*

## D2: Creating mirror symmetry

mirror

*Reflect each shape in the mirror line to create a symmetric pattern.*

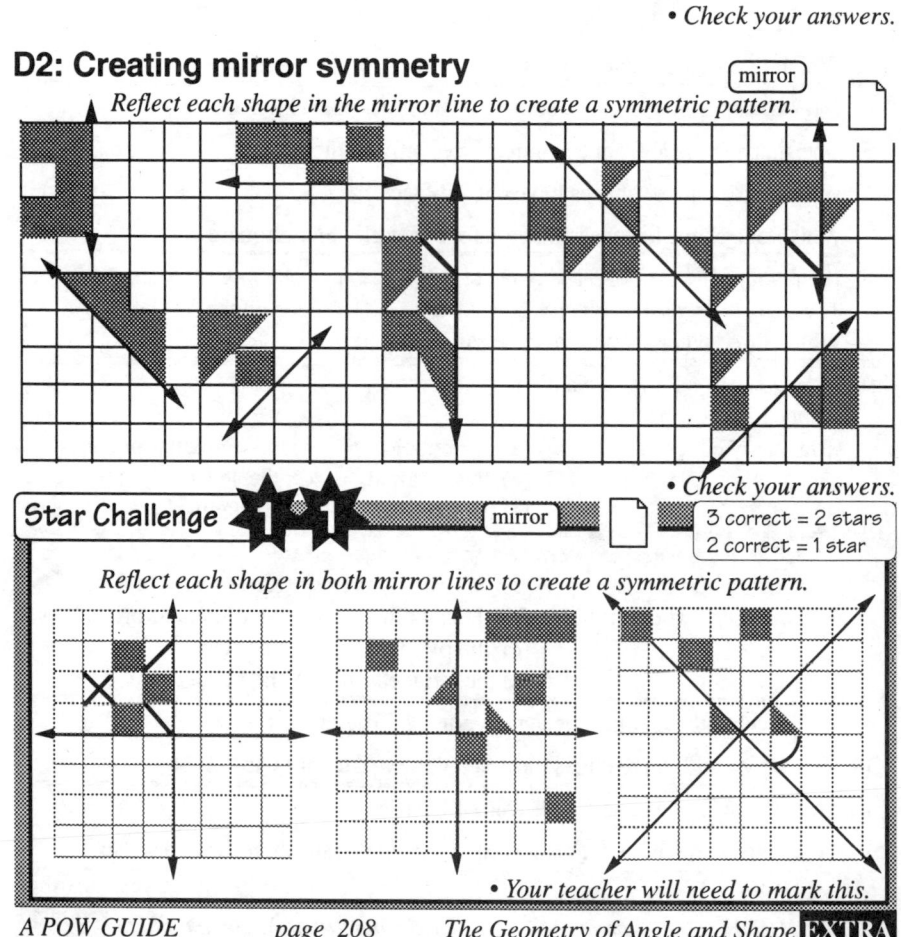

• *Check your answers.*

**Star Challenge**

mirror

3 correct = 2 stars
2 correct = 1 star

*Reflect each shape in both mirror lines to create a symmetric pattern.*

• *Your teacher will need to mark this.*

A POW GUIDE   page 208   The Geometry of Angle and Shape **EXTRA**

# D3: Rotational symmetry

(tracing paper)

Level 4

R  S  P  C  O  T  E

Trace one shape at a time.
Count how many different ways the tracing will fit onto the original shape.
Do not turn the tracing paper over.
Put your results onto a table like this:

| Shape | R | S | P | C | E | O | T |
|---|---|---|---|---|---|---|---|
| No. of ways | | | | | | | |

*Fission*

It helps you keep count if you mark one corner of the shape on the tracing paper.

A tracing of this shape will fit on the shape in 3 different ways.
It has <u>rotational symmetry of order 3</u>.
[Or – its order of symmetry is 3]

• Check your answers.
11-12 correct = 2 stars
8-10 correct = 1 star

## Star Challenge 2 2

Copy and complete this table:

| Shape | A | B | C | D | E | F |
|---|---|---|---|---|---|---|
| Order of rotational symmetry | | | | | | |
| Number of lines of symmetry | | | | | | |

A  B  C  D  E  F

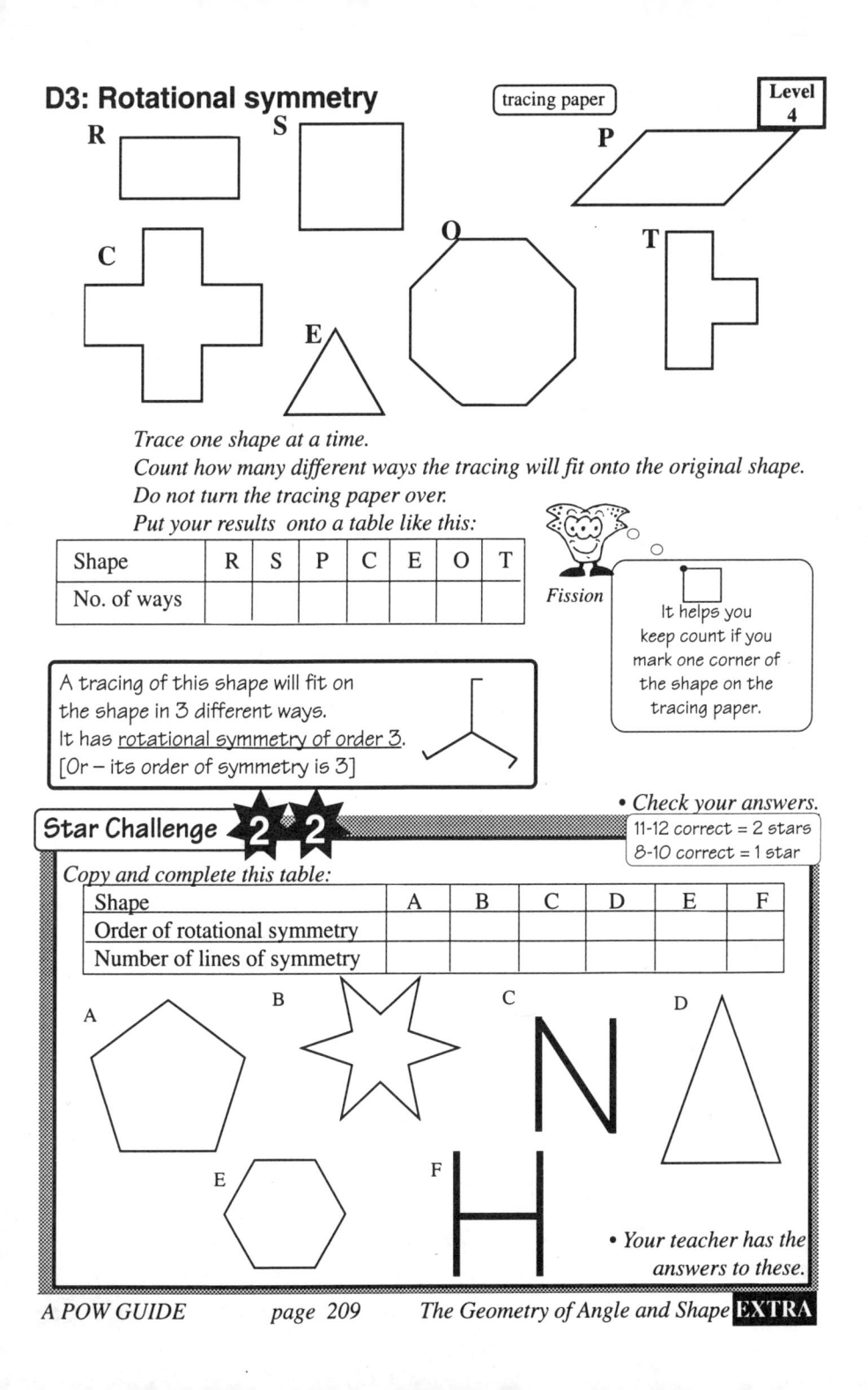

• Your teacher has the answers to these.

A POW GUIDE    page 209    The Geometry of Angle and Shape **EXTRA**

# Section 3: Congruence

Level 4

In this section you will work with congruent shapes.

### DEVELOPMENT

## D1: Congruent shapes

Shapes that are exactly the same shape and size are **congruent**.

*Say which shape is NOT CONGRUENT in each set:*

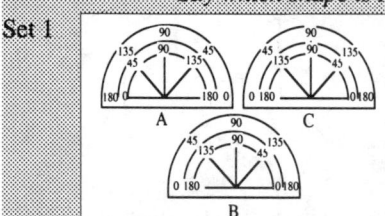

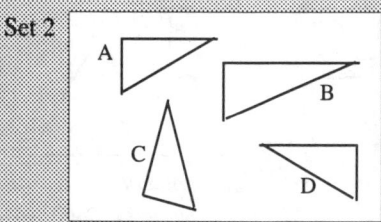

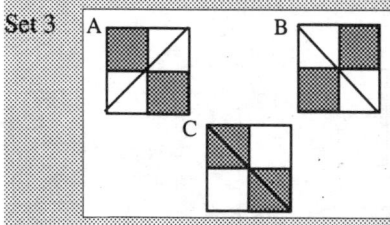

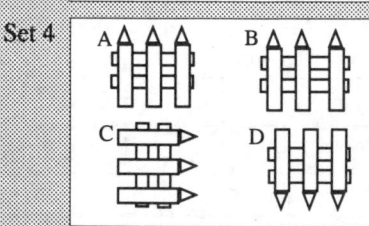

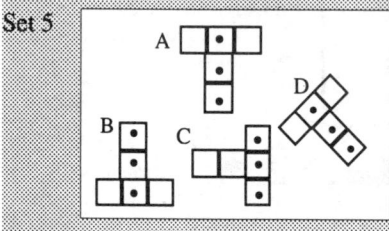

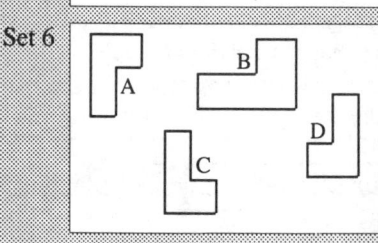

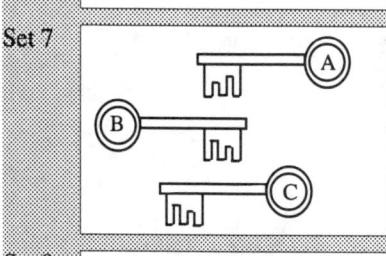

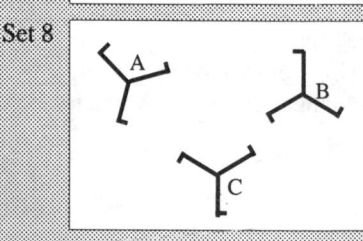

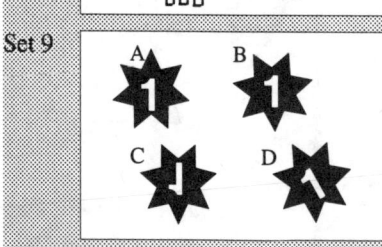

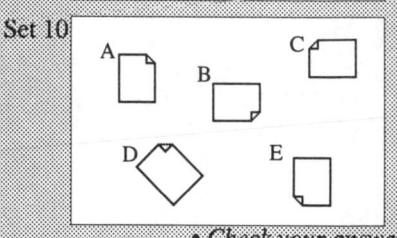

Set 1

Set 2

Set 3

Set 4

Set 5

Set 6

Set 7

Set 8

Set 9

Set 10

• *Check your answers.*

A POW GUIDE       page 210       *The Geometry of Angle and Shape* **EXTRA**

# Section 4: Labelling and measuring lines  [Level 4]

In this section you will:
- review/learn the standard method of labelling lines.
- draw and measure lines.

**DEVELOPMENT**

## D1: Labelling lines

A line is often labelled with CAPITAL LETTERS at each end.
P————————Q   is called the line PQ

1. 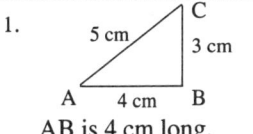  
   5 cm, C, 3 cm, A 4 cm B  
   AB is 4 cm long.  
   (a) How long is AC?  
   (b) How long is BC?

2. PQ = RS means that the lines PQ & RS are the same length. 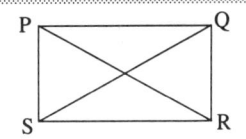  
   (a) Is QR = PS?  
   (b) Is PR = PQ?  
   (c) Is PR = QS?

• Check your answers.

## D2: Measuring lines

1. 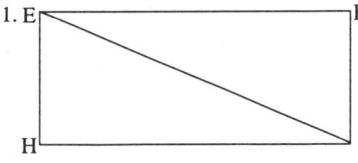 Measure each line:
   (a) EF   (b) FG   (c) EG   (d) EH

2. Measure each line:
   (a) RS   (b) ST   (c) QS
   (d) RT   (e) PT   (f) PR

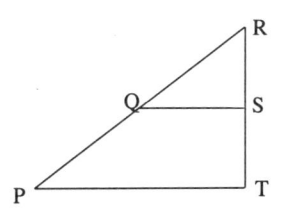

• Check your answers.

## D3: Draw and measure

1. This is a sketch of a rectangle.  
   It is not the correct size.  
   Make an accurate drawing of the rectangle.  
   Measure:  
   (a) WZ   (b) WX   (c) WV   (d) XZ

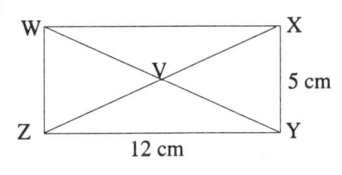

2. This shape is not drawn accurately.  
   Make an accurate drawing of the shape.  
   Measure:  
   (a) GD   (b) DC   (c) BF   (d) AD

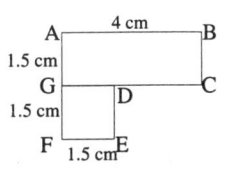

• Check your answers.

A POW GUIDE      page 211      The Geometry of Angle and Shape **EXTRA**

# Section 5: Labelling angles

Level 5

In this section you will read and use labels for angles.

**DEVELOPMENT**

## D1: Labels for simple angles

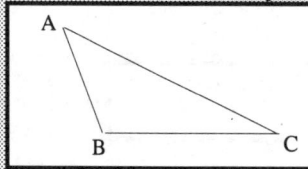

$\hat{A}$ is read as "angle A"

This is used when it is clear which angle is angle A.

1. *Copy and complete:*

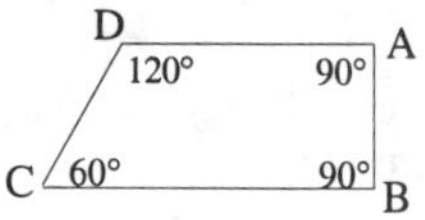

    $\hat{A} = 90°$    $\hat{B} = \ldots\ldots$
    $\hat{C} = \ldots\ldots$    $\hat{D} = \ldots\ldots$

2. *True (T) or false (F) ?*
    (a) $\hat{F} = 40°$    (b) $\hat{D} = 40°$

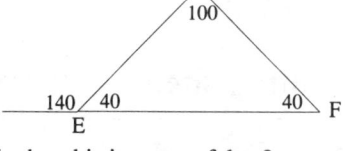

3. $\hat{E} = 140°$

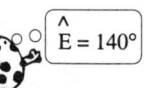

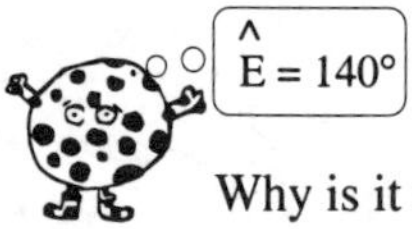

    Why is it not easy to say whether this is true or false ?

*Spottee*

• *Check your answers.*

## D2: Labels for complex angles

The angle marked with a ✗ is called $\hat{CBD}$

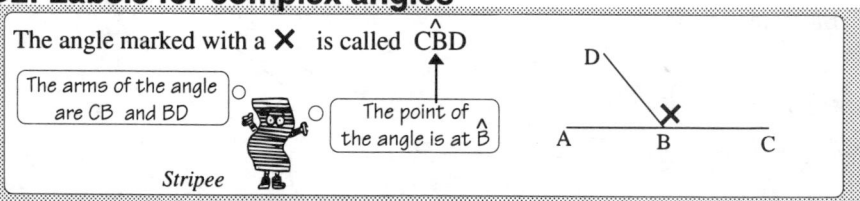

The arms of the angle are CB and BD

The point of the angle is at $\hat{B}$

*Stripee*

*Copy each diagram. Mark the given angle with a ✗*

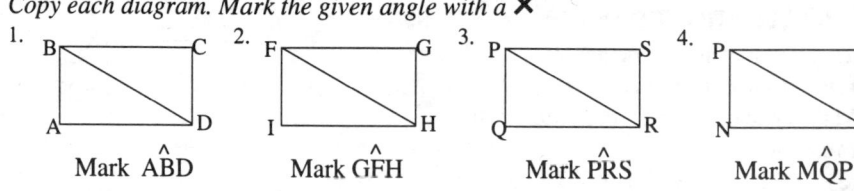

1. Mark $\hat{ABD}$
2. Mark $\hat{GFH}$
3. Mark $\hat{PRS}$
4. Mark $\hat{MQP}$

5. *Copy this diagram.*
    Mark $\hat{UXP}$ with ✗
    Mark $\hat{VPW}$ with ○
    Mark $\hat{PWX}$ with ✓

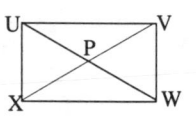

6. *Copy this diagram.*
    Mark $\hat{ACD}$ with ✗
    Mark $\hat{BAC}$ with ○
    Mark $\hat{ADC}$ with ✓

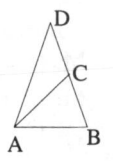

• *Check your answers.*

A POW GUIDE    page 212    The Geometry of Angle and Shape **EXTRA**

# D3: Equivalent angle labels

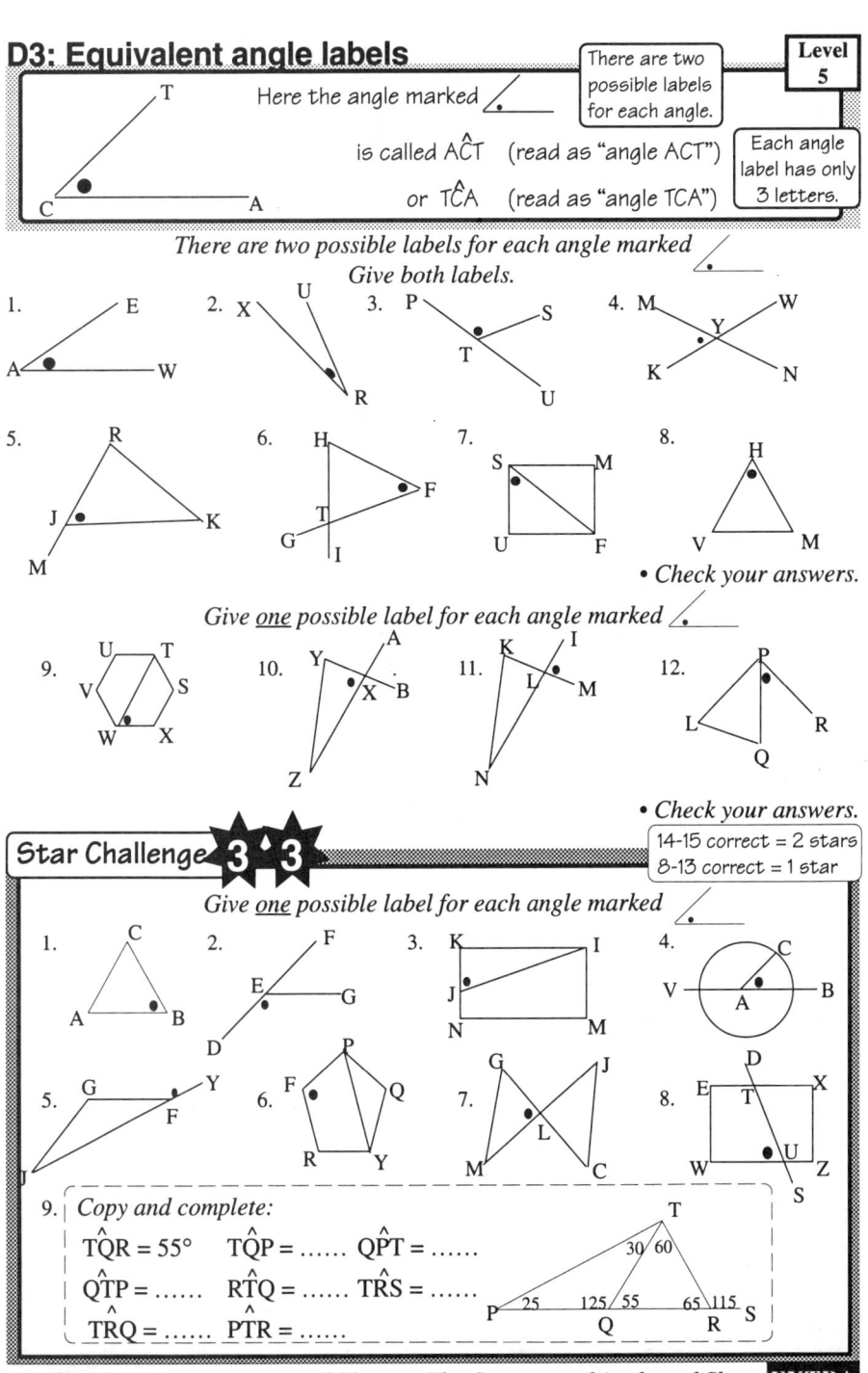

**Level 5**

There are two possible labels for each angle.

Here the angle marked ∠• is called $A\hat{C}T$ (read as "angle ACT") or $T\hat{C}A$ (read as "angle TCA")

Each angle label has only 3 letters.

*There are two possible labels for each angle marked ∠•. Give both labels.*

1. (A, E, W)  2. (X, U, R)  3. (P, T, S, U)  4. (M, Y, W, K, N)

5. (R, J, K, M)  6. (H, T, F, G, I)  7. (S, M, U, F)  8. (H, V, M)

• Check your answers.

*Give one possible label for each angle marked ∠•.*

9. (U, T, V, S, W, X)  10. (Y, A, X, B, Z)  11. (K, I, L, M, N)  12. (P, L, R, Q)

• Check your answers.

## Star Challenge 3★3

14-15 correct = 2 stars
8-13 correct = 1 star

*Give one possible label for each angle marked ∠•*

1. (C, A, B)  2. (F, E, G, D)  3. (K, I, J, N, M)  4. (C, V, A, B)

5. (G, Y, F, J)  6. (P, F, Q, R, Y)  7. (G, J, L, M, C)  8. (D, E, X, T, U, W, Z, S)

9. *Copy and complete:*

$T\hat{Q}R = 55°$  $T\hat{Q}P = ......$  $Q\hat{P}T = ......$
$Q\hat{T}P = ......$  $R\hat{T}Q = ......$  $T\hat{R}S = ......$
$T\hat{R}Q = ......$  $P\hat{T}R = ......$

(Diagram: T at top with 30/60, P—Q—R—S along bottom with angles 25, 125/55, 65/115)

A POW GUIDE    page 213    The Geometry of Angle and Shape **EXTRA**

# Section 6: Classifying angles

Level 5

In this section you will classify angles as acute, obtuse, right or reflex.

**DEVELOPMENT**

## D1: Classes of angles

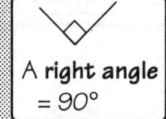

| A **right angle** = 90° | An **acute angle** is less than 90° | An **obtuse angle** is between 90° & 180° | A **reflex angle** is bigger than 180° |

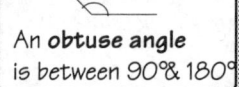

*Say whether each marked angle is acute, obtuse, reflex or a right-angle:*

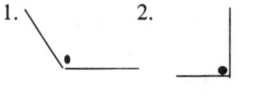

1.   2.   3. 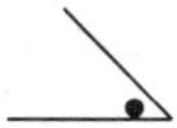   4.    5.    6.  ● = 179°

7.    8. 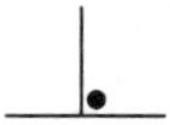   9. 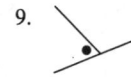   10. 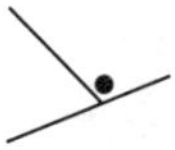   11.    12.  ● = 200°

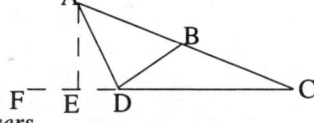

• Check your answers.

### Star Challenge 4

All correct = 1 star

*Say whether each marked angle is acute, obtuse, reflex or a right-angle:*

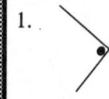

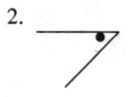

1.   2.   3. 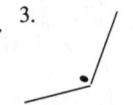   4. ● = 89°   5. 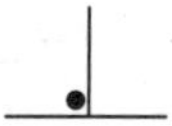   6.

• Your teacher has the answers to these.

## D2: Classifying angles given by labels

*Say whether each angle is acute, obtuse, reflex or a right-angle.*

1. AĈD   2. AÊD   3. DÂE
4. DB̂C   5. DÂB   6. AÊF

### Star Challenge 5

• Check your answers.

5-6 correct = 1 star

Copy and complete each statement. Choose one of the expressions from the box to go in each gap.

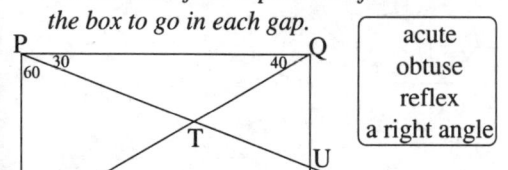

Box: acute / obtuse / reflex / a right angle

1. PT̂Q is ..............
2. PQ̂T is ..............
3. PQ̂U is ..............
4. UP̂Q is ..............
5. RÛT is ..............
6. RÛV is ..............

*A POW GUIDE*     page 214     *The Geometry of Angle and Shape* **EXTRA**

# Section 7: Estimating angle sizes

Level 5

In this section you will estimate the sizes of angles.

### DEVELOPMENT

## D1: Estimating using known angle sizes

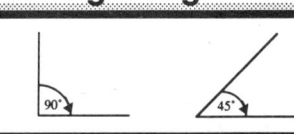

The class were told to compare the angles with the angles in this box. [90°, 45°]

*Pow*

1. The class were asked to estimate the size of this angle.
   Yerwat's estimate was 30°
   It was marked wrong.

   *Yerwat*

   Which of these is the most likely reason why it is wrong?

   **First reason:**
   The angle is about the same size as the 45° angle drawn in the box.

   **Second reason:**
   The angle is bigger than the 45° angle and less than the 90° angle.

2. Plok and Gorbag also estimated the size of the angle in question 1.

   Plok's estimate was 80°  *Plok*

   Both were marked right.

   Gorbag's estimate was 70°  *Gorbag*

   Which of these is the most likely reason why both are right?

   **First reason:**
   Any answer bigger than 45° and less than 90° will do as an estimate here.

   **Second reason:**
   Any answer less than 90° will do as an estimate here.

Compare the angles below with the angles in this box. [90°, 45°, 120°, 60°]

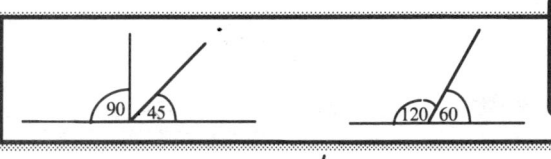

Estimate the size of each angle marked  below:

3.

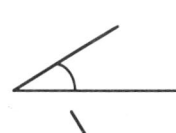

4.

5.

*Pow*

6.

7.

8.

• Check your answers.

A POW GUIDE    page 215    The Geometry of Angle and Shape **EXTRA**

# P1: Estimation practice

**PRACTICE**

Level 5

*Estimate the size of each angle marked with a •*
*At the end of each batch, CHECK YOUR ANSWERS.*

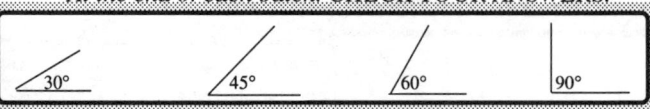

30°   45°   60°   90°

**Batch A:**
1.
2.
3.
4.
5.
6.

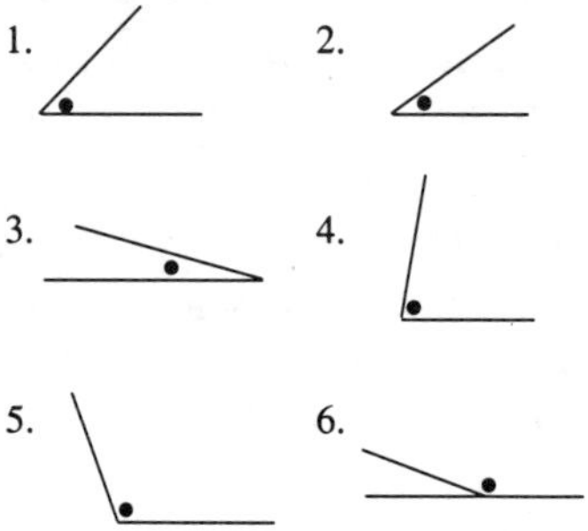

**Batch B:**
1.
2.
3.
4.
5.
6.

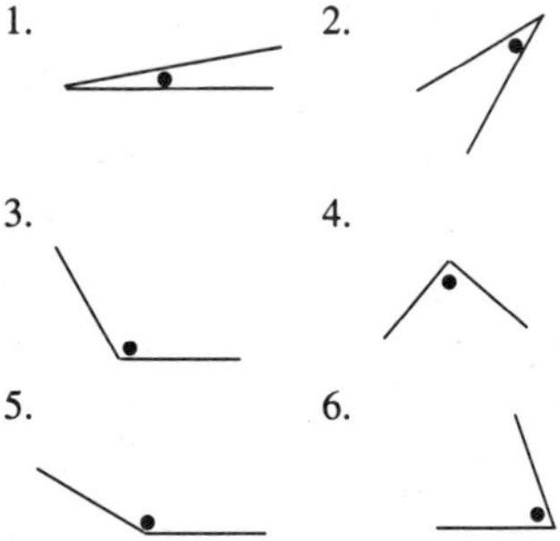

**Batch C:**
1.
2.
3.
4.
5.
6.

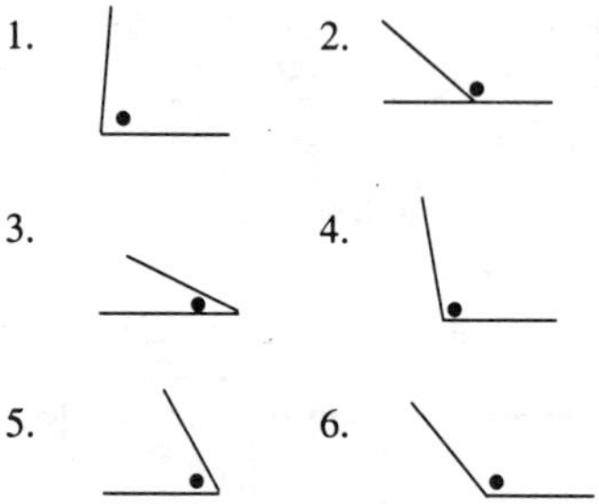

**Batch D:**
1.
2.
3.
4.
5.
6.

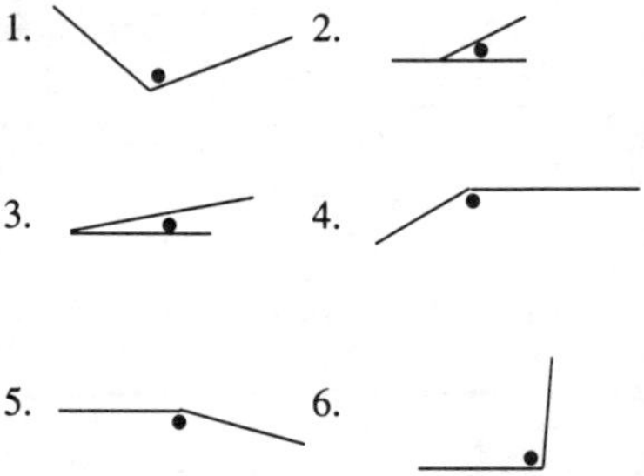

## Star Challenge 6

7-8 correct = 1 star

*Estimate the size of each angle marked with a •*

1.
2.
3.
4.
5.
6.
7.
8.

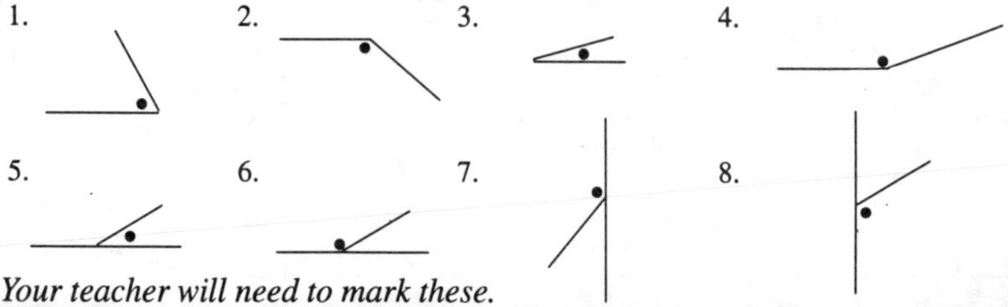

• *Your teacher will need to mark these.*

A POW GUIDE    page 216    The Geometry of Angle and Shape **EXTRA**

# Section 8: Measuring angle sizes

Level 5

In this section you will measure angles.

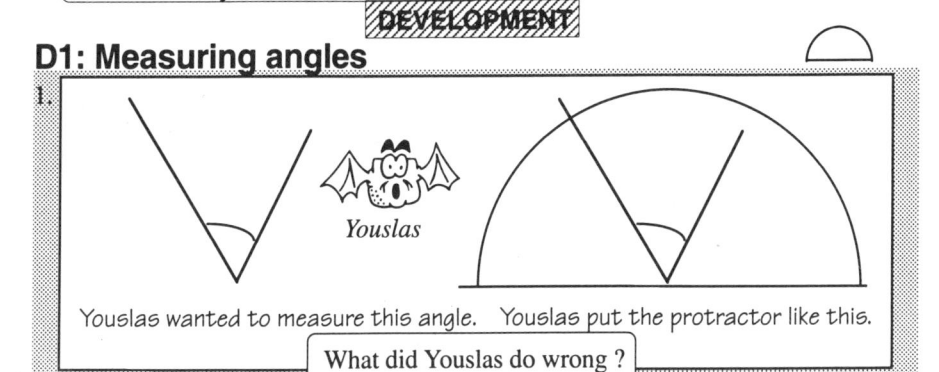

**DEVELOPMENT**

## D1: Measuring angles

1. Youslas wanted to measure this angle.   Youslas put the protractor like this.

   Youslas

   What did Youslas do wrong?

*Measure each angle as accurately as you can.*

2.

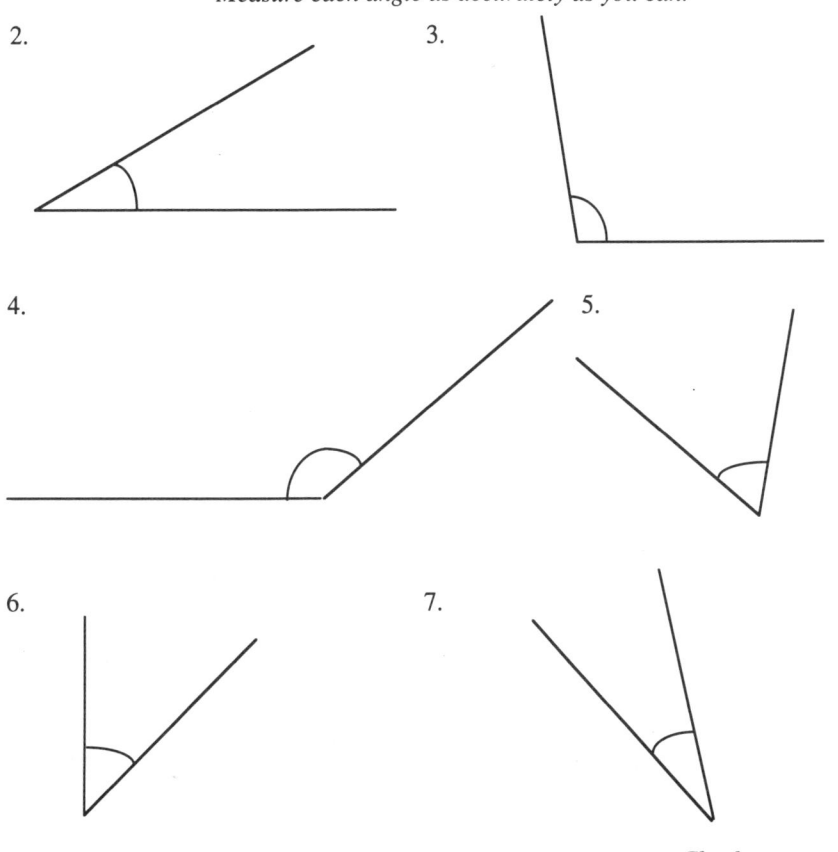

3.

4.

5.

6.

7.

• Check your answers.

A POW GUIDE   page 217   The Geometry of Angle and Shape   EXTRA

**PRACTICE**

Level 5

## P1: Measuring angles practice

**Task 1:** *Measure the acute angles in each diagram. These are marked* ●

1.

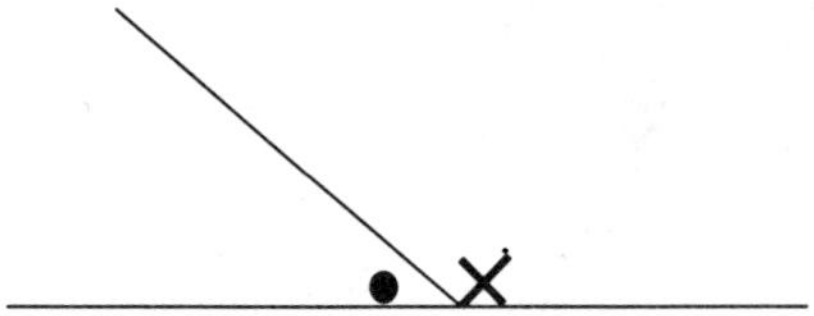

2.

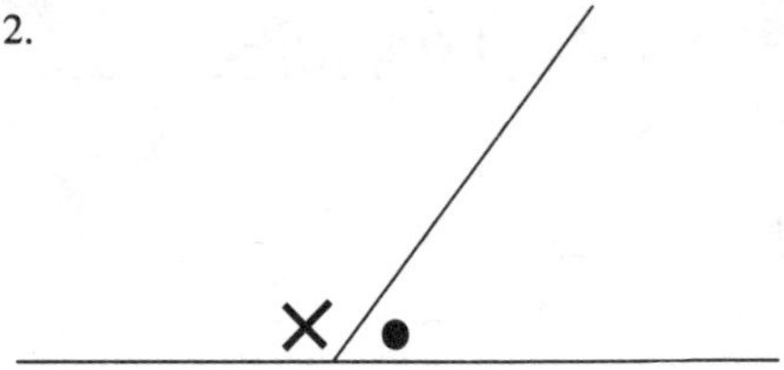

3.

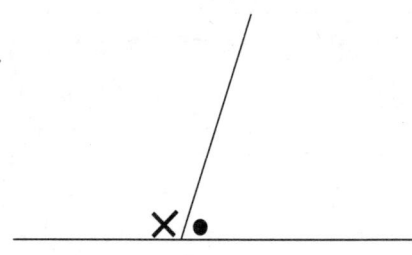

4.

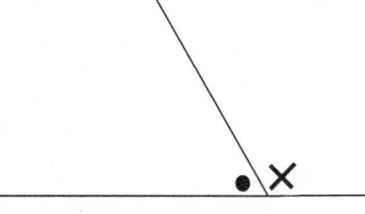

5.

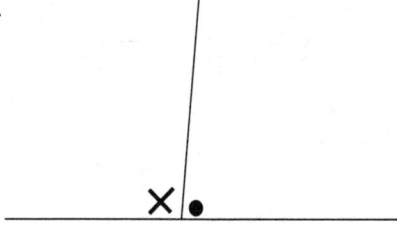

6.

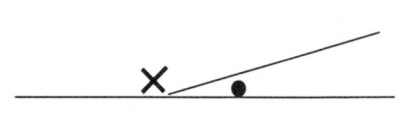

7.

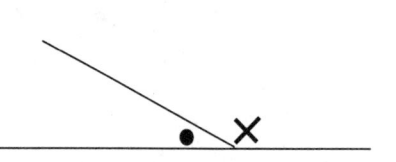

8.

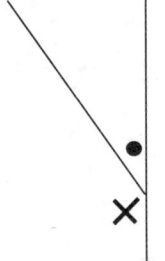

**Task 2:** *Measure the obtuse angles in each diagram. These are marked* ✗

• *Check your answers.*

A POW GUIDE       page 218       The Geometry of Angle and Shape **EXTRA**

# Section 9: Making accurate drawings

Level 5

*In this section you will make accurate drawings from sketches.*

**DEVELOPMENT**

## D1: Accurate drawings of triangles

1. This is a sketch of a triangle. It is not an accurate drawing.
   You are going to draw it accurately using the instructions.

   **Instructions:**
   Step 1: Draw the line PQ.
   Step 2: Draw P̂
   Step 3: Draw Q̂
   Step 4: R is the point where the lines from P and Q meet. Label it R
   Step 5: Measure QR. *CHECK YOUR ANSWER.*
   *If it is reasonably close to the answer, your diagram is correct.*
   *If not, ASK YOUR TEACHER TO FIND OUT WHAT YOU DID WRONG.*

   Triangle PQR: P = 50°, Q = 30°, PQ = 10 cm

   Draw each of the following triangles accurately.
   Measure the line or angle as instructed.
   Check your answer to see if your diagram is correct. If not, **SEE YOUR TEACHER.**

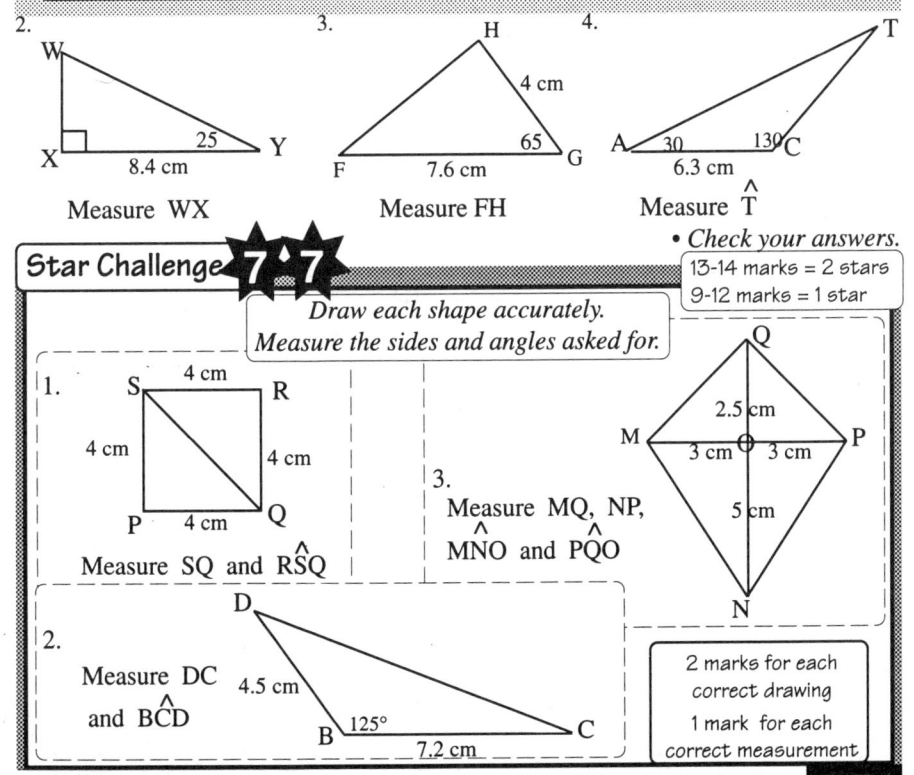

2. Triangle WXY: right angle at X, Y = 25°, XY = 8.4 cm. Measure WX

3. Triangle FGH: GH = 4 cm, G = 65°, FG = 7.6 cm. Measure FH

4. Triangle ACT: A = 30°, C = 130°, AC = 6.3 cm. Measure T̂

• *Check your answers.*

13-14 marks = 2 stars
9-12 marks = 1 star

## Star Challenge

*Draw each shape accurately.*
*Measure the sides and angles asked for.*

1. Square SPQR with SR = 4 cm, SP = 4 cm, PQ = 4 cm, diagonal = 4 cm. Measure SQ and RŜQ

2. Triangle BCD: DB = 4.5 cm, B = 125°, BC = 7.2 cm. Measure DC and BĈD

3. Kite MNPQ with MQ = 2.5 cm, MN = 5 cm, MP = 3 cm + 3 cm. Measure MQ, NP, M̂NO and P̂QO

2 marks for each correct drawing
1 mark for each correct measurement

A POW GUIDE     page 219     The Geometry of Angle and Shape **EXTRA**

# Section 10: Classifying triangles

Level 5

In this section you will:
- recognise and use markings for equal sides and angles;
- classify triangles.

## DEVELOPMENT

### D1: Equal sides and angles

> If two lines have identical markings, they are the same length.

1. Find one line that is the same length as AF
2. Find two lines that are the same length as CI

> If two angles have identical markings, they are the same size.

3. Find one angle that is the same size as $C\hat{D}I$
4. Find one angle that is the same size as $A\hat{F}G$
5. Find one line that is the same length as BC
6. Find one angle that is the same size as $G\hat{F}E$
7. Find two angles that are the same size as $C\hat{B}I$
8. Find one line that is the same length as AB
9. Find one line that is the same length as AC

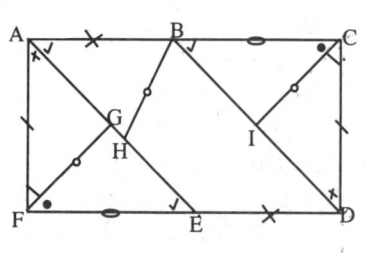

Same markings mean same size!

Icee

- *Check your answers.*

### D2: Classifying triangles

Triangles can be described as:

equilateral (3 equal sides)   isosceles (2 equal sides)   scalene (no equal sides & no right angle)   right-angled

*True (T) or false (F) ?*

1. ΔA is isosceles
2. ΔB is scalene
3. ΔC is equilateral
4. ΔD is scalene

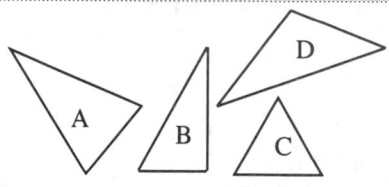

- *Check your answers.*

A POW GUIDE  page 220  The Geometry of Angle and Shape **EXTRA**

## P1: Classifying practice

**PRACTICE**  Level 5

*Copy and complete each statement. Fill each gap with one of these expressions:*

equilateral
isosceles
right-angled
scalene

1. Δ CDE is ...............
2. Δ BCE is ...............
3. Δ AGF is ...............
4. Δ AEC is ...............
5. Δ AFE is ...............
6. Δ OPQ is ...............
7. Δ QOX is ...............
8. Δ PWV is ...............

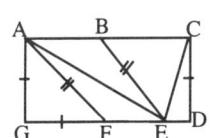

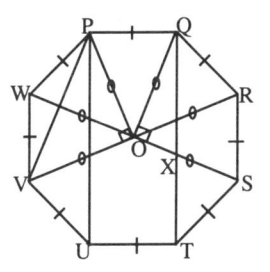

• *Check your answers.*

### Star Challenge 8 8

15-16 correct = 2 stars
11-14 correct = 1 star

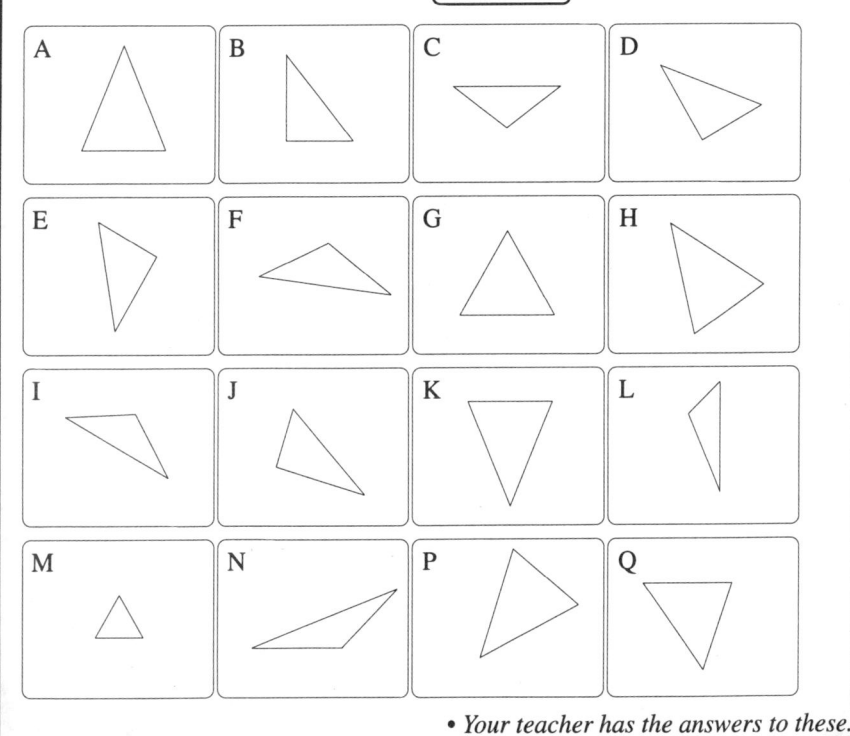

*Classify each of these triangles.
Give each triangle one of these labels.*

equilateral
isosceles
right-angled
scalene

A  B  C  D

E  F  G  H

I  J  K  L

M  N  P  Q

• *Your teacher has the answers to these.*

A POW GUIDE  page 221  The Geometry of Angle and Shape **EXTRA**

# Section 11: Angle properties

Level 6

In this section you will:
- calculate angles on a straight line;
- calculate angles at a point;
- calculate angles on crossed lines.

**DEVELOPMENT**

## D1: Angles on straight lines

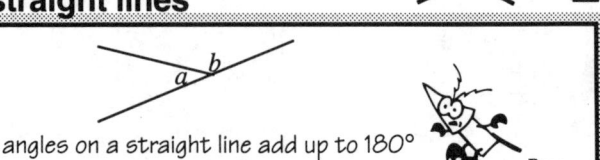

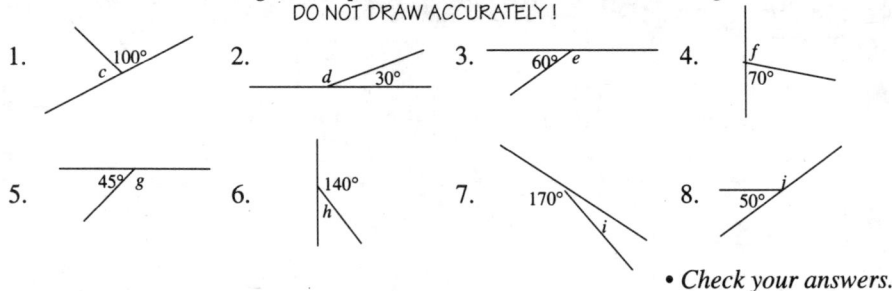

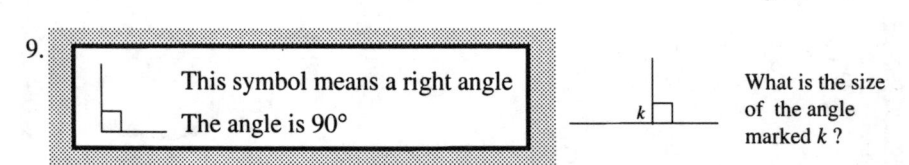

angles on a straight line add up to 180°
$a + b = 180°$

Pow

*Sketch each diagram. Replace the letters with the correct angle sizes.*
DO NOT DRAW ACCURATELY!

1. $c$, 100°
2. $d$, 30°
3. 60°, $e$
4. $f$, 70°
5. 45°, $g$
6. 140°, $h$
7. 170°, $i$
8. $j$, 50°

• Check your answers.

9. This symbol means a right angle. The angle is 90°. What is the size of the angle marked $k$?

*Sketch each diagram. Replace the letters with the correct angle sizes.*
DO NOT DRAW ACCURATELY!

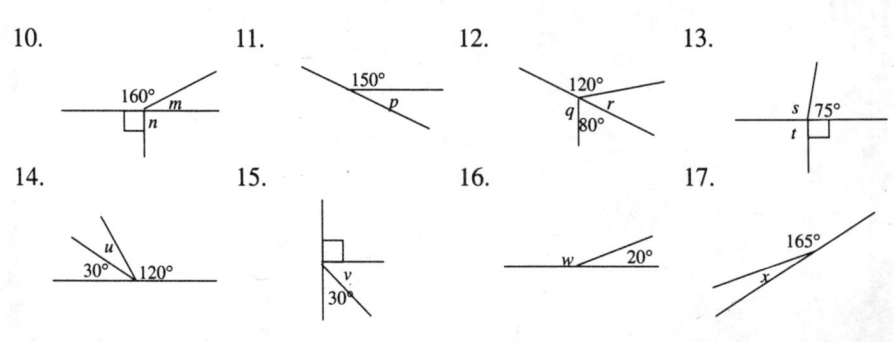

10. 160°, $m$, $n$
11. 150°, $p$
12. 120°, $q$, $r$, 80°
13. $s$, 75°, $t$
14. 30°, $u$, 120°
15. $v$, 30°
16. $w$, 20°
17. 165°, $x$

• Check your answers.

A POW GUIDE    page 222    The Geometry of Angle and Shape **EXTRA**

## D2: Taking shortcuts

**Level 6**

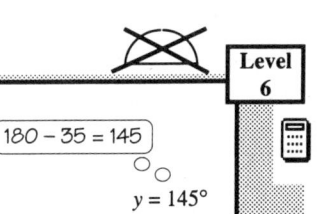

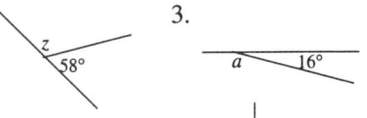

[Diagram: angle y and 35° on a straight line]
Sludge: "I know a shortcut"
180 − 35 = 145
y = 145°

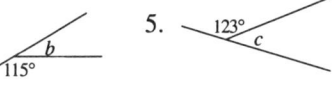

1. Sludge thinks that y = 145°.
   (a) Does 145 + 35 = 180 ?  (b) Does Sludge's shortcut work ?

*Sketch each diagram. Replace the letters with the correct angle sizes.*

2. z, 58°
3. a, 16°
4. b, 115°
5. 123°, c
6. 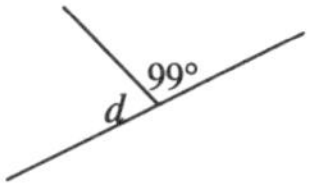 d, 99°
7. 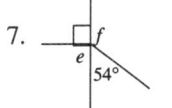 f, e, 54°
8. 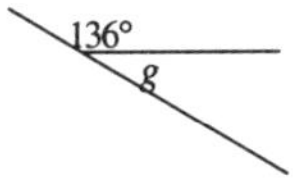 136°, g
9. 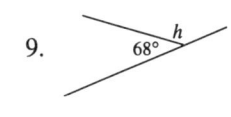 68°, h

• Check your answers.

## D3: More angles on lines

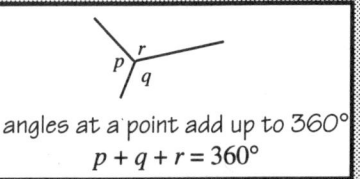

angles at a point add up to 360°
p + q + r = 360°

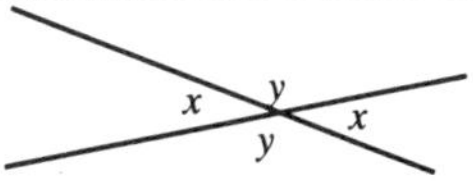

Opposite angles are equal

*Sketch each diagram. Replace the letters with the correct angle sizes.*

1. 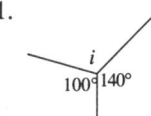 i, 100°, 140°
2. 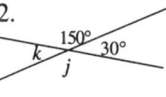 k, 150°, 30°, j
3. 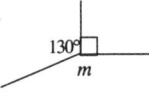 130°, m
4. 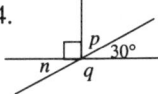 n, p, 30°, q

• Check your answers.

5. 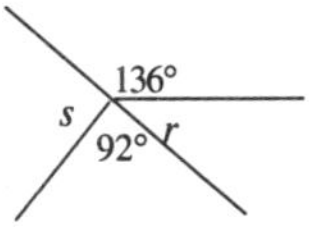 s, 136°, 92°, r
6. 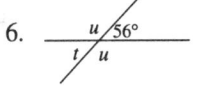 u, 56°, t, u
7. 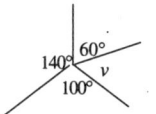 140°, 60°, v, 100°
8. 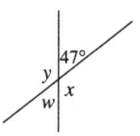 y, 47°, x, w

9. 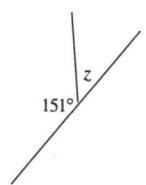 z, 151°
10. 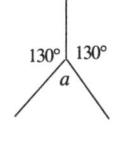 130°, 130°, a
11. 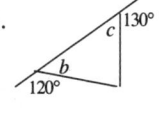 c, 130°, b, 120°
12. 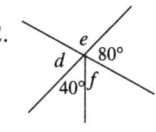 e, d, 80°, 40°, f

• Check your answers.

A POW GUIDE    page 223    The Geometry of Angle and Shape **EXTRA**

# P1: Angle practice

*Sketch each diagram. Replace the letters with the correct angle sizes. CHECK ANSWERS at the end of each batch.*

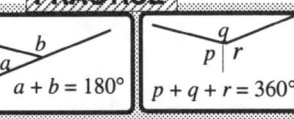

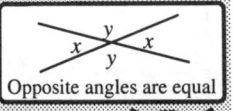

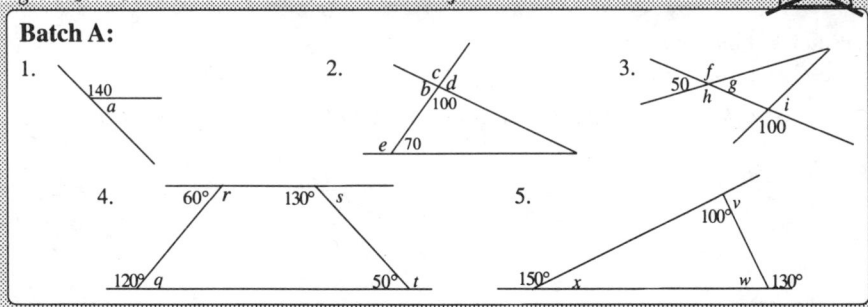

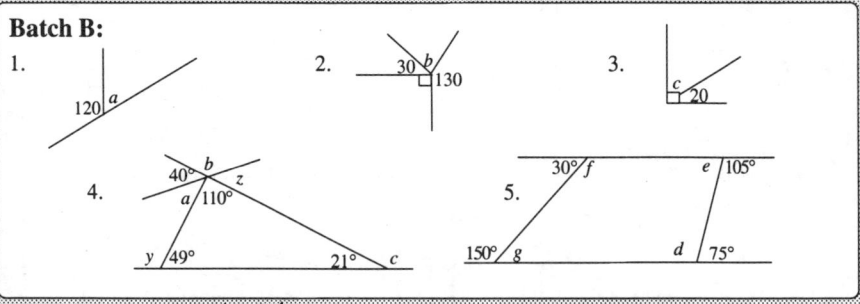

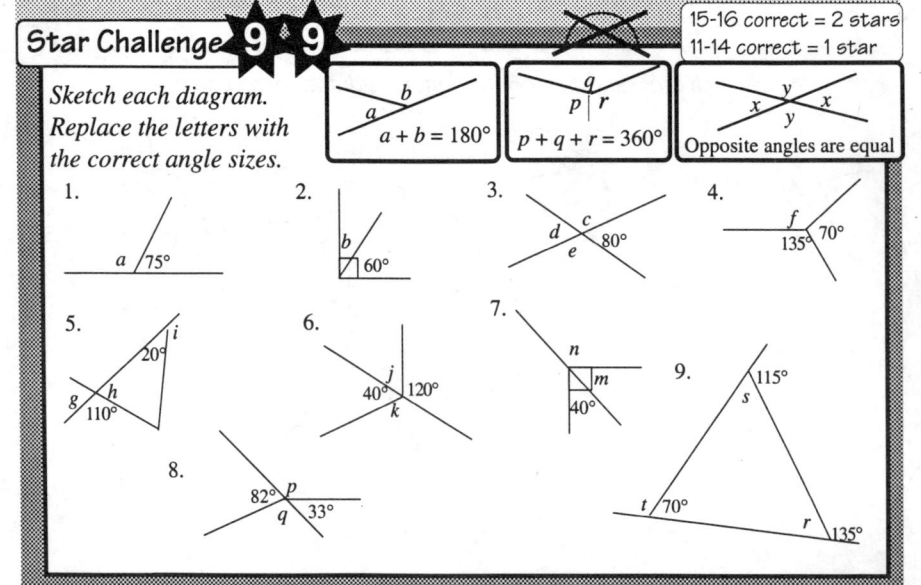

PRACTICE

- $a + b = 180°$
- $p + q + r = 360°$
- Opposite angles are equal

## Batch A:

1. 140, a
2. b, c, d, 100, e, 70
3. 50, f, g, h, i, 100
4. 60°/r, 130°/s, 120°/q, 50°/t
5. 100°/v, 150°/x, w, 130°

## Batch B:

1. 120, a
2. 30, b, 130
3. c, 20
4. 40°/b, z, a/110°, y/49°, 21°/c
5. 30°/f, e/105°, 150°/g, d/75°

## Star Challenge 9 & 9

*Sketch each diagram. Replace the letters with the correct angle sizes.*

- $a + b = 180°$
- $p + q + r = 360°$
- Opposite angles are equal

15-16 correct = 2 stars
11-14 correct = 1 star

1. a/75°
2. b, 60°
3. c, d, e, 80°
4. f, 135°, 70°
5. i, 20°, g, h, 110°
6. j, 40°, 120°, k
7. n, m, 40°
8. 82°/p, q/33°
9. 115°, s, t/70°, r, 135°

*A POW GUIDE*     page 224     *The Geometry of Angle and Shape* **EXTRA**

# Section 12: Triangles

**Level 6**

In this section you will:
- calculate angles in a triangle;
- use the rules for angles in a triangle and on a straight line.

## DEVELOPMENT

### D1: Angles in triangles

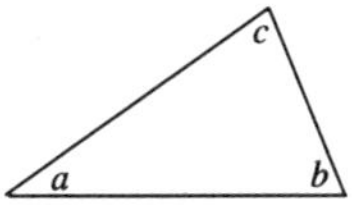

angles in a triangle add up to 180°
$a + b + c = 180°$

*Pow*

Sketch each diagram. Replace the letters with the correct angle sizes.

1. $a$, 40°, 50°
2. $b$, 70°, 70°
3. 30°, $c$, 20°
4. $d$, 60°, 80°
5. $e$, □, 50°
6. $f$, 30°, 110°
7. 30°, □, $g$
8. 50°, 80°, $h$
9. $i$, 50°, 25°

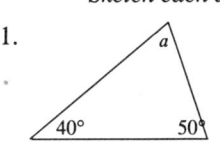

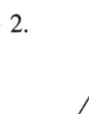

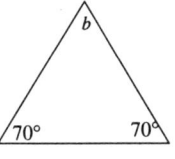

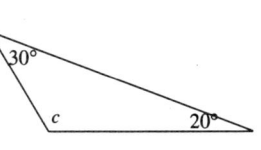

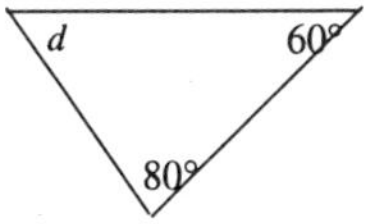

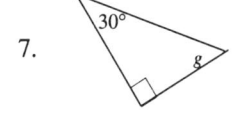

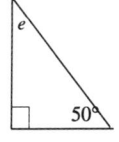

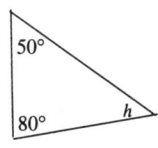

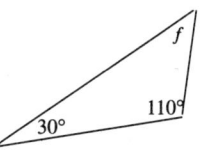

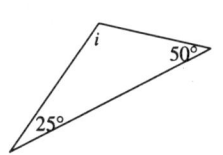

• Check your answers.

### D2: Another shortcut

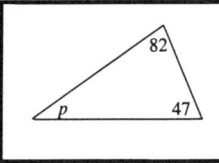

82, $p$, 47

I know a shortcut for this!

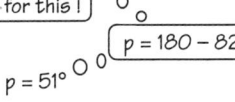

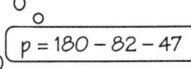

*Modesto*

$p = 180 - 82 - 47$
$p = 51°$

Sketch each diagram. Replace the letters with the correct angle sizes.

1. $j$, 30°, 80°
2. $k$, □, 68°
3. 124°, 43°, $m$
4. 39°, $n$, 42°

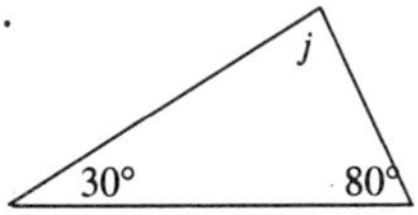

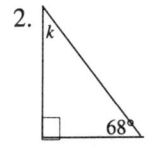

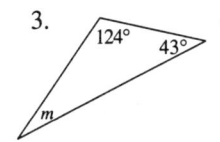

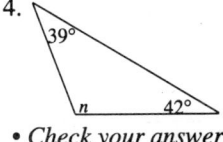

• Check your answers.

A POW GUIDE  page 225  The Geometry of Angle and Shape **EXTRA**

## P1: Angles in triangles practice

**Level 6**

*Sketch each diagram. Replace the letters with the correct angle sizes.*

1. Triangle with angles 36°, 57°, and p.
2. Triangle with angles 15°, 28°, and q.
3. Triangle with angles 25°, 115°, and r.
4. Triangle with angles 50°, 30°, 30°, and u; with s, t at interior point.
5. Triangle with angles 55°, 30°, 15°, 10°, 45°, and v, w, x, y.

• Check your answers.

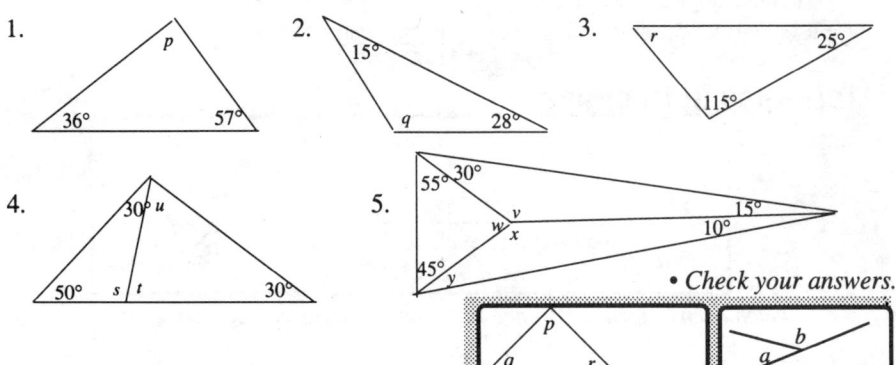

## P2: Triangles and lines

$p + q + r = 180°$

$a + b = 180°$

*Sketch each diagram. Replace the letters with the correct angle sizes.*

1. Triangle with 70°, 85°, a, and b.
2. Triangle with 100°, 35°, c, and d.
3. Triangle with 50°, 80°, 60°, and e, f, g, h.
4. Right triangle with 60°, i, j, k.
5. Rectangle with diagonal, 30°, m, n, p.
6. Triangle with 30°, 20°, 30°, q, r, s.

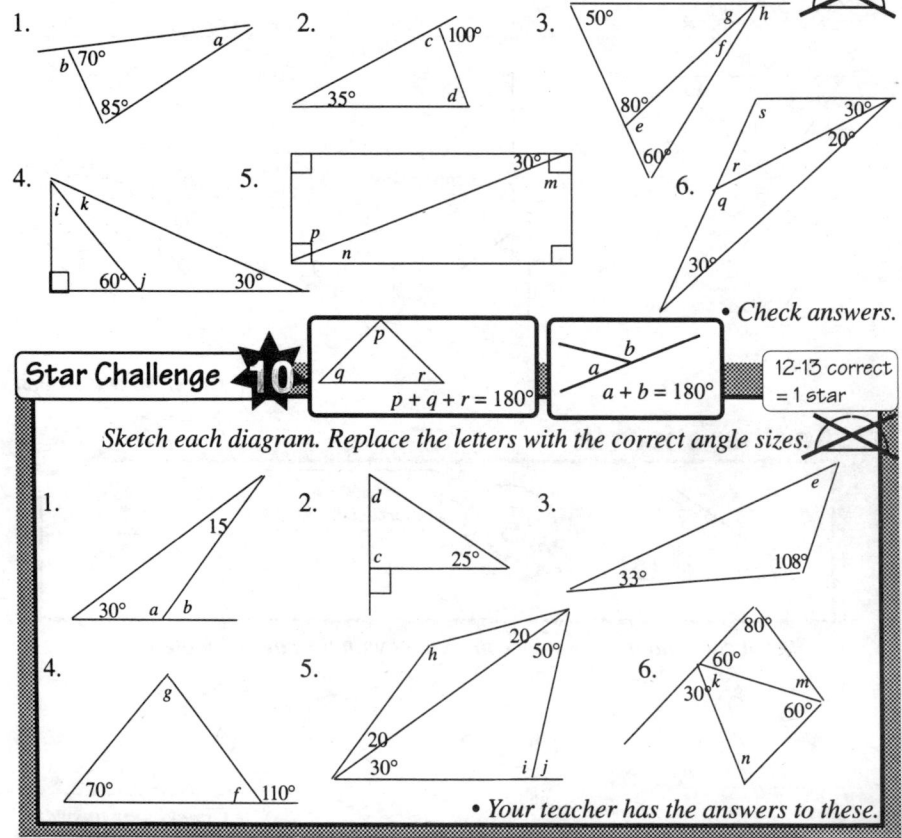

• Check answers.

## Star Challenge 10

$p + q + r = 180°$

$a + b = 180°$

12-13 correct = 1 star

*Sketch each diagram. Replace the letters with the correct angle sizes.*

1. Triangle with 30°, 15, a, b.
2. Right triangle with 25°, c, d.
3. Triangle with 33°, 108°, e.
4. Triangle with 70°, 110°, f, g.
5. Figure with 20°, 50°, 30°, 20°, h, i, j.
6. Figure with 80°, 60°, 60°, 30°, k, m, n.

• Your teacher has the answers to these.

A POW GUIDE    page 226    The Geometry of Angle and Shape **EXTRA**

# Section 13: Special triangles

Level 6

In this section you will calculate angles in equilateral and isosceles triangles.

## DEVELOPMENT

### D1: Equilateral and isosceles triangles

An **equilateral** △ has three equal sides and three equal angles

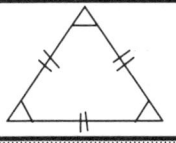

Equal sides have the same markings.
Equal angles have the same markings.
If two angles have sizes given by the same letter, they are the same size.

1. This is an equilateral triangle. Work out the size of each angle.

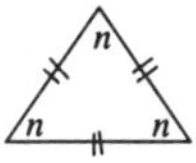

An **isosceles** △ has two equal sides and two equal angles

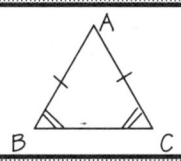

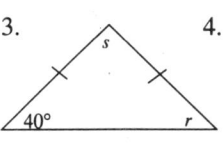

In △ABC
AB = AC
$A\hat{B}C = A\hat{C}B$

Copy each diagram. Replace the letters with the correct angle sizes.

2. (70°, q, p)
3. (40°, s, r)
4. (50°, t, u)
5. (80, q, p)

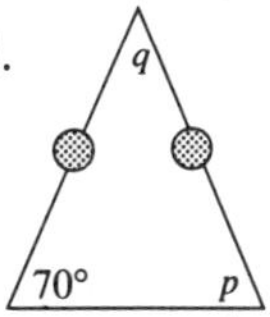

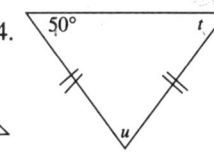

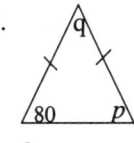

• Check your answers.

How do you know which are the two equal angles?

The two equal angles are at the bottom of the two equal sides.

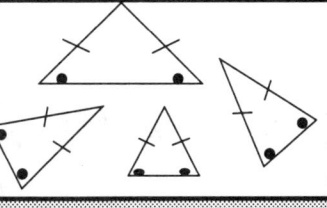

Spoton

Which angles are the two equal angles? [A&B, B&C or A&C?]

6. 7. 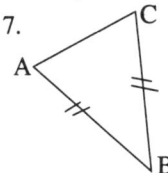 8. 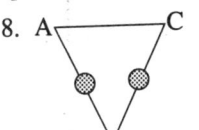 9.

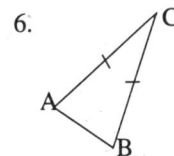

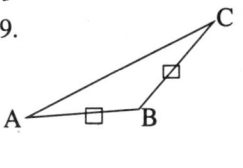

Copy each diagram. Replace the letters with the correct angle sizes.

10. (w, v, 81°)
11. (45°, x, y)
12. (a, 63°, z)
13. (b, c, 20)

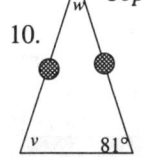

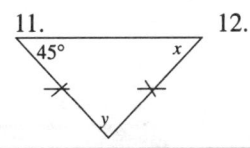

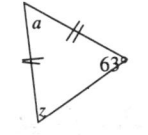

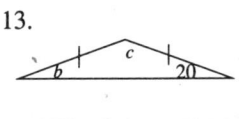

• Check your answers.

A POW GUIDE     page 227     The Geometry of Angle and Shape **EXTRA**

## D2: Working out the base angles (the equal angles)

1. 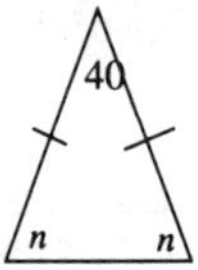 The equal angles are also called the 'base angles'.

   Work out the size of each of the base angles.
   • *If you cannot do this, talk to your teacher.*

*Work out the size of the base angles in each triangle:*

2. 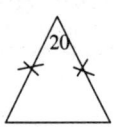    3. 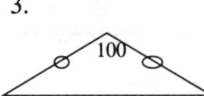    4. 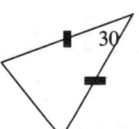    5.

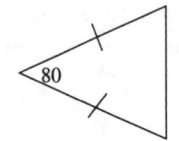

• *Check your answers.*

### PRACTICE
## P1: A mixture of isosceles triangles

*Copy each diagram. Replace the letters with the correct angle sizes.*

1. 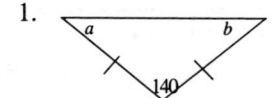    2. 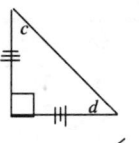    3.

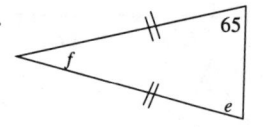

4. 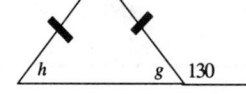    5. 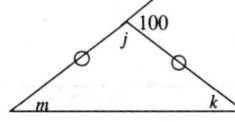    6.

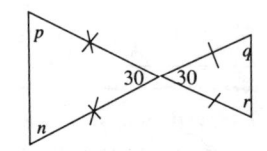

• *Check your answers.*

### Star Challenge ⚡⚡

$a + b = 180°$

20 correct = 2 stars
17-19 correct = 1 star

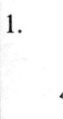

*Copy each diagram. Replace the letters with the correct angle sizes.*

1. 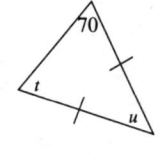    2. 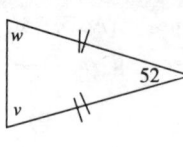    3.

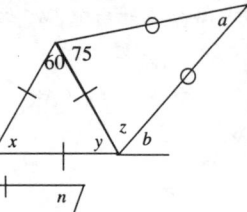

4. 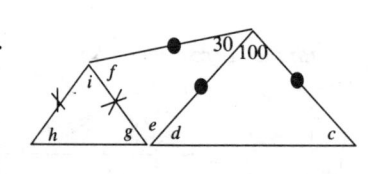    5.

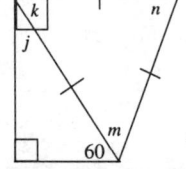

• *Your teacher has the answers to these.*

A POW GUIDE        page 228        *The Geometry of Angle and Shape* **EXTRA**

# Section 14: Parallel and perpendicular lines

**Level 6**

In this section you will:
- review parallel and perpendicular lines;
- calculate angles on parallel lines;

*DEVELOPMENT*

## D1: Naming and labelling

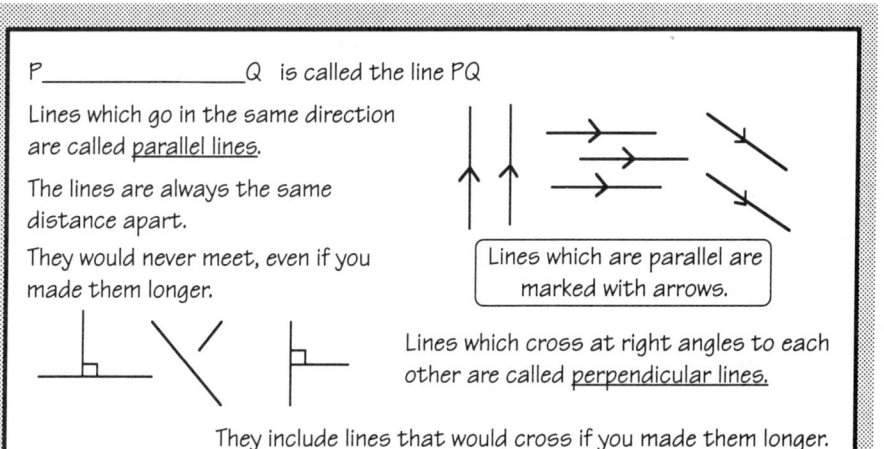

P_____Q is called the line PQ

Lines which go in the same direction are called <u>parallel lines</u>.

The lines are always the same distance apart.

They would never meet, even if you made them longer.

Lines which are parallel are marked with arrows.

Lines which cross at right angles to each other are called <u>perpendicular lines</u>.

They include lines that would cross if you made them longer.

*State whether each of the following is true or false:*

1. PQ is parallel to CD
2. AB is parallel to MN
3. GH is perpendicular to PQ
4. IJ is parallel to KL
5. KL is perpendicular to MN
6. EF is parallel to PQ
7. MN is perpendicular to IJ
8. CD is parallel to KL

*What are the missing words?*

9. AB is ......... to GH
10. AB is ............ to PQ

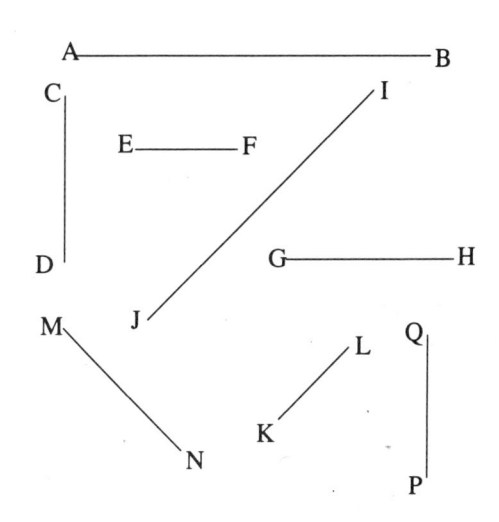

• *Check your answers.*

A POW GUIDE    page 229    *The Geometry of Angle and Shape* **EXTRA**

# D2: Angles on parallel lines

**Level 6**

A line that crosses two (or more) parallel lines is called a **transversal**

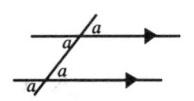

The acute angles along a transversal are all equal

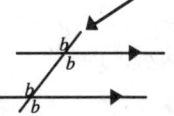

The obtuse angles along a transversal are all equal

*Copy each diagram. Replace the letters with the correct angle sizes.*

1. 140/a, d, e, g, b, c, f

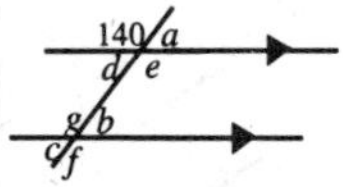

2. h, 110, k, i, j

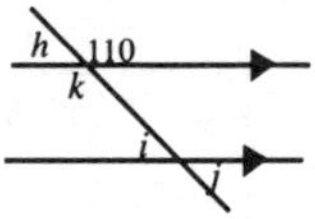

3. p, q, n, m, 30

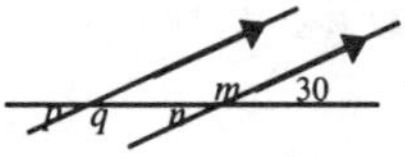

4. 60, u, t, r, s, v

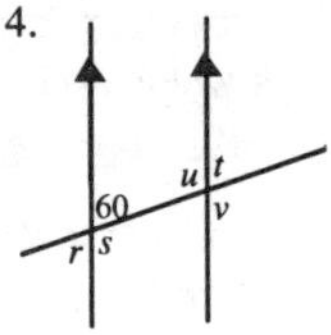

5. z, a, y, x, w, 70

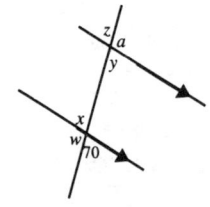

6. f, e, d, c, b, 130

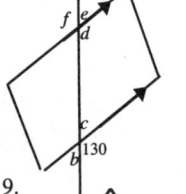

7. 45, g, h, i, k, j, m, n

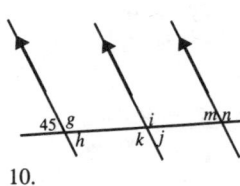

8. a/70, b, c, d, e, f, g, 60, h, i, k, j

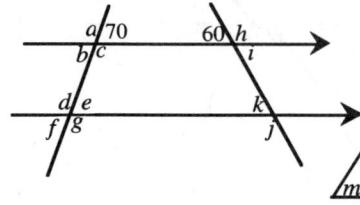

9. 70, 50, n, q, m, p

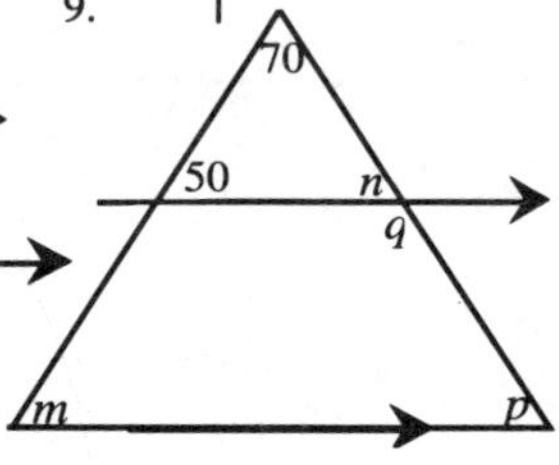

10. t, s, 50, r

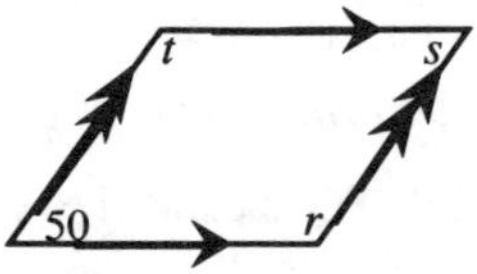

## Star Challenge 12

*12-14 correct = 1 star*

Copy each diagram. Replace the letters with the correct angle sizes.

1. 75, b, a, e, d, c, 105

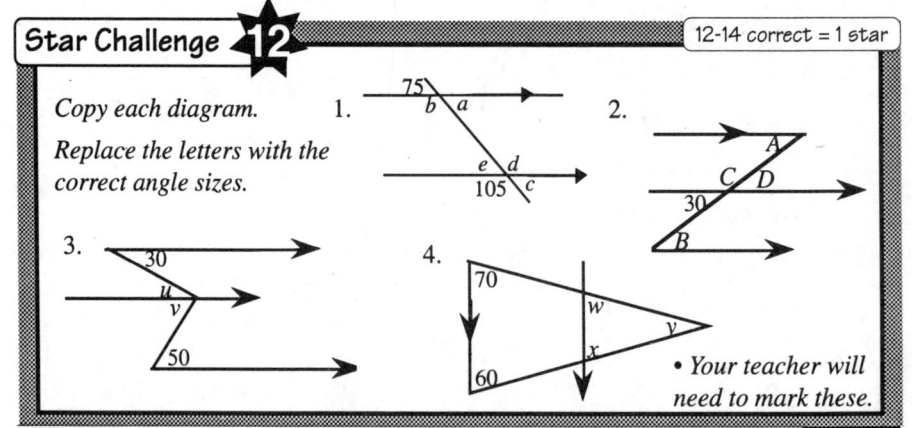

2. A, C, D, 30, B

3. 30, u, v, 50

4. 70, w, y, x, 60

• Your teacher will need to mark these.

*A POW GUIDE*  page 230  *The Geometry of Angle and Shape* **EXTRA**

# Section 15 : Quadrilaterals

Level 6

In this section you will review some properties of quadrilaterals.

## DEVELOPMENT

### D1: Properties of quadrilaterals

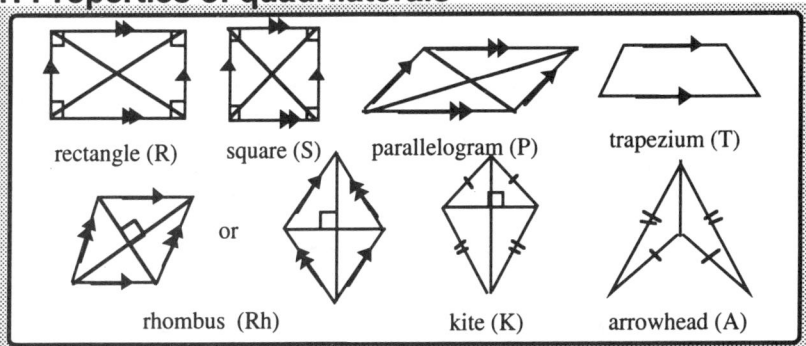

rectangle (R)    square (S)    parallelogram (P)    trapezium (T)

rhombus (Rh)    kite (K)    arrowhead (A)

1. How many sides has a quadrilateral ?
2. How many angles has a quadrilateral ?
3. Which two shapes have four right angles ?
4. Which shape has just one pair of parallel sides ?
5. Which two shapes have four equal sides ?
6. Which shape has four equal sides but does not have four equal angles ?
7. Which shape has two pairs of equal sides and its angles are all right angles ?
8. Which shape has two pairs of equal sides but its angles are not right angles ?
9. Which shape is a squashed square ?
10. Which quadrilateral is described in each case below ?

**Quadrilateral A**
It has two pairs of equal sides.
It has four right angles.
It has two lines of symmetry.

**Quadrilateral B**
It has two pairs of equal sides.
It has one line of symmetry.
It has only one diagonal.

**Quadrilateral C** It has just one pair of parallel sides.

• Check your answers

**Star Challenge 13**

2-3 correct = 1 star

Which quadrilateral is described in each case ?

**Quadrilateral P**
It has two pairs of equal sides. Its diagonals are perpendicular.
It has only one line of symmetry.

**Quadrilateral Q**
It has four equal sides. It has four equal angles. Its diagonals are perpendicular.

**Quadrilateral R** It has two pairs of equal sides.
It has two pairs of parallel sides. It has no lines of symmetry.

A POW GUIDE    page 231    The Geometry of Angle and Shape **EXTRA**

# Section 16: Enlargements

Level 6

In this section you will enlarge shapes using positive scale factors.

## DEVELOPMENT

### D1: Enlarging shapes

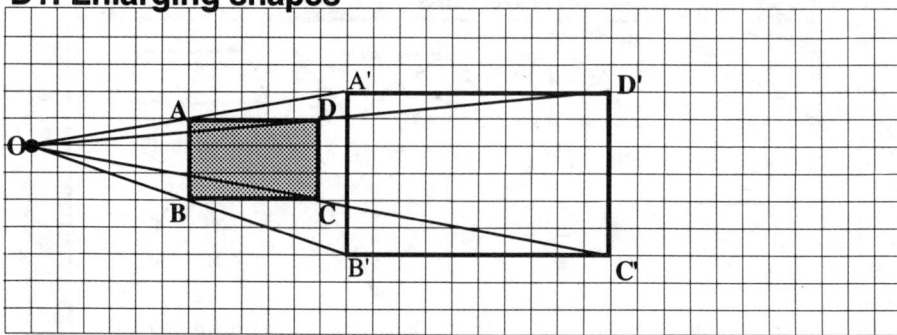

The rectangle ABCD has been enlarged with a scale factor 2 from O (the centre of enlargement). To do this:
- OA is drawn and extended. A' is twice as far away from O as A.
- OB is drawn and extended. B' is twice as far away from O as B.
- OC is drawn and extended. C' is twice as far away from O as C.
- OD is drawn and extended. D' is twice as far away from O as D..

**Task 1:** Use the diagram above. Enlarge rectangle ABCD with a scale factor 3 from O. Label the new rectangle A"B"C"D".

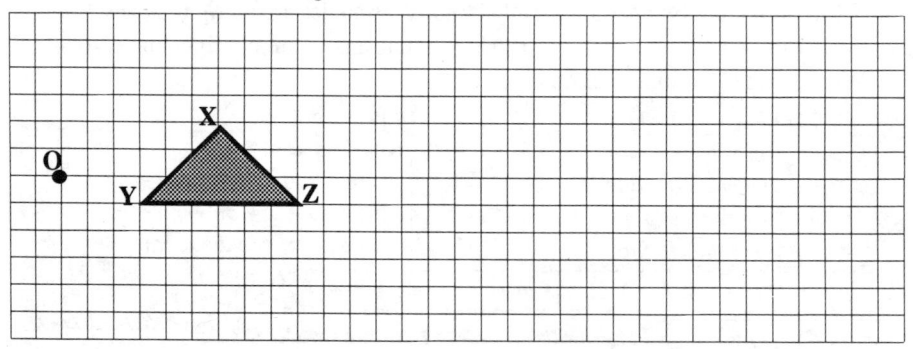

**Task 2:** Use the second diagram. Enlarge △XYZ with a scale factor 2 from O. Label the new triangle X'Y'Z'.

**Task 3:** Use the second diagram. Enlarge △XYZ with a scale factor 3 from O. Label the new triangle X"Y"Z".

**Task 4:** Use the third diagram. Enlarge △RSTUVW with scale factor 2 from O. Label the new triangle R'S'T'U'V'W'

- *Check your answers.*

A POW GUIDE     page 232     The Geometry of Angle and Shape **EXTRA**

# P1: Making enlargements

**PRACTICE**

**Task 1:** Make an enlargement with scale factor 2 of this T shape.
O is the centre of enlargement.

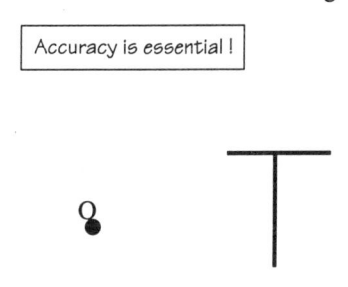

Accuracy is essential!

When you have finished, check that the new T is twice as tall and twice as wide.

**Task 2:** On the same diagram, make an enlargement with scale factor 3
Check that the new T is three times as tall and wide as the first T.

• *Check your answers.*

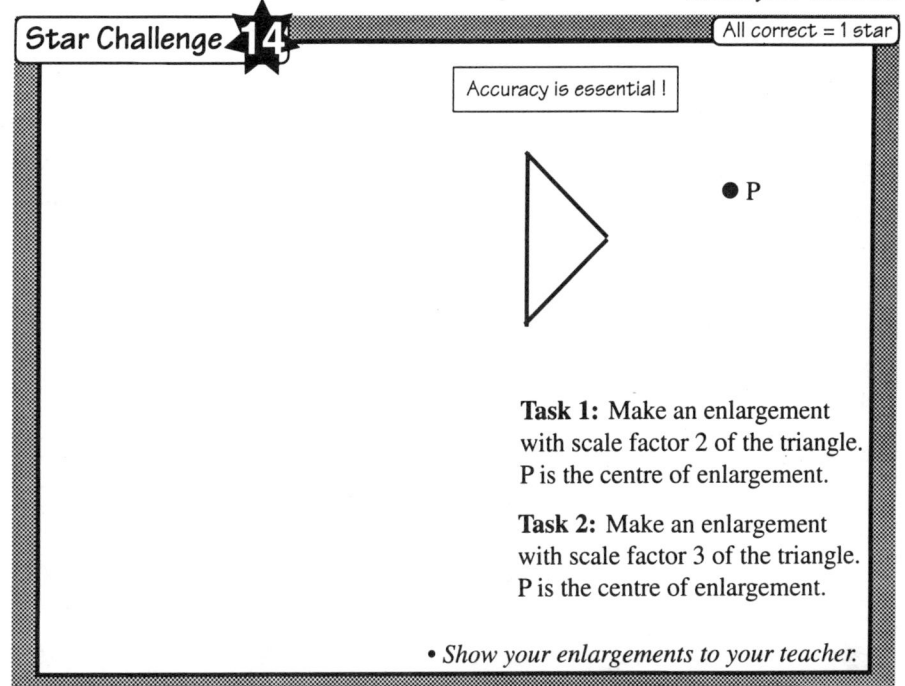

## Star Challenge 14

All correct = 1 star

Accuracy is essential!

• P

**Task 1:** Make an enlargement with scale factor 2 of the triangle. P is the centre of enlargement.

**Task 2:** Make an enlargement with scale factor 3 of the triangle. P is the centre of enlargement.

• *Show your enlargements to your teacher.*

A POW GUIDE    page 233    The Geometry of Angle and Shape **EXTRA**

# Section 17: Technique review

In this section you will review the techniques met in this topic.

Check your answers at the end of each set of problems.

## R1: More congruent shapes     Level 4

Shapes that are exactly the same shape and size are **congruent**.

Say which shape is NOT CONGRUENT in each set :

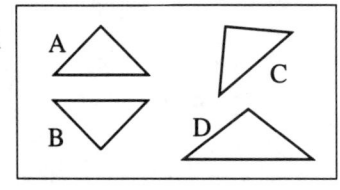

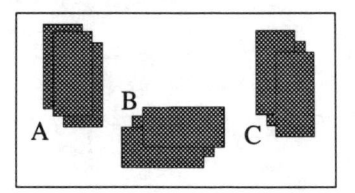

Set 1: A, B, C, D

Set 2: A, B, C

## R2: Mirror and rotational symmetry     mirror / tracing paper     Level 4

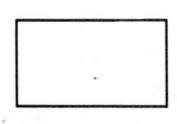

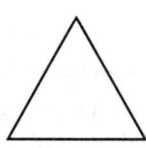

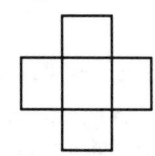

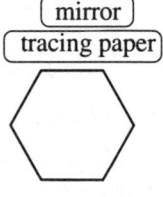

Copy and complete this table:

| Name | | | cross | hexagon | |
|---|---|---|---|---|---|
| Number of lines of symmetry | | | | | |
| Order of symmetry | | | | | |

use mirror
use tracing paper

## R3: Angle labels     Level 5

**Task 1:** Copy and complete:

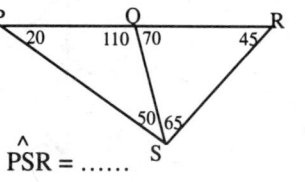

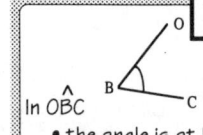

$Q\hat{P}S$ = ......    $Q\hat{R}S$ = ......
$P\hat{Q}S$ = ......    $P\hat{S}Q$ = ......
$R\hat{Q}S$ = ......    $R\hat{S}Q$ = ......    $P\hat{S}R$ = ......

(Angles shown: P=20, O=110/70, R=45, S=50/65)

In $O\hat{B}C$
• the angle is at B
• the arms of the angle are OB & BC

**Task 2:** True (T) or false (F) ?

1. PQS is obtuse    2. QRS is acute    3. RQS is a right angle    4. QSP is reflex

## R4: Estimating angle sizes     Level 5

Estimate the size of each angle below:

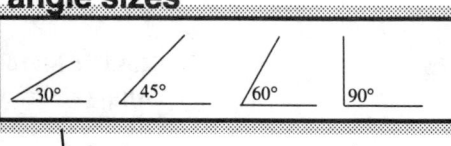

Compare the angles below with the angles in this box.
(30°, 45°, 60°, 90°)

1.    2.    3.    4.

A POW GUIDE    page 234    The Geometry of Angle and Shape    **EXTRA**

# R5: Measuring angles and lines

**Level 5**

Measure each of these angles:
1. EÔD
2. CÔD
3. OB̂E
4. AB̂O

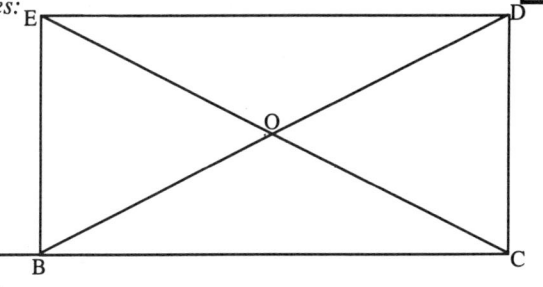

Measure each of these lines:
5. ED   6. DC   7. AC   8. BO

# R6: Classifying triangles

**Level 5**

Copy and complete each statement.
Fill in each gap with one of these expressions:

> equilateral
> isosceles
> right-angled
> scalene

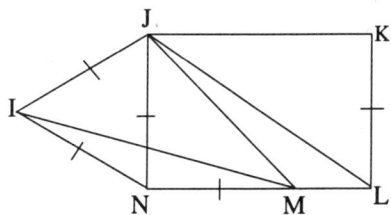

△ JML is ............   △ IJN is ............
△ JKL is ............   △ MNI is ............
△ JMN is ............   △ IJM is ............

# R7: Angles on lines

**Level 6**

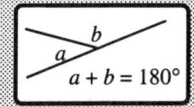

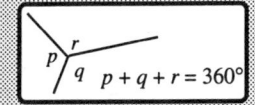

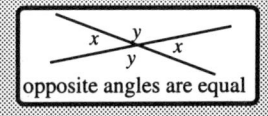

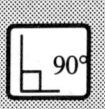

$a + b = 180°$

$p + q + r = 360°$

opposite angles are equal

$90°$

Work out the angle size for each letter. Write each answer in the form "a = ......"

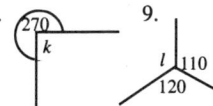

1. 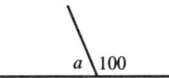 $a \backslash 100$
2. 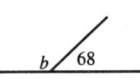 $b / 68$
3.  $30 / c$
4. 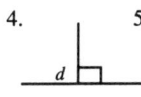 $d$
5. 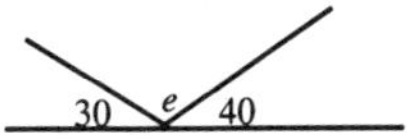 $30 \backslash e / 40$
6. 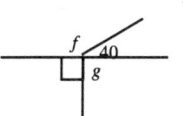 $f \backslash 40 / g$
7. 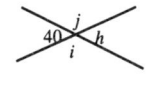 $40 \backslash j / h / i$
8. $270 / k$
9. $l | 110 / 120$
10. 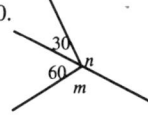 $30 \backslash n / 60 / m$

A POW GUIDE          page 235          The Geometry of Angle and Shape **EXTRA**

## R8: Triangles

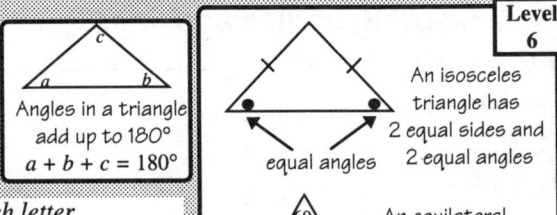

**Level 6**

Angles in a triangle add up to 180°
$a + b + c = 180°$

An isosceles triangle has 2 equal sides and 2 equal angles

An equilateral triangle has 3 equal sides and 3 equal angles

*Work out the angle size for each letter.*
*Write each answer in the form "a = ......"*

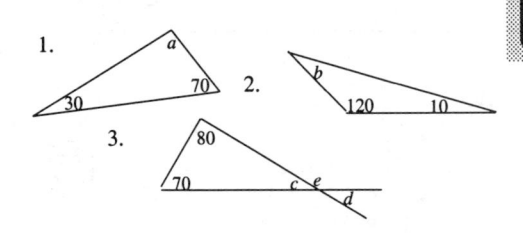

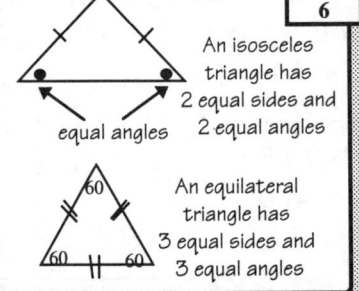

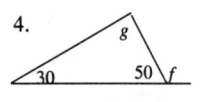

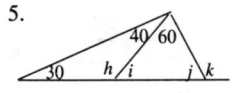

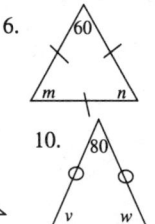

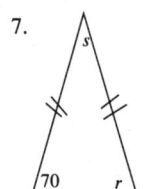

1.  (30, 70, a)
2.  (b, 120, 10)
3.  (70, 80, c, e, d)
4.  (30, g, 50, f)
5.  (30, 40, 60, h, i, j, k)
6.  (60, m, n)
7.  (isosceles, s, 70, r)
8.  (30, right angle, p, q)
9.  (isosceles, 45, u, t)
10. (80, v, w)

## R9: Angles on parallel lines

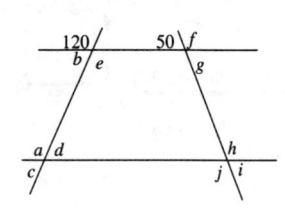

**Level 6**

(diagram with angles 120, 50, labels a, b, c, d, e, f, g, h, i, j)

*Copy and complete:*

a = ......°    b = ......°    c = ......°    d = ......°
e = ......°    f = ......°    g = ......°    h = ......°
i = ......°    j = ......°

A POW GUIDE    page 236    The Geometry of Angle and Shape **EXTRA**

# THE NATIONAL CURRICULUM …
# … AND BEYOND …

*Pow*

# Patterns and Rules
# EXTRA

|  |  |  | |
|---|---|---|---|
| | | | §6 Systematic equation solving |
| | | | §5 Solving equations |
| | | §4 Shape patterns | |
| | | §3 Machines and rules | |
| | | §2 Using letters for numbers | |
| | §1 Rules in words | | |
| Level 3 | Level 4 | Level 5 | Level 6 |

*A POW GUIDE*      page 237

# Patterns and Rules
## Section 1: Rules in words

Level 4

In this section you will :
- work with rules for number chains;
- find rules for tables of related data;
- find and use rules for number machines.

**DEVELOPMENT**

### D1: Rules for number chains

$3 \rightarrow 5 \rightarrow 7 \rightarrow 9 \rightarrow 11$
Rule: Add 2

Write down the first five numbers in each chain:

1. $4 \rightarrow ... \rightarrow ... \rightarrow ... \rightarrow ...$   Rule: Add 3
2. $13 \rightarrow ... \rightarrow ... \rightarrow ... \rightarrow ...$   Rule: Take 2
3. $2 \rightarrow ... \rightarrow ... \rightarrow ... \rightarrow ...$   Rule: Multiply by 2
4. $3 \rightarrow ... \rightarrow ... \rightarrow ... \rightarrow ...$   Rule: Multiply by 2 and add 1
5. $4 \rightarrow ... \rightarrow ... \rightarrow ... \rightarrow ...$   Rule: Add 1 and multiply by 2
6. $32 \rightarrow ... \rightarrow ... \rightarrow ... \rightarrow ...$   Rule: Divide by 2
7. $20 \rightarrow ... \rightarrow ... \rightarrow ... \rightarrow ...$   Rule: Halve it and add 2
8. $4 \rightarrow ... \rightarrow ... \rightarrow ... \rightarrow ...$   Rule: Subtract 1 and double it

Find the rule for each chain:

9. $10 \rightarrow 13 \rightarrow 16 \rightarrow 19 \rightarrow 22$   Rule: ....................
10. $37 \rightarrow 27 \rightarrow 17 \rightarrow 7 \rightarrow -3$   Rule: ....................
11. $5 \rightarrow 10 \rightarrow 20 \rightarrow 40 \rightarrow 80$   Rule: ....................
12. $100 \rightarrow 50 \rightarrow 25 \rightarrow 12\frac{1}{2} \rightarrow 6\frac{1}{4}$   Rule: ....................
13. $1 \rightarrow 5 \rightarrow 13 \rightarrow 29 \rightarrow 61$   Rule: ....................

### Star Challenge 1

- Check your answers.
- All correct = 1 star

Write down the first five numbers in each chain:

1. $25 \rightarrow ... \rightarrow ... \rightarrow ... \rightarrow ...$   Rule: Subtract 4
2. $1 \rightarrow ... \rightarrow ... \rightarrow ... \rightarrow ...$   Rule: Multiply by 5
3. $6 \rightarrow ... \rightarrow ... \rightarrow ... \rightarrow ...$   Rule: Double it and take 5

Find the rule for each chain:

4. $1 \rightarrow 3 \rightarrow 9 \rightarrow 27 \rightarrow 81$   Rule: ....................
5. $3 \rightarrow 5 \rightarrow 9 \rightarrow 17 \rightarrow 33$   Rule: ....................

- Your teacher has the answers to these.

A POW GUIDE          Patterns and Rules **EXTRA**

## D2: From tables to rules

**EXAMPLE 1**  What is the rule connecting the data in this table?

| number of pencils | cost in pence |
|---|---|
| 1 | 10 |
| 2 | 20 |
| 5 | 50 |

Rule:
Cost in pence = 10 × number of pencils

*Find the rule in words for each table:*

1. 
| Number of packets | Number of sweets |
|---|---|
| 1 | 15 |
| 2 | 30 |
| 3 | 45 |

2. 
| Number of letters | Postage (in p) |
|---|---|
| 2 | 40 |
| 3 | 60 |
| 5 | 100 |

3. 
| Number of diamonds | Perimeter |
|---|---|
| ◇ 1 | 4 |
| ◇◇ 2 | 8 |
| ◇◇◇ 3 | 12 |

4. 
| Number of lines | Number of dots |
|---|---|
| •—• 1 | 2 |
| •—•—• 2 | 3 |
| •—•—•—• 3 | 4 |

• *Check your answers.*

## D3: Number machines

*Copy and complete:*

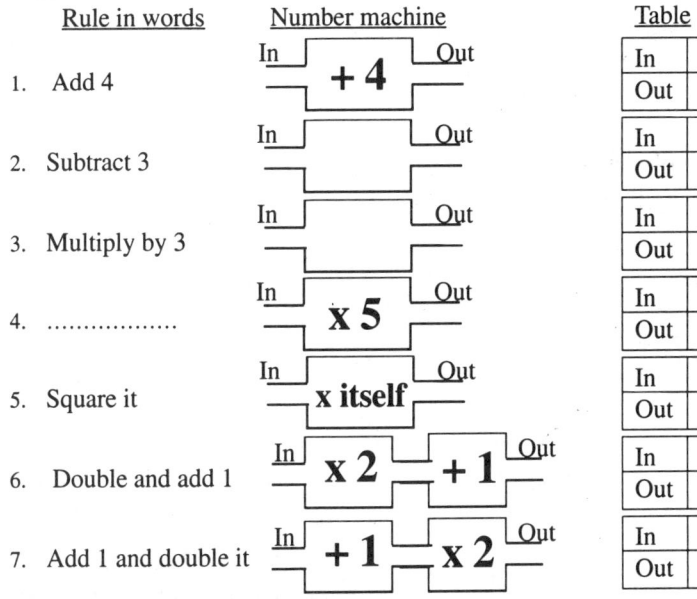

| Rule in words | Number machine | Table |
|---|---|---|

1. Add 4 — In [+4] Out — 

| In | 5 | 10 | 12 |
|---|---|---|---|
| Out | 9 | | |

2. Subtract 3 — In [ ] Out —

| In | 4 | 8 | 10 |
|---|---|---|---|
| Out | | | |

3. Multiply by 3 — In [ ] Out —

| In | 2 | 5 | 7 |
|---|---|---|---|
| Out | | | |

4. ............ — In [× 5] Out —

| In | 2 | 4 | 6 |
|---|---|---|---|
| Out | | | |

5. Square it — In [× itself] Out —

| In | 2 | 5 | 7 |
|---|---|---|---|
| Out | | | |

6. Double and add 1 — In [× 2] [+ 1] Out —

| In | 2 | 4 | 5 |
|---|---|---|---|
| Out | | | |

7. Add 1 and double it — In [+ 1] [× 2] Out —

| In | 2 | 4 | 5 |
|---|---|---|---|
| Out | | | |

8. Does the rule 'double it and add 1' give the same results as 'add 1 and double it'?

• *Check your answers.*

A POW GUIDE   page 239   Patterns and Rules **EXTRA**

# Section 2: Using letters for numbers

Level 5

In this section you will:
- use letters to represent unknown numbers;
- review the meanings of various algebraic expressions.

**DEVELOPMENT**

## D1: Letters for unknown numbers

**EXAMPLE 2:**

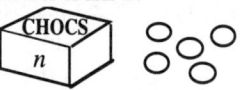

There are $n$ chocolates in a box.
Ellie has 1 box + 5 chocolates
Write an expression to show how many chocolates Ellie has.

Answer: Ellie has $n + 5$ chocolates

*For questions 1 and 2, write an expression for the number of chocolates:*

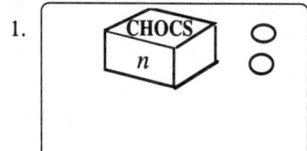

1. [box of $n$ chocs with 2 outside]

2. [box of $n$ chocs — 2 chocolates have been eaten.]

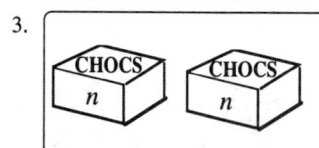

3. [two boxes each with $n$] Which <u>two</u> of these expressions are correct for the total number of chocolates?

   | $n + n$ | $2n$ | $n + 2$ | $n \times n$ |

   • *Check your answers.*

*Write an expression for the number of chocolates in each case:*

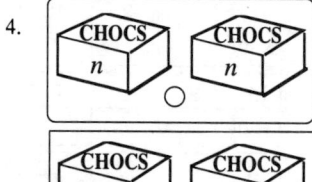

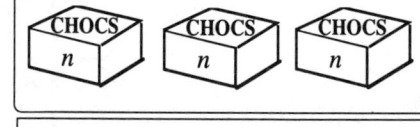

4. [two boxes of $n$, 1 chocolate outside]

5. [three boxes of $n$]

6. [two boxes of $n$, 3 chocolates outside]

7. [three boxes of $n$, 1 chocolate outside]

8. *Match the pictures with the expressions:*

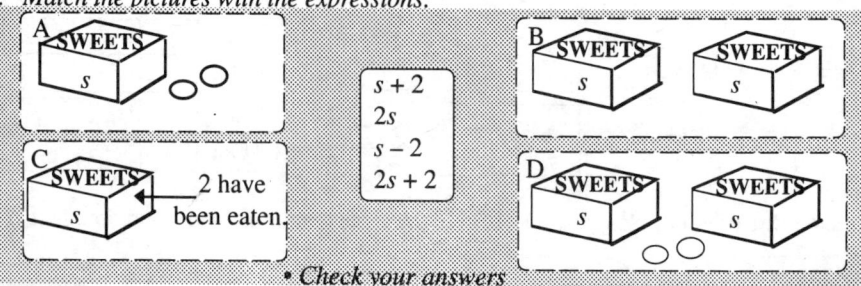

   A. [box of $s$ sweets, 2 outside]
   
   B. [two boxes of $s$]
   
   C. [box of $s$ — 2 have been eaten]
   
   D. [two boxes of $s$, 2 sweets outside]

   $s + 2$
   $2s$
   $s - 2$
   $2s + 2$

   • *Check your answers*

A POW GUIDE    page 240    Patterns and Rules **EXTRA**

# D2: Expressions with brackets

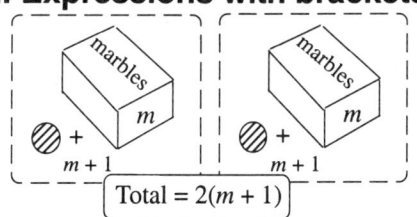

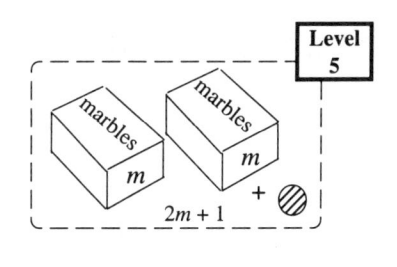

Level 5

Total = 2(m + 1)

1. Is 2(m + 1) the same as 2m + 1 ?
2. Is 2(m + 1) the same as 2m + 2 ?

3. *Copy and complete:* [2 lots of]

Number of sweets = 2 × (... ... ...)
= 2(... ... ...)

and 2(... ... ...) = 2n + ...

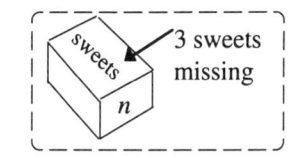

4. 3 sweets missing

(a) There are ...... in one box.
(b) There are 2 boxes. each has 3 sweets missing.

Number of sweets = 2( ... − ...)

• *Check your answers.*

# D3: Matching pairs of algebraic cards

$n + 2$ will always give the same numbers as $\frac{n}{2}$
They are a matching pair.

**Task 1:** Find THREE matching pairs from these algebra cards:

$n + n$   $n^2$   $n + n + 1$   $1 + 2n$   $n \times n$   $2n$

**Task 2:** Find THREE matching pairs from these algebra cards:

$n + n + n$   $2n + 1$   $2n + n$   $1 + 2n$   $2 + n + 3$   $n + 5$

**Task 3:** Find THREE matching pairs from these algebra cards:

$\frac{1}{2}n$   $3n$   $n \div 2$   $2n + 3n$   $2n + n$   $5n$

• *Check answers.*

**Star Challenge 2**  All correct = 1 star

Find SIX matching pairs from these algebra cards:

$n + 2$   $2n$   $n + n$   $2n + 1$   $2(n + 1)$   $2n + 2$

$n + 3$   $2 + n$   $n + n + 1$   $3n + 1$   $2n + n + 1$   $3 + n$

A POW GUIDE          page 241          Patterns and Rules **EXTRA**

# Section 3 : Machines and rules

Level 5

In this section you will work with rules for number machines.

## DEVELOPMENT

### D1: Rules for machines

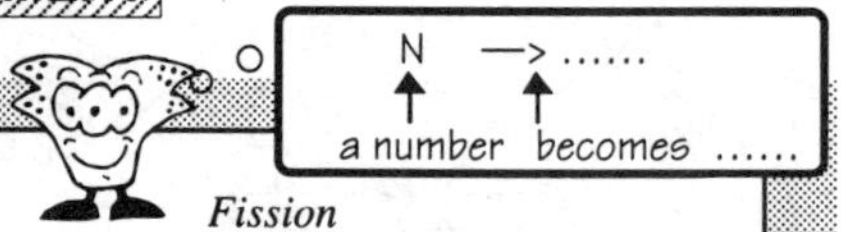

$N \rightarrow \ldots$
a number becomes ......

**EXAMPLE 3**

Q: (a) Find the 'out' value if you put in 3
(b) Find the 'out' value if you put in 4
(c) Find the 'out' value if you put in N
(d) What is the rule for this machine?

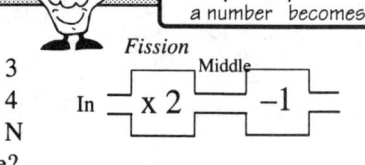

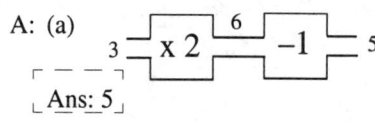

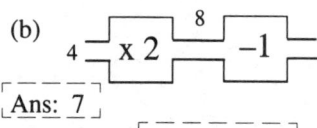

Fission
In — ×2 — −1 —

A: (a) 3 — ×2 —6— −1 — 5
Ans: 5

(b) 4 — ×2 —8— −1 —
Ans: 7

(c) N — ×2 —2N— −1 — 2N−1

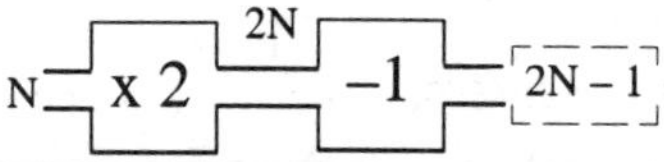

(d) Rule is $N \rightarrow 2N - 1$

Chyps

This rule means "a number becomes twice the number take away 1"

1. In — ×3 —Middle— +2 —Out

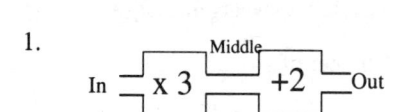

    (a) Find the 'out' value if you put in 4
    (b) Find the 'out' value if you put in 3
    (c) Find the 'out' value if you put in N
    (d) What is the rule for this machine ?

*Write down the rule for each of these machines:*

2. In — ×4 —Middle— −1 —Out

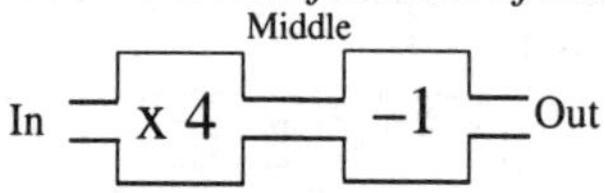

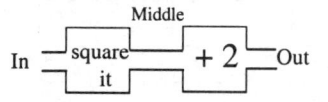

3. In — square it —Middle— +2 —Out

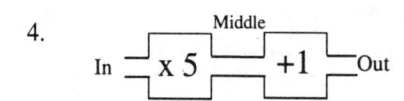

4. In — ×5 —Middle— +1 —Out

5. In — ×5 —Middle— −3 —Out

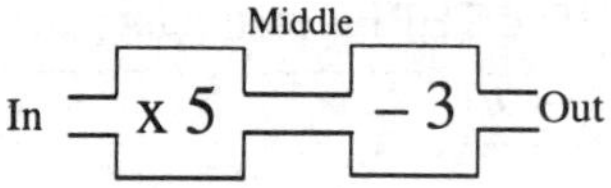

6. Which of these is the rule for this machine?

    $N \rightarrow 2(N + 1)$ or $N \rightarrow 2N + 1$

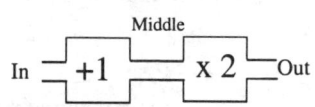

    In — +1 —Middle— ×2 —Out

7. *Draw machines for each of these rules:*

    (a) $N \rightarrow 3N + 1$   (b) $N \rightarrow 3(N + 1)$

8. *Draw a machine for* $N \rightarrow N^2 + 2$

• Check your answers.

A POW GUIDE       page 242       Patterns and Rules **EXTRA**

## D2: Machine instructions

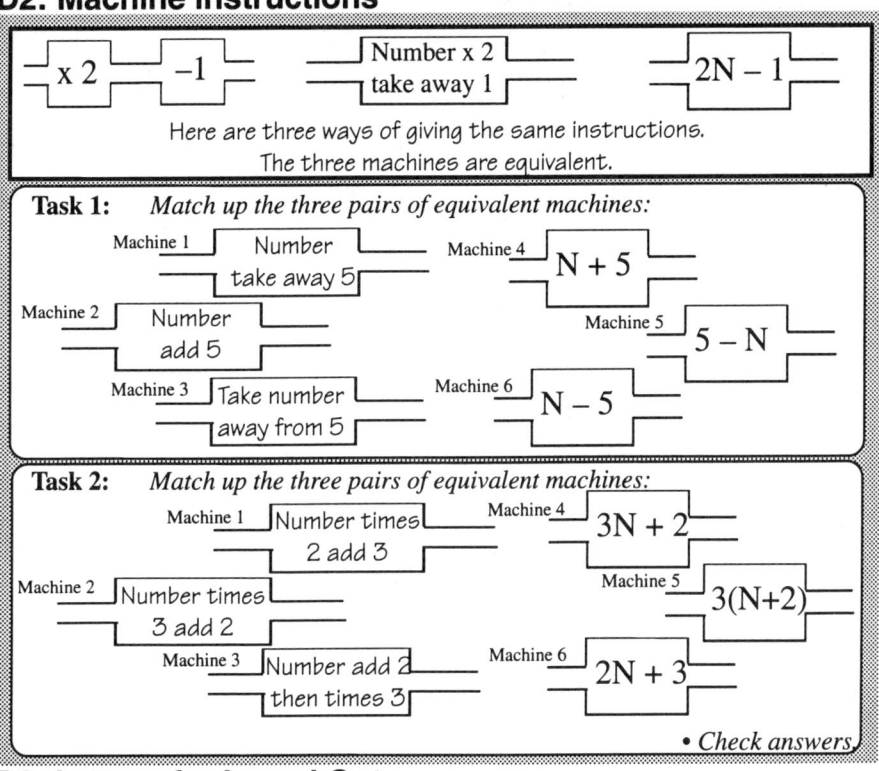

$\boxed{\times 2} \boxed{-1}$     $\boxed{\text{Number} \times 2 \text{ take away 1}}$     $\boxed{2N - 1}$

Here are three ways of giving the same instructions.
The three machines are equivalent.

**Task 1:** Match up the three pairs of equivalent machines:

Machine 1: $\boxed{\text{Number take away 5}}$     Machine 4: $\boxed{N + 5}$

Machine 2: $\boxed{\text{Number add 5}}$     Machine 5: $\boxed{5 - N}$

Machine 3: $\boxed{\text{Take number away from 5}}$     Machine 6: $\boxed{N - 5}$

**Task 2:** Match up the three pairs of equivalent machines:

Machine 1: $\boxed{\text{Number times 2 add 3}}$     Machine 4: $\boxed{3N + 2}$

Machine 2: $\boxed{\text{Number times 3 add 2}}$     Machine 5: $\boxed{3(N+2)}$

Machine 3: $\boxed{\text{Number add 2 then times 3}}$     Machine 6: $\boxed{2N + 3}$

• Check answers

## D3: Letters for In and Out

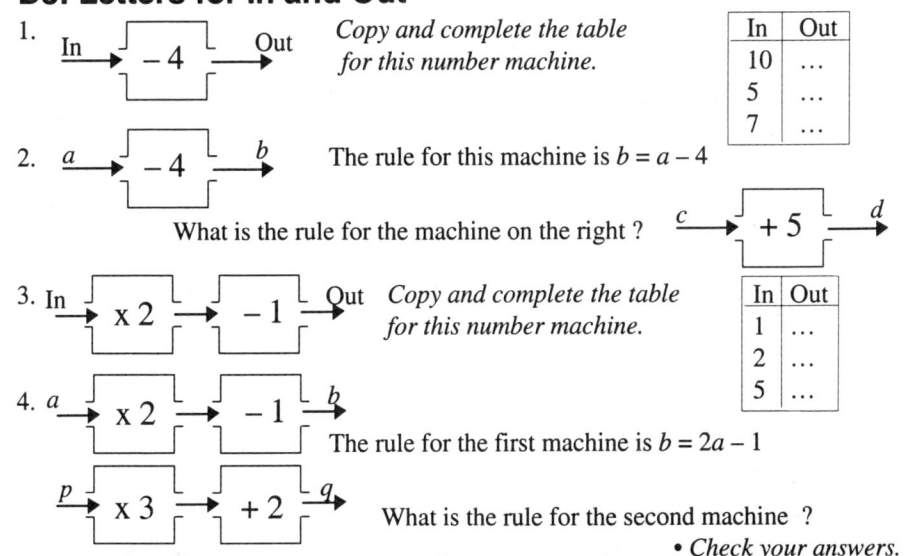

1. In $\rightarrow \boxed{-4} \rightarrow$ Out    Copy and complete the table for this number machine.

| In | Out |
|---|---|
| 10 | ... |
| 5 | ... |
| 7 | ... |

2. $a \rightarrow \boxed{-4} \rightarrow b$    The rule for this machine is $b = a - 4$

What is the rule for the machine on the right?    $c \rightarrow \boxed{+5} \rightarrow d$

3. In $\rightarrow \boxed{\times 2} \rightarrow \boxed{-1} \rightarrow$ Out    Copy and complete the table for this number machine.

| In | Out |
|---|---|
| 1 | ... |
| 2 | ... |
| 5 | ... |

4. $a \rightarrow \boxed{\times 2} \rightarrow \boxed{-1} \rightarrow b$

The rule for the first machine is $b = 2a - 1$

$p \rightarrow \boxed{\times 3} \rightarrow \boxed{+2} \rightarrow q$

What is the rule for the second machine?

• Check your answers.

A POW GUIDE     page 243     Patterns and Rules **EXTRA**

# Section 4: Shape patterns

**Levels 5 & 6**

In this section you will :
- write rules for patterns using algebra (letters instead of words).
- look for patterns in squences of shapes.

## DEVELOPMENT

### D1: Rules for shape patterns

**Level 5**

1. Copy and complete the table:

   | Lines (L) | 1 | ... | ... |
   |---|---|---|---|
   | Dots (D) | 2 | ... | ... |

2. The rule for this pattern is : **Number of dots (D) = Number of lines(L) + 1**
   (a) How many dots will there be with 20 lines ?
   (b) One of these expressions is the rule written using algebra. Which expression is the correct one ?
   
   $D = L + 1$
   $L = D + 1$

3. Copy and complete the table:

   | shape number (S) | 1 | 2 | 3 |
   |---|---|---|---|
   | number of matches (M) | 4 | ... | ... |

4. There is a rule connecting the shape number S and the number of matches M. Give the rule in words.
5. Write the rule using algebra.
6. Work out the number of matches used to make shape number 10.

• Check your answers.

### D2: Choose the right formula

In each case, choose the correct formula for the data in the table.

**A formula is a rule written using algebra instead of words.**

**Level 6**

1. | Lines (L) | Spaces (S) |
   |---|---|
   | 1 | 2 |
   | 2 | 4 |
   | 3 | 6 |

   $S = 2L$
   $L = 2S$
   $S = L + 2$

2. | Squares (S) | Perimeter (P) |
   |---|---|
   | 1 | 4 |
   | 2 | 6 |
   | 3 | 8 |

   $P = 2S$
   $P = 2S + 2$
   $S = 2P + 2$

3. | Squares (S) | Matches (M) |
   |---|---|
   | 1 | 4 |
   | 2 | 7 |
   | 3 | 10 |

   $M = 3S$
   $M = 3S + 1$
   $M = 3S + 2$

4. | Pentagons (p) | Distance round (d) |
   |---|---|
   | 1 | 5 |
   | 2 | 8 |
   | 3 | 11 |

   $d = 3p$
   $d = 3p + 1$
   $d = 3p + 2$

5. Use the formula for question 2.
   Work out the number of spaces in the circle with 6 lines.
6. Use the formula for question 4.
   Work out the distance round the shape with 10 pentagons.

• Check your answers.

A POW GUIDE     Patterns and Rules **EXTRA**

# D3: Matchstick patterns

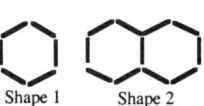

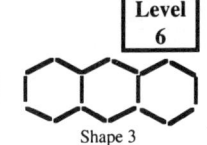

Level 6

1. 

| Shape number | 1 | 2 | 3 | 4 | 5 |
|---|---|---|---|---|---|
| Match sticks | 6 | 11 | 16 | ? | ? |

Shape 1   Shape 2   Shape 3

(a) How many matchsticks will shape 4 have ?
(b) How many matchsticks will shape 5 have ?
(c) How do you find the number of matchsticks in the next shape in the pattern?
(d) How many matchsticks will shape 10 have ?

2. For each set of shapes A, B, C, D and E:
   * copy the first three shapes;
   * draw shape 4;
   * copy and complete the table;
   * explain how you find the number of matchsticks in the next shape in the pattern.

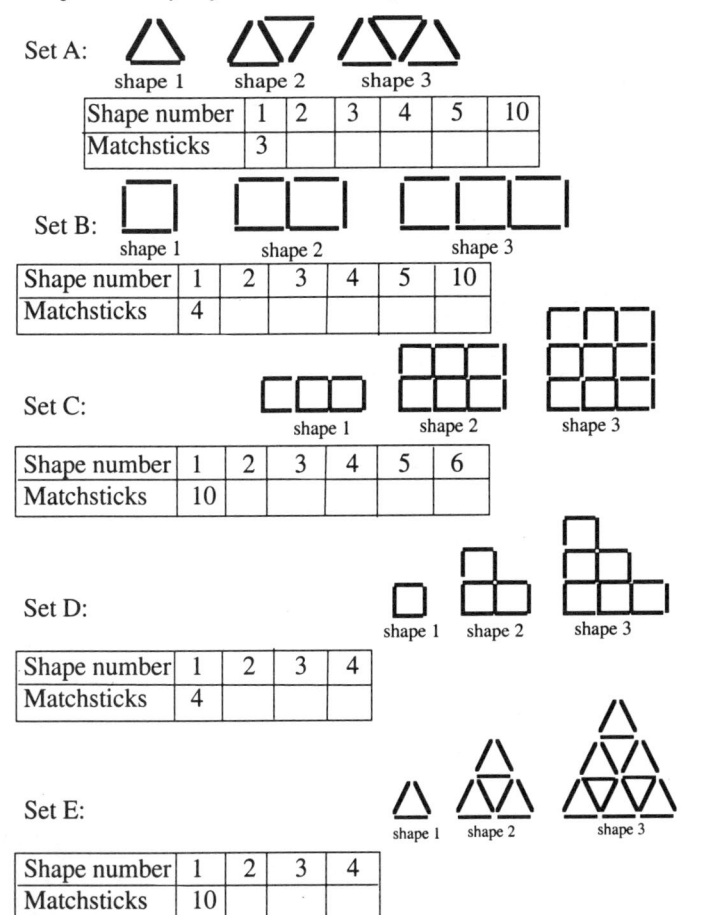

Set A:

shape 1   shape 2   shape 3

| Shape number | 1 | 2 | 3 | 4 | 5 | 10 |
|---|---|---|---|---|---|---|
| Matchsticks | 3 | | | | | |

Set B:

shape 1   shape 2   shape 3

| Shape number | 1 | 2 | 3 | 4 | 5 | 10 |
|---|---|---|---|---|---|---|
| Matchsticks | 4 | | | | | |

Set C:

shape 1   shape 2   shape 3

| Shape number | 1 | 2 | 3 | 4 | 5 | 6 |
|---|---|---|---|---|---|---|
| Matchsticks | 10 | | | | | |

Set D:

shape 1   shape 2   shape 3

| Shape number | 1 | 2 | 3 | 4 |
|---|---|---|---|---|
| Matchsticks | 4 | | | |

Set E:

shape 1   shape 2   shape 3

| Shape number | 1 | 2 | 3 | 4 |
|---|---|---|---|---|
| Matchsticks | 10 | | | |

• Check your answers.

A POW GUIDE   page 245   Patterns and Rules EXTRA

# Section 5: Solving equations

Level 6

*In this section you will solve equations by inspection.*

**DEVELOPMENT**

## D1: What is an equation?

**Expressions and equations**
$2N + 1$ is **an expression**. For each value of N, the expression has a different value.
$2N + 1 = 7$ is **an equation**.
When $N = 3$, it is a true statement. If N is not 3, it is not a true statement.
$N = 3$ is **the solution** of $2N + 1 = 7$
Expressions and equations can use any letters, not just N.

1. $N + 1 = 6$     For what value of N is this true?
2. $a - 2 = 8$     What is the value of $a$?
3. $3b = 18$     For what value of $b$ is this true?
4. $2p + 1 = 7$     What is the value of $p$?

In each question, you have been **solving the equation** or **finding the solution of the equation.**

Solve each of these equations. Write each answer in the form $N = ...$

5. $N + 2 = 9$
6. $2N = 8$
7. $3N = 30$
8. $N + 5 = 8$
9. $2N + 1 = 11$
10. $3N = 12$
11. $2N - 1 = 19$
12. $10N + 1 = 71$

• Check your answers.

## Star Challenge 3 3

34-36 correct = 2 stars
30-33 correct = 1 star

### Solution Pattern

**Solution – colour key**

| Solution | 1 | 2 | 3 | 4 | 5 |
|---|---|---|---|---|---|
| Colour | Red | Blue | Green | Orange | Yellow |

Solve each equation. Colour each rectangle with the solution colour.
(For example: each equation with solution 1 is coloured red.)

| | | | | | | |
|---|---|---|---|---|---|---|
| $p + 3 = 4$ | $2c + 3 = 13$ | $5k = 15$ | $2a + 1 = 7$ | $3p - 10 = 5$ | $3p + 1 = 7$ |
| $2j - 1 = 9$ | $2r + 1 = 3$ | $12 - n = 8$ | $2m = 8$ | $6t = 12$ | $4b - 11 = 9$ |
| $6p + 1 = 25$ | $3x - 2 = 7$ | $5s - 4 = 1$ | $5 + 3p = 11$ | $10c - 5 = 25$ | $3 + 2p = 11$ |
| $2v - 1 = 7$ | $5 + q = 8$ | $3r - 1 = 2$ | $5z - 1 = 9$ | $5 + 2f = 11$ | $4 + u = 8$ |
| $w + 3 = 8$ | $5 + 2b = 7$ | $2n - 1 = 7$ | $3b + 1 = 13$ | $3 + 3d = 9$ | $6 - m = 1$ |
| $9 - 4e = 5$ | $3k + 1 = 16$ | $4y = 3y + 3$ | $10 - g = 7$ | $2y = 10$ | $4n + 3 = 11$ |

• Show your answers to your teacher.

A POW GUIDE     Patterns and Rules **EXTRA**

# Section 6: Systematic equation solving

*Level 6*

In this section you will learn and practice some basic techniques for solving equations.

## DEVELOPMENT

### D1: The basic technique

The rule for solving all equations is *"whatever you do to one side of the equation, you must do the same to the other side"*.

Pow

|       | $2r + 3$ | $= 7$ |       |
|-------|----------|-------|-------|
| $-3$  | $2r$     | $= 4$ | $-3$  |
| $\div 2$ | $r$   | $= 2$ | $\div 2$ |

Copy and complete:

1.
|       | $3p + 2$ | $= 11$ |       |
|-------|----------|--------|-------|
| $-2$  | $3p$     | $= \ldots$ | $-2$  |
| $\div 3$ | $\ldots$ | $= \ldots$ | $\div 3$ |

2.
|       | $2c + 40$ | $= 140$ |       |
|-------|-----------|---------|-------|
| $-40$ | $\ldots$  | $= \ldots$ | $-40$ |
| $\div 2$ | $\ldots$ | $= \ldots$ | $\div 2$ |

3.
|       | $4m + 5$ | $= 13$ |       |
|-------|----------|--------|-------|
| $-5$  | $\ldots$ | $= \ldots$ | $-5$  |
| $\div 4$ | $\ldots$ | $= \ldots$ | $\div 4$ |

4.
|       | $3v - 4$ | $= 11$ |       |
|-------|----------|--------|-------|
| $+4$  | $\ldots$ | $= \ldots$ | $+4$  |
| $\div 3$ | $\ldots$ | $= \ldots$ | $\div 3$ |

• Check your answers.

### D2: A shortcut

A short cut

|       | $2m + 6$ | $= 10$ |
|-------|----------|--------|
| $-6$  | $2m$     | $= 6$  |
| $\div 2$ | $m$   | $= 3$  |

Just write the instructions on *one* side of the equations.

Even though the instructions are only written on one side of the equation, the rule is always: *"whatever you do to one side of the equation, you must do the same to the other side."*

Lubbly

Copy and complete:

1.
|       | $5p + 3$ | $= 18$ |
|-------|----------|--------|
| $-3$  |          | $=$    |
| $\div 5$ |       | $=$    |

2.
|       | $3k - 1$ | $= 11$ |
|-------|----------|--------|
| $+1$  |          | $=$    |
| $\div 3$ |       | $=$    |

3.
|       | $4e - 2$ | $= 18$ |
|-------|----------|--------|
| $+2$  |          | $=$    |
| $\div 4$ |       | $=$    |

Solve these equations. Set out your working as in questions 1 – 3.

4. $3y + 5 = 14$
5. $6p - 3 = 15$
6. $2d + 4 = 20$
7. $7x + 7 = 42$
8. $9a - 2 = 43$
9. $4m + 2 = 14$
10. $8b - 3 = 13$
11. $2p + 1 = 15$
12. $7k - 3 = 18$

• Check answers.

A POW GUIDE     Patterns and Rules **EXTRA**

## P1: Practice Exercises

**PRACTICE**

**Level 6**

*Solve these equations.*
*Set out all working as in D2.*
*Do one batch of questions at a time then CHECK YOUR ANSWERS.*
*You may not need to do every batch.*
*When you feel you are good at this technique, do the Star Challenge.*

**Batch A:**

1.  $3p + 9 = 24$
2.  $8v - 3 = 21$
3.  $2k + 1 = 11$
4.  $5x - 9 = 16$
5.  $7r + 2 = 79$
6.  $6t + 4 = 40$
7.  $8x - 8 = 16$
8.  $7y - 5 = 16$
9.  $5x + 3 = 33$
10. $2w - 2 = 8$
11. $9h - 7 = 11$
12. $7c - 5 = 37$
13. $5s + 3 = 28$
14. $8j + 6 = 46$
15. $3q - 3 = 24$

*STOP ! Have you checked all your answers – and found out where you went wrong ?*

**Batch B:**

1.  $2d + 7 = 15$
2.  $9n - 2 = 25$
3.  $2b - 5 = 11$
4.  $2x + 3 = 19$
5.  $5t - 6 = 19$
6.  $4e + 6 = 50$
7.  $2d - 6 = 10$
8.  $2m - 1 = 29$
9.  $5f + 4 = 49$
10. $8v - 2 = 6$
11. $5y - 4 = 36$
12. $2b - 3 = 17$
13. $5q + 13 = 38$
14. $9n - 7 = 47$
15. $3g - 2 = 13$

It is a total waste of your time if you go onto the next batch of questions without checking your answers first ! You need to know whether what you are doing is correct !

**Batch C:**

1.  $2x + 4 = 20$
2.  $2p - 1 = 9$
3.  $3y - 1 = 11$
4.  $3x + 1 = 7$
5.  $4a - 3 = 13$
6.  $4 + 3s = 16$
7.  $3x - 2 = 10$
8.  $10a - 19 = 1$
9.  $8x + 8 = 24$
10. $6r - 7 = 23$
11. $7q + 2 = 30$
12. $3c - 4 = 5$
13. $2p + 5 = 11$
14. $4z + 3 = 15$
15. $3r - 1 = 20$

Taz

**Star Challenge**

13-15 correct = 1 star

*Solve these equations. Set out all working as in D2.*

1.  $5z - 1 = 9$
2.  $14 + 3m = 20$
3.  $7 + 3n = 13$
4.  $4 + 2r = 6$
5.  $15 + 7p = 29$
6.  $7n - 5 = 30$
7.  $4p - 3 = 13$
8.  $-1 + 5t = 9$
9.  $3 + 4z = 43$
10. $5d - 1 = 49$
11. $3p + 5 = 65$
12. $4m - 3 = 61$
13. $7c + 11 = 81$
14. $3e - 3 = 60$
15. $4f + 16 = 100$

• Your teacher has the answers for these.

A POW GUIDE     page 248     Patterns and Rules **EXTRA**

# THE NATIONAL CURRICULUM ...
# ... AND BEYOND ...

*Pow*

# Coordinates and Graphs
# EXTRA

|  |  |  |  |
|---|---|---|---|
|  | §7 Technique review | | |
|  |  |  | §6 Scatter graphs |
|  |  |  | §5 Related graphs |
|  |  |  | §4 From graphs to rules |
|  |  |  | §3 Coordinates in all four quadrants |
|  |  | §2 Rules and lines |  |
|  | §1 Basic Coordinates |  |  |
| Level 3 | Level 4 | Level 5 | Level 6 |

*A POW GUIDE*

# Coordinates and Graphs
## Section 1: Basic coordinates

Level 4

In this section you will review:
- coordinates in the first quadrant;
- plotting coordinates.

**DEVELOPMENT**

### D1: Coordinates

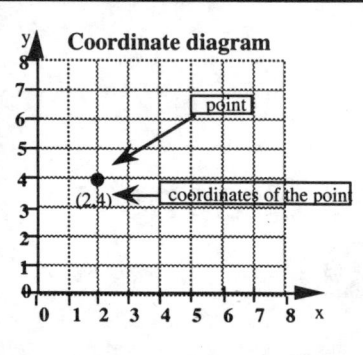

**Coordinate diagram**

In a set of coordinates:
- the first number tells you how far ACROSS to go
- the second number tells you how far UP to go
- the order is important
  – (1,2) is not the same as (2,1)
- coordinates are number parcels. They need wrapping.

Put all coordinates into brackets.

1,2 ✗    (1,2) ✓

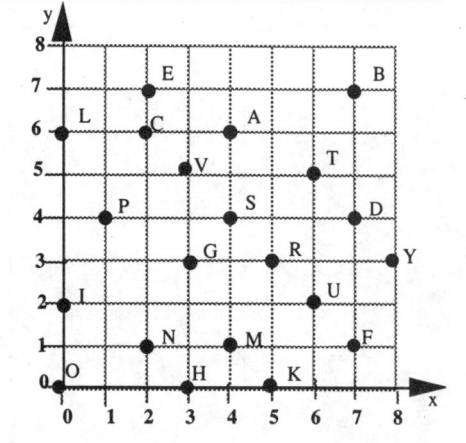

1. The coordinates of the point P are (1,4)
   What are the coordinates of A ?
2. What are the coordinates of U ?
3. The point N is found at (2,1)
   What letter is found at (4,1) ?
4. What letter is found at (3,5) ?
5. What name is given by:
   (1,4) (0,0) (5,3) (6,5)
   (3,5) (4,6) (0,6) (2,7) ?
6. I is at (0,2)
   What are the coordinates of L ?
7. H is at (3,0)
   What are the coordinates of K ?
8. What name is given by : (2,6) (3,0) (2,7) (0,6) (4,4) (2,7) (4,6) ?
9. The origin is at (0,0). What letter is at the origin ?
10. What name is given by : (5,0) (0,2) (2,1) (3,3) – (5,3) (0,0) (0,0) (4,4) (6,5) (2,7) (5,3)
11. Write down the coordinates that spell S U R E – S H O T
12. Write down the coordinates that spell G O L D – F I N G E R
13. What two names are given by
    (7,1) (0,2) (4,4) (4,4) (0,2) (0,0) (2,1) &  (2,6) (3,0) (8,3) (1,4) (4,4)

Check answers.

A POW GUIDE     page 250     Coordinates and Graphs     **EXTRA**

## P1: Buried treasure

**Level 4**

1. What is at (5,2) ?
2. What is at (2,3) ?
3. What is at (1,6) ?
4. What is at (3,2) ?
5. What is at (7,6) ?
6. What is at (6,7) ?

*What are the coordinates of :*

7. Mermaids' beach
8. Death drop
9. Old man's rest
10. Spring
11. Cool pool
12. Seal point
13. Where was gold found ?
14. Where are the tall trees ?
15. Where does the map say that you can find dragons ?
16. Find the point midway between Seal Point and the Marsh. Give its coordinates.

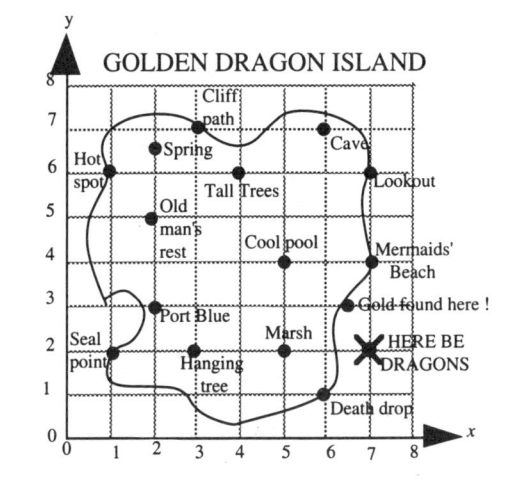

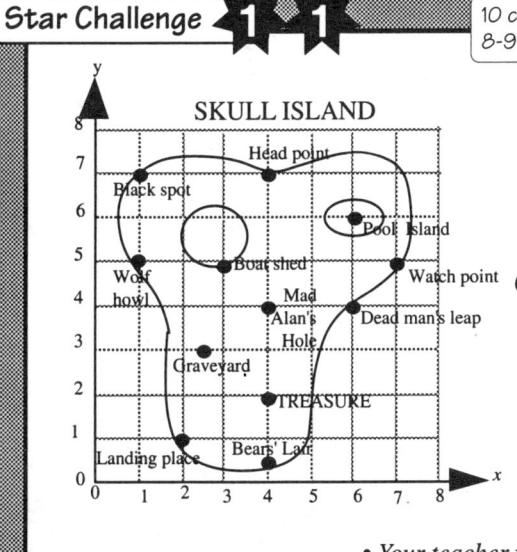

• *Check your answers.*

### Star Challenge

10 correct question-answer pairs = 2 stars
8-9 correct question-answer pairs = 1 star

*Make up ten questions about this map of Skull Island.*

*Give the answers to each of your questions.*

*You must use coordinates in each question-answer pair.*

• *Your teacher will need to mark these.*

A POW GUIDE        page 251        Coordinates and Graphs   **EXTRA**

# D2: Plotting points

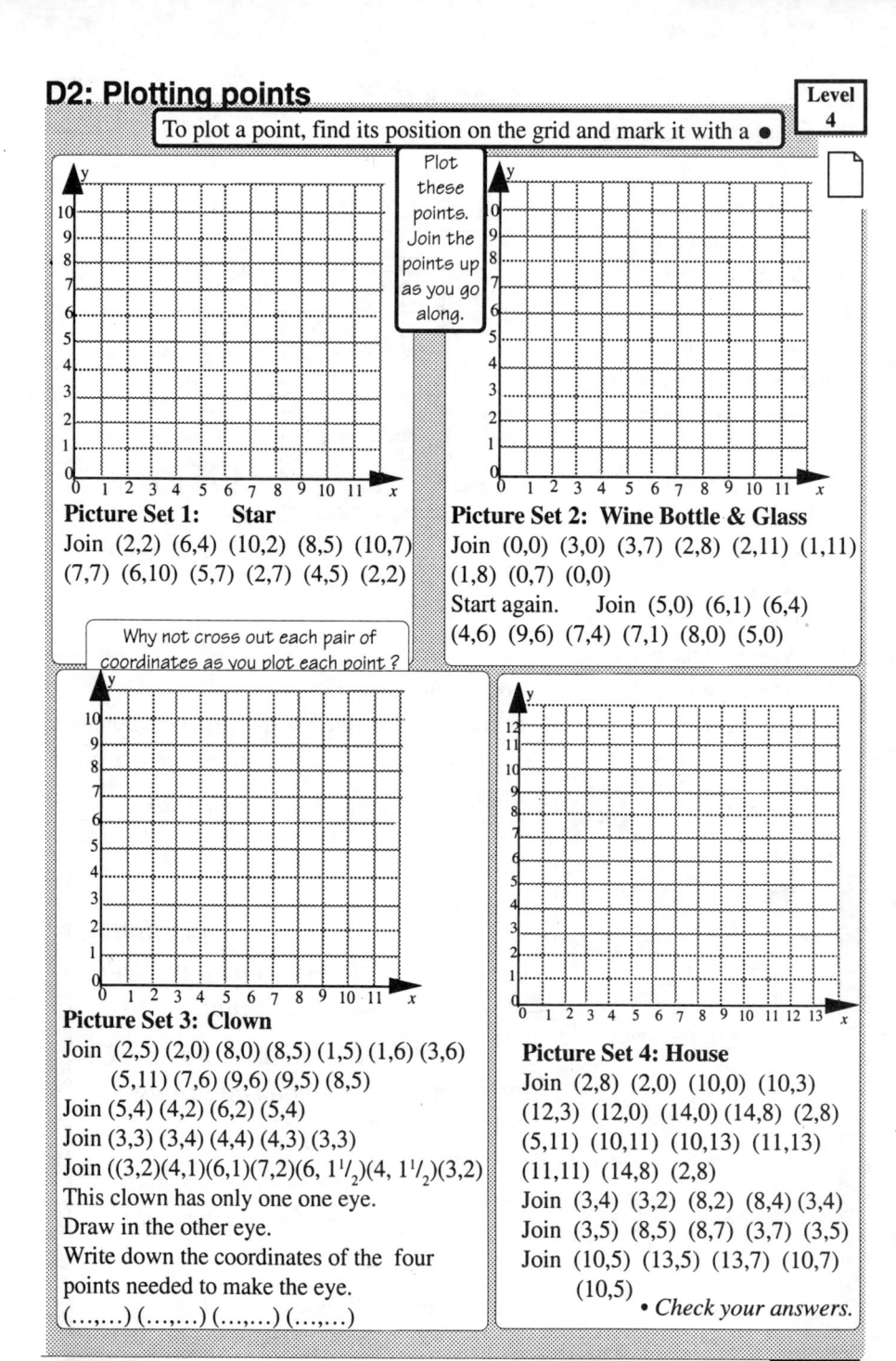

**Level 4**

To plot a point, find its position on the grid and mark it with a •

Plot these points. Join the points up as you go along.

**Picture Set 1: Star**
Join (2,2) (6,4) (10,2) (8,5) (10,7) (7,7) (6,10) (5,7) (2,7) (4,5) (2,2)

*Why not cross out each pair of coordinates as you plot each point?*

**Picture Set 2: Wine Bottle & Glass**
Join (0,0) (3,0) (3,7) (2,8) (2,11) (1,11) (1,8) (0,7) (0,0)
Start again.   Join (5,0) (6,1) (6,4) (4,6) (9,6) (7,4) (7,1) (8,0) (5,0)

**Picture Set 3: Clown**
Join (2,5) (2,0) (8,0) (8,5) (1,5) (1,6) (3,6) (5,11) (7,6) (9,6) (9,5) (8,5)
Join (5,4) (4,2) (6,2) (5,4)
Join (3,3) (3,4) (4,4) (4,3) (3,3)
Join ((3,2)(4,1)(6,1)(7,2)(6, 1½)(4, 1½)(3,2)
This clown has only one one eye.
Draw in the other eye.
Write down the coordinates of the four points needed to make the eye.
(…,…) (…,…) (…,…) (…,…)

**Picture Set 4: House**
Join (2,8) (2,0) (10,0) (10,3) (12,3) (12,0) (14,0) (14,8) (2,8) (5,11) (10,11) (10,13) (11,13) (11,11) (14,8) (2,8)
Join (3,4) (3,2) (8,2) (8,4) (3,4)
Join (3,5) (8,5) (8,7) (3,7) (3,5)
Join (10,5) (13,5) (13,7) (10,7) (10,5)

• *Check your answers.*

A POW GUIDE        page 252        Coordinates and Graphs   **EXTRA**

# P2: Plotting points practice

**Level 4**

Plot these points. Join the points up as you go along.

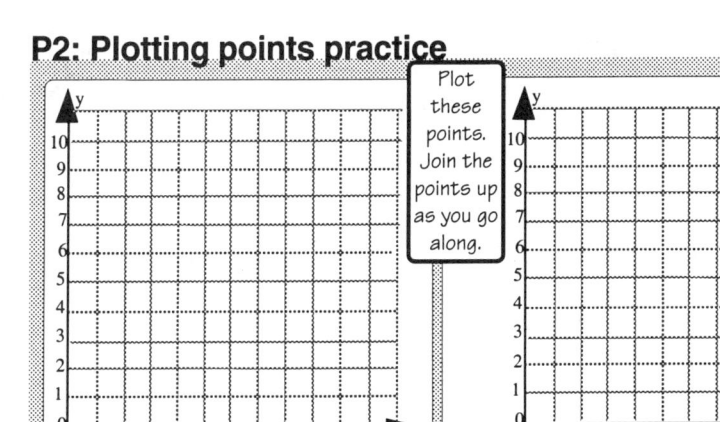

### Picture Set 5: Fighting pin man
Join (3,1) (2,1) (4,4) (5,1) (6,1)
Join (4,4) (4,7) (5,7) (5,9) (3,9) (3,7) (4,7)
Join (6,5) (5,4) (3,6) (5,6) (7,5) (8,6)

### Picture Set 6: Squares inside squares
Join (2,1)(12,1)(12,11)(2,11) (2,1)
Join (7,1) (12,6) (7,11) (2,6) (7,1)
Join (4$\frac{1}{2}$,3$\frac{1}{2}$)(9$\frac{1}{2}$,3$\frac{1}{2}$)(9$\frac{1}{2}$,8$\frac{1}{2}$)(4$\frac{1}{2}$,8$\frac{1}{2}$)(4$\frac{1}{2}$,3$\frac{1}{2}$)
Join (9$\frac{1}{2}$,6)(7,8$\frac{1}{2}$)(4$\frac{1}{2}$,6)(7,3$\frac{1}{2}$)(9$\frac{1}{2}$,6)

• *Check your answers*

## Star Challenge 2-2

1 star for each correct picture

Plot these points. Join the points up as you go along.

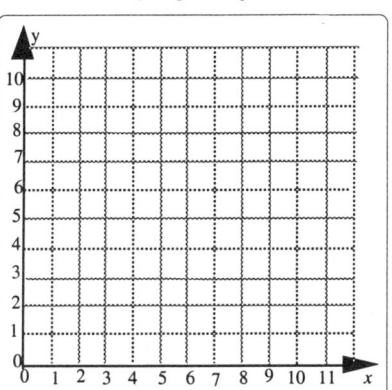

### Picture Set 7: British Rail Logo
Join (3,3) (6,0) (8,0) (5,3) (10,3) (10,4) (5,4) (7,6) (10,6) (10,7) (7,7) (4,10) (2,10) (5,7) (0,7) (0,6) (5,6) (3,4) (0,4) (0,3) (3,3)

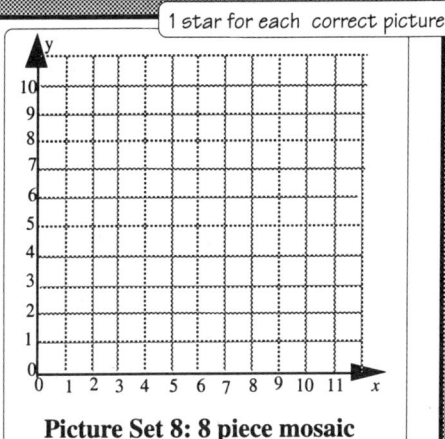

### Picture Set 8: 8 piece mosaic
Join (6,5) (8,4) (9,2) (7,3) (6,5)
Join (5,5) (3,4) (2,2) (4,3) (5,5)
Join (5,6) (4,8) (2,9) (3,7) (5,6)
Join (6,6) (8,7) (9,9) (7,8) (6,6)
Join (4,1) (7,1) (5$\frac{1}{2}$,5) (4,1)
Join (10,4) (10,7) (6,5$\frac{1}{2}$) (10,4)
Join (4,10) (7,10) (5$\frac{1}{2}$,6) (4,10)
Join (1,4) (1,7) (5,5$\frac{1}{2}$) (1,4)

• *Your teacher will need to mark this.*

A POW GUIDE    page 253    *Coordinates and Graphs*   **EXTRA**

# D3: Axes and coordinates

**Level 4**

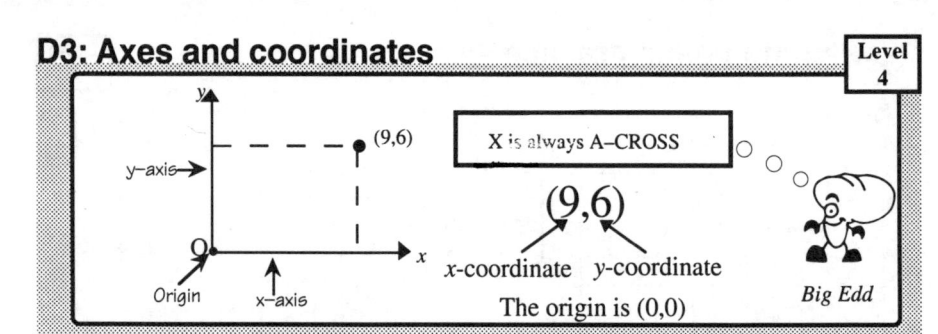

X is always A–CROSS

(9,6)
x-coordinate  y-coordinate
The origin is (0,0)

Big Edd

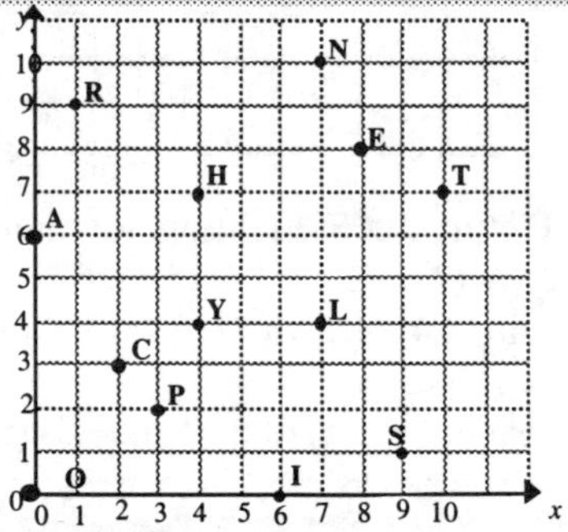

1. Which letter is at the origin ?
2. Which letter is on the x-axis ?
3. Which letter is on the y–axis ?
4. What are the coordinates of R ?
5. What are the coordinates of H ?
6. What is the x-coordinate of S ?
7. What is the y-coordinate of C ?
8. Which letter has the same x-coordinate as L ?
9. Which letter has the same y-coordinate as H ?
10. I choose a letter with x–coordinate 7. Which two letters could I choose ?
11. I choose a letter with y–coordinate 7. Which two letters could I choose ?
12. I choose a letter with x–coordinate 4. Which two letters could I choose ?
13. What word do these coordinates spell
    (3,2) (7,4) (8,8) (0,6)(9,1)(0,6) (7,10)(10,7) ?

• *Check your answers.*
8 correct = 2 stars
6-7 correct = 1 star

## Star Challenge

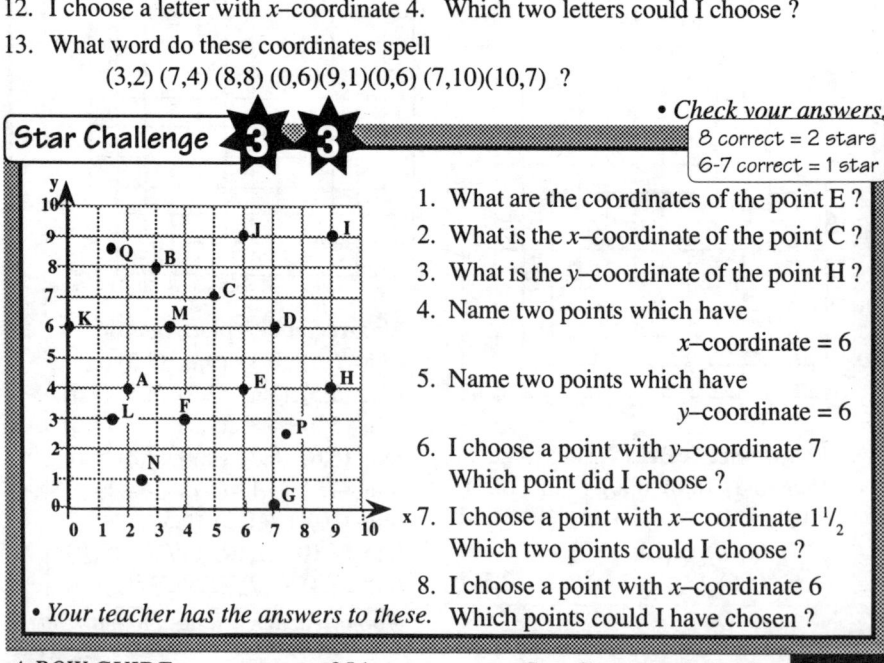

1. What are the coordinates of the point E ?
2. What is the x–coordinate of the point C ?
3. What is the y–coordinate of the point H ?
4. Name two points which have x–coordinate = 6
5. Name two points which have y–coordinate = 6
6. I choose a point with y–coordinate 7. Which point did I choose ?
7. I choose a point with x–coordinate $1\frac{1}{2}$. Which two points could I choose ?
8. I choose a point with x–coordinate 6. Which points could I have chosen ?

• Your teacher has the answers to these.

A POW GUIDE        page 254        Coordinates and Graphs   **EXTRA**

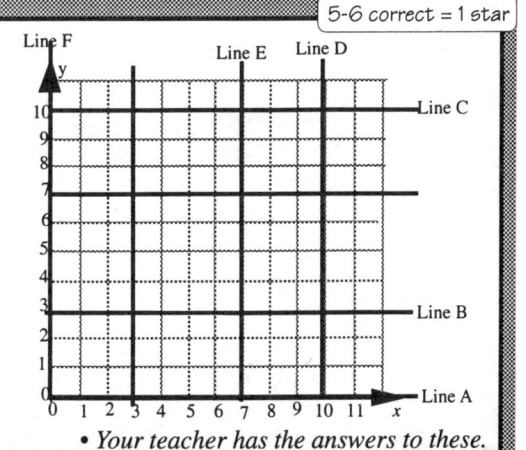

# Section 2: Rules and lines

Level 5

In this section you will :
- learn the equations for some simple lines;
- find sets of points whose coordinates are connected by rules;
- draw lines given the rules connecting the $x$- and $y$-coordinates

### DEVELOPMENT

## D1: Equations of some simple lines

1. *Copy and complete:*
   The $x$-coordinate of A is ......
   The $x$-coordinate of B is ......
   The $x$-coordinate of C is ......
   The $x$-coordinate of D is ......

2. The line through A, B, C, D is called $x = 2$.
   Explain why.

3. *Copy and complete:*
   The $x$-coordinate of E is ......
   The $x$-coordinate of F is ......
   The $x$-coordinate of G is ......
   The $x$-coordinate of H is ......
   Line Q is called $x = ...$

4. What is line R called ?

5. What letter is on the line $x = 8$ ?

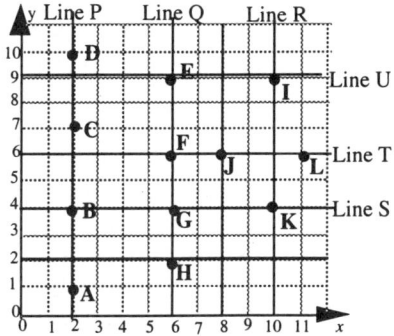

6. *Copy and complete:*
   The $y$-coordinate of B is ......
   The $y$-coordinate of G is ......
   The $y$-coordinate of K is ......
   Line S is called $y = ...$

7. What is line T called ?

8. What is line U called ?

9. Give one letter that is on the line $y = 2$.

- *Check your answers.*

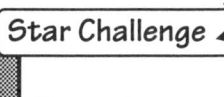

### Star Challenge 4

5-6 correct = 1 star

Choose the correct equation for each line:

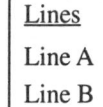

| Lines | Equations |
|---|---|
| Line A | $x = 0$   $y = 0$ |
| Line B | $x = 3$   $y = 3$ |
| Line C | $x = 7$   $y = 7$ |
| Line D | $x = 10$  $y = 10$ |
| Line E | |
| Line F | |

- *Your teacher has the answers to these.*

A POW GUIDE          page 255          Coordinates and Graphs   **EXTRA**

## D2: Connecting rules

**Level 5**

For the points
(0,1) (1,2) (2,3) (3,4)
the connecting rule is
$y = x + 1$

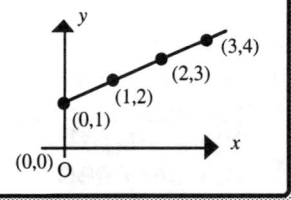

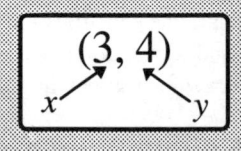

$(3, 4)$
$x \quad\quad y$

*Copy and complete each rule and its set of points:*

| Rule | Set of points for the rule |
|---|---|
| $y = x$ | (0,0) (1, …) (2, …) (…,5) (…, 10) |
| $y = x - 1$ | (2,1) (4, …) (5, …) (8,…) (…, 9) |
| $y = 2x$ | (1,2) (2, …) (3, …) (5,…) (…, 20) |
| $y = x + 2$ | (1,3) (2, …) (3, …) (8,…) (…, 12) |
| $y = x - 3$ | (5,…) (7, …) (10, …) (15,…) (…, 9) |
| $y = 3x$ | (1,3) (2, …) (3, …) (4,…) (…, 30) |
| $y = \frac{1}{2}x$ | (2,1) (4, …) (8, …) (10,…) (…, 10) |
| $y = 2x + 1$ | (1,3) (2, …) (3, …) (4,…) (…, 11) |
| $y = x^2$ | (1,1) (2,4) (3, …) (4, …) (5, …) |

$2x$ means $2 \times x$

$x^2$ means $x \times x$

• Check answers.

### Star Challenge 5

*5-7 correct = 1 star*

Match each rule with the correct set of points:

| Rule | Set of points |
|---|---|
| $y = x$ | Set L: (2,3)(4,5) (8,9) (20,21) |
| $y = 5x$ | Set M: (1,1)(3,3) (4,4) (7,7) |
| $y = x + 1$ | Set N: (6,1)(8,3) (9,4) (15,10) |
| $y = 2x + 3$ | Set P: (1,5)(3,15) (5,25) (2,10) |
| $y = x - 5$ | Set Q: (1,2)(2,5) (4,11) (5,14) |
| $y = 4x$ | Set R: (1,5)(2,7) (3,9) (5,13) |
| $y = 3x - 1$ | Set S: (2,8)(3,12) (4,16) (5,20) |

• Your teacher has the answers to these.

### Star Challenge 6

*7 correct = 2 stars*
*5-6 correct = 1 star*

Find the connecting rule for each set of points:

Hint: Look for a connection between the x- and y-coordinates.

| Set of points for the rule | Rule |
|---|---|
| Set A: (0,3) (1, 4) (2, 5) (5,8) (6, 9) | $y = …$ |
| Set B: (2,0) (4, 2) (10, 8) (6,4) (7, 5) | $y = …$ |
| Set C: (2,4) (3, 6) (5, 10) (6,12) (7, 14) | $y = …$ |
| Set D: (1,1) (2, 2) (4, 4) (5,5) (9, 9) | $y = …$ |
| Set E: (0,0) (1, 5) (2, 10) (4,20) (3,15) | $y = …$ |
| Set F: (0,10) (1, 11) (2,12) (4,14) (10, 20) | $y = …$ |
| Set G: (1,1) (3, 5) (5, 9) (4,7) (10, 19) | $y = …$ |

*Idea*

A POW GUIDE     page 256     Coordinates and Graphs   **EXTRA**

# D3: From rules to graphs

**Level 5**

1.

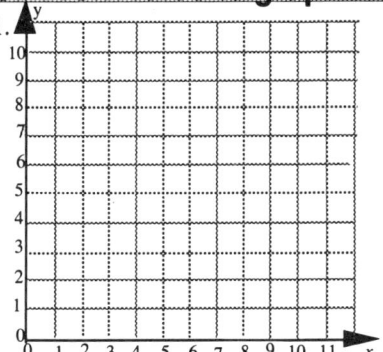

(a) Complete this table:

| Rule | x | 0 | 1 | 3 | 4 |
|---|---|---|---|---|---|
| y = 2x | y | | | | |

(b) Plot the four points on the grid.
Mark each point with a •
Draw a line through the points.
Label the line y = 2x

*If these are not straight lines, check your tables.*

2.

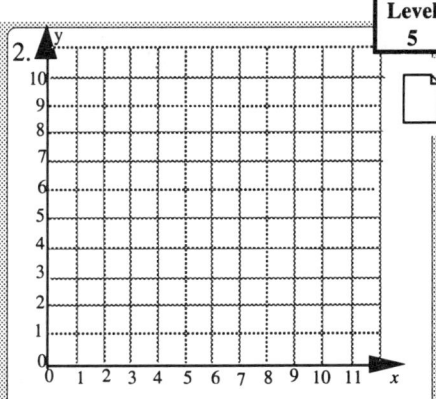

(a) Complete this table:

| Rule | x | 1 | 2 | 4 | 5 |
|---|---|---|---|---|---|
| y = x − 1 | y | | | | |

(b) Plot the four points on the grid.
Mark each point with a •
Draw a line through the points.
Label the line y = x − 1

3.

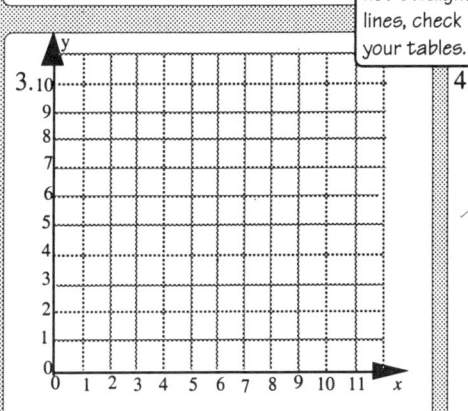

(a) Complete this table:

| Rule | x | 1 | 2 | 3 | 4 |
|---|---|---|---|---|---|
| y = 2x − 1 | y | | | | |

(b) Plot the four points on the grid.
Mark each point with a •
Draw a line through the points.
Label the line y = 2x − 1

4.

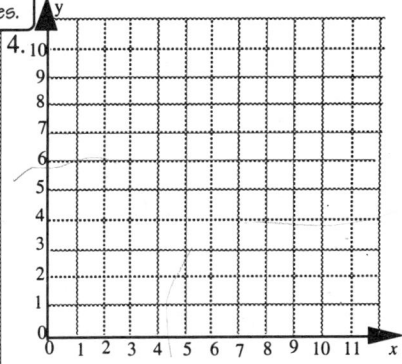

(a) Complete this table:

| Rule | x | 0 | 1 | 2 | 3 |
|---|---|---|---|---|---|
| y = 3x + 1 | y | | | | |

(b) Plot the four points on the grid.
Mark each point with a •
Draw a line through the points.
Label the line y = 3x + 1

• *Check your answers.*

A POW GUIDE          page 257          Coordinates and Graphs  **EXTRA**

**PRACTICE** — Level 5

# P1: From rules to graphs practice

For each question below:
- copy and complete the table
- draw a set of axes with values of x from 0 to 8 and values of y from 0 to 12
- plot the points from that table onto the graph
- draw a straight line through the points
- label the line with its equation.

> You must have a table <u>and a graph</u> for each question - just like in D3!

**Batch A:**

1. Rule $y = x + 5$

| x | 0 | 1 | 2 | 3 | 4 | 5 |
|---|---|---|---|---|---|---|
| y |   |   |   |   |   |   |

2. Rule $y = x - 3$

| x | 3 | 4 | 5 | 6 | 7 | 8 |
|---|---|---|---|---|---|---|
| y |   |   |   |   |   |   |

3. Rule $y = 3x$

| x | 0 | 1 | 2 | 3 | 4 |
|---|---|---|---|---|---|
| y |   |   |   |   |   |

*Big Edd*

• Check your answers.

> EACH GRAPH SHOULD BE A STRAIGHT LINE!

**Batch B:**

1. Rule $y = x + 3$

| x | 0 | 1 | 2 | 3 | 4 | 5 |
|---|---|---|---|---|---|---|
| y |   |   |   |   |   |   |

2. Rule $y = x - 2$

| x | 2 | 3 | 4 | 5 | 6 | 7 |
|---|---|---|---|---|---|---|
| y |   |   |   |   |   |   |

3. Rule $y = \frac{1}{2}x$

| x | 0 | 2 | 4 | 6 | 8 |
|---|---|---|---|---|---|
| y |   |   |   |   |   |

• Check your answers.

## Star Challenge ⭐7 ⭐7

11-12 marks = 2 stars
8-10 marks = 1 star

For each question below:
- copy and complete the table
- draw a set of axes with values of x from 0 to 8 and values of y from 0 to 12
- plot the points from the table onto the graph
- draw a straight line through the points
- label the line with its equation.

1. Rule $y = x + 4$

| x | 0 | 1 | 2 | 3 | 4 | 5 |
|---|---|---|---|---|---|---|
| y |   |   |   |   |   |   |

2. Rule $y = 2x + 3$

| x | 0 | 1 | 2 | 3 | 4 |
|---|---|---|---|---|---|
| y |   |   |   |   |   |

3. Rule $y = \frac{1}{2}x + 1$

| x | 0 | 2 | 4 | 6 | 8 |
|---|---|---|---|---|---|
| y |   |   |   |   |   |

> For each question:
> • 2 marks for correct table (−1 for any mistake);
> • 1 mark for correctly plotted points
> • 1 mark for drawing and labelling line
> Total = 4 marks per question.

• Your teacher has the answers to these.

A POW GUIDE     Coordinates and Graphs    **EXTRA**

# Section 3: Coordinates in all four quadrants

In this section you will review:
- coordinates in all four quadrants;
- plotting coordinates in all four quadrants.

Level 6

### DEVELOPMENT
## D1: Positive and negative coordinates

In a set of coordinates:
- the first number tells you how far ACROSS to go
- the second number tells you how far UP to go

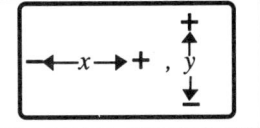

1. What letter is at (4, −1) ?
2. What letter is at (2, −3) ?
3. What letter is at (−3, −3) ?
4. What letter is at (−1, 2) ?
5. What word is given by (3,3) (1,4) (4,1) (−2,−1)?
6. What word is given by (−5,4) (1,4) (−6,−4) ?
7. What word is given by
   (4,−1) (−4,3) (−4,−2) (2,−3) ?

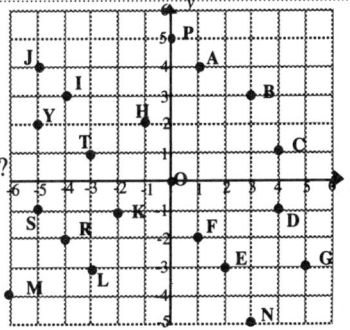

   CHECK YOUR ANSWERS NOW!
   If you are getting them wrong, find out why.

8. What are the coordinates of G ?
9. What are the coordinates of T ?
10. What are the coordinates of L ?
11. Write down the coordinates that spell  S H R I E K
12. Write down the coordinates that spell  C H E S T E R — C I T Y
13. The x–coordinate of D is 4 | What is the x–coordinate of G ?
14. What is the x–coordinate of S ?
15. What is the x–coordinate of J ?
16. The y–coordinate of D is −1 | What is the y–coordinate of G ?
17. What is the y–coordinate of T ?
18. What is the y–coordinate of M ?
19. I choose a point with x–coordinate 3. Which two letters could I choose ?
20. I choose a point with y–coordinate 4. Which two letters could I choose ?
21. I choose a point with x–coordinate −3. Which two letters could I choose ?
22. I choose a point with y–coordinate −2. Which two letters could I choose ?
23. What is spelt by (−5,−1)(0,5)(1,4)(3,−5)(−4,3)(−5,−1)(−1,2)
    —— (−1,2)(0,0)(−3,−3)(−4,3)(4,−1)(1,4)(−5,2) ?

    Check answers.

A POW GUIDE     page 259     Coordinates and Graphs  EXTRA

# P1: Zig's camp

**PRACTICE** — Level 6

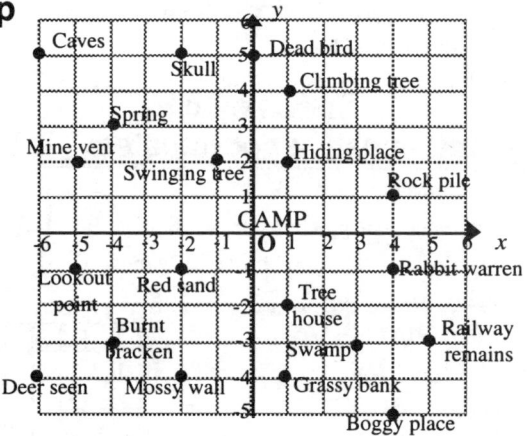

Zig had a camp in the forest. He made a map showing the things he had found.
The coordinates of the place where he saw the deer are (−6,−4).

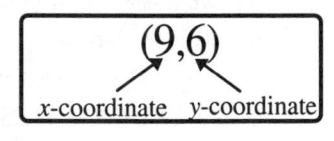

1. What did he find at (4, −1) ?
2. What did he find at (−4, −3) ?
3. Where did he find caves ?
4. He lost his shoe at (3,−3). Where did he lose it ?

(9,6)
x-coordinate   y-coordinate

5. *Copy and complete this table of things and coordinates:*

| Place | Deer | Caves | Rabbit warren | ............... | Look out |
|---|---|---|---|---|---|
| Coords | (−6,−4) | (...,...) | (...,...) | (1,4) | (...,...) |
| Place | ......... | Red sand | ............... | Burnt bracken | ............... |
| Coords | (3,−3) | (...,...) | (1,−4) | (...,...) | (−5,2) |
| Place | Dead bird | ......... | ............... | Swinging tree | Railway remains |
| Coords | (...,...) | (−2,5) | (−2,−4) | (...,...) | (...,...) |
| Place | ............ | Tree house | ............... | Boggy place | ............... |
| Coords | (4,1) | (...,...) | (−4,3) | (...,...) | (1,2) |

6. Which thing has the same x–coordinate as the Spring ?

7. Which two things have the same y–coordinate as the Dead bird ?

8. Which two things have the same x–coordinate as the Boggy place ?

9. (a) Write down the x–coordinates of the Mossy wall, the Red sand and the Skull.
   (b) Which of these equations gives the line through these three points:
      (x = 2)  or  (x = −2)  or  (y = 2)  or  (y = −2) ?

• Check your answers.

A POW GUIDE    page 260    Coordinates and Graphs    **EXTRA**

## D2: Plotting points in all four quadrants

**DEVELOPMENT** — Level 6

For each group of points in a picture set:
- plot the points in the given order;
- join them together with straight lines, as you go along.

Use a new grid for each picture set.

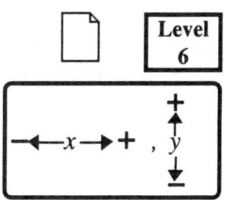

← −x → + , +↑ y ↓−

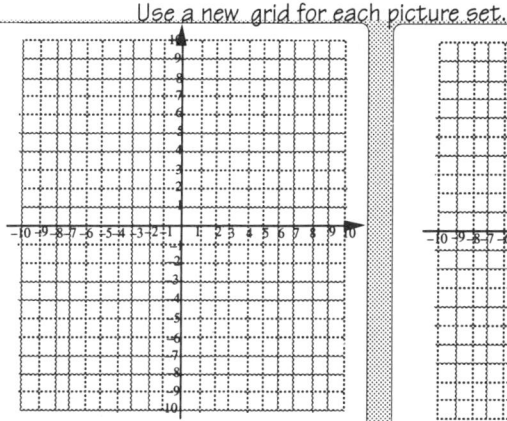

### Picture Set 1: Logo
Join (8,2)(−6,2)(−1,−3)(3,−3)(8,2)
Join (2,2)(6,2)(2,−2)(2,2)
Join (0,2)(−4,2)(0−2)(0,2)
Shade in the triangles made by the last two sets of points.

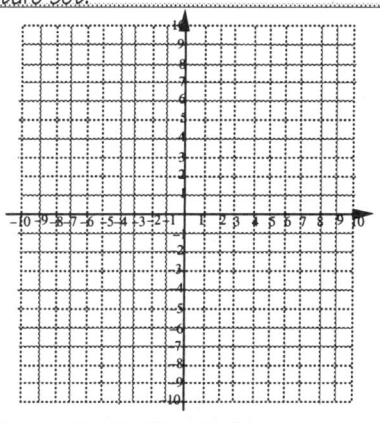

### Picture Set 2: Knock Out
Join (0,−4)(−1,−4)(0,−2)(−2,0)(−6,−4)(−5,−4)
Join (1,2)(0,1)(−2,2)(2,3)
Join (−2,0)(−2,3)(−1,3)(−1,5)(−3,5)(−3,3)(−2,3)
Join (1$\frac{1}{2}$,−3$\frac{1}{2}$)(2,−4)(6,−1)(4,−4)(3.$\frac{1}{2}$,−3.$\frac{1}{2}$)
Join (6,−1)(8,1)(9,0)(10,1)(8,3)(7,2)(8,1)
Join (4,0)(7,0)(5,2)

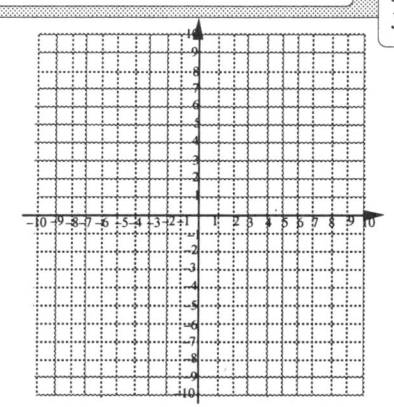

### Star Challenge — 8 — All correct = 1 star

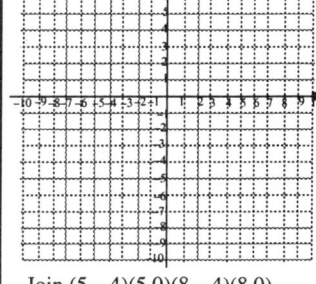

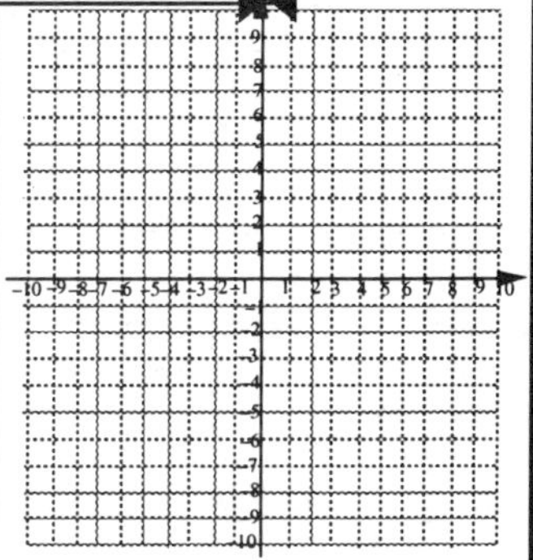

### Picture Set 3: Stacking cubes
Join (0,2)(0,0) (2,−1)(4,0)(4,2)(2,3)(0,2)(2,1)(4,2)
Join (0,−2)(2, −1)(2,−3)(0,−4)(0,−2)(−2,−1)(−2,−3)(0,−4)
Join (4,0) (6,−1) (6,−3) (4, −4) (4,−2) (6,−1)
Join (0,0) (−2,−1)
Join (2,−3) (4,−4)
Join (2,1) (2,−1) (4,−2)

• Check answers.

Join (5, −4)(5,0)(8, −4)(8,0)
Join (0,−2)(2,2)(4, −2)
Join (1,0)(3,0)
Join (−1,0)(−3,0)(−3,4)
Join (−4,2)(−6,6)(−8,2)
Join (−7,4)(−5,4)

A POW GUIDE — page 261 — Coordinates and Graphs — **EXTRA**

# Section 4: From graphs to rules

Level 6

In this section you will :
- draw lines given rules in all four quadrants;
- find the rule that fits a set of coordinates;
- find the rule that fits the coordinates of points on a line.

**DEVELOPMENT**

## D1: From rules to graphs in all four quadrants

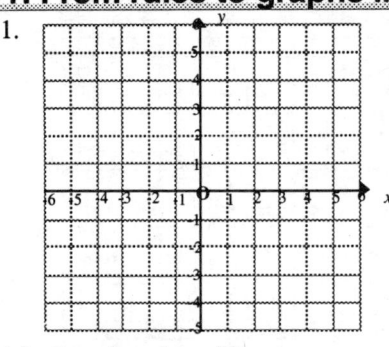

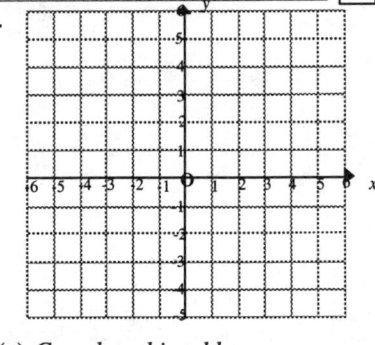

1.

(a) Complete this table:

| Rule | $x$ | –2 | –1 | 2 | 3 |
|---|---|---|---|---|---|
| $y = 2x$ | $y$ | | | | |

(b) Plot the four points on the grid.
Mark each point with a •
Draw a line through the points.
Label the line $y = 2x$

2.

(a) Complete this table:

| Rule | $x$ | –2 | 0 | 1 | 5 |
|---|---|---|---|---|---|
| $y = x - 3$ | $y$ | | | | |

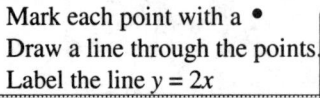

(b) Plot the four points on the grid.
Mark each point with a •
Draw a line through the points.
Label the line $y = x - 3$

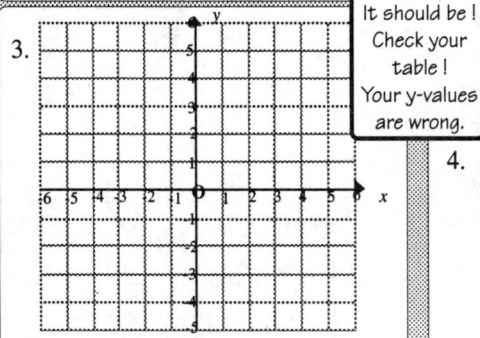

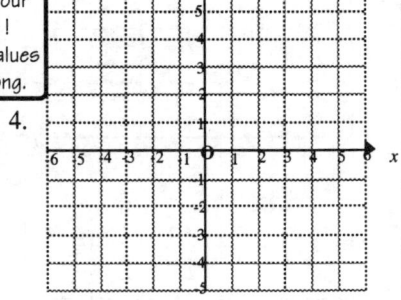

Is each line straight ? No? It should be ! Check your table ! Your y-values are wrong.

3.

(a) Complete this table:

| Rule | $x$ | –5 | –2 | 0 | 2 |
|---|---|---|---|---|---|
| $y = x + 2$ | $y$ | | | | |

(b) Plot the four points on the grid.
Mark each point with a •
Draw a line through the points.
Label the line $y = x + 2$

4.

(a) Complete this table:

| Rule | $x$ | –3 | –1 | 0 | 1 |
|---|---|---|---|---|---|
| $y = 2x + 3$ | $y$ | | | | |

(b) Plot the four points on the grid.
Mark each point with a •
Draw a line through the points.
Label the line $y = 2x + 3$

• Check answers.

A POW GUIDE          Coordinates and Graphs   **EXTRA**

## D2: From coordinates to rules

**Level 6**

1. | Rule | x | 0 | 1 | 2 | 3 |
   |------|---|---|---|---|---|
   | ?    | y | 1 | 2 | 3 | 4 |

   Which of these is the rule for these coordinates?
   $y = x$    $y = x + 1$    $y = 2x$

2. | Rule | x | −3 | −1 | 2  | 3  |
   |------|---|----|----|----|----|
   | ?    | y | 3  | 1  | −2 | −3 |

   Which of these is the rule for these coordinates?
   $y = x − 1$    $y = 2x + 1$    $y = −x$

*Choose the rule for each of these tables of coordinates:*

3. | Rule | x | 0  | 1  | 2 | 4 |
   |------|---|----|----|---|---|
   | ?    | y | −2 | −1 | 0 | 2 |

4. | Rule | x | −1 | 1 | 2 | 3 |
   |------|---|----|---|---|---|
   | ?    | y | −3 | 3 | 6 | 9 |

5. | Rule | x | −2 | −1 | 0  | 3  |
   |------|---|----|----|----|----|
   | ?    | y | −7 | −6 | −5 | −2 |

6. | Rule | x | −2 | −1 | 2 | 5 |
   |------|---|----|----|---|---|
   | ?    | y | 0  | 1  | 4 | 7 |

7. | Rule | x | −3 | 0 | 3 | 6 |
   |------|---|----|---|---|---|
   | ?    | y | −1 | 0 | 1 | 2 |

8. | Rule | x | −2 | 0 | 2 | 4 |
   |------|---|----|---|---|---|
   | ?    | y | −3 | 1 | 5 | 9 |

Choose the rules from:
$y = 2x + 1$    $y = x + 1$
$y = −x$        $y = 3x$
$y = x − 5$     $y = x − 2$
$y = \frac{1}{3}x$    $y = x + 2$

• Check your answers.

## D3: From graphs to rules

For each graph:
(a) copy and complete the table of coordinates
(b) work out the rule

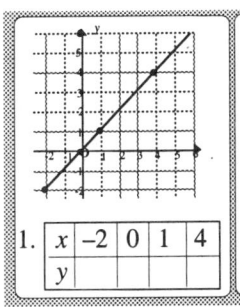

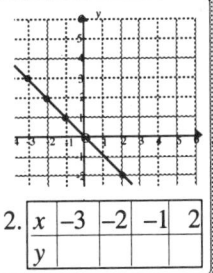

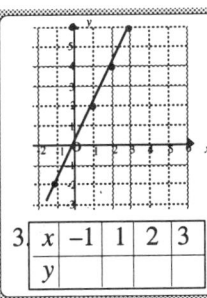

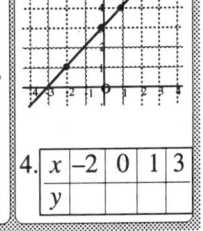

1. | x | −2 | 0 | 1 | 4 |
   |---|----|---|---|---|
   | y |    |   |   |   |

2. | x | −3 | −2 | −1 | 2 |
   |---|----|----|----|---|
   | y |    |    |    |   |

3. | x | −1 | 1 | 2 | 3 |
   |---|----|---|---|---|
   | y |    |   |   |   |

4. | x | −2 | 0 | 1 | 3 |
   |---|----|---|---|---|
   | y |    |   |   |   |

For each graph:
(a) make a table of coordinates    (b) work out the rule

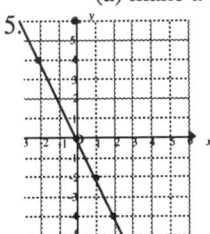

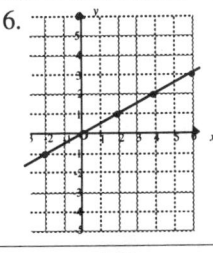

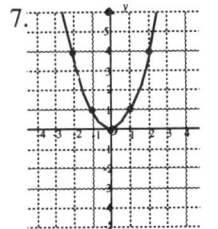

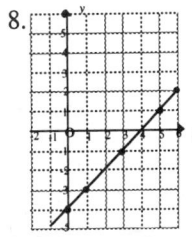

5.   6.   7.   8.

• Check your answers.

## PRACTICE

### P1: Finding rules practice

Level 6

For each graph:
  (a) make a table of coordinates   (b) work out the rule

*CHECK YOUR ANSWERS at the end of each batch.*

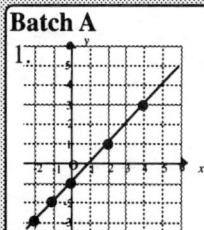

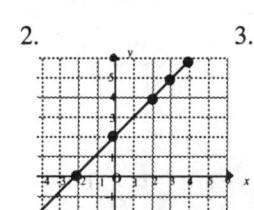

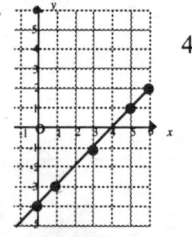

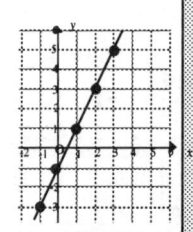

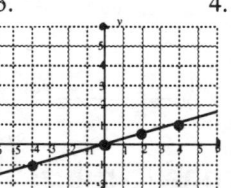

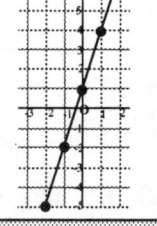

**Batch A**
1.  2.  3.  4.

**Batch B**
1.  2.  3.  4.

### Star Challenge 9

5-6 correct = 1 star

*Match each graph with its equation (its rule)*

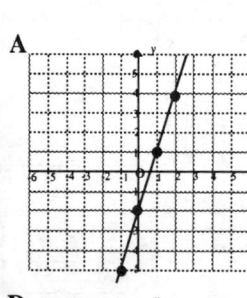

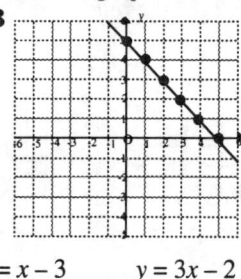

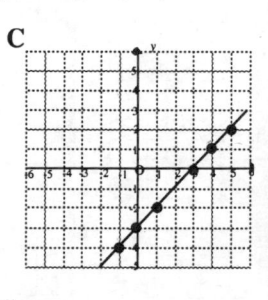

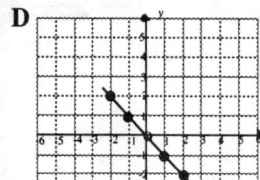

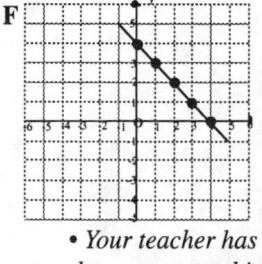

A   B   C

$y = x - 3$   $y = 3x - 2$
$y + x = 5$   $y = 4 - x$
$y = -x$   $y = 2x - 3$

D   E   F

Tables of coordinates would help!

• *Your teacher has the answers to this.*

A POW GUIDE    page 264    Coordinates and Graphs    **EXTRA**

# Section 5: Related graphs

Level 6

In this section you will work with related graphs.

**DEVELOPMENT**

## D1: Parallel lines

1. Copy and complete the table for each graph. Find the equation (rule) for each line.

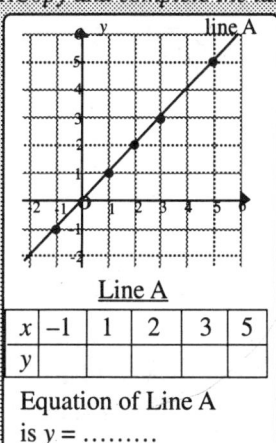

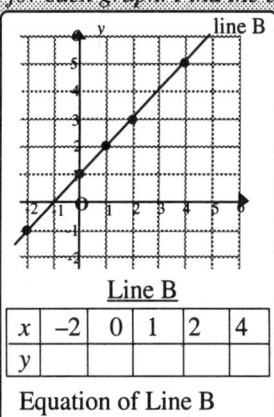

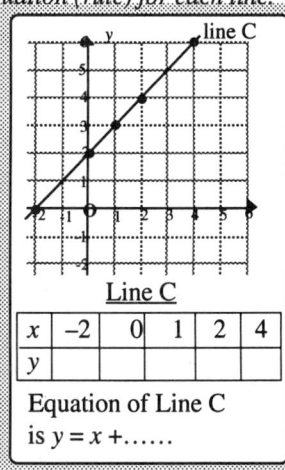

**Line A**

| x | −1 | 1 | 2 | 3 | 5 |
|---|----|---|---|---|---|
| y |    |   |   |   |   |

Equation of Line A is $y = \ldots\ldots$

**Line B**

| x | −2 | 0 | 1 | 2 | 4 |
|---|----|---|---|---|---|
| y |    |   |   |   |   |

Equation of Line B is $y = \ldots\ldots$

**Line C**

| x | −2 | 0 | 1 | 2 | 4 |
|---|----|---|---|---|---|
| y |    |   |   |   |   |

Equation of Line C is $y = x + \ldots\ldots$

2. Copy and complete the table for each graph. Find the equation (rule) for each line.

**Line D**

| x | −1 | 0 | 1 | 2 | 3 |
|---|----|---|---|---|---|
| y |    |   |   |   |   |

Equation of Line D is $y = \ldots\ldots$

**Line E**

| x | −1 | 0 | 1 | 2 |
|---|----|---|---|---|
| y |    |   |   |   |

Equation of Line E is $y = 2x + \ldots\ldots$

**Line F**

| x | −1 | 0 | 1 | 2 |
|---|----|---|---|---|
| y |    |   |   |   |

Equation of Line F is $y = 2x + \ldots\ldots$

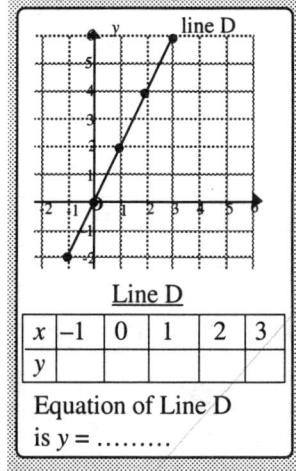

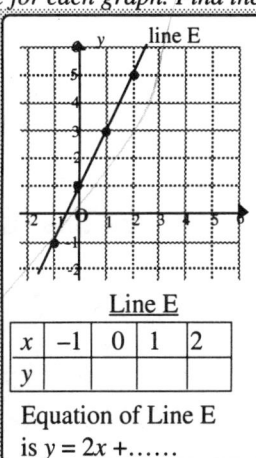

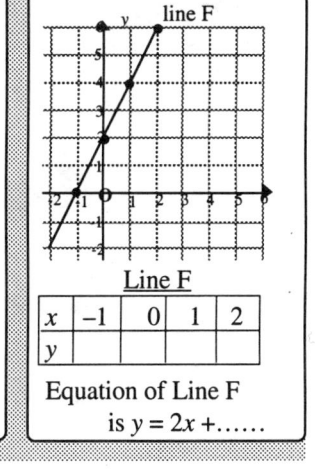

3. Look at the graphs above.
   Find three lines which are parallel to each other.
   Write down the names and the equations of these lines.

4. What is the same about the equations of these parallel lines?

• *Check your answers.*

*A POW GUIDE*     *Coordinates and Graphs* **EXTRA**

## D2: Equations of parallel lines

**Level 6**

These five lines are parallel.
The equations of three of the lines are
$y = x$
$y = x + 1$
$y = x + 2$

1. What is the same about the equations of these three lines?

2. Which of these is the equation of line P?
   $y = x + 3$   $y = x + 4$   $y = 2x + 2$

3. Which of these is the equation of line Q?
   $y = x + 3$   $y = x - 3$   $y = x - 4$

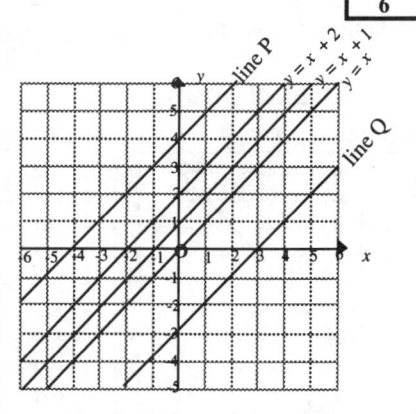

*CHECK YOUR ANSWERS.*

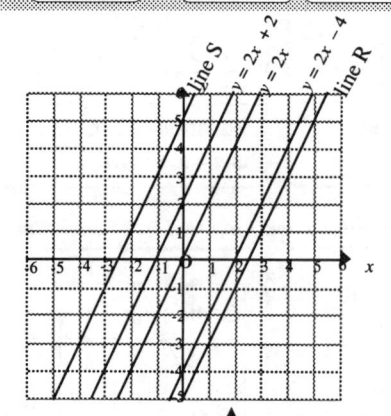

4. Which of these is the equation of line R?
   $y = 2x + 4$   $y = x - 4$   $y = 2x - 5$

5. Which of these is the equation of line S?
   $y = 2x + 5$   $y = x + 5$   $y = 2x - 5$

6. Explain how you would draw the line with equation $y = 2x - 1$ on this diagram.

• *Check your answers.*

### Star Challenge 10

*3-4 correct = 1 star*

*Copy and complete:*

The equation of line W is
$y = \ldots\ldots\ldots$

The equation of line X is
$y = \ldots\ldots\ldots$

The equation of line Y is
$y = \ldots\ldots\ldots$

The equation of line Z is
$y = \ldots\ldots\ldots$

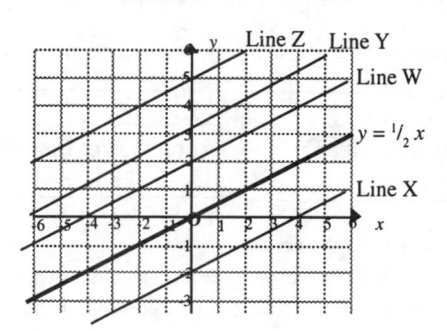

• *Your teacher has the answers to these.*

A POW GUIDE    page 266    Coordinates and Graphs    **EXTRA**

# Section 6: Scatter graphs

Level 6

In this section you will :
 • interpret scatter graphs;
 • develop a basic idea of correlation.

## DEVELOPMENT

### D1: Are they related ?
*Class discussion*

So far, you have worked with graphs of two variables (x & y). The two variables have been connected by a rule (or relationship). Now you are going to look at graphs of two variables which may, or may not, be related.

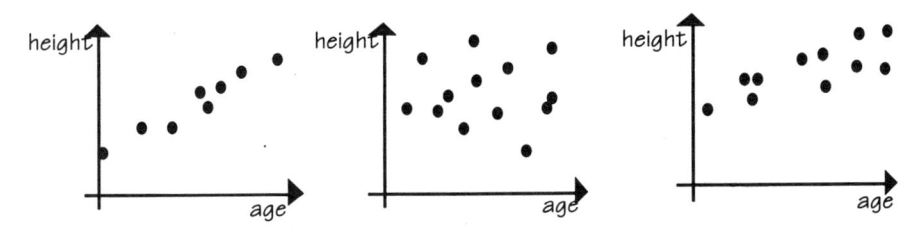

These three graphs show the heights and ages of three groups of people.

> Group 1: aged 40 - 50
> Group 2: aged 13 - 16
> Group 3: aged 1 - 5

**Discussion points**

Think about :
 • for which of these groups does the height rise rapidly as they age ?
 • for which of these groups does the height rise slowly as they age ?
 • for which of these groups is there no relationship between height and age ?

Which graph represents which group ? How can you tell ?

Which graph shows
 (a) a strong relationship    between height and age ?
 (b) a weak relationship      between height and age ?
 (c) no relationship at all   between height and age ?

A POW GUIDE        page 267        Coordinates and Graphs  EXTRA

# D2: Correlation

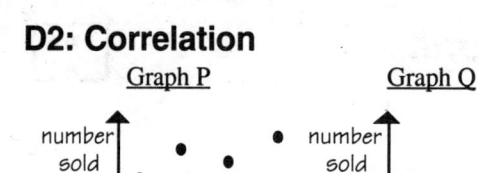

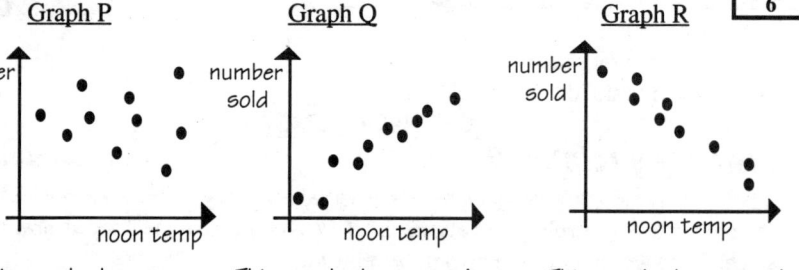

*Individual work*  Level 6

### Graph P

This graph shows **no correlation** between number sold and temperature.

### Graph Q

This graph shows **good positive correlation** between number sold and temperature.

### Graph R

This graph shows **good negative correlation** between number sold and temperature.

---

Vic's Park Café kept a record of the temperature at noon each Sunday. They also kept a record of the number sold of:
  (a) ice-creams
  (b) hot drinks
  (c) packets of crisps

---

1. Would you expect the sale of icecream to increase or decrease as the temperature rises ?

2. Which of these scatter graphs could represent ice-cream and temperature ?
   How do you know ?

3. Which of these scatter graphs could represent hot drinks and temperature ?
   How do you know ?

4. Which of these scatter graphs could represent crisps and temperature ?
   How do you know ?

5. Draw a scatter graph with these axes. Plot ten points to show how you think the number of chilled drinks sold is affected by temperature.

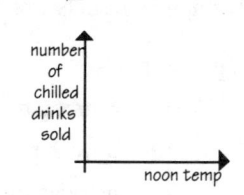

• *Check your answers*

A POW GUIDE    page 268    Coordinates and Graphs **EXTRA**

# Section 7: Technique review

*In this section you will review the techniques met in this topic.*

Check your answers at the end of each set of problems

## R1: Basic coordinates  [Level 4]

1. Youslas says that the letter U is at the point (2,6). Teacher marks it wrong. Explain why.
2. What word is given by:
   (7,7) (2,7) (4,6) (6,5) (0,2) (2,1) ((3,3) ?
3. What are the coordinates of the origin?
4. I choose a point with $x$-coordinate 4. Which three points could I choose?
5. What are the coordinates of the point with letter K?
6. What is the $y$-coordinate of the point P?

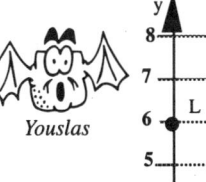

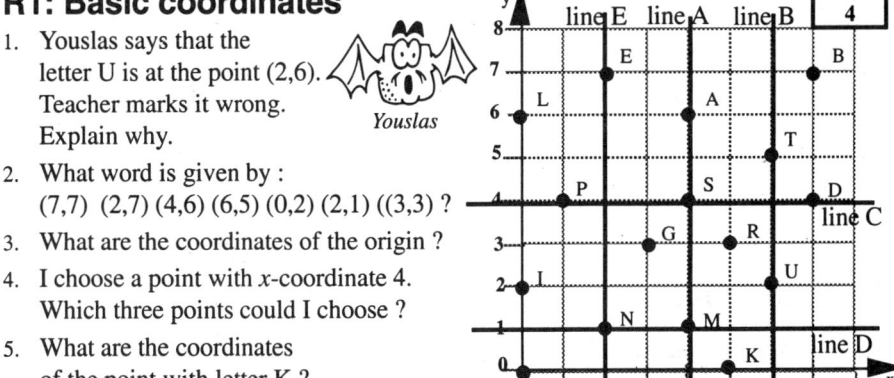

## R2: Equations of some simple lines  [Level 5]

1. | On line A, all the points have $x$-coordinate 4. |
   | On line A, all the points have $y$-coordinate 4. |
   Which of these statements is true, the first or the second?
2. The equation of line A is $x = 4$. What is the equation of line B?
3. The equation of line D is $y = 1$. What is the equation of line C?
4. What is the equation of line E?

## R3: Connecting rules  [Level 5]

*Copy and complete each rule and its set of points:*

1. Rule: $y = x - 3$     Points: (4, ...) (5, ...) (10, ...) (..., 6)
2. Rule: $y = 2x + 1$    Points: (1, ...) (3, ...) (6, ...) (..., 9)
3. Rule: $y = 3x + ...$  Points: (1, 5) (3, 11) (6, 20) (10, ...)
4. Rule: $y = .........$ Points: (1, 6) (2, 7) (5, 10) (7, ...)

## R4: From rules to graphs  [Level 5]

For the rule $y = x + 3$
- copy and complete this table

| $x$ | 0 | 1 | 2 | 3 | 4 |
|---|---|---|---|---|---|
| $y$ |   |   |   |   |   |

- draw a set of axes with values of $x$ from 0 to 4 and values of $y$ from 0 to 8
- plot the points from the table onto the graph
- draw and label the line for $y = x + 3$

A POW GUIDE     Coordinates and Graphs  **EXTRA**

## R5: Four quadrant coordinates

Level 6

1. What letter is at (–6, –4)?
2. What word is given by
   (1, –2) (–4, –2) (–4, 3) (3, –5) (5, –3) (2, –3)?
3. What is the *x*-coordinate of D?
4. What is the *y*-coordinate of D?
5. I choose a point with *x*-coordinate –3. Which two points could I choose?
6. Write down the coordinates that spell DENMARK

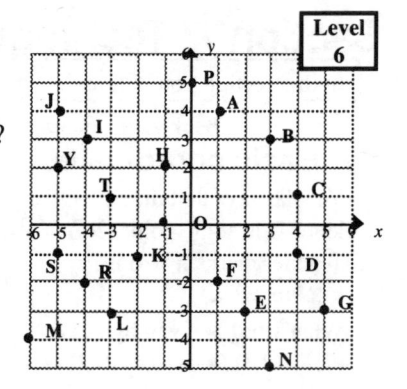

## R6: From coordinates to rules

Level 6

1. 
| Rule | x | 1 | 2 | 3 | 5 |
|---|---|---|---|---|---|
| ? | y | 2 | 4 | 6 | 10 |

   What is the rule for this set of coordinates?
   $y = x + 2$ or $y = 2x$ or $y = 3x - 1$

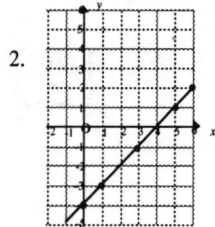

2. (a) Make a table of coordinates for this graph.

   (b) Work out the rule for the graph.

## R7: Related graphs

Level 6

Lines P and Q are parallel to lines with equations
$$y = x$$
$$y = x + 1$$
$$y = x + 2$$

What are the equations of lines P and Q?

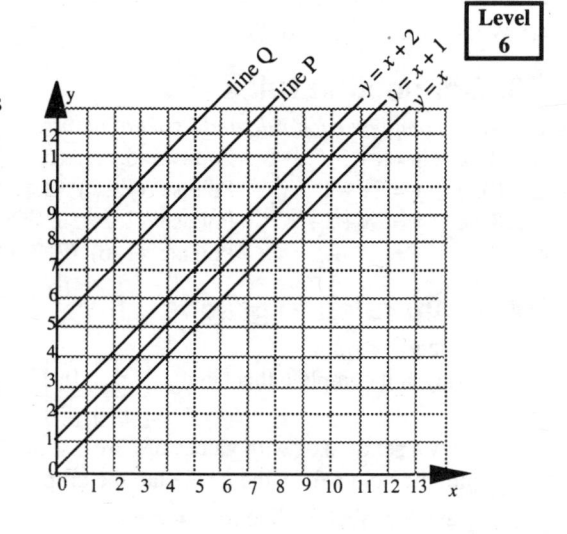

A POW GUIDE            page 270            Coordinates and Graphs    **EXTRA**

# Improving Mental Arithmetic Skills

## Section 2: Practising multiplication skills p8

**D1: Using a table square**
1. 6   2. 42   3. 56   4. 52   5. 182   6. 84   7. 30   8. 96
9. 143   10. 84   11. 54   12. 91   13. 60   14. 154   15. 75   16. 168
17. 72   18. 60   19. 108   20. 54

**P1: Multiplication arithmogons**
(arithmogon puzzle answers)

**P2: Work out the products**
(product grid answers)

## Section 3: Improving multiplication & division p11

**D1: Division is sharing**
1. 3   2. 3   3. 4   4. 2   5. 2   6. 3   7. 5   8. 3
9. 4   10. 2   11. 6   12. 4   13. 3   14. 7

**D2: Division is 'how many are there in '?**
1. 6   2. 8   3. 5   4. 7   5. 3   6. 6   7. 9   8. 4

**D3: Related × and ÷ statements**
1. 6 × 5 = 30   30 ÷ 6 = 5   30 ÷ 5 = 6   2. 8 × 6 = 48   48 ÷ 6 = 8   48 ÷ 8 = 6
3. (a) 9 × 6 = 54   (b) 6 × 9 = 54   54 ÷ 6 = 9   54 ÷ 9 = 6
4. 35 ÷ 7 = 5   35 ÷ 5 = 7   5. 35 ÷ 7 = 5   35 ÷ 5 = 7
6. 54 ÷ 6 = 9   54 ÷ 9 = 6   7. 42 ÷ 6 = 7   42 ÷ 7 = 6

**P1: Multiplication and division**

**Batch A**
1. 7 × 9 = 63   2. 63 ÷ 7 = 9   3. 3 × 8 = 24   4. 30 ÷ 10 = 3
5. 15 × 2 = 30   6. 2 × 9 = 18   7. 6 × 5 = 30   8. 36 ÷ 6 = 6
9. 7 × 8 = 36   10. 4 × 9 = 36   11. 12 × 3 = 36   12. 40 ÷ 8 = 5
13. 6 smarties   14. 5

**Batch B**
1. 5 × 8 = 40   2. 40 ÷ 8 = 5   3. 4 × 11 = 44   4. 80 ÷ 20 = 4
5. 12 × 3 = 36   6. 6 × 8 = 48   7. 9 × 5 = 45   8. 54 ÷ 6 = 9
9. 9 × 8 = 72   10. 7 × 9 = 63   11. 32 ÷ 8 = 4   12. 60 ÷ 15 = 4
13. 6 toffees   14. 4

**D4: Division with remainders**
1. 3 and 1   2. 3 and 1   3. 4 and 1   4. 2 and 2   5. 2 and 1   6. 3 and 2

**D5: Practical division problems**
1. 5   2. 3 and 1 left over   3. 5   4. 3   5. 4   6. 4
7. 4   8. (a) 6   (b) 4 teams of 9 and 2 teams of 10   9. 7
10. 5 (cassettes are approx £2 each and 5 × 2 = 10)
11. 3 (4 × 25p = £1 so 4 × 26p is more than £1 – so can only buy 3)   12. 3

## Section 4: Basic addition and subtraction p14

**D1: Find numbers that add up to ....**

*Strategies for Improving Mental Arithmetic Skills*

## P1: Addition tables
1. 9 | 11
   7 | 9

2. 8 | 11
   11 | 14

3. 15 | 11
   11 | 7

4. 17 | 7
   18 | 8

5. 10 | 14
   11 | 15

6. 18 | 13
   15 | 10

7. 15 | 30
   5 | 20

8. 19 | 12
   20 | 13

9. 21 | 19
   16 | 14

10. 15 | 17
    18 | 20

11. 16 | 19
    11 | 16

12. 14 | 13
    13 | 12

13. 16 | 15
    15 | 14

14. 18 | 16
    17 | 15

15. 15 | 14
    10 | 12

16. 6 | 12
    18 | 16
    17

17. 6
    21
    19 | 18

18. 8 | 12
    11 | 16

19. 8 | 7 | 5
    12 | 11 | 9
    10 | 9 | 7

20. 15 | 17 | 12
    13 | 15 | 10
    11 | 13 | 8

21. 7 | 10
    10 | 11 | 13
    5 | 10 | 12

## P2: Row and column additions

1. 10
   10
   11 9

2. 19
   14
   22 11

3. 29
   13
   23 19

7. 18
   14
   18
   17 18 15

8. 30
   29
   50
   24 25 60

11. 16
    14
    23 31
    14 14

12. 15
    22
    10
    16 12 19

13. 13
    43
    21
    24 25 28

16. 19
    2 17
    12

17. 16
    7
    21

4. 35 5. 36

9. 21 10. 40
   18 5 | 10
   11 25

14. 4 | 20
    6 | 24

15. 11
    8 | 19
    30

17. 17
    19 | 18

18. 11
    21 | 40
    26

22. 6.
23. 3124
28 17

38
27
17

20 23 39

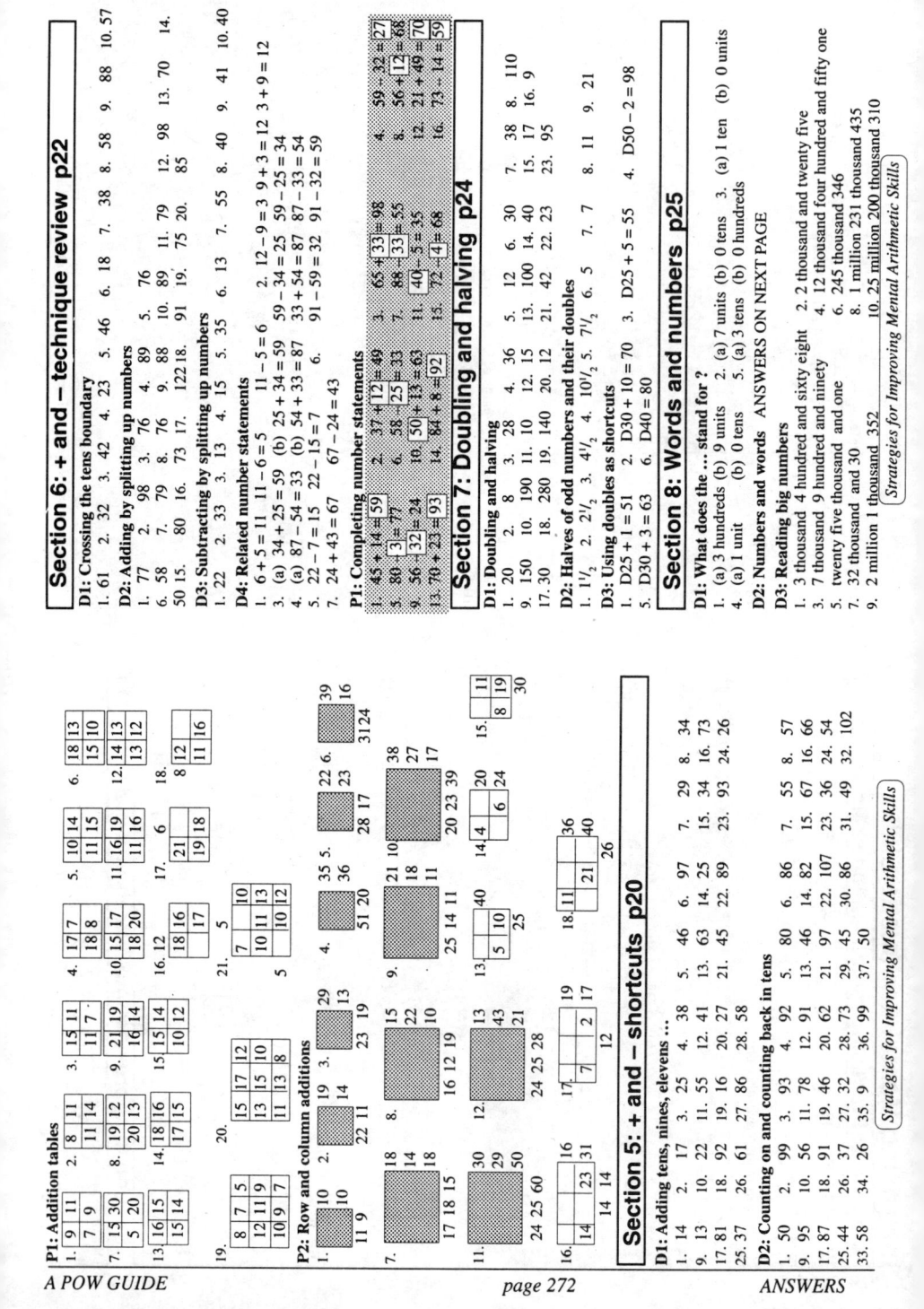

36
40

15.

18.
8 | 12
11 | 16

39
16

## Section 5: + and − shortcuts p20
### D1: Adding tens, nines, elevens …
1. 14  2. 17  3. 25  4. 38  5. 46  6. 97  7. 29  8. 34
9. 13  10. 22  11. 55  12. 41  13. 63  14. 25  15. 34  16. 73
17. 81  18. 92  19. 16  20. 27  21. 45  22. 89  23. 93  24. 26
25. 37  26. 61  27. 86  28. 58

### D2: Counting on and counting back in tens
1. 50  2. 99  3. 93  4. 92  5. 80  6. 86  7. 55  8. 57
9. 95  10. 56  11. 78  12. 91  13. 46  14. 82  15. 67  16. 66
17. 87  18. 91  19. 46  20. 62  21. 97  22. 107  23. 36  24. 54
25. 44  26. 37  27. 32  28. 73  29. 45  30. 86  31. 49  32. 102
33. 58  34. 26  35. 9  36. 99  37. 50

## Section 6: + and − – technique review p22
### D1: Crossing the tens boundary
1. 61  2. 32  3. 42  4. 23  5. 46  6. 18  7. 38  8. 58  9. 88  10. 57

### D2: Adding by splitting up numbers
1. 77  2. 98  3. 76  4. 89  5. 76  6. 18  7. 38  8. 58  9. 88  10. 57
6. 58  7. 79  8. 76  9. 88  10. 89  11. 79  12. 98  13. 70  14.
50  15. 80  16. 73  17. 122  18. 91  19. 75  20. 85

### D3: Subtracting by splitting up numbers
1. 22  2. 33  3. 13  4. 15  5. 35  6. 13  7. 55  8. 40  9. 41  10. 40

### D4: Related number statements
1. $6 + 5 = 11$   $11 − 6 = 5$   $11 − 5 = 6$   2. $12 − 9 = 3$   $9 + 3 = 12$   $3 + 9 = 12$
3. (a) $34 + 25 = 59$ (b) $25 + 34 = 59$   $59 − 34 = 25$   $59 − 25 = 34$
4. (a) $87 − 54 = 33$ (b) $54 + 33 = 87$   $33 + 54 = 87$   $87 − 33 = 54$
5. $22 − 7 = 15$   $22 − 15 = 7$   6.   $91 − 59 = 32$   $91 − 32 = 59$
7. $24 + 43 = 67$   $67 − 24 = 43$

### P1: Completing number statements
1. $45 + 14 = 59$   2. $37 + 12 = 49$   3.   4. 36   5. 12   6. 30   7. 38   8. 110
5. $8 + 3 = 77$   6. $58 − 25 = 33$   7. $88 − 33 = 55$   8. $56 + 12 = 68$
9. $56 + 32 = 24$   10. $50 + 13 = 63$   11. $40 − 5 = 35$   12. $21 + 49 = 70$
13. $79 + 23 = 93$   14. $84 + 8 = 92$   15. $72 − 4 = 68$   16. $73 − 14 = 59$

## Section 7: Doubling and halving p24
### D1: Doubling and halving
1. 20  2. 8  3. 28  4. 36  5. 12  6. 30  7. 38  8. 110
9. 150  10. 190  11. 10  12. 15  13. 100  14. 40  15. 17  16. 9
17. 30  18. 280  19. 140  20. 12  21. 42  22. 23  23. 95

### D2: Halves of odd numbers and their doubles
1. $1\frac{1}{2}$   2. $2\frac{1}{2}$   3. $4\frac{1}{2}$   4. $10\frac{1}{2}$   5. $7\frac{1}{2}$   6. 5   7. 7   8. 11   9. 21

### D3: Using doubles as shortcuts
1. $D25 + 1 = 51$   2. $D30 + 10 = 70$   3. $D25 + 5 = 55$   4. $D50 − 2 = 98$
5. $D30 + 3 = 63$   6. $D40 = 80$

## Section 8: Words and numbers p25
### D1: What does the … stand for ?
1. (a) 3 hundreds (b) 9 units   2. (a) 7 units (b) 0 units   3. (a) 1 ten (b) 0 units
4. (a) 1 unit   5. (a) 3 tens (b) 0 hundreds

### D2: Numbers and words   ANSWERS ON NEXT PAGE

### D3: Reading big numbers
1. 3 thousand 4 hundred and sixty eight   2. 2 thousand and twenty five
3. 7 thousand 9 hundred and ninety   4. 12 thousand four hundred and fifty one
5. twenty five thousand and one
6. 245 thousand 346
7. 32 thousand and 30   8. 1 million 231 thousand 435
9. 2 million 1 thousand 352   10. 25 million 200 thousand 310

*Strategies for Improving Mental Arithmetic Skills*

A POW GUIDE    page 272    ANSWERS

|   | Th | H | T | U | Words: | | 2. Th | H | T | U | Words: |
|---|---|---|---|---|---|---|---|---|---|---|---|
| 1.| | 2 | 0 | 1 | two hundred and one | | | 1 | 2 | 0 | 4 | 1 thousand 2 hundred and 4 |
| 3.| | 2 | 1 | 0 | two hundred and ten | | | 2 | 0 | 0 | 5 | 2 thousand and 5 |
| 5.| | 3 | 0 | 6 | three hundred and six | | | 2 | 0 | 5 | 0 | 2 thousand and fifty |
| 7.| | 5 | 3 | 0 | five hundred and thirty | | | 3 | 1 | 0 | 3 | 3 thousand 1 hundred and 3 |
| 9.| | 6 | 4 | 0 | six hundred and forty | | | 3 | 1 | 3 | 0 | 3 thousand 1 hundred and 30 |
| 11.| | 7 | 1 | 5 | seven hundred and fifteen | | | 3 | 5 | 0 | 4 | 3 thousand 5 hundred and 4 |
| 13.| | 9 | 0 | 6 | nine hundred and six | | | 2 | 5 | 4 | 0 | 2 thousand 5 hundred and 40 |
| 15.| | 9 | 6 | 0 | nine hundred and sixty | | | 3 | 0 | 1 | 0 | 3 thousand and ten |
| 17.| | 7 | 2 | 5 | seven hundred and twenty five | | | 4 | 0 | 0 | 9 | 4 thousand and 9 |
| 19.| | 4 | 0 | 3 | four hundred and three | | | 3 | 1 | 0 | 0 | 3 thousand 1 hundred |
| 21.| | 6 | 7 | 0 | six hundred and seventy | | | 7 | 0 | 2 | 3 | 7 thousand and twenty three |
| 23.| | 7 | 1 | 0 | seven hundred and ten | | | 6 | 0 | 4 | 0 | 6 thousand and forty |
| 25.| | 9 | 0 | 5 | nine hundred and five | | | | | | | |

## Section 9: + and – with 3-digit numbers p26

**D1: + and – single digit numbers to 3-digit numbers**
1. 718  2. 644  3. 264  4. 309  5. 107  6. 429  7. 643  7. 114  8. 202
9. 191  10. 320  11. 352  12. 223  13. 421  14. 669  15. 488  16. 628
17. 267  18. 304  19. 593  20. 954

**D2: Adding 2-digit numbers to 3-digit numbers to multiples of 100**
1. $300 + 43 = \boxed{345}$  2. $100 + \boxed{57} = 157$  3. $65 + \boxed{300} = 365$  4. $68 + 400 = \boxed{468}$
5. $91 + \boxed{700} = 971$  6. $100 + \boxed{45} = 645$  7. $600 + \boxed{45} = 645$  8. $72 + 500 = \boxed{572}$
9. $99 + \boxed{900} = 999$  10. $\boxed{200} + 13 = 213$  11. $\boxed{7} + 200 = 271$  12. $\boxed{100} + 87 = 187$

**D3: Adding 3-digit numbers to multiples of 100**
1. 627  2. 768  3. 961  4. 729  5. 636

## Section 10: Crossing the hundreds boundary p27

**D1: With and without number lines**
1. 101  2. 105  3. 97  4. 99  5. 107  6. 95  7. 97  8. 99  9. 101  10. 94
11. 290 291 292 293 294 295 296 297 298 299 300 301 302 303 304 305 306 307 308 309 310
12. 303  13. 303  14. 297  15. 319  16. 301  17. 299  18. 310  19. 294  20. 296  21. 304
22. 495  23. 402  24. 403  25. 805  26. 802  27. 595  28. 395  29. 397  30. 503  31. 908

**D2: Counting on and back when numbers are close together**
1. $276 + \boxed{6} = 282$  2. $\boxed{7} = 598$  3. $703 - \boxed{696} = \boxed{7}$  4. $419 + \boxed{7} = 426$
5. $487 + \boxed{9} = 496$  6. $824 - \boxed{5} = 819$  7. $658 + \boxed{5} = 663$  8. $893 + \boxed{11} = 909$

## Section 11: + and – techniques for large numbers p28

**D1: + and – 10 to/from 2- & 3-digit numbers**
1. 85  2. 241  3. 114  4. 350  5. 83  6. 740  7. 58  8. 734
9. 705  10. 980  11. 74  12. 468  13. 114  14. 550  15. 188
16. $371 + \boxed{10} = 381$  17. $\boxed{588} + 10 = 598$  18. $743 - 10 = \boxed{733}$  19. $469 + \boxed{10} = 479$
20. $298 + \boxed{10} = 308$  21. $\boxed{696} + 10 = 706$  22. $\boxed{314} - 10 = 304$  23. $898 + 10 = \boxed{908}$

---

## D2: + and – two multiples of 10
1. 90  2. 100  3. 110  4. 160  5. 150  6. 110  7. 110  8. 90  9. 360  10. 320
11. $50 + 60 = \boxed{110}$  12. $90 + \boxed{30} = 120$  13. $120 - 40 = \boxed{80}$  14. $\boxed{90} + 20 = 110$
15. $130 - \boxed{40} = 90$  16. $\boxed{80} + 50 = 130$  17. $\boxed{110} - 50 = 60$  18. $\boxed{70} + 80 = 150$

## D3: + and – multiples of 10 to a 3-digit number
1. 155  2. 194  3. 266  4. 590  5. 875  6. 810  7. 499  8. 885  9. 725  10. 810
11. 225  12. 194  13. 234  14. 702  15. 636  16. 316  17. 342  18. 692  19. 409  20. 688

## D4: + and – 9, 19, 29, ...
1. 346  2. 582  3. 267  4. 666  5. 187  6. 791  7. 346  8. 562
9. 197  10. 707  11. 236  12. 154  13. 544  14. 237  15. 832

## Section 12: Number pairs p30

**D1: Number pairs that add up to 10, 100, 1000**

A: 8—2, 3, 5—5
B: 7—3, 4, 6—4, 5
C: 9—1, 2—8, 5, 7
D: 4—6, 3, 5—7, 5

E: 55—45, 50—50
F: 70—30, 80—20, 40, 25—75
G: 40—60, 100, 70
H: 10, 40, 90, 20—80, 50, 60

I: 11—79, 35—65, 45—89
J: 48, 67—25, 77—52, 33—75, 19—55, 18—72, 28—81
K: 9, 45—25, 81, 70
L: 51—49, 29, 61, 77—23, 59

M: 900, 800, 600, 200, 100, 400
N: 600, 300, 250—800, 750, 200, 700
P: 50, 350—650, 950—400—600, 750
Q: 710—290, 550—650, 960—450, 350—40

R: 15—5, 17, 3, 10, 5—14
S: 13—7, 4, 6—14, 16, 15
T: 25, 26, 8, 5, 14—16, 28, —2
U: 21, 9, 13, 25—5, 17, 15—15

**D2: The number pair shortcut**
A: 25  B: 24  C: 30  D: 32  E: 60  F: 81  G: 107  H: 85
I: 236  J: 280  K: 340  L: 400

## Section 13: Multiplication and division techniques p32

**D1: x and ÷ whole numbers by 10, 100, 100**
1. $5 \times 10 = \boxed{50}$  2. $42 \times 10 = \boxed{420}$  3. $6 \times \boxed{100} = 600$  4. $83 \times 100 = \boxed{8300}$
5. $15 \times 1000 = \boxed{15000}$  6. $17 \times \boxed{10} = 170$  7. $\boxed{23} \times 100 = 2300$  8. $54 \times \boxed{100} = 5400$
9. $9 \times \boxed{1000} = 9000$  10. $\boxed{10} \times 58 = 580$  11. $101 \times 10 = \boxed{1010}$  12. $\boxed{10} \times 10 = 100$
13. $60 \div 10 = \boxed{6}$  14. $350 \div 10 = \boxed{35}$  15. $490 \div 10 = 49$  16. $3100 \div 100 = \boxed{31}$
17. $150 \div 10 = \boxed{15}$  18. $200 \div 10 = \boxed{20}$  19. $1500 \div 100 = 15$  20. $7000 \div 10 = 700$
21. $1100 \div 10 = 110$  22. $\boxed{7000} \div 1000 = 7$

*Strategies for Improving Mental Arithmetic Skills*

A POW GUIDE  page 273  ANSWERS

## D2: × 2-digit multiples of 10 by 2, 3, 4 or 5
1. 50 × 3 = 150   2. 40 × 2 = 80   3. 40 × 3 = 120   4. 80 × 2 = 160
5. 120 × 5 = 600   6. 70 × 3 = 210   7. 90 × 5 = 450   8. 23 × 3 = 69
9. 110 × 5 = 550   10. 70 × 5 = 350   11. 200 × 4 = 800   12. 600 × 3 = 1800

## D3: × 2-digit numbers by 2, 3, 4 or 5
1. 51 × 3 = 153   2. 44 × 2 = 88   3. 31 × 4 = 124   4. 61 × 3 = 183
5. 71 × 5 = 355   6. 32 × 3 = 96   7. 91 × 5 = 455   8. 22 × 3 = 66
9. 62 × 4 = 248   10. 54 × 2 = 108   11. 43 × 4 = 172   12. 72 × 3 = 216

# Section 14: More doubling and halving  p33

## D1: Doubling bigger numbers
1. 80   2. 98   3. 52   4. 84   5. 300   6. 860   7. 8 000   8. 7 400
9. 400   10. 375   11. 14½   12. 22½   13. 30   14. 35   15. 110   16. 18½
17. 35   18. 57   19. 98½

## D2: Repeated doubling and halving
1. 11   2. 5½   3. 52   4. 104   5. 208   6. 21   7. 10½   8. 14
9. 7   10. 132   11. 26   12. 22½   13. 42   14. 120   15. 44

## D3: Adding near doubles
1. 470   2. 810   3. 107   4. 256   5. 296   6. 94   7. 152   8. 920
9. 770   10. 1330

# Section 15: Crossing the thousands boundary  p34

## D1: Hundreds and thousands
1. 2 000   2. 2 400   3. 2 100   4. 1 900   5. 1 700   6. 2 100   7. 1 800   8. 2 500
9. 5 000   5 200   5 400   5 600   5 800   6 000   6 200   6 400   6 600   6 800   7 000
10. 6 100   11. 6 000   12. 5 800   13. 6 300   14. 5 800   15. 5 800   16. 6 300   17. 6 400
18. 8 000   19. 5 200   20. 6 800   21. 3 500   22. 2 900   23. 8 700   24. 7 500   25. 6 800

## D2: Tens and thousands and units
1. 3 020   2. 3 030   3. 3 000   4. 3 000   5. 2 980   6. 2 980   7. 2 960   8. 2 960
9. 5 002   10. 5 003   11. 5 004   12. 5 004   13. 4 997   14. 4 995   15. 5 006   16. 4 996
17. 8 100   18. 4 005   19. 3 300   20. 5 006   21. 1 800   22. 7 900   23. 4 030   24. 7 500
25. 1 400   26. 3 001   27. 4 100   28. 5 900

## D3: Counting on or back when the numbers are close
1. 2 999 + 3 = 3 002   2. 2 596 + 4 = 2 600   3. 1 783 + 5 = 1 788
4. 2 779 + 4 = 2 783   5. 3 003 − 4 = 2 999   6. 3 488 + 7 = 3 495

## D4: Counting on and back with multiples of 10
1. 756   2. 1 295   3. 2 448   4. 845   5. 7 281   6. 4 095   7. 2 579   8. 1 220
9. 7 653   10. 2 217

## D5: Counting on and back with multiples of 100 or 1000
1. 2 773   2. 3 281   3. 6 420   4. 2 395   5. 4 056   6. 2 598   7. 1 559   8. 3 450
9. 5 207   10. 1 857

*Strategies for Improving Mental Arithmetic Skills*

# Section 16: Decimals and rounding  p36

## D1: Decimal number lines
1. 5   5.1   5.2   5.3   5.4   5.5   5.6   5.7   5.8   5.9   6
2. A: 3.5   B: 6.8 or 6.9   C: 8.2 or 8.3   D: 12.8   E: 24.3 or 24.4   F: 1.6 or 1.7

## D2: Fractions and decimals
1. 3.5   2. 7.25   3. 8.75   4. 10.5   5. 5¼   6. 9¼   7. 2¾   8. 25¼
9. 0.3   10. 4.6   11. 0.7   12. 0.9   13. 5³/₁₀   14. ⁹/₁₀   15. 6⁶/₁₀

## D3: + and − decimals to 1 d.p.
1. 2.4 + 0.3 = 2.7   2. 2.5 + 0.4 = 2.9   3. 2.8 + 0.2 = 3   4. 2.8 − 0.6 = 2.2
5. 2.7 + 0.8 = 3.5   6. 3.2 − 0.5 = 2.7   7. 2.9 + 0.6 = 3.5   8. 3.2 − 0.5 = 2.7
9. 3.5 + 0.2 = 3.7   10. 6.1 + 0.8 = 6.9   11. 2.7 + 0.2 = 2.9   12. 4.8 − 0.6 = 4.2
13. 6.9 + 0.4 = 7.3   14. 7.1 − 0.4 = 6.7   15. 8.6 + 0.3 = 9.1   16. 9 − 0.3 = 8.7

## D4: × and ÷ decimals by 10 and 100
1. 2.4 × 10 = 24   2. 4.5 × 10 = 45   3. 6.7 ÷ 10 = 0.67   4. 7.1 ÷ 10 = 0.71
5. 6 ÷ 10 = 0.6   6. 27 ÷ 10 = 2.7   7. 12.4 × 100 = 1240   8. 0.6 ÷ 10 = 0.06
9. 0.04 × 10 = 0.4   10. 3.52 × 100 = 352   11. 5 ÷ 10 = 0.5   12. 2.34 × 10 = 0.234

## D5: Using rounding to work out money problems
1. 5   2. 4   3. £42

## D6: Rounding numbers
1. (a) 2   (b) 3   (c) 3   (d) 3   2. (a) 5   (b) 9   (c) 11   (d) 28
3. (a) 20   (b) 80   (c) 140   (d) 270   4. (a) 300   (b) 600   (c) 500   (d) 800

# Section 17: Fractions and percentages  p38

## D1: Simple equivalents
1. 25%   2. ¾   3. ½   4. 30%

## D2: Fractions and decimals
1. £25   2. £30   3. £30   4. £5   5. £6   6. £12.50   7. £8   8. £15
9. £14   10. £11   11. £5   12. £3   13. £11   14. £21   15. 9p

## D3: Multiples of ¹/₁₀ and 10%
1. £5   2. £10   3. £35   4. 12p   5. 12p   6. 4p   7. 12p   8. 36p
9. £60   10. £120

# Section 18: Measurements of length, weight and time  p38

## D1: Changing between cm and mm
1. (a) 24 mm   (b) 2.4 cm   2. (a) 3 cm 6 mm   (b) 3.6 cm
3. (a) 5 cm 7 mm   (b) 57 mm   4. (a) 4.8 cm   (b) 4 cm 8 mm
5. (a) 91 mm   (b) 9 cm 1 mm   6. (a) 3.8 cm   (b) 38 mm

## D2: Changing between m and cm
1. 2 m = 200 cm   2. 2 m 40 cm = 240 cm   3. 1 m 25 cm = 125 cm
4. 5 m 12 cm = 512 cm   5. 3 50 cm = 3 m 50 cm   6. 405 cm = 4 m 5 cm
7. 701 cm = 7 m 1 cm   8. 275 cm = 2 m 75 cm

*Strategies for Improving Mental Arithmetic Skills*

### D3: Changing between kg and g

1. 2 kg = 2 000 g    2. 3 kg 800 g = 3 800 g    3. 1 kg 500 g = 1 500 g
4. 1 kg 50 g = 1 050 g    5. 1200 g = 1 kg 200 g    6. 2350 g = 2 kg 350 g
7. 1010 g = 1 kg 10 g    8. 7250 g = 7 kg 250 g

### D4: Map scales

1. (a) 2 cm  (b) 5 cm  (c) 8 cm  (d) 5 or 6 cm  (f) 3 cm
2. (a) 2 cm – 2.5 cm  (b) 10 km – 12.5 km  (c) 20 km (accept 17–22 km)

### D5: Fractions of length, weight and time

1. Half a cm = 5 mm         2. half a m = 50 cm           3. half a kg = 500g
4. $1\frac{1}{2}$ cm = 15 mm   5. $2\frac{1}{2}$ m = 250 cm   6. $4\frac{1}{2}$ kg = 4 500 g
7. $\frac{1}{4}$ cm = 2.5 mm   8. $3\frac{1}{4}$ m = 325 cm   9. $1\frac{1}{4}$ kg = 1 250 g
10. $\frac{1}{2}$ hour = 30 min   11. $\frac{1}{4}$ hour = 15 min   12. $\frac{3}{4}$ hour = 45 min
13. 2 hours = 120 min   14. $1\frac{1}{4}$ hours = 75 min   15. $2\frac{1}{2}$ hours = 150 min
16. $\frac{1}{2}$ min = 30 sec   17. $\frac{1}{4}$ min = 15 sec   18. $\frac{1}{2}$ day = 12 hours
19. 3 min = 180 sec   20. 2 days = 48 hours

### D6: Time problems

1. 5.45 or quarter to 6        2. 9.10 or ten past nine        3. 55 min
4. 7.15 or quarter past 7      5. 9.45 or quarter to ten

# Back to Basics

## Section 1: Pencil-and-paper addition  p42

### D1: Addition technique review

1. 429   2. 567   3. 182   4. 710   5. 201   6. 69   7. 279   8. 392
9. 207   10. 336   11. 877   12. 818   13. 126   14. 707   15. 238   16. 987
17. 585   18. 818   19. 1863   20. 570   21. 865   22. 420

### D2: What did they do wrong?

1. Plok put 4 in the tens column. Plok should have put it in the units column.
2. The sum of the units column is 11. Letmewin put 11 as the units total.
   Letmewin should have put 1 in the units column and carried the ten.      3. 61

### P1: getting different totals

1.
```
  25   25   35   35
+ 13 + 31 + 12 + 21
  38   56   47   56
       Totals
```

2.
```
  57   75   78   87   58   85
+ 38 + 38 + 35 + 35 + 37 + 37
  95  113  113  122   95  122
         Totals are 95, 113, 122   Largest is 122
```

3.
```
  67   76   73   37   36   63
+ 38 + 38 + 35 + 68 + 78 + 78
 105  114  108  105  114  141
```
Totals are 105, 113, 122
Totals are 105, 114, 141   Smallest total is 105

## Section 2: Pencil-and-paper subtraction  p46

### D1: Subtraction technique review

1. 14   2. 112   3. 16   4. 46   5. 405   6. 22   7. 19   8. 211
9. 307   10. 318   11. 293   12. 266   13. 415   14. 107   15. 292   16. 521
17. 339   18. 187   19. 584   20. 296   21. 89   22. 396   23. 289   24. 386
25. 461   26. 287   27. 89   28. 518   29. 286   30. 266   31. 384   32. 385   33. 342

### D2: Subtraction mistakes

1. In the units column, Youslas took the top number from the bottom number, instead of the other way round.
2. Zuk put the smallest number on top. The largest number should be on top.   3. 49

### P1: Addition and subtraction problems

1. 63 – 45 = 18           Ans:£18
2. 243 + 28 = 271         Ans:£271
3. 317 – 40 = 277         Ans:£277
4. 645 – 562 = 83         Ans: £83
5. 65 + 87 = 152          Ans: 152 students
6. 27+25+28+28+25 = 129   Ans: 129
7. 97 + 45 = 142          Ans: 142 students
8. 137 – 89 = 48          Ans: 48 students
9. 35 + 87 = 122          Ans: 122 cm
10. 515 – 472 = 43        Ans: 43 cm

### P2: Subtraction snakes

Task 1:
1. 16   13   7   2
2. 22   15   12   8
3. 43   37   28   17

Task 2:
4. 232  218  178   5. 261  248  97
6. 396  234  86    7. 534  267  128

If you get any wrong, ask your teacher to check your working.

### D3: Do you add or subtract?

1. 15 + 10 = 25    2. 41 – 24 = 17      3. 20 – 9 = 11       4. 25 + 10 = 35
5. 20 – 8 = 12     6. 17 + 7 = 24       7. 48 – 30 = 18      8. 33 – 25 = 8
9. 45 + 25 = 70    10. 59 – 42 = 17     11. 47 – 32 = 15     12. 56 + 13 = 69
13. 70 – 39 = 31   14. 51 + 26 = 77     15. 98 – 73 = 25     16. 78 – 65 = 13

Type 3:
```
17 | 25
22 | 31
39   56
```
```
      | 42
17 + 7| 53
53
```

If you get any wrong, ask your teacher to check your working.

### P3: More row and column sums

1.
```
158 |
275 |
169  264
```

2.
```
      | 42
22|31 | 53
56
```

3.
```
37 | 97
81  102
```

4.
```
      | 68
21|47 | 70
23
```

## Section 3: Pencil-and-paper multiplication  p52

### D1: Multiplication technique review

1. 36   2. 92   3. 94   4. 180   5. 448   6. 246

### P1: Multiplication practice

Batch A: 1. 84   2. 162   3. 360   4. 288   5. 738
         6. 42   7. 288   8. 168   9. 413   10. 2592

Batch B: 1. 94   2. 231   3. 354   4. 729   5. 1230
         6. 130   7. 492   8. 603   9. 126   10. 875

Batch C: 1. 246   2. 201   3. 518   4. 145   5. 720
         6. 133   7. 162   8. 315   9. 312   10. 2655

Batch D: 1. 288   2. 430   3. 423   4. 664   5. 735
         6. 660   7. 204   8. 116   9. 486   10. 3900

*Back to Basics*

## P2: Different totals

1. $25 \times 3 = 75$   $52 \times 3 = 156$   $53 \times 2 = 106$   $35 \times 2 = 70$
2. $35 \times 7 = 245$   $53 \times 7 = 371$   $37 \times 5 = 185$   $73 \times 5 = 365$   $75 \times 3 = 225$   $57 \times 3 = 171$
3. $54 \times 4 = 216$   $45 \times 4 = 180$   $44 \times 5 = 220$   3 different totals
4. Largest is 504   [Totals are 288, 504, 228, 498, 204, 258]
5. Smallest is 102   [Totals are 132, 102, 129]
6. There are 24 possible totals. The largest is 2160 [432 × 5]

## Section 4: Multiplication by tens ... p54

### D1: Multiplication by 10, 100, 1000
1. 40   2. 140   3. 370   4. 4170   5. 500   6. 1300   7. 2400   8. 4 000
9. 7 000   10. 29 000   11. 45 000   12. 150 000

### P1: Mixed practice

**Batch A:**
1. $7 \times 10 = 70$   2. $35 \times 100 = 3500$   3. $213 \times 10 = 2130$   4. $9 \times 1000 = 9000$
5. $35 \times 100 = 3500$   6. $17 \times 100 = 1700$   7. $29 \times 10 = 290$   8. $342 \times 10 = 3420$
9. $15 \times 10 = 150$   10. $62 \times 100 = 6200$   11. $73 \times 1000 = 73000$   12. $27 \times 100 = 2700$

**Batch B:**
1. $9 \times 100 = 900$   2. $4 \times 1000 = 4000$   3. $35 \times 10 = 350$   4. $19 \times 100 = 1900$
5. $47 \times 100 = 4700$   6. $83 \times 10 = 830$   7. $75 \times 100 = 7500$   8. $60 \times 10 = 600$
9. $25 \times 100 = 2500$   10. $105 \times 10 = 1050$   11. $222 \times 10 = 2220$   12. $34 \times 100 = 3400$

### D2: Multiplying in your head
1. 120   2. 210   3. 280   4. 240   5. 250
6. 1200   7. 1400   8. 3000   9. 2100   10. 1800
11. 6000   12. 25000   13. 14000   14. 36000   15. 32000
16. 1500   17. 220   18. 15000   19. 180   20. 180
21. 8000   22. 490   23. 300   24. 4000   25. 18000

### D3: Getting more difficult
1. 390   2. 12000   3. 560   4. 4800   5. 3250
6. 3600   7. 7290   8. 22400   9. 36000   10. 1900   11. 12900   12. 3600
3500   13. 750   14. 8000   15. 2160   16. 3720   17. 3600

## Section 5: More multiplication techniques p56

### D1: Little multiplication tables

1. | 12 | 15 |   2. | 70 | 21 |   3. | 20 | 80 |   4. | 12 | 18 |
   | 20 | 25 |      | 400 | 120 |   | 40 | 160 |    | 30 | 45 |

5. | 30 | 100 |   6. | 600 | 210 |   7. | 350 | 200 |   8. | 1200 | 900 |
   | 60 | 200 |      | 40  | 14 |     | 56  | 32  |      | 280  | 210 |

### D2: Another way of setting out multiplication sums
1. Table: 100  20   Ans 120     2. Table: 180  30   Ans 210
   Table: 200  24   Ans 224     4. Table: 180  45   Ans 225
5. 92   6. 364   7. 549   8. 140   9. 234
10. 328   11. 166   12. 228   13. 368   14. 285

*Back to Basics*

## D3: A useful trick
1. 1500   2. 2800   3. 6000   4. 15000   5. 2100   6. 2500   7. 14000   8. 24000

## D4: Multiplying bigger numbers

1. Table: | 200 | 30 |   Ans 345    2. Table: | 800 | 100 | Ans 1035
           | 100 | 15 |                          | 120 | 15  |

3. Table: | 1800 | 60 |   Ans 2294   4. Table: | 1400 | 140 |  Ans 2233
           | 420  | 14 |                         | 630  | 63  |

5. 768   6. 1008   7. 2244   8. 882   9. 2412
10. 1652   11. 564   12. 3780   13. 3071   14. 1207

## D5: Multiplying a 3-digit number by a 2-digit number
1. 1599   2. 5875   3. 13794   4. 13122   5. 20232
6. 21951   7. 49056   8. 24912

## D6: The grating method for multiplication
1. 21315   2. 7688   3. 22672   4. 10064

### P1: Multiplication practice

Batch A:   1. 528   2. 25871   3. 11310
Batch B:   1. 429   2. 4807    3. 7623
Batch C:   1. 300   2. 5764    3. 18522

### P2: Using multiplication to solve problems
1. Shop A: 12   Shop B: 48   Shop C: 60
2. Shop D: 75   Shop E: 135  Shop F: 375
3. (a) $144 \times 18 = 2592$   (b) 5040
4. (a) £177   (b) £1416   (c) £1785   (d) £5355   (e) £26 775

## Section 6: Division techniques p60

### D1: Division using the table square
1. 9   2. 4   3. 4   4. 4   5. 8   6. 7
7. 5   8. 8   9. 9   10. 11   11. 7   12. 15

### D2: It isn't always called division
1. 5   2. £3   3. 5   4. 6   5. 4
7. 5   8. 4   9. 6   10. 8

ANSWERS ONLY ARE GIVEN HERE

### D3: Setting out division sums
1. 5   2. 6   3. 8   4. 4   5. 6   6. 9
7. 7   8. 8   9. 9   10. 4

### D4: More difficult division sums
1. 19   2. 24   3. 51   4. 74   5. 89   6. 105
7. 45   8. 136   9. 92   10. 46   11. 135   12. 81
13. 51   14. 23   15. 14

### P1: Division practice
Batch A   1. 237   2. 123   3. 95   4. 13   5. 24
          6. 150   7. 29   8. 46   9. 17   10. 107

*Back to Basics*

| Batch B | 1. 48 | 2. 119 | 3. 82 | 4. 53 | 5. 127 |
|---|---|---|---|---|---|
| | 6. 62 | 7. 74 | 8. 314 | 9. 135 | 10. 74 |
| Batch C | 1. 157 | 2. 52 | 3. 127 | 4. 318 | 5. 53 |
| | 6. 64 | 7. 17 | 8. 55 | 9. 78 | 10. 78 |

**P2: Using division to solve problems**
1. £9   2. £78   3. £276   4. 45p   5. 18p   6. 28p
7. £116   8. £116

**P3: Division puzzles**
1. 2 answers: 342 & 432   2. 3 answers: 233 & 323 & 332
3. 6 answers: 189, 192, 219, 225, 252, 255

**D5: Dividing by large numbers**
1. 17   2. 23   3. 29   4. 42   5. 56   6. 43
7. 27   8. 21   9. 87   10. 36   11. 32   12. 13
13. 61   14. 37   15. 51

**P3: Large number division practice**

| Batch A | 1. 11 | 2. 46 | 3. 22 | 4. 12 | 5. 45 |
|---|---|---|---|---|---|
| | 6. 29 | 7. 43 | 8. 26 | 9. 17 | 10. 12 |
| Batch B | 1. 51 | 2. 26 | 3. 43 | 4. 71 | 5. 29 |
| | 6. 14 | 7. 13 | 8. 72 | 9. 18 | 10. 23 |

## Section 9: Technique review  p64

**R1: Multiplication and division using a table square**
1. 36   2. 14   3. 72   4. 56   5. 13   6. 84   7. 54
8. 12   9. 13   10. 7

**R2: Pencil and paper addition**
1. 42   2. 387   3. 272   4. 718

**R3: Pencil and paper subtraction**
1. 11   2. 19   3. 128   4. 72

**R4: Pencil and paper multiplication**
1. 72   2. 171   3. 528   4. 574

**R5: Pencil and paper division**
1. 70   2. 68   3. 16   4. 52   5. 59

**R6: Multiplying whole numbers by 10, 100, 1000**
1. 40   2. 520   3. 700   4. 8100   5. 5000   6. 330   7. 2400   8. 340

**R7: Multiplication by 20, 30, ...., 200, 300, ...**
1. 120   2. 150   3. 1400   4. 6900   5. 10200   6. 48000   7. 21600   8. 2820

**R8: Multiplying by 2-digit numbers**
1. 518   2. 1550   3. 4482   4. 10166   5. 13338

**R9: More difficult division sums**
1. 135   2. 81   3. 16   4. 23   5. 14

**R10: Dividing by large numbers**
1. 29   2. 24   3. 38   4. 48   5. 56

*Back to Basics*

# Bar Charts and Beyond

## Section 1: Interpreting tables and diagrams  p 68

**D1: From lists and tables**
1. 9   2. 11   3. 23   4. Officers   5. Crew   6. 28
7. 48   8. 76   9. 50 mm   10. November   11. August
12. Madria   13. Dec – April   14. 674 mm   15. 940 mm   16. June
17.& 18. Either Madria because it doesn't rain for 5 months of the year
or Arro because it has less rain during the year.

**D2: Pictograph review**
1. 10   2. 5   3.

| Zoom | Eros | Zog | Klar | Rima | Other |
|---|---|---|---|---|---|
| 10 | 6 | 5 | 9 | 7 | 8 |

4. 16   5. 45

**D3: Bar chart review**
1. 12   2. 13   3. Frequencies are: 12 14 16 13 5 9 15
4. 84   5. 30   6. Klar   7. 22

## Section 2: Bar charts and pictographs  p 70

**D1: What is missing?**
1. Bar for Chyps should be 5 high – not 6
3. 1 symbol = 2 PGEs
4.

```
Plok     ●●●●
Do-med   ●●●●●
Chyps    ●●●
Idea     ●●
Taz      ●●
Dwork    ●●
```
Key: ● = 2 PGEs

Pan–Galactic Explorers

2.

Number of wins of best Galacton players

Number of wins of best Galacton players (bar chart, Plok Do-med Chyps Idea Taz Dwork, Frequency 0–8)

Pan–Galactic Explorers

**D2: Displaying survey results**

**Task 1:**  Faz 7
Zorbit 4
Limk 8
Sput 6
Mmm 5

**Task 2:** Use the checklist to see if your bar chart is complete.
• equal width bars (1 mark)
• labels in the middle of each bar (1 mark)
• accurate heights of bars (2 marks)
• sensible scale up the page (2 marks)
• labels on both axes (1 mark)
• title (1 mark)

**Task 3:** Use the checklist to see if your pictograph is complete.
• simple symbols (1 mark)
• label on the axis (1 mark)
• KEY (1 mark)
• title (1 mark)
• correct number of symbols on each line (3 marks)

*Bar Charts and Beyond*

## Section 3: Grouped data    p 72

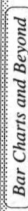

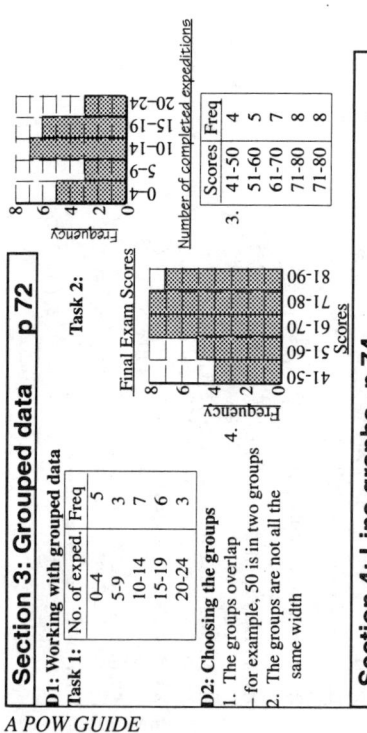

**D1: Working with grouped data**

Task 1:
| No. of exped. | Freq |
|---|---|
| 0-4 | 5 |
| 5-9 | 3 |
| 10-14 | 7 |
| 15-19 | 6 |
| 20-24 | 3 |

Task 2: (bar chart: Number of completed expeditions, Frequency vs ranges 0-4, 5-9, 10-14, 15-19, 20-24)

**D2: Choosing the groups**
1. The groups overlap – for example, 50 is in two groups
2. The groups are not all the same width

3.
| Scores | Freq |
|---|---|
| 41-50 | 4 |
| 51-60 | 5 |
| 61-70 | 7 |
| 71-80 | 8 |

4. (bar chart: Final Exam Scores, Frequency vs 41-50, 51-60, 61-70, 71-80, 81-90)

## Section 4: Line graphs    p 74

**D1: Temperatures on the planet Juno**
1. 8°   2. 18°   3. 20°   4. 6°   5. 00.00 & 10.00
6. 14.00   7. 06.00   8. 26°   9. Rise   10. 8°

## Section 5: Averages and range    p 75

**D1: The mode**
1. 4   2. 4 & 5   3. no mode   4. 6   5. blue   6. 5p & 10p
7. dog   8. no mode   9. 3

**D1: The median**
1. 3   2. 5   3. 5   4. 8   5. 8   6. 12
7. 5   8. 5   9. 9   10. 26   11. 15   12. 12

**P1: Mode and median practice**

**Batch A**
1. No mode   median = 3       3. mode = 8 & 9   median = 8
2. no mode   median = 0       4. mode = 13      median = 11
5. no mode   median = 21      8. mode = 17      median = 18
6. mode = 16 median = 16      9. no mode        median = 65
7. mode = 100 median = 100   10. mode = 9&10    median = 9

**Batch B**
1. No mode   median = 20      3. mode = 19 & 23  median = 20
2. no mode   median = 15      4. mode = 16       median = 12
5. no mode   median = 12      8. no mode         median = 60
6. mode = 13&19 median = 18   9. no mode         median = 200
7. mode = 65 median = 63     10. mode = 0&3      median = 3½

**Batch C**
1. mode = 101 median = 100    3. mode = 4    median = 5
2. mode = 12  median = 12     4. no mode     median = 7½

5. mode = 35  median = 35     8. mode = 8&10   median = 10
6. mode = 21&23 median = 22   9. mode = 150&200 median = 200
7. mode = 83  median = 86    10. mode = 6    median = 6

1. 4   2. 5.8   3. 5    4. 8.5   5. 15
9. 16.5  10. 10.5  11. 5  12. 8  13. 2  14. 3   6. 6
17. 5  18. 21 19. 6. 5 20. 5.7 21. 5.8 22. 7.5 8
7. 7.5   8. 7
15. 6   16. 13

### D2: Mean and range

**P1: Batch A**
1. mean = 5   range = 4       3. mean = 6    range = 6
2. mean = 5   range = 10      4. mean = 9    range = 10
5. mean = 5   mode = 4        7. mean = 4    mode = 1&6
6. mean = 4   no mode        11. mean = 16   mode = 8&10
9. mean = 8   median = 8     12. mean = 50   median = 16
10. mean = 15 median = 17                    median = 4

**P1: Batch B**
1. mean = 15  range = 11      3. mean = 7    range = 10
2. mean = 3   range = 6       4. mean = 9    range = 18
5. mean = 4   mode = 4        7. mean = 9    mode = 6&7
6. mean = 8   no mode         8. mode = 5&6  mean = 5
9. mean = 12  median = 12    11. mean = 16   median = 17
10. mean = 12 median = 11    12. mean = 3    median = 4

## Section 6: Working with averages    p 78

**D1: Average problems**
1. 15.2   2. (a) 26p  (b) 25½p  (c) 3p    3. (a) 220 g  (b) 224g
4. (a) 29  (b) 34  (c) 74          5. (a) 17.1  (b) 16.5  (c) 16.8
6. (a) 2°C  (b) 1.5°C  (c) 1°C  (d) 8°C

**D2: Thinking about averages**
1. (a) 10  (b) £4280  (c) £428  (d) £120  (e) £850  (f) £730
2. (a) Heven 26° (b) Helos 25° (c) 2  (d) range for Heven = 32 − 20 = 12  range for Helos = 30 − 18 = 12  ∴ statement is NOT correct
3. (a) 9  (b) 8  (c) the mode

**D3: Making comparisons**
1. (a) Me  (b) mean  (c) my friend  (d) range
2. (a) 71.4%  (b) 74.2%  (c) Spoton    3. (a) 42%  (b) 11%  (c) Spoton
4. (a) mean  (b) range   5. (a) Tamsin : mean 69, range 26; Peter: mean 68.2, range 14
(b) Peter is more consistent  (c) Tamsin is better – used the mean

**P1: More comparisons**
1. 3   2. 2.4    3 Range = 3  Mean = 2.4
4. The variation in family sizes is much smaller in 1997 than it was in 1967
5. Families are smaller in 1997 than they were in 1967
6. Peter 14  Barry 12.6   7. Peter 5  Barry 27   8. Peter   9. Barry
10. Barry   11. Either: Choose Peter because his average score is only a little less than Barry's and he is more consistent or Choose Barry because his average score is higher and his range of scores shows he can score very highly.

Bar Charts and Beyond

## Section 7: Interpreting diagrams   p 81

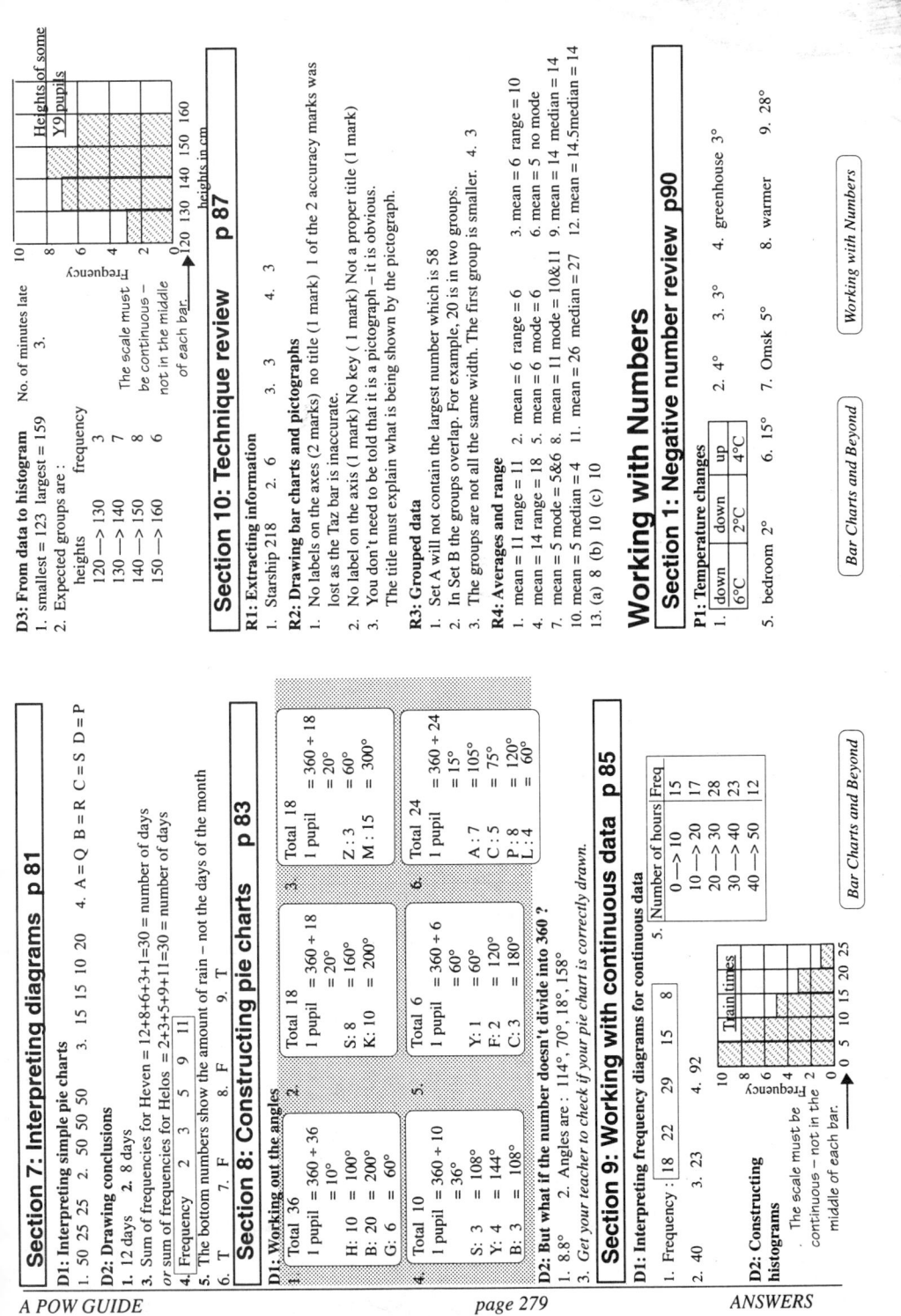

### D1: Interpreting simple pie charts
1. 50 25 25   2. 50 50 50   3. 15 15 10 20   4. A = Q  B = R  C = S  D = P

### D2: Drawing conclusions
1. 12 days   2. 8 days
3. Sum of frequencies for Heven = 12+8+6+3+1=30 = number of days
   or Sum of frequencies for Helos = 2+4+3+5+9+11=30 = number of days

4. | Frequency | 2 | 3 | 5 | 9 | 11 |

5. The bottom numbers show the amount of rain – not the days of the month
6. T   7. F   8. F   9. T

## Section 8: Constructing pie charts   p 83

### D1: Working out the angles

1. Total 36
   1 pupil = 360 ÷ 36
           = 10°
   H: 10 = 100°
   B: 20 = 200°
   G: 6  = 60°

2. Total 18
   1 pupil = 360 ÷ 18
           = 20°
   S: 8  = 160°
   K: 10 = 200°

3. Total 18
   1 pupil = 360 ÷ 18
           = 20°
   Z: 3  = 60°
   M: 15 = 300°

4. Total 10
   1 pupil = 360 ÷ 10
           = 36°
   S: 3 = 108°
   Y: 4 = 144°
   B: 3 = 108°

5. Total 6
   1 pupil = 360 ÷ 6
           = 60°
   Y: 1 = 60°
   F: 2 = 120°
   C: 3 = 180°

6. Total 24
   1 pupil = 360 ÷ 24
           = 15°
   A: 7 = 105°
   C: 5 = 75°
   P: 8 = 120°
   L: 4 = 60°

### D2: But what if the number doesn't divide into 360 ?
1. 8.8°   2. Angles are : 114°, 70°, 18°, 158°
3. *Get your teacher to check if your pie chart is correctly drawn.*

## Section 9: Working with continuous data   p 85

### D1: Interpreting frequency diagrams for continuous data

1. Frequency : | 18 | 22 | 29 | 15 | 8 |

2. 40   3. 23   4. 92

5. | Number of hours | Freq |
   |---|---|
   | 0 —> 10 | 15 |
   | 10 —> 20 | 17 |
   | 20 —> 30 | 28 |
   | 30 —> 40 | 23 |
   | 40 —> 50 | 12 |

### D2: Constructing histograms

*The scale must be continuous – not in the middle of each bar.*

[Train times histogram: Frequency axis 0–10, x-axis 0 5 10 15 20 25]

### D3: From data to histogram

1. smallest = 123  largest = 159
2. Expected groups are :

   | heights | frequency |
   |---|---|
   | 120 —> 130 | 3 |
   | 130 —> 140 | 7 |
   | 140 —> 150 | 8 |
   | 150 —> 160 | 6 |

3. No. of minutes late

[Histogram showing frequency 2,4,6,8,10]

*The scale must be continuous – not in the middle of each bar.*

[Heights of some Y9 pupils histogram: Frequency axis, x-axis 120 130 140 150 160 heights in cm]

## Section 10: Technique review   p 87

### R1: Extracting information
1. Starship 218   2. 6   3. 3   4. 3

### R2: Drawing bar charts and pictographs
1. No labels on the axes (2 marks)  no title (1 mark)  1 of the 2 accuracy marks was lost as the Taz bar is inaccurate.
2. No label on the axis (1 mark) No key ( 1 mark)  Not a proper title (1 mark)
3. You don't need to be told that it is a pictograph – it is obvious.
   The title must explain what is being shown by the pictograph.

### R3: Grouped data
1. Set A will not contain the largest number which is 58
2. In Set B the groups overlap. For example, 20 is in two groups.
3. The groups are not all the same width. The first group is smaller.   4. 3

### R4: Averages and range
1. mean = 11  range = 11   2. mean = 6  range = 6   3. mean = 6  range = 10
4. mean = 14  range = 18   5. mean = 6  mode = 6    6. mean = 5  no mode
7. mean = 5  mode = 5&6   8. mean = 11 mode = 10&11   9. mean = 14 median = 14
10. mean = 5 median = 4   11. mean = 26 median = 27   12. mean = 14.5 median = 14
13. (a) 8 (b) 10 (c) 10

# Working with Numbers

## Section 1: Negative number review   p90

### P1: Temperature changes

1. | down | down | up |
   |---|---|---|
   | 6°C | 2°C | 4°C |

   2. 4°   3. 3°   4. greenhouse 3°

5. bedroom 2°   6. 15°   7. Omsk 5°   8. warmer   9. 28°

*Bar Charts and Beyond*

*Bar Charts and Beyond*

*Bar Charts and Beyond*

*Working with Numbers*

A POW GUIDE            page 279            ANSWERS

**P2: Work these out with and without a calculator**

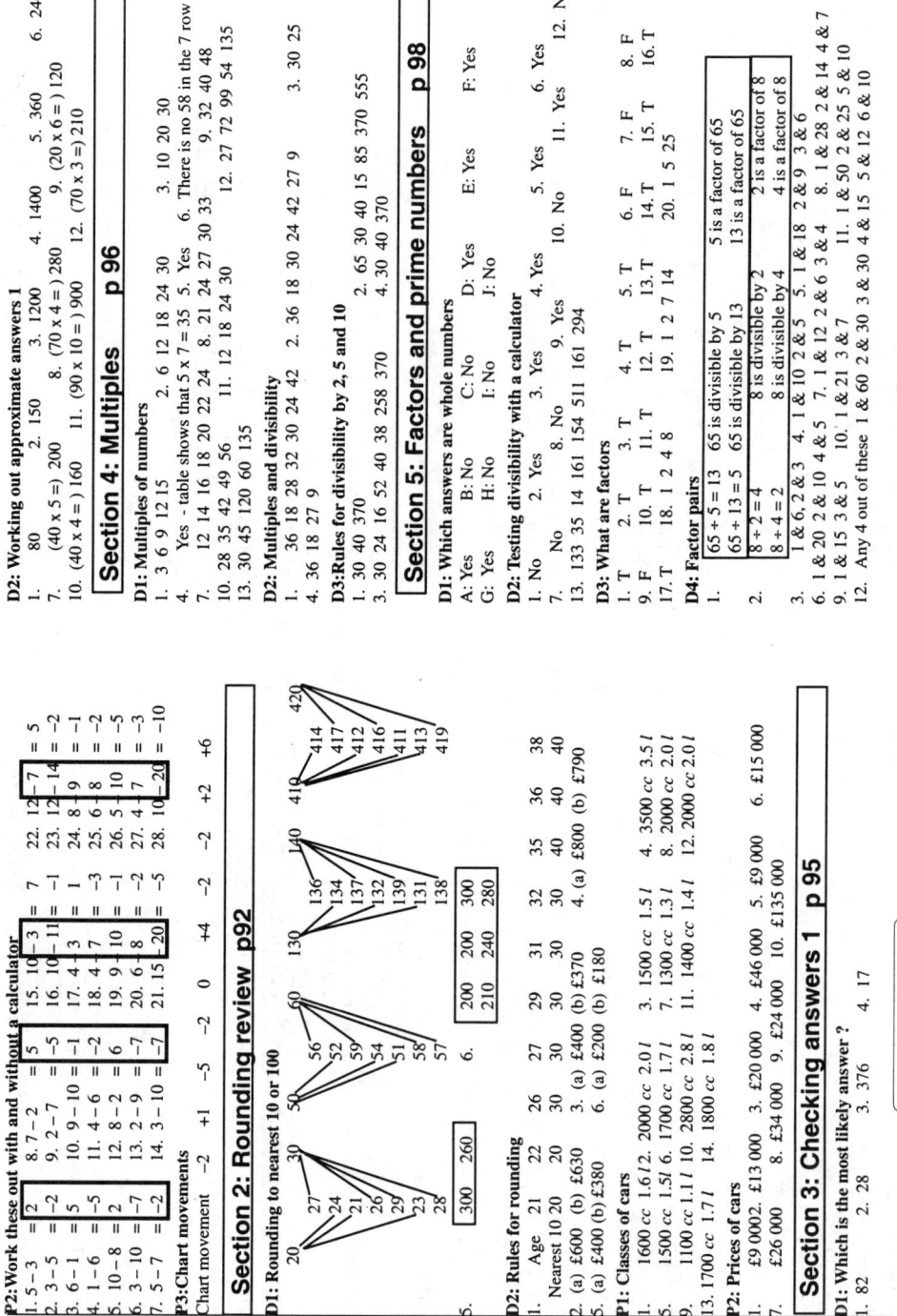

| | | | | |
|---|---|---|---|---|
| 1. 5 − 3 = **2** | 8. 7 − 2 = **5** | 15. 10 − 3 = **7** | 22. 12 − 7 = **5** | |
| 2. 3 − 5 = **−2** | 9. 2 − 7 = **−5** | 16. 10 − 11 = **−1** | 23. 12 − 14 = **−2** | |
| 3. 6 − 1 = **5** | 10. 9 − 10 = **−1** | 17. 4 − 3 = **1** | 24. 8 − 9 = **−1** | |
| 4. 1 − 6 = **−5** | 11. 4 − 6 = **−2** | 18. 4 − 7 = **−3** | 25. 6 − 8 = **−2** | |
| 5. 10 − 8 = **2** | 12. 8 − 2 = **6** | 19. 9 − 10 = **−1** | 26. 5 − 10 = **−5** | |
| 6. 3 − 10 = **−7** | 13. 2 − 9 = **−7** | 20. 6 − 8 = **−2** | 27. 4 − 7 = **−3** | |
| 7. 5 − 7 = **−2** | 14. 3 − 10 = **−7** | 21. 15 − **20** = −5 | 28. 10 − 20 = **−10** | |

**P3: Chart movements**

Chart movement  −2  +1  −5  −2  0  +4  −2  +2  +6

## Section 2: Rounding review    p92

**D1: Rounding to nearest 10 or 100**

1.
20 30 50 60 130 140
27 56 52 59 54 51 58 57 24 21 29 26 23 28
→ 30, 50, 60, 130, 140 (groupings)

136 134 137 132 139 131 138

410 420
414 417 412 416 411 413 419

5.  300  260      6.  200  200  300
                    210  240  280

**D2: Rules for rounding**

1.  Age    21  22  26  27  29  31  32  35  36  38
    Nearest 10  20  20  30  30  30  30  30  30  40  40
2. (a) £600  (b) £630   3. (a) £400  (b) £370   4. (a) £800  (b) £790
5. (a) £400  (b) £380   6. (a) £200  (b) £180

**P1: Classes of cars**

1. 1600 cc 1.6 *l*   2. 2000 cc 2.0 *l*   3. 1500 cc 1.5 *l*   4. 3500 cc 3.5 *l*
5. 1500 cc 1.5 *l*   6. 1700 cc 1.7 *l*   7. 1300 cc 1.3 *l*   8. 2000 cc 2.0 *l*
9. 1100 cc 1.1 *l*  10. 2800 cc 2.8 *l*  11. 1400 cc 1.4 *l*  12. 2000 cc 2.0 *l*
13. 1700 cc 1.7 *l*  14. 1800 cc 1.8 *l*

**P2: Prices of cars**

1. £9 000   2. £13 000   3. £20 000   4. £46 000   5. £9 000   6. £15 000
7. £26 000   8. £34 000   9. £24 000   10. £135 000

## Section 3: Checking answers 1    p 95

**D1: Which is the most likely answer?**

1. 82   2. 28   3. 376   4. 17

**D2: Working out approximate answers 1**

1. 80   2. 150   3. 1200   4. 1400   5. 360   6. 240
7. (40 × 5 =) 200   8. (70 × 4 =) 280   9. (20 × 6 =) 120
10. (40 × 4 =) 160   11. (90 × 10 =) 900   12. (70 × 3 =) 210

## Section 4: Multiples    p 96

**D1: Multiples of numbers**

1. 3 6 9 12 15   2. 6 12 18 24 30   3. 10 20 30
4. Yes - table shows that 5 × 7 = 35   5. Yes   6. There is no 58 in the 7 row
7. 12 14 16 18 20 22 24   8. 21 24 27 30 33   9. 32 40 48
10. 28 35 42 49 56   11. 12 18 24 30   12. 27 72 99 54 135
13. 30 45 120 60 135

**D2: Multiples and divisibility**

1. 36 18 28 32 30 24 42   2. 36 18 30 24 42 27 9   3. 30 25
4. 36 18 27 9

**D3: Rules for divisibility by 2, 5 and 10**

1. 30 40 370   2. 65 30 40 15 85 370 555
3. 30 24 16 52 40 38 258 370   4. 30 40 370

## Section 5: Factors and prime numbers    p 98

**D1: Which answers are whole numbers**

A: Yes   B: No   C: No   D: Yes   E: Yes   F: Yes
G: Yes   H: No   I: No   J: No

**D2: Testing divisibility with a calculator**

1. No   2. Yes   3. Yes   4. Yes   5. Yes   6. Yes
7. No   8. No   9. Yes   10. No   11. Yes   12. Yes
13. 133 35 14 161 154 511 161 294

**D3: What are factors**

1. T    2. T    3. T    4. T    5. T    6. F    7. F    8. F
9. F   10. T   11. T   12. T   13. T   14. T   15. T   16. T
17. T  18. 1 2 4 8  19. 1 2 7 14   20. 1 5 25

**D4: Factor pairs**

1. 65 ÷ 5 = 13      65 is divisible by 5       5 is a factor of 65
   65 ÷ 13 = 5     65 is divisible by 13      13 is a factor of 65
2. 8 ÷ 2 = 4        8 is divisible by 2        2 is a factor of 8
   8 ÷ 4 = 2        8 is divisible by 4        4 is a factor of 8
3. 1 & 6, 2 & 3   4. 1 & 10 2 & 5   5. 1 & 18 2 & 9 3 & 6
6. 1 & 20 2 & 10 4 & 5   7. 1 & 12 2 & 6 3 & 4   8. 1 & 28 2 & 14 4 & 7
9. 1 & 15 3 & 5   10. 1 & 21 3 & 7   11. 1 & 50 2 & 25 5 & 10
12. Any 4 out of these 1 & 60 2 & 30 3 & 20 4 & 15 5 & 12 6 & 10

*Working with Numbers*

## P1: Sums of + and – numbers

| Batch A | 1. 1 | 2. 2 | 3. -3 | 4. 2 | 5. 4 | 6. -6 | 7. 3 | 8. -5 |
|---|---|---|---|---|---|---|---|---|
| Batch B | 1. 2 | 2. -1 | 3. -4 | 4. -2 | 5. 1 | 6. -8 | 7. -8 | 8. 4 |
| Batch C | 1. -6 | 2. -2 | 3. -9 | 4. 4 | 5. 1 | 6. -1 | 7. -5 | 8. 2 |

### D2: Subtracting numbers

1. 4   2. -3   3. 2   4. 11   5. -6   6. 6   7. -5   8. -2
9. 4   10. -4   11. -5   12. -4   13. 3   14. -6   15. -10   16. 7
17. -9   18. -6   19. -4   20. -7   21. 5   22. 4   23. 8   24. -2
25. 8   26. 9   27. -3   28. 0   29. 7   30. 2   31. 12   32. -5

### P2: A mixture of all three types

| Batch A | 1. 3 | 2. -3 | 3. 12 | 4. 12 | 5. 2 | 6. -2 | 7. -12 | 8. 0 |
|---|---|---|---|---|---|---|---|---|
| Batch B | 1. -4 | 2. 6 | 3. -4 | 4. 7 | 5. -8 | 6. -5 | 7. -4 | 8. -3 |
| Batch C | 1. 4 | 2. -4 | 3. -7 | 4. 12 | 5. 4 | 6. 25 | 7. 4 | 8. -3 |
| Batch D | 1. 8 | 2. 4 | 3. -3 | 4. -6 | 5. 2 | 6. 15 | 7. -12 | 8. 7 |

## Section 9: Metric and Imperial equivalents p 108

### D1: Using equivalent values to solve problems

1. 60g   2. 200g   3. 200g   4. 90 cm   5. 21-23 cm   6. a quarter of a kilo
7. three quarters of a kilo   8. (a) 80 min (b) 80 min (c) 120 min (d) 170min
9. 2   10. Frame 4   11. 50 mm by 50 mm , 50 mm by 40 mm, 75 mm by 25 mm
12. 25 miles   13. 16 km   14. Duncan ; 35 miles = 56 km > 52 km
15. 5m because this is ≈ 5.5 yards and will be enough for Mum.

## Section 10: Checking answers 2 p 110

### D1: Checking using inverse operations

1. Ans to sum = 15        Check is 23 + 15 = 38
2. Ans to sum = 32        Check is 14 + 32 = 46
3. Ans to sum = 3         Check is 3 + 15 = 18
4. Ans to sum = 22        Check is 22 + 32 = 54
5. Ans to sum = 41        Check is 41 + 35 = 76
6. Ans to sum = 13        Check is 13 + 36 = 49
7. Ans to sum = 19        Check is 19 + 26 = 45
8. Ans to sum = 38        Check is 38 + 25 = 63
9. Ans to sum = 3         Check is 3 + 9 = 12
10. Ans to sum = 6        Check is 6 + 18 = 24
11. Ans to sum = 108      Check is 108 + 127 = 235
12. Ans to sum = 14       Check is 14 + 48 = 62
13. Ans to sum = 58       Check is 58 – 23 = 35
14. Ans to sum = 178      Check is 178 – 52 = 126
15. Ans to sum = 36       Check is 36 – 24 = 12
16. Ans to sum = 63       Check is 63 – 28 = 35
17. Ans to sum = 82       Check is 82 – 34 = 48
18. Ans to sum = 168      Check is 168 – 42 = 126

*Working with Numbers*

---

### D5: Factor diagrams

1. Numbers in boxes are 1 2 3 6
2. Numbers in boxes are 1 2 4 8 16
3. Numbers in boxes are 1 2 3 4 6 12
4. Numbers in boxes are 1 5 25
5. Numbers in boxes are 1 2 4 5 10 20
6. Numbers in boxes are 1 2 3 4 6 8 12 24

### E1: Sieve of Eratosthenes

The numbers that should be left (the prime numbers) are 2,3,7,9,11,13,17,19,23,29,31,37,
41,43,47,53,59,61,67,71,73,79,83,89,97

### D6: From factors to primes

Task 1:
| 1 | 1 | 1 |
| 2 | 2 | 2 |
| 3 | 1,2 | 2 |
| 4 | 1,3 | 2 |
| 5 | 1,2,4 | 3 |
| 6 | 1,5 | 2 |
| 7 | 1,2,3,6 | 4 |
| 8 | 1,7 | 2 |
| 9 | 1,2,4,8 | 4 |
| 10 | 1,3,9 | 3 |
| 11 | 1,2,5,10 | 4 |
| 12 | 1,11 | 2 |
| 13 | 1,2,3,4,6,12 | 6 |
| 14 | 1,13 | 2 |
| 15 | 1,2,7,14 | 4 |
| 16 | 1,3,5,15 | 4 |
| 17 | 1,2,4,8,16 | 5 |
| 18 | 1,17 | 2 |
| 19 | 1,2,3,6,9,18 | 6 |
| 20 | 1,19 | 2 |
|   | 1,2,4,5,10,20 | 6 |

Task 2: Prime numbers are 2,3,5,7,11,13,17,19

## Section 6: Squares, square roots and cubes   p 102

### D1: Squares and square roots

1. 9   2. 16   3. 6   4. 3   5. 49
6. 12   7. 196   8. 10   9. 17   10. 441
11. 256   12. 625   13. 45   14. 400   15. 8
16. 1600   17. 13   18. 81   19. 1764   20. 1

### D2: Square numbers & cube numbers

1. 1 6 49 81 1 4 64 100
2. 1 4 9 16 25 36 49 64 81 100
3. 1 cubed = 1   2 cubed = 8
4. (a) 27 (b) 64 (c) 125 (d) 216   5. 1 8 27 64 125 216 343 512 729 1000

### D3: Using trial-and-improvement methods

1. A = 17   B = 29   C = 35   D = 7   E = 5   F = 11

The answers to questions 2-7 are given here BUT you must have shown your working as in Q2 & 3. Ans: 2. 41   3. 27   4. 18   5. 32   6. 13   7. 15

## Section 7: Powers  p 104

### D1: Review of powers

1. 16   2. 125   3. 49   4. 1000   5. 32   6. 27   7. 64   8. 625
9. 64   10. 216   11. $2^4$   12. $3^4$   13. $7^3$   14. $9^2$   15. $12^2$   16. $5^4$
17. $8^2$   18. $10^3$   19. $5^3$   20. $15^2$

### D2: More difficult powers

1. 48   2. 108   3. 200   4. 150   5. 45   6. 1029   7. 900   8. 4761
9. 1210   10. 56000   11. 1250   12. 4624   13. 289   14. 49   15. 1024

## Section 8: Working with negative numbers  p 105

### D1: Adding positive and negative numbers

1. 1   2. -4   3. -2   4. -7   5. 8   6. -2

*Working with Numbers*

A POW GUIDE                                        page 281                                        ANSWERS

## D2: Working out approximate answers 2
1. 800  2. 1200  3. 2400  4. 1400  5. 2000  6. 2100
7. (50 x 10 =) 500  8. (80 x 20 =) 1600  9. (70 x 30 =) 2100
10. (90 x 30 =) 2700  11. (60 x 40 =) 2400  12. (90 x 50 =) 4500
13. 10 000  14. 35 000  15. 12 000  16. 12 000  17. 12 000
18. (200 x 50 =) 10 000  19. (500 x 70 =) 35 000  20. (600 x 20 =) 12 000

## D3: Using approximations to check answers
1. Approx number = 1000 (50 x 20) so Sludge is probably right
2. Approx ans = 500 x 90 = 45 000 so Pow is probably right.
3. Approx ans = 300 x 70 = 21 000  24 069 is most likely to be right.
4. 40 x 20 = 800  5. 70 x 20 = 1400  6. 40 x 50 = 2 000
7. 300 x 10 = 3 000  8. 300 x 20 = 6 000  9. 400 x 30 = 12 000

## D4: Multiplying and checking
1. Ans = 336  Check is 30 x 10 = 300  2. Ans = 345  Check is 20 x 20 = 300
3. Ans = 658  Check is 50 x 10 = 500  4. Ans = 7 623  Check is 80 x 100 = 8 000
5. Ans = 1353  Check is 100 x 10 = 1 000  6. Ans = 11 253  Check is 300 x 30 = 9000

## Section 11: Working with ratios    p114

### D1: Applications of ratio
1. 6 ml    2. 2 teaspoons    3.

| 4 ml | 8 ml  | 16 ml | 20 ml |
|------|-------|-------|-------|
| 5 ml | 10 ml | 20 ml | 25 ml |

4. (a) 2 spadefuls of sand and 3 spadefuls of aggregate
   (b) 4 barrowloads of cement and 8 barrowloads of sand
   (c) 6 buckets of cement and 18 buckets of aggregate

5.
| 2½  | 5    | 7½    | 10    | 12½  | 15   | 17½  |
|-----|------|-------|-------|------|------|------|
| 3½  | 7    | 10½   | 14    | 17½  | 21   | 24½  |

6.
| 1  | 2 | 4  | 8  | 10 |
|----|---|----|----|----|
| 1½ | 3 | 6  | 12 | 15 |
| 2½ | 5 | 10 | 20 | 25 |

### E1: Ratio problems
1. 24 cm  2. 144 cm  3. £10 : £15  4. £10 : £40  5. £10 : £25
6. (a) 2 : 1  (b) £2 400  7. (a) five twelfths  (b) £25  8. (a) ³/₈  (b) 15 cm
9. 10p : 20p : 40p  10. £24 : £56  11. ¹/₃  12. 5 : 3

## Section 12: Technique review    p116

### R1: Negative numbers    1. 9°    2. 3°C    3. 7°C
### R2: Rounding numbers
1. 640  2. 600  3. 1090  4. 1100  5. (a) £300 (b) £260  6. (a) £8 900 (b) £9 000
### R3: Checking answers
1. (a) 350 (b) 1800 (c) 1200    2. 210
3. 39 x 23 = 40 x 20 = 800  897 is nearest 899 so 897 is the most likely answer

### R4: Multiples and divisibility
1. 6 12 18 24 30 36   2. 20 25 30 35 40   3. 85 90 375
4. It ends in 0   5. It ends in 0 or 5   6. It ends in 0 2 4 6 or 8   7. Yes

### R5: Whole number answers and divisibility  1. Y  2. N  3. Y  4. Y  5. Y  6. Y

### R6: Factors
1. Yes  2. 1 2 3 6  3. 1 2 7 14  4. 1 2 3 5 6 10 15 30
### R7: Factors    1. 7 17 23    2. 11 13 17 19

### R8: Squares, square roots and cubes
1. 49  2. 36  3. 4  4. 100  5. 3  6. 81  7. 8  8. −27
9. 121  10. 1 4 9 16 25 36 49 64 81 100  11. 16  12. 9

### R9: Powers
1. $5^3 = 125$   2. $6^2 = 216$   3. $2^4 = 16$   4. $10^3 = 1000$   5. $5^3 = 125$
6. $2^3 = 8$   7. $3^4 = 81$   8. $10^2 = 100$   9. $3 \times 6^2 = 108$   10. $(3^3 + 1)^2 = 100$

### R10: Working with negative numbers
1. 3   2. −3   3. 1   4. −5   5. 4   6. −10
7. −4   8. 8   9. −2   10. 4   11. −8   12. −4
13.
| 5  | −1 | 4  |
|----|----|----|
| −2 | −3 | −5 |
| 3  | −4 |    |

### R11: Metric and Imperial equivalents
1. 1 ounce ≈ 25g   2. 1 kg ≈ 2 pounds   3. 1 pound ≈ ½ kg
4. 1 foot ≈ 30 cm   5. 1 metre ≈ 1.1 yards   6. 1 inch ≈ 25 mm
7. 5 miles ≈ 8 km   8. 1 mile ≈ 1.6 km (or 2 km)   9. 24 km   10. 10 miles

# Areas, Volumes and Formulae

## Section 1: Area review    p 120

### D1: What is area ?
1. Area = 3 squares   2. Area = 5 squares   3. Area = 5 squares
4. Area = 6 squares   5. Area = 2 squares   6. Area = 5½ squares

### D2: The most common unit of area
1. Area = 4 cm²   2. Area = 6 cm²   3. Area = 6 cm²
4. Area = 6 cm²   5. Area = 12 cm²   6. Area = 8 cm²
7. Area = 2 cm²   8. Area = 4 cm²   9. Area = 8 cm²

## Section 2: Perimeter review    p 121

### D1: Distance round the outside
A: Distance = 8 cm   B: Distance = 18 cm   C: Distance = 18 cm
D: Distance = 22 cm   E: Distance = 16 cm   F: Distance = 12 cm
G: Distance = 22 cm   H: Distance = 22 cm   I: Distance = 14 cm

### D2: Perimeter
1. P = 8 units   2. P = 12 units   3. P = 12 units   4. P = 14 units
5. P = 14 units   6. P = 8 cm   7. P = 12 cm   8. P = 14 cm
9. P = 14 cm   10. P = 14 cm   11. P = 18 cm

## Section 3 : Areas of rectangles    p123

**D3: Rules for areas of rectangles**

Task 1:
| | | | |
|---|---|---|---|
| A | 5 | 2 | 10 |
| B | 4 | 3 | 12 |
| C | 3 | 3 | 9 |
| D | 6 | 3 | 18 |
| E | 4 | 2 | 8 |
| F | 3 | 2 | 6 |
| G | 10 | 4 | 40 |
| H | 6 | 5 | 30 |

Task 2: area = 7 x 2 = 14 cm²

Task 3: Rule 2
area of rectangle = length x width

**P1: Areas of rectangles using the rule**
1. 40   2. 48   3. 30   4. 25   5. 150   6. 35   7. 80   8. 36

**D2: Units of area**  *Each answer must have the correct unit of area.*
1. 40 cm²   2. 180 m²   3. 42 m²   4. 18 m²   5. 44 m²   6. 40 cm²
7. 10 km²   8. 54 mm²   9. 14 m²   10. 24 mm²   11. 2 km²

**P2: Areas of measured rectangles**
A: 24 cm²   B: 20 cm²   C: 25 cm²   D: 21 cm²   E: 9 cm²   F: 18 cm²

**E1: Keeping area or perimeter fixed**

| | Area = 12 squares | | | Area = 16 squares | | | Area = 24 squares | | |
|---|---|---|---|---|---|---|---|---|---|
| length | 12 | 6 | 4 | 16 | 8 | 4 | 24 | 12 | 8 | 6 |
| width | 1 | 2 | 3 | 1 | 2 | 4 | 1 | 2 | 3 | 4 |
| perimeter | 26 | 16 | 14 | 34 | 20 | 16 | 50 | 28 | 22 | 20 |

## Section 4: Volumes    p128

**D1: What is volume ?**
Volume of A = 8 cubes    Volume of B = 7 cubes    Volume of C = 15 cubes
Volume of D = 21 cubes   Volume of E = 26 cubes   Volume of F = 18 cubes

**D2: Making cuboids with a given volume**

Task 1:
| 4 | 3 | 1 | 12 |
| 6 | 2 | 1 | 12 |
| 12 | 1 | 1 | 12 |
| 2 | 2 | 3 | 12 |

Task 2:
| 20 | 1 | 1 | 20 |
| 10 | 2 | 1 | 20 |
| 5 | 4 | 1 | 20 |
| 5 | 2 | 2 | 20 |

Task 3:
| 24 | 1 | 1 | 24 |
| 12 | 2 | 1 | 24 |
| 8 | 3 | 1 | 24 |
| 6 | 4 | 1 | 24 |
| 6 | 2 | 2 | 24 |
| 4 | 3 | 2 | 24 |

Task 4:
Volume = length x breadth x height

**D3: Volumes of cuboids**
1. 45 cm³   2. 36 cm³   3. 200 cm³   4. 240 cm³   5. 800 m³   6. 400 cm³
7. 240 mm³  8. 54 m³

*Areas, Volumes and Formulae*

---

**P1: Picking the right information**
A  40 cm³   B  72 cm²   C  30 cm²   D  80 cm²   E  96 cm³   F  64 cm³

**E1: Compound cuboids**
1. Vol A is 48 cm³   Vol B is 24 cm³   Vol of solid is 72 cm³
2. 158 cm³   3. 120 cm³   4. 78 cm³

## Section 5: Right-angled triangles    p131

**D1: Squares and half squares**
1. ½ cm²   2.
| A | B | C | D | E | F | G | H | I |
|---|---|---|---|---|---|---|---|---|
| 4cm² | 2cm² | 4½cm² | 6cm² | 5cm² | 3cm² | 2cm² | 3½cm² | 6cm² |

**D2: Rectangles and right-angled triangles**
A and ΔP    B and ΔR    C and ΔS    D and ΔQ

**D3: Areas of right-angled triangles**
1. 9 cm²   2. 6 cm²   3. 2 cm²   4. 5 cm²   5. 8 cm²   6. 7 cm²
7. 14 cm²  8. 6 cm²

**P1: Too much information**
1. 24 cm²   2. 30 cm²   3. 6 cm²   4. 210 cm²   5. 180 cm²

**P2: Areas of measured triangles**
P: 12 cm²   Q: 6 cm²   R: 8 cm²   S: 18 cm²   T: 20 cm²   U: 4 cm²
V: 6 cm²    W: 13½ cm²              X: 14 cm²

**P3: Areas of rectangles and triangles**
1. 24 cm²   2. 25 cm²   3. 48 cm²   4. 7 cm²   5. 12 cm²   6. 18 cm²
7. 9 cm²    8. 20 cm²   9. 45 cm²   10. 9 cm²  11. 10 cm²  12. 12 cm²
13. 30 cm²  14. 50 cm²  15. 99 cm²  16. 16 cm²

## Section 6: Parallelograms    p135

**D1: Areas of some parallelograms**
1.
| A | 1 | 1 | 1 | 1 |
| B | 2 | 2 | 2 | 4 |
| C | 3 | 2 | 2 | 6 |
| D | 2 | 2 | 2 | 4 |
| E | 1 | 3 | 3 | 3 |
| F | 2 | 1 | 1 | 2 |
| G | 3 | 3 | 3 | 9 |
| H | 4 | 2 | 2 | 8 |

2. Area = base x height

**D2 : What have they done wrong ?**
1. *Youslas* added instead of multiplying.
2. *Letmewin* measured the side of the

**D3 : Using the rule to work out the area**
1.
| A | 3 | 4 | 12 |
| B | 2 | 3 | 6 |
| C | 2 | 1 | 2 |
| D | 3 | 1 | 3 |
| E | 3 | 2 | 6 |
| F | 1 | 1 | 1 |
| G | 3 | 2 | 6 |
| H | 3 | 4 | 12 |
| I | 2 | 2 | 4 |
| J | 3 | 3 | 9 |

2. 6 cm²   3. 44 mm²
4. 15 m²   5. 60 cm²
6. 35 mm²  7. 3 m²

8. base = 5 cm    height = 4 cm
   area = 20 cm²

9. base = 10 cm   height = 6 cm
   area = 60 cm²

*Areas, Volumes and Formulae*

---

A POW GUIDE          page 283          ANSWERS

**P1: No measurements given**

|   | A | B | C | D | E | F | G | H |
|---|---|---|---|---|---|---|---|---|
| Base | 2 cm | 3 cm | 3 cm | 2 cm | 4 cm | 2 cm | 4 cm | 3 cm |
| Height | 2 cm | 3 cm | 2 cm | 3 cm | 1 cm | 4 cm | 2 cm | 2 cm |
| Area | 4 cm² | 9 cm² | 6 cm² | 6 cm² | 4 cm² | 8 cm² | 8 cm² | 6 cm² |

## Section 7: Area of any triangle   p 139

### D1: Parallelograms and triangles
A and ΔW    B and ΔX    C and ΔY    D and ΔZ

### D2: Rule for area of a triangle
1. 4 cm²   2. 6 cm²   3. 30 cm²   4. 12 cm²

### P1: Areas of triangles
A: 4 cm²  B: 4 cm²  C: 4½ cm²  D: 3 cm²  E: 9 cm²  F: 6 cm²  G: 3 cm²
H: 2 cm²  I: 3 cm²  J: 6 cm²  K: 2 cm²  L: 6 cm²

### P2: Triangles at all angles
1. 30 cm²   2. 20 cm²   3. 30 cm²   4. 36 cm²   5. 15 cm²   6. 100 cm²   7. 20 cm²

### P3: You will need to measure these

|   | P | Q | R | S | T | U | V | W |
|---|---|---|---|---|---|---|---|---|
| Base | 2.8 cm | 6.1 cm | 4.5 cm | 5.4 cm | 3.7 cm | 3.0 cm | 3.7 cm | 4.2 cm |
| Height | 2.4 cm | 2.0 cm | 2.5 cm | 3.2 cm | 3.3 cm | 2.7 cm | 3.5 cm | 2.6 cm |
| Area | 3.36cm² | 6.1cm² | 5.625cm² | 8.64cm² | 6.105cm² | 4.05cm² | 6.475cm² | 5.46 cm² |

If your base or height is just a little bit different from one of these, ask your teacher to check whether your area is correct for your measurements.

## Section 8: Altogether now ...   p 143

### P1: Areas of rectangles, parallelograms and triangles
1. 40 cm²   2. 50 cm²   3. 40 cm²   4. 25 cm²   5. 20 cm²   6. 30 cm²
7. 8 cm²    8. 25 cm²   9. 40 cm²   10. 24 cm²   11. 27 cm²   12. 15 cm²

## Section 9: The circumference of a circle   p144

### D1: Diameter and radius

**Task 1:**
| Diameter | 2 cm | 3 cm | 1 cm | 5 cm | 4 cm | 2.8 cm | 4.4 cm |
|---|---|---|---|---|---|---|---|
| Radius | 1 cm | 1½ cm | ½ cm | 2½ cm | 2 cm | 1.4 cm | 2.2 cm |

**Task 2:** 1. 20 cm   2. 6 cm   3. 8 cm   4. 14 cm   5. 12 m   6. 3 m

**Task 3:**
|   | P | Q | R | S | T | U | V | W | X |
|---|---|---|---|---|---|---|---|---|---|
| radius | 5 cm | 3 mm | 10mm | 4 m | 7 cm | 50 m | 10 cm | 11 cm | 1 m |
| diameter | 10 cm | 6 mm | 20mm | 8 m | 14 cm | 100m | 20 cm | 22 cm | 2 m |

### D2: Circumference of a circle
1. 31.4 cm   2. 12.56 cm   3. 7.85 cm   4. 15.7 m   5. 37.68 mm
6. 9.42 km   7. 20.096 cm   8. 3.2028 m   9. d = 6 cm   C = 18.84 cm
10. 50.24 cm   11. 28.26 cm   12. 33.284 cm

*Areas, Volumes and Formulae*

## Section 10: Problems involving rounding   p147

### D1: Rounding to the nearest whole number
1. π x 8 = 25.12 which is 25 cm to the nearest cm
2.57 m    3. 8 m    4. 503 m

### D2: Rounding to 2 d.p.
2. 44.77 m
3. (a) 57.28 (b) 179.97 cm

## Section 11: The area of a circle   p148

### D1: Exploring the results of a practical task
2. (a) 50.24 cm   (b) Yes

3.
| radius | 3 | 4 | 5 | 6 | 8 | 10 | 12 |
|---|---|---|---|---|---|---|---|
| measured area | 28 | 50 | 78 | 101 | 202 | 315 | 450 |
| calculated area | 28.26 | 50.24 | 78.5 | 113.04 | 200.96 | 314 | 452.16 |

4. Yusuf    5. 706.5 cm²    6. 132.665 cm²    7. 6cm; 113.04 cm²

### P1: Area practice
2. (a) 615.44 cm²  (b) 1256 cm²  (c) 120.7016 cm²  (d) 19.625 cm²
3. (a) 2 m  (b) 12.56 m²         4. (a) 25 cm  (b) 1962.5 cm²
5. 7850 cm²   6. 706.5 cm²       7. 200.96 cm²    8. 1256 cm²
9. 314 cm²   10. 254.34 mm²      11. 2826 m²
12. The radius is not 8. It is 4.   13. 3.14 x 4 x 4 = 50.24

### P2: Area and circumference practice
**Tasks 1,2 & 3:** Remember: you were asked to give all answers to 2 d.p.
If you didn't do this, go back and do it now !

| A | B | C | D |
|---|---|---|---|
| 43.96 cm | 50.24 cm | 19.47 cm | 25.75 cm |
| 153.86 cm² | 200.96 mm² | 30.18 cm² | 52.78 cm² |

| E | F | G | H |
|---|---|---|---|
| 21.35 mm | 15.07 m | 18.84 mm | 157 km |
| 36.30 mm² | 18.09 m² | 28.26 mm² | 19.63 km² |

**Task 4** Modesto is right. A = 3.14 x 6 x 6 = 113.14

## Section 12: Technique review   p151

### R1: Perimeter
1. 14 cm    2. 20 mm    3. 20 cm    4. 14 cm    5. 8 cm    6. 14 cm
7. 12 cm    8. 8 m

### R2: Areas of rectangles, parallelograms and triangles
**Batch A:** 1. 18 cm²  2. 10 cm²  3. 10 cm²  4. 15 mm²  5. 6 m²  6. 8 cm²
**Batch B:** 1. 18 mm²  2. 18 m²   3. 10 cm²  4. 40 m²   5. 20 cm²  6. 8 mm²

### R3: Too much information
1. 15 cm²  2. 30 cm²  3. 24 cm²  4. 9 cm²  5. 4 cm²  6. 10 m²  7. 50 m²  8. 20cm²

### R4: Volumes of cuboids
1. 30 cm³    2. 50 cm³    3. 120 mm³    4. 30 m³

### R5: Circumference of a circle
1. 31.4 cm   2. (a) 6 cm  (b) 18.84 cm   3. 25.12 cm   4. 31.4 cm   5. 62.8 cm   6. 25.12 cm

### R6: Area of a circle
1. 50.24 cm²    2. 113.04 cm²    3. 78.5 cm²    4. 314 m²

*Areas, Volumes and Formulae*

# Probability

## Section 1: How likely? p 154

**D1: Fair game?**
1. Game 1  2. Game 3  3. Game 3  4. Game 1  5. Game 2  6. Game 2

**D2: Order of likelihood**
1. (a) red (b) red black white green
2 (a) I love Scary Spice – there are most of these badges.
   (b) I hate the Spice Girls – there are least of these badges

## Section 2: The probability scale p 155

**D1: The probability scale of 0-1**

Task 1:
1. Sausage will break
2. Boiled egg must be to the left of Raw egg
   Raw egg must be between $1/2$ and 1

Task 2:

| I hate the Spice Girls | I love Baby Spice | I love Scary Spice | Boiled egg must be to the left of Raw egg | I love at least one of the Spice Girls |
|---|---|---|---|---|
| 0 | | | | 1 |

**P1: Nick's socks**

| 1. White | R |
| 3. Blue | W |
| 5. R | G |
| 6. Orange | Y |
| 7. Red | O |

2.
| Yellow | R or W | R | R or W |
| W | R or G | G or W | B/G/W |
| 4. | B or G | R/G/B | |
| R or B | R or G | R/G/B | |
| W | P | R/G/B | |
| | | P or W | |

## Section 3: Equally likely outcomes p 158

**D1: Are the outcomes equally likely?**
1. Yes  2. No  3. No  4. Yes  5. No  6. Yes  7. No  8. No
9. No  10. No  11. No  12. Yes  13. No  14. No  15. No

**D2: Probabilities of equally likely outcomes**
1. 1 out of 5   p(striped) = $1/5$; 1 out of 5   p(grey) = $4/5$
2. 2 out of 7   p(striped) = $2/7$; 5 out of 7   p(grey) = $5/7$
3. 4 out of 5   p(striped) = $4/5$; 1 out of 5   p(grey) = $1/5$
4. p(striped) = $4/7$; p(grey) = $3/7$  5. p(striped) = 1; p(grey) = 0
6. p(striped) = $5/10$; p(black) = $2/10$; p(grey) = $3/10$
7. p(striped) = $3/10$; p(black) = $2/10$; p(grey) = $1/10$; p(white) = $4/10$

## P1: Random choices

$p(Y) = 1/5$;  $p(A) = 1/5$;  $p(R \text{ or } Y) = 2/5$
$p(G) = 2/7$;  $p(I) = 1/6$;  $p(R \text{ or } G) = 3/6$
3. $p(S) = 2/6$,  $p(T) = 1/11$,  $p(A) = 0$   $p(S \text{ or } P) = 4/11$
4. $p(B) = 1/11$,  $p(D) = 2/9$,  $p(Q) = 0$   $p(L \text{ or } I) = 4/9$
5. $p(S) = 1/13$,  $p(I) = 3/13$,  $p(B) = 2/13$   $p(B \text{ or } I) = 5/13$

**P2: Probability practice**
1. $2/5$   2. $1/100$   3. $5/50$   4. $1/2$   5. 0   6. (a) $1/4$ (b) $2/4$   7. 1   8. (a) $1/12$ (b) $2/12$

**P3: Probabilities with a dice**
1. $1/6$   2. $1/6$   3. $3/6$   4. $2/6$   5. $2/6$   6. $4/6$   7. 0   8. $3/6$   9. $3/6$

**P4: Nick's sock game**
1. (a) $4/10$ (b) $6/10$   2. (a) $9/12$ or $1/2$, (b) $6/12$ or $1/2$   3. (a) $3/5$ (b) $2/5$
4. (a) $5/12$ (b) $5/12$ (c) $2/12$   5. (a) $3/9$ (b) $2/9$ (c) $4/9$   6. (a) $5/10$ (b) $4/10$ (c) 0

**P5: Probabilities with a pack of cards**
1. 52   2. 13   3. 13   4. 26

Batch A:
1. $1/2$  2. $1/4$  3. $1/52$  4. $4/52$  5. $2/52$  6. $4/52$  7. $8/52$  8. $8/52$  9. $12/52$  10. $12/52$

Batch B:
1. $4/52$  2. $1/52$  3. $2/52$  4. $16/52$  5. $4/52$  6. $2/52$  7. $2/52$  8. $1/52$  9. $2/52$  10. $4/52$

## Section 4: Estimating probabilities p 163

**D1: Methods for estimating probabilities**
1. D   2. A   3. B   4. B   5. C   6. C   7. C   8. D   9. A   10. B

## Section 5: Events and non-events p 164

**D1: Sums of probabilities**
1. (a) $4/10$ (b) $6/10$   2. Because you must get either a red or black sock.
The probability of a certainty is 13.   $1/4$   4. $1/3$   5. 0.9   6. 0.2   7. 0.4
8. (a) $1/10$ (b) $9/10$         (c) $9/10$ (d) $4/10$ (e) $8/10$   (f) $2/10$   (g) $8/10$

## Section 6: Combined events p 165

**D1: Listing outcomes of two events**
1. (H,1) (H,2) (H,3) (H,4) (H,5) (H,6) (T,1) (T,2) (T,3) (T,4) (T,5) (T,6)
2. TEA, TEA   TEA, COFFEE   TEA, CHOCOLATE
   COFFEE, TEA   COFFEE, COFFEE   COFFEE, CHOCOLATE
   CHOC, TEA   CHOC, COFFEE   CHOC, CHOC
3. (a) HH   HT   TH   TT
   (b) HHH HHT HTH THH  TTH THT HTT TTT
4. (a) (1,1)       6  (1,5) (2,4) (3,3)(4,2)(5,1)   10  (4,6) (5,5) (6,4)
       3  (1,2) (2,1)        7  (1,6) (2,5)(3,4)(4,3)(5,2)(6,1)   11  (5,6) (6,5)
       4  (1,3) (2,2) (3,1)  8  (2,6) (3,5) (4,4) (5,3) (6,2)   12  (6,6)
       5  (1,4)(2,3)(4,1)(3,2) 9  (3,6) (4,5) (5,4)
   (b) 36   (c) 0   (d) $1/36$

*Probability*

# Let's sort out fractions, decimals & percentages

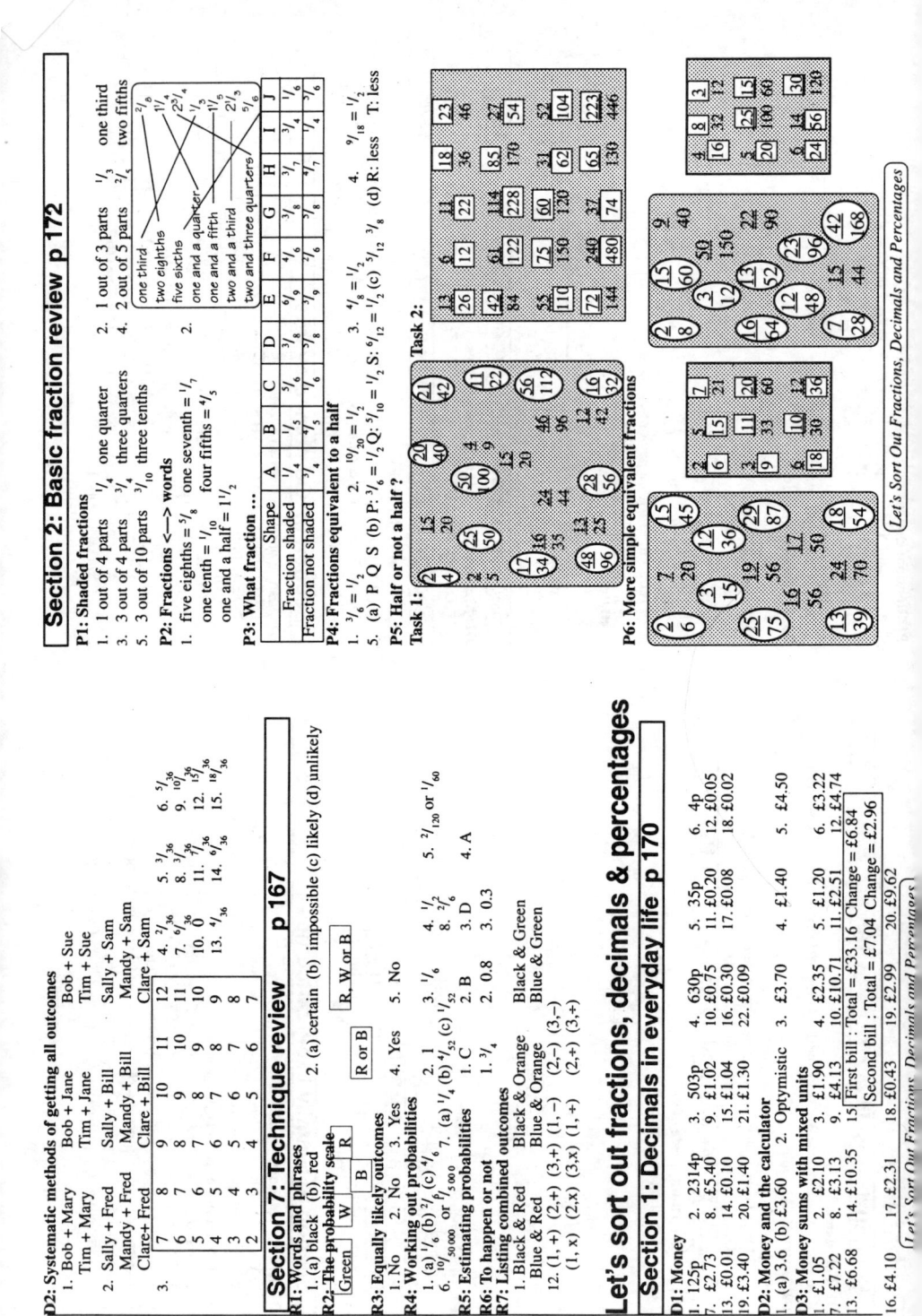

## Section 1: Decimals in everyday life p 170

**D1: Money**
1. 125p
2. 2314p
3. 503p
4. 630p
5. 35p
6. 4p
7. £2.73
8. £5.40
9. £1.02
10. £0.75
11. £0.20
12. £0.05
13. £0.01
14. £0.10
15. £1.04
16. £0.30
17. £0.08
18. £0.02
19. £3.40
20. £1.40
21. £1.30
22. £0.09

**D2: Money and the calculator**
1. (a) 3.6 (b) £3.60    2. Optymistic    3. £3.70    4. £1.40    5. £4.50

**D3: Money sums with mixed units**
1. £1.05    2. £2.10    3. £1.90    4. £2.35    5. £1.20    6. £3.22
7. £7.22    8. £3.13    9. £4.13    10. £10.71    11. £2.51    12. £4.74
13. £6.68    14. £10.35    15 First bill : Total = £33.16  Change = £6.84
Second bill : Total = £7.04  Change = £2.96
16. £4.10    17. £2.31    18. £0.43    19. £2.99    20. £9.62

# Section 2: Basic fraction review

## P1: Shaded fractions
1. 1 out of 4 parts   $1/4$   one quarter      2. 1 out of 3 parts   one third
3. 3 out of 4 parts   $3/4$   three quarters      4. 2 out of 5 parts   two fifths
5. 3 out of 10 parts   $3/10$   three tenths

**P2: Fractions <—> words**
1. five eighths = $5/8$   one seventh = $1/7$
   one tenth = $1/10$   four fifths = $4/5$
   one and a half = $1\tfrac{1}{2}$

2.  one third
    two eighths
    five sixths
    one and a quarter
    one and a fifth
    two and a third
    two and three quarters

## P3: What fraction …

| Shape | A | B | C | D | E | F | G | H | I | J |
|---|---|---|---|---|---|---|---|---|---|---|
| Fraction shaded | $1/4$ | $1/5$ | $5/6$ | $3/8$ | $5/9$ | $4/6$ | $3/8$ | $3/7$ | $3/4$ | $1/6$ |
| Fraction not shaded | $3/4$ | $4/5$ | $1/6$ | $5/8$ | $4/9$ | $2/6$ | $5/8$ | $4/7$ | $1/4$ | $5/6$ |

## P4: Fractions equivalent to a half
1. $3/6 = 1/2$    2. $10/20 = 1/2$    3. $4/8 = 1/2$    4. $9/18 = 1/2$
5. (a) P Q S (b) P: $3/6 = 1/2$ Q: $5/10 = 1/2$ S: $6/12 = 1/2$ (c) $3/8$ (d) R: less  T: less

## P5: Half or not a half?

## P6: More simple equivalent fractions

*Task 1:* (circled equivalent fractions)
*Task 2:* (circled equivalent fractions)

# Section 7: Technique review p 167

**R1: Words and phrases**
1. (a) black  (b) red    2. (a) certain  (b) impossible  (c) likely  (d) unlikely

**R2: The probability scale**

| Green | W | B | R | R or B | R, W or B |
|---|---|---|---|---|---|

**R3: Equally likely outcomes**
1. No    2. No    3. Yes    4. Yes    5. No

**R4: Working out probabilities**
1. (a) $1/6$ (b) $2/6$ (c) $4/6$    2. $1/6$    3. $1/6$    4. $1/2$    5. $2/120$ or $1/60$
6. $10/50000$ or $1/5000$    7. (a) $1/4$ (b) $4/52$ (c) $1/52$    8. $2/6$

**R5: Estimating probabilities**
1. C    2. B    3. D    4. A

**R6: To happen or not**
1. $3/4$    2. 0.8    3. 0.3

**R7: Listing combined outcomes**
   Black & Red     Black & Orange     Black & Green
   Blue & Red      Blue & Orange      Blue & Green
12. (1, +)  (2,+)  (3,+)  (1, −)  (2,−)  (3,−)
    (1, x)  (2,x)  (3,x)  (1, +)  (2,+)  (3,+)

## D2: Systematic methods of getting all outcomes
1.
| Bob + Mary | Bob + Jane | Bob + Sue |
| Tim + Mary | Tim + Jane | Tim + Sue |
| Sally + Mary | Sally + Jane | Sally + Sue |
| Mandy + Mary | Mandy + Jane | Mandy + Sam |
| Clare+ Mary | Clare+ Jane | Clare+ Sam |

2.
| Sally + Fred | Sally + Bill | Sally + Sam |
| Mandy + Fred | Mandy + Bill | Mandy + Sam |
| Clare+ Fred | Clare+ Bill | Clare+ Sam |

3.
| 7 | 8 | 9 | 10 | 11 | 12 | 4. $7/36$ | Bob + Sue |
| 6 | 7 | 8 | 9 | 10 | 11 | 7. $6/36$ | Tim + Sue |
| 5 | 6 | 7 | 8 | 9 | 10 | 10. 0 |
| 4 | 5 | 6 | 7 | 8 | 9 | 13. $1/36$ |
| 3 | 4 | 5 | 6 | 7 | 8 |
| 2 | 3 | 4 | 5 | 6 | 7 |

5. $3/36$   6. $5/36$
8. $3/36$   9. $10/36$
11. $7/36$   12. $1/36$
14. $6/36$   15. $18/36$

A POW GUIDE   page 286   ANSWERS

### P7: Comparing fractions
1. bigger  2. smaller  3. bigger  4. smaller  5. smaller  6. smaller
7. $2^1/_7$  $3/_8$  8. $1/_4$  $2/_9$  $3/_{10}$  $1/_5$  9. $2/_4$  $3/_6$  $4/_8$  $5/_{10}$  10. $4/_6$  $6/_9$

## Section 3: Picturing fractions    p176

### D1: Multiples of simple fractions
1. 4 quarters = 1    5 quarters = $1^1/_4$    6 quarters = $1^2/_4$    7 quarters = $1^3/_4$
   $4 \times 1/_4 = 1$    $5 \times 1/_4 = 1^1/_4$    $6 \times 1/_4 = 1^2/_4$    $7 \times 1/_4 = 1^3/_4$
2. 3 thirds = 1    4 thirds = $1^1/_3$    5 thirds = $1^2/_3$    6 thirds = 2
   $3 \times 1/_3 = 1$    $4 \times 1/_3 = 1^1/_3$    $5 \times 1/_3 = 1^2/_3$    $6 \times 1/_3 = 2$
3. 5 fifths = 1    6 fifths = $1^1/_5$    7 fifths = $1^2/_5$    8 fifths = $1^3/_5$
   $5 \times 1/_5 = 1$    $6 \times 1/_5 = 1^1/_5$    $7 \times 1/_5 = 1^2/_5$    $8 \times 1/_5 = 1^3/_5$

### D2: How many ....?
1. (a) 2 (b) 3 (c) 5 (d) 8 (e) 7 (f) 11     2. (a) 3 (b) 4 (c) 7 (d) 5 (e) 6 (f) 8
3. (a) 5 (b) 7 (c) 9 (d) 10 (e) 13 (f) 15   4. (a) 4 (b) 5 (c) 7 (d) 8 (e) 9 (f) 10
5. (a) 10 (b)11 (c)17 (d) 20 (e) 23 (f) 31

### D3: Whole numbers ——> top heavy fractions
1. (a) $1 = 2/_2$  (b) $2 = 4/_2$  (c) $5 = 10/_2$  (d) $7 = 14/_2$
2. (a) $1 = 3/_3$  (b) $2 = 6/_3$  (c) $3 = 9/_3$  (d) $3 = 9/_3$
3. (a) $1 = 4/_4$  (b) $3 = 12/_4$  (c) $4 = 16/_4$  (d) $5 = 20/_4$
4. (a) $2 = 12/_6$  (b) $3 = 15/_5$  (c) $4 = 30/_5$  (d) $4 = 20/_5$

### D4: Mixed numbers ——> top heavy fractions
1. (a) $1^1/_2 = 3/_2$  (b) $3^1/_2 = 7/_2$  (c) $5^1/_2 = 11/_2$  (d) $7^1/_2 = 15/_2$
2. (a) $1^2/_3 = 5/_3$  (b) $2^1/_3 = 7/_3$  (c) $3^1/_3 = 10/_3$  (d) $5^2/_3 = 17/_3$
3. $5^1/_2$  4. $5^1/_3$  5. $8^1/_3$  6. $7^1/_4$  9. $11/_3$  10. $21/_5$  11. $7/_4$
12. $11/_3$  13. $18/_4$  14. $23/_8$  15. $15/_8$  16. $29/_{10}$  17. $15/_8$  18. $31/_7$  19. $37/_7$  20. $27/_8$

### D5: Top heavy fractions ——> whole or mixed numbers
1. 2   2. 3   3. 3   4. 3   5. 7   6. 4
7. $2^2/_3$   8. $5^1/_2$   9. $2^1/_4$  10. $2^1/_4$  11. $5^2/_4$  12. $1^3/_8$  13. 3  14. $3^1/_4$  15. $3^1/_5$
16. $2^1/_6$  17. $3^3/_5$  18. $3^1/_6$  19. $3^1/_3$  20. $5^1/_5$  21. $1^7/_{10}$  22. $1^1/_{10}$  23. $2^1/_7$  24. $2^1/_6$

### D6: Adding up to whole numbers
1. $3/_4 + 1/_4 = \boxed{1}$   2. $1/_6 + \boxed{5/_6} = 1$   3. $4/_{12} + \boxed{8/_{12}} = 1$   4. $\boxed{3/_7} + 4/_7 = 1$
5. $4/_9 + \boxed{5/_9} = 1$   6. $\boxed{4/_{16}} + 3/_{16} + \boxed{9/_{16}} = 1$   7. $\boxed{19/_{12}} + 3/_{12} + \boxed{2/_{12}} = 1$   8. $\boxed{2/_{20}} + 12/_{20} + \boxed{6/_{20}} = 1$
9. $1^1/_4 + \boxed{3/_4} = 2$   10. $\boxed{1/_4} + 1^3/_4 = 2$   11. $2^1/_3 + \boxed{2/_3} = 3$   12. $2^1/_5 + \boxed{4/_5} = 3$
13. $\boxed{1/_4} + 2^3/_4 = 3$  14. $\boxed{2/_6} + 1^4/_6 = 2$   15. $1^7/_{10} + \boxed{3/_{10}} = 2$   16. $\boxed{5/_8} + 2 + 1^3/_8 = 4$
17. $3 - 2^1/_6 = \boxed{5/_6}$  18. $2 - 2/_3 = \boxed{1^1/_3}$

### D7: Sharing sums with fraction answers
1. $2^1/_2$  2. $3^2/_3$  3. $1^3/_5$  4. $1^3/_4$  5. $3^1/_3$  6. $7^1/_5$  7. $1^1/_5$  8. $1^1/_8$  9. $1^1/_8$
10. $2^1/_4$  11. $1^3/_5$  12. $3^1/_3$  13. $1^3/_5$  14. $1^2/_3$  15. $1^1/_{10}$  16. $2^2/_3$  17. $2^4/_5$  18. $5^1/_3$
19. $5^1/_4$  20. $1^7/_{10}$

### E1: Halves of fractions
1. $1/_6$  2. $1/_8$  3. $1/_{10}$  4. $1/_{12}$  5. $1/_{14}$  6. $1/_{16}$  7. $1/_{20}$  8. $1/_{40}$  9. $1/_3$  10. $1/_4$  11. $1/_5$

## Section 4: Number lines    p 180

### D1: Half and quarter jumps
*The labels should be:*
1. 0  $1/_4$  $1/_2$  $3/_4$  1  $1^1/_4$  $1^1/_2$  $1^3/_4$  2  $2^1/_4$  $2^1/_2$  $2^3/_4$  3  $3^1/_4$  $3^1/_2$  $3^3/_4$  4  $4^1/_4$  $4^1/_2$  $4^3/_4$  5
2. 0  $1/_2$  1  $1^1/_2$  2  $2^1/_2$  3  $3^1/_2$  4  $4^1/_2$  5
3. 0  1  2  3  4  5
4. A: $3^1/_2$  B: $2^3/_4$  C: 4  D: $4^1/_4$  E: 2  F: $3^1/_4$
5. 0  $1/_4$  $1/_2$  $3/_4$  1  $1^1/_4$  $1^1/_2$  $1^3/_4$  2  $2^1/_4$  $2^1/_2$  $2^3/_4$  3  $3^1/_4$  $3^1/_2$  $3^3/_4$  4  $4^1/_4$  $4^1/_2$  $4^3/_4$  5
6. 0  0.25  0.5  0.75  1  1.25  1.5  1.75  2  2.25  2.5  2.75  3  3.25  3.5  3.75  4  4.25  4.5  4.75  5
7. 0  0.25  0.5  0.75  1  1.25  1.5  1.75  2  2.25  2.5  2.75  3  3.25  3.5  3.75  4  4.25  4.5  4.75  5
8. A: 3.5  B: 2.5  C: 2.75  D: 1  E: 2.25  F: 3.25

### D2: Adding the same amount each time
*The labels should be:*
1. 7  7.5  8  8.5  9  9.5  10  10.5  11  11.5  12  12.5  13  13.5  14
2. 23  23.5  24  24.5  25  25.5  26  26.5  27  27.5  28  28.5  29  29.5  30
3. 4  4.5  5  5.5  6  6.5  7  7.5  8  8.5  9  9.5  10
4. 5  5.1  5.2  5.3  5.4  5.5  5.6  5.7  5.8  5.9  6
5. 9  9.1  9.2  9.3  9.4  9.5  9.6  9.7  9.8  9.9  10
6. 3  3.1  3.2  3.3  3.4  3.5  3.6  3.7  3.8  3.9  4
7. 12  12.1  12.2  12.3  12.4  12.5  12.6  12.7  12.8  12.9  13

### D3: Getting closer in
*The labels should be:*
1. 3  3.05  3.1  3.15  3.2  3.25  3.3  3.35  3.4  3.45  3.5  3.55  3.6
2. 7  7.05  7.1  7.15  7.2  7.25  7.3  7.35  7.4  7.45  7.5  7.55  7.6
3. 2  2.05  2.1  2.15  2.2  2.25  2.3  2.35  2.4  2.45  2.5  2.55  2.6
4. 3.6  3.61  3.62  3.63  3.64  3.65  3.66  3.67  3.68  3.69  3.7  3.71  3.72
5. 4.3  4.31  4.32  4.33  4.34  4.35  4.36  4.37  4.38  4.39  4.4  4.41  4.42
6. 6.8  6.81  6.82  6.83  6.84  6.85  6.86  6.87  6.88  6.89  6.9  6.91  6.92
7. 2.7  2.71  2.72  2.73  2.74  2.75  2.76  2.77  2.78  2.79  2.8  2.81  2.82
8. 8.61  8.62  8.63  8.64  8.65  8.66  8.67  8.68  8.69  8.7  8.71  8.72  8.73

## Section 5: Decimals    p 183

### D1: Equivalent decimals and fractions
| | | |
|---|---|---|
| 0.8 | = $8/_{10}$ | |
| 0.02 | = $2/_{100}$ | |
| 0.004 | = $4/_{1000}$ | |
| 3.7 | = $3^7/_{10}$ | |
| 0.29 | = $29/_{100}$ | |
| 0.03 | = $3/_{100}$ | |
| 0.8 | = $8/_{10}$ | |
| 0.003 | = $3/_{1000}$ | |
| 0.61 | = $61/_{100}$ | |

| | | |
|---|---|---|
| 0.054 | = $54/_{1000}$ | |
| 1.7 | = $1^7/_{10}$ | |
| 2.13 | = $2^{13}/_{10}$ | |
| 6.072 | = $6^{72}/_{100}$ | |
| 0.028 | = $28/_{1000}$ | |
| 23.749 | = $23^{749}/_{1000}$ | |

*Let's Sort Out Fractions, Decimals and Percentages*

## D2: Equivalent ways of writing decimals

| Type 1 | ✓ | ✓ | × | ✓ | ✓ | ✓ |  |
|---|---|---|---|---|---|---|---|
| Type 2 | ✓ |   | × | ✓ |   |   |   |
| Type 3 |   | × |   |   | ✓ | ✓ | ✓ |

### D3: Multiplying decimals by 10, 100, 1000

**Set A:**
1. 3.15 × 10 = 31.5
2. 3.02 × 10 = 30.2
3. 
4. 
5. 5.034 × 10 = 50.34
6. 61.357 × 10 = 613.57
7. 5.6 × 10 = 56
8. 37.12 × 10 = 371.2
9. 2.005 × 10 = 20.05
6. 24.56 × 10 = 245.6
9. 1.25 × 10 = 12.5

**Set B:**
1. 0.1 × 10 = 1
4. 0.02 × 10 = 0.2
7. 0.048 × 10 = 0.48
2. 0.25 × 10 = 2.5
5. 0.003 × 10 = 0.03
8. 2.001 × 10 = 20.01
3. 1.003 × 10 = 10.03
6. 0.105 × 10 = 1.05
9. 0.035 × 10 = 0.35

**Set C:**
1. 3.41 × 10 = 34.1
5. 0.356 × 100 = 35.6
9. 11.17 × 1000 = 11170
2. 3.41 × 100 = 341
6. 0.356 × 1000 = 356
10. 3.01 × 100 = 301
3. 3.41 × 1000 = 3410
7. 11.17 × 10 = 111.7
11. 4.5 × 1000 = 4500
4. 0.356 × 10 = 3.56
8. 11.17 × 100 = 1117
12. 19.7 × 100 = 1970

### D4: Dividing decimals by 10, 100, 1000

**Set D:**
1. 12.14 ÷ 10 = 1.214
4. 25 ÷ 10 = 2.5
7. 21.375 ÷ 10 = 2.1375
2. 5 ÷ 10 = 0.5
5. 38.1 ÷ 10 = 3.81
8. 3.1 ÷ 10 = 0.31
3. 0.013 ÷ 10 = 0.13
6. 0.015 ÷ 10 = 0.15
9. 352 ÷ 10 = 35.2

**Set E:**
1. 6 ÷ 10 = 0.6
5. 354 ÷ 100 = 3.54
9. 2.04 ÷ 1000 = 0.00204
2. 35.21 ÷ 100 = 0.3521
6. 0.52 ÷ 100 = 0.0052
10. 0.2 ÷ 1000 = 0.002
3. 0.06 ÷ 10 = 0.006
7. 371 ÷ 100 = 3.71
11. 0.8 ÷ 10 = 0.08
4. 0.04 ÷ 100 = 0.0004
8. 15 ÷ 1000 = 0.015
12. 7.5 ÷ 100 = 0.075

**Set F:**
1. 14.35 ÷ 10 = 1.435
4. 354 ÷ 100 = 3.54
7. 0.356 ÷ 10 = 0.0356
2. 2.35 ÷ 100 = 0.0235
5. 23.6 ÷ 1000 = 0.0236
8. 5 ÷ 100 = 0.05
3. 0.021 ÷ 10 = 0.0021
6. 6.71 ÷ 100 = 0.0671
9. 0.01 ÷ 10 = 0.001

### D5: Multiplying decimals by whole numbers

**P1: Multiplying decimals practice**

**Batch A:** 1. 2.1  2. 1.6  3. 6.5  4. 42.7  5. 30.6  6. 2.4  7. 10.2  8. 43.4
9. 18.06  10. 18.3

**Batch B:** 1. 2.4  2. 10.5  3. 9.2  4. 31.0  5. 7.4  6. 16.8  7. 40.26
8. 20.04  9. 9.24  10. 48.32

**Batch C:** 1. 16.8  2. 21.0  3. 36.9  4. 12.6  5. 3.6  6. 8.68  7. 2.45
8. 18.45  9. 56.88  10. 9.48

**P2: Mixed practice**
1. 72  2. 35.6  3. 0.2  4. 3.456  5. 4  6. 30  7. 0.61  8. 0.02
9. 0.235  10. 0.47  11. 9.42  12. 6.24  13. 1.35  14. 0.12  15. 1.68  16. 2.24
17. 38.52  18. 15.85  19. 1.92  20. 24.4
9. 0.235  10. 0.36570  11. 24.6  12. 9.45  13. 35.07  14. 2.48  15. 31.15  16. 26.5
17. 53  18. 0.53  19. 19. 36.4  20. 0.375  21. 48.66  22. 2.1  23. 1.64  24. 0.041  25. 57.6

*Let's Sort Out Fractions, Decimals and Percentages*

## Section 6: Adding and subtracting decimals p 189

**D1: Simple + and − decimals to 1 d.p.**
1. 2.1 + 0.3 = 2.4
2. 2.8 − 0.5 = 2.3
3. 2.7 + 0.4 = 3.1
4. 2.3 − 0.2 = 2.1
5. 2.5 + 0.5 = 3
6. 2.3 + 0.3 = 3.1
7. 2.7 + 0.3 = 3
8. 3.2 − 0.2 = 3
9. 0.7 + 0.3 = 1
10. 0.1 − 0.8 = 0.8
11. 2.7 + 0.5 = 3.9
12. 4.2 − 0.2 = 4
13. 5.9 + 0.4 = 6.3
14. 2 − 0.9 = 1.1
15. 5.7 + 0.3 = 6
16. 4.1 − 0.2 = 3.9

**D2: Adding and subtracting by stacking**
1. 3.9  2. 9.89  3. 4.1  4. 2.8  5. 6  6. 9.33  7. 3.96  8. 8.9

**D3: Adding and subtracting a mixture of decimals**
1. 10.6  2. 3.52  3. 2.46  4. 5.19  5. 8.35  6. 2.35  7. 0.44  8. 0.45

## Section 7: Fractions & percentages of shapes p190

**D1: The sack race**

| Fraction of race completed | 1/2 | 3/4 | 9/10 | 1/3 | 1/4 | 2/5 |
|---|---|---|---|---|---|---|
| Name | Bill | Tim | Eric | Peter | Sam | Frank |

**D2: What percentage is shaded?**
1. 90% (accept 85-95%)  2. 60% (accept 55-65%)  3. 15% (accept 10-20%)
4. 30% (accept 25-35%)  5. 50% (accept 45-55%)  6. 20% (accept 25-35%)
7. 40% (accept 35-45%)  8. 80% (accept 75-85%)

**D3: Percentages of circles**
1. 50%  2. 25%  3. 40% (accept 35-45%)
4. 10% (accept 5-15%)  5. 70% (accept 60-70%)  6. 90% (accept 85-95%)
7. 20% (accept 15-20%)  8. 55% (accept 50-60%)

## Section 8: Fractions & percentages of amounts p191

**D1: Halves of amounts**
1. £6  2. £18  3. £29  4. 22p  5. £15  6. 8p
7. £39  8. £52  9. 14p  10. £27  11. 36p  12. £23
13. £3  14. 4p  15. 7 sweets  16. £5  17. 9 girls  18. £25
19.
20. 8p  21. £50

**D2: Simple fractions of amounts**
1. £7  2. £22  3. 24p  4. £19  5. 20p  6. £16
7. £24  8. £60  9. 33p  10. 8p  11. 23p  12. £18
13. £24  14. £16  15. £12  16. £8  17. £5  18. 5p
19. £4  20. 7p  21. 2  22. 5  23. 15  24. £5
25. £7  26. 5  27. £3  28. 7  29. 6p  30. £2

**D3: More complex fractions of amounts**
1. (a) £2 (b) £6  2. (a) £7 (b) £14  3. (a) £2 (b) £4
4. (a) £3 (b) £15  5.  (a) £3 (b) £21
6. 9  7. 75  8. 12  9. £5  10. £10  11. 16  12. 6  13. 12  14. 24
15. £40  16. £6  17. 30  18. 6  19. 20  20. 25

*Let's Sort Out Fractions, Decimals and Percentages*

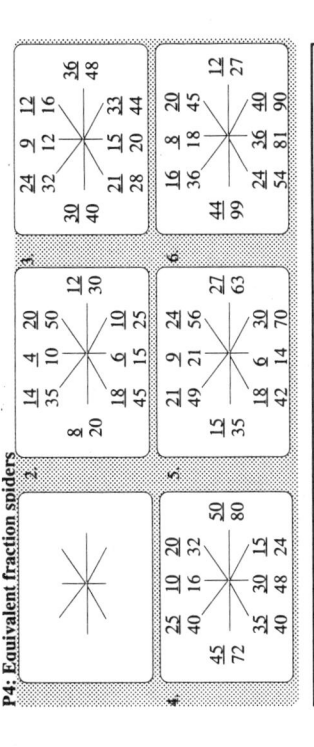

**D4: Using fractions to find percentages of amounts**
1. £10  2. £7  3. £2.50  4. 3p  5. 15p  6. 12  7. £50
8. £5  9. £30  10. 5p  11. £5  12. £10  13. £10  14. £4  15.
£7  16. 20p  17. £20  18. £20  19. 10p  20. 8p

**P1: Practice and extend the ideas**
1. £7  2. £5  3. 4p  4. £20  5. 8p  6. £6  7. £50
8. 45p  9. £12.50  10. 5p  11. £8  12. £11  13. £24  14.
15. £12

**P2: Reducing prices**
1. £3  2. £9  3. £20  4. £40  5. £20  6. £180
7. £1  8. £9  9. £5  10. £4  11. £4  12. £16

**P3: Tricks with 1/10 and 10%**
1. £2  2. £5  3. £20  4. £60  5. £8  6. £28
7. £90  8. £160  9. £10  10. £270  11. £14  12. £900
13. (a) £3 (b) £6  14. (a) £50 (b) £150  15. (a) £6 (b) £42  16. (a) £8 (b) £4
17. £12  18. £24  19. £48  20. £360  21. £21  22. £36  23. £30
24. £210  25. £1200

## Section 9: Making equivalent fractions p195

**D1: A rule for making equivalent fractions**
1. $^6/_{15}$  2. $^2/_8$  3. $^{10}/_{15}$  4. $^{10}/_{12}$  5. $^6/_9$  6. $^2/_4$  7. $^4/_{12}$  8. $^5/_{20}$

**D2: What do you multiply by ?**
1. × 2  2. × 3  3. × 10  4. × 3

**P1: Making equivalent fractions**

Batch A 1. $^6/_8$  2. $^6/_9$  3. $^{30}/_{50}$  4. $^4/_6$  5. $^4/_{16}$  6. $^8/_{10}$  7. $^5/_{15}$  8. $^8/_{18}$
9. $^6/_{21}$  10. $^8/_{40}$  11. $^{20}/_{24}$  12. $^{21}/_{24}$

Batch B 1. $^8/_{28}$  2. $^4/_{10}$  3. $^{15}/_{40}$  4. $^{12}/_{26}$  5. $^{15}/_{24}$  6. $^{24}/_{40}$  7. $^4/_{36}$  8. $^6/_{33}$
9. $^8/_{30}$  10. $^{21}/_{27}$  11. $^{26}/_{36}$

**D3: Using division to make equivalent fractions**
1. $^4/_5$  2. $^2/_3$  3. $^1/_3$  4. $^1/_5$  5. $^2/_5$  6. $^2/_4$  7. $^1/_3$  8. $^2/_3$

**D4: What do you divide by ?**
1. ÷ 3  2. ÷ 4  3. ÷ 5  4. ÷ 2

**P2: Making equivalent fractions using division**
1. $^3/_5$  2. $^1/_3$  3. $^1/_4$  4. $^2/_7$  5. $^1/_8$  6. $^4/_5$  7. $^8/_{36}$  8. $^3/_{75}$

**P3: Mixed practice**
1. $^2/_5$  2. $^{20}/_{35}$  3. $^1/_2$  4. $^3/_4$  5. $^1/_5$  6. $^{14}/_{21}$  7. $^8/_{36}$  8. $^3/_{75}$
9. $^{12}/_{32}$  10. $^1/_4$  11. $^{15}/_{33}$  12. $^{26}/_{30}$

*Let's Sort Out Fractions, Decimals and Percentages*

---

**P4: Equivalent fraction spiders**

1. center $^{45}/_{72}$: $^{25}/_{40}$, $^{10}/_{16}$, $^{20}/_{32}$, $^{50}/_{80}$, $^{35}/_{40}$, $^{30}/_{48}$, $^{15}/_{24}$

2. center $^8/_{20}$: $^{14}/_{35}$, $^4/_{10}$, $^{20}/_{50}$, $^{12}/_{30}$, $^{18}/_{45}$, $^6/_{15}$, $^{10}/_{25}$

3. center $^{24}/_{32}$: $^9/_{12}$, $^{12}/_{16}$, $^{30}/_{40}$, $^{36}/_{48}$

4. center $^{15}/_{35}$: $^{21}/_{49}$, $^9/_{21}$, $^{24}/_{56}$, $^{27}/_{63}$, $^{18}/_{42}$, $^6/_{14}$, $^{30}/_{70}$

5. center $^{16}/_{36}$: $^8/_{18}$, $^{20}/_{45}$, $^{21}/_{28}$, $^{15}/_{20}$, $^{33}/_{44}$

6. center $^{44}/_{99}$: $^{24}/_{54}$, $^{36}/_{81}$, $^{40}/_{90}$, $^{12}/_{27}$

## Section 10: From decimals to fractions p198

**D1: Simplifying fractions**
1. $^3/_4$  2. $^1/_2$  3. $^3/_5$  4. $^2/_5$  5. $^2/_5$  6. $^3/_8$  7. $^4/_5$  8. $^1/_3$

**P1: Simplifying practice**
Batch A:  1. $^1/_3$  2. $^1/_3$  3. $^3/_5$  4. $^2/_3$  5. $^5/_8$  6. $^1/_4$
Batch B:  1. $^1/_8$  2. $^4/_5$  3. $^1/_3$  4. $^1/_3$  5. $^2/_3$  6. $^1/_3$

**D2: Changing decimals to fractions or mixed numbers**
1. $^3/_{10}$  2. $^7/_{100}$  3. $^5/_{1000}$  4. $^{23}/_{100}$  5. $^{13}/_{1000}$  6. $^{37}/_{1000}$
7. $^9/_{100}$  8. $^{36}/_{1000}$  9. $^{126}/_{1000}$  10. $^{57}/_{1000}$  11. $^1/_{1000}$  12. $^{201}/_{1000}$
13. $22^1/_{100}$  14. $13^1/_{10}$  15. $4^{31}/_{100}$  16. $3^{703}/_{1000}$  17. $^{83}/_{1000}$  18. $^{267}/_{100}$
19. $6^{741}/_{1000}$  20. $^{157}/_{1000}$  21. $25^1/_{100}$  22. $7^5/_{10}$  23. $4^7/_{100}$  24. $12^{309}/_{1000}$

**D3: Decimals to fractions in simplest form**
1. $^{35}/_{100} = ^7/_{20}$  2. $^{46}/_{100} = ^{23}/_{50}$  3. $^{44}/_{100} = ^{11}/_{25}$  4. $^{28}/_{100} = ^7/_{25}$
5. $^{45}/_{100} = ^9/_{20}$  6. $^{36}/_{100} = ^9/_{25}$  7. $^{75}/_{100} = ^3/_4$  8. $^6/_{1000} = ^3/_{500}$

**P2: Decimal to fraction practice**
Batch A:  1. $^4/_5$  2. $^1/_5$  3. $^3/_{50}$  4. $^{16}/_{25}$  5. $^1/_{25}$  6. $^{17}/_{50}$
Batch B:  1. $^7/_{25}$  2. $^1/_{25}$  3. $^3/_{50}$  4. $^{22}/_{25}$  5. $^3/_5$  6. $^{17}/_{50}$

## Section 11: Equivalent fractions, decimals and % p201

**D1: Equivalent decimals and percentages**
1. 15% = 0.15  2. 10% = 0.1  3. 5% = 0.05
   23% = 0.23     30% = 0.3     7% = 0.07
   19% = 0.19     70% = 0.7     1% = 0.01
   47% = 0.47     20% = 0.2     6% = 0.06
   68% = 0.68     50% = 0.5     9% = 0.09
   92% = 0.92
   81% = 0.81

*Let's Sort Out Fractions, Decimals and Percentages*

# The Geometry of Angle and Shape

## Section 1: Classifying shapes p206

**D1: Properties of 2-D shapes**
1. A, B, C, E, F, H, I, J, N
2. E
3. D, F, H, K, L, M, N
4. G, I, K, N
5. A, N
6. E, G, J
7. B, E, N
8. K
9. A, H, L, N
10. A, F, H, L, N
11. F
12. I, J
13. I

**D2: Properties of 3-D shapes**
1. square
2. cuboid
3. triangular prism, pyramid
4. triangular prism, pyramid, tetrahedron
5. tetrahedron
6. cone, hemisphere
7. pyramid
8. cube, cuboid, steps
9. (a) 12  (b) 9  (c) 8  (d) 18  (e) 4  (f) 1
10. (a) 8  (b) 6  (c) 5  (d) 12  (e) 4  (f) 0
11. T   12. F   13. T   14. F

## Section 2: Symmetry review p208

**D1: Lines of symmetry**   **D2: Creating mirror symmetry**

**D3: Rotational symmetry**

| Shape | R | S | P | C | E | O | T |
|---|---|---|---|---|---|---|---|
| No. | 2 | 4 | 4 | 3 | 8 | 1 |

## Section 3: Congruence p210

**D1: Congruent shapes**
Set 1: A   Set 2: B   Set 3: C   Set 4: B   Set 5: C
Set 6: B   Set 7: C   Set 8: A   Set 9: B   Set 10: D

## Section 4: Labelling and measuring lines p211

**D1: Labelling lines**
1. (a) 5 cm  (b) 3 cm   2. (a) Yes  (b) No  (c) Yes

**D2: Measuring lines**
1. (a) 6 cm  (b) 2.5 cm  (c) 6.5 cm  (d) 2.5 cm
2. (a) 1.5 cm  (b) 1.5 cm  (c) 2 cm  (d) 3 cm  (e) 4 cm  (f) 5 cm

**D3: Draw and measure**
1. (a) 5 cm  (b) 12 cm  (c) 6.5 cm  (d) 13 cm
2. (a) 1.5 cm  (b) 2 cm  (c) 5 cm  (d) 3.4 cm

---

**D2: Changing fractions into decimals**
1. = 1 + 2 = 0.5
2. = 4 + 5 = 0.8
3. = 1 + 8 = 0.125
4. = 3 + 8 = 0.375
5. 0.02 = 2%
6. 0.47 = 47%
7. 0.13 = 13%
5. = 5 + 16 = 0.3125
6. = 7 + 20 = 0.35
7. = 13 + 50 = 0.26
8. = 11 + 40 = 0.275
9. 0.8 = 80%
10. 0.18 = 18%
11. 0.36 = 36%
9. 0.25
10. 0.625
11. 0.45
12. 0.75
13. 0.38
14. 0.575
12. 0.07 = 7%
13. 0.2 = 2%
14. 0.52 = 52%
15. 0.9 = 90%

**D3: Changing fractions to percentages**
1. 50%   2. 75%   3. 80%   4. 35%   5. 40%   6. 24%   7. 5%

**P1: Percentage test marks**
1. 70%   2. 85%   3. 90%   80%  75%  48%  35%

## Section 12: Technique review p203

**R1: Money sums**   1. £3.03   2. £2.50   3. £4.12   4. £1.51

**R2: How many ...?**   1. (a) 4  (b) 7   2. (a) 3  (b) 7   3. (a) 8  (b) 7

**R3: Mixed numbers <—> top heavy fractions**
1. $5/2$   2. $7/4$   3. $8/3$   4. $7/4$   5. $31/10$   6. $13/2$
7. 3   8. $3^1/3$   9. $3^1/4$   10. $2^3/4$   11. $3^3/5$   12. $3^1/6$

**R4: x and ÷ by 10, 100, 1000**   1. 35   2. 4.135   3. 70   4. 0.006   5. 246.8

**R5: Decimal arithmetic**
1. 2.1   2. 13.5   3. 35.5   4. 0.8   5. 2.2   6. 4.9
7. 2.3   8. 1.6   9. 3.5   10. 7.15   11. 4.6   12. 1.75

**R6: Fractions of amounts**
1. £10   2. £7   3. 6p   4. £20   5. £5   6. £10
7. £30   8. £8   9. £15   10. £12

**R7: Percentages of amounts**   1. £7   2. 4p   3. £8   4. £7   5. £30   R8:

**Equivalent fractions**
1. $4/8$ = $8/16$ = $4/10$   2. $3/4$ = $15/20$ = $15/40$   3. $1/3$ = $9/13$ = $22/30$   4. $6/13$ = $15/24$   5. $1/2$ = $2/5$   6. $9/10$ = $24/40$
7. $1/2$ = $8/16$   8. $2/7$ = $9/33$

**R9: Simplest form**
1. $1/2$   2. $1/3$   3. $3/4$   4. $2/5$   5. $2/5$   6. $1/3$

**R10: Changing decimals to fractions in simplest form**
1. $3/5$   2. $1/50$   3. $3/4$   4. $16/25$   5. $1/5$   6. $31/50$

**R11: Changing fractions to decimals or percentages**
1. 0.6   2. 0.625   3. 0.75   4. 0.35   5. 0.325   6. 0.2
7. 5%   8. 30%   9. 40%   10. 34%   11. 40%   12. 6%

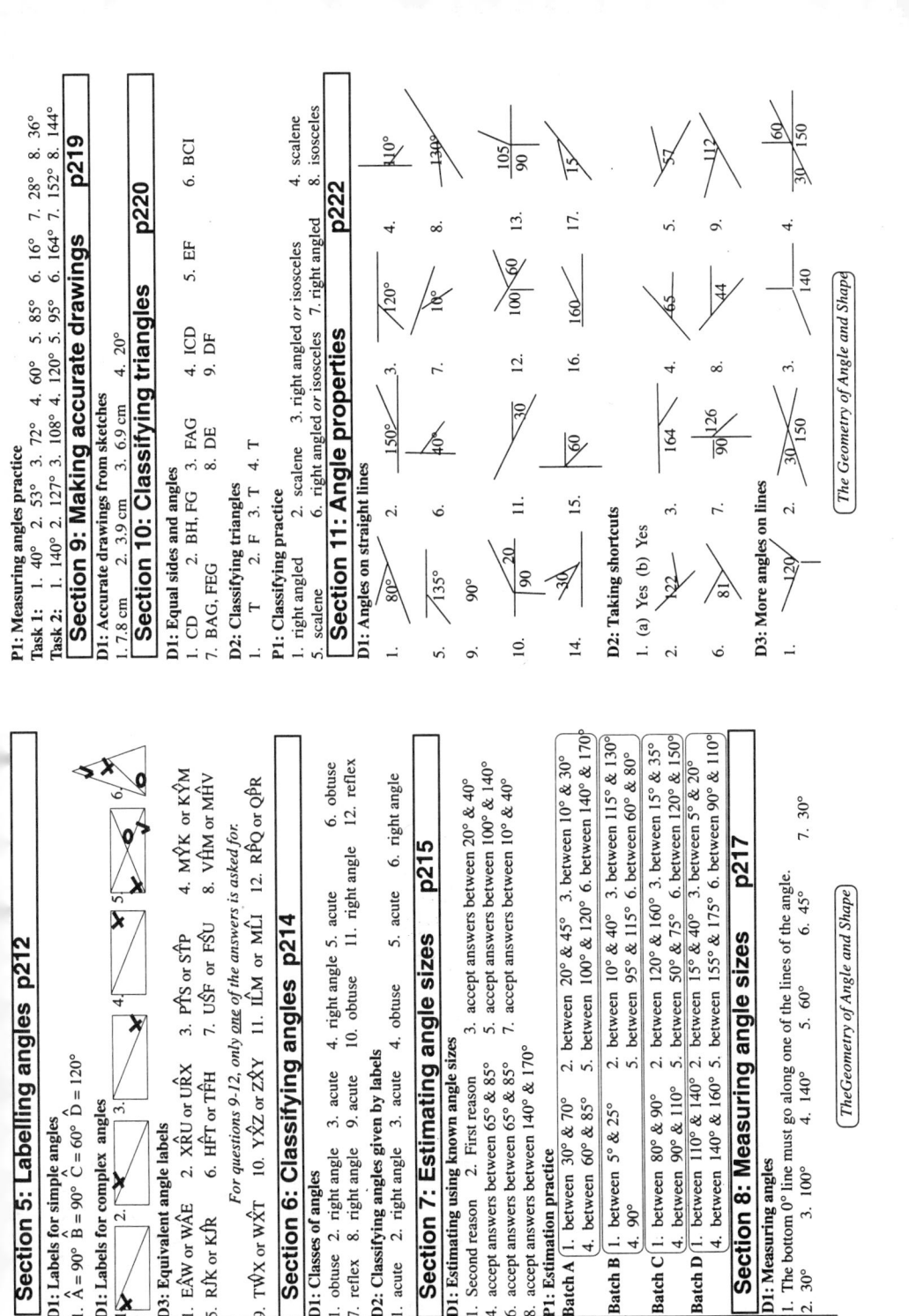

## Section 5: Labelling angles  p212

### D1: Labels for simple angles
1. $\hat{A} = 90°$  $\hat{B} = 90°$  $\hat{C} = 60°$  $\hat{D} = 120°$

### D1: Labels for complex angles
2., 3., 4., 6. (diagrams)

### D3: Equivalent angle labels
1. EÂW or WÂE  2. XR̂U or UR̂X  3. PT̂S or ST̂P  4. MŶK or KŶM
5. RĴK or KĴR  6. HF̂T or TF̂H  7. UŜF or FŜU  8. VÂM or MĤV

*For questions 9–12, only one of the answers is asked for:*

9. TV̂X or WX̂T  10. YX̂Z or ZX̂Y  11. IL̂M or ML̂I  12. RP̂Q or QP̂R

## Section 6: Classifying angles  p214

### D1: Classes of angles
1. obtuse  2. right angle  3. acute  4. right angle  5. acute  6. obtuse
7. reflex  8. right angle  9. acute  10. obtuse  11. right angle  12. reflex

### D2: Classifying angles given by labels
1. acute  2. right angle  3. acute  4. obtuse  5. acute  6. right angle

## Section 7: Estimating angle sizes  p215

### D1: Estimating using known angle sizes
1. Second reason  2. First reason  3. accept answers between 20° & 40°
4. accept answers between 65° & 85°  5. accept answers between 100° & 140°
6. accept answers between 65° & 85°  7. accept answers between 10° & 40°
8. accept answers between 140° & 170°

### P1: Estimation practice

**Batch A**  1. between 30° & 70°  2. between 20° & 45°  3. between 10° & 30°
4. between 60° & 85°  5. between 100° & 120°  6. between 140° & 170°

**Batch B**  1. between 5° & 25°  2. between 10° & 40°  3. between 115° & 130°
4. 90°  5. between 95° & 115°  6. between 60° & 80°

**Batch C**  1. between 80° & 90°  2. between 120° & 160°  3. between 15° & 35°
4. between 90° & 110°  5. between 50° & 75°  6. between 120° & 150°

**Batch D**  1. between 110° & 140°  2. between 15° & 40°  3. between 5° & 20°
4. between 140° & 160°  5. between 155° & 175°  6. between 90° & 110°

## Section 8: Measuring angle sizes  p217

### D1: Measuring angles
1. The bottom 0° line must go along one of the lines of the angle.
2. 30°  3. 100°  4. 140°  5. 60°  6. 45°  7. 30°

### P1: Measuring angles practice
**Task 1:**  1. 40°  2. 53°  3. 72°  4. 60°  5. 85°  6. 16°  7. 28°  8. 36°
**Task 2:**  1. 140°  2. 127°  3. 108°  4. 120°  5. 95°  6. 164°  7. 152°  8. 144°

## Section 9: Making accurate drawings  p219

### D1: Accurate drawings from sketches
1. 7.8 cm  2. 3.9 cm  3. 6.9 cm  4. 20°

## Section 10: Classifying triangles  p220

### D1: Equal sides and angles
1. CD  2. BH, FG  3. FAG  4. ICD  5. EF  6. BCI
7. BAG, FEG  8. DE  9. DF

### D2: Classifying triangles
1. T  2. F  3. T  4. T

### P1: Classifying practice
1. right angled  2. scalene  3. right angled *or* isosceles  4. scalene
5. scalene  6. right angled *or* isosceles  7. right angled  8. isosceles

## Section 11: Angle properties  p222

### D1: Angles on straight lines
1. 80°  2. 150°  3. 120°  4. 110°
5. 135°  6. 40°  7. 10°  8. 130°
9. 90°
10. 90 / 20  11. 30 / 60  12. 100 / 60  13. 105 / 90
14. 30  15. 60  16. 160  17. 15

### D2: Taking shortcuts
1. (a) Yes  (b) Yes
2. 122  3. 164  4. 65  5. 57
6. 81  7. 90 / 126  8. 44  9. 112

### D3: More angles on lines
1. 120  2. 30 / 150  3. 140  4. 60 / 150

*The Geometry of Angle and Shape*

## Section 12: Triangles    p225

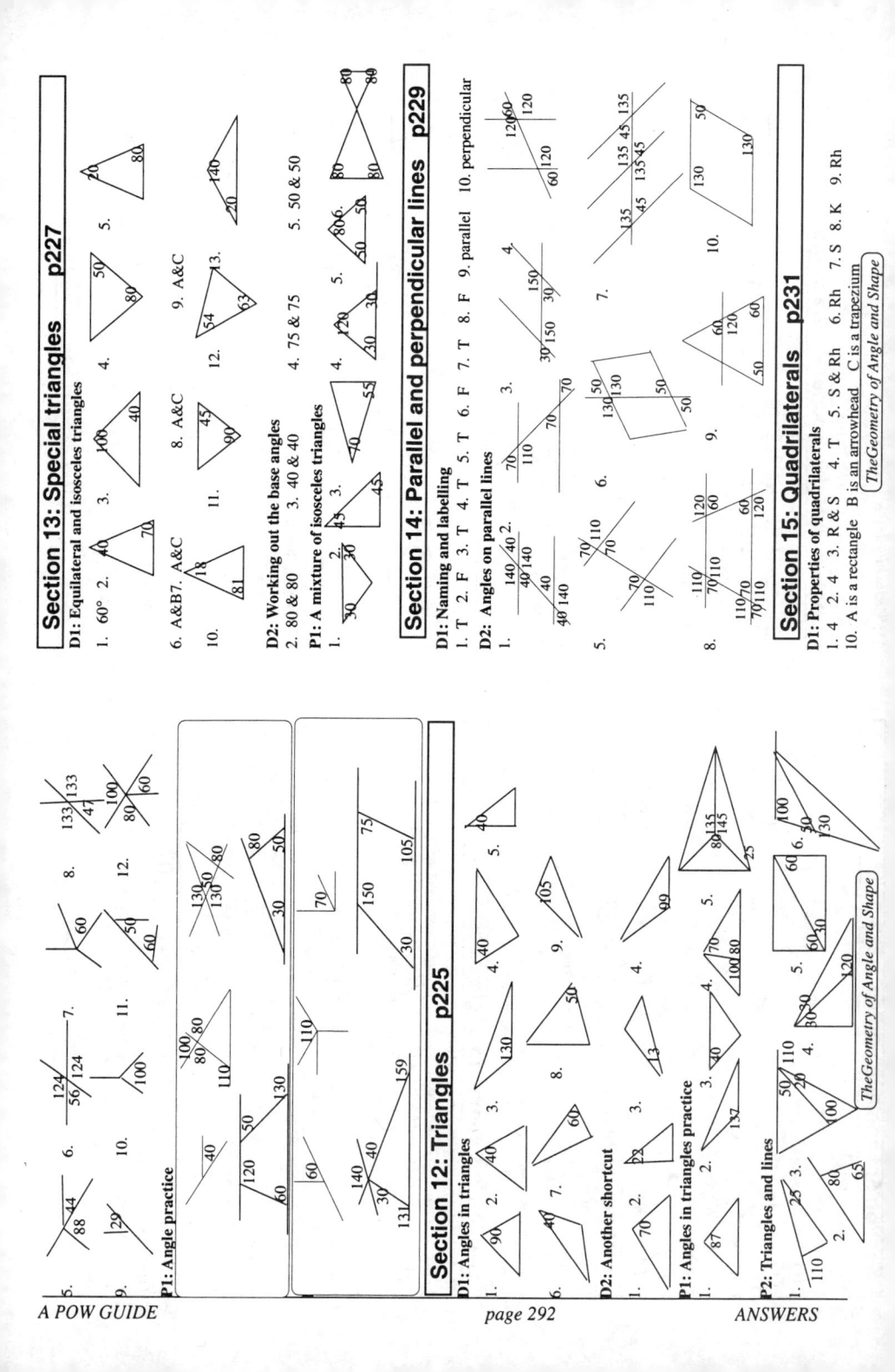

**D1: Angles in triangles**

1. 90  2. 40  3. (130)  4. 40  5. 40

**D2: Another shortcut**

6. 40  7. 70  8. 50  9. 105

**P1: Angles in triangles practice**

1. 87  2. 22  3. 137  4. 13  5. 99

**P2: Triangles and lines**

1. 110  2. 80  3. 25  4. 100, 20, 50, 110  5. 60, 30, 120  6. 50, 130, 100

## Section 13: Special triangles    p227

**D1: Equilateral and isosceles triangles**

1. 60°  2. 40, 70  3. 100, 40  4. 50, 80  5. 20, 80
6. A&B  7. A&C, 18, 81  8. A&C, 45, 90  9. A&C  10. 140, 20  11. (fig)

**D2: Working out the base angles**

2. 80 & 80  3. 40 & 40  5. 50 & 50

**P1: A mixture of isosceles triangles**

1. 30, 2, 30  3. 45, 45  4. 55, 70  5. 30, 30, 120  6. 80, 50, 50, 80  12. 54, 63  13. (fig)

## Section 14: Parallel and perpendicular lines    p229

**D1: Naming and labelling**

1. T  2. F  3. T  4. T  5. T  6. F  7. T  8. F  9. parallel  10. perpendicular

**D2: Angles on parallel lines**

1. 40, 140, 40, 140  2. 140, 40, 40, 140  3. 70, 110, 70, 110  4. 30, 150, 30, 150
5. 110, 70, 70, 110  6. 120, 60, 60, 120  7. 60, 120, 60, 120  8. 50, 130, 130, 50
9. (fig)  10. 135, 45, 135, 45, 135, 45, 135, 45

## Section 15: Quadrilaterals    p231

**D1: Properties of quadrilaterals**

1. 4  2. 4  3. R & S  4. T  5. S & Rh  6. Rh  7. S  8. K  9. Rh
10. A is a rectangle   B is an arrowhead   C is a trapezium

*The Geometry of Angle and Shape*

---

**P1: Angle practice**

5. 88, 44  6. 124, 56, 124  7. (fig)  8. 133, 47, 133, 100, 80, 60
9. 29  10. 100, 80, 80, 110  11. (fig)  12. 130, 130, 80, 30, 50, 50, 60

*The Geometry of Angle and Shape*

A POW GUIDE   page 292   ANSWERS

## Section 16: Enlargements   p232

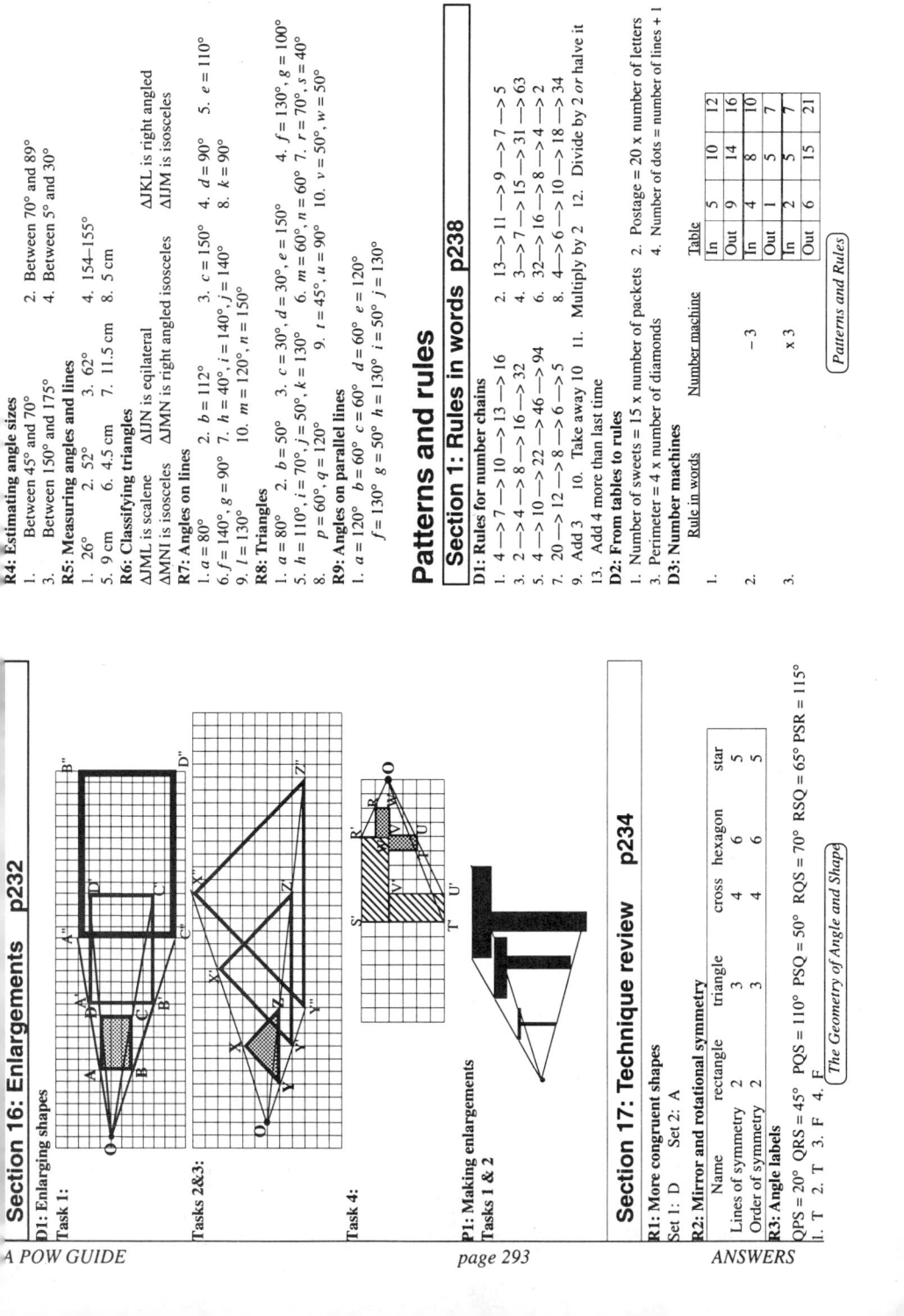

**D1: Enlarging shapes**

**Task 1:**

**Tasks 2 & 3:**

**Task 4:**

**P1: Making enlargements**

**Tasks 1 & 2**

## Section 17: Technique review   p234

**R1: More congruent shapes**

Set 1: D   Set 2: A

**R2: Mirror and rotational symmetry**

| Name | rectangle | triangle | cross | hexagon | star |
|---|---|---|---|---|---|
| Lines of symmetry | 2 | 3 | 4 | 6 | 5 |
| Order of symmetry | 2 | 3 | 4 | 6 | 5 |

**R3: Angle labels**

QPS = 20°  QRS = 45°  PQS = 110°  PSQ = 50°  RQS = 70°  RSQ = 65°  PSR = 115°

1. T   2. T   3. F   4. F

*The Geometry of Angle and Shape*

**R4: Estimating angle sizes**
1. Between 45° and 70°
2. Between 70° and 89°
3. Between 150° and 175°
4. Between 5° and 30°

**R5: Measuring angles and lines**
1. 26°   2. 52°   3. 62°   4. 154–155°
5. 9 cm   6. 4.5 cm   7. 11.5 cm   8. 5 cm

**R6: Classifying triangles**

△JML is scalene  △IJN is eqilateral  △JKL is right angled
△MNI is isosceles  △JMN is right angled isosceles  △IJM is isosceles

**R7: Angles on lines**
1. $a = 80°$   2. $b = 112°$   3. $c = 150°$   4. $d = 90°$   5. $e = 110°$
6. $f = 140°$, $g = 90°$   7. $h = 40°$, $i = 140°$, $j = 140°$   8. $k = 90°$
9. $l = 130°$   10. $m = 120°$, $n = 150°$

**R8: Triangles**
1. $a = 80°$   2. $b = 50°$   3. $c = 30°$, $d = 30°$, $e = 150°$   4. $f = 130°$, $g = 100°$
5. $h = 110°$, $i = 70°$, $j = 50°$, $k = 130°$   6. $m = 60°$, $n = 60°$   7. $r = 70°$, $s = 40°$
8. $p = 60°$, $q = 120°$   9. $t = 45°$, $u = 90°$   10. $v = 50°$, $w = 50°$

**R9: Angles on parallel lines**
1. $a = 120°$  $b = 60°$  $c = 60°$  $d = 60°$  $e = 120°$
   $f = 130°$  $g = 50°$  $h = 130°$  $i = 50°$  $j = 130°$

# Patterns and rules

## Section 1: Rules in words   p238

**D1: Rules for number chains**
1. $4 \to 7 \to 10 \to 13 \to 16$   2. $13 \to 11 \to 9 \to 7 \to 5$
3. $2 \to 4 \to 8 \to 16 \to 32$   4. $3 \to 7 \to 15 \to 31 \to 63$
5. $4 \to 10 \to 22 \to 46 \to 94$   6. $32 \to 16 \to 8 \to 4 \to 2$
7. $20 \to 12 \to 8 \to 6 \to 5$   8. $4 \to 6 \to 10 \to 18 \to 34$
9. Add 3   10. Take away 10   11. Multiply by 2   12. Divide by 2 *or* halve it
13. Add 4 more than last time

**D2: From tables to rules**
1. Number of sweets = 15 x number of packets   2. Postage = 20 x number of letters
3. Perimeter = 4 x number of diamonds   4. Number of dots = number of lines + 1

**D3: Number machines**

| | Rule in words | Number machine | Table |
|---|---|---|---|
| 1. | | | In 5, 10, 12 / Out 9, 14, 16 |
| 2. | | −3 | In 4, 8, 10 / Out 1, 5, 7 |
| 3. | | × 3 | In 2, 5, 7 / Out 6, 15, 21 |

*Patterns and Rules*

A POW GUIDE                page 293                ANSWERS

4. Multiply by 5

| In | 2 | 4 | 6 |
|---|---|---|---|
| Out | 10 | 20 | 30 |

5.

| In | 2 | 5 | 7 |
|---|---|---|---|
| Out | 4 | 25 | 49 |

6.

| In | 2 | 4 | 5 |
|---|---|---|---|
| Out | 5 | 9 | 11 |

7.

| In | 2 | 4 | 5 |
|---|---|---|---|
| Out | 6 | 10 | 12 |

8. No

## Section 2: Using letters for numbers p240

### D1: Letters for unknown numbers

1. $n + 2$ 2. $n - 2$ 3. ☐ & ☐ 4. $2n + 1$ 5. $3n$ 6. $2n + 3$
7. $3n + 1$ 8. A is $s + 2$ B is $2s$ C is $s - 2$ D is $2s + 2$

### D2: Expressions with brackets

1. No 2. Yes
3. Number of sweets = 2 x $(n + 3) = 2(n + 3)$ and $2(n + 3) = 2n + 6$
4. (a) $n - 3$ (b) $2(n - 3)$

### D3: Matching pairs of algebraic cards

Task 1: $n + n = 2n$ $n^2 = n \times n$ $n + n + 1 = 2n + 1$
Task 2: $n + n + n = 2n + n$ $2n + 1 = 1 + 2n$ $2 + n + 3 = n + 5$
Task 3: $\frac{1}{2}n = n \div 2$ $3n = 2n + n$ $2n + 3n = 5n$

## Section 3: Machines and rules p242

### D1: Letters for unknown numbers

1. (a) 14 (b) 11 (c) 3N + 2 (d) N —> 3N + 2 2. N —> 4N – 1
3. N —> $N^2$ + 2 4. N —> 5N + 1 5. N —> 5N – 3 6. N —> 2(N + 1)
7. (a) [x3]—[+1] (b) [+1]—[x 3] 8. [x itself]—[+2]

### D2: Machine instructions

1. Machines 1 & 6 Machines 2 & 4 Machines 3 & 5
2. Machines 1 & 6 Machines 2 & 4 Machines 3 & 5

### D3: Letters for In and Out

1. Out is 7 2 4 2. $d = c + 5$ 3. Out is 1 3 5 4. $q = 3p + 2$

## Section 4: Shape patterns p244

### D1: Rules for shape patterns

1.

| (L) | 1 | 2 | 3 |
|---|---|---|---|
| (D) | 2 | 3 | 4 |

2. (a) 21 (b) D = L + 1

3.

| (L) | 1 | 2 | 3 |
|---|---|---|---|
| (D) | 4 | 8 | 12 |

4. Number of matches = 4 x shape number
5. M = 4 S 6. 40

### D2: Choose the right formula

1. S = 2L 2. P = 2S + 2 3. M = 3S + 1 4. d = 3p + 2
5. 12 6. 32



### D3: Matchstick patterns

1. (a) 21 (b) 26 (c) Add 5 (d) 51
2.

| | | | | | | | |
|---|---|---|---|---|---|---|---|
| Set A: | 1 | 2 | 3 | 4 | 5 | 10 | Add 2 |
| | 3 | 5 | 7 | 9 | 11 | 21 | |
| Set B: | 1 | 2 | 3 | 4 | 5 | 10 | Add 3 |
| | 4 | 7 | 10 | 13 | 16 | 31 | |
| Set C: | 1 | 2 | 3 | 4 | 5 | 6 | Add 7 |
| | 10 | 17 | 24 | 31 | 38 | 45 | |
| Set D: | 1 | 2 | 3 | 4 | | | Add 2 more than last time |
| | 4 | 10 | 18 | 28 | | | |
| Set E: | 1 | 2 | 3 | 4 | | | Add 3 more than last time |
| | 9 | 18 | 30 | 45 | | | |

## Section 5: Solving equations p246

### D1: What is an equation ?

1. 5 2. 10 3. 6 4. 3 5. N = 7 6. N = 4 7. N = 10 8. N = 3
9. N = 5 10. N = 4 11. N = 10 12. N = 7

## Section 6: Systematic equation solving p247

### D1: The basic technique

1. $3p + 2 = 11$, $3p = 9$, $p = 3$
2. $2c + 40 = 140$, $2c = 100$, $c = 50$
3. $4m + 5 = 13$, $4m = 8$, $m = 2$
4. $3v - 4 = 11$, $3v = 15$, $v = 5$

### D2: A shortcut

1. $5p + 3 = 18$, $5p = 15$, $p = 3$
2. $3k - 1 = 11$, $3k = 12$, $k = 4$
3. $4e - 2 = 18$, $4e = 20$, $e = 5$

4. 3 5. 3 6. 8 7. 5 8. 5 9. 3 10. 2 11. 7 12. 3

### P1: Practice Exercises

**Batch A:**
1. 5 2. 3 3. 5 4. 5 5. 11 6. 6 7. 3 8. 3
9. 6 10. 5 11. 2 12. 6 13. 5 14. 5 15. 9

**Batch B:**
1. 4 2. 3 3. 8 4. 8 5. 5 6. 11 7. 8 8. 15
9. 9 10. 1 11. 8 12. 10 13. 5 14. 6 15. 5

**Batch C:**
1. 8 2. 5 3. 4 4. 2 5. 4 6. 4 7. 4 8. 2
9. 2 10. 5 11. 4 12. 3 13. 3 14. 3 15. 7

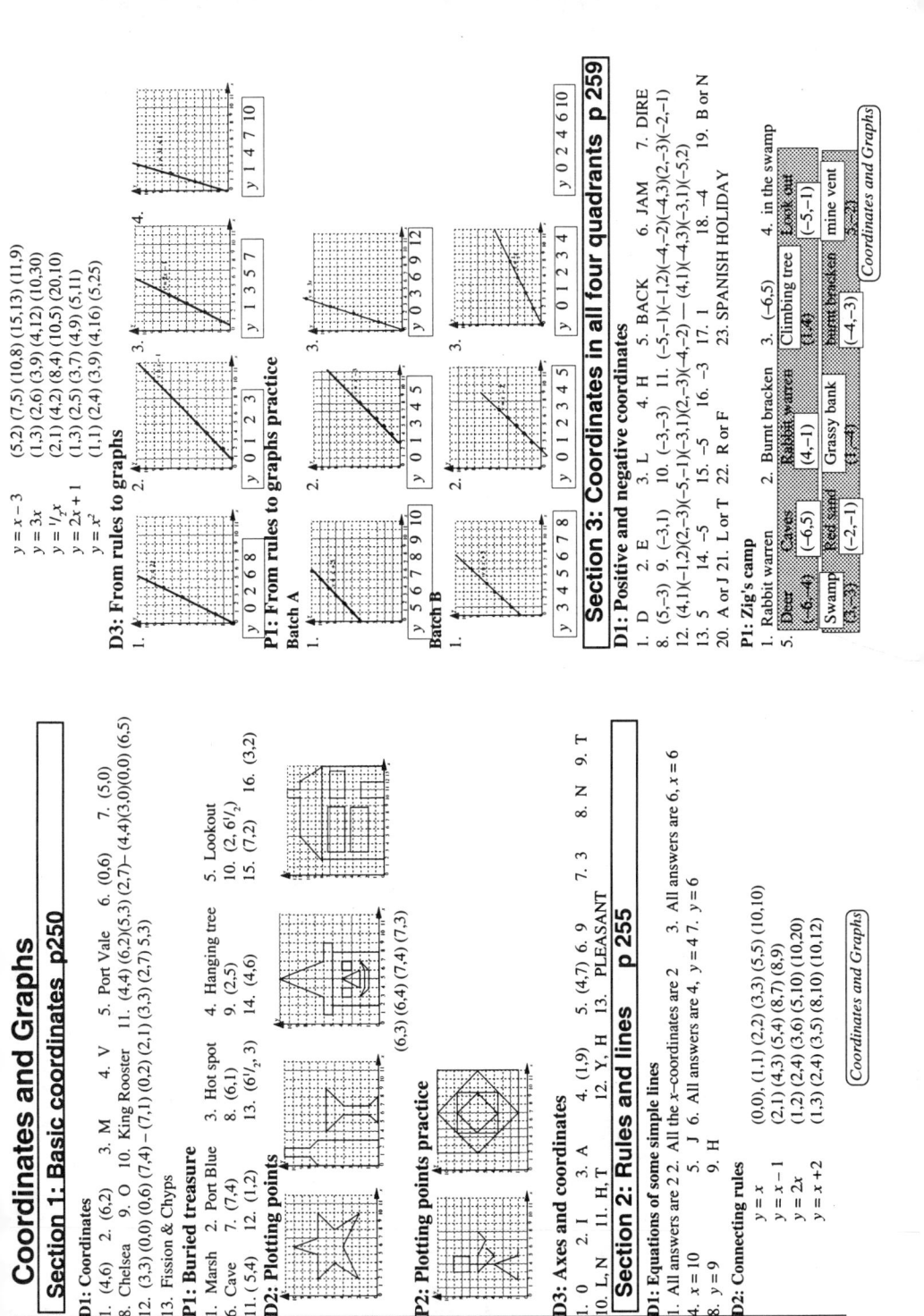

# Coordinates and Graphs

## Section 1: Basic coordinates p250

**D1: Coordinates**
1. (4,6)  2. (6,2)  3. M  4. V  5. Port Vale  6. (0,6)  7. (5,0)
8. Chelsea  9. O  10. King Rooster  11. (4,4) (6,2)(5,3) (2,7)– (4,4)(3,0)(0,0) (6,5)
12. (3,3) (0,0) (0,6) (7,4) –(7,1) (0,2) (3,3) (2,7) 5,3)
13. Fission & Chyps

**P1: Buried treasure**
1. Marsh  2. Port Blue  3. Hot spot  4. Hanging tree  5. Lookout
6. Cave  7. (7,4)  8. (6,1)  9. (2,5)  10. (2, 6½)
11. (5,4)  12. (1,2)  13. (6½, 3)  14. (4,6)  15. (7,2)  16. (3,2)

**D2: Plotting points**

(6,3) (6,4) (7,4) (7,3)

**P2: Plotting points practice**

**D3: Axes and coordinates**
1. O  2. I  3. A  4. (1,9)  5. (4,7) 6. 9  7. 3  8. N  9. T
10. L,N  11. H,T  12. Y, H  13. PLEASANT

## Section 2: Rules and lines p 255

**D1: Equations of some simple lines**
1. All answers are 2  2. All the x-coordinates are 2  3. All answers are 6, $x = 6$
4. $x = 10$   5. J   6. All answers are 4, $y = 4$   7. $y = 6$
8. $y = 9$   9. H

**D2: Connecting rules**

$y = x$      (0,0), (1,1) (2,2) (3,3) (5,5) (10,10)
$y = x - 1$    (2,1) (4,3) (5,4) (8,7) (8,9)
$y = 2x$      (1,2) (2,4) (3,6) (5,10) (10,20)
$y = x + 2$    (1,3) (2,4) (3,5) (8,10) (10,12)

$y = x - 3$    (5,2) (7,5) (10,8) (15,13) (11,9)
$y = 3x$      (1,3) (2,6) (3,9) (4,12) (10,30)
$y = \tfrac{1}{2}x$    (2,1) (4,2) (8,4) (10,5) (20,10)
$y = 2x + 1$   (1,3) (2,5) (3,7) (4,9) (5,11)
$y = x^2$      (1,1) (2,4) (3,9) (4,16) (5,25)

**D3: From rules to graphs**

1.  | $y$ 0 2 6 8 |
2.  | $y$ 0 1 2 3 |
3.  | $y$ 0 1 3 4 5 |
4.  | $y$ 1 3 5 7 |

**P1: From rules to graphs practice**

Batch A
1. | $y$ 5 6 7 8 9 10 |   2. | $y$ 0 1 3 4 5 |

Batch B
1. | $y$ 3 4 5 6 7 8 |   2. | $y$ 0 1 2 3 4 5 |   3. | $y$ 0 3 6 9 12 |   | $y$ 0 2 4 6 10 |

## Section 3: Coordinates in all four quadrants p 259

**D1: Positive and negative coordinates**
1. D  2. E  3. L  4. H  5. BACK  6. JAM  7. DIRE
8. (5,–3)  9. (–3,1)  10. (–3,–3)  11. (–5,–1)(–1,2)(–4,–2)(–4,3)(2,–3)(–2,–1)
12. (4,1)(–1,2)(2,–3)(–5,–1)(–3,1)(2,–3)(–4,–2) — (4,1)(–4,3)(–3,1)(–5,2)
13. 5   14. –5   15. –5   16. –3   17. 1   18. –4   19. B or N
20. A or J  21. L or T  22. R or F   23. SPANISH HOLIDAY

**P1: Zig's camp**
1. Rabbit warren   2. Burnt bracken   3. (–6,5)   4. in the swamp
5.

| Deer | Caves | Rabbit warren | Climbing tree | Look out |
|---|---|---|---|---|
| (–6,–4) | (–6,5) | (4,–1) | (1,4) | (–5,–1) |
| Swamp | Red sand | Grassy bank | burnt bracken | mine vent |
| (1,–3) | (–2,–1) | (3,–4) | (–4,–3) | (5,3) |

*Coordinates and Graphs*

| dead bird | skull | mossy wall | swinging tree | railway remains |
|---|---|---|---|---|
| (5,0) | (–2,–3) | (–2,–4) | (–1,2) | (5,–3) |
| rock pile | tree house | | spring | boggy place | hiding place |
| (–4,1) | (1,–2) | | (–4,3) | (4,–5) | (1,2) |

6. Burnt bracken       7. Caves and Skull
8. Rock pile and rabbit warren    9. (a) All are –2  (b) $x = -2$

**D2: Plotting points in four quadrants**

1.

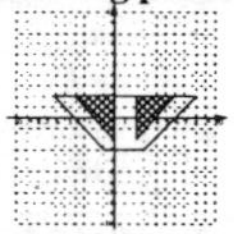

2.

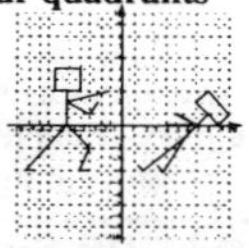

3.

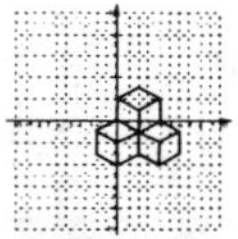

## Section 4: From graphs to rules  p 262

**D1: From rules to graphs in all four quadrants**

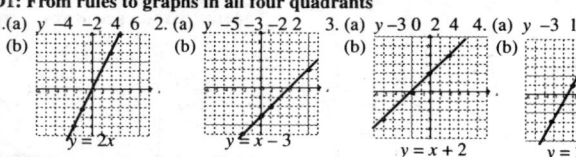

1.(a) $y$ –4 –2 4 6  2. (a) $y$ –30 2 4  4. (a) $y$ –3 1 3 5
      $y = x + 2$          $y = x - 2$          $y = 2x + 3$
   (b) $y = 2x$         (b) $y = -x$         (b)

3. (a) $y$ –5 –3 –2 –2   4. $y = 3x$    5. $y = x - 5$
   (b) $y = x - 3$   8. $y = x^2$

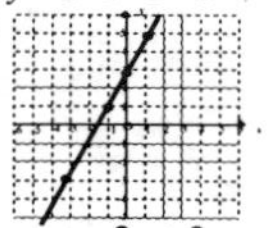

**D2: From coordinates to rules**

1. $y = x + 1$   2. $y = -x$   3. $y = x - 2$   4. $y = 3x$
6. $y = x + 2$   7. $y = \frac{1}{3}x$   8. $y = x^2$

**D3: From graphs to rules**

1.(a) $y$ –2 0 1 4  2.(a) $y$ 3 2 1 –2  3.(a) $y$ –2 2 4 6   4. (a) $x$ –1 3 4 6
      $y$ –3 –2 1 1 2                     $y$ –1 1 2 3             $y$ –1 3 4 6
   (b) $y = x$         (b) $y = -x$        (b) $y = 2x$        (b) $y = x + 3$

5.(a) $x$ –2 0 1 2   6.(a) $x$ –2 2 4 6   7. (a) $x$ –2 –1 1 2  8.(a) $x$ 0 1 3 5 6
      $y$ 4 0 –2 –4       $y$ –1 1 2 3         $y$ 4 1 1 4           $y$ –4 –3 –1 1 2
   (b) $y = -2x$      (b) $y = \frac{1}{2}x$   (b) $y = x^2$        (b) $y = x - 4$

**P1: Finding rules practice**

**A** 1.(a) $x$ –2 –1 0 2 3  2. (a) $x$ –2 0 2 3 4   3. (a) $x$ 0 1 3 5 6  4. (a) $x$ –1 0 1 2 3
        $y$ –3 –2 1 1 2        $y$ 0 2 4 5 6         $y$ –4 –3 –1 1 2      $y$ –3 –1 1 3 5
     (b) $y = x - 1$        (b) $y = x + 2$        (b) $y = x - 4$      (b) $y = 2x - 1$

**B** 1.(a) $x$ –2 –1 0 2 4  2. (a) $x$ –1 0 $\frac{1}{2}$ 1  3. (a) $x$ –4 0 2 4  4. (a) $x$ –2 –1 0 1
        $y$ –4 –3 –2 0 2        $y$ –4 0 2 1        $y$ –1 0 $\frac{1}{2}$ 4     $y$ –5 –2 1 4
     (b) $y = x - 2$        (b) $y = 4x$         (b) $y = \frac{1}{4}x$   (b) $y = 3x + 1$

## Section 5: Related graphs  p 265

**D1: Parallel lines**

1. $y$ –1 1 2 3 5   $y$ –1 1 2 3 5
   Line A is $y = x$   Line B is $y = x + 1$   Line C is $y = x + 2$

2. $y$ –2 0 2 4 6   $y$ –1 1 3 5   $y$ 0 2 4 6
   Line D is $y = 2x$   Line E is $y = 2x + 1$   Line F is $y = 2x + 2$

3. Either A, B & C *or* D, E & F   4. Either they are all $y = x +$ something
                                      or they are all $y = 2x +$ something.

**D2: Equations of parallel lines**

1. They are all $y = x +$ something   2. $y = x + 4$   3. $y = x - 3$
4. $y = 2x - 5$   5. $y = 2x + 5$
6. Parallel to the other lines & cutting $y$-axis at –1

## Section 6: Scatter graphs  p 267

**D2: Correlation**

1. increase  2. Q: sales rise as temperature rises  3. R: sales drop as temp rises
4. P: sales not affected by temperature  5. points go up from left to right

## Section 7: Technique review  p 269

**R1: Basic coordinates**

1. He went up then across – instead of across then up
2. BEATING  3. (0,0)  4. A, S or M  5. (5,0)  6. (1,4)

**R2: Equations of some simple lines**

1. the first  2. $x = 6$  3. $y = 4$  4. $x = 2$

**R3: Connecting rules**

1. (4,1) (5,2) (10,7) (9,6)  2. (1,3) (3,7) (6,13) (4,9)  3. $y = 3x + 2$ (10, 32)
4. $y = x + 5$  (7,12)

**R4: From rules to graphs**

| $x$ | 0 | 1 | 2 | 3 | 4 |
|---|---|---|---|---|---|
| $y$ | 3 | 4 | 5 | 6 | 7 |

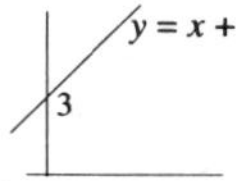

2.

$y = x + 3$

**R5: Four quadrant coordinates**

1. M  2. FRINGE  3. 4  4. –1  5. T or L
6. (4,–1) (2,–3) (3,–5) (–6,–4) (1,4) (–4,–2) (–2,–1)

**R6: From coordinates to rules**

1. $y = 2x$   2. 

| $x$ | 0 | 1 | 3 | 5 | 6 |
|---|---|---|---|---|---|
| $y$ | –4 | –3 | –1 | 1 | 2 |

$y = x - 4$

**R7: Related graphs**

Line P: $y = x + 5$   Line Q: $y = x + 7$